INVESTING

ONLINE

Dealing in Global Markets
on the Internet

STEPHEN ECKETT

FT
PITMAN
PUBLISHING

London · Hong Kong · Johannesburg · Melbourne · Singapore · Washington DC

PITMAN PUBLISHING
128 Long Acre, London WC2E 9AN
Tel: +44 (0)171 447 2000
Fax: +44(0)171 240 5771

A Division of Pearson Professional Limited

First published in Great Britain in 1997

The right of Stephen Eckett to be identified as author
of this work has been asserted by him in accordance
with the Copyright, Designs and Patents Act 1988.

ISBN 0 273 62558 6

British Library Cataloguing in Publication Data
A CIP catalogue record for this book can be obtained from the British Library.

10 9 8 7 6 5 4 3 2 1

Typeset by Phoenix Photosetting, Chatham, Kent
Printed and bound in Great Britain by Bell & Bain Ltd, Glasgow.

The Publishers' policy is to use paper manufactured from sustainable forests.

THE AUTHOR

Stephen Eckett read mathematics at London University and then joined Baring Securities on the Japanese equities and warrants desk. After setting up a futures operation for Barings in Hong Kong, he joined the capital markets division of Bankers Trust and organized the first listing of an index warrant in Asia. He then moved to Tokyo to set up a derivatives desk for S.G. Warburg Securities.

In 1993 he founded Numa Financial Systems Ltd, a training and systems consultancy company specializing in derivatives.

Numa was one of the first financial companies in the UK to set up a Web site. Since then Numa has become involved increasingly with the use of new technologies for investment, in particular investigating the financial applications of the Internet and artificial intelligence systems such as natural language processing.

Contact:

Numa Financial Systems Ltd
PO Box 1736
Bradford On Avon
Wilts
UK
Tel: +44 1225 723072
E-mail: info@numa.com
http://www.numa.com

Contents

Section 4 APPENDICES

PREFACE

There have been many guides to the Internet, but this book is part of the second wave, one that focuses on one particular area and describes how to use the Internet for a specific purpose.

This is the first comprehensive guide to the financial Internet.

The investment services currently available on the Internet are nothing short of remarkable, in many cases they are the equal of expensive services provided for professional investors, but they are free. Today's investors, with just a PC and a connection to the Internet, have the world at their feet.

But this is not an uncritical guide to the Internet. Much time can be wasted looking at different sites, where information turns out to be non-existent, or of little use. This book explores the Net in great detail to find the pith – the real content useful for investors.

Content

This book comprehensively covers all the services available on the Internet for individual and professional investors. All the world's major markets are included for equities, bonds, money markets, currencies, futures and options. Not covered are areas of personal finance (which tend to be country-specific) such as insurance, mortgages, or tax.

The incredible potential of the Internet is not, unfortunately, offered on a plate. There can be problems with:

- how to find information
- how to know if the information can be trusted
- how to use it.

This book provides answers to all three by:

- explaining what the Internet really is, and how it works
- describing in detail the services offered by the world's top financial sites
- demonstrating how to integrate the Internet into all stages of an investment strategy
- providing a comprehensive directory of the global financial Internet.

The major part of this book is an analysis of the investment services on the Internet – the whole multimedia glory of the Net is not covered. However, certain areas of the Internet that are of specific use to investors are covered in quite some detail. These include:

- getting connected to the Internet
- what programs to use, and where to find them on the Internet
- using e-mail
- the World Wide Web
- newsgroups
- using search engines to find information.

Throughout the book, many examples are given of the type of information to be found on different sites, and the appendices contain reference material that should prove of use to any online investor.

Finally, the trends in current Internet development are examined, and the likely implications this will have on the future of investment are explored.

This book is appropriate for individual and professional investors worldwide, with a little knowledge of computing, who want to use the Internet as one of their investment tools.

In addition, the book is aimed at industry professionals who are looking for an overview of what is available on the whole financial Internet, and where things are heading.

How to use this book

This has been written primarily as a reference work, and is not meant to be read through from page one. It is recommended to start with Section 2, which provides the overview and description of the major financial sites. Section 3 provides the definitive directory of the whole financial Internet. When you find yourself asking questions like *why is this free?, how do I know this is right?* and *why is this so slow?*, then Section 1 provides the general background.

Section 1 – INTRODUCTION TO THE INTERNET

This section offers a general introduction to the Internet: what it is and how it works. Details are given on how to connect to the Internet, and the section ends with a look into the likely future direction of the Internet and investment.

Section 2 – MASTERING THE FINANCIAL INTERNET

This provides an overview of the financial Internet, with detailed descriptions of the best sites. Following this there is an in-depth guide to using the search engines to find information, an overview of cyberscams and an eight-point plan demonstrating how to integrate the Internet into an investment strategy. The section closes with an introduction to the Internet *as* an investment (i.e. the Internet-related stocks).

▨ Section 3 – THE DIRECTORY

A reference guide to the whole financial Internet, including addresses, summaries and critical ratings for over 1200 finance-related sites from 45 countries.

▨ Section 4 – APPENDICES

A range of practical reference data to help the investor get online and start using the Internet in earnest.

▨ Glossary

A glossary of over 300 technical terms to aid understanding of topics covered in this book, as well as those used in Internet-related articles and analysts' reports.

A few notes

Rather than repeating certain warnings or information throughout the book, here are the most important points.

▨ **The first, and most obvious, warning is that the Internet is changing very quickly**. This means that the services described in this book will change over time, and that the addresses may alter – or disappear completely.

However, it is not necessary to argue oneself into hopeless paralysis because of this. While bewildering change is a fact if you are interested in the latest browser software or multimedia game, change in the financial Internet is more in appearance than actual reality. Of the major sites identified in this book as being useful for investors (including sites such as the *Wall Street Journal* or *Financial Times*), many of these were in existence from the early days of the Web, and will doubtless be there in the years to come. There will obviously be changes in the services offered, but, again, this is likely to be in incremental improvements, rather than a complete change in direction.

▨ **Be wary of information you see on the Internet.** The Net will be a very fertile ground for scams (see later chapters for advice on how to deal with this). Nothing in this book should be construed as a recommendation for either an investment or an Internet service.

Terminology

A comprehensive glossary is provided at the back of the book. However, there are some words used repeatedly throughout, and for convenience these are briefly explained below:

- **browser:** this always refers to a software program that is used to view Web pages (e.g. Netscape Navigator, Microsoft Explorer); it never refers to users themselves
- **site:** usually refers to a collection of Web pages created and maintained by one individual or organisation
- **service:** used virtually interchangeably with *site*, and meaning any service offered on, or through, a Web site, and
- **URL:** uniform resource locator, the address of a site (or service) on the Internet.

Also throughout the book, the terms *Internet, Net* are used interchangeably, as are *World Wide Web, WWW, Web*. Due to the current profile of the Internet, descriptions here of Web sites commonly divide the world into *North America* (US and Canada) and *International* (rest of the world).

The great advantage of the Internet, and many of the related services and programs, is that they are platform-independent (i.e. it doesn't matter if you are using a PC, a Mac or UNIX system). However, when necessary it has been assumed that the user has a PC, and is running the Netscape Navigator browser.

Finally, in answering the questions *what's on the Internet* and *what use is it?*, the source for everything in this book was the Net.

One practical point: http addresses on the Internet are highlighted in text as follows:

http://www.javasoft.com

Other addresses (mostly newsgroups) are printed as follows:

misc.invest

Addresses should always be input as printed, with no extra spaces or hyphens where the address breaks at the end of a line. Take care not to include any comma, full stop or bracket that may be part of sentence punctuation.

INTRODUCTION

The changes currently taking place on the Internet, where new software and services are announced every week, can be bewildering and distracting. *When is the thing going to be finished?*, one might ask. But the Internet is not a product; it is a method of communication and a powerful tool for those who choose to explore it.

For investors, the Internet is there to be used immediately. The services already online offer a formidable array of powerful tools that do not require the latest, state-of-the-art computer. Right now, investors around the world with an ordinary PC and local telephone call can:

- view closing market prices for most markets in the world
- for many markets, view real-time stock prices and chart price histories
- in the US and UK markets, stock orders can be given via the computer (and, in the case of the US, commissions can be as low as US$12 – irrespective of deal size)
- monitor breaking news stories on CNN and Bloomberg
- read the daily financial papers, *WSJ* and *FT* online, and also most of the other major newspapers worldwide
- monitor a portfolio's value, and receive customized news stories relevant to the portfolio
- view real-time currency movements, with charts and technical analysis
- monitor the value and relative performance of funds
- read investment newsletters specializing in specific sectors
- consult online investment glossaries, read about futures and options, experiment with simulated trading programs and receive buy/sell signals from online trading systems
- analyse company financial information, and view corporate filings as quickly as any professional investor anywhere
- download economics data from government and bank databases and read regular economics reports and forecasts
- discuss all this with other investors online, and monitor what the market is talking about.

And many of these services are free.

The Internet should not be regarded as another technological development. It is not the next consumer product following the radio, television, Walkman, PC, VCR and CD player. And the Internet is not new: it has been around for over

15 years. So, why the sudden excitement? Because the Internet is like a new language, it is a method of global communication, and it is the most significant development since the printing press was invented.

The Internet changes everything?

No, of course not. It won't have much effect on buying oranges in a shop, on health care for the aged, or on car safety design. But, for some areas, and particularly service industries, the changes wrought will be dramatic.

And no industry will be affected more by it than the investment industry.

The Internet will fundamentally affect:

- how we invest
- how we research our investments
- what we actually invest in.

This book deliberately looks at the big picture because the current trends will create a new investment industry out of all recognition to that existing today. The very investment process itself will be transformed, and truly global investment will, eventually, arrive. As the investment, and other, industries move to adapt to the new world, extraordinary opportunities will arise. In fact, we are moving into a period where, as P.J. O'Rourke says,

> *'Opportunity knocks, it jiggles the doorknob, it will try the window if we don't have the alarm system on.'*

But these will be opportunities of the information age, and will not necessarily look like those of the preceding industrial era.

Science fiction?

This book, therefore, is about cyberspace – what's out there, what's on offer, and most importantly how to use it. But what is cyberspace? The term was coined by the Canadian author William Gibson, and he describes it as,

> *'Cyberspace. A consensual hallucination experienced daily by billions. . .unthinkable complexity. . .lines of light ranged. . .in the nonspace of the mind, clusters and constellations of data. Like city lights. . .receding. . .'*

Fine, you may say, but what does any of that have to do with the price of fish, and why should I be interested in it?

Perhaps the words of John Perry Barlow (co-founder of the Electronic Frontier Foundation) are a little more pertinent:

> *'Cyberspace is where your money is.'*

Internet facts

The following is a random selection of data discovered during the research for this book.

- The WWW is doubling in size every four months – a new Web site every four seconds.
- America Online is receiving about 60 000 new subscribers per week in the US, and CompuServe is attracting 10 000 per week in the UK alone.
- Forrester projects that by the year 2000, $45.8 billion in Internet-related revenues will be created in computers, communications, publishing, retail, information services, and entertainment. Additionally, $46.2 billion of financial assets will be managed on the Net.
- Dataquest estimates that 25% of the people who come online do so to get some kind of financial data.
- One in every 100 Web pages contain the word *finance* – slightly more than contain the word *sex*.
- Forrester estimates that 800 000 US investors currently bypass brokers to trade online using Internet brokerages.
- Twenty per cent of US broker Charles Schwab's business is from online orders – it forecasts this will grow to 40% over the next four years.
- PC Quote delivers more than two million delayed and real-time quotes per day to an average of 60 000 users.
- The search engine Infoseek runs seven million searches a day, and as many as 175 searches a second during peak hours.
- The World Wide Web is just five years old.

INTRODUCTION TO THE INTERNET

A general guide to the Internet, including its history and development, its form today, and current issues and possible future developments.

History and development of the Internet

The early history of the Internet is not an exciting one – there are no scientists bursting into rooms gasping, 'I've found it!' Rather, the story is one of organizations with odd acronyms and committees experimenting with different methods of computer communication. But no one knew they were inventing the Internet as such – not as we know it today. The technical foundation for the Internet was laid in the 1960s, but the term *Internet* was not itself even coined until 1982. The early workers on computer networks would have been as surprised as anyone with the resulting system that we call the Internet. The story usually starts with the threat of atom bombs.

By the late 1960s many US government institutions had computers. The data stored on these computers became increasingly important for day-to-day operations, and it was thought it would be useful if the different computers could share data. This would mean connecting the computers; but, appreciating their growing reliance on the machines, there was concern about the form of these connections, and their likely vulnerability to attack. The Advanced Research Projects Agency (ARPA) of the US Department of Defense was given the task of investigating a solution to this. They in turn brought in an independent research company called Bolt Beranek and Newman (BBN), which, in 1969, devised a network that was based on a packet switching protocol (*see* 'How it works' page 10 for more information).

In 1970, the BBN-devised network was installed in four universities in the US, and this can be regarded as the first physical prototype of the Internet – a defining characteristic of which is that it is a packet-switching network.

By 1972, there were 40 different sites linked to the network (called ARPAnet, as ARPA was still funding the project). On this early network, processes were already developing that would be recognized on the later Internet, such as the sending of text files between users (e-mail), or the transfer of large data files between computers (FTP).

But the ARPAnet in 1972 was not the Internet, it was merely one network. Over the following couple of years research went into finding how *different* packet switching networks could be linked together. The result of this was the introduction in 1974 of the TCP/IP protocols, and these are still the foundation protocols for today's Internet.

At this point it is useful to step back a little from talk of protocols to see what was happening elsewhere in the computer world. By the end of the 1970s, personal computers had started appearing, and from these developed the first bulletin board systems (BBS). More important, though, was the tremendous growth of low cost mini-computers, particularly those made by Digital Equipment Corporation (DEC) running a new operating system called UNIX. This multitasking operating system was developed by AT&T Bell Labs and was especially well suited for networking. In 1977, the new version of UNIX was shipped with the UNIX-to-UNIX copy program (UUCP), which allowed any two UNIX computers with modems to transfer files. This led to a great number of irregular, informal networks running over the public telephone system.

> The technical foundation for the Internet was laid in the 1960s, but the term *Internet* was not itself even coined until 1982.

Many universities now had computers and were part of various networks, but only a select few were served by the high-speed ARPAnet. As a result, in 1979 the Computer Science Research Network (CSnet) was formed to provide a network for science researchers. In the following year, a gateway was created between the new CSnet and ARPAnet. Messages could then be sent across the different networks – and the Internet was coming into existence.

Once networks started linking together, new ideas cropped up for how to exploit the potential. One of the first of these was for an electronic newspaper, where anybody could contribute articles which would be distributed automatically to all sites on the network. A process, called Usenet, was devised that used the UUCP facility on UNIX systems. Articles and discussions started appearing in such numbers that topic groups had to be formed, and then yet further sub-groups formed. When DARPA (the new name for ARPA) realized that some of the topics being discussed over ARPAnet were far from being academic or computer-related, a new Usenet protocol had to be devised. This was called Net News Transfer Protocol (NNTP), the protocol still used today for the newsgroups.

Another process developed in these early years was Listserv. Similar in concept to Usenet (i.e. a method for discussing topics on a network), Listserv used e-mail rather than the general broadcasting of Usenet.

The 1980s saw great network activity: new ones sprouted, old ones merged or disappeared. The US Government, determined to retain the lead in scientific research and high-end computing, sponsored the creation of the National Science Foundation Network (NSFnet) – a network of supercomputers connected by the highest grade transmission lines. Each one of the NSFnet computers acted as a focus for the development of further networks. Over the following years, NSFnet came to replace both the ARPAnet (the military part of which formed its own network) and CSnet.

By the end of the 1980s, the Internet was looking good: it had a name, its communication protocols had proved reliable and flexible, academics were exchanging messages around the world, and newsgroups were merrily discussing anything and everything – What more could you want?

But the activity was far from being restricted to the government sector. Anybody could set up a network, and many did when they realized that they could piggy-back on the NSFnet infrastructure.

This period also saw large businesses forming intra-company networks, and, responding to the growth of PC sales in the 1980s, independent services like CompuServe and Prodigy started appearing.

So, by the end of the 1980s, networks were everywhere, and the Internet in particular was looking good: it had a name, its communication protocols had proved reliable and remarkably flexible, academics were exchanging messages around the world, and newsgroups were merrily discussing anything and everything – all together, quite an achievement. What more could you want?

Then the 1990s arrived, and the Internet went stellar.

Before looking at what happened in the 1990s, it's interesting to consider some of the broad trends in computing leading up to this decade. (See Table 1.1.)

The first widespread use of computers in the 1960s saw commands being gathered together, and run through computers (batch processed) in sequential groups. In the 1970s, users operated dumb terminals directly connected to a central computer where the power was all concentrated, and which divided its time between command requests. IBM released its Personal Computer at the beginning of the 1980s, and PC growth dominated computing for the rest of the decade. Companies such as Intel and Microsoft grew massively by offering intelligent machines on the desktop.

Although there was nothing new with the concept of networks, the PC explosion in the previous decade paved the way in the 1990s for the widespread connection of computers. In the middle of the decade, the idea of the Network Computer (NC) was proposed, which appears to offer a return (albeit a multimedia return) to the dumb terminals of the 1970s. Much debate

▨ TABLE 1.1 **The four paradigms of computing**

	Batch	Time-sharing	Desktop	Network
Decade	1960s	1970s	1980s	1990s
Technology	medium-scale integration	large-scale integration	very large-scale	ultra large-scale
Location	computer rooms	terminal room	desktop	mobile
Users	experts	specialists	individuals	groups
User status	subservience	dependence	independence	freedom
Data	alphanumeric	text, vector	fonts, graphs	script, voice
Objective	calculate	access	present	communicate
User activity	punch & try (submit)	remember & type (interact)	see & point (drive)	ask & tell (delegate)
Operation	process	edit	layout	orchestrate
Interconnect	peripherals	terminals	desktops	palmtops
Applications	custom	standard	generic	component
Languages	COBOL, FORTRAN	PL/I, BASIC	PASCAL, C	object-oriented

Source: Scientific American

To the dismay of the Internet old guard, commercial activity did not hang around; just two years later, the number of commercial domains had overtaken the number of academic ones, and the rise of the .COM had begun.

rages as to whether the future of computing is PC or NC. However, this is not a contracting industry looking at consolidation – the PC and NC both offer distinct features, and the future most likely will be PC *and* NC.

At the dawning of the decade in 1990 no one could possibly have anticipated what was about to happen on the Net.

There were two significant developments early in the decade.

The first involved the US National Science Foundation – the body that controlled the NSFnet, the Internet's major backbone. From the beginning, the NSF was fairly relaxed over use of the NSFnet, as long as its Acceptable Use Policy was followed. However, this policy specifically mentioned for-profit activities, and extensive personal and business use, as *un*acceptable. But then in 1992, the NSF changed its stance which effectively meant the dropping of the policy. To the dismay of the Internet old guard, commercial activity did not hang around; just two years later, the number of commercial domains had overtaken the number of academic ones, and the rise of the .COM had begun.

The other significant development was of course the World Wide Web, the introduction of which opened up the Internet to anybody who could point and

The other significant development was of course the World Wide Web, the introduction of which opened up the Internet to anybody who could point and click.

click. In early 1993 there were 50 Web servers in existence; three years later, a new Web site was appearing every four seconds.

The National Center for Supercomputing Applications (NCSA), located at the University of Illinois, released a Web *browser* (see glossary) called Mosaic in 1993, which played an important role in popularizing the World Wide Web. The following year, one of the NCSA developers, Marc Andreesen, left to set up a company called Mosaic Communications Corporation with Jim Clark (ex-chief executive of Silicon Graphics). Its first product was the Web browser Netscape – briefly referred to as Mosaic Netscape – and in November 1994, the company changed its name to Netscape Communications Corporation. At this time, the company's own Web home page welcomed visitors with the following message:

> *Welcome to Netscape*
> *You have just embarked on a journey across the Internet,*
> *and Netscape is your vehicle*

From this time, the Internet entered the popular consciousness, with articles beginning to appear regularly in newspapers. If they weren't aware of it already, the initial public offering of Netscape shares in 1995 alerted the business and investment community to the fact that something big was happening.

And then Microsoft woke up. It had been completely wrong-footed by the pace of Internet growth, and sidetracked into developing its own proprietary network – as had quite a few other companies. In an incredible turnaround, Microsoft restyled itself as an 'Internet' company, and by the middle of 1996 was competing on equal terms with Netscape.

By this time, just two years after its foundation, the home page of Netscape now welcomed people with the message:

> *THE NETSCAPE MISSION*
> *Netscape Communications Corporation intends to be the premier provider of open software that enables people and companies to exchange information and conduct commerce over the Internet and other global networks.*

Not much of the Star Trek flavour left there!

A few significant dates in the Internet's history

[With some general computer developments for reference]

1969   First packet-switched network (designed by BBN using Network Control Protocol).

1970   Four US universities connected by a packet-switching network (attached to ARPAnet).

1971   [Intel introduces the world's first microprocessor.]

1972   Forty sites now connected to ARPAnet, using electronic mail, remote login (an early *Telnet* – see glossary) and file transfer protocol.

1974   TCP/IP protocols introduced.

1975   [MITS Altair 8800 appears on the cover of *Popular Electronics* – world's first mini-computer.]

1977   AT&T starts shipping UUCP with UNIX.

         DES endorsed by the US Government as an official encryption standard.

         Patent filed for the RSA encryption algorithm.

1978   [Microsoft sales first exceed $1 million.]

1979   The US Computer Science Research Network (CSnet) launched.

1981   [IBM introduces its Personal Computer.]

1982   Gateway established between CSnet and ARPAnet.

         The term *Internet* used for the first time.

         [Intel introduces the 286 microprocessor.]

1983   Bitnet (and Listservs) developed at City University of New York, and FidoNet appears in San Francisco.

         Military part of ARPAnet transfers to the private Milnet.

         [Microsoft introduces MS Windows.]

1984   The number of Internet hosts exceeds 1000.

         [The term *cyberspace* first appears in the novel *Neuromancer* by William Gibson.]

1985   [Intel introduces the 386 microprocessor.]

1986   [Microsoft goes public, raising $61 million.]

1987   The number of Internet hosts exceeds 10 000.

1988   The 'Internet Worm' virus temporarily disables 6000 of the 60 000 Internet hosts.

1989   Tim Berners-Lee presents a proposal at CERN – the European Particle Physics Laboratory – for a hypertext system (WWW); the number of Internet hosts exceeds 100 000.

         [Intel introduces the 486 microprocessor.]

▶

1990	Internet membership in the US opens to everybody – leading to commercialization of the Net (previously, sponsorship by a US government agency was required).
	[Microsoft announces MS Windows 3.0, and also becomes the first PC software company with annual sales over $1 billion.]
1991	First working version of the World Wide Web appears at CERN.
	First version of Pretty Good Privacy (PGP) encryption software released.
1992	The first audio and video broadcasts take place over the Internet (MBONE); the number of Internet hosts exceeds 1 000 000.
	[Microsoft ships MS Windows 3.1 and a pre-release version of NT].
1993	50 Web servers in existence.
	First version of the X Mosaic browser released by NCSA.
	WWW traffic 0.1 per cent of the total for the Internet backbone.
	[Intel introduces the Pentium microprocessor.]
1994	The number of domain names for commercial organizations (.COM) overtakes those for educational institutions, and 'Internet in a box' products start to appear to bring the Internet into homes.
1995	Sun releases the Java programming language.
	Debate starts over PCs versus network power (Oracle, Sun v. Microsoft, Intel).
	IPO of Netscape Communications Corp (valuing the company at over $2 billion).
	Microsoft announces a halt of the Blackbird project (an alternative to HTML – see glossary), and opens the proprietary service MSN to all Internet users.
1996	IPO of Yahoo (valuing the company at $860 million).
	The number of Internet hosts exceeds 10 000 000.

The Internet today

This section explains:

- what the Internet is
- how it works
- who uses the Internet
- the major features of the Internet
- further reference sources about the Internet.

DEFINITION (WHAT IS IT?)

The simplest, but perfectly adequate, definition of the Internet is: *The collection of all computers around the world that communicate with each other using a certain set of rules.*

This could be refined to give a slightly more precise description as: *The collection of interconnected networks around the world that all use the TCP/IP protocols to communicate with each other.*

Which itself could be further refined . . . *etc.*

The problem with all definitions is striking the right position on the spectrum of all possible definitions, between accurate and incomprehensible at one end, and simple and misleading (if not totally wrong) at the other.

Any accurate description of the Internet is in danger of only being understood by people who already 'know' what the Internet is. The situation is somewhat comparable to financial derivatives, where the oft-repeated definition, *instruments derived from securities or physical markets*, is most likely meaningless – and certainly useless in practice – to virtually anybody.

The best way to understand futures, for example, is to buy some futures contracts, pay a few margin calls, and pretty quickly you'll be catching on. Similarly, with the Internet, have a look at a few Web sites:

■ the news on CNN financial pages **(http://www.cnnfn.com)**

■ check the current stock price of Intel [INTU] **(http://www.quote.com/)**

■ read about J.P. Morgan's *RiskMetrics* **(http://www.jpmorgan.com/)**

■ use an online options analyser **(http://www.intrepid.com/)**

■ join a discussion about technical analysis programs (misc.invest.technical).

Click on a few hyperlinks and jump to other financial sites, and you'll soon get a feeling for what the Internet is.

Internet terminology

The term '*Internet*' we will take as describing the collection of interconnected networks around the world that all use the TCP/IP protocols to communicate with each other; while '*internet*' (lower case i) is non-specific and merely describes the situation when two or more networks are connected together. Throughout this book we refer only to the former (sometimes simply as the 'Net').

HOW IT WORKS

Starting with our simple description of the Internet as the collection of all computers around the world that communicate with each other using a certain set of rules, the first question we might ask is: what are these computers?

In general these are large computers operating within organizations, such as governments, universities and commercial companies. The computers can be of any type, but many are made by companies like Sun or Digital, and use the UNIX operating system.

Network of networks

The first refinement we will make to our simple Internet definition is to note that the Internet is a *network of networks* rather than a network of individual computers. For example, the commercial online service, America Online (AOL), is on the Internet, but AOL is not one computer but a network of many computers, to which over six million individual subscribers can connect with their own PCs. Similarly, a large company may have its own private network of computers around the world, which will, in turn, be connected to the Internet.

Backbones

These networks are connected by many different methods, including Ethernet cables in offices, telephone lines, fibre-optic cable, micro-wave relays and satellite communication. However, the growth of the Internet has taken everybody by surprise, and, as yet, much of the communication infrastructure is old and unreliable.

If the Internet can be said to have anything like a core, then this would be the *backbones,* which are the primary networks which serve as a framework for the Internet all around the world. At the beginning, in the US, the ARPAnet served as the backbone; now this role is fulfilled by a combination of public and private organizations.

Packet switching

One of the founding guidelines of the Internet was that it had to be robust in the case of disruption (whether this was a result of a nuclear attack or alien road diggers). This requirement would not be satisfied by a network system where messages between two specific computers always travelled by the same route – if that route was closed, the two computers would be unable to communicate with each other.

So, the solution devised was *packet switching*, where the computer sending a message first divides that message into small parts, then packages each part into small electronic envelopes (packets). It includes the address of the recipient computer in each envelope and then fires them off to the Internet. The first computer down the line will receive the first packet, read the address and then forward it to the next computer as best it can. (*See* 'Internet addresses' page 13 for more information about this procedure.)

Thus, all messages become path-independent, and will be routed around the Net until eventually arriving at the correct destination. But inherent in this system is the possibility that different packets of the same message may take different routes to the destination computer.

Some other advantages of packet switching are:

- if one packet is corrupted during transmission then only that particular packet need be retransmitted – not the whole message
- maximum use of bandwidth can be made by allowing other data traffic between the discrete packages.

This simple idea has become one of the principal defining characteristics of the Internet – which can be described as a *packet-switching network*.

TCP/IP

That's all very well, you might think, but some pretty strict rules are going to be needed to control all of this – we don't want stray digital packets casually bumbling around the world taking the scenic route from Tokyo to Osaka via the sea-front casino in Monte Carlo.

Recall that our definition of the Internet had computers communicating *using a certain set of rules*. In fact, there are many layers of different sets of rules, but for the moment we will look at the foundation levels – called the *TCP/IP protocols*.

The rules governing communication between computers are called *protocols*, and can be regarded something like the rules of grammar for the English language (where, for example, sentences generally begin with an upper case letter, end with a full stop and may have various punctuation marks contained within the body of the text).

The Internet Protocol (IP) is the fundamental set of rules that governs communication of *all* data across the Internet (see Figure 1.1).

Internet protocol

1 Every computer on the Internet will have an Internet address.
2 All Internet messages are divided into small packets.
3 Each packet is contained in an IP envelope.
4 The IP envelope will also contain the destination address and the address of the computer sending the message.

▧ FIG 1.1

This is the first level that begins to codify a set of rules to control this packet-switching network. The next level up is called *Transmission Control Protocol* (TCP), and this organizes the separate packets transmitted.

For example, with a large message, TCP will split the data into several packets, each packet will be placed in a TCP envelope (which will also contain information about the size of the packet and its position relative to the greater message being sent), and then the TCP envelope is placed in the IP envelope. So, if the message was split into 15 packets, the TCP envelope with the first packet would contain the information '1 of 15' and the second packet would have '2 of 15' etc. On receipt by the destination computer, the IP envelopes are opened, then the TCP envelopes are opened, and all the packets arranged in order to re-form the original complete message.

When using the Internet it may seem that communication stalls at some points even though the line generally appears fast. This may be caused by individual packets becoming corrupted (and having to be re-sent) or one packet taking a different route and the whole message having to wait to be completed.

If you are using a PC with Windows you will need a program called *winsock.dll*. This translates data from the computer applications into the TCP/IP protocol used on the Internet. (In theory, all of this should be fairly transparent to the user; in practice, however, the *winsock.dll* is a common cause of problems due to incompatibility with certain software programs.)

Internet addresses

We saw in the description above of the *Internet Protocol* that every computer on the Internet must have an Internet address (which is called, oddly, the *Internet Protocol Address*). By convention, this address is composed of four numbers (each less than 256). For example, 205.216.162.12 is an address for the search engine company, Yahoo.

Side notes

- The addressing system has a capacity to reference approximately 4.2 billion (256^4) computers on the Internet – roughly the current human population of the world.

- If you link to the Internet with a PC through an Internet Access Provider (IAP), the provider has an allocation of Internet addresses, one of which will be dynamically assigned to your computer during the period of connection.

Domain Names

As random numbers are difficult to remember (and it is easy to make mistakes transcribing), the Internet provides *Domain Names*, which are simple words representing the actual numerical Internet address.

For example, the Domain Name for the Internet address 205.216.162.12 is surf.yahoo.com.

The Domain Name may have many parts (separated by a stop) and reads from right to left in descending levels of size. The .com signifies that this is a commercial company (the other high-level Domain Names are shown in Figure 1.2). The second level Domain signifies that the company name is Yahoo, and the last that this address belongs to a specific computer called 'surf' at Yahoo.

> ### High-level Domains
>
> com Commercial organizations
> edu Educational institutions
> gov Government entities
> int International organizations
> mil Military (US)
> net Network operations
> org Other organizations

▨ FIG 1.2

Another form of the highest level Domain is a country signifier. For example, the futures exchange in Singapore has the Web site address **http://www.simex.com.sg** where the final 'sg' indicates that this is a Singapore Domain. (Every country in the world has been given a two-letter abbreviation, an index of which can be found in the appendix.)

Each country will have a designated body that looks after the registration of the *Domain Names*. By convention, large US companies usually have just a .com address (as with Yahoo above), and registration of these Domains is controlled by the *Internet Network Information Center* (InterNIC, **http://rs.internic.net**).

These Domain Names are the constituents of what is called the *Domain Name System* (DNS, alternatively called *Domain Name Service*), which uses designated computers around the world as directory *nameservers*. If you send a message to surf.yahoo.com your computer (or IAP) will first send it to a nameserver to convert the text address to 205.216.162.12.

Various facilities exist on the Internet to cross-reference *addresses* (numbers) with *names* (text) or to identify the registered owners of a particular Domain Name. A good list of these can be found at **http://http.demon.net/external/ntools.html**

▨ Routers

To summarize:

1 Messages are packaged into discrete, small packets (governed by *TCP Protocol*).
2 Each packet is placed in another packet containing a unique destination name (*IP Protocol*).
3 If necessary, the destination names (*Domain Names*) are converted to *Internet addresses* (by *nameservers*).

The final part is to explain how these packets find their way quickly and efficiently to the correct destination. This is achieved by computers on the Internet called *routers*, which have stored instructions on how to forward packets in the appropriate direction. There are actually many different routeing strategies that individual routers may use – some might take into account current routeing traffic and which backbone is operational.

Intranet

An intranet is simply a private network that uses the foundation TCP/IP protocols of the Internet to communicate between computers on the network. Hence, for a company, it is like having a mini Internet within its own private network. This has many advantages, including the ability to use off-the-shelf WWW browsers and to create documents as Web pages and make them available company-wide. A company's intranet may, or may not, be connected to the Internet.

(A small point, but it may contribute to confusion: there is one Internet in the world, but there can be any number of intranets. Any two computers connected together and communicating using TCP/IP is an intranet – regardless of whether the computers are further connected to the Internet or not. In addition, intranets are not a proprietary technology, and, thus, do not necessarily need to be spelt with a capital letter.)

Bandwidth and speed

You can never be too rich, too thin, or have too much bandwidth
Information Week 22 January 1996

The Internet comprises millions of linked computers, employing many different mediums of connection: telephone lines, optical fibre, wireless etc. Further, the hardware and method of communication over specific mediums (e.g. a telephone line) are varied as well. Each communication method can be rated by its speed of transmitting data, measured as number of bits per second (bps), and this rating characterizes the bandwidth of the medium.

Table 1.2 summarizes the different communication methods.

■ TABLE 1.2 **Capacity comparison for different communication links**

Communication method	Capacity	Medium	Connection
POTS	< 33Kbps	twisted-pair	switched
56K	56Kbps	twisted-pair	switched/ dedicated
ISDN	128Kbps	twisted-pair	switched
T1	1.54Mbps	twisted-pair	dedicated
ADSL/ HDSL	6Mbps	twisted-pair	dedicated
T3	45Mbps	fibre optic	dedicated
SONET	> 51.84Mbps	fibre optic	dedicated

Notes to Table 1.2:

POTS: 'plain ol' telephone system' – meaning connecting a computer to the telephone network using a modem
twisted-pair: twisted-pair copper wire is the standard telephone line connection
switched: a dial-up connection, enabling different numbers to be called
dedicated: a fixed line, that cannot be used to connect with different numbers

At any time, the speed of sending a message via the Internet will be governed by a combination of the general amount of traffic (data being transmitted) and the path of the message over the various different communication methods.

The World Wide Web is based on the HyperText Mark-up Language (HTML). As the name suggests, it was originally devised as a method for linking *text* documents that contained a basic level of formatting (e.g. bold, italics). Then someone had the bright idea of including images into these pages.

Images were just the start, sound and video files soon followed. With the sudden growth of non-text files being transmitted over the Internet (and accompanied by the general increase in the number of users), the overall bandwidth of the Internet was insufficient, and data transfer times started falling. Much money is now being spent in an effort to improve the Internet bandwidth, by installing higher grade communication channels.

But transfer times will always be governed by the slowest link in the communication chain and the size of the file being transferred. For example, the characters on this page comprise roughly 3K bytes (which is approximately 24 000 bits of data); therefore, a standard modem with speed of 28 800bps can transfer just over a page of this text every second. But, just one good colour image file might have a size of 100K bytes (approximately 800 000 bits), which would take 27 seconds to transfer.

Who is in charge of all this?

The last 100 years have accustomed us to government and organization control, so, despite reading about the history and mechanism of the Internet, people still ask, 'who controls it?'

But the question has as much meaning as asking who controls the English language. The answer is, of course, nobody – but this is a very difficult idea for people to accept.

There are some organizations that have influence within the Internet, but they have no real control. For example, the Internet Society is a voluntary committee composed of the great and the good. They act as a central forum for discussions on protocol amendments (e.g. extending Internet Protocol to allow more addresses), and they also act as a co-ordinating body for sub-committees researching technical issues – but they cannot be said to control the Internet.

WHO IS ON THE INTERNET?

In the Middle Ages, theologians would argue among themselves the question of how many angels could dance on the end of a pin. Some centuries later, we have the new believers arguing how many people are linked to the Internet. And the current debate is just as interesting, obscure, difficult to verify and ultimately irrelevant.

But this is already big business. Surveys are produced, and then attacked by other surveys, which are in turn criticized by reports on the philosophy of Internet measurement. If you are an analyst trying to estimate future revenues of America Online, this might be important, but for the rest, it is likely that anecdotal evidence is as useful as anything; for example, the fact that at the beginning of 1996, CompuServe was signing up 10 000 new clients each week in the UK alone. Or compare the number of people you know who have e-mail addresses today with the number two years ago. As a spokesman at Xerox said, 'Yeah, we're in a hurricane, and they are arguing about whether the wind is blowing 150 miles an hour or 120 miles an hour.'

The current consensus (mid 1996) is that there are 30 million people using the Internet; but with some Web sites seeing activity growing ten per cent monthly, it doesn't matter much if the real Internet population is 25 or 35 million at any one specific time.

COMPONENTS

The Internet is not one homogeneous entity, but merely a collection of computers agreeing to communicate with each other following some basic low-level rules (*TCP/IP protocols*). These base protocols merely look after the addressing and routeing of packets of data to be passed around the Internet. Further rules are required to govern the format of the data within the packets. Without these, computers would not know what to do with data packets they receive from all types of different computers around the world.

At this point, it is helpful to remember that the Internet was not conceived as a method for hyper-jumping between documents or even for sending text messages. The origin of the Net was just a simple method of linking computers, and it is upon this foundation that an amazing digital world has been developed that is a tribute to both the flexibility of the original design and the ingenuity of cyber-architects.

This digital world comprises a whole range of different procedures that have evolved for use over the Internet, with each procedure controlled by its own set of higher level protocols. The more common components of the Internet are:

- *e-mail* – to send electronic messages between networks (SMTP – simple mail transfer protocol)
- *WWW* – the World Wide Web, a system of viewing interlinked documents held on different computers (HTTP – HyperText Transfer Protocol)
- *Usenet* – a method of posting messages to an electronic bulletin board that all people can see and reply to publicly (NNTP – Net News Transfer Protocol).

As these are likely to be the most important functions for investors on the Internet, these are described in some detail below. Some of the other Internet functions are:

- Archie
- FTP
- Gopher
- Hytelnet
- IPhone
- IRC

- MUDs
- Telnet
- Veronica
- VRML
- WAIS

These are not described in detail here, although brief definitions are given in the glossary. Many of these other features are either becoming obsolete, or are increasingly being assimilated into the functionality of the new Web browsers.

Electronic mail (e-mail)

It would be worth connecting to the Internet, and struggling with the hassles of modems, initialization strings, *winsock* conflicts and everything else, if all the Internet offered was e-mail. It is one of the great inventions of the 20th century – one of the simplest, but most powerful of Internet tools.

E-mail is a method of writing messages on a computer, which can then be sent to another computer on a connected network. The network involved might just be a small internal network within a company, or the Internet with its connected user base of millions of people. Strictly, only text messages can be sent by e-mail (meaning just pure text without characters in bold, italics or different fonts); but there are ways of e-mailing documents with formatted text or, indeed, all types of multimedia files (*see 'Encoding'*, page 25).

The benefits of e-mail can be seen as being:

- **Low cost**: the costs incurred with e-mail are the telephone charge to the local Internet node, plus the cost of access to the Internet (the monthly *IAP* charges). Considering that many messages can be sent in just a few seconds (to destinations all around the world), it can be seen that the *per message* cost falls almost to zero. Certainly the cost can be considered negligible compared to the direct communication costs of telephone or fax, or the postal charges for letters.

- **Speed**: messages can be sent around the world in a matter of minutes, although e-mail does not yet offer the immediacy, or reliability, of telephone or fax (and, due to the rapid expansion of the Internet, some e-mail messages can get delayed occasionally for some days). However, this should not be taken as a failure of the e-mail system as such, but rather a symptom of the current inadequate Internet infrastructure.

- **Efficiency**: e-mail messages can be very short (the briefer the better), not requiring the formality of letters or fax, or the five-minute 'weather comment' prelude to a telephone conversation. An even greater benefit than brevity, though, is the organizational capability. This allows for all e-mails to be easily filed into topic areas, and then (very importantly) provides the ability to search automatically all e-mails for particular dates, sender, subject heading, stock mentioned etc. – far better than wading through a filing cabinet of curling paper looking for a fax from that chap with a name like Ngokovsky sent last April (or was it August?).

An advantage over the telephone is that e-mail offers the convenience of receiving communication only when you choose to (although the telephone answering machine, like the video recorder, is one of the most liberating inventions of recent times – while the telephone and television themselves are among the most enslaving). But e-mail also provides an automatic archive of discussions, while details of telephone conversations are easily forgotten.

The death of fax

The facsimile machine is one of the strangest beasts in the techno-jungle. Imagine a delivery lorry with goods arriving at a river; here the lorry is taken apart and re-assembled as a boat which then sails across the river. At the other side the lorry is re-assembled and on it goes. This would be strange behaviour at any time, but if at the same place there was a regular ferry for carrying lorries, the activity would be truly bizarre. But this is the principle of how fax machines work. The majority of faxes are initially created on a computer, and then printed onto paper. The fax machine scans the paper, and creates a picture of the message and this picture is then transmitted. But the picture takes up to ten times longer to transmit than the corresponding text sent direct from the computer as an e-mail would take. Further, the fax must communicate directly with a receiving fax machine (possibly incurring long-distance telephone charges), while e-mail involves just a local call.

This would be bad enough on its own; but the lorry analogy as it stands is too kind to the fax. A better analogy would have the boats arriving at the other side of the river, and then being hauled up onto the dry land and left to rust in the company of hundreds of other boats in a similar predicament. The goods to be delivered are still intact, but there is nothing one can do with them, and the lorry is no more.

Data that is in digital form (as existing in a computer) is very flexible – it can be manipulated and transmitted very easily. But faxes take data and destroy the digital form. Old faxes must be stored in bulky filing cabinets, it is not possible to quickly search thousands of them, and they cannot be directly adapted and incorporated into other documents. All this is possible with e-mail.

One might ask, if faxes are so terrible, why are they so popular and ubiquitous? The answer lies partly with the Japanese: fax machines were eminently suitable for transmitting their character-based scripts (which are more difficult to digitize than Western alphabets), and the Japanese consumer electronics companies mass-produced, and successfully marketed, fax machines worldwide. And the demand was there by a quirk of timing: although e-mail is older than fax, the latter was cheaper and easier to implement in the early days, and the new digital economics (the law of *increasing* returns – otherwise called, for good reason, the *fax effect*) quickly took hold with a large installed user base encouraging further growth. But time has moved on, computers have developed enormously in the last ten years, and fax technology has not. Perhaps in the years to come people will look back at the fax machine (as people do towards the old penny farthing bicycle) and think, *what a wonderful machine, thank goodness we don't have to use it any more.* (Stock tip: sell fax machine companies, but buy scanning technologies – there are a lot of filing cabinets out there to be digitized.)

Does it matter that the fax machine is anachronistic? In practice, not really; but it has probably been responsible for retarding the general acceptance of computer communication, and thereby resulting in a few billion dollars' worth of lost productivity, but this is merely a temporary aberration. More importantly, it is a litmus test: those people who still regard the fax as a pretty neat machine, will have problems understanding the implications of the digital age.

E-mail is not (yet) a complete replacement for the telephone, fax or post, but it is likely that over half of all current communication by those means would be better conducted by e-mail.

Using e-mail

There tend to be four stages of progression when people first start using e-mail:

1 **Confusion**: with the mechanics of the whole thing. How to reply to messages, where to find an e-mail address, losing messages etc.

2 **Delight**: when realizing that messages can be sent to people in countries everywhere, and that people respond! Leading to . . .

3 **Desperation**: as the e-mail in-box begins to fill up with too many messages every day, and replying to them all takes longer and longer.

4 **Acceptance**: the pendulum swings back into the middle when people learn how to deal efficiently with electronic messages, the technology fades into the background and e-mail becomes an ordinary tool.

▓ Effective e-mail

A hundred years ago, letter writing and reading were leisurely affairs – one imagines Sherlock Holmes examining postmarks on his three letters of the day (over the breakfast tea, marmalade toast and cocaine). Today, many people receive over 50 e-mail messages daily, and have only a few minutes to deal with them. It is important, therefore, that for messages to be effective, they must be concise. A few recommendations for writing e-mails are:

▓ The great advantage of e-mails over letters, is that they can be in the form of a memo – no formality is required. Get **straight to the point**, with, if possible, the reason for the message appearing in the first few lines (it can be frustrating scrolling through screens of rambling text).

▓ Text presentation on computer monitors is not one of the great achievements of the modern age – it is awkward and tiring to read. So, compose messages with this in mind: for example, **don't write long paragraphs of text**, break them up into smaller units with each paragraph being just a few lines long. (Should there be any conflict between grammar, and presentation for better comprehension, err on the side of the latter.)

▓ **Don't try to get too clever with the layout** of the messages (e.g. including tabs), as the recipient may well be using a different e-mail program with a different monitor that alters the presentation of the message entirely.

▓ Don't worry about including information about who the message is to, from, its date or subject in the body of the text – all this is included in the message header.

▓ The **subject heading** should be as precise and detailed as space allows. If the editor of a gold investment newsletter receives 50 e-mails daily, it will not be very useful if many of those e-mails carry the subject heading, 'Gold!'.

Reference – e-mail

http://www.webfoot.com/advice/email.top.html – a beginner's guide to e-mail

http://www.uiuc.edu/ccso/other.html#email – list of reference sources

http://www.cis.ohio-state.edu/hypertext/faq/bngusenet/comp/mail/misc/top.html – list of all different FAQs about e-mail

newsgroup: comp.mail.misc

▓ FIG 1.3

E-mail addresses

E-mail addresses are composed of two parts separated by the '@' symbol, for example, 'resu@krowten.irk.ru'. The part to the left of @ is the name of the user, and the right-hand part is the user's location (or, more precisely, the location of the user's e-mail account). The location address is read from right to left in decreasing size: country, network, computer.

An e-mail sent to the above address would be routed to a Russian computer (the final 'ru' signifying Russia), where it would refer to a directory to look up 'irk' (standing for the Siberian town of Irkutsk – although small regional identifiers like this are fairly rare in e-mail addresses). It would further find a directory at some point on its travels to look up 'krowten'. Arriving at the computer 'krowten', the message would be directed to the e-mail account of the user, 'resu'. (*See* 'Domain Names', page 13 for more information about addresses.)

Finding e-mail addresses

If you want to look up the telephone number or address of somebody, it seems obvious that there will be directories to help – after all, what is the point of having a telephone if nobody can find your number (excepting those who specifically want anonymity)? But, one of the results of the decentralized nature of the Internet is that there is no comprehensive official (or even unofficial) directory of e-mail addresses for Internet users. This can be one of the first problems encountered by people new to the Internet, and can prompt reactions like, 'who's in charge here, can't they get their act together?' The answer being, of course, no one is in charge. If you want a directory, how about setting one up yourself – and this is what some companies have done.

There is no one optimal method for finding an e-mail address. Rather, a series of techniques can be tried, that will in most cases eventually reveal the address. These are:

1   By far the easiest solution is to ask somebody for their e-mail address directly (by telephone or letter). Frequently, nowadays, people have their e-mail addresses printed on their business card.

2   The next procedure is to try some of the online directories:
    http://www.four11.com – considering the scale of the problem, this is a surprisingly good service
    http://www.iaf.net
    http://www.whowhere.com – not as comprehensive as the above, but includes a company directory as well.
    http://www.switchboard.com – very comprehensive and provides telephone numbers and addresses, but as yet is only for the US.
    The above, in varying degrees, offer the ability to search for somebody by name, first name, or parts of a remembered e-mail address, and will return close matches. In addition, they offer the possibility of 'anonymous' listing (whereby an e-mail address is not displayed following a search, but it is possible for the searcher to send an e-mail via the system, and the recipient can reply if they wish).

3   One can try one of the Internet general search engines: the best being *Alta Vista* or *DejaNews*. Use these to search on the Web and newsgroups – it is quite possible that if somebody has an e-mail address, their name will appear on a Web page somewhere or they may have written to a newsgroup. The effectiveness of such a search will be determined in part by the exclusivity of the searched-for name (e.g. Smith or Shazbat). (*See* 'Search engines', page 267.)

4   Failing all the above, the final resort is to guess (this is not quite as hopeless as it may appear). First, it helps if you know the company where the person works. If you know this, then you can probably find the *location* part of the e-mail address. For example, you could guess (and be right) that the address of Morgan Stanley is 'ms.com'; alternatively, use a search engine to find the company name and thereby its e-mail address. If the company has a Web page – or shows up in newsgroup searches – it may be possible to determine the style of the *user* name at the company. For example, if you are looking for a Nicholas Leeson, and see that other people in the same company have e-mail addresses such as 'sbrown' or 'jdupont', there is a good chance that an e-mail to 'nleeson' will work. If this fails, an enquiry message to the postmaster at the company may yield something (e.g. postmaster@company.com).

Interpreting message headers

E-mail messages are composed of two parts: the first part is the *header* at the beginning (this displays information about the message), while the rest of the message following is called the *body*. Usually one can ignore the header. Indeed, it can appear a nuisance when the header is 20 lines long and the body just contains, 'OK, go ahead'. However, it can be very interesting to analyse this header sometimes to find out more about the origins of certain messages received.

The best way to understand these headers is to look at an actual example (*see* Figure 1.4).

It can be seen that the header (in Fig 1.4) is similar to any message received over the Internet – albeit a bit longer at the beginning, perhaps. Line numbers have been added (which would not normally be there) for easy reference, and some names and addresses changed. We will look at this header line by line.

▩   **Line 1**: the message was sent by somebody with a user name of resu and an e-mail address, resu@krowten.irk.ru (see above for further information on the address). The 'Sender:' field contains the authenticated identity of the person sending the message, and this should be the same as that in the 'From:' field (line 11). If it is not the same, it might be because the sender was using another computer temporarily, or that the 'From:' field contains a group name. However, it might also indicate that there is something wrong with the message (i.e. that it is a forgery).

Example e-mail message header

```
1    Sender: resu@krowten.irk.ru
2    Received: from relay-1.mail.demon.net (relay-
        1.mail.demon.net [158.152.1.140]) by arl-img-
        5.compuserve.com(8.6.10/5.950515)
        id HAA10793; Sat, 6 Apr 1996 07:02:32 -0500
3    Received: from punt.demon.co.uk ([158.152.1.73]) by
        relay-1.mail.demon.net
        id ad23565; 6 Apr 96 13:02 +0100
4    Received: from ccsoan.irkutsk.su ([193.124.118.177]) by
        punt-1.mail.demon.net
        id aa06395; 6 Apr 96 12:59 +0100
5    Received: from krowten.UUCP by icc.ru with UUCP id
        AA07493(5.65.kiae-1 ); Sat, 6 Apr 1996 20:54:09 -0800
6    Received: by krowten.irk.ru (UUPC/@ v6.13beta, 12Nov94);
        id AA22770 Sat, 6 Apr 1996 19:53:50 -0800
7    To: 73522.1315@compuserve.com
8    Cc: lenin@numa.com
9    Message-Id: <AAUfqPnGs1@krowten.irk.ru>
10   Organization: Private
11   From: "Emantsrif.Resu" <resu@krowten.irk.ru>
12   Date: Sat, 6 Apr 96 19:53:50 -0900
13   X-Mailer: BML [MS/DOS Beauty Mail v1.36h]
14   Subject: Gorbachev?
15   Lines: 6
16   Mime-Version: 1.0
17   Content-Type: text/plain; charset=us-ascii
18   Content-Transfer-Encoding: 7bit
19   Content-Length: 145
```

■ FIG 1.4

■ **Lines 2–6**: these lines describe the route taken, in reverse order, by the message as it was passed from one network to another across the Internet. Line 4 shows the computer, ccsoan.irkutsk.su (still using the old 'su' country identifier for Russia), passing the message onto 1.mail.demon.net, which shuffled it on to another computer in the same organization (line 3) which in turn finally passed it on to a computer at CompuServe (line 2). The time taken by the message can also be tracked – each computer logs the time the message was received in 24-hour format local time. The relationship between local time and Universal Time (UT) is indicated by the four-digit number after the time (so, for example, local time for the CompuServe computer, '-0500', is five hours behind UT).

■ **Line 7**: this should be your e-mail address; if it is something different (for example, eurobigbizwiz@eurobigbizwiz.com) this indicates that your address is on a mailing list, which is being used to send to many recipients at once).

■ **Line 8**: will show a list of addresses to which the same message has been copied. However, this field will be blank (or not appear) if the sender selected to copy messages using 'Blind CC' – which would be a choice in their e-mail program.

■ **Line 9**: every message sent over the Internet is given a unique identifier. This can occasionally prove useful when trying to track specific messages.

■ **Line 10**: the organization name is not necessarily authenticated, but merely relays the name originally input to the e-mail program sending the message.

■ **Line 11**: as above, this information will usually just come from the e-mail program sending the message (with no subsequent verification).

This shows that it would not be too difficult to forge a message from thepope@vatican.org.

■ **Line 13**: you can quite often see header lines beginning with an 'x'. These are not part of the Internet communication protocols, but are merely extra bits of information inserted by the e-mail program. Here, the program Beauty Mail has inserted a little publicity for itself.

■ **Lines 16–18**: these are concerned with defining the type of data being sent. This, as shown, is ordinary ASCII text. (This is covered in detail in the next section).

With the knowledge of the overview given above, it can be interesting to send a message to yourself, and inspect the subsequent header information.

Encoding (sending binary files by e-mail)

Computers cannot send letters (for example, the letter 'D') directly as characters to another computer. Instead, they use a translation method for representing each letter with a number. There are a few different methods for doing this, but by far the most widespread – so much so that it has become a world standard – is the representation code called ASCII (American Standard Code for Information Interchange).

■ ASCII

ASCII is a standard procedure for mapping 128 upper and lower case letters, numbers, punctuation marks and some symbols to the numbers 0–127. (A reference table for all the 128 characters can be found at **http://ei.cs.vt.edu/~netinfo/asciitable.html**.) For example, in ASCII, the letter 'D' will always be represented by the number 68.

However, computers cannot communicate with each other directly using decimal numbers either (if you could look into a communications wire between two computers, you would not see anything looking like a '6' or '8' flying past). So, a further translation occurs, whereby the decimal numbers are translated into binary numbers (the binary representation for 68 being 01000100).

The 0s and 1s of binary numbers *can* be communicated between computers. In fact, this is the basis for all digital communication, and the digital age that is dawning is all about representing 'everything' digitally, leading to the connectivity of everything to everything.

∎ 7-bit

The binary representation for 127 is 1111111; so we need seven binary digits (*bits*) – up to 1111111 – to represent all the decimal numbers 0–127. Because of this, the binary representation of ASCII is called *7-bit*.

When e-mail was first being thought about, in the early days of the Internet, the 128 ASCII characters were considered perfectly adequate for text messages between computers. And so the protocols to control e-mail communications were designed around a 7-bit structure.

Everything works fine up to here. However, the ASCII set does not stop at 128 characters – another 128 characters exist with numerical representations in what is called the 'extended character set'. This includes symbols like '£', '¥' and the special characters used in non-English alphabets, for example, 'é'.

(If you would like to see more of these characters and are using MS Windows, have a look at the Character Map program – usually found in the *Accessories* box. This displays 224 characters: the first three lines are characters 32–127 of the *standard* ASCII set, while the remaining four lines show the 128 characters of the *extended* set.)

A problem that can arise is that, whereas base ASCII is a *standard* standard, the extended set is a *sometimes* standard. Some programs, written in different countries, may decide that they don't need the symbol 'ß' (in the extended set) and decide to replace it in the number representation table with something else. There is no problem with this while the program manipulates data itself, or communicates with other similar programs; but confusion can arise if the program tries to exchange data with another program that does use the 'standard' extended character set.

Thus, while we can be sure that the letter 'D' will always be mapped correctly (to the number 68), we cannot have the same confidence with characters in the extended set.

Another problem that arises is when trying to send messages containing characters from the extended set by Internet e-mail. We saw above that the Internet e-mail procedure is based on a 7-bit structure. But to represent ASCII character numbers 128–255 of the extended set, an extra bit is required (i.e. an 8-digit binary number is needed to represent numbers up to 255 = 11111111). The standard 7-bit Internet e-mail protocols expect messages to be sent and received in blocks of seven bits; the system does not work if an extra bit is added to each block.

An interesting experiment is to send an Internet e-mail to yourself with the body containing, '$$$ – £££ – ¥¥¥ – $$$', and to see what comes back. Often the £ and ¥ symbols will be replaced or missing (the reason being that the £

and ¥ symbols are in the extended set, while the $ is in the base set – after all, this is the *American* Standard Code for Information Interchange). While all this is in the context of e-mail, similar problems may be encountered with messages to Usenet newsgroups.

Therefore, if you are sending a message using extended set symbols (like the £ sign), be aware that the recipient may not see exactly what you have written, and it is always wise to spell out important symbols in words (for example, currencies: 'UK Pounds Sterling' for £, or 'Japanese Yen' for ¥).

Note: messages exchanged within CompuServe (i.e. from one member to another) do not suffer from this problem, as CompuServe, being a private network, uses an 8-bit e-mail system and not the 7-bit Internet e-mail protocol.

Text and binary files

A distinction is made between two different types of computer file: *text* files and *binary* files. The former are centred on the base ASCII character set (strictly, *text files* just contain the printable ASCII characters with codes 10, 13, and 32–126), while binary files are all the other files – usually containing 8-bit characters. So, anything that is not a text file is a binary file: this includes, graphics, sound files and, rather oddly it may seem, some word processor files (this is because the word processor uses the non-text characters to indicate formatting within the document).

▧ UUENCODE

Things have moved on quite a bit since the first Internet protocols were being devised, and now people want to send more than just boring text files by e-mail; they want to include the non-English alphabet characters and to be able to send graphics, documents and all types of multimedia files as well. As described above, it is not possible to send these binary files (with 8-bit characters) directly by Internet e-mail – so a program, *uuencode*, was developed to get around the problem. What this program does is to take the 8-bit binary file and code it into a file containing only 7-bit characters, which can then be transmitted with no trouble; and upon receipt at the other end, the recipient will Uu*de*code the message back to the original 8-bit file.

Figure 1.5 shows the beginning of a file that has been uuencoded; if you receive a message that looks like this, you will have to decode it first. There are a few other methods to code binary files for transfer over e-mail (such as XX or Binhex), but Uuencode is the most common one in use.

Note: this coding (for the purposes of sending binary files by e-mail) is *not* the same as encrypting messages.

Uuencoded file

```
begin 644 7-BIT.WRI
M,;X```"K```````````"%%%0`#0@T`#00````````````````"`%#``````#0@8`
M,,,M9M!1&F+E.&P&L[(P&Q&m$(l3l`L.`V&m*sl$#m%m@1###############################
M<R!W:&5N('1H92"<*$="'4";"!N;:WON("!)=;"!C86XG=`T*<&]S<VEB
```

▉ **FIG 1.5**

▉ MIME

Although the above uuencoding works fine, it is something of an ad hoc 'work-around', that requires both sender and recipient to know that a file has been uuencoded and to understand what to do with it. MIME – *Multipurpose Internet Mail Extensions* – is an attempt to establish a standard for attaching non-text files to standard Internet e-mail, where the files, as they pass across the Internet, will be treated in a consistent manner. Thus, e-mail programs that are *MIME compliant*, will be able to recognize what type of file is being received and know what to do with it. In Figure 1.4 the final part of the e-mail header included MIME information: line 16, line 17 (indicating that the data in the message was ordinary text), and line 18 (showing that the data was already in 7-bit form, so no translation is necessary).

Warning: viruses **cannot** be transferred directly by e-mail, only by programs introduced into a computer. But, uuencoding and MIME are a hybrid e-mail procedure, that can effectively transfer a program onto your computer. Any program will be harmless while it remains as a 'text' message – before it has been decoded. But once decoded it must be treated with all the usual caution accorded to a new program.

Anonymous messages

When an e-mail is sent over the Internet, it carries the address of the sender of the message. As we saw above ('Interpreting message headers', page 23), it *is* possible to forge messages, so that the header information (including the e-mail address of the sender) is false. However, in these cases, it is still sometimes possible to identify the real origins of the message. But what if somebody wants to send a message that is truly untraceable?

The Internet, with its ability to provide an infinitely flexible service for anybody, has the answer with *anonymous remailers*. Somebody wanting to send an untraceable message will post it *via* one of these remailers (which are on a few computers dotted around the world); the remailer receives the message, strips off all the header information identifying the source of the message, and then posts it on to the intended destination.

If the recipient of the message wants to track the route of the message, he will get back to the remailer computer – but no further (some remailers offer the facility to send a message back to original sender).

Why would law-abiding people want to send anonymous messages? Examples are given of employees wanting to blow the whistle on corporate wrongdoing, or people afraid of persecution etc. The service is usually offered by computer operators who believe strongly in the freedom of the Internet and privacy for the individual. These services are currently offered free – although in the future privacy is likely to be big business on the Internet. Despite the laudable aims of anonymous remailers, it is not difficult to see the potential for abuse of such services.

This is obviously a very controversial area, involving some of the same issues as those for encryption.

Reference – anonymous messages

http://www.cs.berkeley.edu/~raph/remailer-list.html

http://www.well.com/user/abacard/re-mail.html – good non-technical introduction by the author of *Computer Privacy Handbook*, Andre Bacard [Peachpit Press]

newsgroups: alt.anonymous, alt.privacy.anon-server, alt.anonymous.messages

---

■ FIG 1.6

World Wide Web (WWW)

> *Ye follow wandering fires*
> *lost in the quagmire*
> *Lancelot and Elaine*, Alfred Tennyson

The original inspiration for the World Wide Web (WWW) cropped up in 1991, and two years later the first working example was created at the physics laboratory CERN, in Switzerland. It was thought a pretty neat idea, and by the beginning of 1993 there were 50 Web servers around the world – and the original WWW proponents were probably quite satisfied with its success. Then it took off. By the middle of 1996 the Web was doubling in size every four months, with new sites appearing every four seconds. For once, it is not hyperbole to say that there was very little precedent for this incredible growth.

Why? In truth the reasons cannot be found in technology (a Web browser is a very simple program, and the Web itself is frequently slow and frustrating). The real explanation must lie deeper, in the fields of psychology and sociology.

However, it is possible to explain why the original concept was warmly received. The 'World Wide Web' describes a collection of files (we might as well call them documents) that sit on computers around the world. All these computers are interconnected, and the documents themselves can be linked to each other, by embedding what are called 'hyperlinks' in the body of the document. These documents must then be viewed with a special program called a browser. To view a certain document, its URL (address of the document location) is given to the browser, which then contacts the remote server (computer), and requests the specified document. The server sends the document to the browser, which then displays it on the screen. Within the document there might be a hyperlink reference to another document, which, when clicked on, will cause the browser to start again and contact possibly a new server to request the new document.

By the middle of 1996 the Web was doubling in size every four months, with new sites appearing every four seconds. There was very little precedent for this incredible growth.

The foundation for the WWW is the HyperText Mark-up Language (HTML). Every document on the WWW is written in this language, and this informs the browser how the document should be displayed on the screen. HTML should not be confused with a programming language (such as C or BASIC), but is rather just a simple formatting code. For example, the HTML code

```
a <b>buy</b> recommendation
```

would produce on the screen something like,

a **buy** recommendation

To see more examples of HTML, the underlying source code for any Web page can be viewed within a browser (command: View | Document Source).

The success of the Web was sealed when the innocuous tag <img. . .> was added to the HTML set. This tag is used to embed images into Web pages, and overnight a million graphic Web designers were born. (It is also from the introduction of this tag that Internet pioneers would date the fall of the Net into a popular, commercial abyss.)

The inspiration for such a system as the WWW can be easily understood when one appreciates that its developers were academics, whose papers commonly contain many references to other papers. Before the Web, consulting these other papers meant requests to a paper-based library, or awkward attempts to find files somewhere on the nascent, and unorganized, Internet.

When the WWW was first introduced, it was just one of many different features on the Internet, and this was a problem with the Internet itself – there were so many different systems being used, each of which required its own program and instructions. Although the subsequent evolution and success of the WWW was not anticipated by its original developers, the technical reasons for its popularity were:

- It provided a simple intuitive, graphical interface, where hyperlinks, within the text itself, was a brilliant idea.
- Increasingly, it was realized that the WWW could integrate all the other disparate functionality of the Internet into the one coherent package.

Hence, a comparison has often been made between the WWW and MS Windows – the killer applications for the Internet and PCs respectively. While the comparison may not be technically accurate, the overall effect was similar: the introduction of MS Windows led to an increased use of PCs, and the WWW finally made the Internet accessible to all.

Tips for using browsers

A few recommendations for using browsers and surfing the Web.

- **No graphics**: the single most effective method of improving the speed of viewing Web pages is to switch off the auto-load of images. If you then want to see a specific image, just click on its graphic icon.
- **Save pages locally**: rather than spending time online reading long Web pages, it is better to save the Web page to your local hard disk (from the menu bar, use File | Save As. . .). Later, to read the page offline, load the file into the browser (using File | Open File. . .). Note: this will just save the text and not any images; if you want to save an image, place the cursor over the image and hold the right mouse button down.
- **Timing**: the speed of accessing certain servers will be greatly affected by the time of the day. The slowest period is always from the time that the US wakes up (this applies worldwide). If you are making heavy use of the Internet, it may be a good idea to use two Internet providers (e.g. CompuServe and another) as their respective connections to the Internet may offer optimal viewing at different times of the day, or for different geographical regions.
- **Error 404**: when retrieving a file, a browser makes contact with the appropriate remote server, and requests the specific file containing the Web page. If the Web server cannot find the file, it returns the dreaded message, 'Error 404 – file not found'. If you get this message, and you want to persevere, try 'walking' up the directory tree. For example, if an Error 404 is received when looking for:

  http://www.ynapmoc.com/abc/def/ghij.html
  try
  http://www.ynapmoc.com/abc/def/
  and then
  http://www.ynapmoc.com/abc/
  etc.

- **Page date**: it can be useful to see when a Web page was last updated: the command, View | Document Info will return information about the Web page (including its last amended date).

▦ **Bookmark contents page**: the home (initial) page of many sites can be a graphic design delight – and a data disaster (i.e. big image files with no useful content). In such cases, it may be preferable to bookmark a more boring-looking, but informative contents page for the site, rather than the home page.

▦ **Open multiple windows**: most browsers allow more than one window to be open at one time (File | New Web Browser). Depending on your network set-up, it may not be possible for more than one window to retrieve a Web page at the same time. However, it can be useful to read one long Web page in one window, while the other retrieves another page; or to keep an index page (or the results of a search engine) in one window, while using the other to look at new pages.

▦ **Taking notes**: if you want to take notes from several pages, open up a text editor (e.g. MS Notepad or Write) and keep it in the background, then on the Web pages themselves simply hold the left mouse button down, drag over the selected text, copy into the clipboard (Ctrl-C), switch to the text editor (Alt-Tab) and paste (Ctrl-V).

Java

The greatest development in the Web world since its original introduction has been the appearance of Java. This is a programming language developed by Sun Microsystems, that has two particular attractions:

▦ It can be used to liven up the otherwise static Web page (for example, with moving images or scrolling bars with updated news or prices).

▦ It works across many platforms (e.g. Windows/DOS, UNIX, Mac).

Most browsers now support Java, and it's likely that some of the most exciting new developments on the Web will be due to Java applications. This may have particular implications for the investor, with the development of more real-time quote and charting services.

> **Reference – Java**
>
> The best examples of Java applications on investment related sites are:
>
> Bulletproof – **http://www.bulletproof.com/**
> Robert's Online Pricers – **http://www.intrepid.com/~robertl/index.html**
> The Conductor – **http://www.HHconductor.com/**
>
> General sources for the Java language can be found at:
>
> Sun's Java company – **http://www.javasoft.com/**
> Gamelan (directory of Java applets – see glossary) – **http://www.gamelan.com/**

 FIG 1.7

Usenet (newsgroups)

They had no conversation properly speaking. They made use of the spoken word in much the same way as a guard of a train makes use of his flags or of his lantern.
Waiting for Godot, Samuel Beckett

One of the strongest forces driving the growth of the Internet is people's desire to communicate and interact. This has led to the development of e-mail, Internet Relay Chat, IPhone and newsgroups. The latter is one of the odder parts of the Internet. Quite often, when you read about problems on the Internet (for example, to do with pornography), it is the newsgroups that are involved. It is a peculiarly anarchic corner of the Internet, that for a long time has looked as if it might collapse under a mass of babbling chit-chat. And yet, somehow, it survives.

The idea behind newgroups is for users to be able to discuss topics of specific interest by using an electronic bulletin board. Someone will post a message to the bulletin board (with a particular subject heading), and everyone else can read and respond to the message, if they want to. Equally, any replies to the original message are public for all to read. If the string of messages about the one specific subject (identified by all carrying the same subject heading) becomes quite long, the messages are called a *thread*. At any time, a user can start a new thread, by posting a message with a different subject heading. At any one time, a newsgroup may have many different subjects being discussed – depending on its popularity.

> Newsgroups are a peculiarly anarchic corner of the Internet, that for a long time have looked as if they might collapse under a mass of babbling chit-chat. And yet, somehow, they survive.

Each individual newsgroup is an interest area within which users wish to discuss similar topics. For example, there is a newsgroup for discussions about the books of George Orwell, there is another for US stocks and another for holidays in Asia. When the newsgroups were first developing, there were just a few different areas of discussion, not surprisingly centred around computing. But then the number of newsgroups started growing and the topic areas broadened, until there are now over 10 000 newsgroups, and it is difficult to think of a subject that is not covered by some newsgroup. The collective term for all newsgroups is Usenet.

▦ Newsgroup names

The title of the newsgroup will usually give a clue to the topics being discussed within it. For example, the three newsgroups mentioned above are called:

    alt.books.george-orwell
    misc.invest.stocks
    rec.travel asia.

The 'alt', 'misc' and 'rec' labels preceding the subjects are an early attempt at classification for all these groups. A list of the major categories appears below.

alt	alternative topics
biz	business related
comp	computer
misc	miscellaneous
news	administrative topics about newsgroups themselves
rec	recreation (arts, hobbies)
sci	science
soc	social issues

This system, however, is not a rigid classification; it all – like so much else on the Internet – just fell into place as time went on. As mentioned before, the first groups tended to discuss computer matters, others started on scientific topics and social issues, and then some topics that didn't seem to fit any category – these were prefixed with 'misc'. Most newsgroups concerned with investment have the prefix, misc.invest. (Why not biz? Good question. Perhaps the computer administrators arranging this in the early days thought that topics like misc.invest.futures was similar to misc.actvism.progressive?)

Then some decidedly weird topics appeared, that did not sit well with the serious groups like misc.education.adult in the 'misc' hierarchy; so a new prefix of 'alt' was created. Needless to say, this latter category has been the fastest growing area of all the newsgroups. The categorization system has now broadened widely, with many different prefixes being used; most significantly, with the internationalization of the Internet, to incorporate identifiers for topics of unique interest to one country (for example, uk.politics.economics).

■ TABLE 1.3 The 20 most popular newsgroups

1	news.announce.newusers	11	rec.arts.erotica
2	alt.sex.stories	12	rec.arts.movies.reviews
3	alt.sex	13	comp.risks
4	rec.humor.funny	14	alt.tv.simpsons
5	news.newusers.questions	15	news.announce.newgroups
6	news.announce.important	16	alt.sex.bondage
7	comp.unix.questions	17	alt.sex.movies
8	alt.binaries.pictures.erotica	18	rec.arts.startrek.current
9	misc.jobs.offered	19	rec.humor
10	comp.lang.c++	20	rec.food.recipes

Source: G. Herbert, http://www.crl.com/~gherbert/ReCount/

▓ How it works

The mechanics of how Usenet works may seem as strange   the content of some of the messages. To receive newsgroups a host (a computer on the Internet) will set itself as a *news server*, and then arrange a news feed from another site. The procedure for all news servers can then be described as 'store and forward'. Each news server will periodically receive a bulk update of messages for newsgroups from another news server; these messages will be stored for a limited period and also forwarded on to other news servers. The messages are transmitted between computers using a set of rules called Network News Transfer Protocol (NNTP).

While the messages are stored on a particular news server, permitted users can access these and read them. If a user wants to add a reply to any message, this will be sent first to their local news server, where it will be stored for a while, and also it will be included in the next bulk transfer of messages onto the next news server. By this method, messages are propagated around news servers all over the world, although it may take some time for any particular message to appear on all news servers.

Thus, at any one time, the same message might be sitting on thousands of news servers worldwide, and megabytes of such messages are being relayed between news servers. This may not appear a terribly efficient system, but, as mentioned before, the Internet was not designed to be efficient.

▓ Usenet control

The above description should explain why the phrase 'Usenet control' is an oxymoron. Control of individual news servers is certainly possible, governed by the server's administrator. And in many cases, administrators *do* decide to limit the range and size of newsgroups that they will allow on their news server. A common restriction applied is to the range of sex newsgroups: this might be for reasons of prudery, but also a necessary restriction if the news server is not very large or fast as the sex newsgroups constitute one of the largest parts of Usenet traffic. If a particular user is irked because their news server does not carry a certain newsgroup, the options are limited: they can remonstrate with the server administrator, or try to access directly one of the free public news servers available on the Internet. However, in the latter case, these public servers are usually very busy and difficult to access.

Although control of individual news servers is therefore possible, such power does not necessarily extend to Usenet as a whole. This is not for the want of trying by many groups who would see society being undermined by the seditious chat of anarchists, vivisectionists (or anti-vivisectionsists) and possibly even currency traders. Putting aside for one moment the rights or wrongs of censorship in particular cases, it is difficult to see, technically, how effective general restrictions could be applied. Certainly a government could pass a law banning sex newsgroups (or a part of them), and this ban would then affect all news servers and the Internet Access Providers that run them. Fine. But what about internationally? The determined seditionist will simply connect to a news server outside the country. Perhaps a Global Conference On the Suppression of Naughty Things would do the trick. Possibly, although it is hard to see such countries as Holland, Iraq, Nigeria, Japan and Cuba agreeing a common policy on morality. Even if this was feasible, and the naughty newsgroups could be banned worldwide, perhaps the traffic will then merely migrate to newsgroups with names like alt.exotic.options. The next stage would therefore be to propose the monitoring of all newsgroups – naughtiness might be anywhere. A slippery slope.

> Although control of individual news servers is possible, such power does not necessarily extend to Usenet as a whole. This is not for the want of trying by many groups who see society being undermined by the seditious chat of anarchists, vivisectionists (or anti-vivisectionists) and possibly even currency traders.

As with much to do with the Internet, this is not an easy question, and there is most definitely no easy answer.

▓ Terminology

A brief word on terminology: the term *newsgroup* derives from the original idea which was to create an electronic newspaper, and the messages within newsgroups are traditionally called *articles*. As Usenet has evolved, both terms are now misleading: there is little news in newsgroups (chat or discussion-groups would be better, although more clumsy, names) and 'articles' is rather a grand term for messages, many of which contain just two lines of jabbering invective, lacking any capitalization, grammar, punctuation or sense. Another old term struggling to maintain the newspaper analogy is *subscribe*, used in the sense of subscribing to a newsgroup – to read the messages. It might have meant something once, but is now unnecessary and pretty much obsolete.

▓ Reading newsgroups

Usenet is still a completely independent part of the Internet – there are people that use e-mail and subscribe to newsgroups who never look at the WWW, and conversely many Web surfers who never read newsgroups. In the past, a dedicated newsreader program was required to read newsgroups, and this may have discouraged some users from looking at Usenet. But the Internet is slowly becoming more integrated, and it is now possible to read newsgroups with some Web browsers (e.g. Netscape Navigator).

If you want to follow a number of newsgroups more seriously, then it might be wise to consider using an offline reader (OLR). This program logs onto the news server, retrieves all new message headings and then logs off (*see* Figure 1.8). You can then look through the headings at leisure (while offline) and mark those messages that look interesting. After this, the OLR can connect to the news server again and download just the message bodies with the marked headings.

A few notes on reading and posting messages to newsgroups:

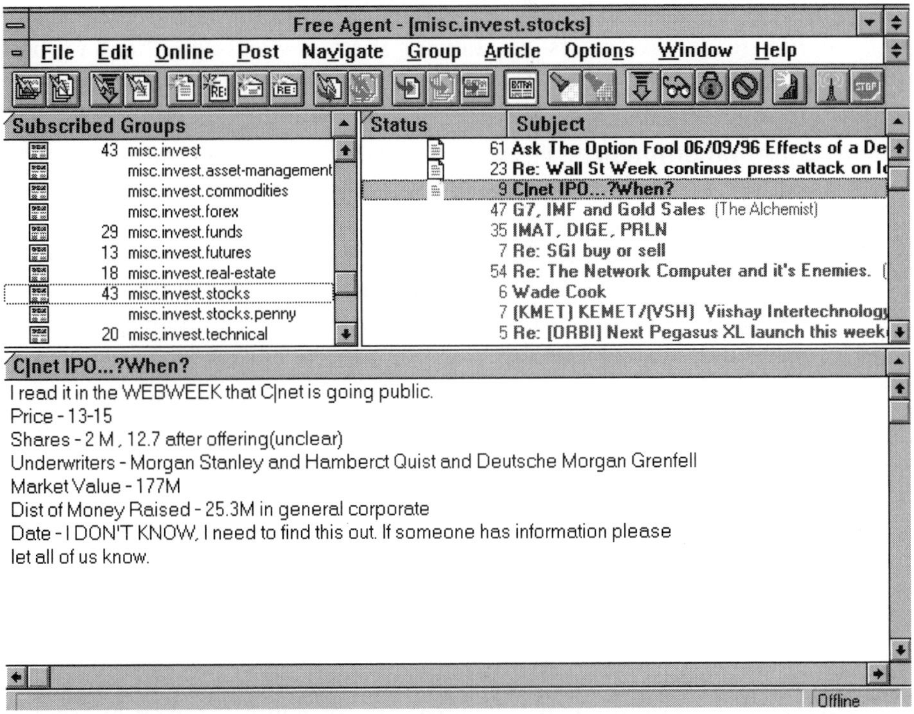

FIG 1.8 Free Agent, an offline reader for newsgroups

■ **Scrolling messages:** due to the bulk of messages being posted to all newsgroups, each news server will limit the period it holds messages. After the expiry limit the message will be deleted from the server.

■ **FAQs:** certain messages are called FAQs and contain frequently asked questions that appear in the newsgroup. It can be a good idea to read these – certainly before posting a question yourself. Because messages scroll off the newsgroup after a period, these FAQs tend to be repeatedly posted at frequent intervals.

■ **Posting messages:** before sending a message to a newsgroup it is strongly recommended to read any associated FAQ (see above) and also to read a few messages to get a flavour of the type of discussions and participants in the newsgroup. It might help to remember that posting a message to a newsgroup is like walking into a bar and shouting, 'My car's broken down outside, does anyone know how to lift the bonnet on a BMW?'. The response you receive would depend greatly on whether that bar was in Harlem, Ireland or Vladivostock.

■ **Subject headings:** if you want people to read a message you have posted, try to make the subject heading interesting and specific. For example, headings like, 'brokers!', or, 'a question' will not attract people to read the message.

■ **Disappearing messages:** it is quite common for new users of Usenet to complain that a message they posted has been removed. The likely explanation of this is that when they log on to the news server, their newsreader program is just showing them *new* messages that have been posted, not all the messages that are actually available (this can be remedied by adjusting the set-up options for the program).

▓ **Cultural differences**: be aware that people all around the world can read your posts. Some of those people will appreciate your subtle, ironic wit, others will not. This problem led to the evolution of emoticons (e.g. :-) the smiling face), in an effort to convey more than was possible in brief text messages to strangers. At first (and even second) glance these may appear childish, but there is no denying that unnecessary problems of misunderstanding frequently do occur in the newsgroups.

▓ **Angry responses**: if you are angered by some message you see, and want to reply to it, it is *always* a good idea never to reply immediately. Leave it for a day, and reply after due consideration in a cool frame of mind.

▓ Moderated groups

The term *signal-to-noise ratio* is used to indicate the number of useful, interesting messages in a newsgroup compared to the rubbish appearing in the same group. The higher the ratio the better. A very few groups are moderated, whereby a person undertakes to filter out the bad posts before they are released to the newsgroup. You may not agree with the editorial policy, but such groups can be more rewarding – although there are not many of them.

As the popularity of a newsgroup grows very large, or interest within a group begins to subdivide, it is common for breakaway groups to form their own newsgroup. For example, at the time of writing this book, there is talk of forming a misc.invest.options newsgroup, to focus talk about options in this new group, rather than in misc.invest.stocks or misc.invest.futures. The process of forming a new newsgroup is not exclusive, anybody can do it, but it is rather mysterious. Briefly, it involves first of all talking (in some existing newsgroup) about forming a new group, gathering a certain critical mass of support, and then lobbying in news.groups. And if that sounds rather woolly – that's Usenet.

As there are so many newsgroups, and millions of messages, it is difficult to track many of them for potentially interesting topics. For this it is better to use one of the search engines: DejaNews is clearly the best, while Alta Vista is a useful backup if the former is too busy. These search engines are very powerful, and allow you to search all messages in nearly all newsgroups for keywords or phrases. In fact, these search engines are alarmingly powerful. DejaNews, for example, offers the ability to track all newsgroup posts by any one user, with a record of how many of those posts were actually replied to (a rather bizarre form of 'interesting person' measurement?). For some search engines, there is the possibility of preventing newsgroup messages being indexed by adding certain qualifiers in the subject heading, but the obvious warning is: *be very careful about the content of any message you send to any newsgroup at any time*.

▓ Netiquette

Netiquette is a rather overplayed term meaning a code of behaviour on the Internet. The term probably came into use when the old Internet hands were alarmed by the sudden growth in popularity of the Internet, and the appearance of 'make*money*fast' posts in the newsgroups. Hence, the enigmatic netiquette was dreamt up to tame the unruly hordes. However, there is no reason to be too worried about contravening some mystic code, just follow the ordinary rules of common sense, bearing in mind that there are a lot of strangers out there, and in the nature of strangers, many of them are very strange.

Reference – newsgroups

New users of newsgroups are usually recommended to have a look at:
news.announce.newusers
news.newusers.questions
news.answers

A useful reference source for newsgroups at SunSITE
http://sunsite.unc.edu/usenet-i/

A comprehensive library of FAQs for many different newsgroups
http://www.is.ohio-state.edu/hypertext/faq/usenet/

Newsgroup search engines
http://www.dejanews.com
http://www.altavista.digital.com

▓ FIG 1.9

Listservs, mailing lists

Listservs are similar to newsgroups in that they are online discussions about specific topics. However, whereas with newsgroups it is necessary to connect to a digital bulletin board (i.e. a news server) to see the collection of messages, Listserv messages are directed straight to your e-mail box.

The administration of Listservs is largely automated: to sign onto one, you send a message to the computer, which enrols you, sends a welcome reply, and then adds your e-mail address to the list. When somebody sends a message to the list, the computer automatically forwards it to the mail boxes of all subscribers on the list.

If you have a few hours to spare every day, and yearn for a more active e-mail box – subscribing to a few Listservs (not necessarily the ones in Figure 1.10) can easily bring in 50–100 messages daily. Compared to newsgroups, the signal-to-noise ratio might be slightly better, but it is still a good thing to find a Listserv that is moderated (i.e. with someone filtering out the uninteresting messages).

Examples of investment Listservs

■ Finance (listserv@vm.temple.edu) – *academic researchers working in a variety of Finance related areas*

■ Stock Market Secrets (smi-request@world.std.com) – *stock market related daily comment*

■ E_INVEST (listserv@vm.temple.edu) – *Electronic Journal of Investing*

■ Oil-gas (oil-gas-request@pavnet.nshore.ncoast.org) – *oil and gas investments*

■ Space-Investors (space-investors-request@cs.cmu.edu) – *space related investment opportunities*

Note: before trying to send any message to the above e-mail addresses, see

http://www.nova.edu/Inter-Links/listserv.html

for further information, instructions on exactly how to subscribe and a searchable index of Listservs.

■ FIG 1.10

In addition, some Listservs offer *digests*, where a selection of messages are aggregated into one daily or weekly post – a method frequently preferable to the individual posts.

Although there are over 5000 Listservs, the vast majority do tend to be oriented toward academic discussions.

Mailing lists are similar to Listservs, in the sense that they are e-mail based, but there is no computer administration. This can have advantages as it means that all posts are filtered first. Not all mailing lists are discussion groups, many are in fact just distribution methods for online journals or newsletters (a good example of the latter is Edupage – a summary of news items on information technology (**http://educom.edu/**).

An index of mailing lists can be found at **http://www.neosoft.com/internet/paml/index.html**

Examples of investment mailing lists

■ OFFSHORE (offshore@dnai.com) – *moderated discussion about offshore investment*

■ WSTN (wall-street-news@netcom.com) – *covers the major financial markets; stocks, bonds, currencies, commodities, precious metals, and the economy*

■ PERSFIN (ikrakow@shore.net) – *a forum where people who have personal finance questions can network*

■ Economic-growth (dse.vanhoudt.p@alpha.ufsia.ac.be) – *for researchers who are working in the field of economic growth*

■ FIG 1.11

Interesting Listservs and mailing lists can be a little difficult to track down, as they are not as easy to index for search engines. Fortunately, some lists have associated Web pages through which they can be contacted. The great attraction of these lists was that they could be set up, and subscribed to, without having to get too deeply involved with Internet protocols and the like.

INTERNET REFERENCES

The following references may prove useful for information about the Internet.

Internet organizations

The Internet has no governing body, but the following institutions play a major role in influencing opinion and guiding development.

W3O – **http://www.w3o.org**
Internet Society – **http://www.isoc.org/**
Electronic Freedom Foundation (EFF) – **http://www.eff.org**
InterNIC – **http://www.internic.net**
CERN – **http://www.cern.ch**

Internet news

The following all carry daily bulletins about Internet developments.

NewsPage – **http://www.newspage.com/**
ZDNet – **http://www.zdnet.com/home/filters/onnet.html**
Pathfinder (Netly News) – **http://pathfinder.com/**
Cowles/SIMBA Media Daily – **http://netday.iworld.com/simba/**
Meckler-M: (NetDay, InternetWorld, WebWeek) – **http://www.mecklermedia.com**
NewsLinx – **http://www.newslinx.com/**
Lycos – **http://point.lycos.com/now/intnews.htm**

Surveys about the Internet

Occasional surveys about the Internet.

CommerceNet – **http://www.commerce.net/information/surveys/cnet-qa3.html**
FindSVP – **http://www.findsup.com:80/findsup/index.html**
Forrester – **http://www.forrester.com**
Gupta – **http://www-personal.umich.edu/~sgupta/**
Killen – **http://www.killen.com/**
Network Wizards – **http://www.nw.com/**
Simba – **http://www.simbanet.com/**

Vanderbilt – **http://www2000.ogsm.vanderbilt.edu/**
WebTrack – **http://www.webtrack.com**

Research about the Internet

Research companies specializing in the Internet.

Aberdeen – **http://www.aberdeen.com/**
Dataquest – **http://www.dataquest.com/**
Delphi Consulting Group – **http://www.delphigroup.com/**
Find/SVP Emerging Technologies – **http://www.findsvp.com/**
Forrester Research – **http://www.forrester.com/**
Frost & Sullivan – **http://www.frost.com/**
Gartner Group – **http://www.Gartner.com/**
Jupiter Communications – **http://www.jup.com/**
Meta Group – **http://www.metagroup.com/**
Patricia Seybold – **http://www.psgroup.com/**

The Internet world

Hip sites to feel the pulse of the Net.

HotWired – **http://www.wired.com**
CNet – **http://www.cnet.com**
Mecklermedia (InternetWorld, WebWeek) – **http://www.mecklermedia.com**
ZDNet (Yahoo Online, PCWeek) – **http://www.zdnet.com/**
Pathfinder's Netly News – **http://pathfinder.com**

Newsgroups: alt.culture.internet, alt.culture.www, cern.www.talk

Getting
connected

Thou seest the world Volumnius, how it goes;
our enemies have beat us to the pit;
it is more worthy to leap in ourselves,
than tarry till they push us.

Julius Caesar, William Shakespeare

The Internet is a collection of networks, and connecting to it means either being part of one of those constituent networks in the first place (e.g. a government institution or university) or subscribing to a network that is. This section will be mainly of interest to the latter group; if you work in a big company it is increasingly likely that Internet access will be provided (if not, ask your computer administrator).

So, to connect to the Internet, the following is required:

- Computer
- Software
- Modem
- Telephone line
- Internet provider

Because the Internet is sometimes marketed as state-of-the-art technology, people might think that connection to it requires the latest, biggest and fastest computer (and possibly computer salesmen do not disabuse customers of that notion). However, the Internet comprises a range of features, some of which will require a powerful computer, while other features (such as e-mail) can be used by a PC with a 386 chip. If you are looking for multimedia entertainment from the Internet, then you must resign yourself to the treadmill of continual upgrades of processor, memory, hard disk and software. If, however, as an investor, you are looking primarily for information and communication, then a 486 PC is perfectly adequate.

CHOOSING AN INTERNET ACCESS PROVIDER

An Internet Access Provider (IAP) is a company that controls a computer that has permanent access to the Internet; it then sells subscriptions for a service, whereby users can connect to this computer, and then through it to the Internet. In the early days of the Internet, the quality of the service offered by different IAPs was very variable. Things are better now, but there still can be quite a difference in the range of services offered, so it can be a good idea to get a personal recommendation, or read a comparative review in a computer magazine.

The best source for lists of IAPs are computer magazines; alternatively, Mecklermedia's iWORLD **http://thelist.iworld.com/** maintains a good list of IAPs worldwide (or see the list in the appendix of this book).

Some factors to consider when choosing an IAP are:

▥ **Location of access node**: upon subscribing to an IAP, it will provide a telephone number that your computer calls each time to connect to the Internet; therefore, the location of this telephone number (and the respective telephone charges applicable) make this one of the most important factors to consider. In addition, if you travel frequently with a portable computer, it can be useful if the IAP has a wide network of access nodes (this is a particular strength of CompuServe globally).

▥ **Type of connection**: nearly all IAPs offer connection via ordinary modems, but it might be worthwhile checking if they also provide ISDN access (you may want to upgrade a connection at a later time, and the mere offering of an ISDN service demonstrates a certain degree of seriousness from the IAP).

▥ **Speed of connection**: most IAPs now offer modem speeds up to 28 000 and even 33 600. (However, don't get too excited about this; general Internet bandwidth problems will prevent you from experiencing such heady rates too often.)

▥ **IAP connection to the Internet**: what type of connection does the IAP itself have with the Internet (e.g. T1, see glossary at the back for description of these speeds).

- **User/modem ratio**: how many subscribers does the IAP have for each of its modems (i.e. what is the likely frequency of getting a busy tone when trying to connect)?
- **Range of services offered**: every IAP should offer WWW access and e-mail, but some do not have Usenet, or only restricted access to certain newsgroups; some IAPs do not allow Internet Phone.
- **E-mail service**: what range of e-mail service is offered – are aliases possible (multiple names for the same e-mail Domain address); is it possible to have e-mail forwarded automatically to another e-mail address? Instead of advertising the services of a Netcom or a Demon in your e-mail address, it can be a good idea to register your own Domain Name (e.g. john-smith.com, with a possible e-mail address, john@john-smith.com); this e-mail address can then stay with you permanently, even if you change Internet providers.
- **What software is provided**: most Internet programs are free or very cheap. However, if you are new to the Internet it can be helpful if you receive these programs initially on a disk (rather than be told cryptically to 'download' these from the /pub directory). Be aware also that programs generously offered by some IAPs may be old versions of the software.
- **What support is offered**: this is difficult to verify, but you might as well ask if technical support is freely available.
- **Web pages**: does the IAP offer a certain amount of hard disk space for your own Web pages?
- **Price**: tariffs tend to be either a fixed monthly rate (for unlimited access time), or a per hour charge. It usually surprises people how much time they spend online, and so, in almost all cases, the former is to be preferred. Price should be one of the last factors to influence a decision here: most IAP charges are not very high, and are far less important than potential telephone charges or slow access speed.

If you have temporary access to the Internet (possibly while visiting a cybercafe) it can be useful to look in newsgroups where the efficiency of IAPs is discussed. In some cases newsgroups exist for certain countries (for example, fr.network.internet.fournisseurs, would be the place for France), while there are also more general newsgroups like: news.answers, alt.internet.access.wanted, alt.internet.services.

Commercial online services

For a number of years there have been private networks to which individuals or companies could subscribe. These networks commonly offered services such as e-mail facilities, files to download and forums to chat in. One of the first of these networks was set up by H&R Block (the tax filing company) and was called CompuServe – which now has some four million subscribers worldwide. The greatest rival of CompuServe is America Online (AOL), which, although established more recently, now has about six million subscribers.

Both these networks had their own proprietary protocols for communication between the computers on their respective networks (but these protocols were not directly compatible with those used on the Internet). However, in 1995, both networks established gateways from their own systems to the Internet, and could henceforth offer subscribers access to the wider Net.

Although these companies now offer Net access, they still offer their own proprietary service as well (e.g. the discussion forums). As such, they have now become hybrid services, and distinct from IAPs (e.g. Netcom or Demon). To distinguish these types of companies from the pure access providers, they are sometimes called *commercial online services*. Their service is more expensive than IAPs, and the great debate is whether they can maintain their higher margins by offering proprietary content.

If you are making fairly heavy use of the Internet, then an IAP will be cheaper but arguments for using a commercial online service, like CompuServe, might include:

▓ **Global network**: CompuServe has access telephone nodes all over the world, and if travelling with a portable computer, these can be very useful.

▓ **Discussion forums**: these are moderated, and the quality of discussion can be far higher than in the public newsgroups.

▓ **Software libraries**: there are vast libraries of files and programs that can be downloaded. Although these files are commonly available for download also over the Internet, CompuServe has a useful search facility ('GO FILEFINDER' – which works well as it is designed to operate on a closed system, and is helpful in finding the latest version of a particular program). In addition, before being made available for download, all files are checked for viruses and to confirm that they actually work – or don't, at least, immediately crash the computer. (This last facility is not fail-safe, but it is at least one extra level of protection.)

In the past, added attractions were that many computer companies offered support via the CompuServe forums, and that there were many specialized databases available. However, many of these same services have now migrated onto the Web and are accessible to all.

COMPUTER CONNECTION

To connect to the Internet, your computer must be physically connected to a telephone line (assuming you are not using an optical fibre connection). There are two possible ways of doing this: via a modem, or using ISDN.

Modems

This is the most common method of connecting computers to telephone lines and thereby to online networks. There are two criteria to consider, when choosing a modem:

▨ **Speed**: in general, faster is always better. However, if you already have a 9600bps modem, this is perfectly sufficient for e-mail and newsgroups. It is possible to view the Web with a 14 400bps modem (and effective transfer rates over the Internet are commonly below this speed anyway). If you are buying a new modem, getting anything less than the fastest available is a false economy. Fastest at the moment is 28 800bps or 33 600bps. Modems are usually backwardly compatible, and will support slower speeds if necessary. A glossary is provided below of the terms used to define the features of modems (i.e. if looking to buy a new modem, it should support V.34).

▨ **Internal/external**: next is the choice of getting a modem that sits inside your computer, or is in an external box. The arguments for the former are that less desk space is occupied, and another external power plug is not required. However, on balance, an external one is probably to be preferred: communication is not always glitch-free and when problems occur, it can be useful to see what lights are flashing on the modem; it is also easy to pass the modem onto someone else if it is external, or to use it on another machine, and for similar reasons is easier to upgrade.

Finally, another factor to consider is if you are likely to use a portable computer with a PCMCIA card. If so, then it is possible to get an attachment for a desktop computer that can use the same PCMCIA modem.

▨ **TABLE 1.4 Modem Glossary**

Abbreviation	Description
ITU-T	The International Telecommunication Union (formerly CCITT), all the standards below are ITU-T standards, unless otherwise stated.
bps	bits per second (standard measure for the speed of data communication)
V.21	data communication standard at 300bps
V.22	data communication standard at 1200bps
V.22bis	data communication standard at 2400bps
V.23	data communication standard at 1200bps (half-duplex; used by Prestel in the UK and France's Minitel)
V.32	data communication standard at 9600bps
V.32bis	similar standard as V.32, but with enhanced speed of 14 400bps

▶

▣ TABLE 1.4 **Modem Glossary** (*contd*)

Abbreviation	Description
V.32ter	unratified extension standard to V.32bis for enhanced speed to 19 200 (sometimes called V.32terbo)
V.FAST	preliminary name for V.34
V.FC	a non ITU-T data communication standard at 28 800bps (developed by Hayes and Rockwell; not the same as V.34)
V.34	data communication standard at 28 800bps
V.35	data communication standard at 48Kbps
MNP	Microcom Networking Protocol: one of the most common modem standards for compression
V.42	error correction standard (also called LAP-M; includes MNP up to level 4)
V.42bis	extension of V.42 to include data compression (Lempel-Ziv)
V.17	communication standard at 14 000bps (mainly for fax)
V.27ter	communication standard at 4800bps (mainly for fax)
V.29	communication standard at 9600bps (mainly for fax)

▣ Note for Windows 3.x users

If you are using an older PC (386 or 486), and the speed of communication does not appear to be as fast as it should be, check the following:

1 Communication faster than V32bis requires a high-speed serial port that uses a 16550-compatible UART. In plain language, the data passed between the modem and the computer must pass through a special chip in the computer. On older machines, this chip does not work fast enough for the modern high-speed modems. To check what type serial port your machine has, type MSD at the DOS prompt and then look at COMM Ports. If it is not a 16550 UART, an inexpensive expansion card with high-speed serial port can be installed. (Note: this only concerns *external* modems; *internal* ones already have suitable serial ports built in.)

2 If your computer does have a 16550 UART port, then check that it has been enabled; the line COMxFIFO=1 (where x = the number of the port being used) should appear in the [386Enh] section of SYSTEM.INI.

The standard Windows v3.1 communication driver (COMM.DRV – found in the \windows\system directory), can be replaced with another driver (CYBERCOM.DRV). This driver is better adapted for high speed (over 14 400bps) communication through a 16550 UART.

Reference – modems

http://www.modems.com
http://www.aimnet.com/~jnavas/modem/faq.html
http://www.best.com/~malch/comfaq.html

▓ FIG 1.12

ISDN

The ordinary telephone system uses an analog technology (continuous sound waves) that is designed for transmitting the human voice. However, this technology is not optimal for transmitting digital signals from a computer. To do this, it is necessary to translate a computer's digital signal into an analog one (done by a modem), transmit over the telephone line, and then untranslate the analog signal (modem again) back into a digital signal, for the receiving computer.

Modem technology has improved over the years: where once modems could transmit data at 2400bps, now they have speeds of up to 28 800–33 600bps. But they are reaching the limits of analog line technology. Even these recent fast speeds require good telephone lines to achieve the high throughput rates – if there is any noise on the line, transfer speeds will fall back to the lower levels.

However, a far superior technology is available. This is called integrated services digital network (ISDN), and it employs a totally different method of using an ordinary telephone line. As the name suggests, this method uses digital rather than analog technology, and although it can still transmit the human voice fine, it is far better suited to computer communication. To use ISDN, your computer needs a terminal adapter, and then you must arrange to connect with a computer also using ISDN at the other end of a telephone line (i.e. with an IAP). (Note: a modem is not required here at all, as no modulation is needed. The digital signal of the computer can be transmitted directly across the telephone line. Another advantage of this is that communication can be established far quicker without requiring the whooshy-squeaky handshaking of modems.)

You can regard ISDN as a temporary stage between 'plain ol' telephone system' and true high bandwidth technology such as cable. But, at the moment, if you are using ordinary telephone lines, it probably offers the best combination of price/performance for Internet access. If this is the case, you might ask, why isn't its use far more widespread? There is no immediate answer to that; it is partly lack of knowledge (ISDN is alternatively held to stand for I Still Don't kNow), but also its use has not been encouraged by the telephone companies. To offer an ISDN service, the local telephone company must make an investment in hardware; however, many were slow to do so, and did not anticipate its demand (encouraged by the use of the Internet). Although many telephone companies are now belatedly offering ISDN, it is rather half-heartedly as they are looking over their shoulders at the expansion of the cable networks.

INTERNET SOFTWARE

Just as different programs such as word processors, spreadsheets and graphics are used on standalone PCs, a range of software must be used for different functions on the Internet. The most important programs will be one for sending and receiving e-mail, and one for looking at Web pages (the latter being called a browser). But there are many other programs that might be used. Fortunately, of late, there has been a trend for browsers to become more powerful, and they are beginning to assimilate a range of functionality within the one program.

A list of recommended programs (and some alternative programs in square brackets) is given in Table 1.5, with an address of where you can download them.

■ TABLE 1.5 **Essential Internet programs with source address**

Function	Program	Source
Winsock (Internet connection)	Trumpet Winsock	http://www.trumpet.com.au/wsk/winsock.htm
E-mail	Eudora/Eudora Lite	ftp://ftp.qualcomm.com/
	[Pegasus Mail]	ftp://risc.ua.edu/pub/network/pegasus/
WWW browser	Netscape Navigator	http://www.netscape.com
	[Microsoft Internet Explorer]	http://www.microsoft.com
Newsreader (OLR)	Free Agent	ftp://ftp.forteinc.com/pub/forte/
FTP	WS_FTP	ftp://ftp.csra.net/pub/
	[Cute FTP]	ftp://ftp.enterprise.net/pub/mirror/winsock-1/ftp/CuteFTP.Betas/
Telnet	EWAN	ftp://ftp.best.com/pub/bryanw/pc/winsock/
	[NCSA Telnet]	ftp://ftpncsa.uiuc.edu/
Compression/archive	PKZip	
	WinZIP	ftp://ftp.winzip.com/winzip/beta/
Virus protection	McAfee V-Shield	ftp://ftp.macafee.com/pub/antivirus/
Encode (binary to text)	XFERPRO	
Image viewer/manipulator	LView Pro	ftp://ftp.std.com/ftp/vendors/mmedia/lview/
	Paint Shop Pro	ftp://ftp.jasc.com/pub/
Document reader	Adobe Acrobat Reader	http://www.adobe.com

Shareware and freeware

The word 'shareware' is somewhat misleading, suggesting some type of program. The term actually applies to a method of marketing and distribution for software. It can best be summarized as a 'try before you buy' approach to selling. The theory is that the programs are available free (to be downloaded via the Internet, or from floppy disks); users try the software for a period (usually up to 30 days), and if they are happy with the program, they pay the registration fee. If they do not want it, they are expected to erase the program from their hard disk.

This method was devised some years ago, to provide the smaller software producers (commonly just one person) with a chance of marketing their programs, when the usual software distribution channels were closed to them. Much of the software is very good quality (and in fact a large number of Internet programs are shareware), but it has to be admitted that the shareware model does not seem to have been a great success, with a very low percentage of users actually registering their programs.

Shareware programs seem to thrive in the nooks and crannies of computing. While the large word processing and spreadsheet packages cater for 90 per cent of a user's requirements, shareware programs are often useful for the smaller tasks (for example, as add-in functions for spreadsheets or converting data from one format to another).

Sites for downloading programs

A common medium of distribution for shareware programs is via 'libraries' on the Internet or bulletin board systems. The best site, with the largest and most up to date collection is undoubtedly Shareware.com which is associated with ClNet; this also has a good introductory guide to the Internet, and reviews and recommends new programs. Another good site for specifically Internet-related programs is at TUCOWS (*see* Figure 1.13).

Internet download sites

Shareware.com **http://www.shareware.com**
TUCOWS **http://www.tucows.com/**
Simtel.Net **http://oak.oakland.edu/simtel.net/**
Coast to Coast Software Repository **http://www.coast.net/SimTel/**
Jumbo **http://www.jumbo.com/**

■ FIG 1.13

Notes on downloading programs

A few notes on downloading files:

▓ Originally, to download files over the Internet it was necessary to use File Transfer Protocol (FTP), but now the capabilities of the Web and browsers are such that it is common to **download directly from a Web page**. Therefore, if there is a file name (for example, 'invest.zip') that is underlined, more than likely it will be possible to simply click on the name to begin the download.

▓ Before starting the download procedure, take a note of the **size of the file**, and the average download speed of Web pages. For example, if the file size is 1273K bytes, and the browser is currently downloading pages at a speed of 900 bytes per second, then you can roughly estimate that download of the file will take over 20 minutes.

▓ If the **connection to the server is slow**, check to see if there are mirror sites. For example, both TUCOWs and Simtel.Net have identical sites on many other computers around the world – it may be that connection to a geographically closer server will improve connection speed.

▓ When downloading a file (either using a browser or using an FTP program) it is always a good idea to create a **special dedicated directory** on your local computer, and download the file into this. Then decompress and de-archive (e.g. unzip) the constituent files into this one directory. If you decide to keep the downloaded program, then transfer it to another directory; if you do not want the program, it is simple to erase all the files in the one directory. (Warning: a program like Netscape might default to download files into the Netscape directory itself, and if a zipped program is then unzipped in this same directory, there is likely to be confusion about which are Netscape files and which are the new ones.)

▓ If the file to be downloaded has '95' or '32' in the title, it is likely that these are programs for **MS Windows 95** – and will not run under Windows 3.x.

▓ If you are a member of a **commercial online service** (such as CompuServe) it may be better to download from a forum library there, rather than over the general Internet. The advantages are that the connection speed may be quicker, some forums are good at ensuring they only have the latest version of a program, and most forums will run some kind of basic virus check on files before making them available. In addition, the forum Sysops usually checks to see that the programs actually work – or at least don't immediately crash a system. Against all this you will have to weigh the extra cost of using the commercial online service.

CONNECTING WHILE *ON THE ROAD*

With small computers truly becoming portable – rather than just *luggable* – more and more people are travelling with their computers and wanting to connect those computers while they are on the road. Some will actually suffer psychological withdrawal symptoms if denied their daily fix of e-mails, while for others it will just be a necessity to be in regular contact while on a long business trip.

However, as Nicholas Negroponte of the Massachusetts Institute of Technology (MIT) indicates below, the global Internet is not quite plug-and-play yet:

> *Connecting around the globe is a black art. The problem is not being digital, but being plug ready. Europe has 20 (count 'em) different power plugs. And, while you may have become used to that small little plastic phone jack, the so-called RJ-11 plug, there are 175 others in the world. . . on a long and circuitous trip a full 25 per cent of my luggage volume is likely to be a combination of phone jacks and power plugs.*

'Being Digital', Nicholas Negroponte

However, for those of you willing to brave the slings and arrows of outrageous hotel telephone bills and cubist-inspired foreign phone jacks, a few points to remember before setting off are listed in Figure 1.14.

Nine points to check if travelling with a computer

1 Power supply
2 Phone jack
3 Electrical screwdriver
4 Access numbers and speed of connection
5 Login scripts
6 AT commands reference
7 Do the hotel rooms have IDD?
8 Try the access phone numbers before you leave
9 Insurance

■ FIG 1.14

■ 1 Power supply

Before setting out check the electric power (voltage, hertz) of the countries you are visiting, and ensure that these are compatible with the computer's transformer. Further, find out the style of power plug and see if you can buy an adapter before leaving, or find out where one can be bought on arrival in the foreign country.

■ 2 Phone jack

As above, try to determine the type of phone jack used in the foreign country before leaving. The standard US phone jack is called *RJ-11*. One useful trick can be to take a *female-to-female* RJ-11 socket. Although the telephone wall sockets in many countries will be of the local design, the jack into the telephone itself may well be an RJ-11 – in which case this can be removed and plugged into the *female-to-female* RJ-11 socket.

In some countries the telephone lead may be *hard-wired* into the wall (i.e. no socket). In these cases the determined cyber-executive may think about using crocodile clips. Also, you might want to consider an *acoustic coupler*, a device that fits over the telephone handset itself, and thus avoids having to mess around with the sockets. These are convenient to fit, but are bulky to carry and the quality of the connection is not reliable.

■ 3 Electrical screwdriver

Despite having all the correct plugs and attachments, these may occasionally need a little 'encouragement' with a screwdriver to get them to fit correctly.

■ 4 Access numbers and speed of connection

This is very important – and easy to forget. Before leaving home make sure you have a list of all possible access numbers and the speed of their connection. If using CompuServe, a list of these can be found at GO PHONES. If staying in a country for longer than a few days, it may be possible to arrange a temporary dial-up service with a local Internet Access Provider (for a list of these *see* **http://www.thelist.com** and the list in Appendix A).

■ 5 Login scripts

It is quite likely that your network provider will not have an access telephone number in the countries you are visiting. In this case it may be possible to use a local network to connect through. For example, if using CompuServe in countries where there is no CompuServe access number, it may be possible to dial locally into a network such as *Infonet* or *Tymnet*.

When you dial into one of these local networks, your computer needs to give instructions to it, saying what destination network it is trying to connect to – these instructions are held in a *script file* (identifiable usually by their .SCR extension).

Your communication program may well come with a collection of such script files (CompuServe's WinCIM program has around 30 login scripts for various networks). However, it is always a good idea to check if there is a new version – a good source for these is the TAPCIS forum on CompuServe.

6 AT commands reference

If, as Nicholas Negroponte says, connecting around the globe is a 'black art', then modem initialization strings are the voodoo heart of the art.

It is a good idea to have a copy of the AT commands in a computer file for reference, as it may be necessary to adapt the modem initialization string for the local telephone conditions. For example, if the modem does not recognize the dial tone (a common problem), an X0 can be added to the string to force the modem to dial regardless of whether there is a dial tone or not.

Tone/pulse dialling systems

Older telephone networks use a system of dialling called *pulse*, while the newer systems use *tone*. It is usually possible to identify which system is being used by listening to the headset: if dialling produces a string of clicks (sounding a little like morse code) this is pulse dialling; more likely, however, you will hear the more familiar 'tuneful' music of tone dialling. If the telephone does appear to use pulse dialling, then the modem string will have to be changed (the initial DT replaced by a DP). If in doubt, try using DP in any case, as pulse dialling will usually work on tone systems, but not vice versa.

7 Do the hotel rooms have IDD?

An increasing number of hotels around the world provide international direct dialling (IDD) from the rooms – thereby avoiding having to place calls through the telephone operator. It is a good idea to check this by calling hotels before leaving on any trip. If you find a hotel that does not have IDD, then it *is* possible to dial manually, but not easy. A better solution might be to ask if you can use the hotel's fax line, as this is usually a direct line to the outside.

If the room has IDD, you have to dial a number (usually a '9') to get an outside line. This number will have to be added to the access number you are calling. A problem can sometimes arise if the modem dials the numbers too quickly; for example, it might be necessary to pause after dialling the '9'. In this case, special characters (check the modem specifications), usually a comma, can be inserted in the number to be dialled, to add pauses. Thus, if you were trying to dial the number 123 4567 from a hotel room that used a '9' for an outside line and required an initial pause, and then a longer pause after the '9', the access phone number should appear as ,9,,1234567.

8 Try the phone numbers before you leave

One of the most useful preparatory exercises is to try logging on through the overseas access numbers before leaving home. If there are any problems, it is better to discover them early (with the possibility of asking for help), rather than later, when sitting on a hotel bed surrounded by wires, screwdrivers, plug adapters, modem and computer manuals, hotel telephone rate card etc.

■ 9 Insurance

Obvious advice: check that the computer is covered by your travel insurance.

Some other miscellaneous advice would include:

■ Remember to re-charge the computer batteries at every opportunity. This is particularly important when you are likely to be searched at airports or wherever, as the usual security check is to ask for the computer to be switched on.

■ If you are travelling with no printer, but would like to produce a hard copy, it might be possible to send the file to the hotel's fax machine, from which it can be photocopied onto decent paper.

■ Before leaving, check the Internet newsgroups and CompuServe forums for information about connecting locally. If you have any questions, this would be the obvious place to post them (*see* Figure 1.15 for details).

Reference – travelling with a computer

Internet newsgroups: rec.travel.asia, rec.travel.europe, rec.travel.latin-america, rec.travel.usa-canada

CompuServe forums: TAPCIS, TRAVSIG

Teleadapt Ltd: **http://www.teleadapt.co.uk/**

It is strongly recommended to look at these pages. The company specializes in advising and selling accessories to help travellers get connected.

Telegroup, Inc.: **http://www.telegroup.com**

A 'traditional' call back operator that is now offering international telephone charge cards. Expensive, but probably cheaper than hotel charges.

■ FIG 1.15

■ Finally, don't forget to pack the modem *and* the modem cable.

Current issues and future of the Internet

It is not necessary to have a detailed knowledge of the workings of the Internet to understand and reflect on the problems that are faced by it, and where all this computer communication is likely to lead. However, it *is* essential to have a general grasp of what the Internet is, and what it is not. Without this non-technical, fundamental appreciation of the Internet, any further analysis is futile.

But there are two great barriers that commonly prevent even a tentative understanding of the Internet.

First, as Bertrand Russell said, people do not want knowledge, they want certainty. And the very last thing the Internet offers is that; almost no statement can be made about the Internet with an honest confidence.

At the beginning of this century the German mathematician, David Hilbert, was asked what he thought the greatest danger facing the human race in the coming century would be. *Over-simplification*, he replied (which, considering this was said before the full flowering of the mass media, must be considered a rather astute prophecy). And, of course, the century *has* been beset with complex problems to which there are no easy answers – despite the over-simplifications and distortions of the media and politicians. So, complicated issues like unemployment, derivatives, genetic engineering and the Internet are simplified and distorted in the misguided search for certainty.

The second problem hindering understanding is the fear of technology (and people's more general fear of change). One of the most bizarre, and worrying, mass demonstrations of this techno-fear was at the time of the capture of the so-called Unabomber in the US. Here was a man who had killed three people and maimed others with randomly targeted bombs – and the popular reaction to his anti-technology manifesto? 'Well, he's got a point.'

Behind many of these fears lies the big one – the fear of losing your job. And the Internet certainly does promise to shake up industries with many levels of intermediaries. But, throughout history, progress and the introduction of new technology has created more new jobs than they have destroyed. In addition, quite often the new jobs are more challenging and interesting than the old ones. One can imagine that with the introduction of the motor car, the people employed in the horse and carriage industry would have been similarly worried. But the motor industry went on to employ many times more people, directly and indirectly, than were ever employed in the transport industry before.

So, there are big questions to be faced regarding the Internet. But to begin to answer them it is necessary to dispel some popular delusions that can lead to confusion. For example:

■ **It's so big**: big – compared to what? At the time of writing there were about 50 million WWW pages, which must roughly equate to the number of dental records in the UK. Is that a lot?

■ **It's so slow**: again, compared to what? This isn't television. Is there some faster service that offers access to *WSJ Online*, the Japan *Nikkei*, real-time Thai stock prices, personalized news and discussion forums on technology stocks?

■ **It's so complicated**: the WWW is remarkable for its 'point and click' ease of use; and the attitude that computers are in general difficult to use belongs to those stuck in a ten-year time warp.

■ **It's very difficult to find anything**: the search engines on the Internet are actually very easy to use, and a brief look at the help files can make any search very powerful and well-targeted. Certainly easier than searching through copies of paper magazines looking for old articles.

■ **There's too much information**: a common refrain is that with the proliferation of news media, there is too much information – leading to data-overload. However, a simple walk down a city street will supply more data to the brain per second than any number of information services. But the brain is ready for this, and over the years has developed some useful filtering processes. In time, similar filtering processes will be available for the flow of news and information data.

■ **It's all in English**: 'It is the ultimate act of intellectual colonialism,' as one Internet service provider in Russia said. Nonsense. One glance at sites in South America, Germany or Japan will show that few are in English. If anything, the Internet is likely to reinforce the strength of national languages, rather than undermine them. With the development of sophisticated translation software, marketers can use their own language, and consumers read it in any language they like. And if you think that translation software is not very accurate (and translated business brochures are?), then rest assured – things are changing fast. One could go further and say that the Internet is likely to lead to a resurgence in local dialects: by providing an efficient cultural forum, and offering a global medium for commerce that does not require the use of some dominant national language.

- **There's too much junk mail**: yes, there is a fair amount of unsolicited mail, as there is with ordinary post. But the incremental cost of receiving this extra mail is rarely significant, and it can be easily deleted. In the future, sophisticated software programs will increasingly be able to filter out unwanted mail.

- **It increases the divisions between rich and poor**: it *is* possible that the Internet will create divisions in society. But those divisions will not necessarily be along the old partitions of geography or wealth. The cost of computers is immaterial, as in the future they will effectively be given away. More importantly, the information age is likely to create opportunities for the third world to compete that would just never have been possible in the industrial age. There will still be poor people, but no one is (or should be) claiming that the Internet is a panacea for the world's ills.

- **It will lead to a dull conformity**: science fiction movies of the 1950s commonly portrayed the future as drab and conformist: serious-faced people walking around in tin-foil Chairman Mao suits. Today, much of our technology actually exceeds the expectations of those films, but compare the variety of fashion, the colour and cosmopolitan mix of people in a city street now with that of 40 years ago. People may, or may not, be happier, but 'dull and conformist' we are not.

- **There's a lot of rubbish**: possibly 85 per cent of everything on the Internet is badly-done rubbish (*read*: subjectively uninteresting), a further ten per cent might be well-done rubbish, while the remaining five per cent is interesting. However, are those proportions any different from the typical selection of magazines displayed on racks in shops? There's no reason why the Internet should be any different.

- **It's all pornography**: yes, there is pornography on the Internet, but you have to look for it. However, there are probably far more financial sites on the Net than pornographic ones. And unsolicited pornographic junk mail is rare, if not non-existent.

- **It can be used by criminals and terrorists**: so can the telephone and postal systems.

Cars kill people, and there is no doubt that if cars were banned, fewer people would be killed; but, on balance, we decide that cars are useful. In the same way, there are many things bad about the Internet, but we will probably decide, on balance, its uses outweigh its downside.

INTERNET ISSUES

The Internet offers ultimate connectivity – *everything* connected to *everything*, and as a result we will have instant access to huge amounts of information, companies will have direct contact with clients, commerce will be friction-free, and there will be responsive electronic democracy. A rosy future for all, then? Perhaps. But there are problems rising to the surface that could upset the digital paradise. A few of these problems are listed below with sources for further reference.

Bandwidth

The current bandwidth of the Internet is perfectly sufficient for the transfer of e-mails, and also probably for 90 per cent of uses for investment purposes. However, for the transfer of multimedia files (images, sounds, video), the Internet is struggling, and everything slows down. Vast resources are now being applied to upgrade the infrastructure of the Internet, and improvements should be noticeable soon.

The progress will be such, in fact, that it will then become apparent that there is a bandwidth problem, not on the Net itself, but in the interface between computers and humans. In addition, data will be supplied to us so quickly and in such abundance, that this will affect the very way we process data, and think.

An interesting point was made by Nicholas Negroponte of the Massachusetts Institute of Technology (MIT), who observed that the bandwidth in fibres under the ground was effectively unlimited, while bandwidth in the air was not. Hence, it would be more sensible if information that was currently sent through the air (e.g. television, radio) was sent instead through the ground, while what was now sent through the ground (e.g. telephone conversations) might be better in the air. The reasoning for this was that the valuable ethereal spectrum for communication should be saved for things that move.

Reference – bandwidth

High Bandwidth Web Page – **http://plainfield.bypass.com/~gzaret/hiband.html**

Yahoo – **http://www.yahoo.com/Science/Engineering/Electrical_Engineering/Telecommunications/**

▓ FIG 1.16

Classifying the Internet

Humans have a great drive for neatness and order, and so when the Internet came along it seemed natural to try to order the thing – in a similar way, perhaps, that a library organizes books. Some companies (e.g. Yahoo) jumped into the breach, and achieved a certain fame for having a plucky attempt. But it is likely that it dawned on these companies, quicker than it did the users, that what they were doing was doomed to failure. The Internet is growing too fast. Furthermore, much of the information just doesn't lend itself to convenient categorization.

The problem ultimately will be that what they are trying to classify is actually the sum of all human knowledge – and that certainly can't be ordered with simple menu trees. Some of the problems the Internet directories will face are:

- The information is not static (as in a book) but changing fast – and the value of information is no longer a snapshot fact at any one time, but rather the process of change itself.
- The usefulness of data is not in the data points (facts) themselves, but rather in the relationships between data. Hence, directories offer the interesting, but useless, data points, but without the important connections.
- How does one classify a human face (without a name)?

It is unlikely that any two humans organize the information in their brains the same way. Following this, a directory that is useful for one person will not be so for another.

The problems outlined here apply to some extent also to search engines. The best that can be achieved with the current technology is for ever more focused Internet directories and search engines. Thus, the current directories' coverage of finance is abysmal, because they are also trying to categorize in the *same* system haflinger ponies and Pearl Jam. Yahoo has obviously realized this and is setting up some specialized directories (e.g. country oriented ones, or directories for children) and Yahoo Finance cannot be far behind.

Information reliability

In the past we trusted a few newspapers and publishing houses to verify the information they presented to us. Now anyone can create a Web site, and potentially broadcast to the world. How do we know any longer if the information we receive is any good?

This demand will lead to a huge service industry for information verification. This will be particularly important in the field of investment, but the demand will be there across all areas.

In some cases, we will look for the equivalent of publishers (or, in effect, editors) on the Net; but the role they will serve will broaden significantly. The field here is wide open for anyone to offer a value-added editorial service, but more than likely quite a few existing publishing houses will also be competing on the Net. For example, if you are thinking of going to Cuba, you might use one of the search engines to look for Web pages with the word 'Cuba' appearing on them. You will likely get returned several hundred references – some very good, many a waste of time. Better would be to visit the site of a travel publisher you trust. On this site, you will find access to its proprietary information, but also it will offer a critical guide to the relevant information elsewhere on the Net. Such sites will become a forum for all potential travellers, and as such will be natural venues for marketing all kinds of extra services to the traveller (e.g. travel insurance, health kits, specialized sunglasses for Cuban sun).

Viruses

It is possible to import a virus onto a computer by downloading a program from the Internet. Unfortunately, viruses are a fact of life, and impossible to avoid completely. However, the chance of attracting a virus are greatly diminished by following a few sensible precautions. But the danger in the future may come from computer viruses that don't look like the ones we have today. Present day viruses are usually fairly crude programs that randomly change data on a hard disk, or destroy it completely. Usually, after a while, the existence of a virus becomes obvious. In the future, viruses may be far more subtle; they might change data 'intelligently'. This could have particularly interesting ramifications in the field of investment, where data could be slightly changed (or changed suddenly at a pre-determined time) that would affect the investment decisions of a critical mass of investors (or the investors' auto-trade personal finance programs).

Security

There is no particular Internet security problem. Rather, there is a general *computer* security problem. So far, very few organizations have linked their main internal computer networks to the Internet (for example, the military certainly haven't, and any break-in to, say, the Pentagon will not be via the Internet). However, as connections to the Internet grow, computer security and Internet security will become pretty much the same issue. This is already leading to the growth of firewalls – a combination of software and hardware that prevents unauthorized users gaining access to a local area network (e.g. a company intranet) via an Internet connection.

In theory it might be possible to create a secure system by spending millions of dollars and not connecting to anything. But in reality, security risk can never be eliminated. It is a matter of economics – how much one is willing to spend to bring the risk below a certain level.

The teenage computer cracker is one of the great demon images of the current age, but the image is overblown (perhaps because so many of the threats of the Internet are intangible, this is one fear that actually has a face). But it is interesting to see that reports on computer security estimate that roughly 80 per cent of all security breaches are by company insiders.

Reference – security

Newsgroups: comp.security.misc, comp.security.unix, alt.security

Security Alert – **http://www.first.org/secalert/**

The Hacker Crackdown, Bruce Sterling [Viking, 1992]
Building Internet Firewalls, D. Chapman [O'Reilly & Assocs, 1996]
Internet Security Handbook, W. Stallings [McGraw Hill, 1996]

■ **FIG 1.17**

Privacy

The Internet was designed as an open system, where messages may be routed via anywhere, and can potentially be read by anyone. And, upon such a foundation, the Internet has grown enormously and has proved useful and entertaining for many people. However, there is a natural problem when one comes to want to send sensitive messages over the system. This is one of the most important issues for the Internet, encompassing problems of private messages and the future of Internet electronic commerce. If a solution to this problem was not available, the Internet would not progress beyond being an amusing toy.

Fortunately, a solution is at hand: out from the dusty cupboards of mathematics departments steps encryption. This offers the ability to code messages, then send them across an open, public network – but where only the message writer and designated recipients can decode and understand the message.

Good, that's it, you might think, so where's the problem? Unfortunately, from here, the problem blossoms from being just a simple technical matter, to a social and political issue involving the conflict between government control and individual liberty.

On the one side, there are people who want to send personal messages to each other, or to send credit card details to a merchandiser via the Net; and on the other side are governments who want to retain the ability to listen in on what's happening. So far, this debate has been carrying on in the US; other countries may not even be aware a problem exists, but the ramifications are global.

In a nutshell, strong encryption techniques already exist (developed in the US) that would allow privacy of messages, and safe electronic commerce; but these techniques are controlled by the US Government (and are even classified as munitions for the purposes of export). The US Government has proposed a medium-strength encryption system for voluntary use (the Capstone Project involving the Clipper chip and key escrow), which allows it to decode any message. Opponents see this as just an intermediary stage to a compulsory government system, where all other encryption techniques are outlawed.

An interesting point is made by Kevin Kelly in his book *Out Of Control*, where he observes that huge amounts of money are being used to connect everything to everything (i.e. linking computers, creating the Internet and improving bandwidth). But having achieved this, the task will then be to control what is *not* communicated (for example, personal information, or business details). Privacy will become big business.

The Electronic Frontier Foundation (EFF) was founded by Mitch Kapor (ex-chief executive of Lotus) and John Perry Barlow, with the aim of alerting people to the threats to civil liberties. Their Web site is one of the most interesting on the Internet and is the primary source for information on privacy-related issues.

Reference – privacy

Newsgroups: alt.privacy, alt.privacy.anon-server, alt.privacy.clipper, comp.society.privacy, alt.society.civil-liberty

EFF – **http://www.eff.org/**

RSA (see glossary) – **http://www.rsa.com/**

The Codebreakers: The Story Of Secret Writing, David Kahn [Macmillan, 1967]
PGP Pretty Good Privacy, S. Garfinkel [O'Reilly & Assocs]

■ FIG 1.18

Payment systems – ecash

For the Internet to continue useful development, the obvious requirement is for commerce to be possible over the Net itself. An amazing number of different systems have been proposed to get around the problem, and it is likely that in the near future these will increasingly be used in practice.

Beyond the simple transfer of funds from one account to another, the Internet offers the possibility of some intriguing new methods of payment. One of these is micropayments, where a customer is only charged small amounts of money for exactly what is used. For example, a reader of a newspaper would only be charged for the specific articles read, which might amount to just three cents a page. This could be very attractive as services offered via the Net would not require previous subscription (a great deterrent for the use of Internet services at the moment). Another possibility would be software programs that are free, and payment is only made when the program is used ('pay-as-you-use').

One of the key issues for electronic commerce is encryption (outlined above). Although the specific details of encryption are wonderfully obscure, the debate is far from trivial. If general, widespread use of uncontrolled encryption happens, this will lead to a significant decline in government power, and the disappearance of much economic activity from public and government view.

It may not be going too far to say that encryption techniques will be the foundation for future communications and society; and in the coming century, they will have the same invisible, but influential, impact that electricity had on the 20th century.

> ### Reference – payment systems
>
> First Virtual – **http://www.fv.com/**
>
> Mondex – **http://www.mondex.com/mondex/home.htm**
>
> Digital Cash – **http://www.digicash.com/**
>
> IBM's Open Market – **http://www.openmarket.com/**
>
> Visa – **http://www.visa.com/**
>
> Mastercard – **http://www.mastercard.com/**
>
> Ecash links (at Exeter University) –
> **http://www.ex.ac.uk/~RDavies/arian/money.html**
>
> *Digital Money*, Daniel Lynch and Leslie Lundquist [John Wiley & Sons]
> *Digital Cash*, Peter Wayner [A.P. Profession]

 FIG 1.19

Censorship

It is extremely easy for anybody to put on the Internet potentially offensive material (e.g. racist literature or pornography) which can be accessed by anybody with an Internet connection. In ordinary life this would be dealt with by constraints applied to the publisher and distribution stopped. But it is not so easy on the Internet, where it may be impossible to find (or reach) the publisher, and, as the Internet is an open network with no central control, it is difficult to prevent distribution.

Various methods are being developed to deal with this, the majority being types of 'opt-in' censorship, primarily for the protection of children. Another initiative has Web sites voluntarily rating themselves, which allows parents to give their children graded levels of access to the Net.

> ### Reference – censorship
>
> Surfwatch – **http://www.surfwatch.com**
>
> Safesurf – **http://www.safesurf.com**

 FIG 1.20

Copyright

This is another of those annoying issues that looks quite straightforward on the surface, but becomes more complex on further analysis. On the one side, there are the creators of material (e.g. authors), who want to be able to create and distribute their work on the Internet and receive remuneration for it. The problem with this is that as soon as anything is placed on the Internet, it can be copied and used elsewhere. The issue is further clouded if the copied work is altered only slightly, but sufficiently to be different from the original work. On the other side, there are people who believe that everything on the Internet is, and should be, in the public domain, and further (and slightly more mystically) believe that *information wants to be free*. Not surprisingly, authors are not usually to be found in this latter group.

The problem here is dealing with ill-defined terms such as *work* or *material*. Since the time of the printing press, it has been natural for people with ideas to write them down on paper and sell them. In the future, however, high value will not be attributed to 'one-dimensional' ideas themselves, but rather to timeliness and a structure that displays the interconnectedness of ideas (not the ideas themselves).

Reference – copyright

Copyright – **http://www.benedict.com/**

Essay by John Perry Barlow at the EFF – **http://www.eff.org**

■ FIG 1.21

Internet economics

Among Web marketers, the most common question asked is not about the best choice of plug-in, or the desirability of using frames, but 'how do we make money from all this?' The majority of Web sites created up to now belong to the 'build it and they will come' school of economic planning. And they've been right. The problem, though, is that while they may come, there is little evidence that people are willing to pay for it yet. There is not so much a

Reference – economics

The Economics of the Internet –
http://www.sims.berkeley.edu/resources/infoecon/

Yahoo – **http://www.yahoo.com/Computers_and_Internet/Internet/Business_and_Economics/**

Commercenet – **http://www.commercenet.net**

The New Internet Business Book, J.M. Ellsworth [Wiley, 1996]
Internet Business Guide 2e, Resnick [Sams.Net]
Internet Commerce, A. Dahl [New Riders Publishing, 1996]

■ FIG 1.22

problem with the online ordering of goods (which is, after all, just a simple extension of mail or telephone ordering), rather with services. All the investment that has currently been made in the Internet has been on the assumption that this attitude will change. It will be interesting to see if, and how soon, it does.

FUTURE DEVELOPMENTS

The most important requirement when looking into the future is a little imagination; avoid being rooted in the here and now. Technology in general, and the Internet in particular, are changing incredibly quickly; and therefore so are the implications of those changes.

Anything one might say about the Internet today will likely be irrelevant in a short while. Yes, in the middle of 1996 the Internet might be said to be very slow, Web page design awful, and good information difficult to find; but the World Wide Web is just five years old and growing ten per cent monthly. Any specific observations made now are not likely to be useful when looking at the big picture.

A rule of thumb for translating computer consultants' time estimates for projects into reality is said to be: increase the unit of time (from days to weeks, weeks to months or months to years), and double the figure (for example, an estimate for a project to take three weeks will mean that it will probably take six months). But the pace of development of technology and the Internet stands this on its head. Developments that people dismiss as science fiction and not likely to happen for the next 50 years or so (e.g. chips in the brain), will probably have prototypes running in ten years; developments thought possible in ten years' time are probably being planned for inclusion in the next Web browser release, and developments thought likely over the next two to five years (e.g. voice recognition and computer language translation) are here already.

> Developments that people dismiss as science fiction and not likely to happen for the next 50 years or so will probably have prototypes running in ten years; developments thought possible in ten years' time are probably being planned for inclusion in the next Web browser release.

It is certainly easy to get distracted and confused by all the new products and services. Every month brings announcements of a new multimedia this or 3D that. But for looking into the future, it is necessary to ignore all this noise, and try to identify some of the main trends that will have a long-term impact.

An important thing is to first consider our attitude to computers themselves. At the moment we probably regard a computer as a box of tricks that sits on a desktop and does things, like formatting a letter or calculating the family budget. As such, it is a little like a car, which can also be useful: one can play with the headlights, listen to the car radio or have a picnic in the back. But the car's potential is not realized until you actually put petrol in it, then you can really go places. A computer is the same, a clever box of tricks whose potential is not realized until it is connected to a network and other computers. At this point, the computer's main function is not as a grand calculator or typewriter, but as a connector. In the coming years, for the majority of people, the boxes will no longer be computers, but *connectors*. An appreciation of this change in role is important to understand its consequences.

None of the following forecasts are proposed as a **good thing** (but not the opposite either). They are merely seen as, in many cases, the natural development of what happens when things become digital and we start using computers that are increasingly interlinked.

Many forecasts for the future sound unappealing and frightening. However, it is quite possible that a vision of our ordinary daily lives would terrify a person who lived 500 years ago. To many, the future promise of virtual existence may not sound like much of a life at all; but the beatnik poet, Timothy Leary, held that most Americans have been living in a virtual reality since the mass acceptance of television anyway – cyberspace simply makes the experience interactive instead of passive.

Technological developments

▓ Connectivity

Some of the most visible developments, helping to improve the Internet bandwidth, will be the digging up of roads and the laying of fibre optic cable. However, it is a rather city-centric view to assume that this will lead to improvements everywhere, as it is unlikely that cable will be laid to country areas. Where cable is not available, modems will be used for a little while yet. But speeds of 33 600bps are reaching the limits of modem development. Thus, wider adoption of ISDN is likely, even though its eventual popularity will be affected by its slow introduction and competition with cable. Beyond this, Internet services may be offered via ADSL or HDSL (see glossary). All together, improvements in the Internet backbone and individual Internet access will lead to a jump in bandwidth many times greater than that seen today.

▓ Hardware

In 1965 Gordon Moore of Intel observed that microprocessor chips doubled in power every one and a half to two years. This did in fact forecast quite closely the subsequent increase in the number of transistors on a chip from 2300 to the 5.5 million of a Pentium Pro processor. There are now indications that this trend might come to an end, as the limits are reached with what can be done with physical components like silica. It's always possible that new mediums or techniques may be invented that allow another surge forward in chip technology. However, the important advances in the future may no longer result directly from increases in raw computing power; they are more likely to come from the increasing interconnectivity of computers and humans themselves.

Interfaces

As mentioned elsewhere, longer term, the most significant development will be the improved interface between computers and humans. This will involve improvements in voice recognition, break-throughs in natural language processing and those chips in the brain.

General Internet developments

The future of the Internet is as a network of private intranets. Each intranet may be defined by being associated with a specific company, and an individual may be temporarily part of several such intranets while he or she works simultaneously for those companies. In addition there will be intranets that are collections of services for a specific activity. For example, an investment intranet may contain some proprietary material, private discussion forums and also offer free access to subscription services such as *WSJ Online*, Disclosure company database, real-time prices and a selection of newsletters and research boutiques.

Computers will be ubiquitous, and people will carry a card (like a credit card) that can be input to any computer, and that will allow access via the computer to the Internet and to their special collection of intranets.

By then, an individual's personality will be defined by the profile of the intranets of which they are a member. There will be many brand name lifestyle intranets, that offer a broad range of services: sports information, entertainment, financial advice, holidays etc. As allegiances to the nation-state (and other geographically extended groups) decline, people will increasingly identify strongly with the intranets of which they are members. This identification will become so strong that they may come to rely on it, and feel threatened by other intranets. This will lead to genuine wars (albeit information wars) between, say, the members of PepsiNet and CokeNet.

An individual's personality will be defined by the profile of the intranets of which they are a member. People will increasingly identify strongly with the intranets of which they are members. This identification will become so strong that they may come to rely on it, and feel threatened by other intranets.

The shorter term will see the development of intelligent agents that can navigate and manage on our behalf all the Internet offers. An example of such would be a personal finance program, which continually monitors the Internet for all types of information, such as portfolio share prices or the best interest rates available.

It is a great mistake to think that the Internet's effect on everything will be similar. Many areas will hardly be touched at all; for example, manufacturing industries (e.g. cars, sports equipment, clothes) will notice little impact. The greatest influence will be seen in service companies.

A random list of general Internet effects might include:

- the rise of virtual companies, where people work for just a short period, but for many overlapping companies simultaneously
- closer company-client relationships
- growth of online ordering
- growth of unsolicited e-mail, but highly focused and cleverly targeted (and as such not regarded as junk)
- growth of black market 'underwire' economies
- problems of tax collecting
- decline in the importance of English as the global language for business
- digital voting for political elections and on individual issues
- decline in importance of the nation-state.

Financial developments

No industry is likely to be affected more by the Internet than investment. However, even without the Internet, there would be strong forces influencing change within the industry.

One of the greatest agents of change is likely to be the humble personal finance program. These have been around for some time (for example, Intuit's Quicken, or Microsoft's Money), but we are starting to see the development of some sophisticated packages. Up to now, these programs have largely concentrated on monitoring bank account information, regular payments (for example, for mortgages or insurance), with perhaps some simple stock portfolio facility.

> One of the greatest agents of change is likely to be the humble personal finance program. These have been around for some time. But, in the future, these programs will know us intimately.

But, in the future, these programs will know us intimately:

- They will know our income and expenditure, our age and life expectancy, details of all our family.
- They will look after the household budget, automatically monitor prices at the online shops and order automatically. If you take up smoking they will find the cheapest cigarettes and recalculate the estimate for the following year's health insurance premium.

- They will advise us how to make provision for future payments (e.g. school fees).
- They will arrange insurance for us (in what the insurance industry becomes: an options market), and, through access to statistical databases, will be able to calculate their own 'fair value' for insurance premiums.
- They will advise which voluntary taxes to pay.
- They will monitor currency movements and hedge potential outgoings (e.g. foreign holidays).
- They will advise on stocks to buy, what level of risk to take, and, if asked, trade the stocks automatically.
- They will warn us against inappropriate investments.
- They will monitor the portfolio, and rebalance when necessary.
- They will monitor news broadcasts and all the world's markets.
- With spare cash they will automatically monitor world interest rates and place the money on deposit, at the best rates for overnight or term according to your forecast cash requirements.

Overall, they will continually monitor the total risk of the portfolio (being the sum of all your current and expected future financial activity), and look to extract maximum value from it by increasing risk in one area and possibly selling option premium in another.

They will, in short, be a full-time financial adviser, that never sleeps, nor (within its terms of reference) ever make a mistake.

The description of such a program might sound intrusive, appalling, frightening or ridiculous. And it may be any of those – but one thing it is not, is science fiction.

One slightly unexpected result of such a program might be that investment would become boring – which is just as it should be. However, investors may decide to liven things up a little by deliberately setting ambitious investment targets. Alternatively, the program may have a facility for manual override, allowing investors to take a certain degree of direct control and trade directly.

Imagine if a personal finance program was released with just some of the features listed above; and consider the likely impact on the banking, insurance and investment industries.

Until recently there was a big divide between institutional and retail investors. The former had:

- investment skill
- computers (or, if not computers, then at least staff for research, portfolio management and trade settlement)
- proximity to the markets (with up-to-date information and immediate trading ability).

The retail investor had pencil and paper, and was detached from the markets. But this is changing irrevocably. The personal computer revolution has brought real computing power into the home. Now investment programs, available for a couple of hundred dollars, are every bit as powerful as those used by many professional investors.

In fact, retail investment programs, in many cases, can be *more* powerful, as much of the exciting computing development in recent years has been at the PC level. New PC programs have been introduced in quick succession, and institutions do not have the flexibility to install and support all the latest packages as they are released.

So, the playing field is levelling: the individual investor's home PC is probably as (if not more) powerful than that of the institutional investor; his or her personal finance program offers general portfolio management; and specialized trading programs offer enhanced investment skill. And just as the individual investor is gaining these powerful tools, the Internet arrives to offer the final piece – easy and cheap contact with the markets.

The combination of all these trends will not merely redefine the relationship between classes of investor, but will also fundamentally influence the whole investment process itself. It will affect:

▓ how we invest (the process of trading)
▓ how we research (the process of analysis)
▓ what we actually invest in.

These three areas are examined further below.

How will we invest?

The highest profile investment development on the Net has probably been the emergence of online brokers. These services are a natural extension for execution-only discount brokerages, and their appearance (despite occasional concerns about bad execution – see the misc.invest newsgroup) can only be seen as a good thing – widening the choice for investors. And with commission rates as low as US$12, irrespective of deal size, an investor is going to have to deal in very small sizes, or incredibly actively, for that to be a significant cost.

It is difficult to see why such online brokerages should not eventually spread to every major world market. The advantage of these online brokers is not just low commissions and quick access, but the potential in the future to link their dealing facility directly into the investor's own portfolio management program running on a local hard disk. This can then avoid mistakes in inputting trade orders or execution details.

International investing

Another advantage, being a natural side-effect of the Internet (but not one that may have been of paramount importance to the brokers initially), is that the online broking facilities can be used equally by anyone around the world. Considering the cost of international telephone calls and faxes, this feature could be extremely attractive for international investors. So, an investor in Japan wanting to buy US$30 000 of Intel shares, has the possibility of trading online and paying commission of, for example, just US$12 (or 0.04 per cent of the trade amount).

Although global investing has been touted for a long time, its practice has really been restricted to institutional investors. Retail clients have confined themselves to investing through funds. But the growth of online brokers could lead to individual investors trading directly around the world at low cost.

ADRs

An intriguing side note can be made here with regard to American Depositary Receipts (ADRs). At the moment, the prime purpose of ADRs is to offer investment in international companies to US (usually institutional) investors. Many of these ADRs are listed on one of the US stock exchanges, and trade just like any other US stock. Therefore, a foreign investor can trade in these stocks just like any US investor, while benefiting from the generally cheaper and more efficient US markets. For example, a South African investor might be interested in Ericsson of Sweden, but find it much cheaper to trade the Ericsson ADR (listed on Nasdaq) via one of the US online brokers. In fact, even Swedish investors themselves might find it easier and cheaper to trade the Ericsson ADR, rather than the stock in their own domestic market. (A few sample brokerage commission rates can be found in the section on online brokers in Section 2, page 213.)

Bulletin boards

Having achieved closer market access, real-time prices and low dealing costs, the next thing individual investors want are better trading prices – the ability to deal within the spread.

This leads to one of the most truly revolutionary changes that is likely to be seen in the stock markets: the introduction of bulletin board trading. In these systems, investors have direct access to the board (for example, on a Web page), and there they can see a list of all the buy/sell orders; if they want, they can add their own order to the board. This system (which can be called a 'crossing system') then matches potential trading partners immediately or at regular intervals. Such systems have been available for some time for institutional investors (e.g. Instinet **http://www.instinet.com/** and Posit **http://www.itginc.com/**), but the individual investor has largely been unaware of this. For such an investor, the crossing system has the advantages of:

▓ lower commissions (dispensing entirely with brokers)

▓ the possibility of dealing within the spread (no market makers or specialists are required)

▓ a more transparent market (by being able to see the orders posted), which can result in greater direct control over the order execution.

These bulletin boards should become quite widespread and popular, especially with retail investors. In theory, anybody can set up a system. In practice, the following are likely to be the major sources:

▓ **Companies themselves**: any company can set up its own WWW system for the trading of its own shares. If it is successful, it is likely that this would attract major liquidity, and become the first place to check for prices (see the example of Spring Street Brewing in Fig. 1.23).

▓ **Specialized Web sites**: there are Web sites setting up now that specialize in particular areas of the market. (The best example is Silicon Investor with technology stocks.) These can become a focal point for many investors. At the moment, they offer the ability to research a company and to talk with other investors. From here, it would seem a natural step to provide a bulletin board system for investors to post orders. (After all, this type of development would seem only to mimic the origins of exchanges themselves.) The key here is to attract a critical mass of users, and the current establishment of chat areas on Web sites would appear to be the result of half an eye towards this opportunity.

▓ **Brokers**: if an online broker has built up a sizeable flow of orders, an obvious progression may be to set up a system for crossing those orders. If they do not, they may see business slowly ebbing away elsewhere. (The online brokers currently investigating such systems are Jack White and E*Trade.)

▓ **Exchanges**: the Arizona Stock Exchange is trying to extend its institutional system for retail orders, and Nasdaq has set up a hybrid system called Naqcess.

Traditionally, the usual problem faced by crossing systems is liquidity, and, apart from regulatory hurdles, the major work here will be in designing systems that get around this problem. However, in some of the above cases, where the site is focused on a particular stock or sector, it may be that this creates sufficient interest for reasonable trading.

One of the obstacles faced by these systems is avoiding being identified as an 'exchange' and thereby having to abide by the strict rules of exchange regulators. But this may not be such a problem for single stock trading systems; and it was significant that the SEC seemed to have no objection in principle to the Wit-Trade system (see Fig. 1.23).

Although there are still quite a few problems to be sorted out, there is a lot of interest in these crossing systems, and the losers could be the retail brokers and exchanges.

Spring Street Brewing Company and Wit Capital

After spending a number of years as a securities lawyer, Andrew D. Klein decided to leave Wall Street and set up a microbrewery called Spring Street Brewing Company. Three years later, in February 1996, the company became the first digital IPO following a public offering of shares via the Internet. The offer was made via the company's WWW site, which carried an official circular; and subscriptions – executed through a subscription agreement attached to each circular – could be e-mailed direct to the company. The offering was qualified with the SEC (Reg. A, Securities Act 1933) and raised nearly $1.6 million from 3500 investors – without the intermediation of Wall Street underwriters.

The day after the IPO, the company announced that secondary trading would commence on its own WWW bulletin board system, which offered buying and selling of the shares without using brokers or paying commissions. Trading duly started, but was halted after a few weeks in response to an informal request from the SEC.

The company's WWW trading system (called 'Wit-Trade') worked by publicly posting buy and sell orders, and then matching prospective trading partners. It was also possible to view a record of recent trading activity and the company's recent financial reports. Settlement of the trades was provided by a form of contract which parties used to execute a binding agreement to trade shares. This required the company to act as its own clearing and transfer agent; and it was this latter part that concerned the SEC.

However, a week later the SEC gave the go-ahead for Wit-Trade – subject to certain modifications, which, in the words of the company's president, Klein, were:

- To ensure careful handling of investors' funds, the Company will use an independent agent, such as a bank or escrow agent, to receive checks from buyers of the securities.

- To prevent confusion about the role of the system, the Company will publish certain warnings on its World Wide Web materials.

- To allow investors to make more informed investment decisions, the Company will disclose through Wit-Trade a complete transaction history showing the price and number of shares for each recent transaction.

- To ensure the quality and integrity of the financial information provided through Wit-Trade, the Company will subject such information to certain SEC oversight.

Following the company's IPO, it was apparently approached by many other companies interested in going public through the Internet. In response to this, the company announced the formation of Wit Capital: an investment bank and stock exchange offering financial advisory services to companies, including the public offering of shares and secondary trading via the WWW.

Source: Wit Capital
http://www.witcap.com/

■ FIG 1.23

▩ Stock exchanges

For a number of reasons one can assume that the exchanges are wary about the Internet. Or, at least, the large established exchanges facing smaller, nimbler competitors are. And it is interesting to note that, among the world's stock exchanges, the New York Stock Exchange, London Stock Exchange and the Tokyo Stock Exchange were among the last to establish a Web site.

Of the three big exchanges, the NYSE was the first to set up a site, but their pages contain many phrases ensuring that no one runs away with the idea that this Net thing is anything too serious:

> *The New York Stock Exchange (NYSE) Web site is designed as an educational tool for investors, students and teachers*

something like a Berlitz language cassette perhaps?, or:

> *The NYSE strives to educate and inform individuals about the capital raising process. The NYSE NET web site is just one of many ways in which we hope to accomplish this goal . . .*

where the 'one of many' wasn't actually in bold, but it may as well have been.

▩ Arbitrage

Arbitrage has never really been viable for individual or corporate investors due to:

- a lack of knowledge: the techniques of arbitrage have been treated like a masonic right, passed from hand to hand only within the dealing room
- lack of access to real-time prices
- transaction costs: investors are separated from the market by commission-charging intermediaries, and this is the prime reason why they will never see arbitrage opportunities wide enough to cover their costs
- lack of access to enough capital to make the arbitrage interesting.

However, all this might change. In the future there might be arbitrage programs that can be bought for a few hundred dollars (or arbitrage modules will be optional add-ins for Quicken v27.0), that will provide all the knowledge and skill to identify, execute and monitor arbitrage opportunities. Low cost access to real-time prices is already here, and online dealing costs are falling. Even if the investor doesn't have the ability to leverage the investment, to make an interesting profit, the strategy will be useful for simple yield enhancement, and may prove particularly attractive for treasury departments within companies. For individual investors, such arbitrage activity could become simply an extension of their personal finance packages, where the highest yield for cash is searched for by the program, either on deposit somewhere – or exploiting some arbitrage opportunity.

In fact, an interesting possibility arises, whereby transaction costs for individual investors could come close to, or possibly even fall below, those of professional investors: the reason being that the former do not have to cover the costs of non-profit making staff, and all the general expenditure of running an office in a city.

Future of trading

Of course, many investors may not like the idea of using computers too much: for researching, or for executing trades and portfolio monitoring. However, they will have to accept that it will be highly likely that a computer will be on the other side of many of their trades; and that increasingly in the future they will be trading against computers.

With the increase in investor education, and more trading controlled by computer, it may result in less emotion-influenced trading, and therefore to a reduction in the effect of crowd psychology. In addition, if there is a decline in the large circulation newspapers and a fragmentation among information vendors, news will no longer be routed though a small number of mediums, but rather a variety of news will be delivered by many different channels.

Many investors may not like the idea of using computers too much. However, they will have to accept that it will be highly likely that a computer will be on the other side of many of their trades; and that increasingly in the future they will be trading against computers.

Against the above, though, one might argue that as computers link together closer, and trading knowledge becomes more widely distributed, the trading programs could start acting more in synch, and the crowd psychology of humans would extend to become the crowd psychology of computers.

However, the forecast that increased computerization of trading would lead inevitably to computers all doing the same thing at the same time was always a fallacy; as the circumstances of the investors benefiting from the programs will always be different: with different cost of funds, investment targets and appetite for risk.

Multimedia and games

Some of the most sophisticated technological developments in recent years have been in the area of multimedia games. And it would be surprising if the techniques developed there had nothing to offer the fields of trading and research. Both these fields have to process large amounts of data, and try to present that data in a form that can be assimilated quickly. But their techniques have not really changed much in decades: largely comprising flashing numbers and line charts on a screen. What about market data that is represented by a combination of three-dimensional colour images and sounds?

And beyond this, there may come a time when the majority of trading activity involves contracts rather than assets, and where a market will constitute the matrix of all such contracts, and an entity's risk will be the aggregate distance from areas of stress within the matrix, and systemic risk measuring will involve the identification of abnormal concentrations of stress. Possibly techniques will be borrowed from physics as traders become stress engineers, continually toying with sub-matrices of contracts to reduce the aggregate stress; and finally markets will lose their objectification as traders become part of, and act within, the matrix itself.

How will we research?

The Internet will offer access to company information worldwide. From which, finally, true global sectors can be created and global investment made possible, as the digitized data can be quickly and easily processed and compared.

Specialized Web sites will appear that offer data and analysis tools for specific market sectors (and these sites themselves may well become the major forums for trading activity in the sector).

Similarly, there should be a huge growth in independent research boutiques and newsletters. This has been a possibility waiting in the wings for a long time – but, until now, such activity was not terribly profitable due to the economics of physically distributing research material and the problems of contacting a critical mass of clients. Now, the Internet offers possible solutions to both those problems. It will be interesting to see whether the demand is actually there for pure research services (with possibly a layered subscription service for different clients, ranging from a base level free service for all, to a value-added full service offering complete portfolio monitoring). As with most things on the Internet, simple economic models rarely apply. Thus, such research boutiques may find the actual research itself a loss leader, compensated for by leveraging off a valuable client base through other services offered (e.g. third party discount brokerage). Or, perhaps revenues will come from subscriptions for access to exclusive online discussion areas with bulletin board trading facilities. Obviously, there will be no one solution here, and different market sectors will support different service models.

> The Internet will offer access to company information worldwide. From which, finally, true global sectors can be created and global investment made possible, as the digitized data can be quickly and easily processed and compared.

Interesting developments should be seen in the techniques of index compilation. The current market indices are nearly all designed for institutional investors, and concentrate on 'investible' (from an institutional viewpoint) securities, with a certain minimum market capitalization and liquidity. But these indices are not particularly representative for individual investors, who tend to invest more in smaller capitalized stocks and may be less concerned about liquidity.

So, there will be a profusion of new indices – covering all types of sectors and portfolio strategy; and tracking all types of market theme, as the turnover cycle for these themes gets ever shorter. While market-capitalization weighted indices are no doubt superior to price-weighted ones for large investors, they may need to be refined for other investors interested in specific small sectors (for example, a sector might contain Microsoft and three other companies with a market capitalization below US$100 million). The indexing industry will become increasingly important as market activity becomes more oriented towards index contracts rather than assets.

And, as mentioned above, new techniques will evolve for representing huge arrays of data, in forms that cannot only be understood quickly, but will also highlight new relationships between the data points.

Technical analysis involves the study of market data, looking for patterns and possible correlations. The price data analysed might include: open, high, low, close, volume and open interest. The techniques used can be fairly sophisticated, and in some ways it seems a shame that the study is limited to such a narrow data set.

This may change. As information becomes more and more digitized, the opportunity arises to apply technical analysis techniques to a huge range of new data.

For example, it would be interesting to study the exact relationship between news reports and price behaviour. But this is difficult, when the majority of investors are reacting to news reports from unrelated newspapers, television commentaries or proprietary information vendors. However, as investors increasingly react to news data that is digitized, it becomes possible to collate the news data more efficiently.

It will be found that there is a mass of data that becomes available, and potentially suitable for analysis. And rather than analysis of the investment directly itself, it will lead to an analysis of investors' behaviour. The ambition here will be similar to that of traditional technical analysis, but the universe of data will be far larger.

It is possible to see the germ of this idea in several places on the Net already. One of the most interesting is at StockMaster. On this site it is possible to view stock prices and charts. But also there is a running investor sentiment survey that offers five buttons to push according to your outlook for the stock: ranging from very bearish through neutral to very bullish. Table 1.6 illustrates the results of such a survey for Apple [AAPL] for a few days in August 1996.

A few notes about the survey:

- The survey sample is statistically very small, so this must be taken as just an illustration.
- On an experimental system like this, there is nothing to stop some investor, long of Apple stock, passing an aimless Sunday afternoon clicking the 'very bullish' button. Possibly on future versions there may be a way of preventing this.

■ TABLE 1.6 StockMaster: Investor Sentiment Survey for Apple

Date (August 1996)	Closing price	Responses	Very negative	Negative	Neutral	Positive	Very positive
20	23.500	167	9	5	11	59	82
21	23.500	113	6	6	15	36	49
22	23.250	759	12	5	16	145	572
23	23.875	379	12	6	9	81	266
24	23.875	178	4	3	10	51	108

Source: StockMaster

■ Despite the above, and although someone might have clicked more than their allotted amount on 22 August, it is interesting to note that the following day, the stock actually did rise. And, further, on 21 August, when the very bullish number fell (from 82 to 49), the following day did actually see the stock fall.

As mentioned above, one should not take too much notice of such a small sample. But this is early days yet. Imagine if this survey grew, to comprise thousands of responses, and imagine that other similar surveys were operating on the Net, and that this data could be quickly and easily collated across the Net and analysed.

Of course, there's no reason to suppose that everybody clicking the buttons does so genuinely (or has even heard of the company Apple), but none of this analysis is expected to offer a quick magic path to easy riches. The analysis will be complex, but it does provide an increasing wealth of raw data to be agglomerated for some serious analysis.

Other sources of such data that will become available for analysis will be the number of requests to see specific stock quotes and charts. Perhaps the online news services (e.g. *WSJ Online*, CNN, *FT*) will analyse the viewing data for their stock reports and commentaries, and make this data available for a fee. And, again, single figures won't be interesting here, but rather data histories will be subject to all the technical analysis techniques currently applied to price data.

■ Text analysis

Virtually all scientific analysis of data is applied to numerical data. But developments in the future hold out the possibility of scientifically analysing text data as well. Although at the moment we have large text databases (an example would be the WWW itself) that can be easily searched on for keywords, when the program finds instances of the keyword all it can do is note its occurrence. It doesn't remotely understand what that word, phrase or sentence actually means. Techniques are being developed at the moment where text is broken down into the components of language, and from here, a start can be made at 'understanding' the actual meaning. This study is called natural language processing (NLP) and although there is much work to do yet, the potential is fascinating.

Virtually all scientific analysis of data is applied to numerical data. But developments in the future hold out the possibility of scientifically analysing text data as well.

It may offer data for a new set of analytical tools (equivalent to those used in technical analysis), where the meaning of text extracts can be charted and correlated. Resulting from this would be the ability for computers to monitor discussion forums and news services automatically – and this would involve far more than simple keyword recognition. The computer would actually understand phrases like, 'I wouldn't say I'm completely unbearish on the other stock' and log the meaning in a database. (Note: whether the text occurs as the spoken voice, written on paper or typed at a keyboard is irrelevant, as all this data can be, or will be capable of being, digitized.)

What will we invest in?

Up to now, most of the discussion in this section has been applicable to investing in stocks, and perhaps some of it is also relevant to other investments such as bonds, currencies, mutual funds, investment trusts, futures and options. However, in the future is this range of investments really what we will be investing in?

We have seen that some companies may take to raising capital directly from investors via the Internet, thereby eliminating the investment banking financial intermediaries. Further, it may be that secondary trading via crossing systems on the Net grows – avoiding another financial intermediary group (brokers). But will we actually want to invest in these companies at all?

Information age companies

As we move into the information age, we can already see companies getting smaller, people working on contract, and the growth of service firms. In this new era, the exciting growth companies are likely to be smaller, hi-tech service companies, rather than the old industrial age, industrial-size corporations.

And these new companies may be difficult to invest in. If they do come to the market at all with a public offering, this will (as always, if possible) be arranged when the hype is at its greatest – and the stocks will subsequently fall from their IPO price. This is demonstrated already to some extent in the Morgan Stanley Internet report which observes that of the 581 hi-tech companies that went public between 1980–94, by the end of this period 45 per cent were below their IPO price. In the future, the popular market themes are likely to turn over ever quicker, and companies may be popular for just a few months, and then fade away.

In addition, the very activity of many of these companies will become ever more esoteric, and investors will be motivated more by the theme rather than fundamentally understanding what the company does. A couple of examples of Internet-related companies illustrate this (taken from the Market Guide reports). One company's activities are described as:

> *develops a family of object-oriented, client/server document management software products that manage intellectual capital across large enterprises.*

while the other

> *develops and markets a suite of customized information services that provide knowledge workers with daily personalized current awareness reports.*

Not only is it difficult to understand what these companies actually do (and if they are any good at it), but the very market they operate in is vague and the future unpredictable. So, often investors find themselves buying companies with products that can't be understood for a market that doesn't exist yet. At best, it seems the investor might find ephemeral management brilliance, rather than long-term earnings growth – there may be no more Texas Instruments or Motorolas.

But it is quite likely that the most interesting companies will not come to the market at all. The later section on M&A and IPOs (page 303), show that M&A activity among hi-tech companies is five times greater than that for IPOs. The company entrepreneurs are finding it easier to capitalize on their developments by simply selling out to another company. This can make it difficult for investors to become involved; and possibly venture capital funds will become increasingly popular because of this.

▨ The role of capital

A fundamental problem for investors, though, might be that the new dynamic companies will not necessarily have a great demand for their capital. These are, after all, information age companies, who may not need the great capital to rent land, build office or factory premises, lease plant and machinery, establish extensive, physical marketing and distribution networks, and employ large departments of personnel and accounts staff. None of this is saying that large capital-intensive companies will disappear, but the returns from these companies may be of decreasing interest to investors.

Thus, there will be huge waves of money trying to invest in essentially small companies, making it almost impossible to get direct exposure at what might be considered 'sensible' prices.

In consequence, investors are likely to get frustrated when they see the evident activity and excitement in a sector (perhaps the Internet itself is an example here), and compare that with the mediocre returns they are seeing in their traditional portfolios. And, in the drive to get a return from their cash, investors will turn increasingly to proxy investment.

Fortunately for them the model already exists for proxy investment – it's called the derivatives market. These instruments will allow one group of investors to bet against another group that, for example, hi-tech stocks are headed up (or down). It will be in this market that investors find that they can get the direct exposure to market themes that they want. And at this point indexing technology will be in great demand, to create a huge dynamic range of indices which can act as the basis for the contracts trading. With the precedent of futures and options contracts on non-assets (such as inflation indices, or market volatility) the path is open to create contracts based on almost anything. For example, it could be M&A activity, the aggregate earnings of a group of companies, the number of times a company's name is mentioned in a selection of news sources, or the relative sales of two competing software programs.

In a trend comparable to digitization, investors will be able to metaphorically take companies apart, and take a view (and investment exposure) on one part of the business, instead of worrying about the complex analysis of the company organism as a whole.

Eventually, all this will lead to a decline in traditional stock market activity, while the *real* action will be taking place elsewhere.

Investment units

At the moment, many investments are homogeneous units trading in separated markets. Thus, we have stocks trading in stock markets, futures in futures markets and currencies in currency markets. The future will see a decline in tradeable instruments being defined by the market they trade in. There will be a great merging and synthesis of these tradeable instruments, and many new ones will be created. Further, these instruments will be trading in all manner of forums and exchanges around the world. Market regulation will become an anachronism as the very word 'market' itself will become an abstract term, difficult to apply to any particular collection of geographically distributed investment activity.

> Market regulation will become an anachronism as the very word 'market' itself will become an abstract term, difficult to apply to any particular collection of geographically distributed investment activity.

However, market regulation may be replaced by individual product regulation. There is not much point in new tradeable investments being created if investors do not understand or are afraid of them. Hence, each investment unit (for short, we will call it an 'invit'), will carry a summary description of its type and contents. This summary might include statistical measures of the investment, including expected return, volatility, correlation with x, and liquidity. A certain group of measures may be possible to aggregate which will allow valid comparison between all types of invit (invits being stocks, funds, futures contracts, or a whole host of new special investment packages).

At this point, it is interesting to briefly compare the similarities between investment and food. Both provide important nourishment for life, and a food diet can be crudely compared to an investment portfolio strategy. In the food industry, one can see that products are increasingly processed and refined. This, together with the large-scale and interconnectedness of the business, seems to create a certain fragility within the system. An example might be the BSE scare in the UK, where one problem affected a large part of the UK food industry. Similarities can be made with finance, where products are also more and more refined and derivative; and as the system becomes more interconnected the systemic risk rises. Anybody, within reason, can set up a stall and sell food; the regulation largely covers the content of the food (not the market). This involves, among other things, a strict control over the labelling of the food: a tin or packet will carry a label with details of constituents and possibly quantities of proteins, carbohydrates and vitamins.

A similar situation may come to exist with the regulation of invits. Anybody can trade these (other mechanisms besides government regulatory ones will control this trading), but the main regulation will be over the content of the invits. Thus, each invit will carry its equivalent of the food label.

When looking for a model for the future investment industry, perhaps the food sector will provide one.

▥ Lifestyle investment

The future will offer access to huge amounts of information and experience, but there will be problems knowing how to filter and select this information. Although there will be computerized expert systems to help, another method will be brand recognition. People will 'buy in' to a certain brand they identify with and that matches their lifestyle. For example, so far on the Internet the best known brand is Yahoo, and as Yahoo sets up associated new sites in other countries, people will use them, because of brand recognition. And these brands obviously become incredibly valuable – too valuable just to leave trapped in a single sector. So, the brand extends to encompass Yahoo T-shirts, Yahoo television, Yahoo – The Movie, and eventually, Yahoo Investments.

A precedent for this already exists in the UK where both Marks & Spencer and Virgin have launched investment products. This trend, although slow to start, should continue. People will be members of the NikeNet, and use the Nike search engine, go on Nike holidays, and buy Nike Mutual Funds and other investments. This is a whole lifestyle thing, investment for the way you are: *Japan Smaller Companies – just do it.*

▥ Gambling

The introduction of uniquely cash-settled futures in the 1970s paved the way for investment that is essentially no different from gambling (the term *gambling* is not being used here in a tabloid pejorative sense). Although the exchanges at the time, seeking to avoid regulatory censure, dreamt up some wonderfully creative descriptions (for example, trading stock index futures is just like buying a basket of stocks), these futures are basically just contracts for differences, and from the investor's viewpoint can be regarded as gambling.

Investment activity is likely to become increasingly focused on contracts rather than assets. The scope of these contracts should broaden considerably, and come to be ever more detached from what are recognizable as investments today.

As described above, investment activity is likely to become increasingly focused on contracts rather than assets. The scope of these contracts should broaden considerably, and come to be ever more detached from what are recognizable as investments today.

An interesting example can be found with City Index, which offers 'spread-betting'. It will quote a bid/offer price, and the gambler buys or sells at so many pounds sterling a point (as specified by the gambler). City Index offers quotes on many sports, but side by side with these are also quotes on stock indices, government bonds, currencies, interest rates and commodities (**http://www.bogo.co.uk/city/text/cityhome.htm**).

As contract trading grows, it seems inevitable that today's boundaries between investment and gambling will blur, and then disappear completely. The investor's portfolio program will monitor the bet on the number of goals in the World Cup Soccer competition alongside the short position in gold.

Reference – gambling

http://www.casino.org
http://www.netexas.com/people/sportbet/casino.htm
http://virtualvegas.com/playground.html
http://www.interlotto.li
http://www.ladbrokes.co.uk
http://www.casino-network.com

■ FIG 1.24

Financial intermediaries

If an investor in the UK, say, wanted to buy some shares in a Japanese company today, the order processing chain might look like this:

client – financial adviser – fund manager – broker – local Japanese broker – exchange

At each stage, the intermediaries take their commission share. And this does not include the other possible costs: the market maker's spread on the exchange itself, bank charges for transferring money, custodian charges, and the government taxes that go to fund the regulatory body overseeing the market.

> Although the changes wrought by the Internet will not be good news for many existing financial intermediaries, this does not mean that the investment business as a whole is somehow going to disappear. If anything, there will be a huge growth, and opportunity, in new financial services – but these will not necessarily look much like the old established ones.

In the future, the investor with a PC might be able to trade direct at the exchange, or, further, on a bulletin board direct with a counter-party. It does not seem hyperbole, therefore, to suggest that the investment industry will be one of those most affected by computers and communication.

There will be huge changes in the industry, many old names will disappear, others will transform and refocus their activities, while completely new competitors will also arrive – competitors not previously associated with finance at all. Some of these may be the brand names (e.g. Coca Cola, BMW or Sony), while other companies may be computer or network-related (e.g. Intuit, Microsoft, Intel, America Online).

Although the changes wrought by the Internet will not be good news for many existing financial intermediaries, this does not mean that the investment business as a whole is somehow going to disappear. If anything, there will be a huge growth, and opportunity, in new financial services – but these will not necessarily look much like the old established ones.

Many financial companies are already actively involved with new technology and the Internet, and a couple of interesting Web sites carry news focused on technology and finance:

Waters Information Services – **http://www.watersinfo.com**

Webfinance (from Investment Dealers' Digest) – **http://webfinance.net**

■ Financial advisers

Financial advisers tend to have a close relationship with their clients (indeed, they are often geographically close as well), and they offer specifically tailored advice. As such, there is no great reason why the Internet should have a strong influence here. However, the increasing sophistication of personal finance software packages will have a great impact in this area.

■ Brokers

Brokerages quite often comprise three units: research, sales and dealing. Up to now, these have been offered as a package – with the exception relatively recently of the appearance of execution-only discount brokers. It looks likely in the future that we will not only have the digitization of data, but also the fragmentation of services. As such, execution-only services will continue to grow (and be offered as components for many different Net services). The research part of brokerages may now be able to standalone and contract out execution to other firms.

> **Selection of headlines from 'Internet in the Markets' at the Web site of Waters Information Services (April–August 1996)**
>
> - Prisma Offers Live Currency Forecast Service on Internet
> - Would-be Instinet, Selectnet Competitor Pushes Harder
> - Telerate Buys Bankers Network
> - EJV Rolls Bondpage, a Net-Based Version of Marketboard
> - Daiwa Securities Moves to Extend Reach; Puts Odd-Lot Trading on I-Way
> - Telerate Closes Deal with Firm Offering Trading Via Intranet
> - DBC to Offer Commodities Service Via Internet and DBS
> - First Union Capital Markets Group Betas Applix 'Anyware' on Internet, Intranet
> - Comstock to Roll 'Net-Based Service for Professionals
> - Hoboken's Derivex Launches Swaps Pricing Service on the World Wide Web
> - First Call to Launch Fixed-Income Version of Research Direct
> - Sungard Futures Systems Plans Internet-Based Version
> - Street Firms Pack Programmers Off to Java Training Course
> - Mortgage Research Firm Rolls Risk Analysis Tools on Web
> - PC Quote Debuts Internet-based Product for Professional Traders
> - Bank of Boston to Provide FX Quotes to Customers via Internet
>
> *Source: Waters Information Services*

FIG 1.25

Fund management

While it may be easy to see that if an increasing number of investors start using either online brokers or even WWW-based crossing systems directly, this will sidestep traditional brokers, it may be thought that the position of fund managers is more secure – as investors will, in the main, still need investment advice.

It is useful to itemize what is offered by fund management to the investor:

- investment skill
- economies of scale
- diversification
- portfolio monitoring
- portfolio management (accounting etc.).

As with brokers, fund managers will not disappear, but their role may change greatly, and plenty of new competitors will arrive on the scene. There will probably be a fragmentation of services in this area as well, with independent companies setting up services focusing just on asset allocation advice or portfolio monitoring. Such ideas may not be new, but the peculiar economics of the Internet may now make them feasible operations.

Looking at the individual fund management services:

- **Investment skill:** this can be replaced partly by an expert system within a personal finance program. There is no doubt that some fund managers are brilliant, but many are not; and, on balance, a program may prove more consistent in the long run, and better able to meet personal investment targets within a specified risk framework.

- **Economies of scale:** fund managers can certainly benefit from dealing in size at better prices. But transaction costs are falling for individual clients (low commission rates and new possibilities of dealing within the spread), and any residual cost advantage the fund manager may have would most likely be offset by their management charges.

- **Diversification:** this can be a real advantage of funds. The size of individual investors' funds are commonly not large enough to enable the economic holding of a broad portfolio. However, it's possible that there might be a trend towards lower dealing units to encourage smaller investors and liquidity. This would not have been feasible when share settlement was largely paper-based; but, as settlement becomes computerized and with electronic payments, there may be little difference between settling a trade of 1000 shares, or 100 trades of ten shares each. This would enable small investors to construct diversified portfolios using only a few shares.

- **Portfolio monitoring:** this may become one of the major services offered via the Internet, where customized prices and news can be fed directly to the individual investor.

- **Portfolio management:** this task should be capable of being dealt with by a personal finance program.

At the very least, with the growth of independent services, and easy portfolio monitoring, the investor will be better able to compare the true cost of different services, or the composite cost of fund management.

Fund managers may well in the future be the best placed to provide custom packages for investors. Thus, an investor's portfolio program may decide that they need an additional investment package with a certain profile, and this will be created specially by a fund management company.

A likely development is that fund managers become brand name managers, (largely marketing operations to attract money) and where the other component fund management activities are increasingly contracted out to third parties.

■ Information services

The major information vendors (e.g. Reuters, Bloomberg) commonly charge thousands of dollars per month for their services. However, they are obviously watching developments on the Internet closely, and will not want to be left behind if financial activity on it grows strongly. As such, they are already setting up small operations on the Internet, partly as an experiment, and partly to stake their claims in cyberspace. Quite a few of these services are already very good, but this is a competitive area on the Net, and it is likely that services will quickly become more sophisticated. Therefore, there will be one trend of a slowly improving service for the professional market, and another trend of a rapidly improving service on the Net, and at some point these trends will begin to converge. But there is still likely to be a huge pricing differential between the two, and the interesting question will be to see how the information vendors try to maintain their high margins at the professional end.

Besides a process of fragmentation towards offering specialized services, there will also probably be an agglomeration of investment services coming together to offer a one-stop supermarket for the investor. One of the most obvious contenders in this field will be Intuit. But many other individual companies or groups could compete in this area; possibly even the *Wall Street Journal* and the *Financial Times*. In the case of these two financial newspapers, their model is to offer perhaps a subscription service, which might be further bundled into many other investment package services on the Net. But their position is such that it would seem a natural step to include an execution broker and other facilities within their own site. In finance, brand names don't come any better than the *WSJ* or *FT*; and while in the non-digital world, brand name exploitation may not be easy or acceptable, the rules may not be the same on the Internet.

Along with much else, news stories themselves will be digitized. An advantage of this is that personalized news services can be created that collate and present stories of particular interest to individual people. An advantage for the vendor (and buyer perhaps) is that stories can be charged for individually. For example, a reader will be charged five cents to read a story on Apple Computer; the accumulated charges for all stories read, might be less than the charge for the whole daily newspaper. There is nothing new with any of this so far. However, as everything becomes digitized and fragmented, everything will have a price; but, further, everything may well have a variable price.

In the case of news stories, there may be a differential pricing structure for different types of news (financial and sports news high, arts news low). But there may also be a differential within the financial news sector itself, and these prices may fluctuate. For example, news stories on a dull stock announcing quarterly figures in line with market expectations will attract a low price. But, consider the case of Iomega at the beginning of 1996: if the chief executive had made a surprise announcement that the Zip drive contained a flaw, there would have been a huge demand for that news, which might therefore have been priced, albeit temporarily, at a premium to all other news.

Going beyond this, there might be continually fluctuating news prices on stocks, that would naturally have some correlation with the stock's market activity. If attention suddenly focused on one stock, the price of immediate news on that stock would start rising. This could lead to an interesting situation where portfolio managers not only hedge their stock values in case of falls, but also long hedge the news component related to their portfolio.

▨ Training

While financial training may not strictly be regarded as an intermediary, some of the most interesting developments will happen in this area. If there is a growth in individual investment, then there will also be great demand for investment education.

We will probably see the appearance of a great many financial training sites on the Internet offering investment education and also awarding professional certificates for the industry worldwide (investment being the prime example of a professional service equally applicable all round the world).

Part of the training on these sites may involve the use of simulated trading programs. These can be very useful for educating new investors, but they may also be used by trading firms to check the performance of their traders – something like the regular checking of airline pilots in simulated flight machines.

Another type of training activity may draw on experience from online games. There are obvious parallels between a trading market and a multi-user game (multi-user Dungeons etc.); the medium of the Internet could create a critical mass of players to make such an operation interesting.

Investment regulation

Financial regulators already have a hard time of it. It seems that when things go well, everything's fine, but when something goes wrong (e.g. Orange County, Barings Bank), all the regulation in place just doesn't seem to help. Each new disaster heralds a new report and possibly a tweaking of existing legislation. But this is just patch-up regulation, pending the next mishap from some unexpected quarter. And the situation will get worse. How are government regulators going to cope with a UK investor with bank accounts in Hong Kong, investing in a Caribbean-registered fund that specializes in Australian stocks and hedges the currency risk in Chicago and the interest rate risk OTC with a Japanese bank? Oh, and the UK investor is a remote-controlled computer. The short answer is that the regulators won't be able to cope.

But we have not lived with government regulation since the time of Moses; it is a relatively recent idea. Before the 19th century, governments were just not expected, and had little inclination, to get involved with watching out, and legislating, for the common man. We should not, therefore, expect regulation to work very well if forcibly applied to radically different environments. But surely regulation is needed, you might ask? Regulation should not be an end in itself, but rather the protection of the public. For a while governments were the best placed to do this, but in the future their role can be ably usurped by computers.

The problems facing regulation of the investment markets in the future are:

- It would cost too much. Like everything this is a matter of economics, and the likely cost of effective regulation and monitoring would outweigh the benefits.

- It would be unworkable. The very nature of future Internet trading will make legislation extremely difficult to draw up – fixed legislation is not appropriate for environments in a continual state of rapid change and evolution. In addition, trading will increasingly be international, and comprehensive agreement on trading regulation among all countries is highly unlikely (and regulation within just one country won't be very useful).

Any regulation will be difficult in the future because the investment world will not be divided into neat compartments of a few different markets and a few different investment products. As mentioned above, markets may lose their defining boundaries (both geographically and product oriented), and as a result, attention will have to concentrate on the investment products themselves.

If regulation did exist, what would it protect against? One of the obvious targets would be share pushers. These already exist on the Internet, and you can frequently receive unsolicited e-mail messages recommending investment in some obscure company. But what about a company that sends unsolicited e-mail advertising holidays in Japan – would that come under any investment regulation? Of course not. What about if that company linked the price of the holiday to the Nikkei Index, or to the US$/¥ exchange rate? What if an excursion on the holiday was free, if JGB futures fell below 115 over a set period, or the Bank of Japan raised the overnight call rate more than x per cent. Perhaps the holiday might include a visit to a Toyota factory and a free souvenir gift of 10 000 Toyota shares. And if not holidays, then books, real estate or yachts. Investment may not look like investment in the future – the very term will become ill-defined.

> Regulation should not be an end in itself, but rather the protection of the public. For a while governments were the best placed to do this, but in the future their role can be ably usurped by computers.

The only realistic solution to all of this will be to provide individual investors with all the tools and information required to carefully assess each investment opportunity themselves. The first reaction to this would be that investments are complex and the investor wouldn't understand it – which is another way of saying that the investor is stupid. As mentioned above, up to now the investor has relied on an outside expert system (comprising professional advice and government regulation); in the future that expert system will be largely available on a computer.

Personal finance programs will either come with an 'investment checking' facility, or have the ability to add in a custom-written module. This module will then continually check the soundness of all investments using pre-programmed routines, and also link directly to online databases for the latest information.

The other important development will be a huge growth in independent services on the Net that offer advice and research on investment soundness in certain areas. Some of these sites may offer a searchable database of all the common scams currently known about on the Net; they will also offer reference material and specialized programs to download. An interesting early example of what such an Internet service might look like is the SEC site, which has a list of current investments known to be scams. One could see this list growing into a large searchable database.

> The other important development will be a huge growth in independent services on the Net that offer advice and research on investment soundness in certain areas. Some of these sites may offer a searchable database of all the common scams currently known about on the Net; they will also offer reference material and specialized programs to download.

Other sites may focus on particular areas of investment, and provide guidelines to follow before making any investment, and, again, databases of problem deals, intermediaries and counterparties. Who might be setting up such services? Well, anybody. The most likely candidates might be companies like Moodys and Standard & Poors, but also it's quite likely that existing market regulators, seeing the writing on the wall, will set up independent consultancies themselves.

Hence, investors will have their personal finance programs which will provide a base level of investment checking. They will also have the choice of a number of independent online advisers: if they are thinking of making a UK investment they may use one adviser (pedigree the SIB), and if making an investment in the US they may be happy with a custom-written add-in module for Quicken.

Not all the share pushing and other unsolicited e-mails are necessarily bad or lose money, just as not all recommendations from regulated brokers make money. Risk is everywhere: it might be a share price declining, a bank going bust, or an intermediary disappearing with client funds. And risk is not binary (on or off), it exists on a spectrum from low risk to high risk, and its analysis is therefore complex. Such analysis is ultimately not helped by attempting to identify and control particular areas of risk, and then claiming risk has been removed due to the activity of some regulatory body. This introduces distortions into the whole analysis. Meaningful risk analysis should be applied to an investor's portfolio as a whole, where the danger of every single investment can be assessed, and its potential effect on the investor gauged.

THE LONG TERM

Histories of the Internet usually start with reference to the US military ARPAnet and the threat of nuclear war in the 1960s. This version has the attraction of providing a firm starting point and not obliging you to delve deeper into the roots of the Internet itself – these being shrouded in military secrecy. Also, this rather James Bond-like version helps to liven up a complex, technical topic, and counter any negative criticism of the Internet 'it's just for looking at dirty pictures' with a demonstration of its useful origins (war and atom bombs).

However, beginning an Internet history in this fashion has two problems.

First, it introduces the Internet as an *it* or a *thing* – an offshoot of a military project, just as Teflon saucepans might have been an offshoot of the NASA space programme. And if a person starts thinking of the Internet as an *it*, then the questions that naturally follow are, *who controls it? why can't it do this. . .?, why doesn't somebody do something about . . .?* But these are the wrong questions to ask, they are inappropriate and have no useful answer.

Second, by starting the history in the 1960s it is not possible to view the development of the Internet in the context of the broader themes that help to explain what the Internet is today, and give a clue to where it is going. It is like starting a history of World War One with the shooting of the Archduke Ferdinand in Sarajevo – this may be factually correct, but any subsequent analysis of the war would be critically hampered by ignorance of the preceding years of imperial power machinations. Similarly, an analysis of the October 1987 stock market crash would be futile if it started with the preceding week's Deutsche Mark rate rise, while ignoring the euphoric price bubble in the months leading up to the crash.

The dangers of taking a simple, short view of evolutionary processes are illustrated in Charles Darwin's *The Origin of Species*, where he says:

> The belief that species were immutable productions was almost unavoidable as long as the history of the world was thought to be of short duration.

A more useful history of the Internet would therefore chart the process of the human race's attempts at communication (right from the grunts), and would include an analysis of the nature of intelligence as well.

The early stages of the human race, from what was recognizable as an ape to what we would recognize today as a human, can be called the age of biological evolution. Towards the end of this period, humans developed a useful range of grunts, and then the ability to grunt about abstract things that they couldn't immediately point at. This ability to abstract led to the idea of numbers and a written language – both being, at the time, abstract representations of reality.

This is a controversial area, but, for the purposes of this book, it can be said that the origin of our intelligence lay in that ability to abstract.

But why did we become intelligent, and what is intelligence? Casting aside centuries of metaphysical musings on the topic, we might consider intelligence as merely the result of reaching a certain threshold of complexity and connectivity. As the human being was evolving in these early years, the brain was enlarging and also developing within itself. And, at some point (a 'point' being a span of thousands of years), the human brain achieved a certain level of complexity and connectivity – which enabled thoughts to interact with other thoughts in a mass of feedback loops. The result of this is what we will call the first level of intelligence.

For some time after this, the brain would have continued to grow and refine itself; until about 12 000 years ago, when humanity entered the cultural evolutionary stage and we became social animals. From that time to the present day (historically a very short period), biological evolution has effectively been static, and while modern individuals may *know* more than their Iron Age antecedents, their actual brains are little different.

Over the following centuries humans increasingly moved to the cities, which, in one sense, can be interpreted as an urge for greater communication. Then the 20th century arrived with telephones, radios and televisions, all of which led to a huge change in the quantity and type of information being received by individual people.

> The medium-term future for the Internet is gossip and gambling. This is not so different from the situation today, where much of human activity can be described as fundamentally gossip and gambling.

And then computers were invented. For a while just a few people used computers, but towards the end of the century their use became widespread, and in the most significant development, these computers began to connect together forming networks, which themselves became increasingly interconnected. The most important collection of networks was the Internet.

Looking into the future briefly, the Internet will offer ample opportunity for people around the world to talk to each other, to conduct business and manage their money. A great many people in fact will have their basic needs provided (from investments or other means) and will spend an increasing amount of time managing their wealth (which becomes a leisure activity) and engaging in an enjoyable range of speculative investments. Thus, the medium-term future for the Internet (and thereby for a great part of the human race) is gossip and gambling. This may sound frivolous, but in fact this is not so different from the situation today, where much of human activity can be described as fundamentally gossip and gambling.

Returning to the present, we now have a situation where, on the one side, there are people who are increasingly comfortable with computers and want to use them to find information and communicate, while, on the other side, individual computers and networks offer access to enormous reserves of data. So, if there is abundant supply and demand, why doesn't information flow more freely? The reason is that there is a bottleneck – the clumsy interface between user and computer. An interface that hasn't changed significantly in 30 years: a small two-dimensional screen (that uses the 100-year-old technology of cathode ray tubes), and a kludgy keyboard derived from a typewriter. Hopeless. So, the most important advances in the coming few years will be the improvement of this interface. Speech recognition may help in a few specific cases but is far from a solution. The human voice is a spectacular tool for conveying abstract ideas, but inefficient for issuing precise detailed commands.

Just imagine, for a moment, controlling a car solely by voice: 'Speed up a bit here – no, not that fast – just a touch slower – flash that idiot in front and . . . blast, missed the turning.'

Just imagine, for a moment, controlling a car solely by voice: 'Speed up a bit here – no, not that fast – just a touch slower – flash that idiot in front and . . . blast, missed the turning.' Or imagine Van Gogh creating his Sunflowers via a voice-operated Microsoft Paintbrush program. Humans are multi-tasking creatures, and trying to process everything through the voice is a waste of that ability.

If not voice recognition, then what? The inevitable development will be the direct communication between the brain and computer. Already, simple experiments have shown that a cursor on a screen can be controlled via electrodes on the brain (think hot/cold and the cursor moves left/right, or bright/dark and the cursor moves up/down). And one can be sure that far more sophisticated experiments are currently being carried out in laboratories around the world. Of course, the usual (and natural) reaction to this is one of distaste. But technological development rarely halts just because the results don't sound very nice.

The direct communication between human and computer may be effected by a microchip implanted in the brain, or a remote device that is able to pick up and read the brain's internal signals. At this point, it becomes possible to communicate very quickly with a computer, and thereby with other computers and through them other humans. One assumes that by this time the infrastructure of the Internet has reached a certain critical quality (with effectively unlimited bandwidth), and that a significant part of the world's population is so connected. What happens then? People start communicating, messages are sent at the speed of light to other people, where the messages are amended and propagated to more people, a message eventually comes back to its starting point, is amended and sent off on

Already, simple experiments have shown that a cursor on a screen can be controlled via electrodes on the brain (think hot/cold and the cursor moves left/right, or bright/dark and the cursor moves up/down).

(probably) a different track. Ideas are generated, and are fed back on themselves to generate further ideas, and . . . well, this is beginning to sound like where we came in; reaching a certain level of complexity and connectivity. But this time, it doesn't involve just the one brain, but billions; and the biological, cultural and technological evolutions will have combined to create a second level of intelligence.

It is interesting to wonder what this second level of intelligence will look like, feel like and what it will think? Unfortunately such speculation is likely to be futile. Just as it would have been impossible for the humanoid apes to contemplate the nature of our intelligence – we simply don't have the intellectual wherewithal. The future is, quite literally, unthinkable.

All this speculation may seem to have slipped over the nutty edge of science fiction. Possibly. But it is interesting to read the works of Pierre Teilhard de Chardin, a Jesuit priest and geologist who had no knowledge of computers or current technology. In the 1930s he was writing about a time in the future when humans become so good at communicating with each other, that this could create what might be called a great Collective Organism of Mind (or, perhaps, an 'Inter-brain'?). He called this the Omega Point, and although the vocabulary may be different, it doesn't take a huge leap of imagination to compare this with the likely destiny of the Internet.

Another interesting parallel may be found in the field of mathematics, much of which concerns the investigation of the logical consequences from an initial set of self-evident truths (axioms). This might be crudely compared with the establishing of the foundation TCP/IP protocols ('axioms') of the Net, and then seeing what further protocols (e.g. the World Wide Web) develop from the simple base ones. And this similarity with mathematics provides another link between the Internet and the human brain (mathematics being largely the process of exploring the abstract reasoning of the brain).

> There has been rapid development of computer technology over the last 40 years but no fundamental change. Yet it will be in the *next* 40 years that computers turn the way we live upside down.

As the century draws to a close, people are wary about the future direction of computing, but they are increasingly comfortable with computers themselves: happy to use them for work and entertainment. In most cases, an initial distrust has been replaced by the benign attitude that computers aren't so bad after all. Quite useful, in fact: cash-till machines, searchable databases, word processors, spreadsheets, multimedia games etc. But, when the history of the 20th century is written, it will be seen that telephones, televisions, cars, and, indeed, even the humble air conditioner, all had a greater impact on people's daily lives than did computers. There has been rapid development of computer technology over the last 40 years, and this has led to incremental modifications (and even sometimes improvements) in many processes, but no fundamental change. Yet. Just as people are finding computers more acceptable, it will be in the *next* 40 years that computers turn the way we live upside down.

Mastering

THE FINANCIAL

INTERNET

A detailed guide to using the Internet for investment

The financial Internet

This section describes in general what is available on the Internet for investors, and illustrates this with detailed descriptions of the best online financial services.

A few notes about this section:

- Addresses for all the services in this section can either be found in the Directory or are included below. Only a small selection of possible sites are described for each category; for a wider range, again see the Directory.

- All the services listed below (and in the Directory) are free, unless otherwise stated.

- Although some sites may require subscription, there is already quite a trend towards aggregation of many services within the one subscription site. Hence, if interested in a particular subscription service, it may pay to look around and see if it is included in a package elsewhere.

- Many sites, although free, may require registration (helping to build up the valuable client databases). Rather than have many different passwords, it is obviously better to fix on one user name and password (a password of six characters seems to satisfy most sites).

Overview

A brief synopsis of the different categories of financial services available on the Internet follows.

News: general, business, economic and financial news bulletins updated through the day; daily and weekly news summaries and comment; the ability to search news archives for keywords or phrases; personalized news services to follow particular stocks or markets.

Newsletters: hundreds of independent newsletters on all market sectors.

Market data: subscription services for real-time prices for indices, stocks, bonds, currencies, commodities, futures and bonds; free delayed prices; daily market summaries; downloadable data for input to local investment program.

Charts: historical charts for stocks, bonds, currencies, commodities and futures.

Exchanges: explanations of how the Exchange works and reference articles on investment; index and specifications of listed securities and contracts; daily closing prices; historic price data.

Regulators and associations: government and market regulators with information about their organizations.

Stocks: company research through corporate filings, annual reports and brokerage research; Internet search tools to find references to companies.

Bonds: prices and market commentary; reference articles; government funding policies.

Currencies: real-time rates; historic values; market analysis and forecasts.

Commodities and precious metals: news, market comments, technical analysis, funds and reference articles.

Futures and options: prices and market comments; analysis; reference articles.

Economic data: access to governments' economic databases; Census data; banks' economic reports.

Discussion forums: read and post messages with other investors around the world.

Funds: read descriptions of funds; funds ranked by performance; search fund databases with specific criteria; read fund analysis, comments and recommendations.

Online trading: send trade orders direct from your own computer; update and monitor personal portfolio; integrate with personal finance programs.

Risk management: find information about risk advisory boutiques and software technology companies; calendars of risk courses and conferences.

Trading systems: subscription services post buy/sell recommendations for market trades.

Software: download demonstration investment software or upgrade packages; order programs directly and get online technical support.

Books: order investment books directly online.

Education and training: calendars of courses and conferences; download and order investment programs; read reference articles on investment.

NEWS

Nearly all the world's major newspapers and news agencies have some service offered on the Internet. In many cases it is not apparent whether the news companies have a clear, coherent strategy for what they are trying to do there. But no matter, these news services form one of the primary resources for investors.

Most countries have national media with Internet news services that offer a combination of all, or some, of the following:

■ up-to-date news bulletins through the day

■ daily general, business and financial news

■ daily market comment

■ daily values for stocks, interest rates, currencies and commodities

■ keyword search facility on current, and archive of past, issues.

Many of the better business newspapers are already virtually one-stop shops for investors (and perhaps this is their future?) offering everything short – for the moment – of an actual dealing facility. But supplying news to a screen is very different from printing on paper, and there are likely to be great changes in the services offered in this sector.

With the above in mind, it is not surprising that the most successful news services on the Internet are Bloomberg and CNN – both companies familiar with providing news on screens.

■ Bloomberg

If you log on to the Internet and just want to find out what's happening in the world, head straight for Bloomberg. The pages and menu structure are refreshingly simple, and, so far, the presentation of useful news has not been impeded by attempts to offer a multimedia visual experience. The service offers:

■ updated bulletins through the day

■ daily general, business, economic and financial stories

■ market reviews

■ market data for equities, treasuries, Muni bonds and futures

■ ranking of most active stocks and major movers

■ digest of top headlines from world newspapers

■ focused news on mutual funds, securities firms and information technology

■ calendar of market holidays.

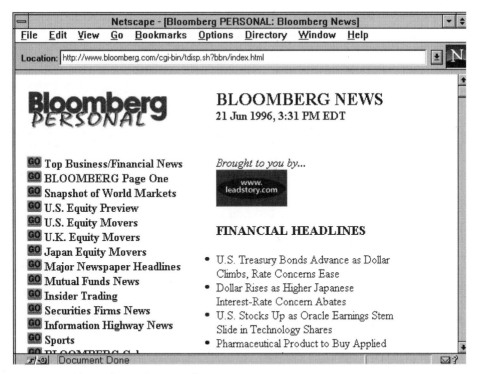

Netscape - [Bloomberg PERSONAL: Bloomberg News]

File Edit View Go Bookmarks Options Directory Window Help

Location: http://www.bloomberg.com/cgi-bin/tdisp.sh?bbn/index.html

BLOOMBERG NEWS
21 Jun 1996, 3:31 PM EDT

GO Top Business/Financial News
GO BLOOMBERG Page One
GO Snapshot of World Markets
GO U.S. Equity Preview
GO U.S. Equity Movers
GO U.K. Equity Movers
GO Japan Equity Movers
GO Major Newspaper Headlines
GO Mutual Funds News
GO Insider Trading
GO Securities Firms News
GO Information Highway News
GO Sports

Brought to you by...

www.
leadstory.com

FINANCIAL HEADLINES

• U.S. Treasury Bonds Advance as Dollar
  Climbs, Rate Concerns Ease
• Dollar Rises as Higher Japanese
  Interest-Rate Concern Abates
• U.S. Stocks Up as Oracle Earnings Stem
  Slide in Technology Shares
• Pharmaceutical Product to Buy Applied

Document Done

▓ **FIG 2.1 Bloomberg Personal**

One of the most interesting features is the daily digest of newspaper headlines from countries around the world.

▓ CNN*fn*

CNN*fn* has a few more bells and whistles than the Bloomberg service, but it is still focused on presenting news stories as clearly as possible, and includes:

▓ updated bulletins through the day

▓ daily general, business, economic and financial stories

▓ daily market reports

▓ global market news from Knight-Ridder

▓ market data updated through the day for: commodities, currencies, interest rates, US/Global stock indices

▓ ranking of most active stocks and major movers

▓ fifteen minute delayed individual quotes available for stocks and mutual/money market funds

▓ glossary of business and financial terms

▓ search facility on news archive.

■ FIG 2.2 CNN financial network

The global market news from Knight-Ridder is very detailed, covering most world markets and includes not only market comments and reports but also forecasts of what will be the major themes in the coming market session.

■ **Wall Street Journal**

The premier cyber emporium for financial news and information. Not only does the *WSJ* comprehensively monitor the US markets, but international markets are also well covered; with market comments and brief outlines of the structure of the international stock markets. The *WSJ Online* includes:

■ daily business and financial news for: global, Asia, Europe, economy, politics and policy

■ personalized news

■ twenty minute delayed US stock quotes

■ personalized stock portfolio monitor

■ daily reports and major closing prices for 25 major world stock markets in: America, Europe, Asia and Africa

■ daily closing market data for financial and commodity markets: grains and oilseeds, currencies, food and fibre, index, livestock and meat, metals and petroleum, interest rates, cash prices, oil statistics

FIG 2.3 *Wall Street Journal*: **Thailand Market Report**

- daily data for credit markets: US/international money rates, Treasury quotes, Federal Reserve statistics; and deposit and loan rate quotes for banking institutions throughout the US

- brief company profiles (*Company Briefing Books*) with information on: company background, financial overview, stock performance, last 20 news articles and press releases

- calendars for US international economic releases and securities offerings

- archive of US economic indicators from government agencies and business research groups

- deposit and loan rate quotes for banking institutions throughout the US

- mutual fund ranking (top 15 and bottom 10)

- search facility on previous 14 issues.

Particularly interesting features on the site are the personalized news and portfolio facilities and also the 'Company Briefing Books'. The site holds a large database of information on individual companies, and when mention of the company occurs in an article or market report, a hyperlink connects to this database. The company information includes:

- **company background**: overview; principal executive officers; address; products and services (*Source: Hoover's Company Profile Database*)

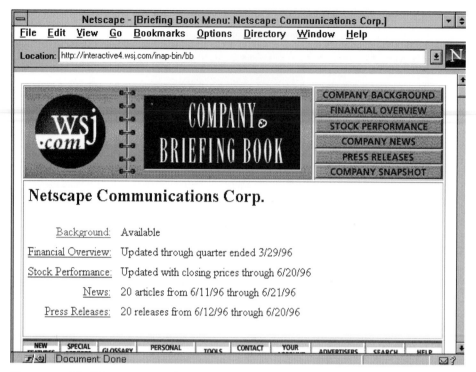

■ FIG 2.4 *Wall Street Journal*: Company Briefing Books

■ **financial overview**: quarterly and yearly revenues, net income, EPS, divs; selected balance sheet ratios and comparisons (*Source: Media General Financial Services*)

■ **stock performance**: eight-month daily and monthly price/volume chart; average daily volume; market value; institutional holdings; total return chart with relatives to sector and market indices (*Source: Media General Financial Services*)

■ **last 20 news articles and press releases.**

This is a very large site, and in these early days of Web site design, (and in common with many other such Web sites), they have a problem with representing the structure of the whole site while retaining a cool, unfussy home page. Hence, this is a good example of a site where it is best to head straight for the contents page (which is admirably well laid out), and possibly even use this as the bookmark page for the *WSJ* site.

■ Financial Times

The *FT* site is similar to that of the *Wall Street Journal* in covering both domestic and international news and markets well. The site mainly consists of a selection of articles appearing in the paper version (a similar strategy employed by the *Economist* Web site – another Pearson newspaper). The *FT* Web site includes:

FIG 2.5 *Financial Times*

FIG 2.6 *Financial Times*: world headlines

- daily general and business news, with updated bulletins through the day
- major stock market indices updated during the day with a 30 minute delay
- daily closing share prices for UK and other major markets
- major stock moves calculated for markets, with basic stock data (yield, PER, dividends, earnings, sales, year high/low)
- daily valuation of UK Unit Trusts, pensions, life insurance funds, and offshore funds
- daily reports on most major stock markets
- regular articles: editorial, comment, analysis; diary of the forthcoming week's world political/economic/business/financial events
- articles on economics and personal finance
- search facility on articles.

There is a fairly large database of daily closing stock prices for major world markets and a search facility to find the correct name of a stock. This database can also calculate the previous day's major stock moves for specific countries or for all countries combined. This latter facility, while not directly useful for investment purposes (the tables consisting largely of volatile, small cap. stocks, as likely to be in the top ten movers as the bottom ten from one day to the next), is nevertheless intriguing to look at now and again. One interesting

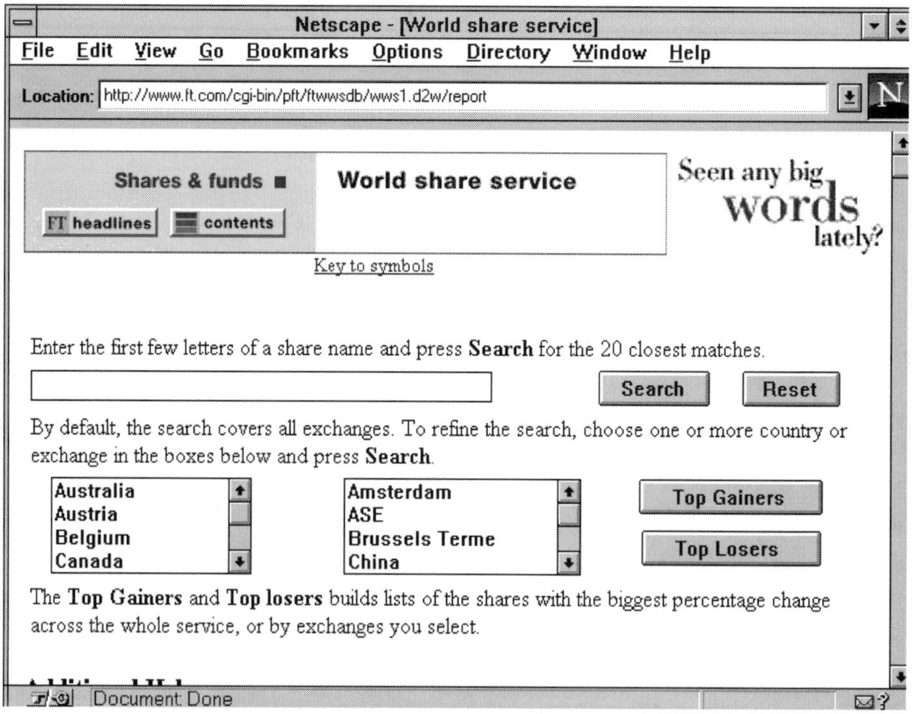

■ FIG 2.7 *Financial Times*: search page for shares and prices

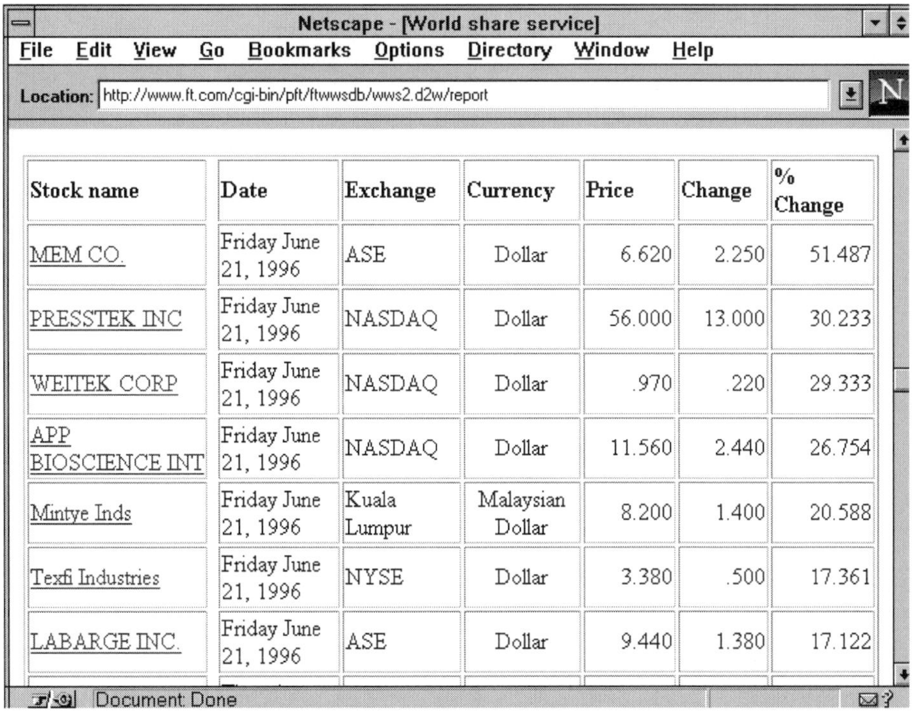

```
┌─────────────────────────────────────────────────────────────────┐
│ ─                    Netscape - [World share service]        ▼ ▲ │
│ File  Edit  View  Go  Bookmarks  Options  Directory  Window  Help │
│ ┌───────────────────────────────────────────────────────────────┐ │
│ Location: http://www.ft.com/cgi-bin/pft/ftwwsdb/wws2.d2w/report  ↓ N │
└─────────────────────────────────────────────────────────────────┘
```

Stock name	Date	Exchange	Currency	Price	Change	% Change
MEM CO.	Friday June 21, 1996	ASE	Dollar	6.620	2.250	51.487
PRESSTEK INC	Friday June 21, 1996	NASDAQ	Dollar	56.000	13.000	30.233
WEITEK CORP	Friday June 21, 1996	NASDAQ	Dollar	.970	.220	29.333
APP BIOSCIENCE INT	Friday June 21, 1996	NASDAQ	Dollar	11.560	2.440	26.754
Mintye Inds	Friday June 21, 1996	Kuala Lumpur	Malaysian Dollar	8.200	1.400	20.588
Texfi Industries	Friday June 21, 1996	NYSE	Dollar	3.380	.500	17.361
LABARGE INC.	Friday June 21, 1996	ASE	Dollar	9.440	1.380	17.122

`Document: Done`

■ FIG 2.8 *Financial Times*: world's top stock price increases

observation to make is that the major mover tables are not necessarily dominated by Hong Kong or Taiwan stocks, as one might have been tempted to think.

▓ AsiaOne

This is a very large umbrella site that has a number of different services, including various newspapers of the region. It is probably the primary resource for information on Asian business and markets. The major sections of interest are: The Singapore *Straits Times* (with general news of the region), the *Business Times* and something they call the Business Center. The combination of these three offer:

▓ daily business and company news and general articles

▓ daily stock market reports for: Singapore, Kuala Lumpur, Bangkok, Jakarta, Manila, Hong Kong, China, Taipei, Tokyo and comment on regional warrants

▓ real-time Singapore (SES) and Malaysia (KLSE) stock prices, with history of all day trades

▓ customized portfolio for SES and KLSE stocks (up to 30 stocks with prices updated every three minutes)

▦ FIG 2.9 Singapore BT StockWatch: SES Summary Page

▦ bi-annual ranking of Singapore-listed companies based on their full-year earnings

▦ daily SIMEX market report and closing prices

▦ daily currency rates

▦ daily Singapore stock market summary data page, with table of most active stocks and major moves

▦ archive of past issues with search facility.

The daily market reports should be of interest to anyone investing in Asia, and the real-time Singapore and Malaysian stock prices are a tremendous service.

▦ Japan Nikkei

The Nikkei Net comprises a digest of news from the daily *Nihon Keizai Shimbun* (Japan's major business newspaper) and a selection of articles from the weekly English language *The Nikkei Weekly*. The Web site includes:

▦ daily market data and comments for: equities, bonds, currencies

▦ daily stories for: general news, economy, finance and companies

▦ summary of news in *The Nikkei Weekly*

▦ archive of past 30 issues of *The Nikkei Weekly*.

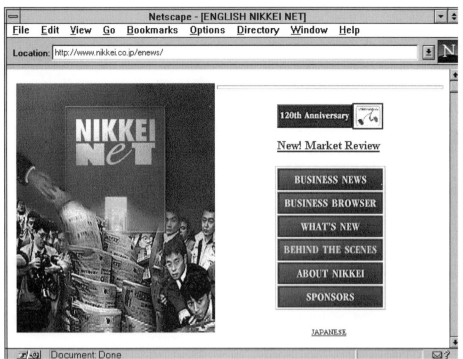

■ FIG 2.10 Japan Nikkei Net

The above six news services are highlighted as some of the finest examples currently on the Internet, but there are many other very good sites, where the news service may well be superior to any of the above for a particular investment or market. The box below lists the other premier newspapers around the world with Web sites, and it is good to glance at some of these to appreciate the impressive depth of what is on offer.

The best newspaper Web sites

■ *Sydney Morning Herald* (Australia)
http://www.smh.com.au/

■ *Financial Post* (Canada)
http://www.canoe.ca/FP/home.html

■ *Hongkong Standard*
http://www.hkstandard.com/

■ *Indonesia Times*
http://www.indocon.com/indotimes/

■ *Corriere della Sera* (Italy)
http://globnet.rcs.it/

■ *Kyodo News* (Japan)
http://www.kyodo.co.jp/

■ *Korea Herald*
http://zec.three.co.kr/koreaherald/

■ *The Star* (Malaysia)
http://www.jaring.my/star/

■ *The Press On-Line* (New Zealand)
http://www.press.co.nz/

■ *Independent Online* (South Africa)
http://www.inc.co.za/

■ *Electronic Telegraph* (UK)
http://www.telegraph.co.uk/

■ *The Times* (UK)
http://www.the-times.co.uk/

■ *Investor's Business Daily* (US)
http://ibd.ensemble.com/

■ *Nando Times* (US)
http://www2.nando.net/

Comparison of news bulletins

As mentioned above, these news services are a great aid for investors, bringing timely business and financial news direct to the desktop computer – for free. Few people could have foreseen this level of service even just a few years ago. And, as such, it seems almost ungrateful to criticize what is being offered for free. But all these services are merely transient stepping stones to a different, and hopefully superior, service in the future.

It is interesting to compare some of the news services, and the box opposite lists the top news stories of three of them, taken at the same time of day. In general, it appears that Bloomberg has the fastest service – news stories are posted here first. But Bloomberg stories are fairly US business oriented; CNN*fn* posts fewer stories, but its coverage is wider. Reuters pops up all over the place on the Web (also offering news services through other sites such as Excite, and it also has a stake in Infoseek). The Reuters stories appearing in the box come from the Yahoo site, and while they are less timely than either Bloomberg or CNN*fn*, they probably have the widest global coverage.

CNN	Reuters (via Yahoo)	Bloomberg
▨ ABB names Janson as new CEO – 2:58 p.m.	*Business*	▨ U.S. Treasury Bonds Advance as Dollar Climbs, Rate Concerns Ease
▨ Triple Witching sparks trading frenzy – 2:50 p.m.	▨ Stocks Rise on Triple Witching	
▨ AOL chief addresses billing issue – 2:34 p.m.	▨ Alleged ValuJet Investigation	▨ Dollar Rises as Higher Japanese Interest-Rate Concern Abates
▨ Judge approves drug $351M settlement – 2:27 p.m.	▨ Manhattan Bagel Stock Drops	
	▨ Oracle Stock Rises	▨ U.S. Stocks Up as Oracle Earnings Stem Slide in Technology Shares
▨ Fidelity curbs employee stock trades – 1:02 p.m.	▨ Fidelity Imposes Trading Curbs	
▨ Lloyd's of London – 12:57 p.m.	▨ Research Merger Announced	▨ Pharmaceutical Product to Buy Applied Bioscience for $467 Million
▨ Stocks strong ahead of the 'Witch' – 12:43 p.m.	▨ Strong Profits in the Movie Biz	
▨ Business Briefs – 12:36 p.m.	▨ HUBCO Acquires Westport	▨ U.S. Judge Approves $351 Million Pharmacist, Drugmakers Settlement
▨ Jazz in Japan – 12:04 p.m.	▨ GM, VW Dispute Gets Rough	
▨ EU to lift ban on British beef – 11:32 a.m.	▨ Classic Toyota Available	▨ LTX Files Lawsuit Against South Korea's Daewoo Over Orders
	World	
▨ Strike ends in South Korea's auto plants – 10:38 a.m.	▨ Israel-Arab Differences Simmer	▨ Manhattan Bagel Shares Fall on Improper Accounting at I&J Unit
▨ SEC looks into Bank of NY – 9:55 a.m.	▨ U.S.-Iran Tensions Growing?	▨ America Online Working to Settle FTC, State and Private Complaints
▨ German house approves evening shopping – 7:41 a.m.	▨ Mad Cow Deal Reached	
	▨ Okinawa To Hold Rare Referendum	▨ SPS Transaction Shares Plunge on Company's 2nd-Qtr Earnings Warning
▨ Tokyo stocks hit four-year high – 7:03 a.m.	▨ Mandela Jail Cell on Exhibit	
	▨ Strawberry Parasite Illness	▨ Harrah's Entertainment Shares Tumble on 2nd-Qtr Forecast
	▨ Cash Shortage Strands Spacemen	
	▨ 260 Dead in India Cyclones	
	▨ Asia-Pacific Spaceport Plans	
	▨ Court Dismisses Condom Case	

Searching

One of the most useful tools offered by sites is the ability to search for information on their pages using keywords. This facility is still fairly new, but it can be expected that it will appear on more and more sites. This search facility can be particularly useful in the cases of:

■ FIG 2.11 *Wall Street Journal*: result of search on 'sumitomo'

■ **Large sites**: if the site has many pages (and in the case of the *WSJ* there might be hundreds, or even thousands, of pages), a keyword search might find relevant information quicker than hacking through a complicated menu structure.

■ **Regularly updated sites**: if the sites are regularly updated (which they will be in the case of newspapers), the ordinary Internet search tools (e.g. Infoseek), will not be able to update their databases quickly enough to index new pages every day. Hence, the sites must be searched individually.

However, having said this, it is likely that in the future the big Internet search engines will become increasingly sophisticated, and one development for them might be to recognize that certain sites are rarely updated, while others change frequently and that therefore the robot indexer needs to revisit possibly daily.

The news sites with useful search facilities are: *WSJ*, *FT*, CNN and Time's Pathfinder. These can prove useful when researching a particular investment or when monitoring a portfolio.

Figure 2.11 shows the result of a search on the keyword 'sumitomo' in the *WSJ* site (clicking on 'DJ' would bring up the full news report).

These search facilities can be very powerful tools, but are an example of a new technology being developed before people really know how to use it. In the future, however, these search tools will become as important to the investor as the study of charts or balance sheets.

As more information becomes digital, new areas of research open up, that would previously have been impractical to study. One such interesting area would be the meta-analysis of a stock or commodity, whereby the correlation between price movement and breaking news stories is investigated. In the past, this type of research was difficult as the news stories affecting a price might have come from a combination of newspapers, radio, TV, ordinary gossip and possibly from foreign sources as well. As all these sources become digital, powerful search tools can track and plot them against price movement. It is most unlikely that any simple correlation would be found, but rather that some complex relationship does exist in a certain number of cases.

It may seem something of a bother to have to independently monitor and search many different news sites – but where a demand exists, the Internet can be very good at fulfilling it. In this case, services are likely to develop that will offer to monitor a range of news services automatically. An example of this is personalized news (or executive news.)

Personalized news

A problem with newspapers is that although you buy the whole paper, you don't necessarily have the time, or the interest, to read all of it. With paper news, there is not much that can be done about this, but with digital news it is another story. With personalized news services we have a glimpse of some of the great changes that computers and the Internet will bring.

A personalized news service offers the ability to only receive news that is of direct interest to you. For example, you may be interested in domestic news, business news and sport, but not interested in art, culture, television and international news (apart from Indonesia, where your son is working). A personalized news service would ensure that you received all articles appearing in your interest area – while not ruling out, of course, the ability to occasionally browse the other areas if so desired. This type of service can be extremely valuable for monitoring news on portfolio constituents.

The personal news services offered on the Internet cannot be regarded as the final product, but rather as very interesting preliminary experiments. There is not just a question of technology here, but also people's own willingness and understanding of how to use the new services.

The two primary personal newspapers at the moment are the *Wall Street Journal* and *The Times* of London. Both of these offer the ability to input special interest subject areas that are used to filter the news presented to individual subscribers.

■ Crayon

A slight variation on the theme is something called Crayon. This provides a front-end to many free news services on the Net, whereby a customized 'newspaper' (Crayon: CReAte Your Own Newspaper) can be generated by setting up key interest areas, and the relevant hyperlinks are created to jump to the appropriate news service.

■ NewsPage

One of the most comprehensive personalized news services is NewsPage from Individual Inc. Every day this scans 20 000 articles from 600 news sources (including newspapers, news wires and magazines) and categorizes the articles into over 2000 international news topics. This includes topics under banking and finance, and also a section called Company Tracking which follows 1400 major companies. Table 2.1 illustrates some of the NewsPage financial categories.

■ **TABLE 2.1 NewsPage: selection of financial news categories**

Financial Services & Investment	*General Economic & Trade Issues*
US Finance Industry Overview	Economic Forecasts
Initial Public Offerings	Economic Indicators
New Bond Issues	Third World Financing
New Stock Issues	Privatization Issues
Major Mutual Funds	International Trade Policy
US Treasury Bonds	Trade Regulation & Tariffs
Currency Markets	
Derivative Markets	
Federal Reserve	*International Banking*
Mortgage-Backed Securities	
Securitization	Asian Banking News
Real Estate Investment Trusts	European Banking News
Venture Capital	Latin American Banking News
Investment Management	US Money Center Banks
Financial Planning	Third World Financing
Brokerage	
Investment Banking	
Securities & Exchange	

NewsPage also has a search facility, which can be useful when looking for particular subjects among so many topic divisions. Within each topic, the day's headlines can be viewed, and relevant article bodies read according to the level of service subscribed to. A further service exists, NewsPage Direct, where users can select up to ten topic areas, and each morning will then receive an e-mail message with all the headlines and news briefs for the topics. Apparently, NewsPage has 200 000 registered users, which is an interesting indication of early interest in these types of services.

Pointcast

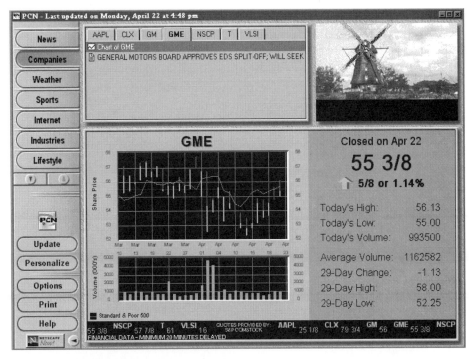

FIG 2.12 Pointcast: company news

One of the most sophisticated personalized news services currently offered, and a pointer to the future of such services, is that of Pointcast. This is a type of screen saver that, when the computer is idle, downloads the latest news direct to the screen and can have a running stock ticker at the bottom of the screen. The information downloaded can be customized and can include: US, international, business, industry and company news, and stock quotes, from sources such as Reuters and S&P Comstock.

There is no doubt that the number and variety of personalized news services on the Internet will grow greatly.

Reference – personalized news

Crayon – **http://crayon.net/**
NewsPage – **http://www.newspage.com/**
Pointcast – **http://www.pointcast.com**
IBM infoSage – **http://www.infosage.ibm.com/**

■ FIG 2.13

NEWSLETTERS

Traditionally, investment newsletters have been independent research carried
out by a few analysts, the results of which were then posted or faxed to paying
clients. Now, the economics of publication on the WWW are proving attractive,
and many investment newsletters are appearing there. The types of service vary
widely: as yet many sites are simply one-page advertisements for a newsletter
that is still only faxed, other sites offer sample newsletters to read, some may
have the whole newsletter available on the Web with password-protected
access, while others still may offer a mixture of free and restricted access pages.

Whatever the format, investment newsletters are likely to be one of the greatest
growth areas in the financial Internet. One of the best sources for a list of

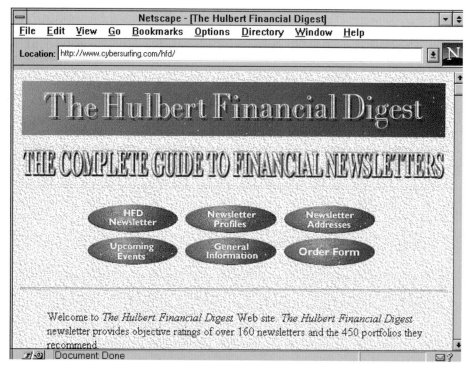

■ FIG 2.14 **The Hulbert Financial Digest**

available newsletters is Yahoo, which currently lists over 150. Each newsletter tends to specialize in a specific topic, the range of which is very broad, as Table 2.2 indicates.

■ TABLE 2.2 Selection of some of the topics for newsletters available via the Internet

▨ mutual funds	▨ expat world
▨ short-term trading of MATIF contracts	▨ municipal finance
▨ mining and mineral exploration stocks	▨ tracking of commodity trading systems
▨ precious metals	
▨ high-growth stocks on NASDAQ	▨ socially and environmentally concerned investments
▨ low-priced NASDAQ stocks	
▨ techniques, methods and tools for derivative markets	▨ insider trading activity
	▨ S&P futures and OEX options
▨ chartist stock picks	▨ small cap public companies
▨ low priced securities	▨ foreign exchange

You are unlikely to find other areas of the financial Internet with such a broad range of topics (the topics listed in the box above are only a small selection), but also such a range of quality and reliability. Some of these newsletters have been established for 30 years and have an impeccable track record, while others may have been recently set up by, for example, a couple of computer consultants who reckon they know a thing or two about hi-tech stocks and can spot the winners.

And perhaps they can. One feature of the financial Internet is that anyone can 'have a go'. Before the Internet, providing a financial service at least required a certain minimum commitment (which might involve capital investment, membership of associations or exchanges etc.). But with the Internet, the line between financial service provider and client becomes thinner in many ways. This may be welcomed when it provides closer client contact for the financial provider, but not so agreeable when it also means the cost of entry for competitors falls.

■ Hulbert Financial Digest

There is already a profusion of newsletters available. The good news is that many are excellent, and that, courtesy of electronic communication, they can be delivered in a timely and cost-efficient fashion. But the number of cyber newsletters will probably grow enormously, and the problems of finding and assessing good ones will become more difficult. However, as always, derivative service industries appear, and in this case one is already to hand in the form of the Hulbert Financial Digest, which is a newsletter that rates 160 other investment newsletters and the 450 portfolios they recommend. Other useful starting points might be: INVESTools, Newsletter Network and Wall Street Online, all of which are umbrella sites with several different featured newsletters.

Reference – newsletters

Yahoo – **http://www.yahoo.com/Business_and_Economy/Companies/ Financial_Services/Investment_Services/Newsletters/**
Hulbert Financial Digest – **http://www.cybersurfing.com/hfd/**
Newsletter Network – **http://www.margin.com/**
Wall Street Online – **http://www.wso.com/wso/**

■ **FIG 2.15**

MARKETS

For some time it has been possible to receive timely information on market activity if one was trading in a local market. This could be supplied by an information vendor (for example Reuters or Bloomberg), or for individual investors there were dial-up or wireless services offering data such as stock prices. But for up-to-date information on foreign markets one was restricted to the expensive, large information vendors. This is now changing.

The most significant characteristic of the Internet is that distance disappears; now there is no difference between accessing data originating from a local town or from the other side of the world. With the Internet, suddenly an enormous amount of market information becomes available to people all over the world.

But it is not just the cost and speed of communication that is changing, but also the nature of the information itself. The data carried by the information vendors naturally tends to be what the majority of investors want to see: for example, data on government bonds, major stock markets, currencies etc. So, for the data to be provided, there must be a demand for the data, and hence hundreds if not thousands of traders are reacting to the same data. But many investors want to make decisions based on either:

- finding new data (that other investors are ignorant of), or
- re-interpreting well-known data that is already 'in the market'.

In the first case, this can be difficult if using information vendors. For example, one might be interested to see a chart of the Danish company Codan Forsikring, or to find a review of the Israeli unlinked shekel bond market, but it is unlikely that one would find this information from the large information vendors if only one of their clients requested it. But this information is available on the Internet (at Aktienyt and Mizrahi Bank respectively). And this is not simply a case for the role of the Internet in emerging markets – all types of data are available on US stocks that would just not be worthwhile broadcasting when only a few traders might be interested. Hence, the very type of financial data that is being communicated around the world will broaden significantly.

Market reports

Some of the best sources for market reports on the Internet are the news sites: *WSJ*, *FT* and *CNNfn*. But also the newspaper sites in each respective country usually carry local stock market reports at least, and these should always be checked. In addition, exchanges quite often compile daily reports. For the US markets specifically, the reports at DBC and Security APL should be useful.

Holt Report

One of the oldest financial services on the Internet must surely be the venerable Holt Report. In 1994 the eponymous Mr Holt started posting a report every day of closing market values to an investment newsgroup. The information was quite wide ranging, including US index levels, international markets, currencies, and a special report on volume activity for stocks that had associated options. Nothing special for any trader with a Bloomberg in front of them, but for ordinary investors (anywhere from Baltimore to Bangkok) this was quite something. Timely market information – and free. In time, the Holt Report migrated onto the Web (although the newsgroup postings still continue), but is showing its age now, and other superior services are available. (Although, on the Web site, there is an archive of all the daily reports from February 1995 that might prove a simple quick reference if one is looking for, say, the price of gold or the Nikkei 225 Index level for 22 April 1996.)

Briefing

The Briefing service is extraordinary, and unique on the Internet – for investors in the US markets it could well on its own justify the price of access to the Net. The service provides constantly updated market data and analysis – the range of which can be seen in Table 2.3. The availability on the Internet of up-to-the-minute data is no longer a novelty, perhaps, but it is Briefing's current comment and analysis that makes the service interesting. For example, a running commentary is made on the progress of the stock market during the trading day:

> *13:40 ET Dow -39 Nasdaq -17 S&P -5.92: Wow, every attempt at a rally just keeps getting slammed back...this is a very difficult environment for the market right now...next up for the markets: MSFT reports earnings after the close today, Bay Networks (BAY)*

comment will be made on earnings announcements:

> *Microsoft (MSFT) reported good earnings Monday after the close, beating estimates by $.02, posting year over year revenue gains of 40%. Costs were well managed. If this isn't good news, nothing is*

■ FIG 2.16 **Briefing from Charter Media**

and the likely reaction in the markets:

> *Watch to see if Microsoft, which fell -1 ¹⁵⁄₆₄ on Monday, can rebound on this report. If not, more tech selling will probably hit.*

forecasts are made for the economy:

> **GDP:** *Consumer spending was flat in June, indicating that economy won't overheat, so we're glad we kept our forecasts moderate. GDP will post slower, but steady growth going forward.*
> **The Fed:** *Greenspan implies Fed isn't leaning towards tightening under current conditions, so we'll back off call of higher short term rates.*

and short, intermediate and long-term forecasts for the stock market:

> *Short Term: Bearish – Poor technicals*
> *Intermediate: Slightly Bearish – Upside limited*
> *Long Term: Slightly Bullish – Weakening but faith still there.*

At the moment this service is completely free, and it is not easy to see how they intend to make money out of it. However, the introductory page seems eager to inform us that the president of Briefing had previously founded MMS International (a real-time analytical service delivered over Telerate, Reuters,

■ TABLE 2.3 Briefing schedule of information update

Stock Market Ticker	9:20 opening call, 9:40 opening indications, 10:00 full open, 11:00 update, 12:00 top stories, 13:30 looking ahead, 15:00 update, 16:15 close
Story Stocks	throughout the day with news on individual stocks
Bond Market Ticker	8:30 open, 9:30 update, 10:30 update, 12:00 morning recap, 14:00 look ahead, 17:00 close
Dollar Market Ticker	9:30 overnight recap, 12:00 mid-day wrap, 17:00 close. Dollar section also contains frequently updated long term outlook.
Economic Data	updated following releases of important statistics
Political Brief	daily commentary
Market Brief	daily commentary
Market Forecasts	reviewed daily, changes as necessary
Market Calendar	as needed
Economic Forecasts	reviewed daily, changes as necessary
Political Forecasts	reviewed daily, changes as necessary

Source: Charter Media

Knight-Ridder, and Bloomberg terminals) and so one assumes that there is some business model behind this, and that therefore the future will see banner ads appearing, or a multi-level subscription service introduced.

■ Dow Jones Telerate (Asia Pacific)

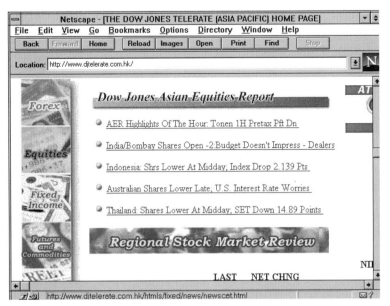

■ FIG 2.17 Dow Jones Telerate (Asia Pacific)

For the Asian markets the best overview of all the markets is provided by Dow Jones Telerate. Its service covers all the stock markets with daily summary reports. For subscribers, it also carries information on currency, fixed income, futures and commodities markets.

■ Yogi – (Polish markets)

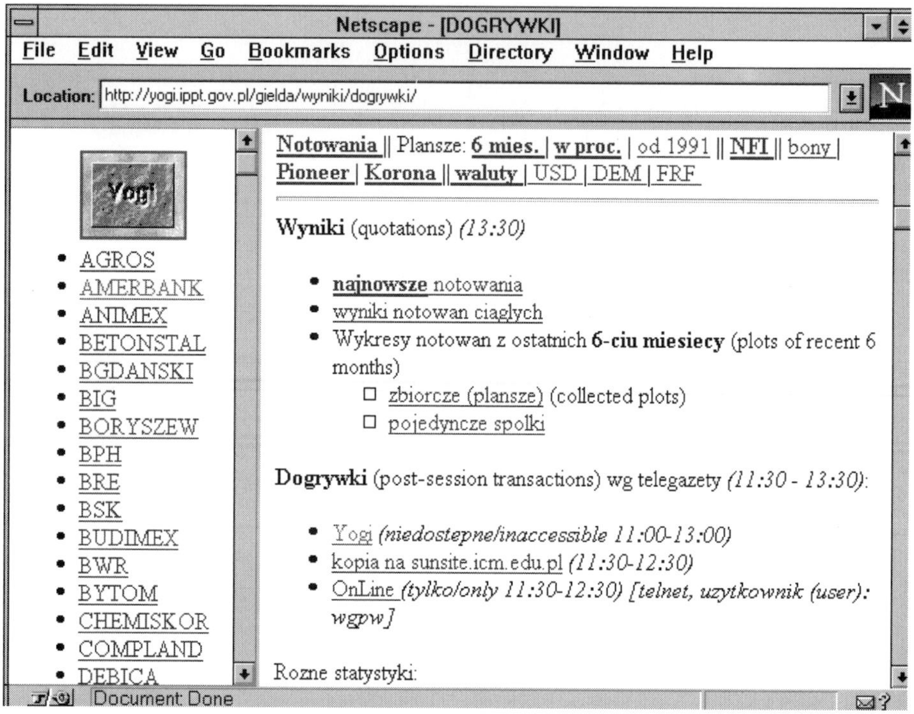

```
┌─────────────────────────────────────────────────────────────────────┐
│ ─                      Netscape - [DOGRYWKI]                      ▼ ≑ │
│  File   Edit   View   Go   Bookmarks   Options   Directory   Window   Help │
│ Location: http://yogi.ippt.gov.pl/gielda/wyniki/dogrywki/          ± N │
```

Notowania || Plansze: **6 mies.** | **w proc.** | od 1991 || **NFI** || bony |
Pioneer | Korona || **waluty** | USD | DEM | FRF

Yogi

Wyniki (quotations) *(13:30)*

- AGROS
- AMERBANK   ● **najnowsze** notowania
- ANIMEX   ● wyniki notowan ciaglych
- BETONSTAL   ● Wykresy notowan z ostatnich **6-ciu miesiecy** (plots of recent 6
- BGDANSKI   months)
- BIG   □ zbiorcze (plansze) (collected plots)
- BORYSZEW   □ pojedyncze spolki
- BPH
- BRE   **Dogrywki** (post-session transactions) wg telegazety *(11:30 - 13:30)*:
- BSK
- BUDIMEX   ● Yogi *(niedostepne/inaccessible 11:00-13:00)*
- BWR   ● kopia na sunsite.icm.edu.pl *(11:30-12:30)*
- BYTOM   ● OnLine *(tylko/only 11:30-12:30) [telnet, uzytkownik (user):*
- CHEMISKOR   *wgpw]*
- COMPLAND
- DEBICA   Rozne statystyki:

Document: Done

■ **FIG 2.18 Yogi: Polish market information**

An attractive characteristic of the Internet is that anyone can offer a service that is globally available. A result of this is that one quite commonly comes across sites where it is not immediately obvious either what it offers, or who is maintaining the site. An example here is the Polish Yogi site. After a little digging around it appears that this is run by some Polish academic department. It can be worth exploring these types of sites as the information can be very good – and so it is with this site. Although much of the text is in Polish, the pages are also a good example of how it is not so difficult to understand non-English sites if the subject matter is quite technical. In this case it does not take long to realise that *waluty* is something to do with currencies, that *zbiorcze plansze* leads to five-year and six-month stock and index charts updated daily, and that the menu on the left of the screen leads to intraday tick data for the stocks listed. Sites like this may not win any design awards, but they certainly have a wealth of data freely available for investors interested in the Polish market.

Institute for Commercial Engineering

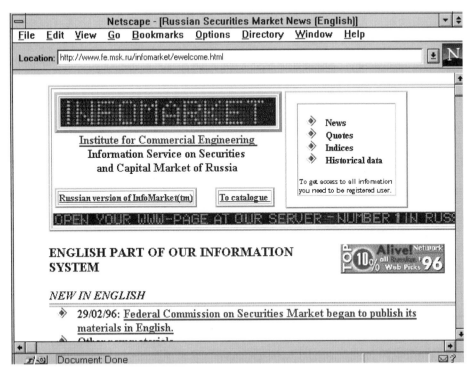

Netscape - [Russian Securities Market News (English)]

File Edit View Go Bookmarks Options Directory Window Help

Location: http://www.fe.msk.ru/infomarket/ewelcome.html

Institute for Commercial Engineering
Information Service on Securities
and Capital Market of Russia

News
Quotes
Indices
Historical data

To get access to all information you need to be registered user.

Russian version of InfoMarket(tm)   To catalogue

OPEN YOUR WWW-PAGE AT OUR SERVER - NUMBER 1 IN RUSS

ENGLISH PART OF OUR INFORMATION SYSTEM

NEW IN ENGLISH

29/02/96: Federal Commission on Securities Market began to publish its materials in English.

Document: Done

FIG 2.19 Institute for Commercial Engineering: Russian capital markets

A similar site to the one above is at the Institute for Commercial Engineering in Russia, which has set up a large service for the capital markets there. Indeed, like INO Global Markets in the US or Interactive Investor in the UK, this site seems to be cornering a substantial part of a specific market, as one realizes that many different financial services in Russia are in fact based at this server. This includes: the Russian Exchange, the Federal Commission on Securities and the Capital Markets and RINACO Plus (a securities broker). The latter service provides:

- updated daily prices/charts for stocks and indices
- daily stock bid/offer prices
- summaries of industry analysis reports
- overview of the stock and fixed income markets
- institutional investors' guide to emerging market funds in Russia.

The Institute for Commercial Engineering Web site as a whole is very professionally designed, with a large amount of data on the Russian markets (but one does wonder how much academic work can be continuing at some East European engineering and physics departments while they are setting up these first-rate financial Internet services).

Stocks

This section examines the facilities available for stock investors in the following categories: exchanges, quotes, charts and research. The ESI Web site, however, straddles all of those areas, so is described first.

■ **Electronic Share Information (ESI–UK)**

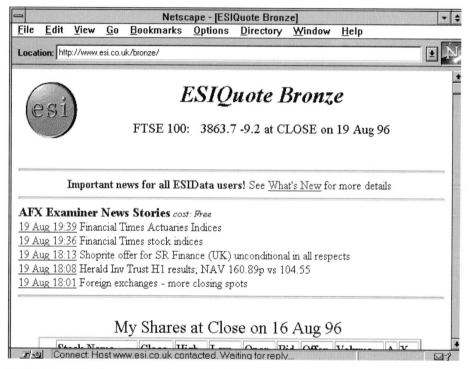

■ FIG 2.20 ESI: Bronze service with AFX news and custom portfolio

ESI provides information on the London share market and is the most innovative and interesting Internet site in the UK. At the beginning of 1995 it signed a contract with the London Stock Exchange (LSE) to distribute share prices. A few months later, on the eve of launching the ESI Web site, the longer term implications of the Internet seemed to have dawned on the LSE, which tried to withdraw its licence. Following a brief series of comments in the press (in support of the little guy), the LSE relented and the service went ahead.

The ESI site now provides a wide range of service, including: real-time share prices, portfolios, custom charts, access to company information, a news ticker, and, perhaps most importantly, a 'trading gateway' which links to the Sharelink MarketMaster share dealing service and to the Stocktrade Dealing Service.

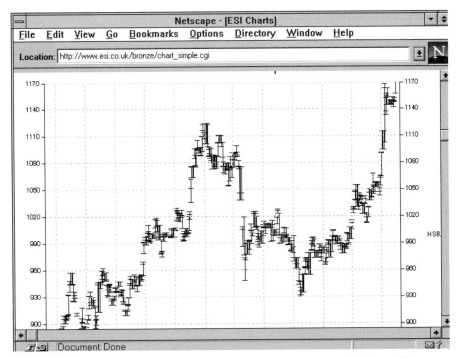

FIG 2.21 ESI: share price of HSBC Holdings PLC, Aug 95–Aug 96

In greater detail, the service comprises three levels:

- **Free**: top 400 LSE stock prices updated eight times a day, full LSE market prices updated after midnight, FTSE100 Index updated through the day.

- **Bronze service**: everything in the free service, plus: personalized portfolio for tracking up to 100 shares, portfolio valuation e-mailed overnight, custom stock charts for 4500+ shares, Unit Trust daily prices, downloadable five-year OHLCV price histories, news stories from AFX, company profiles from Hemmington Scott, access to trading gateway. (Cost from £5 per month.)

- **Silver service**: everything in the Bronze service, plus: unlimited real-time prices, a self-updating page of real-time prices for up to 25 different stocks, real-time multiple portfolios evaluation, stockwatch limit minding. (Cost £20 per month.)

For any particular company it is possible to view comprehensive details on:

- real-time price
- stock information: relevant codes, sectors and indices
- custom charts
- price history data
- RNS news stories on the stock: Regulatory News Service from the London Stock Exchange (also provided is the Examiner news stories from AFX News)
- company information from Hemmington Scott.

One of the most useful features is the ability to download daily share price data (formats: Metastock, ASCII, CSV, Indexia) for use in portfolio and technical analysis programs. The custom charts are really quite powerful, offering the facility to plot stocks with a configurable moving average, and with a relative plot of another stock, or the Relative Strength Index or Momentum lines.

Exchanges

The overall quality of exchange Internet sites is very high, and these should always be one of the first sources that an investor should check. But the major exchanges have been relatively slow to establish Internet sites; this may be due to internal lethargy, befuddlement, or a vague feeling of unease with the trend towards increasing computational power and connectivity at the investor end. The vanguard of exchange Web sites is dominated by the smaller exchanges around the world, such as those of Geneva, Taiwan, and Stockholm, which are among the most professional of all financial sites on the Web. Other first-rate sites are the Australian, Caracas, Madrid, Singapore and Tel-aviv exchanges.

The structure of many exchange Web sites is quite similar: they all tend to include a history of the exchange, and then have information about its practices, publications, data, rules and members. Beyond this, the better exchanges carry closing prices for all issues traded, comprehensive market reports and perhaps even intraday delayed quotes. Figure 2.23 outlines the structure of the NYSE Web site, which can act partially as a base model for all the other exchanges.

■ New York Stock Exchange (NYSE)

■ FIG 2.22 New York Stock Exchange: home page

As the NYSE is the largest stock exchange in the world, it is surprising to find its Web site a rather modest affair. However, one assumes that this is something of an initial trial and it will be developed further in the future. Data that might be of particular interest on the site includes:

- the daily updated **listing of all issues traded**, with the stock symbol, company name, specialist name, trading post, and trading panel of each issue

- **historical data archive** of daily market volume (from 1879) and daily closing values for the NYSE indices (from 1966).

Summary of contents on the NYSE Web site

NYSE News
- News Releases (incl. new listings, suspensions, and delistings; trading records, program trading, and trading halts; annual and quarterly financial results; disciplinary actions taken by the NYSE due to violations of NYSE rules and Federal securities laws.
- Information Memos.
- Positions and Statements (incl. Preferencing Dealers; payment for order flow).
- The Exchange Newsletter.

About the NYSE
- History of the NYSE.
- Today's Exchange (incl. Facts and Figures; The Organization; Annual Report; Latest Quarterly Results).
- Going forward (incl. Overseas Investing; New Technology).
- The Auction Market (incl. The NYSE Floor: Layout and Participants; Order Transmission; Trade Reporting and Dissemination; Quote Reporting and Dissemination; Audit Trail; Order Flow Concentration and Rule 390; The SuperDOT System; Intermarket Trading System; Stopping Stock and Crossing Orders; Block Trades and the Upstairs Market; Unusual Market Conditions).
- How a stock is bought and sold.
- Floor Professionals (incl. Specialists; Commission brokers; Independent brokers).
- Listed Companies.
- Member Firms.

Publications
- Books of General Interest.
- Directories and Reference Books.
- Research Papers.
- Pamphlets and Information Kits.

Data
- Listed Company Symbol Guide.
- Historical Statistics Archive.
- Trade and Quote (TAQ) Database CD.
- Market Data Products.

Glossary of Financial Terms

▓ FIG 2.23

■ Nasdaq

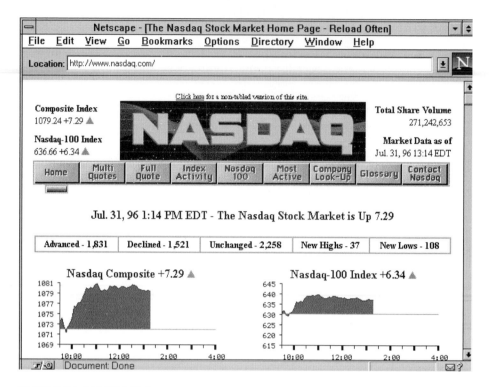

■ FIG 2.24 NASDAQ: home page

Befitting an exchange that lists companies like Microsoft, Intel and Sun Microsystems, the NASDAQ home page – with its brushed metal button bar and continually updated charts, statistics and coloured icons – looks like it might be the control panel of the Starship Enterprise. This home page carries a useful summary of the market, and beyond this, the site has 15 minute delayed quotes and some brief reports on index and stock activity.

■ Stock Exchange of Thailand

The Web site of the Stock Exchange Thailand is an example of the many excellent smaller exchange Internet services around the world. Besides the standard information on the history and structure of the exchange, this site also has:

■ general information: beginners' guide to the Exchange; information on investor protection, taxation and the SET50 Index

■ prices: real-time prices for stocks, sector and market indices

■ listed company information: company profile, trading history, financial statement, directors

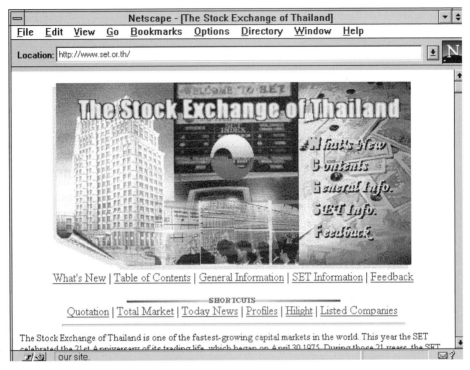

FIG 2.25 Stock Exchange of Thailand: home page

- listed company news: database from news sources and searchable by date or company name
- monthly report from the Bank of Thailand: downloadable as Thai/English and in text/Excel format.

All in all, a very impressive range of information.

Quotes

This must be one of the most exciting new areas opening up on the Internet – the ability to see real-time, or marginally delayed, stock quotes from around the world. Until recently, or, in fact, still now, professional investors are paying thousands of dollars a month to data vendors for information that is increasingly available via the Internet.

The range of services already available is very broad, including closing prices from most exchanges in the world, delayed prices for some markets, and in some cases real-time quotes and intraday charts. As is usually the case with the Internet, there is no one particular site that offers everything, so it is necessary to shop around to find the most appropriate service.

Previously, using different data vendors might have involved installing all types of different proprietary software, possibly installing dedicated cards in the back

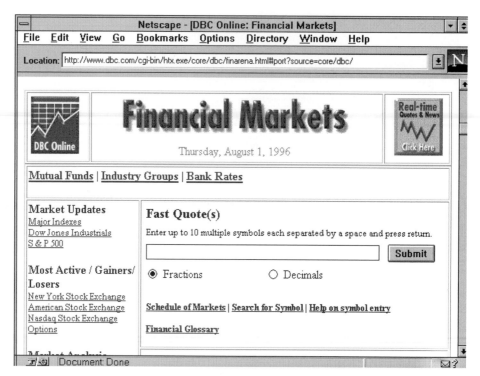

FIG 2.26 Data Broadcasting Corporation: home page

of a PC, and then receiving data by a combination of wireless or telephone line. A major advantage of the Internet is that it provides a standardized means of communicating data; and so it is possible to use many different vendors (if desired) without having to reconfigure the whole computer. Furthermore, up to now it has not been practical to try out many different data vendors for comparison purposes, and most investors must choose one service that satisfies most of their requirements, but not all. In the future with the Internet, investors may independently subscribe to many different data vendors but only using (and paying for) one small component of a service.

The quote services offered over the Internet are very varied, in order to describe them this section divides them into:

▓ free quote services, and

▓ subscription services.

The former tend to offer delayed quotes and the latter have real-time ones, but this distinction does not follow in every case.

This section focuses on Internet services that either specialize in providing quotes, or where a major part of the site provides prices. If looking for quotes for a particular market, the other important sources to check will be the Internet sites of the exchanges or newspapers – which are not necessarily included in the lists here.

Free quotes – North American exchanges

People are, in general, obsessed by things that are free, and things that are new. And why not? Falling fair and square into this category are free stock quotes. The first time one logs on to one of these services, and retrieves an almost current quote, and perhaps a chart, there is the niggling thought, where's the catch? But, as yet, there isn't one: the quotes are there and are free.

Table 2.4 lists the major suppliers of free quotes for the US and Canadian exchanges.

TABLE 2.4 Free North America stock quotes

Service	Markets	Delay (mins) Portfolio
CNNfn	US	15 no
DBC	US	15 yes
Lombard	US	20 no
NETworth	US, Canada	15 yes
PC Quote	US, Canada	20 no
Quote.com	US, Canada	15 yes
Research	US	20 yes
Security APL	US, Canada	15 no
Silicon Investor	US (technology)	15 no
Stockcenter (Virgil)	US	20 no
StockMaster	US	15 no
Telenium	Canada	D/C no

D/C: daily closing prices

Most of the services in Table 2.4 require the simple input of the stock **ticker symbol**; if you do not know the symbol for a stock, there is usually a facility for looking up the correct symbol (or if you are interested in technology stocks, some symbols are listed in Appendix K at the back of this book).

The quotes returned by each service will be **delayed** by something like 15 or 20 minutes. This delay is actually required by the exchanges (the ultimate providers of the data), who stipulate the minimum delay required for the prices to be distributed for free. Table 2.5 lists the delays required by the respective exchanges; and although the figures shown in the delay column of the above table vary, in practice the delays for all services will probably conform to that shown in the table.

■ TABLE 2.5 **Delays for price quotes from actual trade time required by N. American exchanges to be distributed at no cost**

Delay (mins)	Exchanges
No delay	Some NYSE and AMEX index data
10	Chicago Mercantile Exchange (CME) Chicago Board of Trade (CBOT) Kansas City Board of Trade (KCBT)
15	American Stock Exchange (AMEX) NASDAQ Stock Market (NASDAQ) NASDAQ Bulletin Board (BB) Canadian exchanges (ASE, TSE, ME, VSE, WCE)
20	New York Stock Exchange (NYSE)
30	Commodities Exchange Center (CEC) COMEX (COMEX) New York Mercantile Exchange (NYMEX)

Source: Quote.com

Note: it is important to have a basic understanding of how Web browsers work and, particularly in this case, the operation of the browser **cache**. If viewing stock quotes (and this, of course, equally applies to many other financial Web sites), make sure that you are viewing the latest page – and not one that has been cached by your browser. This can be done by using the browser reload button (which will compare the cached document with that on the remote server and display the latest); or, if making quite heavy use of the quote service for a period, it might be an idea to set the memory cache to zero.

Besides returning the last traded price (delayed) the quote services will commonly return a fair amount of other information as well. Figures 2.27, 2.28, 2.29 compare the output from three such services: CNN*fn*, DBC and Security APL.

These screen shots are for quotes for Oracle Corp., and were taken almost simultaneously. You can see that the range of data differs between the services. For example, DBC carries the day's percentage change and bid/ask size, which does not appear in the CNN*fn* screen. (DBC also provides another screen with extended information). The other thing to note is that there can be some inconsistency in data between the services. This will mainly occur with the financial information such as P/E ratios and earnings per share figures.

There are now many Web sites that offer delayed quotes such as these, but most of these services derive their data from just a few sources. For example, in Table 2.4, CNN*fn* and StockMaster source their data from S&P Comstock while Silicon Investor uses PC Quote.

The portfolio facility offered by some quote servers can be interesting, and this is described in greater detail later in the section.

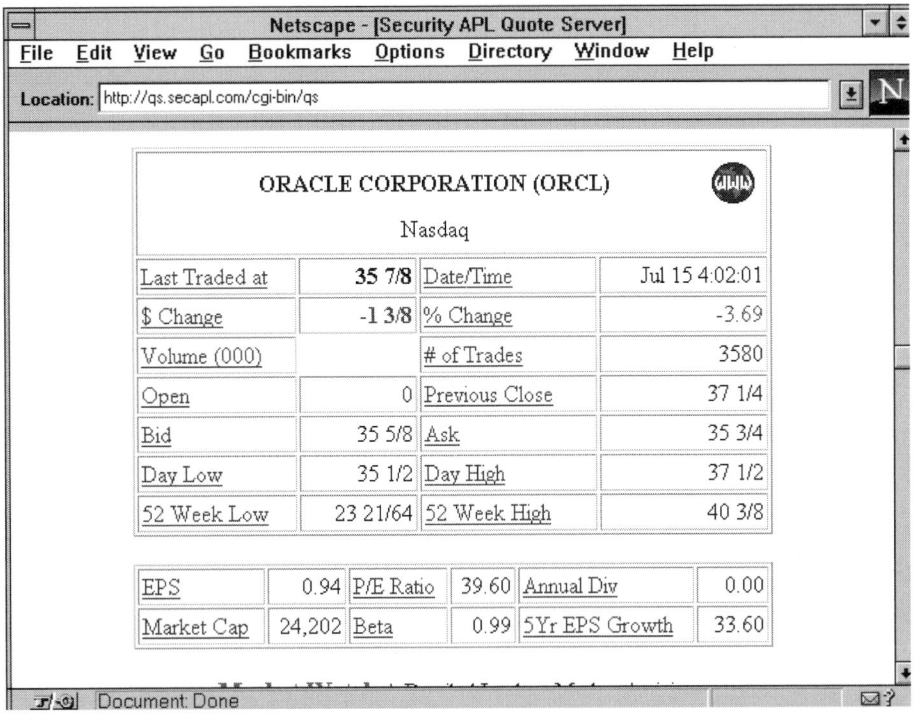

FIG 2.27 Security APL free stock quote service

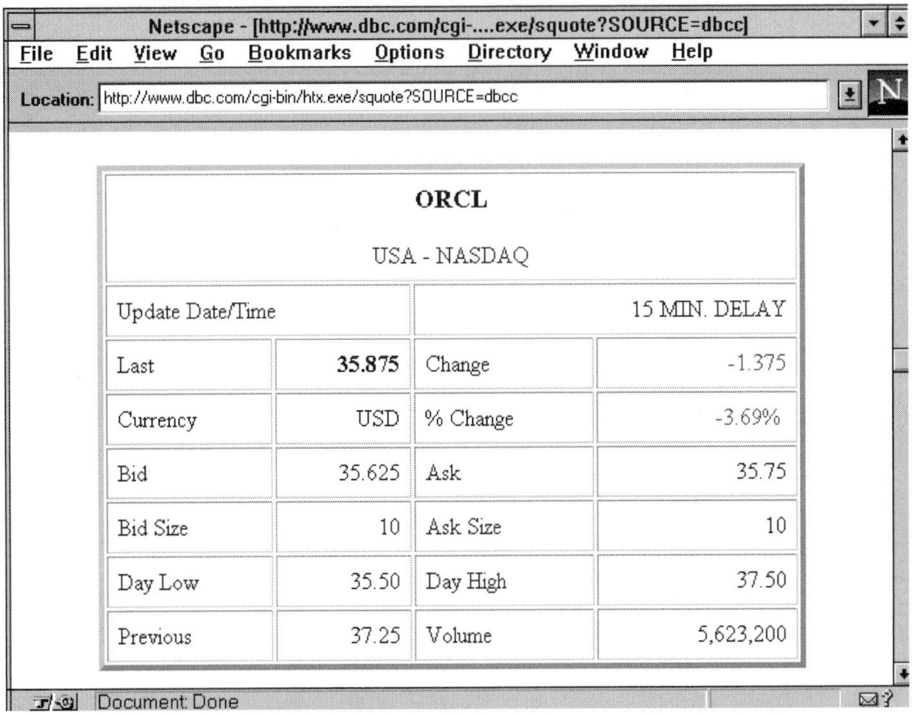

FIG 2.28 DBC free stock quote service

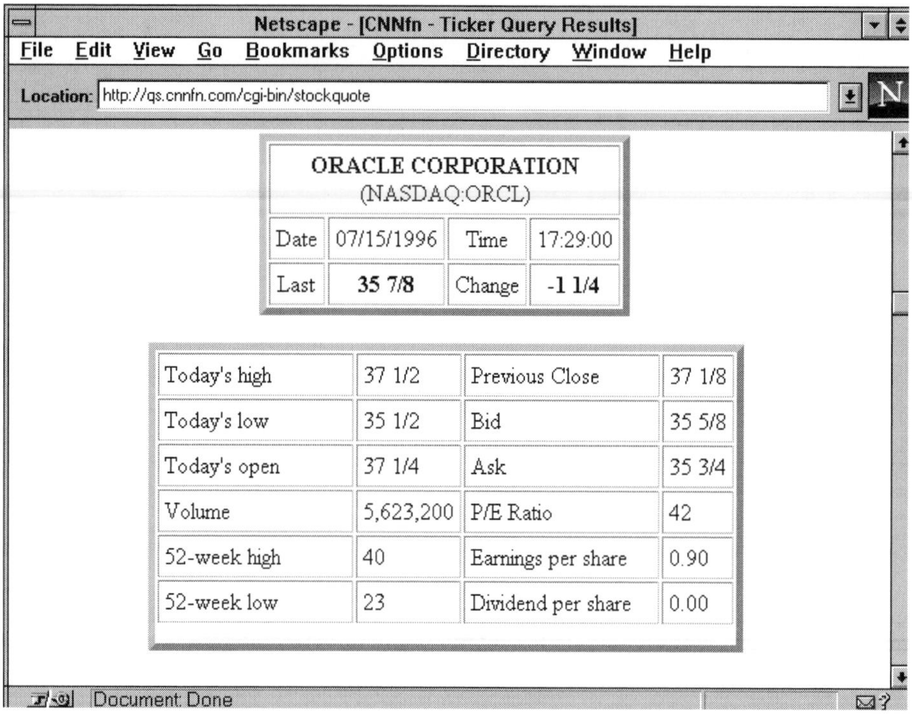

Netscape - [CNNfn - Ticker Query Results]		
File **Edit** **View** **Go** **Bookmarks** **Options** **Directory** **Window** **Help**		

Location: http://qs.cnnfn.com/cgi-bin/stockquote

ORACLE CORPORATION
(NASDAQ:ORCL)

Date	07/15/1996	Time	17:29:00
Last	**35 7/8**	Change	-1 1/4

Today's high	37 1/2	Previous Close	37 1/8
Today's low	35 1/2	Bid	35 5/8
Today's open	37 1/4	Ask	35 3/4
Volume	5,623,200	P/E Ratio	42
52-week high	40	Earnings per share	0.90
52-week low	23	Dividend per share	0.00

Document: Done

▪ **FIG 2.29 CNN*fn* free stock quote service**

▪ Free quotes – international exchanges

With much of the Internet, it seems that the North American services are somewhat ahead of the rest of the world – but this is not always the case. Certainly there is a greater range of services concentrating on the US market, but elsewhere very good services exist also, such as the real-time, or near real-time, quote servers in Singapore, Malaysia and Norway. Table 2.6 lists some of the major free quote servers around the world, outside North America.

As can be seen in Table 2.6, the majority of these international quote servers carry end-of-day quotes. A few of the services (i.e. DBC, FT, PC Quote Europe and TeleStock) have data on a number of different markets – which are detailed separately in Table 2.7.

■ TABLE 2.6 Free stock quotes for international markets

Service	Market	Delay (mins)
DBC	(see note)	
Financial Times	(see note)	D/C
PC Quote Europe	(see note)	D/C
TeleStock	(see note)	D/C
NetQuote	Australia	D/C
Weblink	Australia	D/C
Vienna University of Economics	Austria	D/C
Internet CZ, Alvera	Czech Republic	D/C
Financial Information Warehouse	Germany	D/C
Hoppenstedt Börseninformationen	Germany	D/C
Hong Kong Star	Hong Kong	D/C
Hongkong Standard	Hong Kong	D/C
Fornax	Hungary	D/C
Walla	Israel	D/C
TexNET	Italy	D/C
Korea Directory	Korea	D/C
Malaysia Online	Malaysia	1
The Star	Malaysia	D/C
Infosel	Mexico	D/C
NOS Teletekst	Netherlands	R/T
Global Register	New Zealand	D/C
Iguana Information Services	New Zealand	D/C
ABSNET	Norway	5
Yogi	Poland	D/C
RINACO Plus	Russia	D/C
Financial Interactive Services Hub (FISH)	Singapore	D/C
Stock Web	Singapore	R/T
BT StockWatch	Singapore, Malaysia	R/T
Affärsvärlden	Sweden	30
Linewise Information Services	Sweden	30
ESI	UK	60

Note: for details of markets covered by DBC, FT, PC Quote Europe and TeleStock see Table 2.7
D/C: daily closing prices
R/T: real-time

▨ **TABLE 2.7 Free end-of-day international stock quotes**

DBC	Financial Times	PC Quote Europe
Asia Pacific	*Africa*	*Africa*
Bombay	Johannesburg	South Africa
Colombo		
Karachi	*Asia Pacific*	*America*
New Zealand	China	Brazil
Philippines	Hong Kong	Canada
Seoul	India	Mexico
Shanghai	Indonesia	
Shenzhen	Korea	*Asia Pacific*
Taipei	Kuala Lumpur	Australia
	Manila	Hong Kong
Europe	New Zealand	Indonesia
Athens	Osaka	Japan
Istanbul	Singapore	Korea
Lisbon	Sydney	Malaysia
Luxembourg	Taiwan	New Zealand
Prague	Thailand	Philippines
Warsaw	Tokyo	Singapore
		Taiwan
Latin America	*Europe*	Thailand
Buenos Aires	Amsterdam	
Bogota	Copenhagen	*Europe*
Caracas	Czech Republic	Denmark
Lima	Frankfurt	Germany
Montevideo	Greece	Finland
	Helsinki	France
	Hungary	Italy
TeleStock	Lisbon	Netherlands
	Luxembourg	Norway
Europe	Madrid	Portugal
Athens	Milan	Spain
Berlin	Munich	Sweden
Bremen	Oslo	Switzerland UK
Dusseldorf	Paris	
Frankfurt	Poland	
Hamburg	Stockholm	
Munich	Turkey	
Stuttgart	Vienna	
Switzerland	Zurich	

Source: DBC, TeleStock, Financial Times, PC Quote Europe

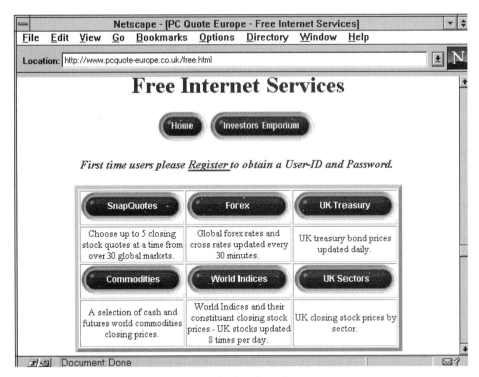

FIG 2.30 PC Quote Europe: Menu for free Internet

FIG 2.31 PC Quote Europe: End-of-day quotes for two French stocks

All of the quotes from the four vendors in Table 2.7 are end of day. The *Financial Times* has the interesting facility to create a table of the top or bottom stock movers each day. The data for the *FT* site comes from Telekurs **http://www.Telekurs.com,** which on its own pages provide some end-of-day prices – these are displayed in tabular form for the whole market, so they may be convenient if looking for many quotes at one time. TeleStock is one of the few quote servers that provides historical data (*see 'Charts'*, page 145).

PC Quote Europe is probably the most extensive international free quote server. In addition to offering up to five quotes simultaneously, it also carries a brief price and financial summaries, which includes:

■ 52 week high/low

■ EPS

■ P/E ratio

■ dividend amount

■ dividend yield

■ dividend frequency

■ dividend date

■ number of shares outstanding.

■ Subscription quotes – North American exchanges

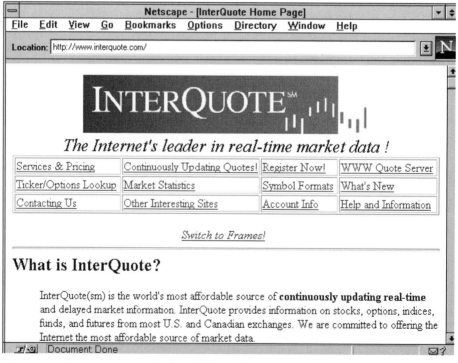

■ FIG 2.32 Interquote: real-time US stock quotes

The provision of real-time quotes on the Internet could be one of the most interesting areas of development for investors. Most real-time quote services at the moment require a subscription – although, as shown above, not all servers around the world do. The major subscription quote servers for the North American markets are shown in Table 2.8.

▨ TABLE 2.8 Subscription North America stock quotes

Service	Markets	Delay (mins)	Portfolio	Basic Monthly Price ($)
DBC	US, Canada	R/T	yes	29.95
Interquote	US, Canada	R/T	yes	29.95
PC Quote	US, Canada	R/T	yes	23.00
Quote.Com	US, Canada	15	yes	n/a
Security APL	US, Canada	R/T	yes	50.00
Telenium	Canada	15	yes	15.00
TIPnet (Telescan)	US, Canada	R/T	yes	n/a

R/T: real-time

Many of these companies also provide a free delayed quote service as well (*see* Table 2.4). Comparing the services offered here is, unfortunately, not easy, because few of the sites offer the same thing. There are technical differences and different pricing structures.

Technically, the more straightforward real-time services are those accessible by ordinary browsers (or those, at least, that support tables and perhaps cookies). Examples of this service are offered by DBC, InterQuote and PC Quote. Subscription to these allows simple access to pages looking much like any other Web page – except with real-time quotes. However, the current Web browser/server technology does not allow the easy communication of *continuously* updated prices – to view the latest quotes, the page must be reloaded by pressing a button (i.e. a new request sent to the Web server). This is not the greatest hardship, though, and many investors may be perfectly satisfied with this.

However, InterQuote and PC Quote also offer another option, which is to use a proprietary program to download and display the quotes, instead of using a browser (in fact, a browser is not needed at all here). With these special programs, it *is* possible to display continuously updated real-time prices. The PC Quote program seems to be the state of the art here, with dynamic quotes, charts, and DDE links to Excel.

The prices in Table 2.9 are included to give a rough idea of the cost of real-time data (all prices are for the basic service offering real-time quotes). And, as can be seen, the prices are fairly modest. However, the full pricing structures can be rather awkward to compare. The simplest is for a service such as the DBC MarketWatch, which has a flat rate fee. By comparison, Interquote has five levels of subscription service (varying according to access method and length of quote delay). The Quote.com service is very comprehensive, but also has one of the most involved charging structures. It offers a great range of discrete services (detailed in Table 2.9), which can be subscribed to individually, or there are

▥ TABLE 2.9 **Quote.com: subscription services**

Subscription service	Description	Monthly Charge ($)
Charts	custom charts (100 per day)	9.95
Reuters News	breaking news	9.95
Business Wire	media relations wire service	9.95
PR Newswire	media relations wire service	9.95
S&P News	focused news on 6500 actively traded public companies	12.95
Nelson's Domestic Earnings Outlook	company, exchange and consensus information on North American stocks	12.95
Ultra Trading Analytics Options Services (Level 2)	options strategy analysis screens	14.95
S&P MarketScope	commentary and analysis of market developments	14.95
Vickers Insider Trade Reports	insider trading information from SEC filings on over 10 000 US companies	14.95
Zacks	overview of stock recommendations and EPS estimates from 2500 analysts at 185 US brokerage firms	14.95
Freese-Notis Weather	weather predictions and trading advice for commodity traders	18.95
Nelson's Research Headlines	database of research firms following stocks with report headlines	19.95
S&P Stock Guide	balance sheet data for over 5000 US stocks	24.95
Trendvest	rating service for projecting the future performance of investment markets, common stocks, and stock mutual funds	24.95
Nelson's Global Earnings Outlook	company, exchange and consensus information on global stocks	24.95
Nelson's Global Research Headlines	database of research firms following global stocks with report headlines	34.95
Disclosure	basic US company reports	34.95
Ultra Trading Analytics Options Services (Advanced Level 3)	advanced options strategy analysis screens	99.95

Source: Quote.com

four levels of packaged service. Another factor to take into account is exchange fees; sometimes these are included in the prices quoted and sometimes they must be added separately.

When people first start using e-mail or the wider Internet, one of the first things they look for is the print button. Of course, the huge advantage of digital information is that it is flexible and efficient – both qualities being lost when information is transferred to smeared ink on dead trees. But this atavistic urge for hard copy is very strong, and will take us some time to overcome. However, in this one case, due to the variety and complexity of quote services and prices, if you are looking to compare the latest services and prices, the best approach might be to print out the help pages from the respective sites.

▓ Subscription quotes – international exchanges

▓ FIG 2.33 WebLink: Australian stock quotes

Table 2.10 lists services offering subscription (usually real-time) quotes on international markets. As yet, there are not so many of these, but this area should grow quickly. Although these services are frequently established with the domestic market *and* the domestic investor in mind, thanks to the technology of the Internet they can be equally useful to interested investors on the other side of the world.

▓ **TABLE 2.10 Subscription International stock quotes**

Service	Market	Delay (mins)
Weblink	Australia	60
BorsaOnWeb	Italy	1
Malaysia Online	Malaysia	R/T
Iguana Information Services	New Zealand	R/T
Financial Interactive Services Hub (FISH)	Singapore	R/T
ESI	UK	R/T

R/T: real-time

With so much data being given away on the Internet, one can understand the importance that exchanges and data vendors attach to real-time quotes. With the diminishing role and power of stock exchanges, real-time prices are one of the few genuine products they have left to sell; and for data vendors, their Byzantine pricing structures are tortuous efforts to preserve margins on these services. But it is a little odd that there is such an obsession with real-time prices among investors; if you've got them, great, but many investors feel paralysed and incapable of trading without them. For traders, these real-time prices are obviously essential, but for the far larger group of investors this is not necessarily the case. Two developments that might help to change this attitude are:

▓ **Technical ('scientific') investing**: a whole book could be written on this one topic, but using real-time prices can lead to emotional investing, and investors can start chasing prices up and down. Consistently successful investors tend to stand back a little from the market, designate price entry and exit points before getting involved, and then use limits or other orders to control the execution. The development and use of more sophisticated trading programs by investors will encourage a more rational approach to investing, where many orders can be left with brokers (or automatic execution programs) awaiting execution when pre-set triggers are hit. This sounds rather dull, but investors should be aware of their *primary* motive for investing: is it genuinely to make money or for the thrill? In the future – indeed, it is already happening – brokers will supply their clients with real-time data, not as some vague package to entice new clients, but principally to encourage their existing clients to trade actively. And there are few sound investment books that recommend active trading as the secret path to consistent profits.

▓ **Global investing**: in the future, investors are likely to invest more in international markets, and invest more directly themselves. Unless they are prepared to stay awake around the clock, real-time prices will not be very useful when trading in markets on the other side of the world.

Internet quote servers certainly look interesting and seem useful, but it is questionable whether investors really do use these services, or are they the 'free airline washbags' of the financial Internet? Figures from PC Quote show that its Web site delivers more than two million delayed and real-time quotes every day to an average of 60 000 users. This suggests that each user is retrieving on average 33 quotes per day – which appears rather high, but perhaps not, if many investors are running portfolios and updating these several times a day. Whatever, the order of magnitude is high, and PC Quote is just one of the quote servers available. So it does look as though a significant number of investors are beginning to use these already.

In addition to providing its own proprietary dynamic quotes program, PC Quote is also developing special Visual Basic tools for manipulating quotes. This is very interesting, and could lead to a mini-industry in all types of specialized quote and portfolio programs.

Portfolios

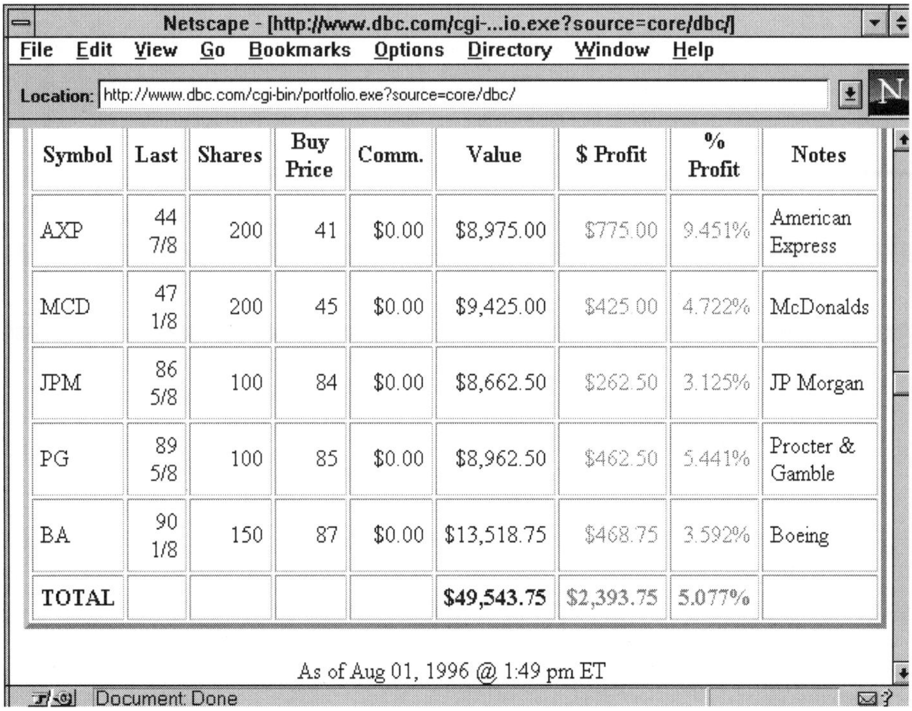

Symbol	Last	Shares	Buy Price	Comm.	Value	$ Profit	% Profit	Notes
AXP	44 7/8	200	41	$0.00	$8,975.00	$775.00	9.451%	American Express
MCD	47 1/8	200	45	$0.00	$9,425.00	$425.00	4.722%	McDonalds
JPM	86 5/8	100	84	$0.00	$8,662.50	$262.50	3.125%	JP Morgan
PG	89 5/8	100	85	$0.00	$8,962.50	$462.50	5.441%	Procter & Gamble
BA	90 1/8	150	87	$0.00	$13,518.75	$468.75	3.592%	Boeing
TOTAL					$49,543.75	$2,393.75	5.077%	

As of Aug 01, 1996 @ 1:49 pm ET

FIG 2.34 Data Broadcasting Corporation: custom portfolio valuation

The majority of the free quote servers require ticker symbols to be input singly, or in batches of, say, five, each time a request is made. This can be a nuisance if you are following the same set of stocks for a while. There are ways of getting around this (*see* custom WWW Portfolio Monitors, page 296), but a more convenient solution is quote servers that offer portfolios. At the moment this includes the free DBC, NETworth, Quote.com and Research, and virtually all the subscription quote services.

Figure 2.34 shows the portfolio valuation screen of DBC. The portfolio is created by inputting stock symbols, price and commission paid, and quantity bought, and then a valuation can be retrieved at any time. This facility is quite simple and does not have any advanced portfolio management features. Nevertheless, it can be a very handy method of tracking a few stocks, and also potentially very useful for novice investors.

Symbol		Price	Quantity	Volume	High	Low	Last	Change	%	Value	Gain
CCUUY	Cervecerias Unidas [CL]	24.500	200.000	166	24.000	23.500	24.000	0.125	0.52%	£4,800.00	-£100.00
DBRSY	De Beers Cons Mines [ZA]	33.250	200.000	99	31.875	31.625	31.750	-0.625	-1.93%	£6,350.00	-£300.00
FLH	FILA Holdings [IT]	83.875	100.000	938	78.500	76.750	77.875	0.875	1.14%	£7,787.50	-£600.00
FUJIY	Fuji Photo Film [JP]	30.188	200.000	153	29.375	29.125	29.250	0.375	1.30%	£5,850.00	-£187.60
GLX	Glaxo Wellcome [UK]	27.625	200.000	24289	27.750	27.375	27.500	-0.500	-1.79%	£5,500.00	-£25.00
REP	REPSOL SA [ES]	33.750	200.000	2277	33.625	32.750	33.000	-0.750	-2.22%	£6,600.00	-£150.00
RP	Rhone Poulenc "A" [FR]	25.000	200.000	352	25.125	24.875	25.125	0.500	2.03%	£5,025.00	£25.00
TRIBY	Trinity Biotech PLC [IE]	4.000	2,000.000	163	4.000	3.813	3.875	-0.125	-3.12%	£7,750.00	-£250.00
DIS	Walt Disney [US]	57.375	150.000	30888	54.750	53.500	54.125	-0.250	-0.46%	£8,118.75	-£487.50
	Total									£57,781.25	-£2,075.10
	Grand Total									£57,781.25	-£2,075.10

▦ FIG 2.35 Internet StockTracker: portfolio of international ADRs

A more sophisticated portfolio program is called Internet StockTracker and can be found at the StockCenter Web site of Virgil Corp. This program can track equities, options, mutual fund and market index prices, and offers:

▦ twelve different portfolios and up to 150 stocks per portfolio

▦ individual portfolio valuation plus a grand total of selected portfolios

▦ updates on request, or programmed automatically for every few minutes, on all or selected days

▦ upper and lower price that alerts can be set for each stock

▦ columns that can be customized

▦ portfolios exported in ASCII format.

After the portfolio stocks have been input, and an Internet connection made, the program will automatically connect to the StockCenter Web server and download the delayed quotes for the portfolios. All this can happen in the background, while the user views other sites with a browser. As with the DBC facility above, this is not a fully featured portfolio program, but it does what it sets out to do well, and is a great little program for tracking some stocks, for learning the basics of portfolio investing or for simply exploring one of the Internet's new innovations.

Although most portfolio services on the quote servers are, so far, restricted to North American markets, there are many international ADRs trading, particularly on the NYSE and Nasdaq. The portfolio displayed in Figure 2.35 is composed of such international ADRs, and is probably the simplest method of tracking an international portfolio valued in US dollars automatically. (For more information about ADRs, *see* Appendix J.)

(Internet StockTracker is just one of several similar programs available that make use of the quote servers. For more information *see* investment software and shareware, page 253.)

Charts

Many of the sites that offer price quotes also have charting facilities.

▦ Free charts – North American exchanges

Table 2.11 lists the major charting services for North American exchanges.

▦ **TABLE 2.11 Free stock charts – North America**

Service	Covers	Time Period	Customize
DBC	US	180 day	no
INVESTools	US		time period, bar/line/candle, moving average, size
Lombard	US		time period, (incl. intraday), size
NETworth	US, Canada		time period, moving averages, comparisons
Quote.Com	US, Canada	intraday, 360 day, 50 week, 12 month	no
Research	US	52 week	no
Remedies	Dow 30, Indices	360 day	no
Silicon Investor	US (technology)	180 day, 100 week, 60 month	no
Stockcenter (Virgil)	US	360 day	no
StockMaster	US	360 day	no
The Stock Room	Indices	720 day	no

■ FIG 2.36 **Free chart service from INVESTools: Silicon Graphics Inc [SGI]**

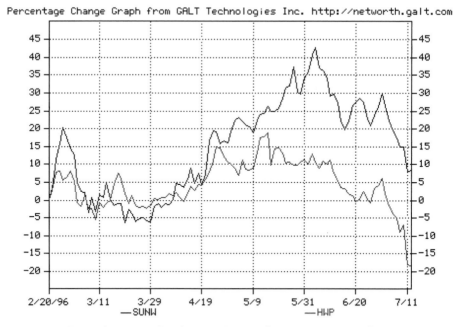

■ FIG 2.37 **Free chart service from NETworth: comparative chart, Sun Microsystems [SUNW] v. Hewlett Packard [HWP]**

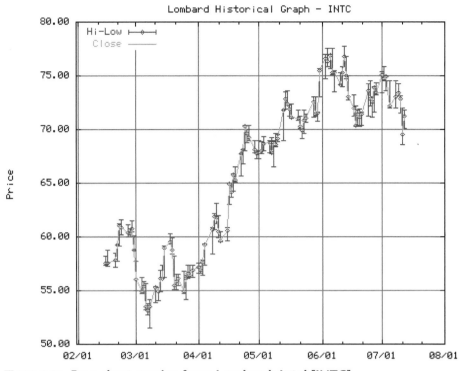

FIG 2.38 Free chart service from Lombard: Intel [INTC]

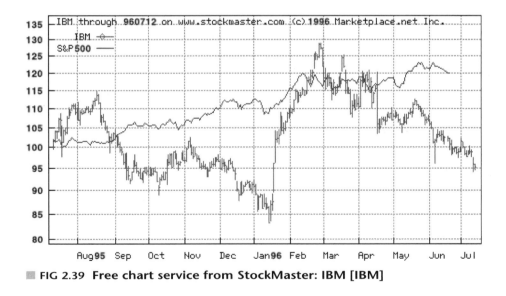

FIG 2.39 Free chart service from StockMaster: IBM [IBM]

None of the above services offer any sophisticated technical analysis (most being simple daily HLC bar charts), but it is undoubtedly useful to be able to quickly view historic price behaviour. Figures 2.36 to 2.39 illustrate the output charts from four of these services.

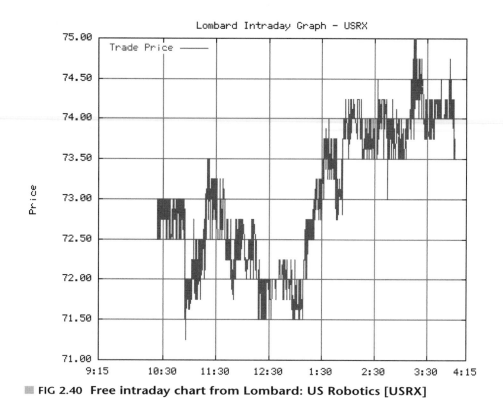

▧ FIG 2.40 Free intraday chart from Lombard: US Robotics [USRX]

The majority of sites do not allow any customizing of the charts – requiring merely the input of the ticker symbol, whereupon a standard chart will be returned (being, in most cases, a chart of daily prices for the previous one year). However, INVESTools, NETworth and Lombard *do* allow a certain degree of customization, usually allowing control over the time period and size and style of the display graphic. INVESTools has the ability to produce line, bar or candlestick charts, while Lombard is about the only service that can produce intraday charts.

The most advanced service is NETworth, which offers control over up to three moving averages, and, most importantly, the facility for producing comparative charts for up to four securities. This really can be most useful, as it is always interesting to compare a price performance with the market as a whole, or with companies in the same sector.

There are a couple of other charting sites that deserve a mention. The first is Stock Room: this offers some fairly sophisticated charts that can be customized on US and international market indices, bond yields, metals, currencies, interest rates, producer price indices and the Fidelity Sector Fund Relative Strength. The other, Kuber's Trading Desk, has some fairly advanced technical analysis charts on intraday and historical data for stocks, indices, futures, options and funds.

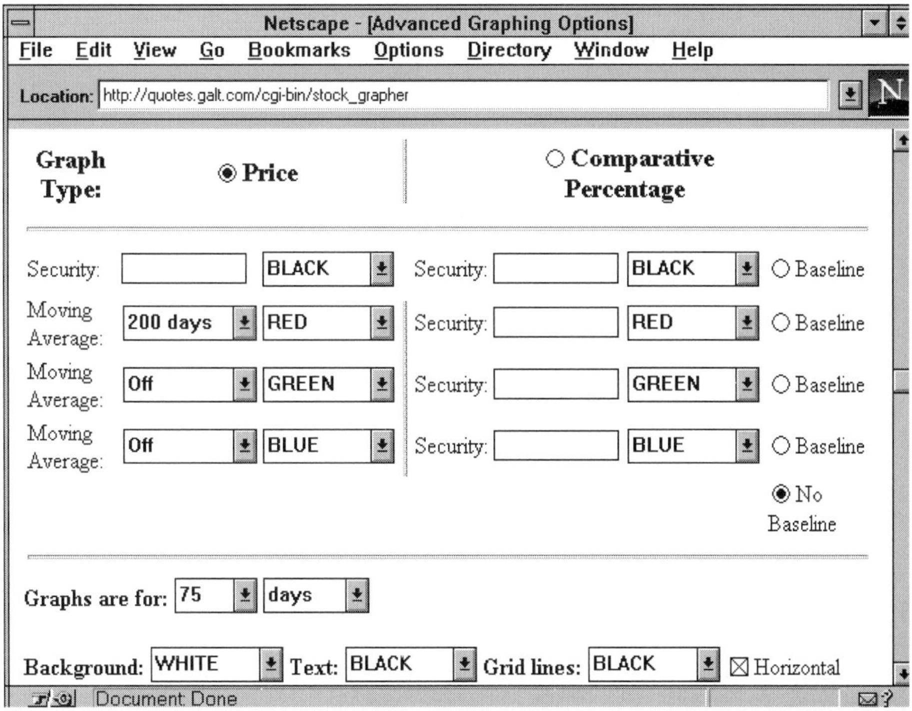

FIG 2.41 Input screen for NETworth free chart service

Note: if you would like to create a number of charts and then compare them offline, don't forget that it is possible to download images from Web pages. (In the case of Netscape, position the mouse arrow over the image and press the right mouse button.) These images can be stored on your local hard disk, and easily combined onto one page for printing out by using some simple graphics program (e.g. Paintshop Pro).

While charts such as the ones described above are nothing remarkable for professionals in trading rooms, or ordinary investors who subscribe to information providers (e.g. Telescan in the US, or Fairshares in the UK), the Internet services are fairly high quality, free and do not require proprietary software or hardware to use. Beyond this, however, these Internet services themselves are beginning to provide some fascinating information that was previously impossible to collate and analyse. For example, have a look at Table 2.12.

Table 2.12 shows statistics generated by StockMaster, with the number of requests its server received for charts of specific companies for the one day, Saturday 13 July 1996. On that day, the figures show that the price chart for Motorola was the most popular, being requested 663 times. A few observations on the data:

▓ TABLE 2.12 Most frequently requested charts from StockMaster
(Saturday 13 July 1996)

No. requests	Stock	No. requests	Stock
663	Motorola Inc [MOT]	299	Sun Microsystems Inc [SUNW]
581	Apple Computer Inc [AAPL]	254	Iomega Corp [IOMG]
511	Intel Corp [INTC]	253	Bay Networks [BAY]
486	Hewlett–Packard Co [HWP]	251	General Electric Co [GE]
481	Microsoft Corp [MSFT]	250	Fidelity Magellan Fund Inc [FMAGX]
407	Cisco Systems Inc [CSCO]	243	Oracle Corporation [ORCL]
347	IBM Corp [IBM]	238	Coca Cola Co [KO]
322	Netscape Communications [NSCP]	203	Compaq Computer Corp [CPQ]
311	P B H G Growth Fund Inc [PBHGX]	197	U S Robotics Inc [USRX]
305	Micron Technology Inc [MU]	196	20th Century Ultra [TWCUX]

Source: StockMaster

▓ It is difficult to know how to interpret these figures as there is no real precedent or benchmark. Is the fact that 663 charts were requested for Motorola really significant? Considering that all these financial services on the Internet are only a few months old, and that this data is just for one day, perhaps it *is* surprising that quite so many people are using this one service.

▓ There is obviously a bias towards technology stocks that no doubt reflects the user profile of the Internet. But it is also interesting to observe that the table is dominated by fairly mainstream technology stocks, and there are few specifically Internet-related stocks (e.g. Cascade, Cybercash, Netcom, Raptor, or Yahoo) which one might have expected. In fact, just four of the companies in the table are in the Hambrecht & Quist Internet Index (of 46 stocks).

As the figures are just for one day, it is possible the table is not at all representative of the general situation. So let's compare the table with Table 2.13, which shows similar figures produced by the Silicon Investor site.

The main differences from the StockMaster data are that Silicon Investor only follows technology stocks, and that the chart viewing figures cover the whole period from the beginning of 1996 to 14 July 1996. The figures displayed show the total number of requests made for the seven and a half months and also the daily average. Some comments on the table:

▓ Not only do these figures suggest that the StockMaster data *is* fairly representative (both sets of figures being the same order of magnitude), it is

■ **TABLE 2.13 Most frequently requested charts from Silicon Investor (1 Jan 96–14 Jul 96)**

Total Request	Avg/ Day	Stock	Total Request	Avg/ Day	Stock
136 171	698	Iomega [IOMG]	56 844	292	Microsoft [MSFT]
107 906	553	Amati [AMTX]	55 181	283	Netscape [NSCP]
100 470	515	Micron Technology [MU]	55 115	283	Applied Materials [AMAT]
84 455	433	Intel [INTC]	54 717	281	C-Cube Microsystems [CUBE]
73 151	375	Sun Microsystems [SUNW]	51 866	266	Ascend [ASND]
70 540	362	Bay Networks [BAY]	45 348	233	Integrated Device Tech [IDTI]
70 044	359	Cisco Systems [CSCO]	43 894	225	Hewlett-Packard [HWP]
66 285	340	Oak Technologies [OAKT]	43 671	224	IMP [IMPX]
64 122	329	LSI Logic [LSI]	43 246	222	Quarterdeck [QDEK]
60 856	312	Novell [NOVL]	42 942	220	S3 [SIII]

Source: Silicon Investor

a little extraordinary quite how close these figures are. (E.g. StockMaster had 407 requests for Cisco, while Silicon Investor had an average of 359.)

■ While it was not easy to tell if the viewing figures on the one day for Motorola were high, to have an average of 700 people over seven months looking at the Iomega chart every day *does* seem high.

■ It is likely that the market capitalization of the hardware section of the technology sector is greater than that for either software or services, but it is interesting to see the overwhelming dominance of hardware stocks in this top 20.

Many more observations could be made. Imagine if one collated this data every day (from other sources as well), and then compared it with daily stock price movements – it could be the basis for some interesting research, forming part of the new meta-analysis of investor behaviour.

■ Free charts – international exchanges

As yet, there are not many free charting services for international markets, but some of the better ones are listed in Table 2.14.

The most advanced of all of these is TeleStock (*see* Figures 2.42 and 2.43). This covers quite a few markets, and can produce data in table or chart form, where the time period can be customized. The excellent feature of this site is that historic price data can be displayed for all securities – there are very few sites

FIG 2.42 Free chart service from TeleStock: input screen

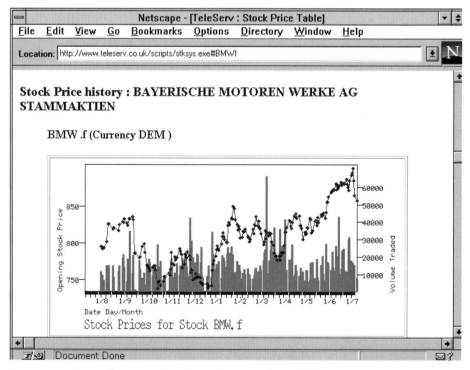

FIG 2.43 Free chart service from TeleStock: BMW

TABLE 2.14 Free stock charts – international markets

Service	Market	Service	Market
TeleStock	(see note)	Delphi Economics	Norway
Finstocks	Finland	RINACO Plus	Russia
BorsaOnWeb	Italy	Financial Interactive Services Hub (FISH)	Singapore

Note: see Table 2.7 above for markets covered

that offer this. And further, this data can be downloaded in Intuit's Quicken format, which might be useful for some North American stocks as well (which are covered by TeleStock, although not included in Table 2.7).

Research

The Internet offers tremendous opportunities to track down company information, but this information is not necessarily as structured or as easy to find as, for example, stock quotes. The online services available tend to divide into two categories:

- **corporate information** (derived from government required corporate filings, or investor relations material)
- **independent analysis** by brokers or specialized research companies.

This is one of the few major areas of the financial Internet where many of the services require a subscription. This may be due to much of the information being genuinely original. However, quite a few services act as a front-end package for much material that is freely available elsewhere on the Internet (examples of this might be the SEC EDGAR filings and PR Newswire). For these, the investor has to balance the time involved in searching for information on many different sites, with the convenience of having everything in one package with a consistent structure.

EDGAR Database of corporate information

In common with many countries, companies in the US must file regular reports about their activities and financial health. These reports are very detailed and should form the starting point for any serious fundamental research on US companies. Obviously, for decades these reports were filed on paper, and one can imagine that just processing all that paper must have been a small industry in itself. Then a little while ago the US Securities and Exchange Commission (SEC) set up a trial system called EDGAR (Electronic Data Gathering Analysis and Retrieval), whereby companies could file their reports electronically. This trial must have been a success, as from 6 May 1996 all public, domestic companies have to file electronically, and the SEC will no longer accept any paper submissions (beyond a few hardship exemptions).

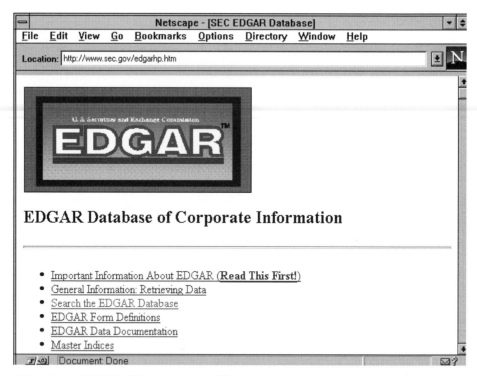

▓ **FIG 2.44 EDGAR: US corporate filings**

The great advantage of this procedure is not only that the filings can be retrieved and viewed electronically, but also the turnaround time between the date of filing and being available on the database is very short. All this would be fine, but of little use to the investor if the database was then only accessible through awkward and expensive proprietary systems. But, in a remarkable display of open government, the SEC has made the whole EDGAR system freely available via the Internet using the WWW or FTP (of which only the former will be dealt with here). This leads to a significant levelling of the playing field with the data being equally accessible to institutional or individual investors – worldwide.

The EDGAR site now carries all corporate filings made electronically to the SEC from January 1994, and new filings are available on the database just 24 hours after the date of filing. Table 2.15 lists the forms that companies file and which can be found on the SEC EDGAR Web site.

■ **TABLE 2.15 Description of forms filed with EDGAR**

EDGAR Corporation Finance Forms

Securities Act Registration Statements
- ■ **S-1**: Registration Statement, General Form
- ■ **S-3**: Registration Statement, Certain Issuers
- ■ **S-4**: Registration Statement, Business Combinations
- ■ **S-8**: Employee Benefit Plan Securities Offering
- ■ Rule 424 Prospectus Filings – specific section of Rule 424B3

Proxy Materials
- ■ **PRE 14A**: Preliminary Proxy Statement
- ■ **PREC14A**: Preliminary Proxy Statement, Election Contest
- ■ **PREM14A**: Preliminary Proxy Statement, Merger or Acquisition
- ■ **DEF 14A**: Definitive Proxy Statement
- ■ **DEFC14A**: Definitive Proxy Statement, Election Contest
- ■ **DEFM14A**: Definitive Proxy Statement, Merger or Acquisition

Annual, Quarterly and Periodic Reports
- ■ **ARS**: Annual Report to Security Holders (voluntarily filed on EDGAR)
- ■ **8-K**: Current Report
- ■ **10-Q**: Quarterly Report
- ■ **10-K**: Annual Report, S-K Item 405 Box is not checked
- ■ **10-K405**: Annual Report, S-K Item 405 Box is checked

Williams Act Filings
- ■ **SC 13D**: General Statement of Beneficial Ownership
- ■ **SC 13G**: Statement of Beneficial Ownership
- ■ **SC 14D1**: Tender Offer Statement
- ■ **SC 14D9**: Solicitation/Recommendation Statements

Source: US Securities and Exchange Commission

Note: the forms above are for corporations, but there is another set of forms for investment management (e.g. for mutual funds).

EDGAR does not cover all possible corporate filings, as some forms are not yet permitted to be filed electronically, while some other forms are voluntary. For example, the company annual reports to shareholders need not be filed, but some companies do file them voluntarily (although much of the same information can be found in the 10-K report).

Of all the forms that companies file, the most useful are probably the 10-Q and 10-K (the quarterly and annual reports). The components of the 10-K report can be seen in Table 2.16.

▓ **TABLE 2.16 Components of the 10-K form (available on the SEC EDGAR database)**

EDGAR 10-K Form

▓ **Item 1.** Business (incl. Industry; Products; Manufacturing; Employees; Sales; Backlog; Competition; Research and development; Intellectual property and licensing; Compliance with environmental regulations; Executive officers)

▓ **Item 2.** Properties

▓ **Item 3.** Legal proceedings (incl. Litigation; Environmental proceedings)

▓ **Item 4.** Submission of matters to a vote of security holders

▓ **Item 5.** Market for the registrant's common equity and related stockholder matters

▓ **Item 6.** Selected financial data

▓ **Item 7.** Management's discussion and analysis of financial condition and results of operations

▓ **Item 8.** Financial statements and supplementary data

▓ **Item 9.** Changes in and disagreements with accountants on accounting and financial disclosure

▓ **Item 10.** Directors and executive officers of the registrant

▓ **Item 11.** Executive compensation

▓ **Item 12.** Security ownership of certain beneficial owners and management

▓ **Item 13.** Certain relationships and related transactions

▓ **Item 14.** Exhibits, financial statement schedules and reports on Form 8-K

Source: US Securities and Exchange Commission

Of all the items in the 10-K report, it is the final part (Item 14, with the financial statements) that takes up the bulk of the report. Needless to say, for investors who like digging into dense, fact-intensive reports, the ones here are as good as it gets. For example, if you were interested in Intel, its 29 March 1996 10-K filing reveals:

▓ the amount Intel spent on research and development for the previous three years

▓ what it did with a Greek drachma borrowing in Ireland

▓ the size of the three properties Intel owns in Japan – and what it is doing with them

▓ details of the Intel step-up warrant.

As can be expected, some of the files on EDGAR are very large – the 10-K report is typically some 180K bytes in size. Thus, these are the type of files where it is a very good idea to save to your local hard disk for reading offline later on. If you are downloading quite a few files, it may be possible to automate this to some extent with some batch routine to operate late at night (if you try to download during a time when the Internet is busy, and receiving speeds are, say, at 300 bytes per second, one 10-K will take ten minutes to download). If you are looking for a direct bulk feed of the data, the general dissemination of the EDGAR data is looked after by Lexis/Nexis **(frank.cory@lexis-nexis.com)**.

Foreign companies with securities trading in the US are not required to submit filings to EDGAR. However, some do so voluntarily, and if this becomes more widespread, the intriguing possibility opens up where corporate information could be more accessible and detailed on EDGAR, than in the companies' own domestic market.

Although the flashing screens of the live quote, charting and real-time news services of the Net attract attention and have a high profile, in some ways it is this under-designed, image-starved EDGAR site that seems the greater demonstration of not only the immediate power of the Internet, but also the ways in which the investment process will be changed by it. After all, live quotes and up-to-date news have been previously available to investors via telephone or television (albeit more expensively and less efficiently than today with the Net), but now, investors in Siberia or Zimbabwe can directly access extremely detailed US company information at the same time, and for pretty much the same price, as a fund manager in Boston.

These are early days yet for the SEC EDGAR system, however, and the service is still a little rough in places:

▓ The search system is rather clumsy (instead of indexing all the companies and reports, a keyword search is required on the header information at the beginning of each report).

▓ The format of the reports is crude, and to find specific information within the report requires a fairly detailed knowledge of the structure of the filings.

These drawbacks may well disappear in the future (and the SEC site does offer a small program that will convert the text reports into WordPerfect format, making them readable by MS Word and others). However, with the potential demand for ready access to these reports, it would be extraordinary if some third-party services did not set up to offer a smoother interface – and, indeed, two have already done so: Smart Edgar and Edgar Online. Such services cost about US$10 per month and can offer all, or a combination of, the following:

▓ better structured indexing and searching facilities for finding specific company reports

▓ a daily list of new reports filed

▓ extending the above, a monitor service to alert investors when companies they are following file reports

▓ improved formatting of the reports, with better display and printing options

▓ direct access to specific sections of reports (for example, the Management's Discussion part of the 10-Q and 10-K reports can be interesting but tedious if it is necessary to download a 180K byte file for just a few paragraphs).

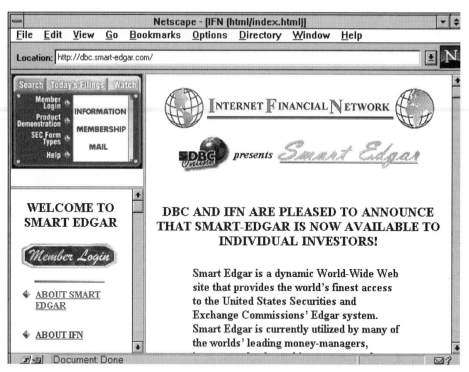

The majority of all US company information services base their research on the SEC filings, so investors can retrieve similar data themselves for free from EDGAR. However, if time is valuable, one of these independent services can prove useful for accessing exactly the desired data quickly.

Disclosure and I/B/E/S

For some time, Disclosure has been one of the main sources for all corporate filings in the US. It now has an archive of all SEC filings from 1968 and recently formed a partnership with Wright Investors' Service to distribute Worldscope – a database of international corporate information.

It's obvious that Disclosure bit the CD ROM bug very big, and much of its Web site used to be just an advertising pitch for these. (And, incidentally, its site must also have been one of the few on the hi-tech, multimedia Internet that proudly boasted of a *microfiche* service). However, it has now launched Global Access, which is a subscription database, accessible via the Internet, for viewing or ordering four million filings from over 29 000 US and international public companies. This service offers all of the facilities listed for the third-party EDGAR vendors above, plus:

▓ access to *all* SEC filings (not limited to just the EDGAR ones)

▓ an archive of all SEC filings from 1968

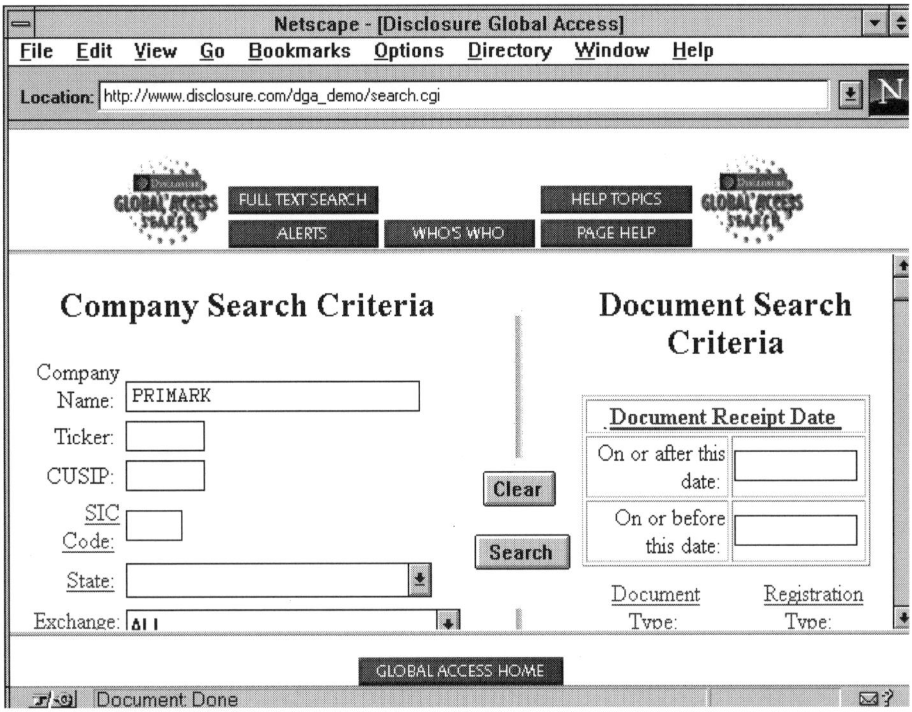

FIG 2.46 **Disclosure Global Access: retrieve SEC corporate filings**

- powerful search facilities across all EDGAR filings
- the ability to download EDGAR financial statements in Excel format.

The Web site also offers something called *Tearsheets*, which are downloadable PDF files described as, 'one page graphic representations of a company's fundamental, management, earnings and pricing data'. These are priced at $3.00 each and can be paid for using either the *CyberCash Wallet* or the *CheckFree Wallet*.

There are also some pages that Disclosure has compiled from its database that rank the top US and international companies by: net sales, total assets, net income, number of employees and five year growth in EPS (an extract of which is shown in Table 2.17).

In a section explaining why investors should subscribe to the Disclosure service, rather than get the information free from the SEC, there appears the following:

> *All of Disclosure's products (including our Internet products) are and will be secure from 'eavesdroppers.' Hackers can tell your ordering patterns at NYU and the SEC site which may have implications for certain users.*

■ TABLE 2.17 Disclosure rankings of top 20 international companies by: 5 yr growth in EPS, number of employees and net income

Rank	Company	Country	5 yr EPS Growth	Company	Country	Employees ('000s)	Company	Country	Net Income ($m)
1	Varig, S.A. – Viacao Aerea Rio	Brazil	1125	General Motors Corporation	US	709	General Motors Corporation	US	6881
2	Companhia Vale Do Rio Doce	Brazil	1019	Wal-Mart Stores, Inc.	US	675	General Electric Company	US	6573
3	Souza Cruz S.A.	Brazil	722	Pepsico, Inc.	US	480	Exxon Corporation	US	6470
4	Aracruz Celulose S/A	Brazil	671	Siemens Ag	Germany	373	Philip Morris Companies, Inc.	US	5450
5	Companhia Suzano De Papel	Brazil	650	Ford Motor Company	US	347	Kon Nederlandsche Pet	Netherlands	4367
6	National Bank Of Greece SA	Greece	463	Hitachi, Ltd.	Japan	332	IBM	US	4178
7	Industrias Villares S.A.	Brazil	246	Sears, Roebuck And Co.	US	314	Ford Motor Company	US	4139
8	Saes Getters spa	Italy	228	Daimler-Benz Ag	Germany	311	HSBC Holdings plc (HK $)	Hong Kong	3885
9	Christian Dior SA	France	226	Unilever N.V.	Netherlands	308	HSBC Holdings plc	UK	3823
10	Merloni Elettrodomestici spa	Italy	225	Unilever Plc	UK	308	Intel Corporation	US	3566
11	Gubre Fabrikalari T.A.S.	Turkey	218	AT&T Corp.	US	300	Citicorp	US	346
12	Resource Mortgage Capital	US	205	Mercantile Stores Company	US	300	Seagram Company Ltd.	Canada	3381
13	Rhone-Poulenc Rorer Inc.	US	202	Unilever Indonesia P.T.	Indonesia	300	Merck & Co., Inc.	US	3335
14	Turk Tuborg Brewing & Malting	Turkey	199	Istituto Finanziario Industria	Italy	269	Du Pont (E.I.) De Nemours	US	3293
15	Lockheed Corporation	US	198	Matsushita Electric Industrial	Japan	265	Nippon Life Insurance Co.	Japan	3077
16	Heilit + Woerner Bau-Ag	Germany	180	Philips Electronics N.V.	Netherlands	265	Coca-Cola Company	US	2986
17	Waagner-Biro Ag	Austria	176	Stone Container Corporation	US	259	Chase Manhattan Corp	US	2959
18	Amgen, Inc.	US	164	Fiat spa	Italy	248	Roche Holding Ag	Switzerland	2922
19	Miyata Industry Co., Ltd.	Japan	159	Volkswagen Ag	Germany	242	British Telecommunications	UK	2806
20	Semperit Ag Holding	Austria	158	Columbia/Hca Healthcare	US	240	Wal-Mart Stores, Inc.	US	2740

Source: Disclosure/Worldscope database

Obviously there is an element here of marketers' scaremongering and, at the moment, a largely spurious warning. But what an interesting idea!

Disclosure is owned by Primark, which also owns Datastream, TASC, Vestek and I/B/E/S. This collection of companies should ensure that Primark is one of the major providers of company information worldwide.

I/B/E/S is an interesting company: it collects earnings forecasts from 7000 analysts at over 750 brokerage and investment firms for 16 000 companies in 47 countries; it then collates and calculates the consensus forecasts, which it then provides to the investment community. The company has two main products: EPS Surprise Reports, and EPS Consensus Forecasts; both of which can be ordered from its Web site, where the latest Surprise Report is published and updated five times daily.

Hoover's

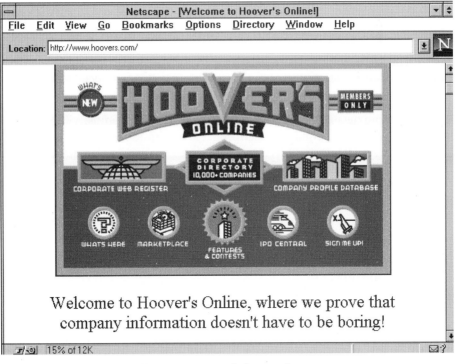

FIG 2.47 Hoover's Online: company information

Hoover's provides basic information on about 15 000 companies worldwide and detailed information on about 2600 companies. The former is available on its MasterList Plus database, which can be accessed for free at the Hoover's Web site. Search facilities are offered on: ticker symbol, company name, location, industry or sales. A sample MasterList entry for Allied Signal is shown in Figure 2.48.

Allied Signal

Phone:	201-455-2000	Fiscal Year End:	December
Fax:	201-455-4807	Sales Year:	1995
Web Site:	http://www.alliedsignal.com	Sales ($ millions):	14,346.00
CEO:	Lawrence A. Bossidy	1-Yr. Sales Change:	11.90%
CFO:	Richard F. Wallman	Employees:	88,500
HR:	Donald J. Redlinger	Ticker Symbol:	ALD
Fiscal Year End:	December	Exchange:	NYSE

Description:
Allied Signal is a diversified industrial powerhouse. Its 3 segments – Aerospace, Automotive, and Engineered Materials – produce advanced technology products and services for military, commercial and general aviation, and space markets. Principal products include airplane engines, environmental control systems, airborne weather avoidance, wind shear detection systems, wing ice detection systems, and collision avoidance radar systems. Allied also makes products for missiles and spacecraft. Cutting much of its stake in the automotive market, the company decided in 1996 to sell its brake unit to Bosch for $1.5 billion.

▓ **FIG 2.48 Hoover's free MasterList Database: Allied Signal**
Source: Hoover's Online

The Hoover's MasterList is in the process of being extended to include a European companies section as well.

The more detailed reports are held in the Hoover's Company Profile database, access to which requires subscription ($9.95 per month or $101.49 per year). These reports are about five pages long and comprise the following sections about each company:

▓ Description

▓ History

▓ Officers

▓ Location

▓ Competitors

▓ Financials

The Hoover's reports are very popular, and are currently also available online through America Online, Bloomberg, CNN*fn*, CompuServe, Dow Jones, IBM infoMarket, LEXIS-NEXIS, Microsoft Network, and Reuters. For example, the CNN*fn* site has links to the Hoover's company descriptions which is the same as the MasterList reports; and the *Wall Street Journal* in its Briefing Books has links to a major excerpt from the Hoover's Company Profile (including *verbatim* sections 1-4 and just missing the Competitors and Financials sections).

The Hoover's Online site is really quite lively, and it seems to have grasped the concept of the Web better than many other financial sites. Besides the company databases, there is also:

- a daily in-depth focus on a company
- an industry focus report
- a weekly digest of the major company news
- a list of business book bestsellers
- a compilation of the latest earnings reports filed with the SEC
- Who's On Top? (previously called The List of Lists), Figure 2.49.

Hoover's Who's On Top (List of Lists)

The Hoover's site maintains a page of links to dozens of lists elsewhere on the Net that rank companies by size, sales, compensation, reputation and other criteria. While not strictly anything to do with corporate information, these lists can be diverting, and particularly appealing to list devotees. A sample of the links to lists is given below:

- The *FORTUNE 500* Largest US Corporations
- The *Forbes* 500 Largest Private Companies in the US
- The *Forbes* 400 Richest Americans
- 35 Greatest Fortunes in the US
- *Forbes* 40 Top Money Entertainers
- Top Patent Winners in the United States
- Top 20 in CEO Compensation
- The Inc. 500 (Emerging Companies)
- 100 Biggest American Computer Companies
- 10 Largest: Personal Computer Manufacturers, Software Companies,
- 40 Largest Management Consulting Firms in the US
- Top 20 CPA Firms in the US
- 10 Leading World Advertisers
- *Ad Age's* Top 200 Brands
- 20 Most Advertised Brands in the US
- Most Valuable/Underutilized/Best Managed Brands
- Sports Franchises That Increased the Most in Value
- *Financial World's* 20 Best Brokerages
- *Financial World's* Best/Worst 25 Analysts
- America's 100 Most Admired Companies
- *Multinational Monitor's* 10 Worst Corporations

FIG 2.49
Source: Hoover's Online

Market Guide

Market Guide has quite a large range of company information services available via the Internet, given in Table 2.18.

▦ TABLE 2.18 Market Guide: description and prices of reports
Note: the two prices are per report or monthly subscription

Report	Description	Price Single/ Mnthly (US$)
Company Snapshot Report	Provides a quick view of a company's key financial ratios, pricing data, earnings announcements, industry and sector information, plus description of the company's line of business, recent operating results and address.	Free
Quick Facts Report	Company Snapshot Report *plus* operating results, institutional and insider ownership, and historical quarterly revenues and earnings data.	1.00 3.95
Company Profile Report	Quick Facts Report *plus* quarterly and annual income statement, balance sheet and cash flow statement items, capital structure, key officers, and a comparison of the company to its industry, sector and market.	2.50 9.95
Ratio Comparison Report	Detailed report of key ratios, statistics and growth rates, comparing the company to its industry, economic sector and the market.	1.00 4.95
Earnings Estimates Report	First Call consensus EPS estimates for the current and next quarter and the current and next fiscal year. Plus, estimates vs. actual EPS results for the previous five quarters. Also includes price, volume, and earnings data from Market Guide.	2.50 n/a
Detailed Financial Statements	Historical quarterly and annual income, balance sheet, and cash flow statements. These Detailed Financial Statements are shown in company specific line item description formats, virtually identical to the way each company reports providing invaluable insight into the operations of the company.	5.00 n/a
ProVestor Report	Market Guide's most comprehensive report. Includes Detailed Financial Statements, the Ratio Comparison Report, the company's business description, recent operating results, historical pricing, institutional ownership and insider trading data, price performance, short interest information, capital structure, key officers, and address	6.95 n/a
StockQuest TM	A software application which provides screening on over 8,200 publicly traded companies. There are over 50 pre-defined variables to screen for companies that meet investment criteria.	19.95 7.95

Source: Market Guide

The basic Company Snapshot Reports are free, and apart from the Market Guide Web site itself, these reports can also be accessed from DBC and Hoover's Online. Whereas the latter's own MasterList reports (*see* Figure 2.48) concentrate on the company's basic information, Market Guide has more about share price, earnings and financial ratio data. So, the two services complement each other fairly well.

Besides the information shown in Figure 2.50, the free Company Snapshot Reports also carry the data shown in Figure 2.50a.

FIG 2.50 Market Guide: Company Snapshot Report for Allied Signal

Allied Signal

Complete Financials: Mar 1996   **Earnings Announcement: Jun 1996**

Business Summary
Allied-Signal Inc. designs, develops, manufactures and markets products in three business segments: Aerospace, Automotive, and Engineered Materials. For the 3 months ended 3/31/96, sales increased 11% to $3.78B. Net income increased 14% to $225M. Revenues benefited from increased aerospace and engineered materials sales from the consolidation of recent acquisitions. Earnings also reflect productivity improvements and lower foreign exchange costs.

Earnings Announcement: For the quarter ended JUN 1996, revenues were 3,347; after tax earnings were 272.

Ratios and statistics at a glance (as of 08/02/96)

Price $	62.5	EPS (TTM) $	3.35
52 Week High $	62.5	P/E Ratio (TTM)	18.69
52 Week Low $	41.13	Book Value (MRQ) $	13.05
3 Month Avg Daily Vol (Mil)	0.67	Price/Book (MRQ)	4.79
Beta	0.99	Sales Per Share (TTM) $	50.95
Market Cap (Mil) $	17 673.13	Return on Assets (TTM) %	7.7
Shares Outstanding (Mil)	282.77	Return on Equity (TTM) %	26.93
Float (Mil)	231.87	Cash Per Share (MRQ) $	1.97
Indicated Annual Dividend $	0.9	Current Ratio (MRQ)	1.29
Dividend Yield %	1.44	Total Debt/Equity (MRQ)	0.58

Note: Mil = Millions; MRQ = Most Recent Quarter; TTM = Trailing Twelve Months

FIG 2.50a Market Guide: free Company Snapshot Report for Allied Signal
Source: Market Guide

The StockQuest program offered by Market Guide might be interesting to some investors. This is a Windows program that allows screening on over 8000 companies (listed on the NYSE, AMEX, Nasdaq and OTC exchanges). Screening is possible on 50 predefined variables, or others can be customized.

▓ Zacks Investment Research

▓ FIG 2.51 Zacks Investment Research: home page

Zacks Investment Research has become something of a standard for stock research for the investment industry. Its Web site has two interesting features:

■ **Research Watch**: this is a free service that offers an index to all current brokerage research reports produced by over 235 US and Canadian brokerage firms.

■ **Analyst Watch**: this is the main subscription service ($150 per year) that monitors analysts' earnings estimate revisions and brokerage buy/hold/sell changes.

The latter service itself has three components:

■ **Portfolio Alerts**: a daily e-mail report summarizing changes to stocks in a portfolio.

- **Zacks Company Reports**: eight-page reports on over 5000 companies.
- **Custom Equity Screening**: screen the equity database using any combination of 5000 investment criteria.

Business Wire and PR Newswire

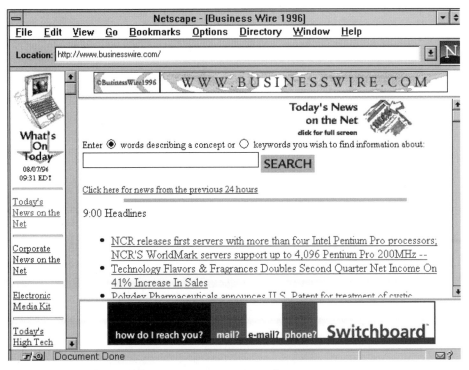

FIG 2.52 Business Wire: company news releases

These are two media relations services that disseminate company news releases. As such, and despite their names, they should not be confused with ordinary news services. Every day they post hundreds of company releases; however, it will rarely be worthwhile just browsing through these releases (as many tend to be of the 'Meganational Corp. announces coffee sales in the staff room up 2.3 per cent on previous Qtr' variety).

Both these Web sites are well organized and have good search facilities, so they can prove very useful if looking for information on one particular stock. Also, the news releases are categorized by sector, so, if you are following technology stocks, it might be interesting to check the latest releases in that one sector.

These types of company news service are quite common in North America (Canada also has Canada NewsWire, Canadian Corporate News, and Carlson On-line Services), but, as yet, not so active in the rest of the world.

References

Business Wire **http://www.businesswire.com/**
PR Newswire Home Page **http://www.prnewswire.com/**
NEWSdesk **http://www.newsdesk.com/**

▓ FIG 2.53

▓ Wall Street Research Network (WSRN)

▓ FIG 2.54 **Wall Street Research Net: custom research links to other sites**

This site has almost no original material at all, but rather a collection of clever customized links. For example, if you were looking for information on Eastman Kodak, after inputting the ticker symbol (EK), or company name, a Web page is returned that has customized links for Eastman Kodak to:

▓ the Eastman Kodak home Web page

▓ a current price quote (from DBC)

▓ the EDGAR filings (at the SEC)

▓ stock charts (from StockMaster and NETworth)

- press releases (from PR Newswire, Business Wire and/or its own Web page)
- the *Wall Street Journal* Briefing Book
- company news and profile (from Yahoo).

If this service is kept updated, and you are fairly new to the Internet, then it could be quite a useful short cut to access many of the different Internet sites. The WSRN pages also have links to sources on the economy, markets and news.

Hemmington Scott [UK]

```
Netscape - [Vodafone Group PLC]
File   Edit   View   Go   Bookmarks   Options   Directory   Window   Help

Location: http://www.hemscott.co.uk/hemscott/equities/company/cd01906.htm
```

UK Equities Direct

Vodafone Group PLC

OLD NAME: (16 Sep 91) Racal Telecom PLC. **ACTIVITIES:** Mobile telecommunications services **STATUS:** Full; Lon option; ADR. **INDEX:** FT-SE 100. **SECTOR:** Telecommunications.

| Corporate data | Share Price Graph | Outlook | Broker Forecasts |

| Contacts | Key Dates | Registrars |

Annual Reports are also available

```
Document Done
```

FIG 2.55 Hemmington Scott: company information on London Stock Exchange stocks

Hemmington Scott is the publisher of the Hambro Company Guide, which is one of the major sources for information on UK stock market companies. It has now set up a Web site, and a service called UK Equities Direct, which contains pretty much all of the data from the Hambro Company Guide (*see* Table 2.19 for an outline of this information).

About the only difference with the paper Company Guide is that this carries five-year financials, while the Web pages have just the latest two years. All the data comes from the companies themselves (who pay to appear), and some pay to have more information about the company displayed than the basic format

■ **TABLE 2.19 Hemmington Scott: outline of information available on each company**

■ **Summary**: activities; listing status; index constituent; sector.

■ **Corporate data**: financials (summary of balance sheet and profit/loss account); ordinary capital (including major shareholders holding over 3% and directors' holdings); gearing, ROCE and interims; names of directors, number of employees and total remuneration; company's bankers, financial advisers, brokers, auditors, solicitors, and financial PR advisers.

■ **Share price graph**: 4-year line chart, with FTA relative.

■ **Outlook**: extracts from the company annual/preliminary reports.

■ **Broker forecasts**: consensus figures from brokers compiled by Hemmington Scott.

■ **Contacts**: head and registered offices.

■ **Key dates**: year end; int/fin ex-div; annual report, AGM.

■ **Registrars**.

Source: Hemmington Scott

shown above. Hemmington Scott is also building a database of company annual reports, which will be properly formatted in HTML, and not scanned images of the report pages, or in Adobe's Portable Document Format (PDF).

There is obviously much potentially useful information here. An interesting section details the major shareholders with over a three per cent stake. For example, in the figures for Vodaphone, one can see that 30.1 per cent of the shares are held by Bank of New York (Nominees) – from which one can assume that a third of Vodaphone shares are trading as ADRs in the US.

The site also has sections on:

■ Companies Removed (from the HS Corporate Information Database)

■ Mergers and Acquisitions

■ Name Changes

■ New Issues

■ ADR Stocks

■ Traded Options

■ AIM Companies.

Every quarter, Hemmington Scott compiles a ranking of the top corporate advisers under various criteria:

■ the most number of stock market clients

■ clients making the most profit

■ fastest growing clients

■ clients with the fastest growing earnings.

An example of the ranking for the 'fastest growing clients' category is shown in Table 2.20.

■ TABLE 2.20 Ranking of corporate advisers with fastest growing clients (Qtr Oct 95–Jan 96)

Corporate adviser	(%)		Corporate adviser	(%)	
Auditors			*Solicitors*		
Grant Thornton	20.6	(5)	Herbert Smith	22.6	(1)
BDO Stoy Hayward	19.9	(2)	Pinsent Curtis	17.4	(3)
Deloitte & Touche	18.2	(1)	Clifford Chance	15.5	(4)
Price Waterhouse	14.9	(8)	Slaughter & May	14.5	(7)
KPMG	14.1	(3)	Nabarro Nathanson	11.8	(2)
Ernst & Young	12.1	(9)	Eversheds	10.7	(5)
Coopers & Lybrand	9.7	(6)	Linklaters & Paines	10.3	(6)
Robson Rhodes	9.1	(6)	Ashurst Morris Crisp	9.6	(8)
Arthur Andersen	7.5	(4)	Freshfields	7.5	(9)
Binder Hamlyn	5.3	(10)	Simmons & Simmons	3.2	(10)
Financial advisers			*Stockbrokers*		
HSBC Samuel Montagu	25.4	(2)	James Capel	134.6	(1)
Hill Samuel	23.7	(1)	Hoare Govett	32.0	(2)
Morgan Grenfell	22.0	(10)	NatWest Wood Mackenzie	21.4	(5)
Schroders	18.2	(3)	Panmure Gordon	19.7	(3)
Baring Brothers	18.0	(6)	Credit Lyonnais Laing	19.5	(7)
Hambros	16.6	(11)	UBS	11.7	(4)
Robert Fleming	12.9	(9)	Greig Middleton	11.6	(6)
NM Rothschild	12.8	(5)	de Zoete & Bevan	11.5	(8)
Kleinwort Benson Ltd	10.0	(4)	Cazenove	11.1	(11)
Barclays de Zoete Wedd	8.7	(12)	SBC Warburg	7.7	(10)

Source: Hemmington Scott

■ Dongwon Securities [Korea]

An excellent example of a broker's site with company information is that of Dongwon Securities in South Korea. For each of 600 companies listed on the Korea Stock Exchange, the site has a very detailed page with:

■ company profile

■ share price and ratios (including price high/low; EPS; book value/share; P/E ratio)

■ share price chart (daily)

┌───┐
│ ═   Netscape - [Korea Company Handbook]   ▼ ▲ │
│ **File   Edit   View   Go   Bookmarks   Options   Directory   Window   Help** │
│   │
│ Location: http://www.dws.co.kr/hs_hbook.htm   ⬇ N │
│   │
│ *Korea Company Handbook*   │
│   │
│ Korea Company Handbook includes *600 listed company* in the Korea Stock Exchage, so you │
│ can get any investment information from here and are able to jump to any company's home page. │
│   │
│ *Alphabetical Order*   │
│   │
│   ● A - Aluminium of Korea...   ● J - Jaeil Engineering...   ● S - Sae Han Electronics... │
│   ● B - Beak Kwang Mineral   ● K - Kabool...   ● T - Tae Bong Electronics... │
│   Products...   │
│   ● C - Central Investment &   ● L - Lamy Cosmetics...   ● U - Ulsan Investment & │
│   Finance...   Finance... │
│   ● D - Dacom...   ● M - Mando Machinery...   ● V : Non-Available │
│   ● N Noo Woo   │
│ ⬛ Document: Done   ✉ ? │
└───┘

■ FIG 2.56 Dongwon Securities Co

■ balance sheet summary (with five-year history)

■ earnings record (with five-year history).

■ Global Register [New Zealand]

Another interesting site is the ambitiously titled Global Register of New
Zealand. The data is not comprehensive, as it only carries information on
subscribing companies, but for these companies it has excerpts from the annual
report, news announcements and share price history.

Bonds

By the middle of 1996, Yahoo listed 224 Internet sites under the 'stocks'
category, while just ten sites were listed for 'bonds'. These are far from being
definitive figures for sites on the Internet, but they do offer a quick overview of
the situation, and, if anything, may underestimate the differential between
stock and bond services on the Net. However, what they lack in quantity, they
gain in quality, with the average bond site being superior to many stock sites.

US

For indicative prices of US bonds, two useful sites are:

- **Bloomberg**: US Treasury yield curve; PSA/Bloomberg National Muni Bond Yields

- **DBC**: corporate, mortgage backed, CMO (data from Capital Management Sciences).

And **Briefing** has a scrolling bond commentary.

Public Securities Association (PSA)

FIG 2.57 PSA: The Bond Market Trade Association

The PSA is a trade association for the bond markets, which includes: municipal bonds, US Treasury securities, Federal Agency securities, mortgage and other asset-backed securities, corporate debt securities, money market instruments, and repos. In 1980 its operations were merged with the Government National Mortgage Association (GNMA) Dealers Association; and again in 1983, with the Primary Dealers Association. The association now has some 360 members, including domestic, and international, securities firms and banks that underwrite, trade and sell debt securities.

The PSA Web site can be very useful; beyond the expected information on legislative and regulatory issues, market practices, upcoming conferences, news and press releases, there is a section with research reports on the bond markets and a collection of statistical tables (see Figure 2.58).

Reports provided at the PSA Web site

Cross-Market
- Debt Markets Represented by PSA in 1995
- Outstanding Level of Public/Private Debt

Municipal
- Trends in the Holdings of Municipal Securities
- Long/Short term
- Tax-exempt Interest Earnings
- PSA Swap Index History
- Municipal Default Rate

Mortgage and Asset-Backed
- Issuance of Agency MBS
- Outstanding Agency MBS
- Issuance of Agency CMOs
- Outstanding Agency CMOs
- Outstanding ABS by Credit Class
- Outstanding Mortgage Debt

Treasury
- Issuance of US Treasury Marketable Securities
- US Treasury Securities Outstanding
- Average Daily Trading Volume of US Treasury Securities
- Estimated Ownership of US Debt Securities

Funding/Repos
- Financing by US Government Securities Dealers Reverse Repurchase and
- Repurchase Agreements

Money Markets
- Outstanding Money Market Instruments

■ FIG 2.58

A sample of one of these reports (on Treasury securities trading volume) is given in Table 2.21

■ **TABLE 2.21 Average daily trading volume ($bn) of US Treasury Securities by Primary Dealers with: brokers, customers.**

Year	Broker/ Dealer	Customer	Total	Year	Broker/ Dealer	Customer	Total
1980	11.4	6.9	18.3	1988	63.0	39.2	102.2
1981	13.3	11.2	24.5	1989	69.8	43.1	112.9
1982	17.4	14.8	32.2	1990	68.7	42.5	111.2
1983	23.3	18.8	42.1	1991	78.5	49.0	127.5
1984	28.5	24.3	52.8	1992	95.7	56.4	152.1
1985	39.6	35.8	75.4	1993	107.7	65.9	173.6
1986	53.3	42.3	95.6	1994	116.1	75.2	191.3
1987	64.6	45.6	110.2	1995	112.7	80.5	193.2
				1996:Q2	121.4	88.4	209.7

Source: PSA and Federal Reserve Bank of New York

GovPX

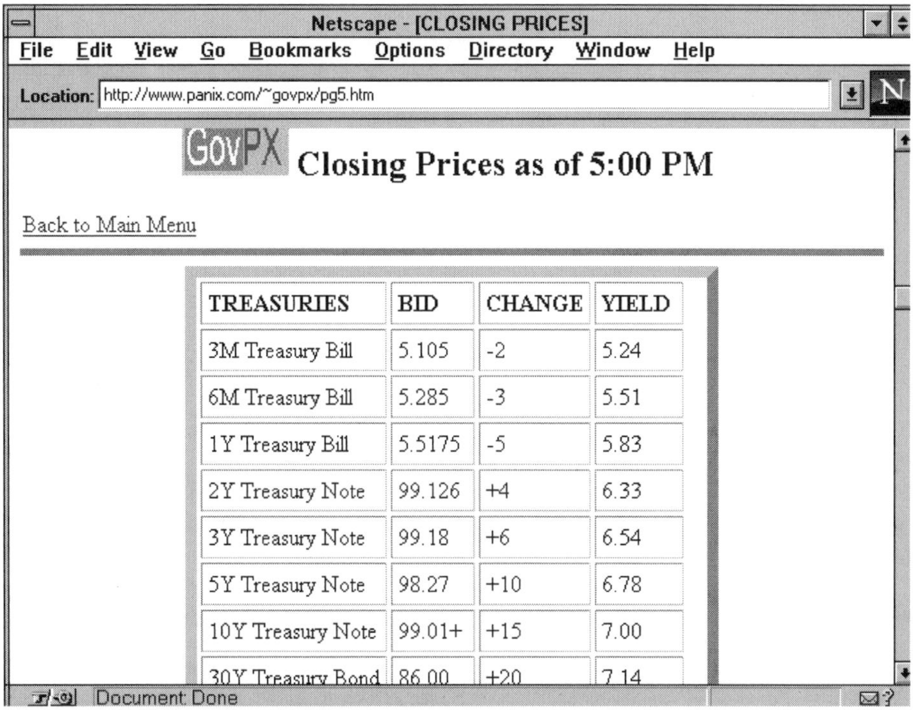

TREASURIES	BID	CHANGE	YIELD
3M Treasury Bill	5.105	-2	5.24
6M Treasury Bill	5.285	-3	5.51
1Y Treasury Bill	5.5175	-5	5.83
2Y Treasury Note	99.126	+4	6.33
3Y Treasury Note	99.18	+6	6.54
5Y Treasury Note	98.27	+10	6.78
10Y Treasury Note	99.01+	+15	7.00
30Y Treasury Bond	86.00	+20	7.14

FIG 2.59 GovPX: benchmark prices treasuries

GovPX provides Treasury benchmark prices that are based on the global trading activity of all the primary dealers, as reported by five of the six inter-dealer brokers. Its Web site posts daily benchmark prices and a summary data treasury report as well as a quarterly treasury report.

In addition, it offers a subscription service to download text files with end-of-day prices for active and off-the-run Treasuries and Zero Coupons. These are posted at 10-15 minutes after the hour (3:00pm, 4:00pm and 5:00pm), and in the format shown in Table 2.22.

Besides the Web sites mentioned above, there are a few others that provide a combination of market comment and reference articles. The best of these are:

- **Bonds-Online**: treasuries, corporate, municipal, funds
- **Municipal Resource Center**: (RR Donnelley Financial)
- **The Blue List**: (Standard & Poor's) municipal, corporate
- **Bondtrac**: municipal, corporate.

Other sites that should be useful would include, **The Board of Governors of the Federal Reserve**, and **The US Department of the Treasury**.

■ TABLE 2.22 GovPX: format for downloadable text file with end of day
Treasuries prices

Field	Example	Comment
Record Number	0019	
Cusip	912810EH7	
Maturity	15/01/99	
Coupon	7.250	
Product Type	T,N,B or Z	T-Bill,N-Note,B-Bond,Z-Zero
Alias	10Y	Identifies security trading sector
Active code	N,A or W	N-Off-the-run,Active,When issued
Settlement	C,N,W,or R	C-Cash,N-Next Day,W-When issued
R-Next Day		
Last Trade Date	28/02/95	
Last Trade Time	16:46:28	
Last Trade Side	H or T	Hit or Take
Last Trade Price	101.3984375	All prices carried to 8 decimal places
Aggregate Volume	71	In millions
Bid Price	101.3671875	
Ask Price	101.4296875	
Mid Price	101.3984375	
Mid Yield	5.198	3 decimal places
Change Sign	+ or −	Change from same day yesterday
Price Change	0.0390625	8 decimal places
Yld Change Sign	+ or −	
Yield Change	40	Basis points are in 1/10ths of a basis point
High Price	101.5000000	
Low Price	101.3828125	
Open Price	101.5000000	Tokyo Open

Source: GovPX

International

There are no particular sites that cover international bond markets as a whole,
rather there are many sites within countries that cover their own domestic
markets. A couple of good examples of these are:

■ **Toronto-Dominion Bank**: daily morning market update for money and
bond markets

■ **Daiwa Institute of Research**: with monthly data on its proprietary indices
for bonds, CBs and warrants.

J.P. Morgan

Having said above that no sites cover international markets, an exception must be made for J.P. Morgan which has an excellent site for government bond markets.

In recent years international investors have invested increasingly in government bonds, and the bank has developed the J.P. Morgan Government Bond Index to act as a benchmark for these investments. The Index is calculated daily, and comprises traded, fixed-rate, domestic government bonds from 15 countries. To ensure that the Index is relevant to investors, only truly liquid bonds are selected. The Index measures the total, principal, and interest returns of the markets, and can be reported in 67 different currencies. The Web site has a full description of the Index and its composition. In addition it is possible to download:

- **daily data files**: daily returns for the global bond index, (available from 10pm EST)
- **monthly summary files**: monthly index returns on a global, country and non-country basis
- **The Government Bond Index Monitor**: a monthly analysis of world government bond markets (PDF format).

(Note: the first two sets of files are in text, tab-delimited format for import into spreadsheets.)

The J.P. Morgan site also offers an outline of some 22 government bond markets around the world, listed in Figure 2.60.

Government bond markets outlined by J.P. Morgan

Australia	CGBs	Germany	Bobls
Austria	Bund	Ireland	IGBs
Belgium	BGBs, OLOs	Italy	BTPs, CTOs, CCTs, CTEs
Canada	Canadas	Japan	JGBs
Denmark	DGBs	The Netherlands	DSLs
Europe	ECUs	New Zealand	NZGs
Finland	Markkas	Spain	Bonos, Obligaciones
France	OATs, Emprunts	Sweden	Stats
France	BTANs	Switzerland	SGBs, SGNs
Germany	Bund	United Kingdom	Gilts
Germany	Schätze	United States	Treasuries

FIG 2.60

These outline reports can be viewed in HTML format on the Web site, or all of the reports can be downloaded in one PDF file. An example of one of these reports can be seen in Figure 2.61, which describes the German Government bond market. Another page on the site explains the conventions of each respective market (for example, with respect to accrued interest and the trading procedures).

German Federal Government Bonds 'Bund'

Characteristics

Brief description: Bonds (Anleihen) are issued by the Federal Government (Bund), and have been issued by the German Unity Fund (Unities), the Treuhandanstalt (Treuhand), the Federal Railway (Bundesbahn), the Federal Post Office (Bundespost), and the Economic Recovery Program (ERP). The privatization of the Federal Railway (Bahn AG), the telecommunication part of the Federal Post Office (Telekom), and the inclusion of Treuhand debt and German Unity Fund debt into the so-called Debt Inheritance Fund has led to an explicit debt service of outstanding issues through the Federal Government. It cannot be determined at this time whether these new entities will issue bonds or finance themselves through other means. The most common maturity for new bonds is 10 years. Outstandings (as of February 17, 1995) were approximately DM673 billion (US$452 billion), of which Bunds accounted for 58%.

Issuers: Federal Government, Debt Inheritance Fund (possibly).

Typical issue size and maturity: Under the new issuing procedure (see System of issue), the typical size for Bund issues is DM10-15 billion. Original maturities range from 8 to 30 years, and are typically 10 years.

Form: A 'collective debt-book entry' system is maintained by the Kassenverein (Central Depository Bank for securities). There are no physical bond certificates.

Typical denomination: DM1,000 is the minimum denomination.

Listing: Seven days after issuance, German bonds are traded on all eight of the domestic stock exchanges (Frankfurt is the most important one). Prices are fixed once during stock exchange hours; however, as of October 3, 1988, variable trading was introduced at the German Stock Exchanges for Bund, Bahn, Post issued after January 2, 1987 with a minimum size of DM2 billion. The new Unity Fund issues participate in this, too.

At the Stock Exchange, the Bundesbank makes a market in Bund, Unities, and Post issues, while the Railway Bank makes a market in Bahn issues. The Bundesbank takes up a variable amount of every new Bund to provide a liquid market during the fixing. In addition to the stock exchange transactions, substantial OTC trading occurs.

Structure: All recent issues have been bullets.

Transactions

Trading basis: Bonds trade on a price basis (clean). Usually, prices on screens move in increments of DM0.01.

Typical transaction size: DM25 million. The minimum size for variable trading on the Stock Exchange is DM1 million, but the turnover is negligible. Smaller amounts can be traded at the Stock Exchange fixing.

Bid/offer spread: The price spread is normally DM0.06 for liquid issues and up to DM0.10 for others.

Commission, transactions costs: No commission is charged for OTC trades. Commissions for stock exchange transactions are usually negotiated and the Kursmakler (brokerage) fee is charged as a percent of the nominal value which is included in the net price for clients.

Tax: Since January 1, 1993 there has been a withholding tax on coupons. Since January 1, 1994 withholding tax is also charged on accrued interest. A solidarity surcharge tax on witholding tax amounts went into effect on January 1, 1995. Banks and non-German taxpayers are exempt from this tax.

Settlement date conventions: Stock Exchange settlement takes place two market days after the trade date. International settlement takes place seven calendar days after the trade date, and is now the most common settlement for all trades with foreigners. As of June 1995, international settlement will take place 3 business days after trade date.

Clearing system: Bonds are usually cleared via the Kassenverein; however, for those having custody outside Germany, Bund, Unities, Bahn, Post are eligible for clearing through Euroclear and Cedel. Settlement is usually delivery versus payment.

Liquidity: The most recent Bund issues are the most liquid. Unity Fund issues are as liquid as Bund, while agency issues are less liquid than their Bund counterparts.

Benchmark: The most recently issued Bund serves as the 10-year benchmark. Currently, it is the 7.375% Bund of January 3, 2005 with DM17 billion outstanding.

■ **FIG 2.61**
Source: J.P. Morgan

System of issue: There is a closed-shop Federal Bond Syndicate (Konsortium) composed of formerly 109 financial institutions (including foreign banks). Recent developments aim at a reduction of this number. In the traditional system of issue, all members are allocated a fixed percentage of total issue size irrespective of the issue terms. Up to 25% of the initial offering is retained by the Bundesbank for intervention and market-making purposes.

Since July 1990, a new issuance procedure has been implemented for Bunds and Unities. This procedure was a combined effort by the German Ministry of Finance, the Bundesbank and federal agencies to promote a more global distribution of government bonds, and consists of two tranches which combine the traditional syndicate procedure with a competitive Dutch tender auction.

The first tranche has fixed terms, including issue price, and is allocated along traditional guidelines among syndicate members. As compensation for reduced selling commissions (now 7/8%), the control numbers which had been used in the past ('Schalterprovision') to foster sales to non-speculative investors were abolished.

The second portion is auctioned with bids made via consortium banks in DM0.01 increments for bonds with the same conditions, except issue price, as the first tranche. No selling commissions are paid on this tranche. Bids may be placed until the morning (10:00 a.m. to 11:00 a.m.) after the launch date, with the allocation by the Bundesbank taking place within two hours thereafter.

The two tranches plus the Bundesbank quota form one single issue with identical terms and one security code. The total issue volume is announced by the Bundesbank after allocation. The proportions of total volume raised through either of the two tranches are flexible in order to capitalize on prevailing market conditions at the time of issue.

Trading hours: (local time, GMT + 1)

OTC:	8:30 a.m. to 5:30 p.m.
Stock Exchange Fixing:	11:00 a.m. to 1:30 p.m.

Interest and yield calculations

Coupon payment: Interest is paid annually.

Coupon accrual: Interest usually accrues from the previous coupon date (inclusive) to the settlement date (exclusive). The value date is always the same as the settlement date.

Ex-dividend date rule: As of January 1, 1994, German Federal Government Bonds no longer trade ex-dividend.

Year basis: 30E/360; the rule that always treats the 31st of the month as the 30th.

Yield calculation method: In Germany, there are three different yield calculation methods: 'ISMA,' 'Braeß/Fangmeyer,' and 'Moosmüller'. The differences between these methods are based on their assumptions about how to calculate the compound interest in a broken-year period. The Braeß method is the most popular for domestic transactions, while ISMA is used internationally.

Special rules concerning interest calculations: In the Braeß and Moosmüller methods, simple interest is calculated for partial coupon periods, while compound interest is calculated for full periods. In the Braeß method compounding is annual, while the Moosmüller method compounds at the same frequency as coupon payments on the bond. Therefore, for Bund, Bahn, Post, the two methods are identical.

Special or unusual features

Ten-year bond futures contract on LIFFE and DTB
Daily fixing at the Stock Exchange
Control numbers (for bonds issued until July 1990 only)
Alternative yield calculations
Coupon custody depends on trade date, not value date

Screens

Reuters		Telerate	
JPDE	Government benchmarks	38248	Government benchmarks
JPDF-L	Government bonds	38249-53	Government bonds
JPDM	Euro-DM benchmarks	38254	Euro-DM benchmarks
JPDN-Q	Euro-DM bonds	38255-7	Euro-DM bonds
JPDR	Warrants	38258	Warrants
AVSA-H	Prices-Bund (Stock Exchange fixings)		
AVSN-P	Prices-Bahn (Stock Exchange fixings)		
AVSQ-S	Prices-Post (Stock Exchange fixings)		

▦ **FIG 2.61 continued**

J.P. Morgan has also constructed an index called the Emerging Markets Bond Index Plus (EMBI+), to track the total returns for traded external debt instruments in the emerging markets. This index includes external-currency-denominated Brady bonds, loans and Eurobonds, as well as US dollar local markets instruments. Supporting this index, it is possible to download:

■ **Introducing the Emerging Bond Index Plus (EMBI+):** description of the Index (PDF file)

■ **Emerging Markets Bond Index Monitor:** monthly analysis of emerging market bonds (PDF file)

■ **historical data:** 1994 to current (text file in comma-delimited format).

■ **BradyNet**

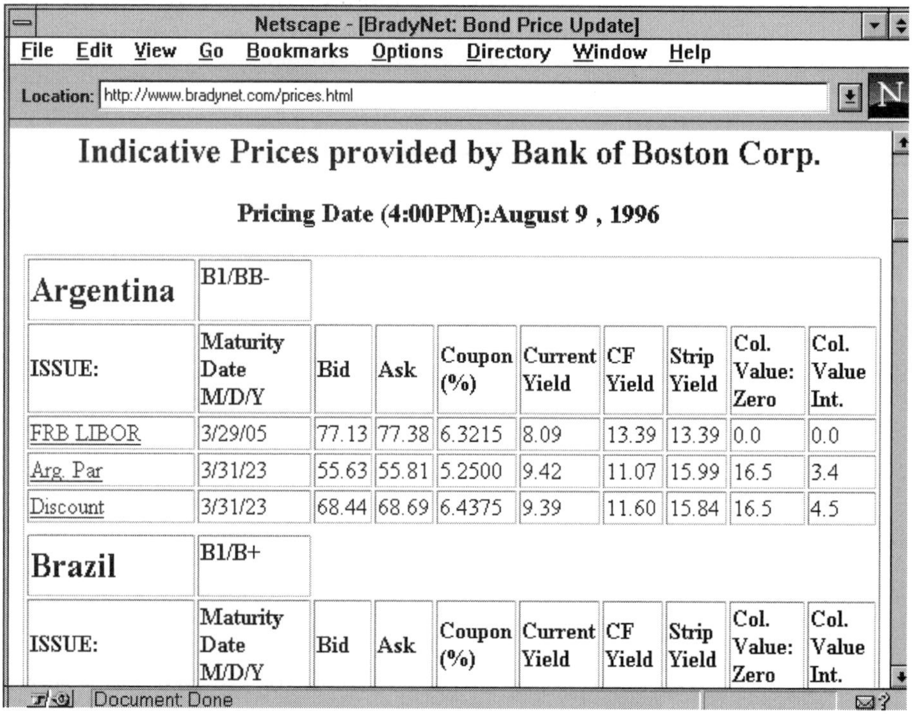

Netscape - [BradyNet: Bond Price Update]

File   Edit   View   Go   Bookmarks   Options   Directory   Window   Help

Location: http://www.bradynet.com/prices.html

Indicative Prices provided by Bank of Boston Corp.

Pricing Date (4:00PM):August 9 , 1996

Argentina	B1/BB-								
ISSUE:	Maturity Date M/D/Y	Bid	Ask	Coupon (%)	Current Yield	CF Yield	Strip Yield	Col. Value: Zero	Col. Value Int.
FRB LIBOR	3/29/05	77.13	77.38	6.3215	8.09		13.39	13.39	0.0	0.0
Arg. Par	3/31/23	55.63	55.81	5.2500	9.42	11.07	15.99	16.5	3.4
Discount	3/31/23	68.44	68.69	6.4375	9.39	11.60	15.84	16.5	4.5
Brazil	B1/B+								
ISSUE:	Maturity Date M/D/Y	Bid	Ask	Coupon (%)	Current Yield	CF Yield	Strip Yield	Col. Value: Zero	Col. Value Int.

Document: Done

■ **FIG 2.62 BradyNet: resource centre for Brady bonds**

The original J.P. Morgan Emerging Markets Bond Index covered just Brady Bonds, and a site that now concentrates on these bonds is called BradyNet. This site provides:

■ **prices:** with analytics such as current yield, yield to maturity, stripped yield (from Bank of Boston Corp)

- **descriptions:** amount issued, date issued, coupon, amortization, denomination, maturity date, day count, schedule, currency, enhancements, credit rating
- **forums:** for discussion of issues by market professionals.

Finacor [France]

```
┌─────────────────────────────────────────────────────────────────────┐
│         Netscape - [Welcome to FINACOR Home Page]                     │
│ File  Edit  View  Go  Bookmarks  Options  Directory  Window  Help     │
│ Location: http://www.finacor.fr/                                      │
└─────────────────────────────────────────────────────────────────────┘
```

Warning : Bold indicates running trades - Italic shows losing trades exited - Normal indicate

Paris Future Desk

- Notionnel
- Pibor
- Bund
- CAC 40

Paris Arbitrage Desk

Paris Emerging Markets

Annual report 1995

Finacor Rahe

MAJOR GOVERNMENT BONDS & CROSS-CURRENCY SPREADS
10-year Government Bond Benchmark   2-year G

Country	Yield	vs GER	Day-1	Wk-1	Spread Outlook	Yield	vs GER
USA	6.61%	34	38	33	↗ Tget near 65 bp	6.01%	212
Japan	3.20%	-307	-309	-300	⇔	1.13%	-276
Germany	6.27%					3.89%	
France	6.34%	7	3	0	↗ Tget near 15 bp	4.63%	74
UK	7.95%	168	164	-165	⇔	6.32%	243
Ecu	6.80%	53	51	44	↗ Tget at 56 bp	4.77%	88
Italy	9.52%	325	312	308	⇔ Buy 300 bp	8.69%	480
Spain	8.94%	267	256	245	⇔	7.67%	378
Belgium	6.62%	35	36	35	⇔	4.07%	18
Holland	6.22%	-5	-6	-5	⇔	3.95%	6
Sweden	8.24%	197	192	190	⇔	6.56%	267
Denmark	7.24%	97	96	98	↘	4.46%	57

MAJOR YIELD CURVE SPREADS : GOVERNMENT BENCHMARK
2-yr / 10-yr Bond Spread   3-mth Future

Country	Spd	Day-1	Wk-1	Target	Spread Outlook	Spd	Day-1
USA	60	61	60	55	↘ Sell 2s vs 10s	0.25	0.26
Japan	207	206	201	200	⇔	0.52	0.51

Document Done

FIG 2.63 Finacor: daily government bond report

Finacor, a broker based in Paris, has a site that is a very good example of what can be done by a broker on the Web.

For the purposes of this section, Finacor has an interesting set of pages called the Finacor Arbitrage Group, which contains a daily European bond commentary with a market comment, an update on running trade strategies, a table of major government bond prices and cross currency spreads, and major yield curve spreads and three-month futures.

In addition to this, the pages also have:

- Paris Future Desk (with comments and charts on the MATIF: notionnel and PIBOR)
- Daily Press Digest from France, Germany and Italy

- Weekly Global Calendar
- Long Term Economic and Political Global Calendar
- Global Election Calendar
- Global Holiday Calendar.

Currencies

Currencies were the most natural market for the first financial Internet services. Unlike, for example, earnings per share figures (the interpretation of which will change from country to country), exchange rates are equally relevant to everybody around the world.

▓ GNN Koblas Currency Converter

The first useful service that appeared was on the GNN (Global Network Navigator) site, and was called the Koblas Currency Converter. Although this is looking rather old now and is irregularly updated, it is interesting to mention from a historical view that this was one of the first truly global Internet sites that took notice of users outside the US. Rather than simply having a list of currencies relative to the US$, all cross rates could be displayed as well (for example, all the rates relative to the Deutsche Mark).

▓ Lund University and Xenon Labs

There are several services on the Internet that post daily exchange rates, one example being the University of Michigan. But these pages are often fairly basic, and just show rates relative to one currency (usually the US$) and not cross rates. Seeing an opportunity here, a couple of services developed which automatically download the raw currency data available onto their own sites, input it into a database, and present an easy to use front-end interface. Examples of this type of site are the Department of Computer Science at Lund University in Sweden, and the Xenon Labs Universal Currency Converter. Having input the data to a database, they can then calculate cross rates as well: the former will output the basic cross rate, while the latter is slightly more sophisticated and will calculate the answer to, 'I want to convert x Canadian Dollars to Thailand Baht'. These services are a clever idea, and a good example of Internet technologies, but at best their data is only as accurate and timely as the underlying source. However, for tourists, or if you are contemplating buying an investment book priced in Australian Dollars, or for people who get confused whether, £1.5 = US$1 or US$1.5 = £1, these provide a good quick reference.

▓ Bloomberg and CNN*fn*

Bloomberg and CNN*fn* are more serious, and probably the best quick source for currency rates. Both of these provide tables of US$ rates updated through the day; the former has a very comprehensive list of currencies and also has major cross rates. Another interesting service is provided by INO Capital Markets: this

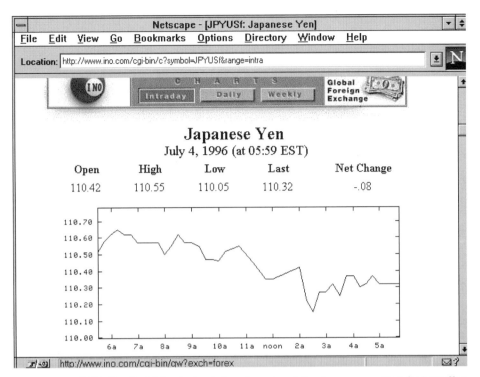

■ **FIG 2.64 INO Capital Markets: intraday chart for Japanese Yen/US Dollar**

has US$ rates for about 30 currencies updated through the day (although Bloomberg and CNN*fn* are quicker to refer to), but also intraday, daily and weekly charts are available as well, with data supplied by S&P Commstock.

In Asia the best sites are Dow Jones Telerate, Hong Kong Star, Asia Inc Online and Singapore's AsiaOne.

■ Forex Watch

The services up to this point are useful, but nothing to excite investors more actively involved with currency dealing. Now we come to some more sophisticated foreign exchange sites. Forex Watch provides:

■ major cross rate trading levels (updated every five minutes)

■ technical levels for the above, including major and minor support/resistance and moving averages

■ intraday hourly technical charts

■ scrolling bulletin board of currency comments

■ short, medium and long term trading signals from an automated technical system

■ European cross rates and ERM table (updated every 15 minutes)

■ description of charts and technical analysis.

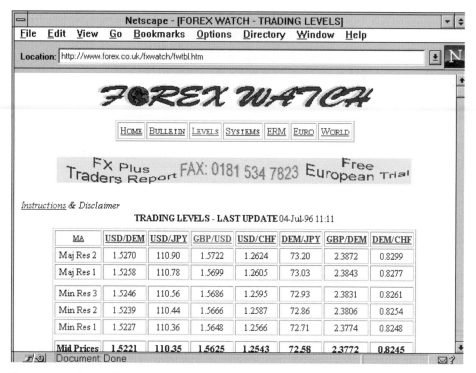

FIG 2.65 **Forex Watch: major cross rates with technical levels**

Information Internet/Currency Management Corporation

Another site, Information Internet, was the first service to actually offer real-
time currency rates broadcast over the Internet, as well as providing comparison
graphs to illustrate currency movements over the past 24 hours. To view this it is
necessary to first download its free proprietary Windows program. An associated
company, Currency Management Corporation (CMC), is a foreign exchange
dealer that has a daily currency market report with fundamental and technical
outlooks and also general information on FOREX dealing.

CME and PHLX

If you are interested in currency **futures and options** then general information
and daily settlement prices can be found at the Web sites of the two major
exchanges, CME and PHLX; otherwise, always check if there is a local domestic
exchange (for example, look at the MATIF if interested in French Franc
contracts). The CME is particularly useful, with intraday currency futures and
options prices updated every ten minutes, a currency IQ quiz, trading simulator
and free videotape.

For **commentary on the currency markets** the best services are the Knight-Ridder
news at CNN*fn*, Briefing, the bulletins at Forex Watch and the daily comment at
CMC; while there are subscription newsletters at INO and Forex Watch.

▦ Olsen and Assocs.

Finally, a Swiss company called Olsen and Assocs. (a kind of research boutique) provides quite a wide range of historical data (daily currency rates from 1990), analysis, forecasts and reports from its proprietary currency trading model.

Futures and options

In some ways, the nature of futures and options lends itself far more to the new possibilities of the Internet than is the case with stocks. Many contracts are of truly international interest, and as they are traded, rather than invested in, speed of information is of the essence. And indeed, there probably is a disproportionately high number of futures sites, relative to the number oriented towards stocks. However, while the technical quality of many futures sites is very high, the overall impression of this sector is rather lacklustre.

Futures services were among the very first WWW sites to appear in early 1994 and 1995, and credit must go to them for seeing the long-term potential here. But, after adding their glossaries, contract specifications and links to worldwide exchange sites, they appear to have run out of steam, and are perhaps now wondering where to go next. This whole sector lacks the innovation or vitality of sites such as: INVESTools, NETworth, Silicon Investor, or ESI in the UK.

No doubt this will change in the future (and in fact the very distinction between stocks, futures and options will disappear), but a few reasons for the current difference might be:

- **Online dealing:** while it is now possible to trade stocks online, this is not yet possible with futures. The influence of the exchanges is greater in the world of futures than it is with stocks, and these exchanges cannot yet decide whether, on balance, the Internet is a threat or an opportunity.

- **Research:** futures investors tend to follow a small number of contracts and, once they have their data feeds and charts, are more independent than stock investors, who are always looking for new rumours or tips.

- **Discussion:** following on from the above point, everyone can listen and contribute to a chat about Motorola or Apple and enjoy it, but futures discussions tend to the esoterica of economics or technical analysis. Some professional traders (for example, Stanley Kroll) actively shun all interaction and regard all outside information as largely white noise.

- **Similarity of sites:** virtually all exchanges and contracts around the world followed the models set by the big Chicago exchanges. Hence, the characteristics of the worldwide exchanges, and the contracts traded on them, are very similar. (A rare example where this didn't happen was the odd case of the Tokyo Stock Exchange introducing futures, but treating them almost identically to stocks trading on the Exchange.) Because of this smaller universe, and similarity of institutions and instruments, it is no surprise that all the Web sites tend to resemble each other.

■ *Futures* Magazine

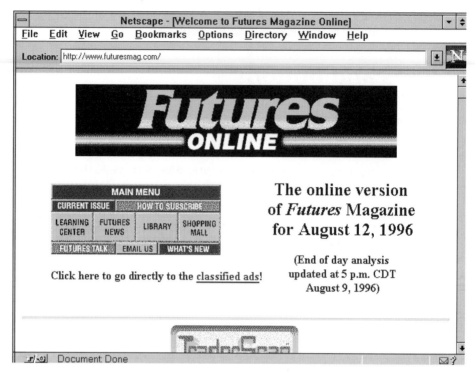

This is the Web site for one of the major US futures magazines, *Futures*, and includes selected articles from each month's issue, with an archive of these selections from October 1995. Fortunately the articles they have put on the Web site include the book and software reviews and the Computerized Trader column – all of which are usually well written and useful to refer to.

The site has started a *Futures Talk* forum, which encourages readers to discuss online various topics concerning futures. Having only just started, the talk is rather fitful, but as the forum is moderated it may develop to become more stimulating than the misc.invest.futures newsgroup.

Apart from this, the site has the expected assortment of links and shopping mall with books, videos for sale and notices of seminars and conferences.

Exchanges

The collection of futures exchange sites are among the most professional on the Web. Even if they are all rather similar (see the Sydney Futures Exchange below for a representative menu structure), they do offer a tremendous amount of information that was previously awkward or expensive to discover. Beyond the four exchanges illustrated below, other good examples of futures sites are: the Finnish SOM, Hong Kong Futures Exchange, SIMEX (Singapore), MEFF Renta Fija (Spain) and OM Group (Sweden, UK).

Chicago Mercantile Exchange (CME)

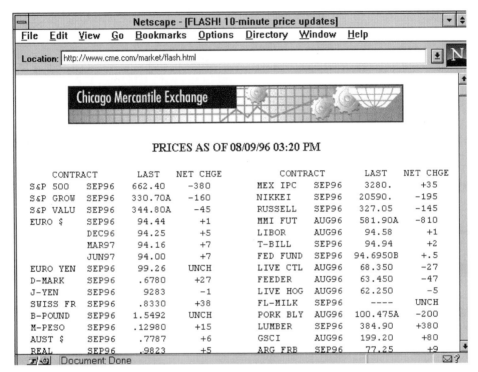

CONTRACT		LAST	NET CHGE		CONTRACT		LAST	NET CHGE
S&P 500	SEP96	662.40	-380		MEX IPC	SEP96	3280.	+35
S&P GROW	SEP96	330.70A	-160		NIKKEI	SEP96	20590.	-195
S&P VALU	SEP96	344.80A	-45		RUSSELL	SEP96	327.05	-145
EURO $	SEP96	94.44	+1		MMI FUT	AUG96	581.90A	-810
	DEC96	94.25	+5		LIBOR	AUG96	94.58	+1
	MAR97	94.16	+7		T-BILL	SEP96	94.94	+2
	JUN97	94.00	+7		FED FUND	SEP96	94.6950B	+.5
EURO YEN	SEP96	99.26	UNCH		LIVE CTL	AUG96	68.350	-27
D-MARK	SEP96	.6780	+27		FEEDER	AUG96	63.450	-47
J-YEN	SEP96	9283	-1		LIVE HOG	AUG96	62.250	-5
SWISS FR	SEP96	.8330	+38		FL-MILK	SEP96	----	UNCH
B-POUND	SEP96	1.5492	UNCH		PORK BLY	AUG96	100.475A	-200
M-PESO	SEP96	.12980	+15		LUMBER	SEP96	384.90	+380
AUST $	SEP96	.7787	+6		GSCI	AUG96	199.20	+80
REAL	SEP96	.9823	+5		ARG FRB	SEP96	77.25	+9

FIG 2.67 Chicago Mercantile Exchange: flash market quote

Most futures exchanges take their information and education roles very seriously, and for a long time they have been a source of prodigious quantities of, usually free, brochures and other material. Let loose on the Web (with its favourable publishing economics), the CME and CBOT in particular have created vast sites that must be among the largest and most polished of all financial sites.

The information available on the CME site can be grouped into the following areas:

- **About the CME:** history; listing of contracts, trading hours and contract specifications; new contract details (e.g. Nasdaq 100, Mexico's IPC stock index, Brady bonds, Euroyen).
- **Education:** guide to getting started in trading; guide to finding a futures broker; glossary.

■ **Professional resources**: daily information bulletins; quote vendor directory; calendar of key economic and agricultural reports; industry Web links.

■ **Other topics**: description of GLOBEX; Risk Management (including description of SPAN); Emerging Markets (a new division at the CME).

The most useful information on the site is probably the price data, and the CME makes this available in a number of different ways:

■ **Flash quotes**: one-screen summary of intraday prices updated every ten minutes for a range of the most active contracts (continues after hours with GLOBEX session).

■ **Intraday currency prices**: currency futures and options prices updated every ten minutes (continues after hours with GLOBEX session).

■ **Daily settlement prices**: settlement prices for all futures and options contracts posted shortly after markets close (with final adjustments posted by 7.15pm). Estimated volume and the previous day's volume and open interest are also listed.

■ **Time and sales data**: complete price history for each contract for the previous trading day.

▓ Chicago Board Of Trade (CBOT)

The CBOT Web site covers similar ground to the CME, but is, if anything, even larger with more educational material on futures and options. As with the CME, the most important section is probably the price data, and a menu for this can be seen in Figure 2.68.

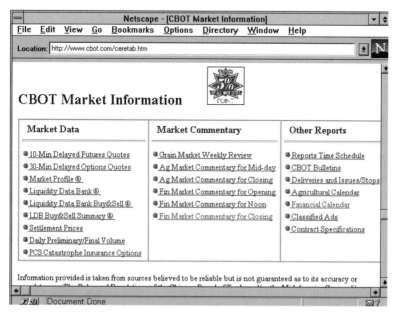

▓ FIG 2.68 CBOT: market information menu

The CBOT site has created a whole sub-section, called Marketplex, which is the area for all price data, and for marketing third-party futures services, some of which are:

- **Market Research Inc (MRI)**: global futures markets charts
- **Chartwatch**: financial futures charts and technical analysis
- **Lombard Street Research**: economic research and forecasts of major industrial nations (particularly the UK economy)
- **MJK**: global commodity exchange data (see below)
- **Hart-Bornhoft, Inc.**: managed futures source
- **Managed Futures Association**: excerpts and articles from the current issue geared to the managed futures industry.

Plus, as would be expected, numerous services for the agricultural markets.

London International Financial Futures and Options Exchange (LIFFE)

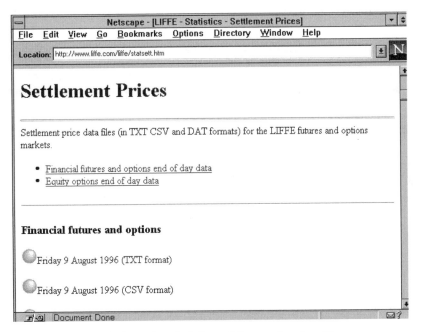

FIG 2.69 LIFFE: download daily settlement price files

The London exchange's site is a match for the Chicago ones in size and quality of material present. There is a very comprehensive library of publications, with technical articles and guidelines for managing derivatives risk. The education section has details of training software, calendars of courses, and an interesting table (*see* Table 2.23) illustrating the growth in attendance at these courses.

■ TABLE 2.23 **Attendance at LIFFE's education courses**

	1991	1992	1993	1994	1995
Courses	34	52	101	137	169
Delegates	900	1500	4200	5500	6200

Source: LIFFE

The most impressive section of the LIFFE site is the statistics department, from where it is possible to download:

■ settlement prices (*see* Figure 2.69)

■ time and sales (tick by tick data)

■ price histories (end-of-day data)

■ SPAN risk arrays

■ annual volumes and open interest

■ volume and open interest charts

■ contract records (in table form)

■ contract inception/deletion dates.

Many of the above are available in TXT, CSV or DAT format.

LIFFE also offers a free CD ROM with HLCV and OI for the equity products, the data on which can then be updated directly with downloads from the Web site.

■ Sydney Futures Exchange (SFE)

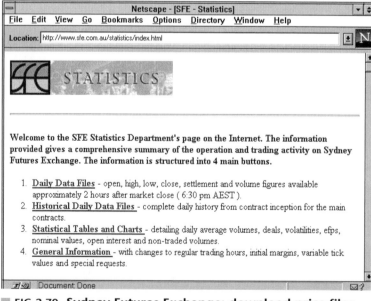

■ FIG 2.70 **Sydney Futures Exchange: download price files**

The SFE has a simple site, but what it does, it does extremely well. And that is to offer an excellent range of data through clear, uncluttered screens.

A detailed outline of the SFE site structure is given below, as a model for what can be expected at many futures exchange Web sites.

Structure of Sydney Futures Exchange Web Site

Overview
- History
- Regulations
- Members
- Facilities
- Structure
- New Zealand F.O.E.
- Clearing House

News
- News for SFE
- Newsletters
- Media Releases

Private Clients
- Introduction to Futures
- SFE FAQ

Products
- Agriculture
- Interest Rates
  - (90 Day Bank Bills
    - Background
    - Margin Rates
    - Quoting Conventions
    - Quote Vendor Access Codes
    - Trading Hours
    - Contract specifications
  - 3 & 10 Year Government Bonds)
- Equity
- SFE COMEX Gold
- Trading Hours, Margins

Statistics
- Daily Data Files (OHLCV, whole exchange)
- Historical Daily Data Files (OHLCV, by contract)
- Statistical Tables and Charts (vol, OI, etc)

Links to other sites

FIG 2.71

Brokers

As yet, it is not possible to trade futures online, so most broker Web sites satisfy themselves with a combination of contract details, economics calendars, end-of-day prices, market comments and links to industry sources.

Jack Carl Futures

Jack Carl is one of the largest discount futures brokers in the US and is part of E.D.&F. Man International Inc. Its site has daily settlement prices for a wide range of markets, contract specifications and margins, and its daily MarketLine Commentary.

Phillip Alexander Securities and Futures Limited [UK]

■ FIG 2.72 Phillip Alexander: daily interest rate futures charts

The Phillip Alexander site includes explanations of the mechanics of the markets it is trading, with contract specifications and margin requirements. It also has an interesting set of futures charts (*see* Figures 2.72 and 2.73).

Futures charts provided by Phillip Alexander Securities and Futures Limited

Stock Index Futures
- FTSE 100 & Nikkei
- NYSE & S&P
- CAC 40

Interest Rate Futures
- Eurodmark & Bund
- Sterling & Gilt
- MATIF & French Govt Bonds
- Eurodollar & US Treasury Bonds

IMM Foreign Currency Futures
- IMM pound and IMM German mark
- IMM Swiss franc and IMM Japanese yen

Energy Futures
- Crude Oil & Gas Oil
- Heating Oil

Softs and Grains Futures
- Soyabeans & Soyabean Meal
- Soyabean Oil & Wheat
- Cocoa & Coffee
- Corn & Cotton
- Sugar NY

Base Metals
- Copper & Lead
- Zinc & Tin
- Nickel

Precious Metals
- Gold & Silver
- Platinum & Palladium

Meats
- Cattle & Hogs
- Pork Bellies

■ FIG 2.73

Quotes and charts

There are not as many quote providers for futures as there are for stocks, but it is still possible to get slightly delayed quotes for all US futures and options (for the extent of the delays see Table 2.5 in the quotes section on stocks), and at least settlement prices for all international contracts.

As with stocks, the first place to always look for quotes is the exchanges themselves – most will provide at least end-of-day prices, and some, for example the CME, have intraday flash quotes as well.

US Stock and Index Options Quotes

Table 2.24 lists four servers that provide delayed quotes for US stock and index options.

■ TABLE 2.24 US stock/index options quote providers

WWW Service	Example symbol
INO Global Market	(select from list)
Lombard	AOQUE
PC Quote	.AOQUE
Quote.com	+AOQUE

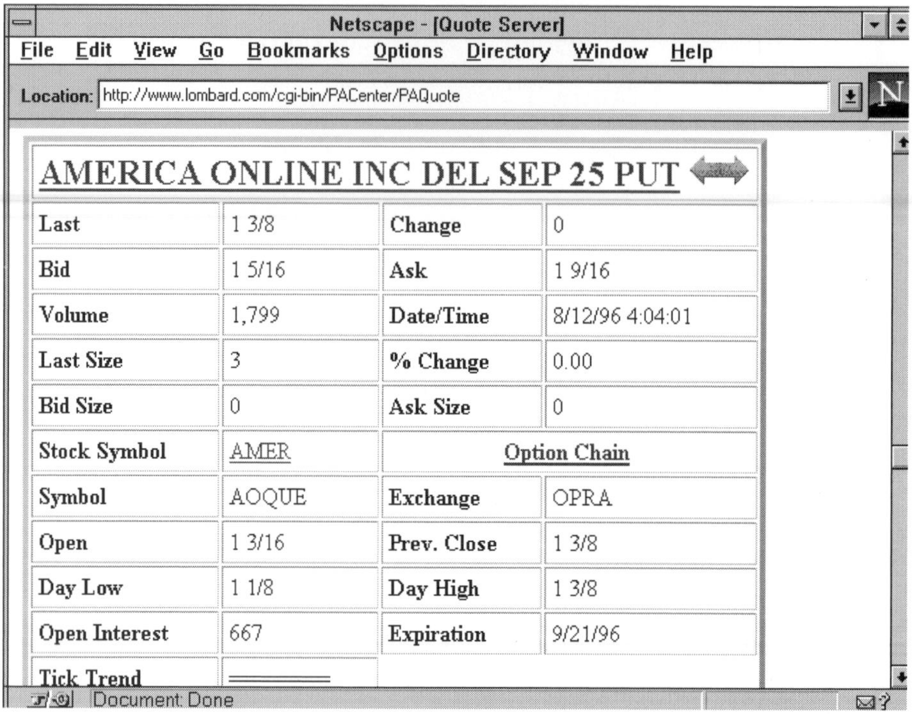

■ FIG 2.74 Lombard: quote for September 25 put on America Online

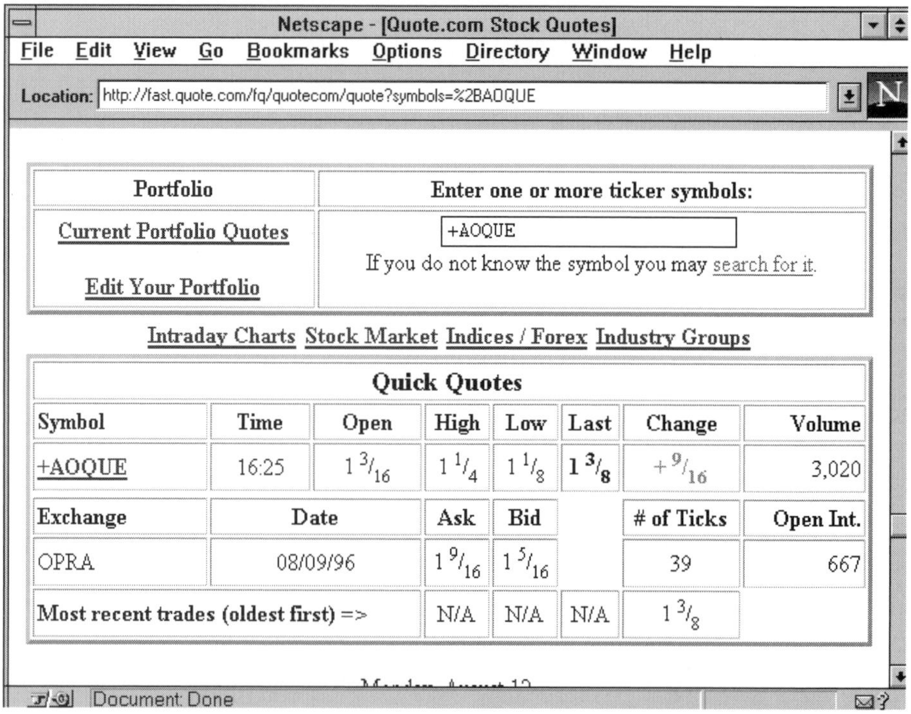

■ FIG 2.75 Quote.com: quote for September 25 put on America Online

```
┌─────────────────────────────────────────────────────────────────────────┐
│ ▬                    Netscape - [INO: AMER Options]                  ▼ ♦ │
│  File  Edit  View  Go  Bookmarks  Options  Directory  Window  Help       │
│  ┌──────┐┌───────┐┌──────┐ ┌────────┐┌──────┐┌──────┐┌──────┐┌──────┐┌──────┐│
│  │ Back ││Forward││ Home │ │ Reload ││Images││ Open ││ Print││ Find ││ Stop ││
│  └──────┘└───────┘└──────┘ └────────┘└──────┘└──────┘└──────┘└──────┘└──────┘│
│  Location: http://www.ino.com/cgi-bin/getopt?symbol=AMER            ▲ │ N │
└─────────────────────────────────────────────────────────────────────────┘
```

AMERICA ONLINE(NASDAQ)

Symbol Open   High   Low   Last   Time

AMER 0.3125 0.31375 0.2875 0.2925 16:19 8/9/96

Click on Symbol for more information

Option	Symbol	Bid	Ask	Time of Bid/Ask	Last	Last Traded
Aug 17.5 Call	AOQHW	11.375	12.125	5:29 8/11/96	11.75	5:29 8/11/96
Aug 20 Call	AOQHD	9.0	9.5	19:44 8/10/96	10.625	13:13 7/23/96
Aug 22.5 Call	AOQHX	6.625	7.0	5:29 8/11/96	6.625	14:52 7/15/96
Aug 25 Call	AOQHE	5.875	6.125	11:40 8/9/96	8.875	15:42 8/2/96
Aug 30 Call	AOQHF	1.0	1.125	16:07 8/9/96	1.125	16:07 8/9/96
Aug 35 Call	AOQHG	0.25	0.375	14:32 8/9/96	0.25	15:00 8/9/96
Aug 40 Call	AOQHH	0.125	0.3125	17:42 8/8/96	0.1875	9:59 8/9/96
Aug 45 Call	AOQHI	0.0625	0.0625	5:28 8/11/96	0.0625	16:18 8/2/96

Document Done

▬ FIG 2.76 INO: option quote series for America Online

Figures 2.74 and 2.75 display the output options quote screens for Lombard and Quote.com. The fiddly part of these options quotes is often getting the ticker symbol correct. (*See* Appendix H.) But getting the symbol itself correct is not the end of the matter, as the different services then have various input methods.

Table 2.24 includes in each case an example of the input for finding a quote for a September put option on America Online stock with a strike of 25. From Appendix H, one can see that the symbol is AOQUE (AOQ = option code for America Online; U = September; E = 25 put), and that is what is input to the Lombard service; but PC Quote requires a period to precede the symbol and Quote.com a '+' sign.

Both INO and Lombard have a useful facility where the whole option chain is displayed on the screen (see Figure 2.76), and individual contracts selected from it. In addition, the latter accepts input parameters for the option in 'near' English. Thus, the America Online option could be entered as,

AOQ sep 25 put

If you are looking at options for the first time, it can be interesting to follow some prices for a while. (Rather than inputting a longish symbol code each time, it might be an idea to think of using one of the online portfolio facilities for this, or the WWW Portfolio Monitor – described in Appendix M.) For many options, of course, there will be little or no trade many days, and so these may not be useful to follow. To quickly find the most active options, DBC has a good page showing those with the highest turnover each day.

US Futures/Commodities Quotes

Table 2.25 shows the WWW quote providers for US futures and commodities.

■ TABLE 2.25 US futures/commodities quotes

WWW Service	Example symbol
DBC	SP=Z7
INO Global Markets	(select from list)
MJK (CBOT)	(select from list)
PC Quote	/SP7Z
Quote.com	SPZ7

Source: Scientific American

Appendix I at the back gives the codes and guidelines for forming the ticker symbol. In Table 2.25, input examples are given for the S&P500 Dec 97 futures contract (SP = code for S&P futures trading at the CME, Z = December, 7 = 1997). As can be seen, these differ slightly for the servers.

International Quotes

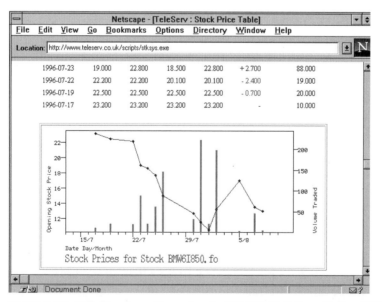

■ FIG 2.77 TeleStock: option charts (BMW Call Sep Strike 850)

■ **TABLE 2.26 International futures/options quotes**

Web site	Covers	Delay
Austrian futures	Austrian futures, options	D/C
Grupo Financiero Serfin	Mexican options	D/C
Hong Kong Star	Hong Kong futures/options	D/C
The Star	Malaysian futures	30 min
TeleStock	German, UK, US options	D/C

D/C: daily closing

Table 2.26 lists some quote servers around the world providing futures/options quotes. The most useful is that of TeleStock, which not only has quotes for Germany, UK and the US but also features the ability to chart option prices – which is fairly unusual (*see* Figure 2.27).

■ **INO Global Markets**

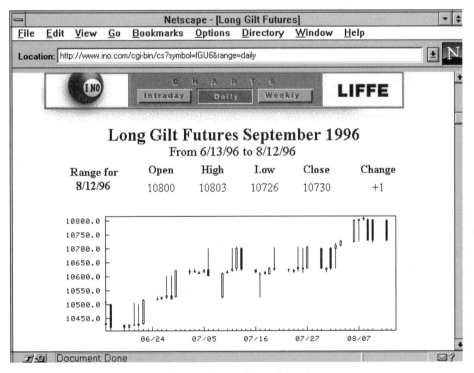

■ **FIG 2.78 INO: free intraday, daily and weekly charts**

INO is probably the largest and most impressive of all futures sites; it is not so much one service, as an umbrella site for many, including:

▨ The Options Clearing Corp

▨ The Options Industry Council

▨ Lind Waldock (discount futures brokerage)

▨ Optionomics Corp (option analysis and risk management software)

▨ Market Bookstore (order futures books online).

Besides these, the sites feature:

▨ Global Exchanges: directory of worldwide futures exchanges

▨ Stark Research: research on CTAs

▨ World Market Reports from KRF/Global News

▨ Press Release Center for the futures industry.

The site also offers quotes on: stocks, options, and futures on the following exchanges:

▨ CBOT	▨ MATIF	
▨ CME	▨ MGEX	
▨ CSCE	▨ NYCE	
▨ FOREX	▨ NYMEX	
▨ LIFFE	▨ SIMEX	

The chart service is very good, covering stocks, futures and currencies, with a choice of intraday, daily or weekly displays.

▨ Prophetdata

▨ FIG 2.79 Prophetdata: daily continuous contract charts

Prophetdata specialises in providing data and charts from over 230 worldwide markets, with some data histories going back to 1959. An outline of its services and prices is given in Figure 2.80.

Futures data packages from Prophetdata

Futures Updates: daily data updates in MetaStock, TTD, ASCII formats.

Basic Markets (top 25 futures markets) – $9.95/month
Major Markets (top 37 futures markets) – $14.95/month
All Worldwide Markets (over 230 markets) – $19.95/month
Note: continuous contracts for all the above – plus $5.

FTP-Based Updates: daily OHLCV OI for 200+ worldwide futures updates via FTP (ASCII format)

$14.95/month

Web-Based Charts: view charts on the Web, includes bar, line, and candlestick chart types; arithmetic and semi-log charts; moving averages; open interest; custom portfolio

Worldwide Futures – $14.95/month

QuickCharts System: full-featured technical analysis package that runs on local PC and downloads data from the Web site

Unlimited Access to Futures Contracts and Cash – $19.95/month

Note: most of the above services also offer comparable data for stocks, funds and indices.

■ FIG 2.80

The first service, **Futures Updates**, is aimed at investors using programs such as SuperCharts or MetaStock, where formatted data is required. The **FTP** service is for investors possibly writing their own software, and an automated download may be possible. **Web-Based Charts** gives access to a program where futures charts can be viewed, and portfolios can be compiled very usefully (this saves inputting all the symbol codes and chart parameters every time). The **QuickCharts System** uses the WWW to download data onto a local hard disk, where a provided technical analysis program can then be used. Most of these updating services complement the CD ROM historical database of futures prices marketed by Prophetdata.

A very useful feature of the Prophetdata site is the complementary charts of back-adjusted continuous futures contracts. The start and end dates of these can be adjusted, and the database in some cases goes back a couple of decades. The charts available are in the following markets:

- Bond Statistics
- Currencies
- Energies
- Financials
- Foods and Grains
- Indices and Indicators
- Industrials and Metals
- Meats
- International
- UK

As examples, specific charts for the International and UK markets are listed in Table 2.27.

▓ **TABLE 2.27 Prophetdata free charts: continuous contracts**

International	UK
CCAAO: All Ordinary Index	CCEUL: Euro Lira
CCAIR: 90-Day Bank Acc Bill	CCFTM: FTSE Mid 250
CCASX: Australian 10-Year Bond	CCITC: Brent Blend Crude Oil
CCASY: Australian 3-Year T-Bond	CCITS: Gas Oil
CCBT: Japanese 10-Year Govt Bond	CCLAG: London AM Gold Fix
CCIT: 3 Month Euro-Yen	CCLAP: German Bund APT
CCJGP: Japanese Govt Bond APT	CCLBP: Ital. Govt Bond APT
CCMN: Notional	CCLBR: London Barley
CCMP: Pibor	CCLCC: London Met Cocoa
CCMU: ECU Long Bond	CCLEC: 3 month Euro Curr. Unit
CCMX: CAC-40 Index Futures	CCLES: Euro-Swiss Franc
CCSEY: 3 month Euro-Yen	CCLFA: German Bund
CCSNI: Nikkei Index	CCLFG: Long Gilt (20-Year)
CCSSF: Sulphur Fuel	CCLFL: Shrt Sterling (3 month)
CCTTX: Tokyo Stock Price Index	CCLFU: Euro-DMark
CCTUS: US Treasury Bond	CCLFX: FTSE 100 Index
CCWCB: Canadian Barley	CCLGF: London PM Gold Fix
CCWO: Winnipeg Oats	CCLGP: Long Gilt (20-Year) APT
CCWR: Canola Rapeseed	CCLIB: Ital. Govt Bond
CCWW: Winnipeg Wheat	CCLKC: London Met Coffee
CCWWB: Canadian West Barley	CCLLP: Shrt Sterling (3 month) APT
CCWX: Winnipeg Flaxseed	CCLPO: London Potatoes
CCWY: Winnipeg Rye	CCLSB: London Sugar #5
CCYL: Japanese 20-Year Govt Bond	CCLSI: London Silver Fix
	CCLSP: Euro-Swiss Franc APT
	CCLSS: London Sugar #7
	CCLUP: Euro-DMark APT
	CCLW: London Wheat
	CCLXP: FTSE 100 Index APT
	CCU: Unleaded Gas

Source: Prophetdata

▓ FutureSource

FutureSource supplies real-time data on the futures, cash and options markets; its Web site gives details of its quite extensive range of products. The site also

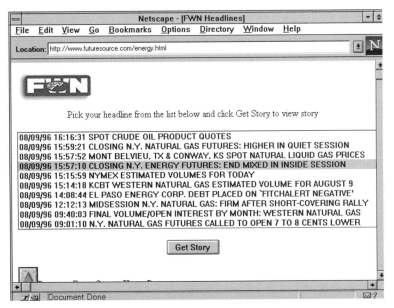

FIG 2.81 FutureSource: Futures World News headlines

offers a look at Futures World News (which, like *Futures* magazine and FutureSource itself, is owned by Oster Communications). By selecting a keyword from the following list, news stories – delayed six hours – are displayed (*see* Figure 2.81 for a sample from 'Energy').

Currency, Economy, Energy, Federal, Fiber, Financial, Food, General, Government, Grain, Meat, Metals, Stocks, Treasury, USDA, Weather.

To demonstrate its server, charts and intraday quotes can be viewed for 20 contracts (listed in Table 2.28).

TABLE 2.28 FutureSource: contracts available with free intraday quotes and charts

US Treasury Bonds	Unleaded Gas Futures
Corn Futures	Natural Gas Futures
Soybean Futures	Cotton Futures
Soybean Meal Futures	Coffee Futures
Soybean Oil Futures	Orange Juice Futures
Japanese Yen Futures	Gold Futures
Canadian Dollar Futures	High Grade Copper Futures
British Pound Futures	Silver Futures
Crude Light Oil Futures	Dollar-Yen Forex Spot Prices
Heating Oil Futures	Pound-Dollar Forex Spot Prices

Source: FutureSource

■ MJK

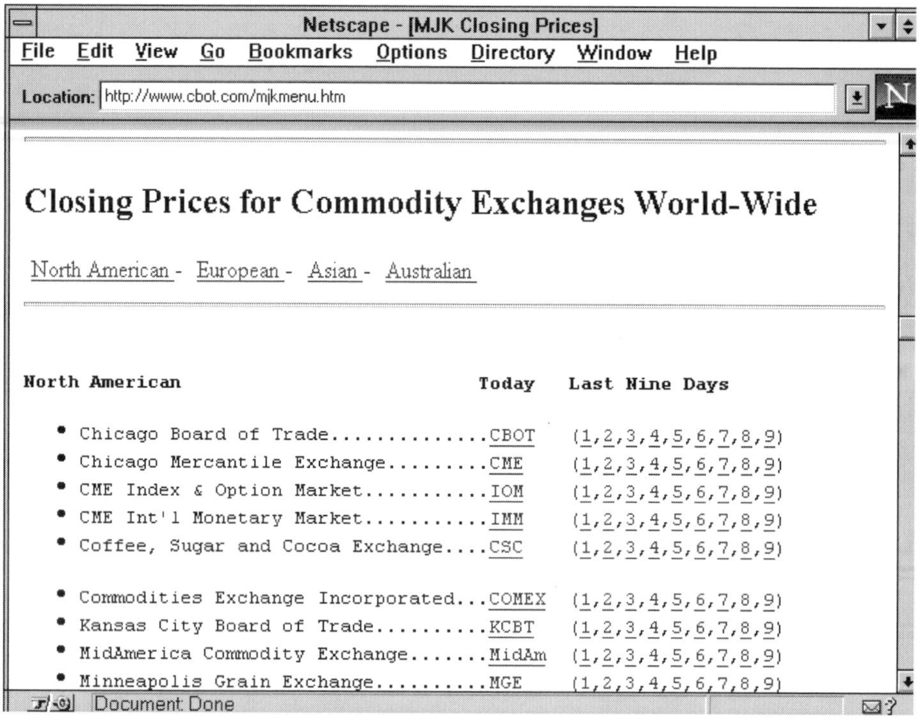

Netscape - [MJK Closing Prices]

File   Edit   View   Go   Bookmarks   Options   Directory   Window   Help

Location: http://www.cbot.com/mjkmenu.htm

Closing Prices for Commodity Exchanges World-Wide

North American - European - Asian - Australian

North American	Today	Last Nine Days
• Chicago Board of Trade.............CBOT		(1,2,3,4,5,6,7,8,9)
• Chicago Mercantile Exchange........CME		(1,2,3,4,5,6,7,8,9)
• CME Index & Option Market..........IOM		(1,2,3,4,5,6,7,8,9)
• CME Int'l Monetary Market..........IMM		(1,2,3,4,5,6,7,8,9)
• Coffee, Sugar and Cocoa Exchange....CSC		(1,2,3,4,5,6,7,8,9)
• Commodities Exchange Incorporated...COMEX		(1,2,3,4,5,6,7,8,9)
• Kansas City Board of Trade.........KCBT		(1,2,3,4,5,6,7,8,9)
• MidAmerica Commodity Exchange.......MidAm		(1,2,3,4,5,6,7,8,9)
• Minneapolis Grain Exchange.........MGE		(1,2,3,4,5,6,7,8,9)

Document Done

■ FIG 2.82 MJK: menu for closing prices

For a number of years MJK has provided historical data. Its Web site is part of the CBOT's MarketPlex, and is one of the most convenient sources for closing prices for many futures exchanges around the world (a list is given in Table 2.29). In fact, its pages contain a rolling ten-day history of closing prices.

Commodities and precious metals

Most commodities information would be found on sites mentioned in the above section on futures and options. However, a few sites specialize in precious metals and so are worth mentioning separately.

A good quick source for commodities prices (metals, livestock/meat, petroleum, and lumber) is CNN*fn*, which has 20-minutes delayed data. The CBOT, COMEX, MIDAM, HKFE, SIMEX and SFE exchanges trade gold (and the US ones also silver) contracts, and their Web sites carry prices and information resources.

Not surprisingly, Gold is a popular topic on the Internet (potentially of interest to anybody around the world) and there are quite a few independent Net

▓ TABLE 2.29 MJK free closing prices: commodity exchanges worldwide

US Exchanges		Canadian and International	
▓ Chicago Board of Trade	CBOT	▓ Montreal Exchange	ME
▓ Chicago Mercantile Exchange	CME	▓ Winnipeg Commodity Exchange	WCE
▓ CME Index & Option Market	IOM	▓ Int'l Petroleum Exchange	IPE
▓ CME Int'l Monetary Market	IMM	▓ London Commodity Exchange	LCE
▓ Coffee, Sugar and Cocoa Exchange	CSC	▓ London Int'l Financial Futures Exchange	LIFFE
▓ Commodities Exchange Incorporated	COMEX	▓ Marche a Terme Int'l Exchange	MTI
▓ Kansas City Board of Trade	KCBT	▓ Singapore Int'l Monetary Exchange	SIM
▓ MidAmerica Commodity Exchange	MidAm	▓ Tokyo Int'l Financial Futures Exchange	TIFF
▓ Minneapolis Grain Exchange	MGE	▓ Tokyo Stock Exchange	TSE
▓ New York Cotton Exchange	NYC	▓ Sydney Futures Exchange Ltd	SFE
▓ New York Futures Exchange	NYF		
▓ New York Mercantile Exchange	NYM		

Source: MJK

newsletters on the topic. Eagle Wing Asset Management has an interesting overview of gold funds, and Australia's *The Privateer* has charts, market reports and attitude.

▓ Kitco Minerals & Metals

Kitco is a precious metals dealer based in Montreal, Canada, and has created an amazingly comprehensive site, particularly for information on gold and silver. There is a fair amount of material here for goldsmiths and jewellers (discussion groups and assay results checks), and a very good index of links to Internet sites; but it is the gold and silver data that is most interesting.

Paramount must be the 'near-live' prices for gold, silver, platinum, palladium and rhodium, collated from sources around the world. This could well be the best source on the Internet for such prices. In addition, the site has a good range of charts for gold and silver:

- **ten year historical:** including relative changes
- **monthly:** ten minute intervals beginning with February 1996
- **24-hour:** ten minute intervals including current and last two days
- **gold lease and forward rates:** 1988 to date.

■ FIG 2.83 Kitco: 'near-live' precious metal prices

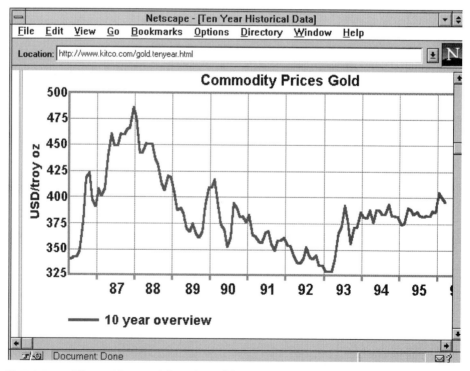

■ FIG 2.84 Kitco: 10 year historic gold price

Finally, it is possible to view (and download in zip format) historic price data in ten-minute intervals for whole trading days (data from February 1996).

Although it is something of a cliché to talk of 24-hour trading nowadays, apart from currencies and gold, not that many contracts or assets are actively traded around the clock. For this reason, it is interesting to view these 24-hour, ten-minute price files, and to see the overlapping exchanges opening and closing (*see* Figure 2.85) to get a real sense of a market that never closes.

The 24hr Trading Clock for Gold and Silver (New York time)

00:10	Hong Kong (HKFE) closes for 2½ hours
02:10	Approximate time Sydney spot market closes
02:30	Hong Kong (HKFE) re-opens for the day
02:40	Tokyo (TOCOM) closes until next trading day
03:00	Approximate time London spot market begins trading
05:30	Singapore (SIMEX) closes
05:40	Hong Kong (HKFE) closes until next trading day
08:10	New York Electronic access market closes
12:10	Approximate time London spot market closes
14:40	New York (COMEX) and Chicago (CBT) close
14:40	— All markets are closed —
16:00	New York Electronic access market opens
18:30	Approximate time Sydney spot market begins trading
20:00	Tokyo (TOCOM) opens
21:00	Hong Kong (HKFE) opens
21:00	Singapore (SIMEX) opens
22:10	Tokyo (TOCOM) closes for 1½ hours
23:30	Tokyo (TOCOM) re-opens for the day

FIG 2.85
Source: Kitco Minerals & Metals Inc.

Chamber of Mines of South Africa

It is difficult to commend this site too highly; it probably is, 'the world's largest repository of mining and minerals-related information on the Net' as it describes itself. Although the information here covers the broad range of mining, much of it is gold related. Some features of the site are:

- **news**: daily digest of mining news
- **prices**: daily precious metals prices, with links to other price sources and mining/commodity stocks
- **statistics**: gold production and analyses (what percentage of the world's gold or platinum resources are in South Africa? It's all here)
- **Kruggerrands**: general and technical information
- **resources**: policy documents, press releases, speeches, industry agreements, South African and World Mining directories of links.

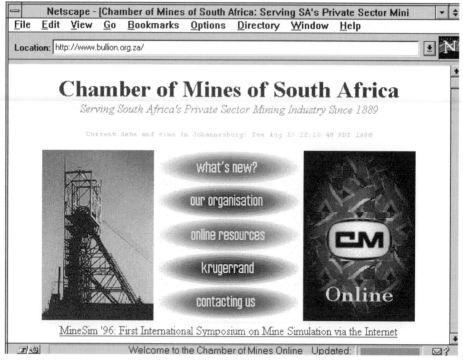

■ FIG 2.86 **Chamber of Mines of South Africa: home page**

Its directory of links is particularly comprehensive, and includes a special section on mining-related commodities and investment information.

■ CPM Group

The CPM Group is an independent research boutique specializing in the metal commodity markets. It has an online subscription service ($21 per month for the complete service) that includes:

- **daily analysis**: e-mail market report
- **monthly Web newsletter**: markets review, options and futures strategies, charts, graphs, metals equities and mutual fund information, a model portfolio and trading strategies.

CPM also provide a free, daily, price-only e-mail summary for the gold, silver, copper and platinum markets.

ECONOMICS DATA

There is no shortage of economics information on the Internet. Economics departments at academic institutions might see the Net as a useful method of raising their global profile; while banks, unable to decide what to do with their piece of cyber real estate, frequently fill up the space with an *Economic Review* or suchlike.

Because of the educational interest, this area benefits from several academically rigorous indexes of Net economics resources; the best being **FinWeb** or the index compiled by **Bill Goffe** at the University of Southern Mississippi. **NetEc** is a good starting point for University economics papers.

Also due to the academic presence, this is one of the few remaining areas on the Internet where you are likely to stumble across gopher resources. However, this is no problem as modern browsers can deal with gopher menus and most of the resources here are purely textual or tabular data – losing nothing by not being hyperText. (In fact, with the proliferation of over-designed, image-intense Web pages, it can be something of a relief to come across a simple, well-organized gopher menu.) One of the best gopher resources up to now has been the **Economic Bulletin Board** (at the University of Michigan), although this is now largely being superseded by STAT-USA.

If you are investigating a country's economy for the first time, the best quick overview is probably the **CIA Factbook**. This may not have the most up-to-date figures, but it is well organized, and has the great benefit of presenting a consistent set of data for all countries (making the data more suitable perhaps for comparative studies rather than as a source for absolute figures for any one particular country).

One of the remarkable developments of the Web has been how quickly governments around the world have established good quality sites with socio-political and economic statistics. Some of the best examples are:

- Brazilian Embassy in London
- Department of Finance, Canada
- Ministry for Foreign Affairs, France
- Statistics Finland
- Central Bureau of Statistics, Indonesia
- Jaring, Malaysia
- Central Bureau of Statistics, Netherlands
- Reserve Bank of New Zealand
- Government Information Office, Taiwan
- Central Bank of Turkey

As mentioned above, another source for economics data is the domestic bank Web sites, good examples of which would include **Rabobank** (Netherlands), **ABSA** (South Africa), **WestPac** (Australia) and **Thai Farmers Bank** (Thailand).

On a more global scale, **Morgan Stanley** and **Bankers Trust** showcase their economics prowess with regular reports on their Web sites.

■ World Bank

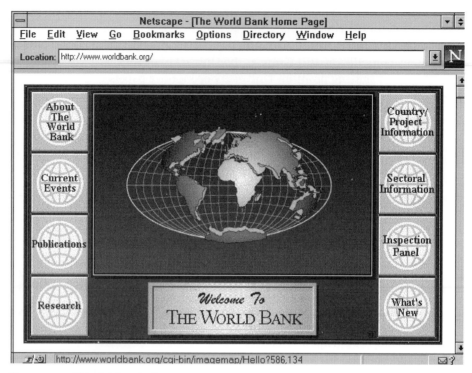

■ FIG 2.87 World Bank: home page

The World Bank site concentrates mainly on development economics, and incorporates a quarterly Finance and Development report (IMF/WB) and access to the Development Economics database. In addition, there are World Bank briefs; research reports, records of speeches and press releases. There is also a useful section on the World Bank Global Bonds.

Possibly of more immediate interest to investors is the United Nations server which acts as an umbrella site for, among others:

- International Monetary Fund
- International Trade Centre
- United Nations Industrial Development Organization
- World Trade Organization.

■ US Federal Reserve Board

The US has been leading the world in practising open government on the Internet, and there are a number of Federal servers that provide useful economics data. However, as the information is spread around, it can be

FIG 2.88 Federal Reserve Board: home page

difficult to track down the correct server quickly. Of help here might be the **FedWorld** server, which is the central access point for US Government servers and has a search facility. If looking specifically for data, then **STAT-USA** might be more useful. This is a subscription service run by the US Department of Commerce and collates data from many other government departments. It includes, among other things, daily economic news; Survey of Current Business, Global Trade Outlook, Economic Report of the President, and the Budget of The United States. Some data on the STAT-USA server comes from the **Federal Reserve Board** and is also available on its own Web site, which features the Beige Book and a database of Federal Reserve statistical releases. For information on tax policy, or T-Bill, Note and Bond auction results, the **US Department of the Treasury** server is the place to look.

HM Treasury [UK]

It is possible that HM Treasury might have surprised even itself with the size and quality of this site (although it does bear the hallmark of an enthusiastic IT department, and it's possible that many Treasury mandarins are unaware even of the site's existence). The best place to start here is with the 'Treasury News' page, which carries the latest releases and statements.

Elsewhere, the site contains:

■ FIG 2.89 HM Treasury: official news on the UK economy

■ **annual budget information**: Chancellor's Budget Statement, FSBR (Budget Red Book), The Budget Snapshot, The Budget in Brief Index of News Releases – archive from 1994

■ **annual debt management report**: including comments on the gilts markets

■ **minutes** of the Chancellor's monthly monetary meetings with the Governor of the Bank of England (*see* Figure 2.90), with updated background economic information (archive from January 1994)

■ **annual Summer economic forecast**: with the official assessment of UK economic prospects

■ **occasional economic papers and briefs**

■ reports of the **Panel of Independent Forecasters** with archive from October 1993

■ **record of speeches**.

Excerpt from the Monthly Monetary Meeting: 3 July 1996

22. The Chancellor said that he and the Governor were still slightly apart on the decision to cut rates last month, but that there was no difference between them on the conclusions for rates this month.

It can be interesting to read the minutes of the Chancellor's monthly monetary meetings with the Governor of the Bank of England (example above), and compare the soothing tone there, with the subsequent newspaper headlines.

■ FIG 2.90

▓ Political and Economic Risk Consultancy (PERC)

PERC is based in Hong Kong and specializes in strategic business information and analysis for companies doing business in East and Southeast Asia. Its Web site is interesting principally for its library of Country Risk Reports, which comprise an executive summary, near-term outlook and economic indicators. The countries covered are:

- China
- Hong Kong
- Indonesia
- Malaysia
- Philippines
- Singapore
- South Korea
- Taiwan
- Thailand

FINANCIAL ADVISERS

One of the major themes of this book is the blurring of the boundaries between the financial services. This has been happening for some time, but the trend is being accelerated under the influence of computers and communications. The category, 'Financial advisers' here is not meant to be well defined (and any attempt at a definition would in any case be inappropriate in different countries); and the institutions mentioned here (e.g. Merrill Lynch) might easily belong in other sections as well, such as brokers or fund managers.

So the purpose of this section is to group together either those large financial institutions that span many categories and offer a comprehensive service, or those very small operations that purely offer financial advice.

In the UK there are a couple of Web sites, **MoneyWorld** and **MoneyWeb**, that largely offer personal finance advice (the latter can be interesting to look at occasionally, as its opinionated comments make a refreshing change from the usual corporate-think sites elsewhere).

There are an increasing number of UK Independent Financial Advisers (IFAs) on the Net – most of which can be found through Yahoo or the UK Web directories. The majority of these sites simply describe services offered, although some have reference articles and even offer financial advice via e-mail. A useful service is offered by **Interactive Investor** (*see* the Fund Managers section, page 222, for more information), where people can search on a database of 6000 IFAs to find one close to where they live, and can also send a financial question to a panel of advisers.

▓ Merrill Lynch

It appears that Merrill Lynch is taking the Internet very seriously. Its Web site is very well organized and obviously much thought has gone into its planning. There are three sections of potential interest:

- **Investor Learning Center**: introductory articles on investment with an investment glossary (a little above the standard-feature Web site glosssary)
- **Personal Finance Center**
- **Financial News and Research Center**: this is the most interesting section with some research reports on Investment Markets Environment, Equities, Taxable Fixed Income and Tax-Exempt Fixed Income, two daily market comments, a daily key market indicators report (although it's better to look at CNN*fn* or DBC for this) and a Washington Watch report.

The information provided here is mainly personal finance advice, so there is not too much of interest here for the more advanced investor.

▓ Prudential Securities

The Prudential Securities site is aimed at a similar audience to the Merrill Lynch one above, and has investment quizzes, financial calculators, and glossaries. Of more interest to the investor might be:

- three times daily stock and bond market commentaries
- weekly strategy report
- municipal-bond market comment.

The main feature of this site is a facility where clients can, at any time, review their accounts online: account balances, transaction history, and investment allocation.

ONLINE BROKERS

As seen elsewhere in this book, the Internet can offer much to the modern investor: generate ideas from news stories, research and analyse possible investments, or monitor the value of a portfolio etc. Having made use of all this, at the moment there may be no pressing need to actually give orders online as well; if you trade only occasionally then an ordinary broker, or discount broker, may be satisfactory. However, in a sense, online trading is the central core of everything this book is about. The financial Internet brings investors closer to markets, and thereby closer to other investors. Although online trading, as it exists at the moment, still goes through the (possibly human) intermediary of the online broker itself, this is merely a stage before direct access to markets.

Online brokers have sprung up remarkably quickly in the US, and there are now quite a few Web sites through which one can give trading orders and view account status. Elsewhere in the world, things are a bit slower. The main trailblazer outside the US is Sharelink in the UK, which offers a full online broking service, while a few other brokers (e.g. Pont Securities in Australia) are starting to accept orders by e-mail.

Table 2.30 outlines some commission charges for online brokers around the world – an 'online broker' being taken to mean a broker that will accept orders via computer.

(Note: in this chapter, where US Dollar equivalent values are given for comparison purposes, the rates used are £/US$=1.54; US$/A$=1.3.)

■ TABLE 2.30 **Sample broker commissions worldwide**

US	
Aufhauser	1 < S < 399 : $22.49 400 < S < 1700 : $30.60 S > 1700 : $0.018 * S
CompuTEL	S < 5000 : $19.75
eBroker	$12
eSchwab	S < 1000 : $29.95 S > 1000 : S * $0.03
*E*Trade*	S < 5000 : $14.95 S > 5000 : $14.95 + (S * $0.01)
Lombard	S < 5000 : $14.95 S > 5000 : S * $0.01
NDB	S < 5000 : $28 S > 5000 : $28 + (S * $0.01)
UK	
Sharelink	V < £2500 : V * 1.00% plus £2500 < V < £4500 : (V – 2500) * 0.75% plus £5000 < V < £75 000 : (V – 5000) * 0.10% [max £50] V > £75 000 : £25 + (V * 0.10%)
*Typical dealing only**	V * 1.00%
*Typical full-service**	V * 1.65%
Australia	
Pont Securities	V < A$6000 : A$54 A$6000 < V < A$120 000 : A$108 V > A$120 000 : V * 0.1%

S: number of shares; V: transaction value
* not online

A few notes on Table 2.30:

■ The table should not be taken as the definitive reference table, but is included for general comparative purposes only. All the rates are taken from the brokers' own Web sites, which are freely accessible for viewing the latest details.

■ All the above rates are for orders given online for equities listed on the major exchange (for example, the NYSE for the US brokers).

▩ These rates should not be taken as the whole story: quite often there are other charges (government duties etc.) that may apply.

▩ For comparison purposes, the UK figures include representative rates for a dealing only and a full-service broker.

▩ Pont Securities does not have a full online trading service via the Web, but it accepts orders by e-mail (which attract a ten per cent discount off standard rates).

With the approximate rates from Table 2.30, it is interesting to compare the charges levied for similar sized deals around the world (*see* Table 2.31).

▩ TABLE 2.31 **Comparison of brokers' commissions worldwide for a transaction deal of US$10 000**

Broker		Commission on US$10 000 deal
US		($)
Aufhauser		30.60
*E*Trade*		14.95
Lombard		14.95
NDB		28.00
CompuTel		19.75
eBroker		12.00
eSchwab		29.95
*(FBS)**		109.50
UK	(£)	($)
Sharelink	45.75	70
*Typical dealing only**	64.93	100
*Typical full service**	107.14	165
*(FBS)**	60	92
Australia	(A$)	($)
Pont Securities	120	92
*(FBS)**		208

* not online

Notes on Table 2.31:

▩ In each case the commissions are calculated for a transaction deal of US$10 000 or equivalent (and, where the assumption was necessary, the deal comprised 500 shares at US$20 each).

▩ Although Fidelity Brokerage Services (FBS) do not yet take orders online, as it offers possibly the most comprehensive global service of any standard brokerage, its commission figures are included here for comparison. (*See* 'Fidelity Brokerage Services' (FBS) below.)

The most immediate observation on comparing the information in the two tables is obviously the wide range in charges: US$12-208. However, one should be wary of drawing too many conclusions from this simple comparison. Some of the brokers' commissions are flat rate (rather than percentage), and so the comparative ranking might change greatly for deals of different sizes.

Most importantly, the services offered here are not all the same. For example, Fidelity Brokerage Services appears expensive, but one of its advantages is that it offers the ability to trade in all markets, from just the one account (which avoids opening multiple accounts and maintaining minimum balances at all of them).

The commission rates should be just one factor to be considered in choosing a broker. Others should be:

Dealing

- efficiency of trade execution
- minimum dealing size
- types of order accepted (limit, others?)

Account

- minimum initial deposit to open account
- minimum account balance
- interest paid on balances
- margin account availability, and rates
- treatment of dividends and interest paid
- what online reports are available (account balance, portfolio summary, transaction summary)
- are there detailed statements (are these posted)?
- is the account protected/insured?
- how can money be transferred to/from the account?

Miscellaneous

- range of markets covered
- range of securities covered (equities, options, futures, mutual funds, bonds, OTC)
- research available
- contact options (e-mail, Web, fax, telephone)
- what is the backup if the computer is down?

Of all the above criteria, the first one, trade execution, can be just as important as the commission charges. In the above example (for Table 2.31), if the execution slipped just ⅛ of a Dollar (or 0.00625 per cent) this would add $62 to the effective transaction cost – at which point the commission rate differential begins to look less significant.

The choice of broker will ultimately depend on one's own circumstances. An investor who deals rarely and has a long investment holding period will not (and should not) place paramount importance on commission rates or execution efficiency, whereas the situation would be very different for an active investor.

▨ Brokerage services (FBS)

The FBS service is aimed at both UK expatriates wanting to invest in the UK and international investors wanting to invest internationally. It does not yet offer online dealing, but, as the most comprehensive global brokerage, it is a useful benchmark service. One of the main attractions of the service is the ability to deal in multiple markets from the one account. An outline of its commission charges is given in Tables 2.32, 2.33 and 2.34 for international clients dealing in the UK, US, or other world markets. This only includes the rates for equities, and other small charges may apply, so for further details it is best to check the FBS Web site. (Note: the US Dollar equivalent rates are included merely as a guideline and are not provided by FBS itself.)

UK markets

▨ TABLE 2.32 FBS brokerage commissions for UK equities

Transaction value (V) (£)	Commission (£)	Transaction value (V) –Approximate US Dollar Equivalent–	Commission
0–2500	25	0–3850	39
2501–3500	35	3851–5390	54
3501–5000	50	5391–7700	77
5001–7500	60	7701–11 550	92
7501–10 000	65	11 551–15 400	100
10 001–15 000	70	15 401–23 100	108
15 001–20 000	75	23 101–30 800	116
20 001–30 000	85	30 801–46 200	131
> 30 000	0.28%	> 46 200	0.28%
Maximum Commission:	250		385

US markets

■ TABLE 2.33 **FBS brokerage commissions for US equities**

Transaction value (V) ($)	Commission ($)
0–2500	29.50 + (V * 1.70%)
2501–6000	55.50 + (V * 0.66%)
6001–22 000	75.50 + (V * 0.34%)
20 001–50 000	99.50 + (V * 0.22%)
50 001–500 000	154.50 + (V * 0.11%)
500 001 plus	254.50 + (V * 0.09%)

International markets

■ TABLE 2.34 **FBS brokerage commissions for international markets**

Transaction value (V) (£)	Commission (£)	Transaction value (V) –Approximate US Dollar Equivalent–	Commission
0-2500	100	0-3850	154
2500-5000	125 plus	3851-7700	192 plus
on next 10 000	0.7% plus	on next 15 400	0.7% plus
on next 90 000	0.50%	on next 138 600	0.50%

Note: the international markets covered by the above rates are:

■ **European markets:** *Austria, Belgium, Denmark, Finland, France, Germany, Holland, Italy, Norway, Spain, Sweden, Switzerland.*

■ **World markets:** *Australia, Hong Kong, South Africa.*

US market

There are quite a few services offering online dealing facilities for the US markets, and, like standard discount brokers, there is little to choose between them, as their Web services are all fairly similar. If you are trying to select one, it might be an idea to view some of the messages in financial forums (e.g. misc.invest newsgroup) as online brokers' services (or lack thereof) is one of the most popular topics of discussion. It's likely that in the future, some online brokers will attempt to distinguish their services from competitors by bundling other services into the account (for example, free access to the *WSJ Online*, Zacks analysis service etc.).

Beyond that it is always wise to check carefully the account conditions. For example, quite a few of the online brokers will require a US$10 000 initial deposit and then a US$1000 minimum account balance.

▦ Lombard

```
┌──────────────────────────────────────────────────────────────────┐
│ ─        Netscape - [Trade Executions for John Macilwaine]    ▾ ◆ │
│ File  Edit  View  Go  Bookmarks  Options  Directory  Window  Help │
│ Location: http://www.lombard.com/Demo/tradeexec.html        ± N   │
└──────────────────────────────────────────────────────────────────┘
```

Trade Executions for John Macilwaine

Trade Activity in Margin Account:

Trade Date	Side	Quantity	Description	Buy/Sell Price	Value
Friday, May 26, 1995	Buy	40	Call H J Heinz Sep 45	4	$16000.00
Friday, May 26, 1995	Sell	100	IBM Corp.	93 3/4	$9375.00

Document Done

▦ FIG 2.91 Lombard: online trade execution report

Lombard was one of the first brokers to offer online trading. The site offers free general access to delayed quotes and one of the more sophisticated charting servers on the Internet. Opening an account with Lombard offers:

▦ online trading of stocks, options and funds

▦ a form for inputting trade order

▦ a report form for trade executions

▦ a report form for real-time portfolio valuation

▦ real-time stock quotes

▦ stock research.

E*Trade

```
┌──────────────────────────────────────────────────────────────────────┐
│          Netscape - [E*TRADE - Trading Demo - Stock Order]             │
├──────────────────────────────────────────────────────────────────────┤
│ File   Edit   View   Go   Bookmarks   Options   Directory   Window   Help │
├──────────────────────────────────────────────────────────────────────┤
│ Location: http://www.etrade.com/html/demo/stock.htm                    │
└──────────────────────────────────────────────────────────────────────┘
```

Account: IRA 252-99980-11   ▼ = Help

▼ **Transaction:**   ▼ **Number**   ▼ **Stock**   ▼ **Price:**
   ○ Buy   of shares: symbol: ◉ Market
   ◉ Sell   [6000]   [BORL]   ○ Limit: [   ]
   ○ Sell Short   Get Symbol   ○ Stop: [   ]
   ○ Buy to Cover   ○ Stop Limit: [   ]

☒ ▼**All or none** (only for orders over 300 shares)   ▼ **Term:** [Good Until Cancelled ▼]

Trading password: [xxxx]   Review the order carefully.   [**Preview Order**]

   Home ◆ **Visitor Center** ◆ **The E*TRADE Advantage** ◆ **Open An Account**

Document Done

▓ **FIG 2.92 E*trade: online trade order form**

E*Trade was one of the pioneers in online trading, having offered for some time the facility to pass orders electronically either directly, or via an online service like CompuServe. It has now established itself as one of the major WWW brokers, with one of the lowest commission rates. Unlike other brokers (e.g. Lombard), who may offer account holders some research, or traditional discount brokers (e.g. Schwab) who view their Internet activity as a natural extension of their broking service, E*Trade is primarily a computer operation, that aims to offer an efficient dealing service at one of the lowest costs; its Web site is probably the most professional of all the online brokers. In common with these other services, E*Trade offers clients online dealing with real-time prices and reports that include: account balances, portfolio summary and transaction history.

CompuTEL

CompuTEL is a division of Thomas F. White & Co and yet another operation building the new Cyber Wall Street in San Francisco. As with the other sites, CompuTEL offers demonstration pages showing what the online trading service looks like in practice.

UK market

▓ Sharelink

Netscape - [Order Entry]
File   Edit   View   Go   Bookmarks   Options   Directory   Window   Help

Location: http://www.esi.co.uk/sharelink/buysell.html

Select Buy or Sell : ◉ Buy ○ Sell

Enter EPIC : `HNSN`

Quantity : `10000` shares.
-- or--
Value : `_____` (as share currency) This is **exclusive** of charges.

Deal at : ○ Best ◉ Limit

Limit Price : `166` (as share currency)
Limit expires on : `1995/09/28` (YYYY/MM/DD)

Closing Bargain Reference : `_____` Please enter the bargain reference of the bargain you wish to close against. This is shown in the top left corner of the relevant contract note. You may not close against a bargain which is less than 2 business days from its settlement date.

▓ FIG 2.93 Sharelink: online trade order form

Sharelink was formed in 1987 with the backing of British Telecom and broker Albert E. Sharp; in 1995 it merged with the US discount brokerage Charles Schwab. According to its Web site, Sharelink has over 600 000 clients and handles up to one in ten of all deals on the London Stock Exchange.

In co-operation with ESI, Sharelink has now extended its telephone MarketMaster account to include a full dealing facility via the WWW. In practice, this means that investors can subscribe to the ESI Bronze service for real-time share prices, and give orders for trades via the MarketMaster Web page. The service includes:

▓ online trading

▓ account balance on request

▓ safe custody service: shares, investment trusts, unit trusts, corporate bonds, gilts, and cash.

The MarketMaster site is a no-frills one, but it does carry a comprehensive description of the service, including:

- dealing facilities
- portfolio administration: valuations, dividends, tax certificates, capital events, shareholder rights
- cash management: deposits, withdrawals, statements, interest on balances
- commission and charges: stamp duty, contract levy, reinvestment of dividends
- MarketMaster security.

FUNDS

It seemed to genuinely surprise some fund management companies, that when they first put up a Web site, people from all over the world could look at it, and might even accept the invitation to 'Contact Us'. Of course, in many countries fund management is one of the most regulated of industries, but on the Net no one is yet sure what regulation applies – indeed, if there is any applicable regulation at all. Hence, the fund management companies tend to be extra cautious and this is made manifest on their Web sites with pages of warnings in size 8-pitch. In addition, the large international fund management companies have resorted to setting up a number of parallel sites for investors in different regulatory environments – even though the funds being offered are very similar.

The categories in this section (US, UK and International) are therefore fairly loose. For example, GAM appears in the UK section (due to an interesting Unit Trust feature), but it is an international management company for international investors.

As yet, there is nothing terribly exciting happening in this area. Most of the sites here are purely informational (e.g. fund descriptions, daily fund prices, market comment, contact details), all of which can be found in newspapers or brochures; but the Web sites make this information at least more accessible and immediate. Further, the information is usually free, and the few interactive databases of funds and their performances might be useful.

US Funds

The fund management industry in the US is very large and highly developed, and this is reflected in the range and quality of Web sites dealing with funds investment. Sites such as **Mutual Funds Interactive**, **Mutual Fund Research** and **INVESTools** offer a combination of: performance rankings, quotes and charts, market analysis and, possibly, recommendations.

NETworth

The best site in this sector is NETworth, which features:

```
┌─────────────────────────────────────────────────────────────────────┐
│ ─         Netscape - [The NETworth Mutual Fund Market Manager]   ▼ ◆ │
│  File  Edit  View  Go  Bookmarks  Options  Directory  Window  Help   │
├─────────────────────────────────────────────────────────────────────┤
│ Location: http://networth.galt.com/www/home/mutual/mfmm.html   ◆  N  │
├─────────────────────────────────────────────────────────────────────┤
│                                                                   ◆   │
│                    Visit Your Personal Portfolio                      │
│                                                                       │
│  Fund Atlas                        Top 25 Performing Funds            │
│                                                                       │
│  An easy to use directory of mutual fund families'  ┌─────────────┐◆  │
│  presentations.                    │All Categories        │      │   │
│                                    │Aggressive Growth     │      │   │
│  ─────────────────────             │Equity-Income         │      │   │
│                                    │Growth                │      ◆  │
│                                    └─────────────────────┘          │
│                                    ○ YTD ○ 3 Month ● 1 Year          │
│  Fund Search                       ○ 3 Year ○ 5 Year ○ 10 Year       │
│                                                                       │
│  Use Fund Search to discover which mutual funds     ┌────────┐       │
│  meet your investment criteria.                     │ Submit │       │
│                                                     └────────┘       │
│  ─────────────────────             ─────────────────────             │
│                                                                       │
│   Fund Profiles from:              Fund Prices                        │
│   ┌──────────────────────────┐     ┌──────────────────────────┐      │
│   │      MORNINGSTAR         │     │    Net Asset Values      │  ◆   │
│   └──────────────────────────┘     └──────────────────────────┘      │
├─────────────────────────────────────────────────────────────────────┤
│  ▓/◙  Document: Done                                            ✉?   │
└─────────────────────────────────────────────────────────────────────┘
```

■ FIG 2.94 NETworth: The Mutual Fund Market Manager

■ **ranking**: the top 25 performing funds for each sector

■ **fund search**: on a number of criteria, including a keyword in the fund description, size of fund, maximum sales charge, and performance

■ **funds profile from Morningstar**: net assets, yield, three-month and YTD returns, fund description, minimum purchase, fund manager details

■ **fund prices**

■ **NAV data**: charts, last five days values.

NETworth also has a section on the site that specializes in equities as well; and the charting and quote server for both equities and funds is one of the best on the Internet. Also, for both equities and funds, there is the facility to create your own customized portfolio, avoiding the need to input individual ticker symbols each time.

UK funds

■ Interactive Investor (III)

This is probably the largest and most useful site for investors in the UK. It is big because it acts as an umbrella site for many independent services, including

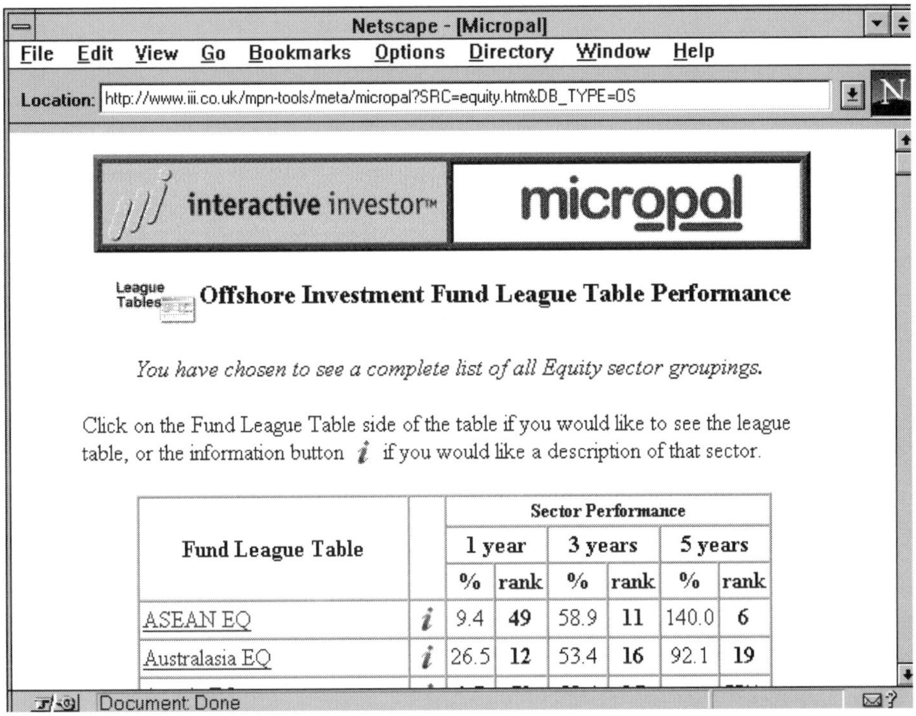

FIG 2.95 Interactive Investor: Micropal funds performance ranking

fund management groups, magazines and industry associations. Unlike the US NETworth site above, III has almost no coverage of equities, but concentrates on funds and personal finance. The site contains:

- **News:** the *FT* magazines, *Financial Adviser, Product Adviser, Investment Adviser* and *Offshore Financial Review* all have their own sub-sites here.

- **Micropal funds performance:** covers all Unit Trusts, Investment Trusts, PEPs and SIB authorized Offshore funds in the UK; individual fund performances over one, three and five years and comparisons with the sector average; also ranking of all funds. A subscription service offers more details. There is also a listing of the Micropal fund awards.

- **Unit Trusts:** the association body **AUTIF** has a sub-site, while there are also links to the pages of Micropal and a selection of fund managers.

- **Investment Trusts:** the association body **AITC** has a sub-site, while there are also links to the pages of Micropal and a selection of fund managers.

In the case of Unit and Investment Trusts, several fund managers have sub-sites on III, including **Gartmore, GAM, M&G**, and **Fidelity**.

■ M&G

An example of one of the fund manager sub-sites on III is M&G, which, founded in 1931, is the oldest Unit Trust group in the UK, having imported the idea of mutual, open-ended funds from the US. The M&G site gives details on its range of funds, a description of its investment philosophy and a daily table of fund prices.

■ GAM

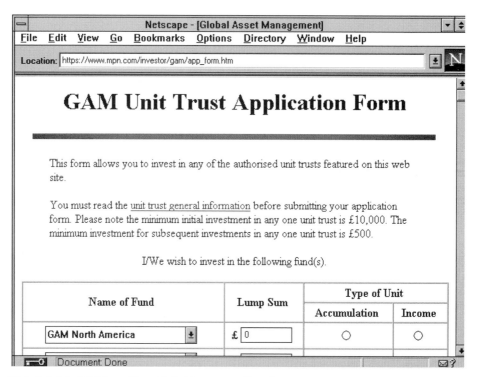

■ FIG 2.96 GAM: online Unit Trust application

Of all the fund management sites aimed at UK investors, GAM is probably the most go-ahead. Its site has well-presented details on all the funds (illustrated with charts and fund manager comment) and daily price and performance figures. But the interesting feature on its site is an application form to buy or sell GAM Unit Trusts. All the details are there to be completed in an ordinary Web form – fill in the form and click to send off (although payment must still be made by posted cheque). Now, looking at this sensibly, this is no big thing, merely a copy of the ordinary paper Trust application form sent by computer; but, given the strictness of UK funds regulation, this must be seen as a significant development.

TrustNet

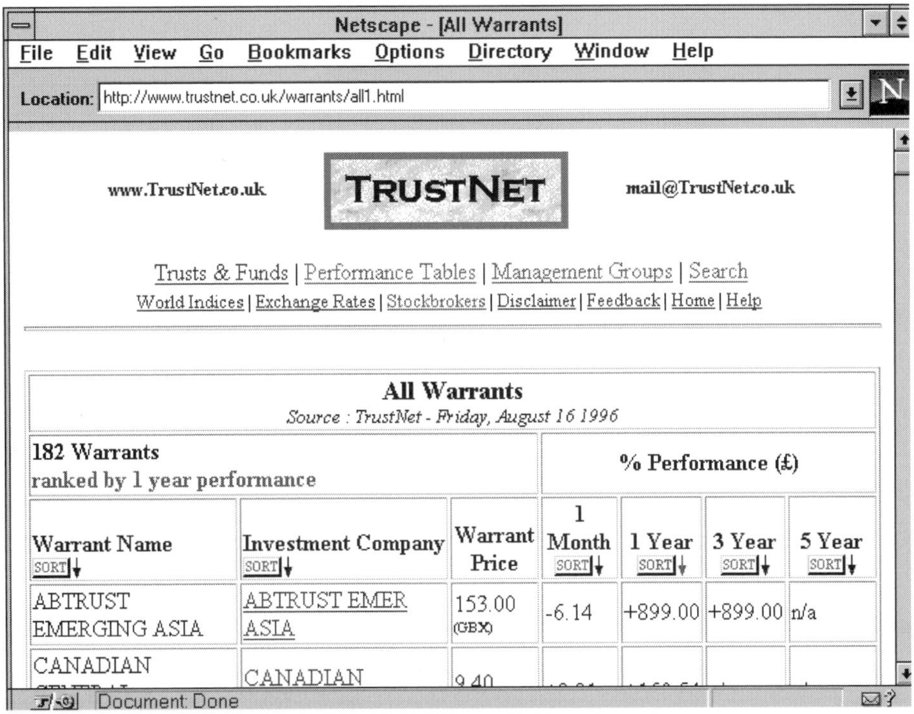

Netscape - [All Warrants]

File   Edit   View   Go   Bookmarks   Options   Directory   Window   Help

Location: http://www.trustnet.co.uk/warrants/all1.html

FIG 2.97 TrustNet: ranking of investment trust warrants

TrustNet covers over 600 UK Investment Trusts and closed end Offshore Funds. As one would expect, the site has:

- **Trust profiles**: performance chart, price, performance, discount to NAV, capital structure, portfolio summary etc.
- **Management group profiles**: Trusts managed, with total gross assets, contact details.

There is also a fairly powerful facility to rank Trusts within sectors by:

- fund or manager name
- performance: over one, three and five years (the performance of warrants can also be ranked)
- discount to NAV.

International

■ Fidelity

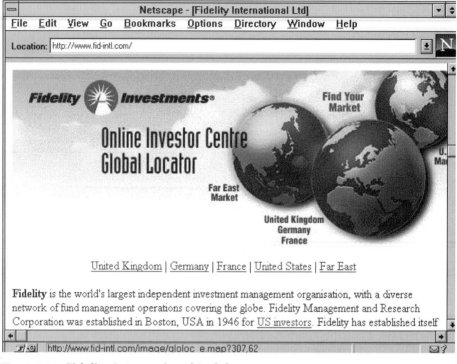

■ FIG 2.98 **Fidelity International Ltd: home page**

Fidelity was established in Boston in 1946 for US investors; later, in 1969, Fidelity International Ltd (FIL) was set up for international investment and international investors. After the first page, the Fidelity site divides into separate sites, according to the nationality/residence of the investor.

The Fidelity sites, while not spectacular are functional. Nevertheless, in some ways, they are among the most interesting on the whole Internet, if only by reason of having been created by the world's largest investment manager.

The sites contain information about the very wide range of Fidelity's investment products, and there is a section called Investors Tools in which one finds:

■ market commentaries

■ fund prices

■ investment calculator

- Investor First Steps: interactive introduction to mutual funds
- an investment competition.

None of the above individually are particularly sophisticated or rare; but, taken together, they begin to form the crude basis of an expert system to automatically advise clients on investment.

Flemings

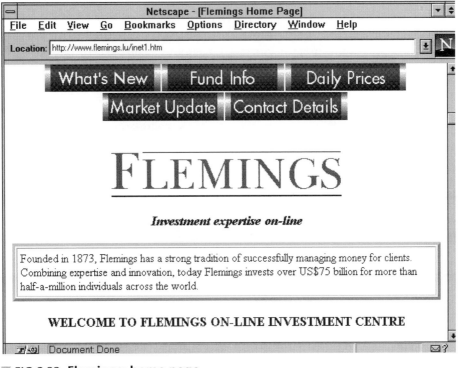

FIG 2.99 Flemings: home page

The Flemings international site is based on a server in Luxembourg, and, in common with the other fund management sites, the first page is written for the regulators to read rather than investors. The rest of the site is principally concerned with the Flemings Flagship Fund which is an umbrella fund for European investors. There are regular reports about the performance of this fund, weekly market reports (US, Europe, Far East and Emerging Markets) and daily fund prices are posted.

Credit Lyonnais International Asset Management (HK)

This site is based in Hong Kong and concerns funds investing in Asia. On the pages you can find:

- monthly report on fund performance: asset allocation and top five holdings, dealing information, chart relative to benchmark index, fund manager comment and performance history
- weekly market comments
- regional strategy notes.

DISCUSSION FORUMS

Online forums allow users to discuss with others around the world topics on investment. The most widespread of these forums are the Internet newsgroups. Table 2.35 below lists the current newsgroups available.

▥ TABLE 2.35 **Financial newsgroups**

Newsgroup name	Description	Activity	Quality
aus.invest	Australian investments	1	1
comp.os.ms-windows.apps.financial	PC Windows financial programs	2	1
misc.invest	General investment	5	2
misc.invest.canada	Canadian investments	2	2
misc.invest.funds	US mutual funds	5	4
misc.invest.futures	Futures and options	3	4
misc.invest.real-estate	Property worldwide	3	1
misc.invest.stocks	US stocks	5	3
misc.invest.stocks.penny	US low-priced stocks	2	1
misc.invest.technical	Technical analysis	3	4
sci.econ	Economics	2	2
uk.finance	UK personal finance	3	3

Notes:

- The activity column gives a general indication of the number of messages posted to each group. ('5' indicates the most active groups.)
- The quality column is a subjective assessment of the interest and calibre of messages posted. ('5' indicates the highest quality; note, this is only a comparative assessment.)

There is also a collection of newsgroups in ClariNet which carry financial topics – access to these groups will depend on the news server you use, as these carry a subscription fee.

Most of the general financial newsgroups are still fairly US oriented, although in the case of some (e.g. misc.invest.technical) this is not important. Those groups which are more country focused (e.g. uk.finance) tend towards narrow personal finance topics (e.g. tax, mortgages, insurance) rather than general investment.

> I'M GOING TO JAIL, ON MY WAY, HERE'S THE OEX FORECAST.

Message heading seen in the misc.invest newsgroup

Types of newsgroup messages

The ideal for newsgroups is a free discussion of ideas between investors all around the world. The potential is inspiring; for example, an investor residing in Kuwait could post a question about investing in a specific Chilean company, and receive an informed response from investors in Chile itself – information which was unlikely to be in any newspaper, library or analyst's report. In practice, the majority of posts to financial newsgroups tend to fall into the following categories.

▨ Questions

The newsgroups can be a good place to post a question – there are, after all, thousands of people reading these messages every day. When the newsgroups were starting there was a stalwart band of people imbued with the sense of building a co-operative online community, and these people would rush to answer questions and help if they could. But they soon became overwhelmed by the flood of new onliners, who treated the forums as merely free answer bureaux.

Today, if you have a question, you can try posting it (e.g. 'where can I find historic data for Spanish stocks?') but the chances of receiving a response are diminishing. Where questions *are* answered, be careful as the reply might be genuine, well-written and plain wrong (certain topics – for example, derivatives – do seem to encourage a type of 'have-a-go' punditry).

The types of question that do attract some attention are those asking for recommendations for brokers, data feeds or programs. The replies can be interesting, but must be treated warily: disgruntled clients of a broker are always more likely to write about their grievances than the 1000 satisfied clients.

Occasionally a question will lead to a thread of several messages with a more extended discussion of the topic (this tends to happen in the more focused newsgroups, like misc.invest.futures or misc.invest.technical). This could be good – this is what the spirit of the newsgroups is about. In practice, however, these discussions frequently degenerate into bad-tempered squabbling, with all the vehemence of religious fundamentalists arguing some obscure doctrinal point.

Sample message thread from misc.invest.technical

Guru 1   "You can talk all you want about the fundamentals of Iomega but the charts always prove to be right..For every impluse wave there is a corrective wave. So get ready for a corrective wave."

Guru 2   "The stock 'corrected' almost 40% in last two weeks. I believe this was the 'impulse' wave and it will correct back up."

Guru 1   "Your knowledge is just unbelievable...To start with you can not have an impulse wave DOWN! Let alone a Corrective wave UP! Unless you consider Iomega in a BEAR market??????????"

▧ New service announcement

There will frequently be announcements of new services being offered on the Internet; this might include new WWW pages, newsletters, data feeds or whatever. This can be quite useful, as there are few outlets to alert investors to new services coming online.

▧ Scams

Not surprisingly, the newsgroups are not short of scams; this includes all the 'MAKE MONEY FAST' posts. What *is* surprising is the extraordinary crudity of these scams. They can usually be identified quite easily, some distinguishing features being: over-use of upper case characters, the use of repeated '>' and '*' characters to highlight the heading, the offering of some guaranteed return above the current risk-free rate, and a contrived e-mail address. The usual, and best, advice is to ignore these posts and hope they will go away; but, given the persistent nature of some of them, one can only assume that a certain number of people *do* respond to these. Occasionally, the set-up can be more sophisticated, whereby a leading question will be deliberately posted (e.g. 'can anyone recommend a good training course?'), with staged answers.

▧ Puffing (stock trash-talk etc.)

Sometimes messages will appear with headings like, 'THE DOW WILL CRASH TODAY', or 'IIXX it's going UPPPPP!!!!!!!', where one can safely assume that the writer has a position in the stock or contract and is indulging in some puffery. For the most part these are mildly amusing to see, but one series of posts in 1995 was both sad and fascinating. An investor had obviously shorted a hi-tech stock and then posted some lightly spurious tale about the company. The stock nudged up. Another knocking post followed from the short. However, the stock then surged up; and as the stock continued to climb over the following two weeks, the posts from the investor became ever more frantic and the stories about the company more outlandish and malicious.

Why the financial newsgroups don't work

The general ideal of newsgroups (being online conversations) is fine, but there is no reason why they should work in all areas of human activity. Newsgroups seem to work best with topics of communal interest or for hobbies. For example, newsgroups about television programmes, butterflies or old Jaguar cars are likely to be successful, as people can become enthusiastic and engage in good-natured conversation. But investors are too selfish – quite rightly. On a one-to-one basis, investors might discuss the markets and swap stock tips, but there is no reason why this model of activity should extend to broadcasting to thousands of people worldwide. Further, investors tend to form networks of useful contacts, but networks do not always follow the rule: the bigger the better. Networks are by their nature exclusive, and the problem with newsgroups, in this case, is that there is no exclusivity – they are open to all.

It is interesting to observe that travel newsgroups have a similarity to the financial ones. At first glance, both seem likely candidates for active newsgroups – but they both involve selfish activities. The travel groups are also dominated by 'me, me, me' posts: on the one side people trying to find cheap hotels in Paris or the best beaches in Asia, and on the other, travellers boasting about bouncing around the Hindu Kush on a pogo stick for a dollar a day. But there is no real discussion here.

The more focused financial newsgroups (e.g. misc.invest.futures) tend to be more successful than the more general misc.invest groups, but this is only a small matter of degree. It's possible that after the newsgroups have fragmented and specialized down to groups such as misc.invest.options.exotic.binary, then the potential of newsgroups will be realized.

Financial discussion forums exist, apart from on the Internet, in commercial online services like CompuServe and America Online, and there is no doubt that these are far better than the newsgroups. One important reason being that these groups are moderated, with designated people in charge of filtering useless messages. However, they still suffer from the contradictions of non-exclusive groups talking about selfish and personal topics.

Hence, a summary for newsgroups could be that it is best to avoid them, the signal-to-noise ratio is just too low and life too short. And, if this book had been written at the end of 1995, that would indeed have been the concluding summary on the topic.

But then ... have a look at the chart in Figure 2.100.

Iomega, a maker of storage disks, developed a removable disk for PCs that was vastly superior to old floppy disks. That was a good story, but by March 1996 the stock had already risen many fold in the previous year and a half, and there was every reason to believe the stock was fully valued. And then it rose five times over the next two months. What happened?

The sudden strong rise has been attributed to thousands of messages that appeared in the Motley Fool investment forum on America Online. This forum is not some online backwater, but is famous for the number and dedication of its participants; it prides itself on providing good research to the 'little guy'. In the case of Iomega, messages poured in from everybody, including, it was suggested, even Iomega employees logging-in under pseudonyms.

The *Wall Street Journal* reported Iomega's local SEC district administrator as saying,

> '*Obviously there is some concern with what is going on over the Internet generally — not to say there is anything illegal going on. This is a new world for everybody.*'

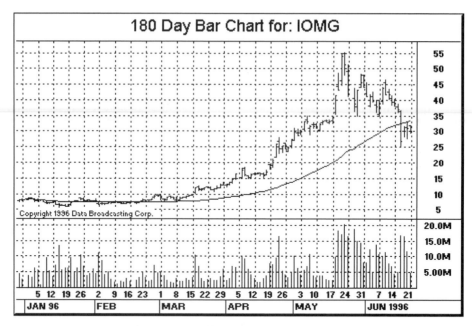

■ FIG 2.100 Iomega (IOMG) stock chart
Source: Data Broadcasting Corp.

You can say that again. Until now the financial intermediation industry and media have had the monopoly on effective rumour and gossip, but if this type of thing grows, matters are liable to get out of hand.

The *WSJ* went on to report that Iomega was planning to issue more stock, and that, despite the possible difficulties of the underwriters' analysts justifying the high share price,

> ...*Wall Street's cold shoulder won't affect the underwriting, because the real promotion is happening on-line. Underwriters have one set of estimates; on-line Iomegans have another.*

This is powerful stuff, the ramifications of which are significant: Wall Street becoming marginalized?

Not yet, but does this mean at least that the dismissive summary of online discussion forums needs to be revised? Yes, although not quite as much as it might at first appear.

Such incidents as Iomega are still isolated events. It will be some time yet before the chatter has any influence on many large capitalized stocks. In terms of looking for positive investment advice, it is likely that the forums will remain unrewarding, not being able to see the wood for the trees. However, it would seem that they should be incorporated into the ordinary checking procedure before taking any action in the markets, and for monitoring portfolios. As far as the Internet newsgroups go, this can be best achieved by periodically using the search engines to check on stocks being monitored.

So, don't expect to find useful ideas (quickly) in the newsgroups, but it might be important to know if there is discussion of a particular stock before taking any action in it.

The real future of discussion forums, however, would appear to be in more private areas than the open newsgroups (this re-introduces the idea of exclusive networks). There are already many of these starting up on Web sites, and companies are beginning to realize that discussion areas on their Web sites might be one of the best ways of adding value and attracting people to a site. After all, this is no different from the beginnings of a market or stock exchange – a critical mass of people interested in a certain activity, meeting together and exchanging opinions. After a while, if the market, exchange or forum is a success, its owner is in a powerful position.

Hence, many discussion forums are now setting up on Web sites, where, in some cases, a certain exclusivity is offered (by way of registration or subscription). One of the most successful forums can be found at the Silicon Investor site – where the quality of discussion is certainly superior to that found in any newsgroup. Other forums are being established by the sites of Euromoney, *Futures* magazine and Omega Research (and Motley Fool itself also has a Web site).

Of course it doesn't take a huge leap of imagination to see how things may develop from here. A critical mass of people are attracted to a forum, they discuss stocks, one investor may be bearish and another bullish, one thing leads to another, and a stock exchange may develop within the forum itself. Whether companies setting up forums within Web sites are actually looking this far ahead is difficult to say, but it's possible that in the future some sites may offer a whole array of very sophisticated, free investment services, where subscription is only required for participation in the forums (which is not unlike the subscription paid by brokers to stock exchanges now).

MARKET REGULATION

This area is, as yet, under-represented on the Internet, but should grow strongly in the coming years to become the most important of all sectors of the financial Internet. About the only presence at the moment is by US regulators, such as the SEC, CFTC and also the **Financial Crimes Enforcement Network (FinCEN)** at the US Treasury Department, which is concerned with electronic payments and money laundering. Another useful site might be the **Federal Trade Commission** (http://www.ftc.gov/bcp/scams01.htm) which has a special section on scams. It has also been reported that the National Association of Securities Dealers (NASD) is setting up a site, where sanctions and complaints against dealers can be viewed.

An interesting development will be the establishment of independent 'regulators', or 'scam checkers'. These will be sites where individuals or associations take it upon themselves to monitor and report on the probity of participants in various markets. An early proto-example of such a site is called **Municipal Bond Market Scandals** (http://lissack.com/), which keeps interested readers up to date on the latest scandal developments. Another example can be found at http://www.webcom.com/~lewrose/, which concentrates on advertising law in relation to the Internet.

▮ US Securities and Exchange Commission (SEC)

In the elegant language of government, the SEC is described as an 'independent, nonpartisan, quasijudicial regulatory agency' whose responsibility is to administer the Federal securities laws. As such, the SEC is concerned with:

▮ protecting investors

▮ ensuring that investors have access to disclosure of all material information concerning publicly traded securities

▮ regulating securities dealers, investment advisers and investment companies.

Besides being the repository for the EDGAR database, the SEC Web site contains:

▮ information about the SEC

▮ advice to investors

▮ news digests and public statements

▮ SEC Rules

▮ SEC Enforcement Division.

The most interesting of these sections is the final one on enforcement, where there is information on current civil suits in Federal Court and administrative proceedings. There is also a list of investor alerts (*see* Figure 2.101), information about bounties for persons who report insider trading violations, and details on how to file a complaint by e-mail.

Investor alerts at the SEC – August 1996

▮ Frequently Asked Questions About Better Life Club of America
▮ Investment Fraud and Abuse Travel to Cyberspace [An extraordinarily convoluted title, but this is about the Internet, and incorporates some of the most useful few pages anywhere on the WWW]
▮ Notice: PaineWebber Direct Investments Claims Fund
▮ Fraud in the Sale of Unregistered Securities of Telecommunications Technology Ventures
▮ So-Called 'Prime' Bank and Similar Financial Instruments

▮ **FIG 2.101**

This is an important site to follow, as it is likely that other countries will be strongly influenced by it when setting up their own regulatory sites.

■ US Commodity Futures Trading Commission (CFTC)

The CFTC was created in 1974 by the US Government as an independent agency to regulate the commodity futures and option markets. The format of the Web site is somewhat similar to that of the SEC. There is information about the Commission, a 'Sanctions in Effect' list, and a Proceedings Bulletin which has details on particular individuals or firms found liable for violating federal commodities law. There is also quite a large section explaining the CFTC reparations program, and the facility to make a complaint by e-mail. Finally, the site holds the regular Commitments of Traders Report (with details of, for example, the number of traders long/short in particular markets and their percentage of open interest), with an archive of old reports from 1986.

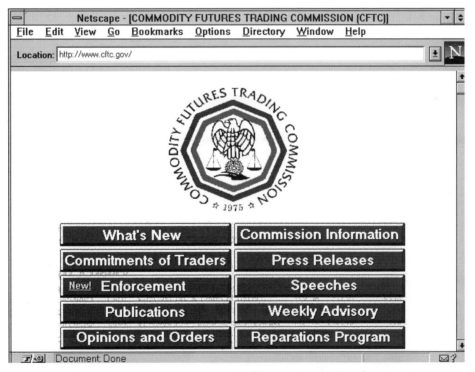

■ FIG 2.102 **US Commodity Futures Trading Commission, home page**

OTHER RESOURCES

Asset pricing and analysis

There are not many sites that specialize in asset analysis or allocation, but this whole area is increasingly merging with general risk management (*see* below). A couple of consultancies, **Wilshire Associates** and **Ibbotson Associates**, have introductory Web sites, while **Morgan Stanley** on its site has information about the MSCI Indexes and a selection of charts with performance updates.

■ BARRA

BARRA was formed in Berkeley, California, in 1975 to 'turn theoretical financial research into practical investment technology'. Initially, it was involved mainly in asset allocation, but has now broadened to generally offer analytical models, software and services to investors and traders worldwide. Its Web site covers three areas:

- ■ **Products**: services for fixed interest and equity markets.
- ■ **Market/Index**: BARRA has developed quite a few market indices in co-operation with other financial institutions, and a database of these is

■ FIG 2.103 BARRA: home page

available from the site – updated monthly. This database includes: explanation of beta, S&P/BARRA Growth and Value Indices, BARRA Canadian Indices, Sharpe/BARRA Growth and Value Indices, and BARRA Emerging Market Index.

- **Research publications**: there is a searchable database of all articles that have been written by BARRA, with many of the articles available in HTML format. These are quite academic, but certainly interesting to give a glimpse of the state of the art here.

Risk management

There are several risk companies on the Web, including those concerned with:

- **risk consultancy**: Lindquist, Stephenson & White, RISC (of Price Waterhouse), Peartree Limited
- **risk technology**: C·ATS, Infinity, Brady, Glassco Park and Cambridge Risk Dynamics.

The majority of these are corporate information sites, with just product and contact details. A few of the software sites have demonstration programs available for download. Perhaps in the future there will be more interactive sites where risk programs can be assessed online.

J.P. Morgan and *RiskMetrics*

The major site in this area is without doubt that of J.P. Morgan, in which it introduces its approach to quantifying global market risk with *RiskMetrics*.

J.P. Morgan provides the methodology and the calculated data each day, and companies are free to do what they like with this data.

Supporting the *RiskMetrics* work, the Web site has:

- **numerous articles (PDF for download)**: explaining *RiskMetrics*, including a quarterly *RiskMetrics Monitor* with information on any changes
- **datasets**: two sets of files for download (volatilities, correlations), available daily/monthly and in Mac/DOS/UNIX formats
- **regulatory dataset**: volatility and correlation estimates meeting the requirements of the BIS/Basel Committee proposal on the use of internal models
- **Excel Macro Add-In**: for easy access to, and manipulation of, the *RiskMetrics* data in a Mac/Windows Excel spreadsheet
- **third-party support directory**: several consultants and software houses have developed risk systems based on *RiskMetrics*
- **conferences calendar**: primarily about Value at Risk and internal risk controls.

RiskMetrics

RiskMetrics is a methodology to estimate market risk based on the Value-at-Risk approach. It comprises a set of consistently calculated volatilities and correlation forecasts for use as inputs to estimate market risks, and covers:

- government bonds
- money markets
- swaps
- foreign exchange
- equity indices

for the following markets:

- Australia
- Belgium
- Canada
- Denmark
- European currency units
- France
- Germany
- Great Britain
- Italy
- Japan
- Netherlands
- Spain
- Sweden
- Switzerland
- United States.

In addition, it includes volatility estimates on the term structure of 11 commodities futures contracts as well as on fixed income, equity and currency markets in Austria, Finland, Ireland, Norway, Portugal, Hong Kong, New Zealand, and Singapore (bringing the total number of countries to 23).

Source: J.P. Morgan

The site also has details on:

- **FourFifteen**: besides third parties developing independent systems based on *RiskMetrics*, J.P. Morgan has developed its own tool, called FourFifteen. This provides a Value-at-Risk (VaR) calculator and report generator, and runs on Windows or Mac platforms.

J.P. Morgan is a global financial services firm that serves governments, corporations, institutions, individuals and privately held firms with complex financial needs through an integrated range of advisory, financing, trading, investment, and related capabilities.

August 15, 1996 - features

Year 2000 problem J.P. Morgan has recently published an industry analysis of the so-called "Year 2000 Problem," which highlights the potentially devastating results of programming written since the dawn of the computer age that was not designed to handle any dates beyond 1999. (8/9/96)

Degas Exhibition Next month, the Art Institute of Chicago unveils a remarkable collection

■ FIG 2.104 J.P. Morgan: home page

■ **Risk Management Advisory**: description of J.P. Morgan's expertise and consultancy services offered for risk management.

In summary, it is a little disappointing that this site does not have more general articles and discussion on risk (i.e. this is not a general resource centre for risk management), but the support services for its own *RiskMetrics* methodology is superb, and the data download via the Internet makes the technique readily accessible worldwide.

Trading systems

For some time now there have been a number of independent subscription services that offer trading advice (and indeed actual buy and sell signals). Up to now the preferred method of delivery for these services has probably been the fax; but the Internet offers obvious advantages for distributing time-sensitive trading signals to a wide audience – so many of these services are beginning to migrate onto the Web. Subscription to such a trading system may offer a daily/weekly/occasional e-mail signal report, or access to password-protected pages on a Web site.

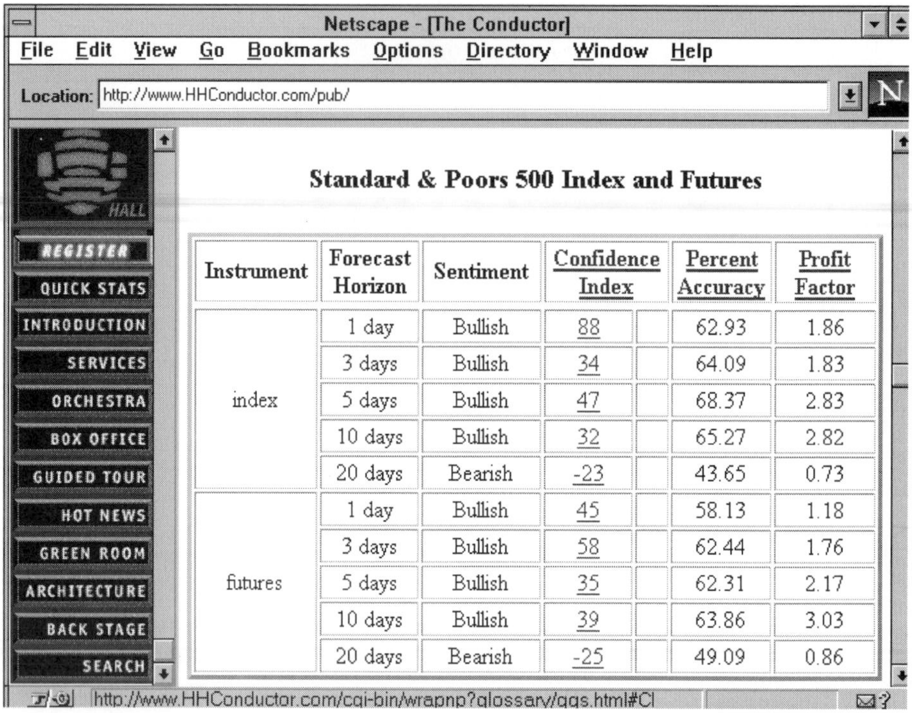

Instrument	Forecast Horizon	Sentiment	Confidence Index	Percent Accuracy	Profit Factor
index	1 day	Bullish	88	62.93	1.86
	3 days	Bullish	34	64.09	1.83
	5 days	Bullish	47	68.37	2.83
	10 days	Bullish	32	65.27	2.82
	20 days	Bearish	-23	43.65	0.73
futures	1 day	Bullish	45	58.13	1.18
	3 days	Bullish	58	62.44	1.76
	5 days	Bullish	35	62.31	2.17
	10 days	Bullish	39	63.86	3.03
	20 days	Bearish	-25	49.09	0.86

■ FIG 2.105 **The Conductor: analysis of S&P500**

The trading systems on offer fall, very crudely, into three categories:

- **stock picks**: where a few daily stock recommendations are made on the basis of a combination of fundamental and technical analysis
- **technical analysis**: offering buy/sell signals typically on a smallish range of commodities and futures contracts, where the signals are solely generated by classic charting techniques (and in many cases still analysed manually)
- **computer program**: where signals (usually for commodities and futures contracts) are generated completely automatically by a computer program. The more basic services in this area will refer to 'artificial intelligence' (AI) systems, while the more advanced (realizing that the general idea of AI is widely perceived as not having lived up to its initial hype) refer to neural networks, fuzzy logic, genetic algorithms, and knowledge-based systems.

The Conductor

The most sophisticated service in the latter category of computer program trading systems is called The Conductor, which is certainly one of the most advanced sites on the financial Internet.

For each market followed, the system produces bullish/bearish sentiment indicators (for specified time horizons) and also an analysis of the likely accuracy of the forecast (*see* Figure 2.106).

Extract from a forecast report by The Conductor

Historical Perspective	...Today's bullish Confidence Index (94) predicts that the Major Market (index) will move higher over the next 5 trading days. Based on past performance, this model's Confidence Index produced winning signals 77% of the time based on 35 signals.
Bottom Line	...Historically, this model has made $3.51 for every dollar it's lost
Risk Experience Index	...From a risk versus reward perspective, Thursday's forecast shifts the trading odds in your favor on a risk-adjusted basis by a ratio of 1.08 to one...Today's forecast indicates that the reward over the next 5 trading days is 8.01% greater than the downside risk on average.
Trivial Predictor	...Today's forecast has outperformed a trivial predictor by a factor of 4.13 to one.
Model Trend	...The Confidence Index has generally trended higher over the past 10 trading days. In addition, today's signal is 2 Confidence Index points above its 21-day simple moving average. The model's signals have ranged from a low of 77 to a high of 99 over the past 21 trading days.

■ FIG 2.106

The description of the service offered is very thorough, and every day the system is demonstrated by displaying the trading signals for a randomly chosen market. (Subscription ranges from US$14.95–185 per month).

This is the face of technical analysis when it grows up, where technical analysis is recursively applied to its own results. It is about as far removed from cash-flow and ROCE analysis as one can get, and fundamental investors are likely to be baffled and stubbornly sceptical about the whole thing. But for technically-oriented investors, this is a glimpse into the future; it is probably as advanced as any system being used by professional managers anywhere – and it is available to anybody on the Internet. Whether it works or not is, of course, an entirely different matter; the concept may be good, but independent assessment and time will tell if it has its sums and application methodology right.

Online financial calculators

Some of the simplest applications of Internet interactivity are Web-based financial calculators. With these it is possible to input parameters and calculate the result directly. The attractions of these are that instead of reading a fixed example of a calculation (e.g. a retirement plan), the example can be made directly relevant by inputting the user's own details.

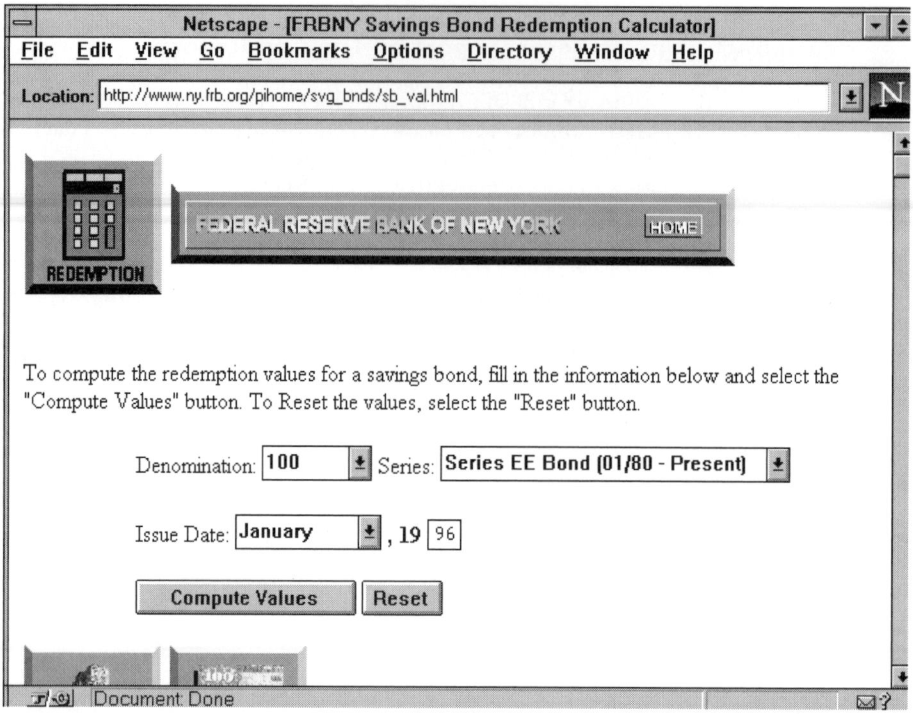

FIG 2.107 Federal Reserve Bank of New York

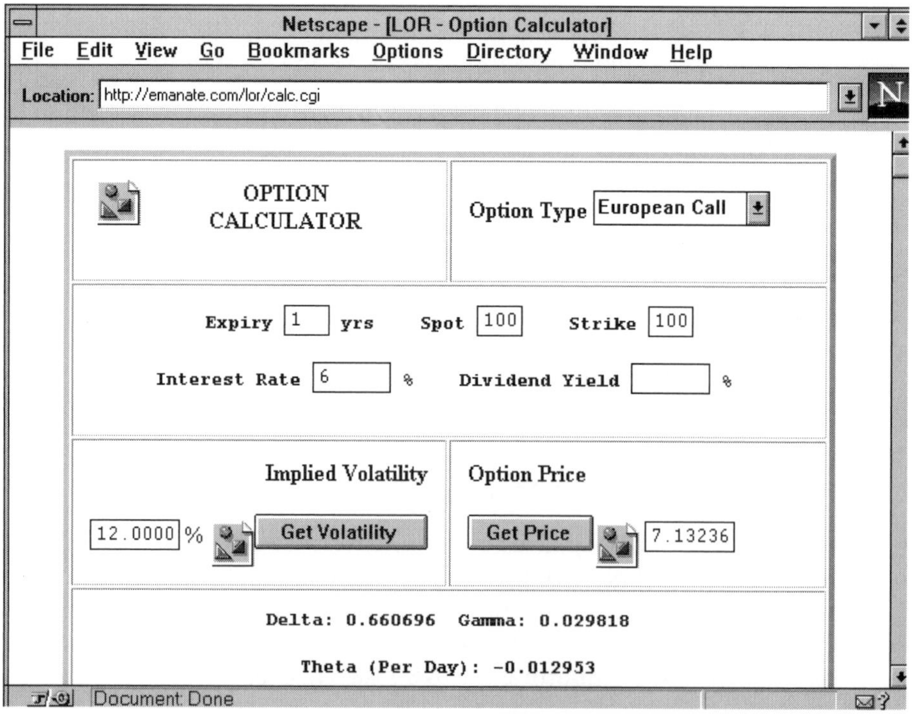

FIG 2.108 Leland O'Brien Rubinstein Associates

So far, the range of online financial calculators is mainly focused on personal finance, with calculators for mortgages, savings, retirement etc., and these naturally tend to be fairly country-specific. But there are others that include, derivatives, fixed income yield calculations and general statistics. The calculators are there partly as an advertisement for the company running the Web site, and partly as an experiment with the new Internet technology.

The **Royal Bank of Canada** has a commission calculator for its discount brokerage services. This calculates the commission charged for trading Canadian or US equities as well as options, mutual funds, and gold/silver certificates. **Robert's Online Pricers**, is similar but will determine the rates charged by over 30 different brokerages.

The **Federal Reserve Bank of New York** offers a calculator that computes the redemption values for Savings Bonds, and the **Sallie Mae** Web site has a good collection of calculators, including:

- estimating the cost of college education
- savings calculators
- expected family contribution
- net assets
- estimate borrowing needs
- calculating the cost of a deferment
- monthly budget calculator
- estimating monthly student loan payments.

There is also no shortage of retirement planners on the sites of investment advisers – no doubt hoping to attract customers when they realize the problems they will have paying for their Internet bills if they live to be 100 years old.

Although the majority of these sites are US based, the calculations themselves are often currency independent, and the results can be mentally translated into a local currency.

For slightly more complex calculations, a number of universities have statistical models online, and there are calculators to analyse convertible bonds, warrants and options. An example of the latter is the Web site of Leland O'Brien Rubinstein Associates (a risk management company), where a Web calculator will determine the implied volatility or fair value, delta, gamma and theta for American/European style options.

A word of caution: although it will be rare that any of the programs are actually wrong, confusion can occur over the interpretation of the results of many programs.

As a test, identical values were input into four online option calculators, and the resulting outputs compared. The values input were:

Option type   : European call
Stock price   : 50
Strike   : 100
Maturity   : 5 years
Volatility   : 35%
Interest rate   : 7.0%
Dividend yield   : 0%

The results are shown in Table 2.36.

▒ TABLE 2.36 Comparison of online option calculators

	Option value	Delta	Gamma	Theta
LOR	6.762712	0.355322	0.008659	−0.00435
Numa	9.564	0.475	0.010175	−2.519
OptionVue	11.71	48.1	1.02	0.89
Robert's	9.7312	0.4812	0.0102	−0.007

On first inspection, it appears there is quite a variation in the calculations, and the obvious question is, which is the correct one? The answer is that they are probably all correct *within their specific parameters of reference*.

Many differences can occur due to the assumptions made and definition of units. (In fact, the problem with many option calculations is not that they are difficult – it is that they are too *simple*. What they are trying to model is complex, and it can be deceptively attractive to input five or six figures into a calculator. The complexity of option models is not in the mathematics of the calculation, but, rather, determining what units to input and then how to interpret the output results. As such, due to their deceptive simplicity, options models (such as Black Scholes) must be regarded as among the most dangerous inventions of recent years.)

Technical: how the programs work

In many computer programs, only a small part – frequently just a few lines of code – are required for the mathematics of the problem. The other 90 per cent of the program is concerned with the user-interface (for example, the layout on the screen, and preventing the program from crashing if the user experiments by pressing alt-F12). The advantage of the Web is that an easy, cross-platform interface is readily available with the use of forms (fill-in boxes on a Web page).

All the calculators require the browser to support *forms* – but most do so today in any case. Beyond that, the programs are of three types:

- **CGI**: these are programs (written, for example, in C or Perl) that run on the remote Web server. If, for example, you are using the Merrill Lynch Net Worth calculator, after filling in the required parameters and clicking *Calculate*, the data is sent to the Merrill computer, where a program will operate on the figures, write a new Web page on-the-fly and then send that back to the browser, to be displayed on the user's screen. This is still the most common type of Web calculator, and nearly all browsers will support this.

- **Java Applet**: the problem with the CGI is that if traffic on the Internet is high, and there is a great strain on the remote Web server, there can be a delay as data is sent back and forth between the user and the remote computer. A Java Applet is a small program that is downloaded onto the user's computer at the same time as the Web page is viewed. This program can be faster than CGI as it runs locally and may not need to contact further the remote computer. Only the latest browsers support these Java Applets.

- **JavaScript**: this is similar to the above, but here the program code is embedded into the Web page itself. Again, only the latest browsers will be able to support this feature.

In the list of programs in the Directory, all are the basic CGI type, unless otherwise indicated.

Reference

Some simple, and misleading, descriptions of the Internet would have it as a huge library of information. Books, however, have publishers who filter and edit the material before publication (and then libraries add yet another filtering stage, with their own selection procedures). With the Internet, it is like having instant access to a million first drafts – where one might come across a Warren Buffet on asset turnover, or a Nick Leeson on risk management.

There is no shortage of potential reference material on the Net: there are many online dictionaries and every serious site has its assortment of educational articles and glossaries; but it has to be admitted that the general quality is poor. Many sites seem to get carried away with the technology and the idea of broadcasting to a world audience, such that, amid the excitement of HyperText and frames, the content tends to be forgotten.

Of course, there are some good sites about (for example, those listed below and the academic journals), but if you are looking for a clear and reliable explanation of a financial topic, a standard textbook will prove superior to anything currently on the Net.

■ Finance Wat.ch

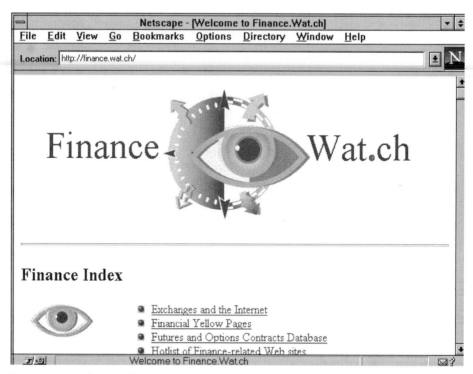

■ FIG 2.109 Finance Wa.tch: home page

Finance Wat.ch is one of those bewildering sites you come across on the Internet, where it is not immediately obvious: what it is, what's there, or even who's doing it. After some lengthy investigation, it appears this is a type of joint effort between a software consultancy and some Swiss (hence the rather clever punning 'Wat.ch') financial industry associations. However, despite initial confusion, this site is involved in some very interesting areas.

Firstly, it has a number of reference pages:

- a directory of all **exchanges** on the Internet
- a fairly comprehensive database of world **futures contract specifications**
- a database of specifications for **market indices**
- a **multilingual financial glossary** (although the concept is better than the actual execution)
- a collection of IFCI Geneva papers on **Derivatives and Risk Management.**

But potentially more interesting is the activity in financial training. One of the participating institutions is the International Finance & Commodities Institute (IFCI), which is described as a 'non-profit foundation created in 1984 under the supervision of the Swiss government with the objective of promoting the understanding of both commodity and financial derivatives throughout the world'. The IFCI offers traditional seminars and workshops (details on the site), but is also involved in financial computer-based training courses. (*See* 'Education and training', below.)

Derivatives Research Unincorporated

Occasionally, when surfing the Web, one comes across a site that stands out strongly from the rest. Such a site is Derivatives Research Unincorporated. This holds the archives of a series of articles posted regularly to the misc.invest.futures newsgroup written by Don Chance, Professor of Finance at Virginia Tech, US. The articles are non-technical discussions of various topics in derivatives, and are examples of some of the best original and value-added content to be found on the WWW. (A sample of some of the topics covered is given in Figure 2.110.)

Sample articles from Derivatives Research Unincorporated

- Tree Pricing of Bonds and Interest Rate Derivatives
- No-Arbitrage Models of the Term Structure
- Implied Volatility
- Stock as an Option
- A Brief History of Derivatives
- Asset Allocation with Derivatives
- Risk Neutral Pricing of Derivatives
- Digital Options
- Credit Risk in Derivatives
- Misconceptions About Covered Call Writing

FIG 2.110

University of Exeter, UK

Similar to the site above, this is devoid of 100K byte home page imagemaps, or jerky JavaScript scrolling messages – and is also one of the most fascinating on the Internet. The page is about Money, and presents a collection of links to information about the history of money, modern developments, and the prospects for electronic money. Some of the topic areas are:

- **History of Money**
- **Barter**: a new life with the Internet
- **Numismatics**: information on coins and paper money
- **E-Money**
- **Libertarian Views on Money**
- **The Internet and Economics**

▓ **Financial Scandals**: Barings, Daiwa, Sumitomo, BCCI, European Union, Whitewater, US Municipal Bonds, etc. (there's no shortage of subjects in this area).

The high quality of organization and depth of research in these pages demonstrates that there is far more to creating a good links page than simply listing some cool sites; and it is not such a great surprise to learn that the page author is the Science Librarian at Exeter University.

▓ misc.invest FAQ

Most newsgroups have an associated file called a FAQ, which is a collection of questions – and answers – that have been frequently posted in the forum. These FAQs will usually have been compiled by an enthusiastic volunteer. Such a FAQ exists for the misc.invest newsgroup (and also for the misc.invest.funds and misc.invest.futures groups).

The FAQ for misc.invest is large and covers a wide range of investment topics. The messages can be very interesting to read, and have a certain raw and immediate quality that makes a change from the studied, and staid, prose of books or newspapers. But you should be aware that these messages might be written by anybody, and that there is very little editing or checking.

An example might be found in the section on hedging. This topic is dealt with in three paragraphs, the first of which mentions something about risk reduction, but the finale is:

> *In my opinion, the best (and cheapest) hedge is to sell short the stock of a competitor to the company whose stock you hold. For example, if you like Microsoft and think they will eat Borland's lunch, buy MSFT and short BORL. No matter which way the market as a whole goes, the offsetting positions hedge away the market risk.*

Now, this is actually a very interesting trading strategy, but it should not necessarily be recommended as a prime hedging method for a stock holding. Certainly a novice investor holding Syquest [SYQT] stock at the beginning of 1996 and shorting Iomega [IOMG], would have been puzzled by the description of hedging as 'risk reduction'.

Therefore, though this FAQ can be an interesting reference source, treat it as entertaining but dubious. Don't forget that the messages appearing on public or private forums (e.g. newsgroups) will frequently be sincere, interesting, and wrong.

Education and training

Along with market regulation and 'scam-checking' sites, one can expect to see a huge growth in the number of Internet sites in education and training though there is not much to see at the moment.

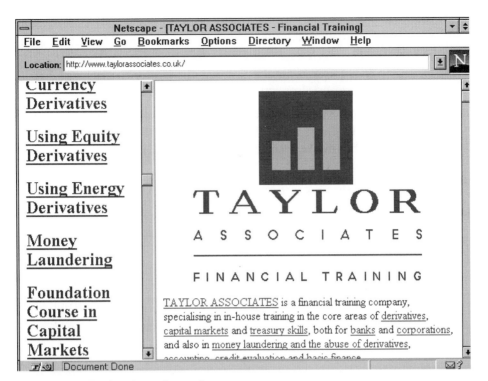

Netscape - [TAYLOR ASSOCIATES - Financial Training]

File   Edit   View   Go   Bookmarks   Options   Directory   Window   Help

Location: http://www.taylorassociates.co.uk/

Currency
Derivatives

Using Equity
Derivatives

Using Energy
Derivatives

Money
Laundering

Foundation
Course in
Capital
Markets

T A Y L O R
A S S O C I A T E S

F I N A N C I A L   T R A I N I N G

TAYLOR ASSOCIATES is a financial training company,
specialising in in-house training in the core areas of derivatives,
capital markets and treasury skills, both for banks and corporations,
and also in money laundering and the abuse of derivatives,
accounting, credit evaluation and basic finance.

Document: Done

FIG 2.111 Taylor Associates: home page

As a group, the futures exchanges probably have the best pages with
educational material (usually offering, books, videotapes, courses and
sometimes online teaching programs). The educational role of futures
exchanges has always been very strong, and they have found the initial
exploitation of the Internet obvious and relatively straightforward.

The IFCI development of computer-based courses (mentioned above under
Finance Wat.ch) could be an interesting site to follow. There is a training
consultancy, **Taylor Associates**, specializing in derivatives, that has a Web site
which, while clearly designed, is largely just a description of a non-digital
service (*see* Figure 2.111).

And quite a few sites list financial courses and conferences available, but apart
from this, there is surprisingly little on the Internet that can be regarded
directly as educational.

Simulations

Together with the two sections above, 'Reference', and 'Education and training',
these are all evidently closely linked and should be complementary. One of the
best methods of financial training should be simulated trading, and there is
great potential for this via the Internet.

There are already a few services in this area, but the majority are still at the experimental stage. The principal subscription service is **Auditrack**, a 'full-service simulated brokerage', where Auditrack determines the most likely execution level for each simulated order. The service is used by professional and private investors and also, apparently, universities.

The Swiss Center for Scientific Computing has established a server called **ART** – The Artificial Trading Room, which is a continuing experiment in real-time trading. Another example can be found at the **CME** which has a simulated currency trading program.

Trading simulation is another area that should see strong growth in the future; probably in two areas:

- **Programs**: where trading is simulated using a specially designed computer program.
- **MUDs (Multi-user Dungeons)**: derived from the games arena, multi-user games have an obvious parallel with the structure and interaction of any market. An interesting future development will be the extension of these games from slaying dragons to pitting one's wits against a number of online opponents in a trading environment.

Investment software

Not surprisingly, the Internet can prove very useful when researching and using investment programs. Already many software companies have Web sites, through which they offer information on their programs, technical support and the facility to download demonstration programs and upgrades. In future, it is likely that if you want to buy a program, it will be paid for and downloaded immediately via the Internet – thereby avoiding the extra cost and time currently incurred using floppy disks, CD ROMs and other physical media.

Appendix C at the back of this book has a list of investment software companies (many of which have Web sites) that cover portfolio management, technical analysis, options and neural networks. Although many of these companies are based in the US, with the opening of international markets through the Internet, this should encourage many other countries to begin marketing globally their investment programs. This inherent internationalization is one of the great features of cyber commerce: if an investor in Finland sees an interesting program developed by a New Zealand company, the program can be ordered directly without worrying about a lack of local distribution.

■ Equis International

One of the best examples of a software manufacturer's Web site is that of Equis – the developer of Metastock, the technical analysis program. This is a good

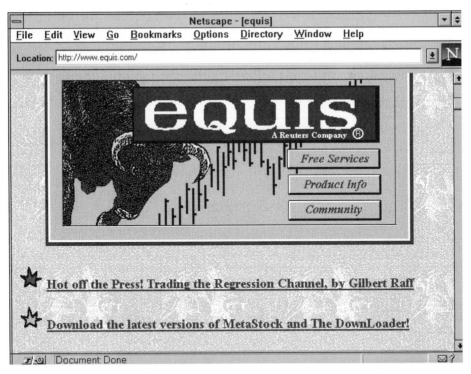

FIG 2.112 Equis International

model of a Web site being used for far more than just a digital glossy brochure. The site features:

- several regular market comments by industry experts
- a weekly investment events calendar
- regularly updated lists of 'hot stocks' generated by the Explorer feature in Metastock (this includes several lists, such as stocks with bullish/bearish engulfing pattern, stocks up over 20 per cent on double average volume, stocks breaking out of consolidation (upside), most oversold stocks etc.)
- information about the programs, including the ability to download demonstration versions
- support for existing clients including newsletters, custom formulas, systems tests, and files to download.

A common initial reaction to the Internet is that it is a great marketing tool, where one Web site can be seen by potential buyers all over the world. This is possibly true. But one of the more recent business models places greater emphasis on existing client support, rather than continual advertising to attract new clients. It is in this area of maintaining contact with existing clients that the power of the Internet is likely to lie – not necessarily with new sales. The Equis site shows the possibility of offering global support to a large client base.

Other good examples of software sites are those for MathWorks (engineering and scientific software) and OptionVue (PC options trading software). The latter additionally offers online forums for users to discuss programs and trading techniques.

■ Microsoft and Intuit

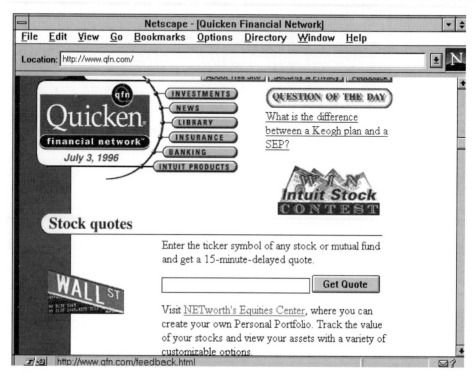

■ FIG 2.113 Intuit's Quicken Financial Network

Obviously the two heavyweights in this field are Microsoft and Intuit, with their respective programs, Money and Quicken. Although these packages until now have concentrated on personal finance, they are beginning to incorporate more and more advanced investment features. As yet, the Microsoft site offers little more than some standard product details on the Money program. By contrast, Intuit has established a Web site called the Quicken Financial Network, which looks set to become one of the major financial sites in the world. Its purchase and incorporation of the Galt NETworth site was a very shrewd move, and certainly adds muscle to its service. The Quicken site now offers:

■ Fifteen-minute delayed stock and mutual fund price quotes

■ links to the Newspage news service

■ daily investment articles

■ library of investment topics.

This will certainly be one of the most interesting sites on the Internet to watch, as it builds into what could be the first global financial supermarket.

To accompany the growth in general and specialist investment programs offered over the Internet, there will probably be a small service industry analysing and comparing these programs. Two sites that are already operating in this field are The Computerized Trader (a collection of articles from *Futures* magazine about trading and technology), and a guide to treasury technology by computer consultant Bob Browning.

Ordering software

So, we can read information about investment programs over the Internet, and we can download demonstration versions to try. The next step is to order them. In the future it is likely that software will be ordered direct from the producer, and, further, that both payment and receipt of the program will be via the Internet. For the client this has the advantage of allowing them to get hold of the program quickly, while the producer can develop direct contact with the client.

Anderson Investors Software

There are a few software retailers on the Net that distribute investment programs and will post internationally. One such, Anderson Investors Software, Inc. (on the Wall Street Directory site, *see* 'Books' below) has a fairly large selection, including data packages, personal finance and financial and stock market analysis. It's certainly worth comparing the prices at these sites with local distributors.

Shareware and freeware

The technology of the Internet does lend itself to all sorts of small utility type programs, and there has been an explosion of software in this area. An example of this is where Web sites provide free quotes (e.g. Security APL). It is possible to visit these sites, input a ticker symbol, click the button and receive the quote. This works because the browser sends a command to the Web server, to collect the quote for the specific security. However, that command does not necessarily have to originate from the one specific Web page. In fact, although many sites offer quotes from their pages, there are very few original source servers, with all the others merely routeing their quote requests to these external servers. But the quote requests to the servers do not necessarily have to originate from a Web page at all. One of the limitations of quote services has been that only a limited number of quotes can be retrieved at one time. However, some small programs are available (running independently of any browser) that will retrieve any number of quotes automatically from servers. Another attraction of these programs can be that their interface is superior to that offered on many

Web pages. A selection of these and other types of financial shareware is given in Table 2.37 (all these programs are currently just for US, and possibly in some cases Canadian, stocks).

▓ TABLE 2.37 Internet financial shareware programs

Program name / file name / location	Description
Netquotes netq13.exe (Win 3.x) http://ourworld.compuserve.com/ homepages/sejohnson	Automatically downloads and displays 15-minute delayed stock and mutual fund quotes from the Internet. A configuration entry specifies the time period between updates. The program provides detail, summary, and ticker displays for the list of stock symbols supplied by the user
NetStock nets0602.zip (Win 3.x) http://www.jaxnet.com/~henrik	A simple little stock and mutual fund Internet quote retrieval program with export functionality for Quicken users.
Personal Stock Monitor psm12.zip (Win 95) http://telogy.com/~aivasyuk/	Time delayed (10-15 minutes) stock quotes.
ProStream psinst.exe (Win 95) http://www.ps-group.com/	An Internet Broadcasting Service which delivers free stock quotes directly to the user's workstation.
Quote Ticker Bar qtb21.zip (Win 3.1) qtb.zip (Win 95) http://www.connix.com/~randy/	A program that delivers time-delayed stock quotes
Stocktrack32 stktrk11.zip (Win 95) http://www.flinet.com/~emeyers	Retrieves stock information, such as the current value, the day high, the day low etc.
WinStock winstk16.zip (Win 3.x) ws32r1v12b.zip (Win 95) http://www.teleport.com/~magoldsm/ winstock/	A stock tracking program that provides 15-minute delayed stock quotes in a configurable window. It will also track portfolio values.

Besides the programs in Table 2.37, there are many other financial shareware programs available (a list of over 100 of these can be found in Appendix D at the back of this book). Most of these programs can be found in the large shareware libraries (see Figure 2.114), which also include thousands of computer utility programs for all purposes, including, for example, statistics, which might be useful. Most of the shareware programs in Table 2.37 can also be found at the TUCOWS site.

▨ Shareware.com

The best source for all types of shareware (including financial) is probably Shareware.com. It does not have a directory of programs but uses a search engine: if you know the specific name of the program you are looking for this can be input directly. Alternatively, input a keyword such as 'finance', and all the financial-related programs will be listed.

Some financial shareware is very good, but much is not. Browsing through the programs is really like a jumble sale – a few possible nuggets among the rest. The true cost of these programs is not monetary (the registration fee for many is of the order of $15 and rarely over $50), but rather the time spent in downloading, installing, testing, crashing and then finally deleting the software. Having said that, if you are looking for some small vital program that converts Metastock data to Quicken format – the shareware libraries are the places to look.

Financial software download sites

Shareware.com **http://www.shareware.com**
TUCOWS **http://www.tucows.com/**
Simtel.Net **http://oak.oakland.edu/simtel.net/**
Cal. State University Finance Shareware Archive
http://coyote.csusm.edu/cwis/winworld/finance.html
Coast to Coast Software Repository **http://www.coast.net/SimTel/**
Jumbo **http://www.jumbo.com/**

▨ FIG 2.114

Books

▨ Amazon.com

A number of mail-order book companies have services on the Internet, the most impressive of which is Amazon.com, which claims to have one million books available. Its financial section is worth looking at, and the books may well be cheaper than in shops. They post internationally, with a scale of three delivery methods (the cheapest of which has charges of approximately US$4 per order and then US$2 per book). Another online bookshop is the Internet Bookshop, which is based in the UK.

▨ Wall Street Directory

A more specific service for investors is that offered by the Wall Street Directory. This has a collection of products for 'computerized traders and investors' including books and software.

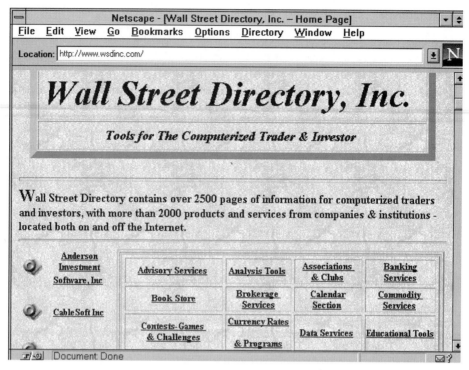

■ FIG 2.115 Wall Street Directory

These online services can certainly be useful for investors living outside large cities – and even within cities, a US$6 postal charge may be less than the cost of a taxi ride and the time spent journeying to a bookshop on the other side of town.

However, the future of books on the Internet (as far as paper-based technical books have a future at all) is likely to be on specialized sites, rather than online mega-bookstores. For example, if a site exists that specializes in information about risk management, mail-order book companies, or publishers themselves, will do better to market relevant books about risk through this site, rather than on general Web sites.

Journals

As the majority of economics and finance journals are produced by academic institutions, it is not surprising to find many with pages on the Web. However, the majority of these pages, as yet, tend to carry information about the journals rather than include any content. Their sites will typically have details on:

■ **subscriptions**: details of subscribing to the paper journal

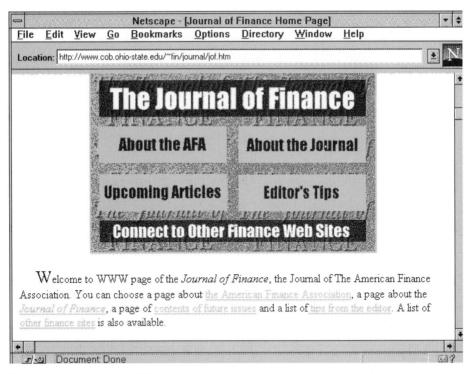

FIG 2.116 *Journal of Finance,* home page

- **submissions**: guidelines and style requirements for submitting papers for publication
- **contents**: titles (and possibly abstracts) of papers in previous, current and forthcoming papers.

There are a few journals, however, where papers can be read: *Journal of Applied Econometrics* (with an archive of many papers back to 1988), *Journal of Financial and Strategic Decisions* and the *Journal of Finance.*

On the sites where papers can be read, these must usually be downloaded as PDF files.

Journal of Finance

The *Journal of Finance* is the journal of The American Finance Association and is based at Ohio State University. Not only is this one of the leading finance journals, but it also offers the full text version of papers (in PDF format) from previous issues (archive from March 1995) and some forthcoming papers as well (*see* Figure 2.117).

> **Sample of articles appearing in *Journal of Finance***
>
> ▓ Impact of the 1988 Basle Accord on International Banks
> ▓ Transparency and Liquidity: A Study of Block Trades on the London Stock Exchange under Different Publication Rules
> ▓ Third Market Broker-Dealers: Cost Competitors or Cream Skimmers?
> ▓ Price Limit Performance: Evidence from the Tokyo Stock Exchange
> ▓ The Valuation of Complex Derivatives by Major Investment Firms: Empirical Evidence
> ▓ Good Timing: CEO Stock Option Awards and Company News Announcements
> ▓ Corporate Governance and Equity Prices: Evidence from the Czech and Slovak Republics
> ▓ Cash Flow and Investment: Evidence from Internal Capital Markets
> ▓ General Properties of Option Prices
> ▓ Limit Order Trading

▓ **FIG 2.117**

Offshore banking

As mentioned at the beginning, this book is more about investment rather than personal finance or banking. However, it might be useful to mention a few sites with information about offshore banking.

The best directory of offshore banking sites is at the Institute of Finance and Banking, University of Göttingen (**http://www.gwdg.de/~ifbg/bank_off.html**); while a couple of other online resources are Offshore (**http://www.dnai.com/offshore/offshore.html**), and Offshore Tax Haven, Trust, Asset Protection and Banking Reference Page (**http://www.nolimits.com/nolimits/offshore.html**).

▓ Flemings Offshore Bank

Flemings has an offshore bank based in the Isle of Man, UK, called Robert Fleming (Isle of Man) Limited. This offers the Flemings Offshore Reserve Account with: high interest rates, cheque book (available for Sterling, US Dollars, Deutsch Marks and Yen accounts only), Gold Visa Card, commission-free foreign exchange transactions, and Faxbanking (**http://www.flemings-offshore-bank.com/**).

▓ Barclays Offshore Banking

Barclays offers offshore banking facilities through offices in Ireland, Isle Of Man, Channel Islands and London; and is designed for UK expatriates and international investors, with liquid assets in excess of £50 000. The usual range of banking facilities is offered: money transfers, cheque and savings accounts, fixed term deposits, and investment advice. As with Flemings above, the Web site just carries information about the services (**http://www.offshorebanking.barclays.com/**).

Top ten financial Internet sites

An entirely subjective list of the top financial sites on the Internet is given in Figure 2.118. Of course, the sites listed will not necessarily be equally relevent to all investors, but it provides an overview of the current state of the art.

Note: arbitrarily, the news sites (such as CNN*fn*, *WSJ Online*, Bloomberg, *FT Online* and AsiaOne) have deliberately been excluded from the list – otherwise they would have dominated (the top of) the list.

Top ten Internet financial sites

1 DBC – market data
http://www.dbc.com/

2 Dow Jones Telerate – Asian market news
http://www.djtelerate.com.hk/

3 Charter Media – market news
http://www.briefing.com/

4 CBOT – futures exchange
http://www.cbt.com/

5 CME – futures exchange
http://www.cme.com/

6 US Securities and Exchange Commission – regulatory body
http://www.sec.gov/

7 J.P. Morgan – investment bank
http://www.jpmorgan.com/

8 Fidelity International – fund manager
http://www.fid-intl.com/

9 The Conductor – online trading system
http://www.HHConducor.com/

10 TeleStock – US stock quotes and charts
http://www.teleserve.co.uk/

▓ FIG 2.118

Top ten financial umbrella sites

The function of many sites is quite straightforward. For example, the Bloomberg site provides up-to-date business and financial news, while the US Census Bureau site provides information about, and access to, a selection of Census data. Other sites, however, are more complex. There might be a wide range of information and services provided by the company controlling the Web site itself, or there might be an agglomeration of services provided by different companies. The thinking behind the latter type of site is to achieve a critical mass of services (similar to a shopping mall), so that users find it useful to bookmark the site to return to it.

These sites can hold much good information, and the level of page organization can be higher than average, but frequently their breadth of content can lead to problems when coming to categorize them. Hence, the

Top ten financial umbrella sites

1 *MarketPlex* – (at the CBOT, umbrella site for a collection of futures-related services) technical charts, research reports; select articles from journals; access to subscription MRI service: daily charts/data; access to MJK closing prices for commodity exchanges worldwide
   http://www.cbot.com/mplex.htm

2 *PAWWS Financial Network* – (subscription general investment resources: brokerage and research services)
   http://pawws.com/

3 *Pathfinder* – (Time's umbrella site for: Fortune, Hoover's Business Profiles and Money) general information on personal finance and investment
   http://www.pathfinder.com/

4 *INO Global Markets* – Options Industry Council; CTAs; Stark Research: performance tracker of CTAs; intraday/daily/weekly charts/data for the world's major futures and options markets; journal articles; conference calendar; reference articles; bookshop
   http://www.ino.com/

5 *NETworth* – mutual fund information from Morningstar: search facility for funds, fund rankings, prospectus database, articles and market outlooks; directory of company Web sites
   http://networth.galt.com/

6 *Interactive Investor* – (UK) umbrella site for information on: IFAs, UK Unit Trusts, investment trusts, PEPs and offshore funds, with pages maintained by fund managers; news service with the following journals: *Financial Adviser, Product Adviser, Investment Adviser* and *Offshore Financial Review*; Micropal fund performance figures; site search facility; links
   http://www.iii.co.uk/

7 *Nest Egg* – (umbrella site for financial services) Smith Barney Wall St Watch: daily market info; New York Institute of Finance Center; general articles on equities/funds
   http://nestegg.iddis.com/

8 *Finance.Wat.ch* – futures/options contracts specs; world indices specs; financial education/training resources; four-language glossary on derivative instruments; IFCI Geneva papers on derivatives and risk management
   http://finance.wat.ch/

9 *Institute for Commercial Engineering* – (Russia) includes: Russian Exchange; REDGAR; Federal Commission on Securities and the Capital Market; RINACO Plus (broker)
   http://www.fe.msk.ru/

10 *INVESTools* – collection of investment newsletters; news/research resources; charts; Morningstar reports; bookstore; investment articles
   http://investools.com/

▨ FIG 2.119

term *umbrella* is sometimes used to describe these sites that do not fit neatly into any one financial service.

An example of such a site is the UK Interactive Investor, which contains a number of independent fund managers and financial magazines, all sharing the same root Web address.

It is possible that these financial umbrella sites will fade away or evolve into something else, as services on the Internet become more specialized (in a similar way that radio and TV transmissions become more targeted). Also, it is now easier for companies to create their own Web sites and the usefulness of a common URL diminishes as addresses and location become increasingly transparent to the user.

Finding
information

After the first few days on the Internet, of looking at cool sites, stumbling across a Hungarian homage to Hendrix, and possibly even finding the CNN Web site, the time comes to do something serious. The immediate problem encountered is how to find anything. Fortunately, the best guides to the Internet are, as yet, free and on the Net itself.

When looking for information, there are broadly two different types of service that can be used:

■ **directories:** human-written catalogues of selected sites
■ **search engines:** programs that automatically search for keywords.

These are described in some detail below, and a summary at the end of this chapter offers guidelines for how to find specific information.

DIRECTORIES

Internet directories are attempts to classify services on the Net into certain categories. The top general categories may have headings such as Art, Business, Computers, and then below these will be a tree-like structure of sub-categories (thus Business might divide into Markets and Investment, which might further sub-divide into Currencies, Futures and Options etc.). Using these directories is quite simple and you find information in a method similar to any book or travel guide: by identifying the broad area you are interested in and then focusing on more specific topics.

One of the first of these directories to become established was Yahoo. Other directories have subsequently appeared, the majority of which have the apparently added advantage of 'objectively reviewing' sites and frequently assigning a rating for quality. A list of the major directories is given in Table 2.38.

■ **TABLE 2.38 General Internet directories**

Internet directory	location
A2Z (Lycos)	http://a2z.lycos.com/
Excite NetDirectory	http://www.excite.com/
GNN Select (Webcrawler)	http://www.webcrawler.com
InfoSeek Select	http://guide.infoseek.com/
Magellan	http://www.mckinley.com/
Point	http://www.pointcom.com/
Yahoo	http://www.yahoo.com/

If you were looking for a mutual fund site at one of the rating directories in this table, there might be a Business and Economics category to choose at the top level, and below this perhaps a Mutual Funds category, where there would be reviews of the selected sites, and a rating score.

However, there are a couple of problems here:

■ **Directory organization**: in practice it can be difficult to find some subjects, as the general world of finance does not necessarily fit into any neat classification system (for example, *risk management* can be an awkward topic to categorize). Further, the classification systems used by different directories are not consistent, hence ill-defined terms such as *markets, investment, finance or economics* tend to become woolly category headings for a random collection of sites.

■ **Objectivity**: it is difficult to know on what basis ratings of particular sites are assigned, and a reviewer's idea of 'coolness', may not coincide with what investors find useful.

Hence, these directories may serve a purpose for the complete Internet neophyte, or when exploring areas other than finance, but they offer little to an investor after an initial introductory period.

■ Yahoo

An exception to the above dismissal of directories must be made for Yahoo. Its database of sites is relatively small (at the time of writing it had indexed roughly 500 000 sites, compared to the 50 million URLs indexed by Excite), but its categorization is reasonably accurate, and its international coverage broader than the other directories.

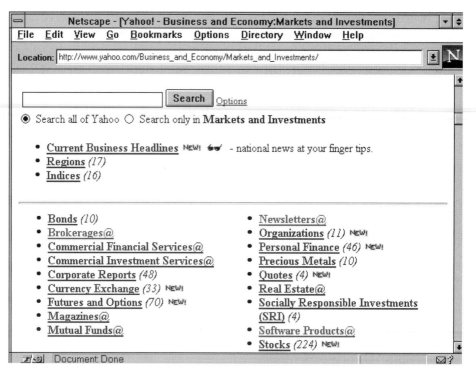

■ FIG 2.120 Yahoo Internet directory: Markets and Investments section

For each site in its database Yahoo includes information on the site name, the URL and a short description of the service – *as provided by the service provider itself.* As such, it is no use for looking for obscure references likely to be buried in Web pages, but if you are looking for a corporate entity's Web site (e.g. Deutsche Bank) or a well-defined category (e.g. German banks) then Yahoo is a good place to start looking. In addition, the coverage of general computing and Internet matters is very good, so that if, for example, you are looking for information on:

■ a demographic survey of the Internet

■ how to set up a Web site and register a Domain Name

■ the latest information about Internet security

■ information about Java,

the 'Computers & Internet' category of Yahoo should be the place to start.

Although Yahoo has a keyword input, this should not be confused with the powerful search engine keyword searches explained later. Yahoo's keyword search simply acts as an index to its directory.

In some ways, Yahoo is becoming more an Internet brand machine than a mere directory, and as such the directory and the company itself act as a convenient touchstone for what is happening with the Internet. An interesting example is to examine the number of references in some of Yahoo's finance categories (*see* Table 2.39).

■ TABLE 2.39 **The change in WWW references in selected Yahoo categories over 20 weeks in the middle of 1996**

Yahoo Section Name	URLs listed 10 Mar 96	URLs listed 26 Jul 96	Increase (%)
Bonds	7	10	43
Currency Exchange	21	33	57
Futures and Options	50	70	40
Personal Finance	31	46	48
Stocks	126	224	78

The table shows that over a 20-week period in the middle of 1996, the number of Web sites listed, for example, under the heading, 'Stocks', rose from 126 to 224 (an increase of 78 per cent). While Yahoo is not an exact mirror of the Internet, the figures above are probably a fair representation of general Internet development in these categories. (Ignoring the fact that the most misleading of forecasts can be produced by straight-line extrapolation from limited data, it is amusing to calculate that if the growth rate continued as in the table, in two years there would be more stock-related Internet services than there are stocks listed on the NYSE.)

Specialized finance directories

Almost all financial Web sites have a page or so of links to other related sites. Unfortunately, the vast majority of these are rather dismal affairs. They are frequently created in the first place as 'me-too' efforts with no particular aim; the URLs are copied from another page, with one or two new ones added, and then the list is not updated and is left to rot like a cabbage patch – a trap for the unwary surfer. (The cycle continues when this page is in turn itself copied and reproduced on a new Web site.) Indications that links pages are not updated include the presence of links to the MIT Experimental Stock Server (now moved to the StockMaster site) or the GNN Koblas Currency Converter (the financial Internet equivalent of the old video table tennis game). These are link viruses that spread ceaselessly – every time one page is updated, two new sites appear and copy an old set of links.

Another problem is that few of these links pages are well organized, with the worst being just a huge list of URLs added in chronological order (a 60K byte URL pile-up on the information highway). One can admire the dedication required of the page compiler, but also wonder at the folly of pursuing such a meaningless activity.

▓ Dept of Finance, Ohio State University

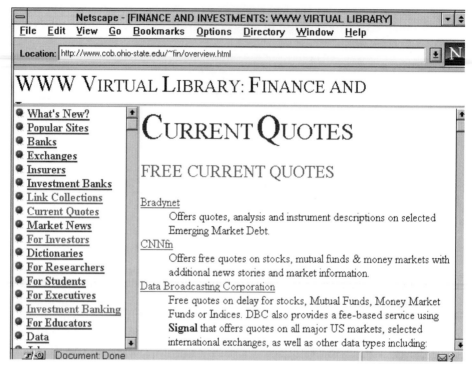

▓ FIG 2.121 Dept of Finance, Ohio State University

However, there are some links pages that have had some thought applied to them. First and foremost is the Virtual Library of Finance and Investments at the Department of Finance, Ohio State University. This is one of the superior sites on the Internet, where, beyond the expected links to banks, exchanges and market news sources, there are also very good sections for researchers and sources of financial data. This book generally avoids hip phrases like 'check it out', or 'bookmark this', but if you are going to bookmark just one site – this should be it.

Besides the Ohio University site, other good pages with financial links are ranked in Figure 2.122.

Top ten financial pages of links

1　Virtual Library of Finance and Investments – (Dept of Finance, Ohio State University)
　http://www.cob.ohio-state.edu/~fin/overview.html

2　Institute of Finance and Banking – (University of Göttingen)
　http://www.wiso.gwdg.de/ifbg/ifbghome.html

3　Investment SIG
　http://cpcug.org/user/invest/

4　Wall Street Directory
　http://www.wsdinc.com/

5　The Treasury Management Pages
　http://www.mcs.com/~tryhardz/tmp.html

6　Findex
　http://www.findex.com/

7　Gibbons Burke's Wahoo
　http://www.io.com/~gibbonsb/wahoo.html

8　invest-o-rama!
　http://www.investorama.com/

9　NETworth
　http://networth.galt.com/www/home/insider/insider.html

10　IFCI Financial Yellow Pages
　http://Finance.Wat.ch/YellowPages/

■ FIG 2.122

SEARCH ENGINES

Although search engines and directories commonly appear at the same sites, they are completely different. Where the latter have actual people who visit, categorize and rate Web sites, search engines are almost completely computerized.

The difference between directories and search engines can be crudely compared to that between tourist guides and atlases: if you were looking for the address of the Hotel Bristol in Paris or a list of good beaches in Thailand, you would use a guidebook, whereas if you wanted to know if there was a town in the world called Parsnip, an atlas (with index) would be more useful. (However, this parallel collapses fairly quickly on closer inspection: Internet search engines are far more powerful than atlases, while tourist guides are far superior to any Internet directory.)

A search engine has two components:

■ **Spiders (or robots)**: programs that automatically visit Web sites. They will record what information is on that page, and then possibly follow a link onto another page and record that, etc. These spiders can be continually roaming the Web visiting new, and updating old, sites.

▓ **Database**: the information found and recorded by the spiders (comprising URLs and text from Web pages) is stored in a database.

When somebody uses a search engine, their search request can be dealt with quickly as all the information is readily available in the one database. So, a search engine is a software program that allows very detailed searches of the whole Web. If the word, 'regoondling' exists anywhere on the Internet, it is likely that one of the more powerful search engines would be able to find it, and return the location.

A couple of characteristics of search engines that can be useful to know are:

▓ **Updating delay**: obviously due to the size of the Internet, it is not possible to revisit sites frequently to update them, and for many Web pages this does not matter. However, for certain sites (particularly news sites that may be changing every day), the search engines will not carry up-to-date references. Further, some sites are password-protected for subscription-only users, and the search engines may not be able to reference these. It would certainly be useful to have one search program with an up-to-the-minute index of the latest articles from the *WSJ*, *FT*, CNN and other news services. Perhaps in the future special (subscription) services will offer this; for the moment, the best that can be done is to individually search each site using the proprietary search tools on the site itself.

▓ **Written-on-the-fly pages**: evidently the search engines can only index pages that exist, but not all do – or rather, some are just temporary. For example, the home page for the World Bank is on a computer with the address as www.worldbank.org and the page itself is probably a file called something like index.html. This page (or file) sits on that computer and waits for people to look at it. However, some pages are only created when a specific request is made to the server. An example of this would be the MarketGuide service on the Data Broadcasting Web site. This service provides summary information on US companies, where the user inputs a ticker symbol and is then given the summary page. But the page comes straight from a computer database, and was written as a Web page on-the-fly – it did not exist before the request was made. Hence, search engines would have difficulty indexing these types of pages.

▓ **Restricted access**: some Web sites specifically prevent search engines from accessing their site and indexing their pages.

With knowledge of the above, one can see that although search engines are very powerful, they will not in all cases return the best information possible.

The major target for Internet searching is the World Wide Web, but there are also programs that search for messages on Usenet, and look for e-mail addresses. The rest of this chapter investigates search engines for the WWW and Usenet (for e-mail addresses *see* 'Electronic mail', page 22).

World Wide Web

There are quite a few different search engines, with new ones (such as HotBot) appearing all the time. This section concentrates on investigating six of the major search engines, to try to discover what their respective strengths are, and how to choose which one to use.

The following six characteristics are examined:

1 size of the database (i.e. the number of Web pages that are indexed)
2 how often the database is updated
3 flexibility of input search criteria
4 output summary information
5 how the output URLs are ordered
6 search engine response time (i.e. its speed).

Although the specific findings here will become out of date, the framework for comparison should remain valid for some time, and allow continual updating of the results.

1 Database size

A simple test was carried out to investigate the size of the different search engine databases. For this test, various finance-related keywords were input to each search engine and the number of documents found recorded. The results are presented in Table 2.40.

A few notes on the test procedures:

- All the words were input in **lower case** (thereby catching all occurrences of the word, regardless of the upper/lower case combination within the word as it appears on the Web page).

- Words were chosen in an effort to test specifically **finance-related terms**, hence, in general, only finance-related pages were found. This helps to give an indication of the size of the 'financial Internet'. (An interesting side note here is that although the financial world is frequently held to be jargon-ridden, there are actually few words that are unique to that world – for example, *bonds*, *futures* and *options* all have other meanings outside finance, *eurodollar* will also include the car hire company, *quanto* is an Italian word, etc. Many esoteric terms do exist, but these are usually combinations of ordinary words, for example, *implied volatility* or *convertible bond*.) For this reason, J.P. Morgan's term 'RiskMetrics' is very well suited for a test of this sort. As a fabricated term, all occurrences of it are likely to be exactly the intended meaning. Further, the word appears enough times – and, importantly, on a range of different sites – to make it statistically interesting. Similarly, any other completely fabricated word (e.g. invesco) is useful for this test.

- Only **single words** were input to avoid any confusion between the treatment of multiple words by different search engines.

▨ For each test word, an average of the numbers of URLs found for all the search engines was calculated. Each search engine was then assigned a rating relative to that average. For example, the six search engines found an average of 1495 URLs for the word *bundesbank*; Alta Vista (having found 2000) is therefore assigned a rating of 134, and Lycos (which found 89) is assigned a rating of 34. To increase the sample size, another eight words – *equities, eurobond, ftse, futop, garch, liffe, nyse, nzfoe* – were analysed in a similar way. Each search engine therefore had 18 individual ratings: one for each word tested. An overall **average rating** was then assigned to each search engine, being the simple average of all the 18 individual ratings.

▨ Alta Vista only returns an approximate number of documents found for each search, so this is why all its figures in the table are rounded.

▨ TABLE 2.40 **Comparison of search engines: number of documents found in keyword searches**

Keyword	AltaVista	Excite	Infoseek	Lycos	Open-Text	Web-Crawler
finance	400 000	651 872	35 529	71 542	52 665	14 843
economics	300 000	536 844	52 112	68 752	41 751	9160
soros	8000	9180	418	1395	662	179
bundesbank	2000	6052	89	513	264	50
invesco	1000	2168	162	336	118	141
riskmetrics	600	874	63	207	100	44
euroyen	200	350	19	52	31	10
swaption	40	96	14	14	7	5
hibor	32	49	0	7	6	1
krugerrand	2	10	1	1	1	1
Average Rating	175	308	36	42	28	11
URLs catalogued (m)	30	50	4	50	1.5	0.5

Source for URLs catalogued: Calafia Consulting

The test highlighted the following points:

▨ **Alta Vista** and **Excite** were ahead by a very wide margin in the number of documents they found. They were so far ahead, in fact, that their performance tends to skew the rankings of the others. For example, WebCrawler could prove perfectly satisfactory in many searches, but the ranking of 11 suggests it would not be worth using.

- Excite found 651 872 Web documents that contained the word *finance*. Considering that when this test was done, there were approximately 50 million Web pages, this implies that over **one in every 100 Web pages contains the word *finance***. This is not impossible, but it does seem extraordinarily high, particularly when you realize how few finance-related pages actually contain the word *finance* at all. (Just look at some of the larger sites, such as the CBOT to confirm this.) If one conservatively assumes that one in five finance pages actually contains the word itself, this puts the total size of the financial Internet at 3.2 million pages, or some 6.5 per cent of the total World Wide Web. (Alternatively, perhaps all those music Web pages of the X Generation contain song lyrics about getting jobs and financial planning?)

- An odd feature of Excite was that occasionally it gave **different results** for the same search request; this characteristic was not noticed with any of the other engines.

- Besides the surprising result that there were so few references for *krugerrand*, the four single URLs found by the four engines were all different.

- The final row of the table includes estimations from an external source of each engine's size (i.e. number of URLs indexed). Despite the crude nature of this test, it is interesting to observe that there is a rough **correlation between the average ratings and this total number of URLs catalogued**. The major exception to this is for Lycos, which suggests that either the URLs-catalogued estimation is wrong, or the index/search procedure of Lycos is not very efficient.

Although both the size of the Web and the search engines' capabilities will change dramatically, Table 2.40 suggests a very simple test that can be conducted at any time to assess the current situation.

2 Frequency of database update

As many Web pages change frequently, it is useful for search engines to revisit all pages regularly and re-index them. However, this is evidently a large task (think how slow some pages are to download, then imagine visiting a few million of them), and it is difficult to assess how up to date individual search databases are. With new Web pages appearing continually, there is likely to be a greater emphasis on indexing these new pages, rather than updating old ones.

It has been suggested that the (perhaps deliberate) advantage of the smaller databases, such as WebCrawler, is that they are more up to date by being able to frequently revisit their smaller universe of pages covered. But there is little hard evidence to support this.

3 Flexibility of input search criteria

Table 2.41 summarizes the advanced search techniques offered by each search engine.

■ TABLE 2.41 Search techniques available from the search engines

Search feature	Alta Vista	Excite	Infoseek	Lycos	Open-Text	Web-Crawler
Use of +/-	yes	yes	yes	no	no	no
Boolean	yes	yes	no	yes	yes	yes
Truncation	*	no	no	stemming	no	no
Adjacency	" "	no	" "	no	yes	" "
Proximity	NEAR (10)	no	[ ] (100)	no	NEAR (80)	NEAR (x)
Specify search fields	yes	no	no	no	yes	no
Bookmark	yes	yes	yes	yes	no	no

As can be seen, each search engine offers slightly different searching facilities, and the respective help pages should be referred to for understanding the usage by each engine, as they will not all necessarily use the techniques in the same fashion.

Explanation of the table:

- **Use of +/- :** terms that must be present in the documents are pre-fixed with a '+', while terms that must not appear are pre-fixed with a '-'. For example, +oat -agriculture might be an attempt to find references to the French Government bond and not the cereal.

- **Boolean:** a set of terms can be used to control the conjunction of the keywords (typically these are: AND, OR, NOT). For example, takeover AND nasdaq will only return references where both terms are present; while Microsoft OR msft, will find documents containing either, or both, Microsoft or its ticker symbol. NOT will preclude words from appearing. These Boolean operators can be combined: for example, takeover AND (Microsoft OR msft). It may be preferable generally to use '+/-', as they are easier to understand with less ambiguity. For example, Oracle NOT prophesy is, in most cases, syntactically wrong and should be Oracle AND NOT prophesy; but is probably easier as +Oracle -prophesy. However, the precise syntax used in each case may differ between engines, so this must be checked.

- **Truncation:** this offers the facility to search for all words with the same stem. For example, speculat* will find speculation and speculating. These wild characters (e.g. '*') can usually only be placed at the end of a word, and not the beginning. Lycos automatically searches for all 'stem-similar' words.

- **Adjacency:** inverted commas are frequently used to keep words together. For example, "Dow Jones" will only find documents where the phrase Dow Jones appears. If Dow Jones was input without the inverted commas, then all documents would be found where either the word Dow or Jones appeared somewhere. Further, if Dow AND Jones were used, then this would just find documents where *both* the words appeared – but not necessarily together.

- **Proximity**: an example above had the search enquiry: takeover AND Microsoft, in an attempt perhaps to find any documents associating Microsoft with takeovers. However, such a search will find documents where the words *takeover* and *microsoft* appear anywhere – not necessarily relevant to each other at all. For example, it might find a news brief where story number one covers a takeover involving Sony, and story number nine has news of the resignation of Bill Gates. Some search engines offer the very useful facility of finding documents where words appear close to each other. For example, Alta Vista, OpenText and WebCrawler use the NEAR operator, and inputting, takeover NEAR Microsoft to Alta Vista will find all documents where the two words appear within ten places of each other. WebCrawler has the unique superior facility of determining exactly the proximity range, thus a WebCrawler search on Paul NEAR/4 Cabot, would find occurrences of Paul Cabot, Paul C. Cabot or Cabot, Paul C.

- **Specify search fields**: all search engines will search for keywords in the body of text on Web pages. In addition, Alta Vista and OpenText offer the potential to search on other fields (e.g. the page title, or the URL). For example, with either engine it is possible to search for Web pages where *Goldman Sachs* appears in the page title (in Netscape the page title appears in the blue bar at the top of the window). Alta Vista's search criteria in this area are very advanced and also allow searches specifically on: anchor, applet, host, image, and link.

- **Bookmark**: it is possible to save some search requests as bookmarks, to save having to re-input common search requests. For example, one might build a fairly complex request for Alta Vista such as:

  ("Morgan Stanley" NEAR IPO) AND NOT Netscape

to find all mentions of Morgan Stanley associated with IPOs, but where Netscape is not mentioned. The browser will send this request to Alta Vista in the following form:

```
http://www.altavista.digital.com/cgi-
bin/query?pg=aq&what=web&fmt=.&q=%28%22Morgan+Sta
nley%22+NEAR+IPO%29+AND+NOT+Netscape&r=&d0=&d1=
```

This may look rather convoluted at first, but a closer look quickly reveals the gist of what is going on (helped once you realize that many Internet protocols do not like transmitting spaces between characters, so these are sometimes replaced by a '+' character which is stripped out later on). When the above type of script appears in the browser location window (after a search enquiry), it indicates that this search can be bookmarked for later use, thereby avoiding having to retype the search criteria. (For more information on this, *see* 'WWW Portfolio Monitors', page 296.)

Here are a few other general notes on structuring input criteria that are valid for most search engines:

■ **Implied OR**: if disjointed words are input, for example, Exxon Repsol ELF, in one search request, then the Boolean operator OR will be implied. In other words, this will have the same effect as inputting, Exxon OR Repsol OR ELF.

■ **Capitalization**: upper case characters in the search criteria will only find similar in documents, whereas lower case characters will find occurrences of both upper and lower case. For example, an input of NASDAQ will only find occurrences of *NASDAQ*, but an input of nasdaq will find nasdaq, *NASDAQ*, *Nasdaq*, *NasdaQ* etc.

■ **Natural language**: some search engines boast an ability to accept search requests formulated in ordinary language. For example, some engines might have an attempt at:

I am looking for info about Cisco and if it has any connection with British Telecom

However, natural language processing as used by search engines is still a fairly crude science, and it is likely that the above would be processed simply by stripping out the small conjunctions and similar. Therefore it is far easier and simpler to take five minutes to read the Help file explaining the structured language of searches, and input the above as:

Cisco AND "British Telecom".

■ 4 Output summary information

Following the processing of a search request, search engines will display a summary of the documents found matching the criteria. Table 2.42 summarizes this information.

■ **TABLE 2.42 Comparison of output search result information**

Feature	Alta Vista	Excite	Infoseek	Lycos	OpenText	WebCrawler
Matching score	no	yes	yes	yes	yes	yes
Extract	2-3 first lines	3-5 lines [see note]	3-5 first lines	2-3 first lines	3-4 first lines	3-4 lines [see note]
File size	yes	no	yes	yes	yes	no
Date catalogued	yes	no	no	no	no	no

Notes on Table 2.42

- **Matching score**: the majority of search engines assign a rating to each document found according to 'how closely it satisfies the search criteria'. However, it is not always easy to discover the methodology of how these ratings are calculated (they appear to involve some arbitrary collection of factors such as the number of times the keyword appears in the document, or the 'popularity' of the page). Of the five search engines analysed with this feature (*see* Table 2.42), when tested with the word kruggerrand, they returned the following scores for the first URL: 72 per cent, 67 per cent, 100 per cent, 1.84 per cent. But all the documents found equally contained the keyword, correctly spelt, and occurring about once – so the variation in scores is confusing. As such, there seems little purpose in displaying these matching scores with their mysterious computation (is anyone going to decide they will only accept references with a score over x per cent?) and a mere ordering of results is the only sensible use (*see* 'Ranking of the URLs', below). These scores would seem to be an example of supply-side 'we have the technology to calculate some obscure statistical measure that will be meaningless to just about everybody' data, rather than demand-driven information.

- **Extract**: for every URL found, the search engines can display an extract from the document, to give a small taste of the style and content of the whole page. (Some of the engines refer to this extract misleadingly as a 'summary'.) The majority of engines simply quote the first two or three lines of the whole page (see table). In practice this is rarely useful, as the top few lines frequently just have some menu hyperlinks. Excite appears to make a valiant effort at displaying something useful, attempting to identify a major cluster of the keywords in the document and quoting a passage from the surrounding text. It is not always possible to determine the strange ways of these search engines, and WebCrawler's behaviour certainly defies rational analysis, as its approach seems to be to quote three or four lines from the document completely at random (which, incidentally, may on occasion prove more useful than the information in the first few lines). In the coming years there will be many great technological advances, but the ability to usefully summarize a document in two or three lines will not be one of them; if bandwidth is a problem it is probably better to use the facility of Alta Vista or WebCrawler to dispense with the extracts and just have a condensed URL list displayed.

- **File size**: an indication of the size of the referenced document can obviously prove quite useful before deciding to view the page.

- **Date catalogued**: this indicates when the file was last visited by the search engine and added to the database. This can be very useful and it is unfortunate that this feature is not more common.

▨ 5 Ranking of the URLs

If 2000 references are found for a keyword search, the method in which they are ordered for display is important. Or rather, the ordering of the first ten or 20 is very important (as this is quite often all that people look at). Knowing this, designers of Web sites sometimes employ bizarre methods to improve the 'placing' of their pages in search rankings, the most common of which is to pepper the pages with what they consider will be common keywords. For example, you can sometimes see words such as 'stocks, shares, equities, investment' repeated many times over, at the top or very bottom of a Web page. There is much discussion in certain areas of the Internet by Web designers of the mechanisms of specific search engines and how it is possible to improve the indexing and position of their pages; and some of the tactics discussed would seem to stray beyond the margins of acceptable behaviour.

At present, following a search, the found URLs are listed according to some matching score calculation, but there are problems with these calculations (*see* note above).

OpenText attracted some controversy when it actually started selling keywords, so that 'ownership' of such a word ensures that one's Web page will be at the top of the list of URLs following a search on that word. For example, a company might 'buy' the word finance, which would result in its Web page being listed first when any user searched on that keyword. This type of activity naturally raises all sorts of concerns; but an argument *can* be made that if a company is willing to pay for a word to attract people, then it is demonstrating a certain level of commitment (and sharpness) that warrants its pages being looked at as much as anyone else's. And, after all, as yet these search engines are free, and no one is paying OpenText to provide a completely consistent, scientific service. But this possible selling of keywords raises further questions about the applicability of keyword matching scores.

Also, the uncertainty around the matching scores makes it difficult to assess the effectiveness of the ranking for each search engine. A number of tests were carried out on search engines involving the following keyword phrases:

> *pharmaceutical stock recommendation*
> *interest rate swap*
> *new oil discovery*
> *stock hedging techniques*
> *implied volatility*
> *stock market guide*
> *german interest rates*
> *fixed interest swiss franc*
> *India investment*

but no patterns were identified in the return results and the ordering appeared random and inconsistent between all the engines. An example of the top ten URLs found for the keywords *implied volatility* is shown in Table 2.43.

▪ TABLE 2.43 Top ten ranking by search engines on the keywords: *implied volatility*

Alta Vista	*Excite*	*Infoseek*
1. Excel Q&A – Implied Volatility www.financialcad.com	1. Implied Volatility www.wat.ch	1. Futures Options Analysis www.flash.net
2. Option Implied Volatility Demo www.eight.com	2. Implied Volatility www.wat.ch	2. Volatility www.familyinternet.com
3. The Market News Service r www.economeister.com	3. Implied Volatility www.wat.ch	3. Stewart-Peterson Options hnet.west-bend.wi.us
4. The Market News Service www.economeister.com	4. Implied Volatility www.wat.ch	4. Stewart-Peterson Options hnet.west-bend.wi.us
5. Vol. 58 No. 75 Wednesday, http://fr.counterpoint.com	5. Implied Volatility www.wat.ch	5. The OEX Advantage www.cboe.com
6. Quoteline GmbH – http://194.209.35.99	6. Implied Volatility www.wat.ch	6. Stewart-Peterson Options hnet.west-bend.wi.us
7. Stewart Mayhew's Vita haas.berkeley.edu	7. Implied Volatility www.wat.ch	7. Stewart-Peterson Options hnet.west-bend.wi.us
8. Learn About Financial www.e-analytics.com	8. TVol Snapshots www.camtech.com.au	8. The Option Strategist : www.dirs.com
9. The Market News Service www.economeister.com	9. Options Function Reference www.financialcad.com	9. Recovering Probabilistic gopher.ag.uiuc.edu
10. OPTION SIMULATOR sports.dbc.com	10. TermFinance – historical www.wat.ch	10. Advances in Pacific Basin bos.business.uab.edu

Lycos	*OpenText*	*WebCrawler*
1. Implied volatility rates for una.hh.lib.umich.edu	1. TermFinance – implied finance.wat.ch	1. Risk Explorer: Risk www.riskex.com
2. A source of unbiased implied netec.mcc.ac.uk	2. Volatility/The section below, www.familyinternet.com	2. Portfolio Insurance www.telebyte.nl
3. Historical Volatility and www.e-analytics.com	3. Options Function Reference www.financialcad.com	3. INVESCO Equity Products www.invesco.com
4. Implied Volatility Patterns in klaatu.oit.umass.edu	4. Stewart-Peterson Options hnet.west-bend.wi.us	4. INVESCO Equity Products www.invesco.com
5. OPTION MASTER® www.options-inc.com	5. FEN ABSTRACTS 11/4/95 munshi.sonoma.edu	5. Numaweb : derivatives : www.numa.com
6. Volatility Handbook, The www.wsdinc.com	6. Fuqua Finance Working Paper www.duke.edu	6. LIFFE – Education – Core www.liffe.com
7. Implied Volatilities for FX www.ubs.ch	7. Bradford Raschke MTA www.mta-usa.org	7. PMpublishing's Professional www.pmpublishing.com
8. Implied Volatilities for FX www.ubs.ch	8. Options & Alternatives www.wsdinc.com	8. PMpublishing's Professional www.pmpublishing.com
9. The Option Strategist : stocks www.dirs.com	9. ECON999/Weimin Wang qed.econ.queensu.ca	9. PMpublishing's Professional www.pmpublishing.com
10. Implied Binomial Trees mitpress.mit.edu	10. Fuqua Finance Working www.duke.edu	10. Kingswood Associates – www.snapshot.com

Considering the simplicity of the search, one would assume that all the search engines would find the same URLs for *implied volatility* (within the constraints of the size of their databases), and would then assign an appropriate matching score to each URL. It is therefore surprising that there is so little correlation between any of the top ten results, suggesting that the scoring techniques employed are wildly different.

The first test on *pharmaceutical stock recommendation*, was interesting, where, considering just the first URL found in each case, only Excite, Infoseek and OpenText actually found pages with information on pharmaceutical *stocks* – the others found general articles on pharmaceutical companies. And, although OpenText does not perform well in some of the other tests, it was the only one that actually did discover a Web page with a specific recommendation for a pharmaceutical stock.

■ 6 Speed

During all the tests carried out, no discernible difference was noticed for the response time between any of the search engines. In all cases, results were returned in about one to two seconds. This is quite impressive when you consider the heavy use of these search engines – Infoseek alone claims to process seven million searches a day, reaching 175 searches per second at peak times.

It is possible that a difference in speed might exist if one was using some kind of batch program to feed a large number of requests to the engines automatically, but in this case the great determinants of speed would more likely be the time of the day and general Internet traffic conditions, not the internal processing speed of the search engine computer.

■ Alta Vista

On balance, the search engine of choice must be Alta Vista, as it combines the largest database with flexibility of search language. Tables 2.44 and 2.45 summarize the search language for Alta Vista and provide some examples of its use.

■ TABLE 2.44 Alta Vista: search language for simple queries

Operator	Use	Example	Finds documents...
+	document must include this word	+Vietnam,	with the word *Vietnam*
-	document must not include word	-war	without the word *war* appearing anywhere
*	truncation	broker*	with *broker, brokers, broker's,* or *brokering etc.*
'...'	whole phrases	'efficient market theory'	with exactly the phrase, *efficient market theory*

FIG 2.123 Alta Vista, the premier search engine for the WWW

TABLE 2.45 Alta Vista: search language for advanced queries

Operator	Use	Example	Finds documents where...
AND	Boolean and	Iomega AND newsgroup	the words *Iomega* and *newsgroup* both appear
OR	Boolean or (non-exclusive)	gearing OR leverage	either *gearing* or *leverage* appear (non-exclusive)
NEAR	words are close together	earnings NEAR disappointing	the word *earnings* appears within ten words of *disappointing*
NOT	Boolean not	NOT technology	the word *technology* does not appear
(...)	combines search features	Cray AND (Hitachi OR Fujitsu)	*Cray* appears and so does either *Hitachi* or *Fujitsu*

Few of the examples in these tables would yield interesting results on their own; the real power of the search engines lies in the more complex searches made possible by combining different elements of the search language. The amazing scope of search engines such as Excite and Alta Vista makes it actually quite easy to find information, however obscure; but the problem is not in finding the information, but rather filtering out all the other irrelevant information found. Therefore, nearly all the more complex search enquiries are concerned with narrowing searches rather than broadening their scope to find hidden data nuggets in secluded Web pages.

The examples in Figure 2.124 include some ideas on combining search elements to narrow the criteria using Alta Vista's search language.
(Note: the other search engines all use languages similar to that of Alta Vista – see the above section on *Flexibility of input search criteria* for a comparison – but their respective use of the operators will not necessarily be identical. So, check the search engine Help file first).

Examples of Alta Vista simple queries

■ +"stock market guide" -beginner*
  Finds documents with the whole phrase *stock market guide* appearing, but the word *beginner* or *beginner's* does not appear.

■ +derivatives -warrants -"convertible bonds"
  Finds documents with *derivatives* appearing but no mention of *warrants* or *convertible bonds*.

■ +Philippines +stock* +investment* -"golf courses"
  Finds documents with *Philippines*, *stock* or *stocks* and *investment* or *investments* appearing, but no mention of *golf courses*.

Examples of Alta Vista advanced queries

■ (DuPont OR DD) AND Dow AND NOT "Dow Jones"
  Finds documents with a mention of *Dupont* or its ticker symbol, and *Dow* (for the chemical company) but excludes documents with the word Dow appearing as *Dow Jones*.

■ losses NEAR (Daiwa OR Sumitomo)
  Finds documents with the word losses appearing within ten words of either *Daiwa* or *Sumitomo*.

■ (profits NEAR warning) AND (Compuserve OR csrv OR "America Online" OR amer)
  Finds documents with either *CompuServe* or *America Online* mentioned (or their ticker symbols) and where also the word *profits* appears near *warning*.

■ Internet AND ("securities transactions" NEAR regulation)
  Finds documents with the word *Internet* and where also *securities transactions* appears close to *regulation*.

■ (recommendation NEAR Pepsi) AND NOT (recommendation NEAR buy)
  Finds documents with the word *recommendation* near the word *Pepsi*, but excludes all occurrences where the word *buy* is close to the word *recommendation*.

■ merger AND NOT (merger NEAR denied) AND ("Credit Suisse" OR CS) AND ("Union Bank of Switzerland" OR UBS)
  Finds documents with the word *merger* appearing (but not close to *denied*) and also mention of the two Swiss banks.

■ FIG 2.124

Usenet

As with the World Wide Web, it is possible to search for keywords occurring in the newsgroups of Usenet. The search engines offering this facility are: Alta Vista, Excite, Infoseek, and DejaNews. The latter is a specialized service for searching only Usenet and is probably the best.

DejaNews

FIG 2.125 DejaNews: the premier search engine for newsgroups

Like the Web search engines, use of DejaNews is fairly straightforward: input a number of keywords and the program will search its historic database of messages that have been sent to newsgroups, and return any matches found. One small difference is that if more than one keyword is input with spaces between them, DejaNews assumes an implied Boolean AND operator (i.e. it looks for messages that contain all the words). By contrast, Web search engines usually assume an implied Boolean OR operator between words.

More complex searches with DejaNews are also possible and these are summarized in Table 2.46.

■ **TABLE 2.46 Reference guide for DejaNews search language**

Operator	Use	Example	to find messages with....
&	Boolean AND	unemployment & Japan	both *unemployment* and *Japan*
|	Boolean OR (non-exclusive)	aluminum | aluminium	either the American or English spelling of the metal
&!	Boolean AND NOT	bonds &! government	*bonds*, but not *government*
^x	NEAR x number characters	sell ^8 toshiba	the words *sell* and *toshiba* are within eight characters of each other
'...'	whole phrases	'strong buy recommendation'	exactly the phrase – *strong buy recommendation*
*	wildcard	equit*	*equity, equities* etc.
(...)	combines search features	undervalued & (shares | stocks)	*undervalued, shares* or *stocks*
{...}	truncation	{trad trading}	*trade, trader, traders, trading* etc.
~a	author search	~a wclinton@white*	an author with e-mail address beginning wclinton@white
~s	subject search	~s (ICI & losses)	ICI and losses in the subject heading
~g	specify newsgroups	~ g misc.invest*	Only appearing in newsgroups with root name misc.invest
~dc	specify message date	~dc 1996/10/30	Sent on 30 October 1996

One can see that the principle in many of these operators is similar to that used by the Web search engines, and, like them, the operators can be combined into increasingly complex queries.

A useful feature with DejaNews is the context searches; these restrict the search to some subset of all the messages (a subset defined by: author, subject heading, newsgroup or date). For example, a straight search on the word *Pepsi* will produce a set of messages from newsgroups such as: alt.teens, alt.tv.commercials, alt.consumers etc., which may well produce interesting anecdotal information on the drinks corporation. However, if one is more directly interested in discussion about Pepsi stock, then it can be a good idea to restrict the search to just the investment-related newsgroups. Hence, an input criteria of:

~g misc.invest* & Pepsi

will restrict the search to newsgroups with names beginning misc.invest, and will thus just produce messages from groups such as, misc.invest, misc.invest.funds or misc.invest.stocks.

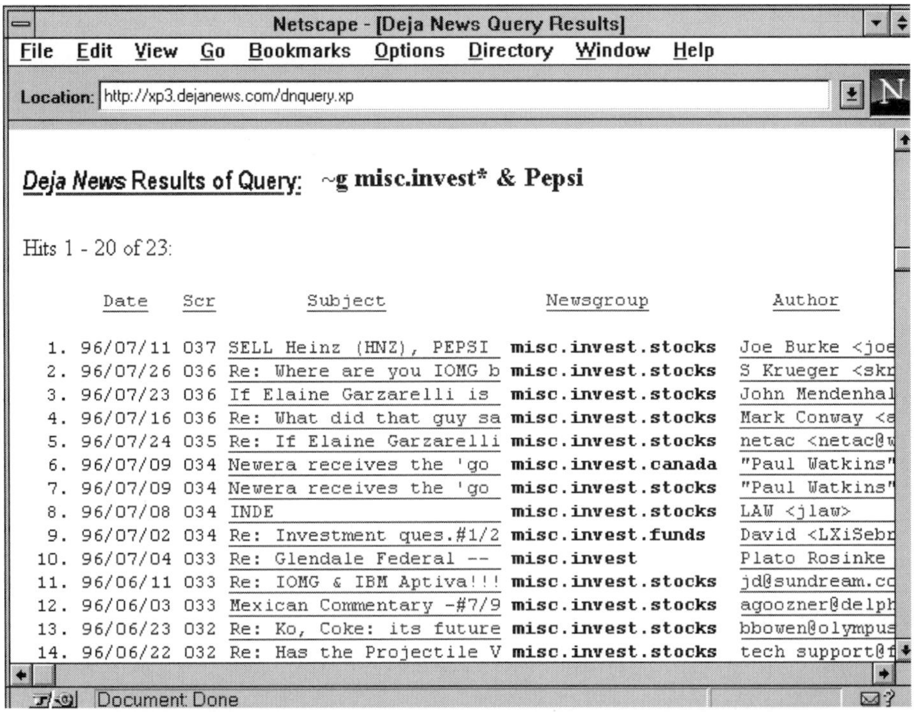

```
┌─────────────────────────────────────────────────────────────────────┐
│ ─        Netscape - [Deja News Query Results]            ▼ │ ◆ │
│ File  Edit  View  Go  Bookmarks  Options  Directory  Window  Help      │
├─────────────────────────────────────────────────────────────────────┤
│ Location: http://xp3.dejanews.com/dnquery.xp              ▣  N        │
├─────────────────────────────────────────────────────────────────────┤
│                                                                    ▲  │
│ Deja News Results of Query:  ~g misc.invest* & Pepsi                  │
│                                                                       │
│ Hits 1 - 20 of 23:                                                    │
│                                                                       │
│      Date    Scr      Subject            Newsgroup          Author    │
│                                                                       │
│  1. 96/07/11 037 SELL Heinz (HNZ), PEPSI misc.invest.stocks Joe Burke <joe│
│  2. 96/07/26 036 Re: Where are you IOMG b misc.invest.stocks S Krueger <skr│
│  3. 96/07/23 036 If Elaine Garzarelli is  misc.invest.stocks John Mendenhal│
│  4. 96/07/16 036 Re: What did that guy sa misc.invest.stocks Mark Conway <a│
│  5. 96/07/24 035 Re: If Elaine Garzarelli misc.invest.stocks netac <netac@w│
│  6. 96/07/09 034 Newera receives the 'go  misc.invest.canada "Paul Watkins"│
│  7. 96/07/09 034 Newera receives the 'go  misc.invest.stocks "Paul Watkins"│
│  8. 96/07/08 034 INDE                     misc.invest.stocks LAW <jlaw>    │
│  9. 96/07/02 034 Re: Investment ques.#1/2 misc.invest.funds  David <LXiSebr│
│ 10. 96/07/04 033 Re: Glendale Federal --  misc.invest       Plato Rosinke  │
│ 11. 96/06/11 033 Re: IOMG & IBM Aptiva!!! misc.invest.stocks jd@sundream.cc │
│ 12. 96/06/03 033 Mexican Commentary -#7/9 misc.invest.stocks agoozner@delph │
│ 13. 96/06/23 032 Re: Ko, Coke: its future misc.invest.stocks bbowen@olympus │
│ 14. 96/06/22 032 Re: Has the Projectile V misc.invest.stocks tech support@f▼│
│ ◄                                                                  ►  │
├─────────────────────────────────────────────────────────────────────┤
│ �277▼| Document: Done                                        ☑?       │
└─────────────────────────────────────────────────────────────────────┘
```

FIG 2.126 DejaNews: results of searching for 'Pepsi' in investment newsgroups

When returning the results of a search, DejaNews displays a list of all relevant messages with date, subject heading, newsgroup and author. Clicking on the subject heading will retrieve the message found, with the ability to read the other messages in the thread. (As such, DejaNews can be used as a type of proto-newsreader for newsgroups.) It is also possible to click on the author name and view a profile of all messages sent to newsgroups from that e-mail address.

Summary

When looking for information on the Internet there is no single method to use; each search should be assessed according to the type of data being looked for.

Here are a few general guidelines.

▨ If you are completely **new to the Internet**, and just want a general look around to see what is available, then have a look at the University of Ohio site (and perhaps some of the other specialist financial directories listed above: *see* page 265).

▨ If looking for a **corporate entity's** home page (e.g. Morgan Stanley) or, for example, a **list of investment banks** try Yahoo first. (In the case of Morgan

■ TABLE 2.47 Major Internet search engines

Search engine	URL	WWW	Usenet
Alta Vista	http://altavista.digital.com	yes	yes
DejaNews	http://www.dejanews.com	no	yes
Excite	http://www.excite.com/	yes	yes
InfoSeek	http://guide.infoseek.com	yes	yes
Lycos	http://www.lycos.com/	yes	no
OpenText	http://www.opentext.com/	yes	no
WebCrawler	http://www.webcrawler.com/	yes	no
Metasearch engines			
search.com	http;//www.search.com	yes	
MetaCrawler	http://www.metacrawler.com	yes	
Savvysearch	http://guaraldi.cs.colostate.edu:2000/	yes	

Stanley, Yahoo returns two references – both being the MS site – whereas Alta Vista returns 7000).

■ At the other end of the spectrum, if you are looking for something **very obscure** (something for which there might be just a handful of references on the Web), then Excite and Alta Vista are the search engines to use.

■ Finally, if you are looking for some information that doesn't fit into the above two categories, then any of the six search engines listed here could potentially be useful. The real choice will be in balance between size of database and flexibility of search language, and broadly, Alta Vista scores highest. However, search engines are optimized for certain types of search.

Reference – searching for information

http://www.netskills.ac.uk/resources/searching/ – Searching for Information on the Internet (Netskills at Newcastle University)

http://calafia.com/webmasters/whatsnew.htm – Webmaster's Guide (Calafia Consulting)

Books:
Finding It On The Internet, Paul Gilster [John Wiley & Sons]

Web Search Strategies, Bryan Pfaffenberger [MIS Press, 1996]

■ FIG 2.127

The general summary for the search engines must be that they all do a good job, but they have different strengths and it does pay to learn how to use each one. There are a few Web sites, Metasearch engines, that act as a front-end to the search engines listed here (and others), and can present queries to many different engines at one time. This may sound a good idea, but as mentioned above, it is rarely difficult to find information. The problem is in eliminating the irrelevant data, and for this it is better to use the powerful search language of one specific search engine to narrow the search, rather than a more general search on many engines.

Cyberscams

The Internet is a very fertile ground for scams. However, despite the alarmist announcements from regulators, nearly all of these scams are extremely crude, and can be spotted very easily. Three vital things to remember:

- **Common sense**: don't leave home without it. Both the investment and computer worlds are rife with jargon, but that doesn't mean that either is beyond sensible analysis. Never invest in something you don't understand, and if in doubt, try explaining an Internet-derived investment idea to someone else.

- **If something sounds too good to be true, it probably is**: at any one time around the world, there are hundreds of banks and investment institutions employing thousands of people whose sole job it is to spot investment opportunities. The smaller investor can compete on an increasingly level playing field when it comes to taking a view on a stock or market. But, it is most unlikely that a genuine 'low-risk', 'high-return', 'guaranteed', 'arbitrage' opportunity would get within a million miles of the public Internet, before being spotted by professional investors.

- **Don't assume that anything appearing on the Internet has been checked or edited by anybody.**

Setting up a financial Web site

Just because something appears on a Web site does not make it trustworthy. Anybody can set up a Web site, it takes very little time or money, they can call the site anything they like, and the only current restriction on its address is whether the address has previously been reserved or not. An Internet novice and budding shares tipster, wanting to set up their own financial boutique on the Web, could learn everything they needed to know in a few minutes' perusal of the sites listed in Yahoo. For example, the three-point guide to an instant global financial Internet service:

1 Contact a Web provider to register a Domain Name (e.g. prudential-fidelity.com). (Approximate cost: US$150, time: one week)

2 Arrange to rent hard disk space from Web provider for the WWW pages. (Approximate cost : US$20 per month, time: two days)

3 Take a little time to learn HTML programming to write some Web pages, using a freeware/shareware HTML editing program (time: five days).

So, for a cost of less than US$200 and taking less than two weeks, a financial Web site can be created. If you wanted the page to be quickly in the top ten per cent of all financial Web sites, you could further:

- Visit CNN, *WSJ Online* and Point.com to see what they considered were the foremost financial Web sites, look at these pages, freely borrow ideas, download their HTML pages and amend.

- Create instant content by 'borrowing' pages from other sites (e.g. their page of links, glossaries).

- Simultaneously register on multiple Internet directories and search engines by using a service like Submit-It.

- Send a few messages to the financial newsgroups announcing the new financial service.

- Visit other financial Web sites and request a link to your site in exchange for adding them to your prestigious list of links.

And with very little effort, in a short time, the new financial Web site will be up and running. As far as viewers are concerned, they would not know if this page had been created by a 16-year-old pizza parlour assistant, an ex-Daiwa Bank trader, or a Taiwanese monk.

Obviously, the actions listed above are not condoned, but neither are they sententiously condemned (apart from, perhaps, the crass copying of other Web sites' pages). The point is not to canvass for unenforceable laws to stop unscrupulous people, but to illustrate to Internet users why care should be taken in reading anything on the Net.

Examples of scams

The North American Securities Administrators Association (NASAA) identified the following types of cyberscam:

- **Manipulation of obscure, thinly-traded stocks**: this includes all the messages sent to online forums and Web pages with stock tips. Don't forget that what might look like several people writing messages to a forum may turn out to be just one. A popular target for this is Canadian gold, silver and diamond mining stocks.

■ **Misconduct by phoney or unlicensed brokers/investment advisers.**

■ **Undisclosed interests of promoters.**

■ **Promotion of 'exotic' scams**: this covers the range from investments that are just bad and should be filtered out by any sensible research (e.g. wireless cable television 'build-out' schemes, ostrich farming, cyber casinos and viatical settlements), to the blatant and crude (e.g. pyramid schemes, Ponzi scams).

The SEC describes on its pages the five enforcement actions it has so far taken against financial cyberscams. These include:

■ an ethanol plant in the Dominican Republic (offering a 50 per cent return)

■ investments offering annual returns in excess of 200 per cent, backed by 'Prime Bank Guarantees'

■ worldwide telephone lottery (which raised over US$3 million)

■ two Costa Rican enterprises (where a bank guaranteed principle and a 15 per cent annual return)

■ an eel farm.

And, one assumes, they were the subject of enforcement actions because they had enjoyed some success in raising money. Sad, but true.

Indicators of possible fraud

A few possible signs to watch out for:

■ words or phrases like 'guaranteed return', 'limited offer', 'high yielding', 'inside information', 'no risk'

■ unsolicited e-mail messages with investment recommendations

■ the e-mail signature not matching the message header information (*see* 'Identifying the source of Web pages or e-mail' below)

■ overseas investment.

General advice to protect yourself

This may be a rather cynical approach, but it doesn't hurt to be sceptical of everything seen on the Internet. Other advice would include:

■ Download a copy of the Web page, or message (from the browser menu bar: File | Save as), and print a hard copy. Make a note of the URL.

■ Try reviewing messages in the forums about the investment (use DejaNews to search the newsgroups). Think about sending a message to a forum, asking if anyone else knows anything about the investment.

■ Don't expect to get rich quick.

■ Don't assume that anybody, or any institution, is checking what is put on the Internet.

The SEC has additionally listed ten questions that should be asked about any investment seen on the Net (*see* Figure 2.128).

SEC ten questions to ask about any investment opportunity

1 Is the investment **registered with the** SEC and the state securities agency in the state where I live or is it subject to an exemption?
2 Is the person recommending this investment **registered with my state securities agency?** Is there a record of any complaints about this person?
3 How does this investment match my **investment objectives?**
4 Will you send me the **latest reports** that have been filed on this company?
5 What are the **costs** to buy, hold, and sell this investment? How easily can I sell?
6 Who is **managing the investment?** What experience do they have?
7 What is the **risk** that I could lose the money I invest?
8 What **return** can I expect on my money? When?
9 How **long has the company been in business?** Are they making money, and if so, how? What is their product or service? What other companies are in this business?
10 How can I get **more information** about this investment, such as audited financial statements?

FIG 2.128
Source: Securities and Exchange Commission (SEC)

Identifying the source of Web pages or e-mail

If you receive an e-mail message and you want to check where it came from:

- Analyse the message header information (the boring bit at the top of all Internet e-mail messages). (*See* 'Interpreting message headers', page 23.)
- Search DejaNews for any messages sent by the author to newsgroups.
- Use Alta Vista or Excite to see if the author's name appears in any Web page anywhere.

If trying to identify the owner of a Web site, and/or the registered owner of a Domain Name (e.g. prudential-fidelity.com):

- For .com Domains, try InterNIC (which looks after registering these names).
- For other Domains, it may be possible to track down the appropriate registration body through Yahoo, and search through its site. Some services exist that provide general search facilities over multiple high-level (i.e. country) Domain names, the best of which is Demon in the UK (**http://www.demon.net/external/ntools.html**).

Resources

Virtually all the useful resources in this area are based in the US. Most other regulators elsewhere are probably keeping their heads down, to see what happens there. However, the lead taken by the US will probably eventually be adopted in other countries, so the information here may well be globally relevant.

The prime reference source is the SEC. It seems quite excited by cyberscams and its coverage should grow accordingly.

References – Cyberscams

Securities and Exchange Commission (SEC) **http://www.sec.gov**
Commodity Futures Trading Commission (CFTC) **http://www.cftc.gov**
National Fraud Information Center (NFIC) **http://www.nfic-inter.net**
Federal Trade Commission **http://www.ftc.gov**
Consumer Information Catalog **http://www.pueblo.gsa.gov**

■ FIG 2.129

The eight-point plan
for online investing

Having provided a reasonably comprehensive directory of world financial sites, and explained some of the better services in detail in Chapter 5, this chapter aims to bring everything together, and demonstrate how all the parts are available on the Internet to form a coherent investment approach.

The eight-point plan for online investing

1 Idea generation
2 Identify investment vehicle
3 Current price and chart
4 Investment research
5 Economics background
6 Investment verification
7 Investment transaction
8 Portfolio monitoring

The role that the Internet can play in each stage is explained below.

It should be said that the very first stage would be **educational**, learning about investment, followed by analysis of one's own financial situation: future requirements, investment objectives and asset allocation. There are certainly bits and pieces on the Internet that can offer some help in these early stages,

but this is not really a strong part of the Net, and it offers no particular
advantage – as yet – over good books and a financial adviser in the flesh.

1 Idea generation

The Internet can play a very strong role in generating ideas for investment. Just
as discussions within an office or browsing through books in a library might
suggest particular investment targets or strategies, so can browsing through
forums or Web sites.

An obvious starting point is the news sites such as CNN*fn* or *WSJ Online*, then
all the news sites for the local domestic markets. Independent newsletters can
be good for giving ideas on specific stocks, while market reports may well
suggest an interesting development. In general, perhaps, the newsgroups are
not a good source here, as the signal-to-noise ratio is too low (unless you have
limitless time). However, the 'private' forums, on sites such as Silicon Investor,
or the Motley Fool, could be more rewarding. And just random 'surfing' can
turn up interesting topics; for example, Hoover's has a special section on major
business of the week (BizBuzz).

Example sources

▓ News: CNN*fn*, Bloomberg, *WSJ Online*, *FT Online*, AsiaOne, Economist
▓ Market reports: Briefing, DBC, Knight-Ridder at CNN*fn*
▓ Newsletters
▓ 'Private' forums: Silicon Investor, Motley Fool.

2 Identify investment vehicle

Having found an interesting idea or strategy, the next stage is to identify a
suitable investment vehicle. At its simplest this might just be a stock, or
perhaps an option. If interested in a wider theme or market sector, then a fund
may be more appropriate, or if looking at an overseas investment, the
possibilities would include investment directly in a foreign stock, in an ADR if
one exists, in a foreign market fund, or in a listed or OTC index option. Further,
if there is currency exposure, one might want to look at some strategy for
hedging the risk – perhaps with options or futures.

For all these possibilities, the Internet can prove helpful. The first place to start
would usually be with the local exchange. For example, if interested in
Thailand, the Thai stock exchange has a very comprehensive site, and from
here, one will often see useful links to other sources. Through an exchange one
can usually find a list of all securities that are listed, or at a futures exchange
one will find the contract specifications. If interested in a fund, then many
fund sites offer searches on keywords to find an appropriate list.

If there is no success with exchanges or particular sites, it might be worth trying
a general search using Alta Vista or Excite. For example, if you are interested in

an investment in Korea, try searching on 'Korea AND investment', or 'Korea AND investment AND fund'. (*See* 'Search engines', page 267.)

Example sources

■ Exchanges: stock, futures

■ Fund Web site.

3 Current price and chart

Once an investment vehicle has been identified, you need to know if it is possible to track its price easily, what the current price is, and hopefully view some charts of historic behaviour. If the investment is a US, or UK stock, option or fund there should be no problem – there are quite a few servers offering quotes and charts. Elsewhere, again the first place to look is the local exchange, as this will usually at least have end-of-day prices for all securities listed. The other very common source is news sites. For example, FT Online covers many markets, AsiaOne has quotes for Singapore and Malaysia, the Hongkong Star for Hong Kong and the Nikkei for Japan.

Example sources

■ Quote servers: DBC, Quote.com, ESI, TeleStock

■ Exchanges, stock, futures

■ News sites: FT.

4 Investment research

It is in this area that the Internet may well have the most to offer. However, as there are likely to be many possible sources here, the problem will be in identifying the most appropriate.

Assuming that you are interested in a particular company, there are the specialist research databases such as Hoover's, Zacks in the US or Hemmington Scott in the UK. Then you might want to check any news stories, by searching the archives of sites like *WSJ Online*, *FT Online*, CNN*fn*, or a local newspaper. Similarly, you can search the archives of the media relations sites like PR Newswire or Business Wire, or look up a newsletter covering the stock.

For certain stocks there may well be a focused Web site (such as Silicon Investor on technology stocks) offering information. It is also increasingly likely that the company will have a Web site itself, which may provide financial information. And, at this point, don't forget the power of the humble e-mail. Many companies are still in the honeymoon period with the Internet, and an e-mail question direct to the finance director may well get a response (in the near future, expect most companies to have automatic e-mail responders which will send replies customized to keywords in your original message).

If you want to be extremely thorough, search engines could be used to check for every mention of the company on any Web page, and DejaNews could be used to search for any mention in the newsgroups.

Example sources

- Company research/information: Hoover's, Zacks, Disclosure, Hemmington Scott
- News archives: CNN*fn*, *WSJ Online*, *FT Online*, Pathfinder, local newspapers
- Media relations: PR Newswire, Business Wire
- Focused investment site: Silicon Investor
- Company's own Web site
- Search engines: Alta Vista, Excite, DejaNews.

5 Economics background

You may wish to research the economics background to the investment. Internationally, the Internet scores highly here, with much economic and socio-political data available on government servers. The supra-national servers like the World Bank or the United Nations can also be useful, but it can be more a matter of pot luck with what data might be available. A good starting point when researching a new market is the CIA World Factbook.

Many banks and investment institutions publish a great range of economic reports and forecasts – in some cases it seems that the smaller the economy, the more active the economists.

Also there are interesting economic articles appearing in newspapers like the *FT Online* and *Economist*, which should usually have site search facilities.

Example sources

- Government statistics servers: CIA World Factbook
- Supra-national servers: World Bank, United Nations
- Banks: global investment and local banks: Morgan Stanley, Bankers Trust
- Newspapers: *Economist, WSJ Online, FT Online.*

6 Investment verification (scam check)

This is probably the most underdeveloped area of the Internet for investors at the moment – but expect this to change in the future. The best sites at the moment are all in the US (*see* 'Cyberscams', page 286), with good general advice, but not likely to be helpful on investment outside the US. Fairly soon there should be 'scams registers' (government and privately operated) where investors can check the probity of investments and intermediaries.

Currently, the best options are probably general Internet searches on the Web or newsgroups, to check for any comment on the investment or intermediary.

Example sources

- Government regulators: SEC, CFTC, TFC, NASD
- Private scam registers (not yet available)
- Search engines: Alta Vista, Excite, DejaNews.

7 Investment transaction

Having satisfied yourself with the research, the time will come to actually give the trade order. As yet, full online brokerages are only available in the US and the UK, but standard brokers in other markets may increasingly begin to accept e-mail orders. If you are looking for a suitable broker to transact the trade, the local exchange will usually have a list of members.

Example sources

- Online brokers: Lombard, E*Trade, CompuTEL, Sharelink.

8 Portfolio monitoring

After the trade, you will want a method of monitoring the price, the general market and any breaking news stories about the particular investment or market. Here again, the Internet can play a very strong role.

First, there are many quote servers to get prices ranging from real-time to end of day (the latter facility existing for most markets in the world now). In addition, many of these servers offer the facility to value portfolios, which can be very useful.

To keep abreast of breaking news, services like the newspapers, CNN*fn*, and Briefing can be scanned regularly – where their site search facilities can be put to good use. In addition, the search engines can be used to regularly monitor pertinent Web pages or messages in newsgroups. (For more information about automating this, *see* 'Create your own WWW portfolio monitor, below.)

The first news services on the Web were fairly crude, but there have been interesting developments in the customizing of news – and this is perfectly suited for monitoring a portfolio. So, there are quite a few services available that can channel specialized news; for example, PointCast or NewsPage. Other services will monitor all news wires and alert by e-mail any development in a specified key area.

Example sources

- Quote servers: DBC, PC Quote, Quote.com, NETworth, TeleStock

■ Newspapers: CNN*fn*, *WSJ Online*, *FT Online*, Briefing

■ Customized news services: PointCast, NewsPage.

Create your own WWW portfolio monitor

The files that comprise the World Wide Web (the ones displayed when using a browser like Netscape) are constructed using a language called HTML. This language is very flexible, and allows links to be made from one page to another (the link usually appearing as underlined blue text). Writing your own Web page is perfectly feasible, and in this page it would be possible to add links to those services you found most useful on the Internet. Of course, this exercise alone might not be very helpful, as most Web browsers have a bookmark facility to do this very thing.

However, with a little knowledge of HTML, it is possible to write pages that are far more complex and flexible than bookmarks. This section explains how to construct your own Web page, using HTML, that can be used to monitor information on the Internet relevant to your own particular portfolio.

The URL for the Knight-Ridder Asia Markets reports on CNN*fn* is:

http://cnnfn.com/markets/knight-ridder/asia.html

and if you visit the page and bookmark it, that is the address that will be recorded. If later you want to change the bookmark to the European reports instead, it is necessary to visit the CNN*fn* site, find the KR Europe page, bookmark it and delete the old Asia bookmark.

But it is also easy to create a Web page yourself, where the page contains the following HTML code:

```
<a href="http://cnnfn.com/markets/knight-
ridder/asia.html">Market Report</a>
```

When this page is viewed with a browser, the above code will appear as the two underlined words, 'Market Report', which when clicked on, will cause the browser to jump to the KR Asia markets page on CNN*fn*.

You might have thought that URLs were bad enough already, without complicating the matter further; but HTML is really very easy (it is nothing like as complex as a programming language), and it is not even necessary to fully understand what '<a href' might mean. For example, if you wanted to change the above link to the KR Europe reports page, after a little inspection you might guess that by changing the word 'asia' to 'europe' would achieve the desired effect. And you would be right.

Neat, you might say, but seems like a lot of effort to just save a few seconds over bookmarks – which seem to do a pretty good job otherwise. Take a look at the code below:

```
<a href="http://qs.secapl.com/cgi-bin/qs?tick=XON">XON Quote</a>
```

This is a little more daunting than the Knight-Ridder link above: first there is a question mark character that looks a little worrying, and then (if you are used to seeing a few URLs) there doesn't seem to be any proper '.html' page referenced here. However, you might notice the 'secapl' in there and guess that this has something to do with its quote service.

This code produces an underlined 'XON Quote', that when clicked on automatically retrieves the quote for Exxon from the Security APL quote server. (Incidentally, this technique is used by many public Web sites, whereby the site appears to offer stock quotes directly themselves, but in fact there are just hyperlinks – like the one above – to a proper quote server elsewhere.)

This code in your own Web page then has two advantages:

- Retrieving a quote becomes a **'one-click' procedure**, rather than arriving at the main page of a quote server and then navigating several levels of menu to reach the quotes page, only to then forget the symbol code.

- If you have constructed a fairly large personal Web page with many hyperlinks as above to different services, then it is a simple matter to simultaneously **change all the links if you want to follow a new stock**. For example, if you want to change from following Exxon [XON] to DuPont [DD], then by using the Edit | Replace facility in all text editors or word processors, all occurrences of 'XON' can be replaced with 'DD' in two seconds. Now that is more flexible than bookmarks.

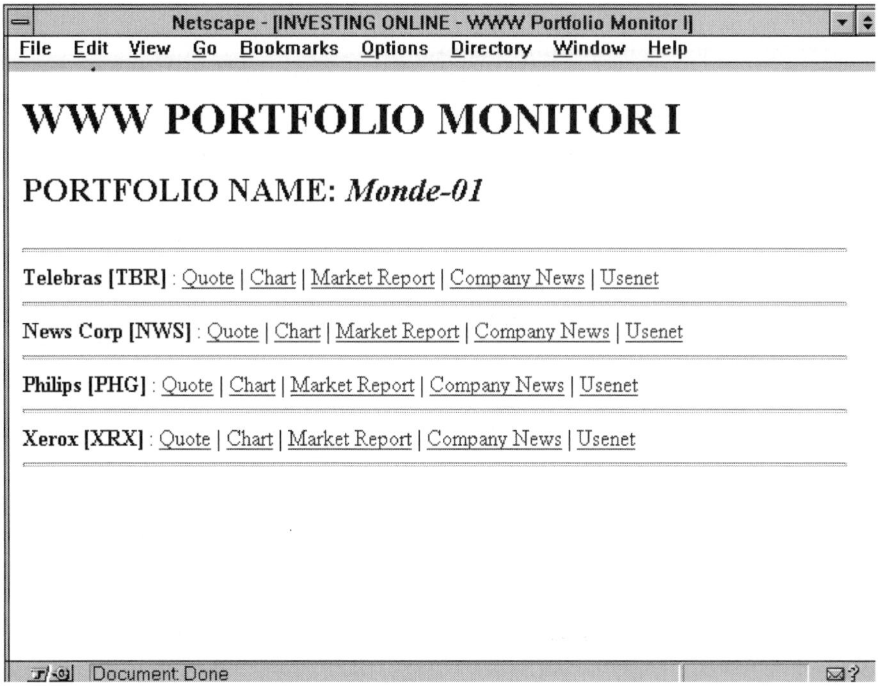

Netscape - [INVESTING ONLINE - WWW Portfolio Monitor I]	▼	◆

File   Edit   View   Go   Bookmarks   Options   Directory   Window   Help

WWW PORTFOLIO MONITOR I

PORTFOLIO NAME: *Monde-01*

Telebras [TBR] : Quote | Chart | Market Report | Company News | Usenet

---

News Corp [NWS] : Quote | Chart | Market Report | Company News | Usenet

---

Philips [PHG] : Quote | Chart | Market Report | Company News | Usenet

---

Xerox [XRX] : Quote | Chart | Market Report | Company News | Usenet

---

Document Done

■ **FIG 2.130 WWW Portfolio Monitor I**

Figure 2.130 displays a Web page that demonstrates some of the potential for creating your own Portfolio Monitor. The underlying HTML code for this page is Appendix M at the back of the book.

This Web page is designed to help an investor quickly find up-to-date information on four stocks that they are following: Telebras ADR (Mexico), News Corp ADR (Australia), Philips ADR (Netherlands) and Xerox (US). For each stock there are five links:

- **Quote**: the code underlying this is as given above (for XON), and when the word 'Quote' is clicked on, the latest quote for Telebras (in the first case) will be retrieved automatically from the Security APL service.

- **Chart**: this automatically calls the StockMaster service, and will immediately retrieve a chart of the stock.

- **Market Report**: this link jumps to the appropriate Knight-Ridder page for the domestic market. (For example, in the case of Telebras, the Americas index page will appear, from which the specific Brazil report can be selected.)

- **Company News**: this retrieves the latest news about the specific company from the Yahoo business database.

- **Usenet**: this link jumps to DejaNews (a Usenet search engine) and then automatically searches the newsgroups for any mention of the stock.

Obviously many stocks can be followed with such a system, which saves finding and navigating around sites and then remembering, and inputting manually, symbol codes. From just a few simple building blocks, some fairly complex pages can be built. For example, Figure 2.131 shows a more sophisticated version of the WWW Portfolio Monitor. (The underlying code for this page can be found in Appendix N – although just the first two stocks have been included as the code is similar for all.)

This page offers customized links to information on:

- **General Market**: in the box to the right of the title are some links to news services about the general market. The first is the Bloomberg summary of global equity, currency and commodity markets; then news bulletins from CNN and Reuters; then Bloomberg's digest of domestic headline news for the major markets, and finally the currencies ticker comment from Briefing.

- **Quotes**: this is similar to the previous page, and calls a quote directly from the DBC quote server.

- **Charts**: intraday charts from Lombard, and 100-day charts from NETworth. Hence, if you clicked on 'Intraday' for News Corp., a minute-by-minute chart would appear. It is possible to customize both Lombard and NETworth charts, so that, for example, in the case of the latter, the time period could be changed to 200 days, a 30-day moving average added or a chart comparing the ADRs of Telebras with Telefonica de Argentina always plotted.

```
┌─────────────────────────────────────────────────────────────────────────┐
│ ─        Netscape - [INVESTING ONLINE - WWW Portfolio Monitor II]   ▼ ▲  │
├─────────────────────────────────────────────────────────────────────────┤
│ File   Edit   View   Go   Bookmarks   Options   Directory   Window   Help │
├─────────────────────────────────────────────────────────────────────────┤
```

WWW PORTFOLIO MONITOR II	World market snapshot
	News: CNN | Reuters
	World newspaper headlines
PORTFOLIO NAME: *Monde-01*	FX ticker with comment

Company	Quotes	Charts	Markets	Company News	WWW / Usenet	Currencies
Telebras [TBR]	DBC	Intraday 100 Day	Knight-Ridder WSJ	Briefing | CNN FT | Yahoo	Alta Vista DejaNews	Bloomberg
News Corp [NWS]	DBC	Intraday 100 Day	Knight-Ridder WSJ	Briefing | CNN FT | Yahoo	Alta Vista DejaNews	INO chart
Philips [PHG]	DBC	Intraday 100 Day	Knight-Ridder WSJ	Briefing | CNN FT | Yahoo	Alta Vista DejaNews	INO chart
Xerox [XRX]	DBC	Intraday 100 Day	Knight-Ridder WSJ	Briefing | CNN FT | Yahoo	Alta Vista DejaNews	

```
│ 🖼 Document: Done                                              ✉? │
└─────────────────────────────────────────────────────────────────────────┘
```

▓ FIG 2.131 WWW Portfolio Monitor II

▓ **Markets**: this retrieves the reports from Knight-Ridder and further adds the excellent specific market reports from the *Wall Street Journal*.

▓ **Company News**: many news sites offer the facility to search their archives for keywords; these links call four such services (Briefing, CNN, the *Financial Times* and Yahoo), and inputs the keywords automatically. Each one of these sites works slightly differently and should be investigated individually. For example, Briefing usually includes mention of the stock code in reports, and this code can be used to search on. This is preferable to searching on the company name, as many names are not very specific. For example, the words 'News Corp' may pick up many articles that mention the two words separately, but have no relevance to the company. In this case, if possible, a search on the ticker code 'NWS' is likely to be more successful. CNN and the *FT* do not commonly mention ticker codes so the company name must be used as the keyword. The success of any searches will also largely depend on the efficiency of the respective search programs used by each site.

▓ **WWW/Usenet**: Alta Vista offers the facility to search all the Web for mentions of a word (i.e. the company name) appearing on Web pages created since a certain date. You can use this to see if any new pages have recently appeared with comments on a portfolio stock. Unfortunately, it seems that a specific 'From' date must be input to Alta Vista, rather than 'in the last *x* days', so this would have to be changed manually every now and then. The simple

Portfolio Monitor I page included a DejaNews search on the newsgroups for the company name. One problem you might encounter is that with a company name like Philips, this could return thousands of messages from people chatting about problems with their Philips vacuum cleaners. For the ultra conscientious fundamental stock analyst this 'client feedback' could prove interesting (and in the future may even prove quantifiable?), but the ordinary investor is probably more interested in gossip about the directors' dealings. Therefore, the link in this page limits the search to just the investment newsgroups (the misc.invest hierarchy), and further refines the keywords to look for either the company name or ticker symbol.

▧ **Currencies**: for the non-US stocks some currency information is included. For News Corp. and Philips, the link calls the INO Capital Markets server for latest quotes and charts for the Australian Dollar or Netherlands Guilder. The INO server does not carry this for the Brazilian Real, so the link calls the Bloomberg currency page for this.

Note that for some of these services (i.e. Lombard, *WSJ* and the *FT*), previous registration is required.

Concerning the WWW or Usenet searches, it could be possible to combine all the searches into one composite request, which would then allow a total portfolio search to be effected with just one click.

As mentioned above, a portfolio change can be carried out quite easily by using the find and replace feature of text editors. For example, if you wanted to replace Philips [PHG] with Alcatel [ALA] of France, then it is a matter of ten seconds to replace all occurrences in the page of Philips with Alcatel and PHG with ALA.

These pages are not necessarily meant to be used exactly as presented, but merely to give a demonstration of what is possible. No doubt services will change and the links in these pages will have to be adapted accordingly. There is not enough space here to go into too much detail about HTML, but a good source of further information are the links at Yahoo (follow the directory tree down – Computers and Internet I Software I Data Formats I HTML I Guides and Tutorials) or there are now plenty of books on HTML. As a rough starter to getting a Web page going, you might like to try the following steps:

1 **Copy the code** in the appendix using a text editor or dedicated Web editor. (A word processor *can* be used, but remember to always save the file in text format.)

2 **Save the file** into a work directory (such as c:\test) and call the file something like 'pm1-test.htm'.

3 Run the Web browser and **load the created HTML** page. For example, with Netscape, from the menu bar select File and then Open File – this will bring up the usual File dialog box.

4 If you are happy with the file, you can then **bookmark it**, to retrieve it easily in the future.

Investing *in* the Internet

It is difficult to open a newspaper today and not see something about the Internet. A two-year-old company with no history of earnings is valued at US$2 billion in the market; we are told that Bill Gates wakes up in the morning and thinks of browser market share; a company providing access to the Internet markets a 'lifestyles' image and makes headline news when its network stalls for a few hours; this book forecasts the convergence of investment and gambling; and your father has an e-mail address.

Obviously, something is happening, and, it looks like it is here to stay. So, if this is the next big thing, there should be some useful investments to ride the theme, shouldn't there? Perhaps another IBM or Intel, Microsoft or Lotus. Well, perhaps not.

At the end of 1995, Morgan Stanley produced an investment report about the Internet (available at its Web site and also published by HarperCollins). In this report, Morgan Stanley recommends an Internet portfolio consisting of Cisco [CSCO], Ascend [ASND], Cascade [CSCC], America Online [AMER], and Intuit [INTU]. While these are possibly fine companies, it is difficult not to feel a little dissatisfied with the selection. Who's Cascade? What are, 'high performance, multi-service wide area network switches'? Switches? Is that the best there is? Isn't there some proper hardware manufacturer somewhere that's going to put an Internet box of something in every Chinese household? If the Internet is the biggest thing since the PC explosion, are these really the new Intels and Microsofts?

But the mistake is to regard the Internet as a theme that can be played. In fact, this chapter shouldn't really exist at all; the Internet is not principally a new technology (like VCRs or CD players were) to be wrapped up and marketed to the public. It is more like a language that people all over the world adopt and start speaking. In such a case there are peripheral service companies that benefit, but the theme quickly becomes too broad and diverse to mean anything.

So, the uninspiring portfolio is not due to any fault with Morgan Stanley – the companies just aren't there. Or rather, there aren't listed stocks with an adequate market capitalization to be interesting to institutional investors. The MS report makes an interesting comment, that there are some 150 million PCs in the world but only seven per cent connected online. There is clearly tremendous potential for growth here, but not growth that will necessarily translate immediately into massive hardware sales (beyond a few modems). In other words, besides the Internet backbone, much of the infrastructure for Internet growth with the consumer is already in place.

The winners from the PC boom were largely big semiconductor, computer or software manufacturers, and large capital investment was required for entry to the industry. This time, however, the cycle of profitability is likely to be much shorter, and the companies exploiting this smaller and ephemeral. One can see already that the real winners in the Internet are not the large computer companies, but the smaller entrepreneurs, who set up the Netscapes and Yahoos (an interesting list of Internet-made millionaires is available on the Net – *see* URL at the end of this chapter). This is great for them, but makes it hard for the investor to get exposure to the action.

Not only is it difficult to find good companies to invest in here, it is even difficult to identify superior and sustainable technology or products. Hence, about all the investor has to fall back on is trying to identify good management. Neither Netscape nor Yahoo have sophisticated products, but they are interesting purely because their management has so far shown a greater acuity in anticipating Internet developments than the competition.

A few Internet themes are briefly described below.

Themes

■ **Hardware**: the majority of people do not need state-of-the-art equipment to connect to the Internet; and much of the hardware required for Internet connection (e.g. PCs) is already a commodity business with low margins. Further, as mentioned above, initial Internet growth will be driven by users who already have PCs (the major equipment required). Hence, it is necessary to look to the companies producing equipment for upgrading the general Internet backbone.

■ **Software**: the most difficult area in which to carve out a sustainable niche. Any new program can be reproduced by competitors, and at any moment, profitability (or even just survival) requires constant and rapid innovation.

■ **Content providers**: the only area looking in the long term likely to provide high(ish) margins – but, as yet, still awaiting further developments in electronic payments systems (e.g. micropayments).

Beyond these there will develop hundreds of other small niches encouraged by the Internet (although they may not offer any interesting investment opportunity). A slightly random selection of these would include:

■ **Human-computer interface**: on the one hand there is a tremendous amount of data available on the Internet, and on the other, there are people who want access to that data. Between them is a bottleneck – a kludgy interface comprising 100-year-old technology (cathode ray tubes and keyboards). In some small cases, the situation can be improved with voice recognition technology, but this is an intermediary stage before chips in the brain and other science fiction horrors.

■ **Cryptography**: an open network, such as the Internet, has many benefits, but cryptography techniques are essential to take the Net beyond a plaything.

■ **Delivery companies**: eventually, widespread online ordering of merchandise will be commonplace – but the non-digital products will still have to be physically delivered to consumers.

■ **Scanning technology**: the next few years will see a massive digitizing and transferral of information on paper to computer files.

■ **Adult training**: continuing adult education will be an important priority, and in many cases the perfect medium will be the Internet.

IPOs and M&A

The scale of recent IPO activity has not been seen since the PC industry flourished in the early 1980s (*see* Table 2.48), and the launching of companies like Netscape have become the stuff of legend. However, an interesting view on this is given by Morgan Stanley in its Internet report. It observes that of the 581 hi-tech companies that went public between 1980–94, by the end of this period 45 per cent were below their IPO price.

▣ TABLE 2.48 Hi-tech IPOs

Year	Proceeds (US$m)	No. Issues
1982	680	49
1983	4048	227
1984	784	93
1985	463	71
1986	2852	136
1987	1999	117
1988	774	51
1989	1051	64
1990	914	47
1991	3948	128
1992	6906	176
1993	4446	167
1994	3983	163
1995	8613	226
1996*	5493	79

* to 4 April 1996
Source: Securities Data Company

It can be seen in Table 2.49, that Morgan Stanley maintains a hefty lead in the ranking of investment banks with regard to IPO activity. However, this is due to a relatively small number of large deals. The Web sites of these banks can be useful sources for information about IPOs.

▣ TABLE 2.49 Hi-tech IPO managers January–28 June 1996

Manager	Proceeds (US$m)	Market share (%)	No. of issues
Morgan Stanley	3032	29	9
Alex, Brown & Sons	1140	11	19
Goldman, Sachs & Co.	792	7	7
Donaldson, Lufkin & Jenrette	700	6	8
Merrill Lynch & Co.	453	4	4
Hambrecht & Quist	444	4	12
Robertson Stephens	415	4	12
Salomon Brothers	313	3	4
Montgomery Securities	304	2	8
CS First Boston	261	2	3

Source: Securities Data Company

Although IPOs attract all the publicity, the primary activity in this sector is M&A – which is the main provider of cash to entrepreneurs. In 1995 there were 226 hi-tech IPOs, compared to 1052 private company transactions; which is fully in line with the average over the last eight years, where there have been five times more M&A than IPO transactions. This has ramifications, of course, for the stock investor, who would find it difficult to participate in this off-market activity. For the ordinary investor, the best solution would probably be venture capital funds.

With the Internet growing so quickly, companies found it impossible to develop market share and presence fast enough themselves, so strategic alliances became the order of the day. By the beginning of 1996 the pace of these new alliances was particularly frenetic, as can be illustrated in the collation of headline announcements in Figure 2.132.

Sample of technology corporate activity, January–March 1996

AT&T To Acquire Stake In Satellite TV Company; Netscape Cuts Deals With Verifone, AOL; GEnie Sold To Yovelle Renaissance; Cisco Will Acquire TGV Software; Bell & IBM Close To Deal In Canada; Microsoft & MCI Form Internet Alliance; IBM Buys Tivoli Systems; Visa, Mastercard Agree On Electronic Payment System; Netscape Agrees To Buy Insoft; Another Global Telecom Alliance; Approval For Disney Merger With Capital Cities/ABC; MCI And AT&T Talking Of An Alliance; Netscape, Silicon Graphics Team Up For 3-D; IBM Alliance With Italian Telecom; Apple Inks Deals With Adobe, Disney; Visa And Microsoft To Develop Home Banking System; Electronic Wallet From Oracle And Verifone; Silicon Graphics Planning To Buy Cray Research; Microsoft Wooing AOL; Netscape Nails Down Compuserve Deal, Microsoft Miffed; HP, Microsoft Team Up To Market PCs; AOL, AT&T, And Netscape Strike Deals; AOL Turns To Microsoft For Browser Software.

■ FIG 2.132

An intermediate climax, of sorts, for this activity was seen in the final few announcements, when AOL announced a deal with Netscape, and the very next day announced another deal with Netscape's competitor Microsoft (following a midnight call from Bill?).

Stocks

In *The Money Masters*, John Train lists 11 characteristics that Warren Buffet associates with 'wonderful businesses'. Among the 11 are:

- they have a good return on capital
- they are understandable
- they see their profits in cash
- their earnings are predictable.

180 Day Bar Chart for: $IIX

▩ **FIG 2.133 IIX Internet Index**
Source: DBC

It is probably safe to assume that there are few Internet stocks lurking in the Berkshire Hathaway portfolio.

This illustrates the difference between what might be called company investors and stock investors. The former (typified by Warren Buffet) analyse a company in-depth, take a long-term view, and are relatively unperturbed by short-term share price fluctuations. On the other hand, stock investors play the market, and try to judge what the share price will do. One of the commonest causes for confusion is when somebody thinks they are a company investor, but acts like a stock investor.

It is unlikely that company investors would find anything interesting in the Internet (and if they did, more than likely it would be illiquid, or not listed at all). For the stock investor, the Internet offers challenging volatility, and ample scope for discussions on support/resistance levels and notions of stock value.

There is a problem with identifying Internet-related companies, and what might be the general activities of such companies. If there is a consensus for the latter then it would divide as:

▩ **hardware**: infrastructure companies such as Cisco [CSCO] and Ascend [ASND]

▩ **software**: programs written for use on the Internet, such as Netscape [NSCP] or Macromedia [MACR]

▩ **service/content providers**: access providers or a company offering some service over the Internet, for example, America Online [AMER] or CNET [CNWK].

But it doesn't take long to realize that many companies don't fall neatly into these categories, and that fairly soon such a classification scheme will be unworkable.

A number of Internet indices have been formed to try to track overall performance here. (Five of these indices, with their constituents, are listed in Table 2.50). And, as can be seen, there is remarkably little agreement over what is an Internet stock.

The five Internet indices in the table are briefly described below.

1   Inter@ctive Week Internet Index [IIX], developed by AMEX and Inter@ctive Week (Ziff-Davies), options traded on the AMEX. (*See* Figure 2.133 for 180-day chart.)

2   ISDEX Internet Index: developed by iWORLD (Mecklermedia Corp.).

3   H&Q: Hambrecht & Quist Internet Index. (Note, on its Web page it still indicates H&R Block as being in the index. This is not included below, and this will most likely be replaced by CompuServe at some time.)

4   GSTI Internet Index (GIN); one of the seven Goldman Sachs Technology Indexes traded on the CBOE.

5   CBOE Internet Index [INX].

Note: contract specifications for the two options (trading on AMEX and CBOE) can be found in Appendix L.

■ TABLE 2.50 **Constituents of Internet indices**

Stock	IIX	ISDEX	H&Q	GSTI	CBOE
	1	2	3	4	5
3Com [COMS]	1		1		
Accent Software [ACNTF]		1			
Adobe [ADBE]	1		1		
America Online [AMER]	1		1	1	1
Ascend [ASND]	1		1	1	
Avid Technology [AVID]	1				
Bolt Beranek and Newman [BBN]	1		1		
Broadband Technologies [BBTK]	1		1		
C-Cube Microsystems [CUBE]	1				
Cabletron Sys Inc [CS]	1				
Camelot [CAML]			1		
Cascade [CSCC]	1		1	1	1
CheckFree Corp [CKFR]			1		
Cisco [CSCO]	1		1	1	1
CMG Information Services [CMGI]	1	1	1		

Stock	IIX	ISDEX	H&Q	GSTI	CBOE
	1	2	3	4	5
CNET [CNWK]		1			
Compression Labs [CLIX]	1				
CompuServe [CSRV]	1				1
CUC International [CU]	1		1		
CyberCash [CYCH]	1	1	1		
Dataware Technologies [DWTI]			1		
Excalibur Technologies [EXCA]			1		
Excite [XCIT]	1	1			
Forefront [FFGI]		1			
FTP Software [FTPS]	1	1	1		
Fulcrum Technologies [FULCF]			1		
Gandalf Technologies [GANDF]		1	1		
Global Village Communication [GVIL]			1		
Individual [INDV]		1	1		
Infoseek [SEEK]		1			
Intuit [INTU]	1		1		
Lycos [LCOS]		1			
M.A.I.D PLC [MAIDY]			1		
Macromedia [MACR]	1		1		
McAfee Assoc [MCAF]					1
Mecklermedia Corp [MECK]		1	1		
Metricom Inc [MCOM]	1				
Microtouch Sys Inc [MTSI]	1				
Mindspring [MSPG]		1			
Netcom Online Com. [NETC]	1	1	1		1
NetManage [NETM]	1	1	1		1
Netscape [NSCP]	1	1	1	1	1
Netstar [NTSR]	1				
Newbridge Networks [NN]	1				
Novell [NOVL]	1				
Open Market [OMKT]		1			
Open Text [OTEXF]		1	1		
Optical Data Sys [ODSI]	1				
Oracle [ORCL]					1
Picturetel Corp [PCTL]	1				
Premenos Technology [PRMO]	1		1		
PSINet Inc. [PSIX]		1	1		1
QUALCOMM [QCOM]	1				
Quarterdeck [QDEK]	1	1	1		

Stock	IIX	ISDEX	H&Q	GSTI	CBOE
	1	2	3	4	5
Raptor Systems [RAPT]	1	1	1		
Secure Computing [SCUR]	1		1		
Security Dynamics [SDTI]	1				1
Silicon Graphics [SGI]	1		1		1
Softquab Intl [SWEBF]			1		
Spyglass [SPYG]	1	1	1		1
Sterling Software [SSW]			1		
Stratacom [STRM]	1		1		
Sun Microsystems [SUNW]	1		1	1	1
Sunriver [SRVC]			1		
US Order [USOR]			1		
US Robotics [USRX]	1		1	1	
UUNet [UUNT]	1	1	1	1	
Verity [VRTY]			1		
VocalTec [VOCLF]	1	1	1		
Yahoo [YHOO]	1	1			1
TOTAL	44	25	45	8	15

Other Internet indices (not shown above) actually include companies like AT&T, Intel and Microsoft. Is Microsoft an Internet-related stock? The company itself would probably claim that it is; but if that is so, then where are the boundaries drawn? Already one can feel the Internet as a coherent market theme beginning to shimmer and disperse.

Appearing in four or more of the indices (in fact, Netscape is the only stock appearing in all of them) are:

- America Online [AMER]
- Cascade [CSCC]
- Cisco [CSCO]
- Netcom Online Com. [NETC]
- NetManage [NETM]
- Netscape [NSCP]
- Spyglass [SPYG]
- Sun Microsystems [SUNW]
- UUNet [UUNT]

And, if one had to identify a 'hard core' of Net stocks, it might as well be these.

UK stocks

Whereas the investor in the US market seems spoilt for choice, elsewhere, there is very little indeed. What at first might appear an Internet play, turns out to be a multimedia CD ROM software house with a Web page.

The UK has a few interesting companies (*see* Table 2.51) but was deprived of potentially one of the more attractive plays when Unipalm PIPEX was bought by UUNet.

▓ **TABLE 2.51 UK Internet-related stocks**

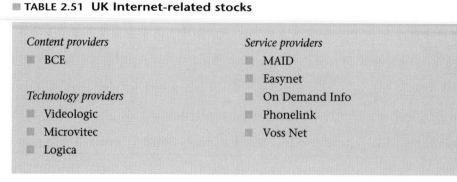

Content providers	Service providers
▓ BCE	▓ MAID
	▓ Easynet
Technology providers	▓ On Demand Info
▓ Videologic	▓ Phonelink
▓ Microvitec	▓ Voss Net
▓ Logica	

Source: Charles Stanley

Funds

Given the extra volatility of Internet stocks, and the frequently esoteric nature of the underlying business, investors may prefer to invest in a fund. This may also open up the opportunity to invest in venture capital projects.

▓ US

Of course, there is no shortage of general technology funds, but few, as yet, specialize in purely the Internet. Such Internet funds are likely to be classified in the 'Speciality-Technology' sector. A search in NETworth reveals the following four funds that are the most likely candidates:

▓ EV Traditional Information Age [ETIAX]

▓ EV Marathon Information Age [EMIAX]

▓ Robertson Stephens Information Age [RSIFX]

▓ Seligman Communications and Information Fund [SLMCX].

In addition, Prudential Securities on its Web site has information about a unit investment trust – the Van Kampen American Capital Internet Trust.

The most interesting development was the announcement in mid 1996 of the launch of the WWW Internet Fund. This is a fund that invests in the Internet (no big surprise there), but information about the fund, and application for purchase, is only available *via* the Internet. Consequently, its Web site **http://www.Internetfund.com** has:

▓ fund description

▓ fund performance

- details of online trading
- Internet news
- information about WWW Advisors Inc.
- a prospectus.

International

Elsewhere, it is still a little early for funds to be set up – a fact not unrelated to there being few Internet stocks to invest in outside the US. In the UK one might keep an eye on Interactive Investor and TrustNet for any developments.

Options

Of the five Internet indices listed above, two have index options trading:

- Inter@ctive Week Internet Index on AMEX
- CBOE Internet Index.

Contract specification for these can be found in Appendix L.

Strategies

Due to the problems of identifying good Internet-related stocks with sustainable earnings (or any earnings at all), and the volatility in the sector, it may be more interesting to look at arbitrage opportunities that may occur.

One could study the behaviour of the indices and analyse how often they are updated. The sector is changing so quickly that the difference in updating between two indices could offer an opportunity. For example, when a new Internet company starts trading, is it added immediately to the index, and if so at what price?

If an investor preferred the hardware component of an Internet index, the hardware stocks could be bought and the index sold. Or an Internet index could be shorted against a technology index.

A word of warning on shorting Internet stocks. It is a common cry among investors that the Internet is over-valued, and in similar situations particularly high-flying stocks might be considered candidates for shorting. But, in other sectors, the rationale for this is that the stock is over-valued, and that after some time, a critical mass of investors will see sense, appreciate the over-valuation and act accordingly. But, despite everything one might read, 'value' is not well-defined, and there is even less common agreement as to its meaning in the Internet sector. In fact, valuation for stock investors (not company investors) is a relative, rather than absolute term, and the problem with the Internet is that there is very little to relate it to. Morgan Stanley in its report accepts that the Net 'breaks rules of Wall St analysis'.

Resources

Not surprisingly, some of the best sites on the Internet are concerned with the Internet itself and investment in the Internet. A couple of these, Silicon Investor and Red Herring, are described below.

▨ Silicon Investor

▨ FIG 2.134 **Silicon Investor: comparison groups – communications**

Silicon Investor provides quotes and charts, company information and links, and discussion groups on hi-tech stocks. This is one of the most important investment sites on the Internet, and an indication of its popularity is given by the fact that the site receives 40 000 messages and 20 million hits every month.

About 400 hi-tech companies are followed on the site, and for each one there is a page with:

▨ quotes

▨ charts: 100-day, 100-week, 60-month

▨ comparison groups: comparisons with other companies active in similar areas

▨ StockTalk: online discussions about the company

- company links: links to the company's own Web site and pages with financial information and press releases
- company description: from the 10-K
- competition: from the 10-K
- recent quarter results.

The strong features here are the comparisons of similar stocks and the interactive discussions – probably the most popular part of the whole site. For a flavour of the discussions, *see* Figure 2.135.

Examples of comments (August 1996) about Cascade [CSCC] on Silicon Investor

...Also at a projected 5yr growth of 47% and next years estimate of around $1 per share the stock should not be trading at more than $47 in order for the growth ratio to be at least 1. Notice how it hit that level and bounced last

...This stock seems to have severe resistance at 64

...OK... broke through serious resistance. If this stock opens up in the morning, watch out for the 'short' squeeze up to ~72. But, with such low volume, it seems too much like a false rally

...Ouch... The 'shorts' are getting it in the shorts!

...cabot says buy at 4:00 pm est

...Cabot also manipulated Iomega and Presstek, among others. He has lost credibility.

...Watch out, it will be down to 50's soon.

...I could dig that, – I shorted the gap.

...All this short sentiment is interesting. I guess you didn't get hit bad enough at the end of July. I'm LONG on their ability to translate Frame Relay success into ATM success for large customers. This one is and will continue to be a monster

...PE is just too high ... Too risky to hold this stock.

...ASND and SHIVA and USRX are falling. Why not CSCC. SOLD and will buy again in the 40's or 30's.

FIG 2.135
Source: Silicon Investor

The discussion is made more interesting by the appreciation that the participants might be anybody: an individual investor from Omaha, a physicist in Moscow, an employee of Cascade or a broker in Korea. The comments can easily be dismissed as rambling chat. But these are early days yet, and as these discussion groups grow, it will be strange to realize that the market actually has a voice and can be read, and that in fact this voice *is* the market.

This Web site is interesting for many reasons, partly because of the useful information on hi-tech stocks, but more importantly as an example of a Web site that is really exploring the possibilities of the new medium, and not just trying to extend the presence of a product from another medium (e.g. paper magazines).

■ Red Herring

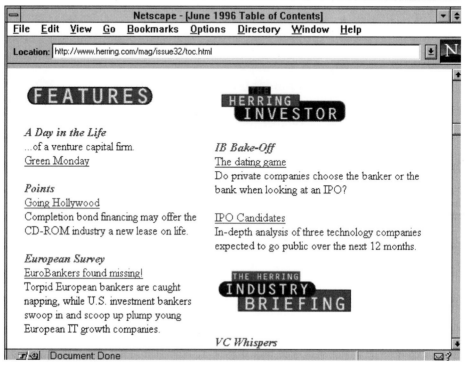

■ FIG 2.136 **Red Herring Magazine: June 1996 contents**

Red Herring also looks at technology (and entertainment) companies, but unlike Silicon Investor, it is more focused on corporate, rather than stock market, activity. Hence, it can be a useful source for information on IPOs and M&A activity. The Herring is also a monthly magazine, and the Web site provides information about the current issue, and, more usefully, an archive of full previous issues (from July 1994). The magazines usually feature interviews with industry players (e.g. Steve Case of AOL), company profiles (e.g. Quote.com) and analysis of industry trends (e.g. multiplayer online gaming).

Also on the site:

■ an index and ordering facility for **independent specialized reports** (e.g. ATM, California Technology Stock Letter, Electronic Gaming News, High Tech Hotsheet & High Tech Hotwire, Internet Business Report, and Semiconductor Industry Business Survey)

■ **company profiles**: mainly descriptive, but more detailed than those found, for example, in the Hoover's free database

■ a useful **links directory** of, among others, investment banks, law firms and venture capital firms.

Useful Web sites

URLs for Web sites that may prove useful when researching investments in the Internet are given below.

Technology stock information

■ Briefing – **http://www.briefing.com**

■ Silicon Investor – **http://www.techstocks.com**

■ Red Herring – **http://www.herring.com/**

■ TechInvestor (CMP) – **http://techweb.cmp.com/investor/**

■ iWORLD (Mecklermedia) – **http://netday.iworld.com/stocks/index.shtml**

■ NewsPage – **http://www.newspage.com/**

Internet Indices and stock quotes

■ Hambrecht & Quist Internet Index – **http://www.hamquist.com/research/stats/indices/internet.html**

■ Interactive Week (ZDNet) – **http://www.hydra.com/interactive_week.html**

■ iWORLD (Meckler-M) – **http://fast.quote.com/groups/isdex.html**

■ Virgil StockCenter – **http://www.stockcenter.com/**

Technology news

■ Computer News Daily – **http://computernewsdaily.com**

■ Upside – **http://www.upside.com/**

■ Yahoo – **http://www.yahoo.com/headlines/compute/**

■ Bloomberg – **http://www.bloomberg.com/**

■ CNN – **http://cnnfn.com/**

■ Nando – **http://www.nando.net/nt/info/**

■ USAToday – **http://www.usatoday.com/**

■ TechWeb (CMP) – **http://techweb.cmp.com/**

■ ZDNet – **http://www.zdnet.com/**

■ CNET – **http://www.cnet.com/Content/News/**

■ Techwatch@Pathfinder – **http://pathfinder.com/**

■ PR NewsWire – **http://www.prnewswire.com/**

■ San Jose Mercury – **http://www.sjmercury.com/news/scitech/**

■ Infotech Weekly – **http://www.infotech.co.nz/current/**

■ Japan Nikkei – **http://www.nikkei.co.jp/enews/TNKS/High-Tech.html**

Technology sites with search facilities

■ TechWeb (CMP)

■ ZDNet

■ iWORLD (Mecklermedia)

■ Nando

■ Red Herring

[All URLs given above]

Investment banks

■ Hambrecht & Quist – **http://www.hamquist.com/**

■ Montgomery Securities – **http://www.montgomery.com/**

■ Morgan Stanley – **http://www.ms.com/**

■ Robertson, Stephens & Co. – **http://www.rsco.com/**

Miscellaneous

■ DBC (for technology indices: NASDAQ High Technology Index [$IXCO], AMEX High Technology Index [$XHT], PSE High Technology Index [$PSE], Morgan Stanley High Tech Index [$MSH], Semiconductor Index [$SOX] – **http://www.dbc.com/**

■ Top Vendors: record of top computer companies in Silicon Valley – **http://www.netvalley.com/netvalley/top100am_vendors.html**

■ Net Millionaires: tracking the people made millionaires from the Net – **http://www.pulver.com/million/**

The FINANCIAL INTERNET DIRECTORY

A directory of Internet resources for investors, comprising over 1200 references from 45 countries.

INTRODUCTION

There are a number of problems which might be encountered when looking for information on the Internet:

- A **keyword search** with a service like Lycos may well return 2000 references, with nothing to choose between them.

- An **Internet index** like Yahoo may be better, but these general indices do not necessarily categorize data in the best way for each subject area. In addition, the description of the service is commonly provided by the Web site itself (which can lead to odd anomalies – in one case, several University departments claiming to be the Russia Stock Exchange). Finally, many international sites do not bother to register with Index services as they regard them as too US oriented.

- Having found a likely financial Web service, it may take a significant amount of time scrambling around a **badly organized site** before you realize that there is nothing of interest there.

- And perhaps you find a site with relevant information – is it the best site? Perhaps there is another site with more up-to-date figures, or one that allows the easy download of the data to your own computer.

The Financial Internet Directory goes some way to solving these problems.

The Directory is the result of visiting and assessing over 1500 finance-related Internet sites – virtually all the financial sites in the world. It is the result of hours spent fighting through a jungle of badly constructed HyperText and tepid 'cool sites', and of ages spent waiting for imagemaps to download (where it would have been quicker to receive them as colour photos in the post).

Most importantly, the Directory is the result of the great search for pith – the quest for content on the Internet. And the good news is that it does exist. But it can be difficult to find, hidden among all the other services on the Internet vying for attention.

Of the 1500 sites assessed the best were selected for inclusion in the Directory, which offers:

- a **guide to over 1200 finance-related Internet sites**, from 45 countries
- a **categorization system** devised specifically for investors
- in every case a **concise description** of the resources actually available at the site (and not merely as promised on the sites' home pages)

■ a **rating system** to measure the usefulness of the information on sites for investors

■ a **URL** (Internet address) that has been checked in every case to be valid at the time of compilation.

The structure of the Directory is designed to enable you to find information as quickly as possible. In many cases, the information you are looking for may not be on the Internet, in which case the Directory should be the quickest method of confirming this. As examples, the Directory should be the fastest way if you are looking for:

■ a four-language glossary on derivative instruments

■ a site to download the Metastock technical analysis demonstration program

■ a bookshop to order investment books online

■ a monthly report on the Spanish economy

■ a local Independent Financial Adviser in the UK

■ the daily price of a fund that invests in the Indian market

■ daily closing prices of the Rio de Janeiro Stock Exchange

■ a searchable index of South African news stories from 1994

■ the latest announced company results in Japan.

The Lycos search engine has currently indexed roughly 50 million Web pages. This Directory covers about 0.04 per cent of those pages. But they are the most useful pages. And 0.04 per cent is 20 000 pages of investment information available directly from your own computer.

NOTES TO THE DIRECTORY

The criterion for inclusion in the Directory was that the sites must include information useful for investors. For the majority of countries included, the listing of financial sites can be considered as fairly comprehensive. The main exception is for the US, where the process of selection was more rigorous due to the very large number of Internet sites there.

The Directory is divided into four (unequal) sections:

A. Global: this includes sites that are equally useful to investors all over the world, regardless of what specific market they may be interested in. For example: world news, currency rates, commodity and gold prices, international fund management groups and risk management.

B. Regional: this covers sites that specialize in specific regions such as Asia or East Europe, and also includes a section on Emerging Markets.

C. Countries: this is the largest part of the Directory, with references for investment resources for 45 of the largest economies.

D. Stock and futures exchanges: references for the Web sites of over 65 exchanges worldwide. (Further details on the exchanges can be found under the respective country headings – this section merely provides a compilation of all the exchange URLs for quick reference.)

A more detailed index for the Directory can be found in the next section.

Categorization

At the top level of (geographical) classification, there is no great problem assigning sites on the basis of whether they are globally, regionally or nationally relevant. For example, the Central Bank of Turkey site is relevant purely to Turkey, while that of *Euromoney* is globally pertinent. In a few cases, sites are listed under both the global and national category – for example, the *Financial Times* is listed in the 'Global' and 'UK' sections.

The listings within the 'Regional' and 'Stock and futures exchanges' sections are grouped by continent.

The 'Global' section largely follows the News, Markets, Economy model of the 'Countries' section, but also has categories for general services and reference.

The categorization model employed for the 'Countries' section (and also part of the 'Global' section) may not be immediately obvious, so this is explained below.

Classification within the Countries section

The easiest method of compilation for the Directory would have been simply to aggregate all sites according to institutional type. For example, all banks grouped together, all stockbrokers, all fund managers etc. But there are already quite a few listings of banks on the Internet, so another one would not add very much. Besides, finding banks is not very difficult; if you are looking for a bank in Chile, then simply look up the 'Chile: Finance' section in Yahoo, or use Infoseek to search on 'bank Chile'.

There is a problem also with listing, say, all banks together: banks are no longer a homogeneous group. Some while ago such a grouping might have made sense, but now, after many years of reorganization, globalization, specialization, regionalization, fragmentation, deal-orientation, client-orientation and reorganization of the initial reorganization, – banking activities are increasingly diverse. So a grouping of Swiss banks might list UBS Bank next to Zürcher Kantonalbank – nominally both banks, but with very different activities from the point of view of an international investor.

For this Directory the sites are categorized according to function and resource type, rather than by the form of entity providing the resource. From this scheme, the resources available on the Net for investors fall into three main categories:

- News
- Markets
- Economy.

These are the categories that are directly useful to investors, and the approach for each country was to identify the specific resources that provide, for example, a table of daily stock prices or a daily comment on the Government bond market. As a result of this approach, one might find a bank listed under the 'Markets' section (if it provides a currency market report), or a bank may be in the 'Economy' section if it provides a monthly economic bulletin.

This method of categorization may initially be slightly confusing, and sites do not always fall neatly into the categories, but it is a mistake to think that the Internet *should* fit conveniently into any classification scheme that can currently be devised.

It is also the case that the method of categorization used here is in tune with one of the themes running through this book, which is that the structure and role of corporate entities, and the nature of the relationship between them and other companies and clients, will be irrevocably changed by the Internet – to the extent that terms like 'bank', 'broker', and 'fund manager' will no longer be useful categorizations.

Therefore, each country is divided into the following five sections:

News

This lists the news services available about the country, with details on the type of news (whether it is only of a general nature, or more specifically oriented towards business and finance), and whether archives and a search facility exist.

Markets

This is usually the largest section for each country, and will include any market data that is available. Further sub-classifications may be made into specific markets (for example, sub-dividing into: stocks, bonds, currencies, commodities, futures and options).

If a site specializes in, for example, currencies, then it will be listed under a 'Currencies' classification. If, however, a site covers quite a few different markets (e.g. interest rates, currencies, and commodities) then it is listed higher in the classification tree, under 'Markets'.

Economy

Includes sites with useful economics data about the country. Appearing here will be Central Bank sites (if existing), other government servers, and bank sites with economic reviews.

Miscellaneous

For completeness, this is to aggregate all those other sites that don't fall into the above categories. (And despite the explanation above of the futility of classifying banks together, such a category does occasionally appear here, more for reasons of stylistic neatness than anything else).

Other URL lists

The situation is changing all the time, and online directories are always likely to be updated more frequently than paper versions. This section usually includes one or two of the best URL directories found for each country, with good finance sections.

Note: while the US section broadly follows the above schema, due to the large number of sites there, the number of sub-categories existing is far greater than for any other country.

Individual site descriptions

Each site description attempts to detail as precisely, and concisely, as possible exactly what resources are available on the site.

An opening parenthesis might be used to explain the nature of the site, if this is not readily apparent. For example, to explain that the company is a stockbroker, or that the Web pages are merely an advertisement for a subscription newsletter.

For brevity, the text description is rather condensed and possibly slightly cryptic. For example, the character '/' is used as an abbreviation for 'and', so 'daily/weekly/monthly reports' is to read as 'daily, weekly and monthly reports are available'.

Colons are used to aggregate all services of a similar nature, or frequency, so:

> 'daily market data: major stock moves, major stock indices, popular shares, inflation/interest/Sterling rates, business comment'

should be read as, market data is available every day with tables of major moves by stocks, tables of the major stock index values, data on some popular shares, data for inflation, interest rates and Sterling rates and a business comment.

A few comments about the descriptions:

■ All the sites listed are in **English**, unless otherwise stated. (However, in the case of foreign language sites, it is frequently possible to understand these, particularly in the case of data pages.)

■ All the services listed in the Directory are **free**, unless otherwise stated.

■ One can assume that all sites will have the minimum of **contact details** for the company and possibly also product details; therefore this is not explicitly stated for each site.

■ In addition to the above, nearly all **stock and futures exchanges** sites have information about the exchange, its history, contract specifications, trading hours, educational courses and, if you're lucky, a message from the Chairman. Hence, again, this is not stated explicitly for each individual exchange.

■ Some care has been taken to determine the frequency of services offered (e.g. for market reports). In certain cases, reports appear irregularly, or an archive of reports appears to abruptly terminate at some previous date. In these cases, the services are described as being 'occasional'.

■ Some sites prepare reports in Portable Document Format (**PDF**). These reports must be downloaded onto your local computer and then read using Adobe's Acrobat Reader.

Ratings

Each site appearing in the Directory has been accorded a star rating on a scale of 1 to 5. This rating has nothing to do with the quality of the site or its 'coolness', it is purely a measure of how useful the information on the site is likely to be for investors.

Rating system

1 Nothing useful on the site, beyond the company contact details (and possibly other corporate information).

2 As above, but some effort has been made, and there might be, for example, a glossary of terms or a brief explanation of the local market.

3 A site with a good effort made to present a range of useful information for investors.

4 A very good site, with a critical mass of useful information, and well organized.

5 Excellent, a model of its class. The company has obviously put some original thought into the Internet and is taking it very seriously.

This rating system, along with so many others, might seem hopelessly subjective – and that cannot be completely denied. But as a comparative rating, it turns out to be more objective than might be thought. For example, at one end of the scale it is easy to see that the Chicago Mercantile Exchange and the Chamber of Mines of South Africa sites deserve 5-star ratings, as they both contain a huge wealth of information. At the other end, however, there are many large sites, with many pages and numerous, well-designed graphic images, that nevertheless have no useful content – and it is therefore not difficult to assign a low rating.

So, the yardstick for every site was 'is there any useful content for investors here'; and while 'useful content' is itself a subjective measure, at least this is easier to judge than a more general attempt to grade the 'quality' of a site.

A couple of further notes about the ratings:

- Sites accorded a rating of '1' may still be useful for some purposes, if all the user wants is information about that specific company.
- Some sites may be very large and useful in general, but their financial component alone merits only a low rating.
- Not all sites are rated – this is usually due to the site being in a non-English language, or it offers only a subscription service that was not assessed.

Economics data

For each country, the following economics data are given:

- Gross Domestic Product (GDP) ($)
- GDP per capita ($)
- GDP growth (%)
- External debt ($)
- Exports ($)
- Imports ($)
- Domestic currency name and abbreviation.

Note: GDP dollar estimates for all countries are calculated on a purchasing power parity (PPP) basis.

All figures come from the CIA 1995 World Factbook available online at **http://www.odci.gov/cia/**

In addition to the economics data, each country's two-letter Internet Domain Name is also listed.

These figures are not included as an up-to-date source for country economic data (that should be available online – see the 'Economics' section of the Directory for each respective country); but the data might prove useful for quick reference, and it can also be interesting to compare the range of financial

Web sites existing with the scale of economic activity.

Pursuing this a little further, Table 3.1 lists: the number of financial Web sites for each country, their GDP ($billion), GDP per capita ($) and then an index to measure the respective financial 'wiredness' of each country. This final 'Wired index' figure is calculated by normalizing the number of Web sites with the country GDP figure and then multiplying by 100:

Wired index = 100 * number of Web sites / GDP ($bn)

■ TABLE 3.1 Ranking of financially wired countries

	Country	No. Web sites	GDP ($bn)	GDP/ capita ($)	Wired index
1	Estonia	12	10	6460	120.0
2	Luxembourg	8	9	22 830	88.9
3	Croatia	10	12	2640	83.3
4	New Zealand	29	56	16 640	51.8
5	Singapore	17	57	19 940	29.8
6	Hong Kong	24	136	24 530	17.6
7	Israel	12	70	13 880	17.1
8	Czech Republic	13	76	7350	17.1
9	Finland	13	81	16 140	16.0
10	Chile	15	97	7010	15.5
11	Norway	14	95	22 170	14.7
12	South Africa	25	194	4420	12.9
13	Sweden	21	163	18 580	12.9
14	Greece	11	93	8870	11.8
15	Malaysia	18	166	8650	10.8
16	Austria	15	139	17 500	10.8
17	Hungary	6	58	5700	10.3
18	Switzerland	15	148	22 080	10.1
19	Australia	37	374	20 720	9.9
20	Denmark	8	103	19 860	7.8
21	Portugal	8	107	10 190	7.5
22	Philippines	12	161	2310	7.5
23	Canada	47	639	22 760	7.4
24	United Kingdom	67	1045	17 980	6.4
25	Poland	12	191	4920	6.3
26	Venezuela	11	178	8670	6.2
27	Netherlands	16	275	17 940	5.8
28	Belgium	10	181	17 040	5.5
29	Taiwan	14	257	12 070	5.4
30	South Korea	21	508	11 270	4.1
31	Thailand	14	355	5970	3.9
32	Argentina	10	270	7990	3.7
33	Mexico	26	728	7900	3.6
34	Russia	24	721	4820	3.3
35	Brazil	27	886	5580	3.0
36	Germany	36	1344	16 580	2.7
37	Turkey	8	305	4910	2.6

▶

▓ TABLE 3.1 **Ranking of financially wired countries (*contd*)**

	Country	No. Web sites	GDP ($bn)	GDP/ capita ($)	Wired index
38	France	28	1080	18 670	2.6
39	United States	157	6738	25 850	2.3
40	Spain	11	515	13 120	2.1
41	Indonesia	13	619	3090	2.1
42	Japan	34	2527	20 200	1.3
43	Italy	13	998	17 180	1.3
44	India	14	1254	1360	1.1
45	China	22	2978	2500	0.7

Notes on Table 3.1:

▓ It must be said immediately that the table is not meant to be taken as a rigorous academic study. The economic data is not the most recent available, but worse than that, the figure for the number of Web sites is a very dubious figure: being merely the number of sites found for inclusion in this Directory.

▓ For nearly every country, much effort *was* expended in tracking down all financial-related Web sites, except in the case of the US, where the number of Web sites in the above table underestimates the true figure, and is the cause of the lowly position.

▓ At the other end of the table, the top three countries must be taken as statistical outliers, due to their small absolute GDPs.

The *caveats* could continue. However, despite everything, it might be possible to accept some broad orders of magnitude reflecting the current situation. In which case, a couple of observations would be:

▓ At the **top of the table**, the presence of Hong Kong and Singapore may be no surprise, but New Zealand, Israel, Czech Republic, Norway and South Africa form an interestingly diverse group. Or perhaps not; one could regard these as isolated countries, either geographically or – until recently – politically, and possibly they see the Internet as a tool for overcoming that isolation.

▓ While at the **bottom end**, one might be surprised to find technologically advanced countries such as France, Spain, Japan and Italy.

By arbitrarily removing countries with a GDP of less than $50 billion (a minor attempt to remedy some of the statistical shortcomings of the study), a list of the Top Ten Financially Wired Countries can be drawn up.

Top Ten financially wired countries

1 New Zealand
2 Singapore
3 Hong Kong
4 Israel
5 Czech Republic
6 Finland
7 Chile
8 Norway
9 South Africa
10 Sweden

In the same week that these figures were being calculated, an international study of businessmen found that New Zealand was the least corrupt country with which to do business. And the same country is top of this financially-wired ranking. No doubt a coincidence. But it is tempting to draw some crude parallel between the two, and even hypothesize about the links between the openness of a society, lack of corruption and the conditions existing to allow the development of an Internet industry. The presence of the Scandinavian countries also in the 'Top Ten' would support this.

INDEX TO THE DIRECTORY

Global

NEWS

▥ *CNNfn Financial News* – (*see* US section) [5]
http://www.cnnfn.com/

▥ *Wall Street Journal* – (*see* US section) [5]
http://update.wsj.com/

▥ *Financial Times* – (*see* UK section) [5]
http://www.ft.com/

▥ *Bloomberg Personal* – (*see* US section) [5]
http://www.bloomberg.com/

▥ *Reuters News (via Yahoo)* – (*see* US section) [3]
http://www.yahoo.com/headlines/

▥ *NewsPage* – database of daily business news headlines from 600 sources; indexed in categories and keyword search facility; company tracking facility; subscription for: full news stories, daily personalized news sent by e-mail [5]
http://www.newspage.com/

▥ *Television Corporation of Singapore* – news updates: world, world financial, Asia-Pacific financial [4]
http://tcs.com.sg/whaton/news/

▥ *World News Connection* – (subscription foreign news alert service from the US Government) [5]
http://wnc.fedworld.gov/

▥ *The Economist* – list of contents in the weekly paper version; selected articles and surveys online; leader; politics/business summary; Britain In Brief; archive of past issues [3]
http://www.economist.com/

MARKETS

- *Euromoney* – selection of articles from paper version; archive of past issues with keyword search facility; capital markets league tables; discussion forums; preview of coming year; world financial calendar [3]
  http://www.emwl.com/

- *Global Market Network* – (subscription daily markets analysis from IDEA: bonds, money, currency, commodities, Latin America, Emerging markets)
  http://www.idea-globalmarket.com/

Quotes, charts and information

- *DBC Online* – (market data from the major global exchanges) quotes from North/South American, European and Asian exchanges [5]
  http://www.dbc.com/

- *PC Quote Europe* – (European representatives for PC Quote Inc.) price data; bookshop [5]
  http://www.pcquote-europe.co.uk

- *TeleStock* – (selection of US/European exchanges) daily closing stock/bond/options data/charts; data downloadable in Quicken/MS Money format [5]
  http://www.teleserv.co.uk/

- [Also: *CNNfn, Bloomberg Personal, Financial Times*]

- *MarketWatch at Calpoly* – historical data/charts for: precious metals, bonds, commodities, currencies, stock indices, US hi/lows, US advance/decline [4]
  http://www.busfac.calpoly.edu/pub/marketwatch.html

- *Primark* – (global financial data) contact details for subsidiaries: Datastream, Disclosure Incorporated, I/B/E/S Inc, Worldscope [1]
  http://www.primark.com/

- *The Financial Data Finder* – (Dept of Finance, Ohio State University) directory of financial/economic data available on the Internet [5]
  http://www.cob.ohio-state.edu/dept/fin/osudata.htm

Stocks

- *InterNet Bankruptcy Library* – (worldwide troubled company resources) [3]
  http://bankrupt.com/

- *Stock Club* – online discussion forum for all stocks; links [4]
  http://stockclub.com/

Bonds

- *US Public Securities Association* – (bond market trade association) legislative/regulatory issues; market practices; conferences; research

reports/stats; press releases; site search facility [4]
http://www.psa.com/

▓ *Bloomberg Personal* – international yield curves [3]
http://www.bloomberg.com/markets/

▓ *J.P. Morgan* – daily updates to: government bond indices, Emerging Markets Bond Index Plus, currency indices, and RiskMetrics volatility and correlation data sets; monthly analysis reports; reference outline on government bond markets; glossary; world holiday and time guide [5]
http://www.jpmorgan.com/

▓ *BradyNet* – (info on Brady bonds) daily indicative prices and analytics for: Brady bonds, options on Brady bonds, eurobonds, exotics and exchange traded futures and options on futures; bond descriptions [4]
http://www.bradynet.com/

▓ *B & P Partners* – (broker/dealer) daily market update; discussion forum; subscription for bond portfolio analysis, market quotes [3]
http://www.bondtrader.com/

Currencies

▓ *Bloomberg Personal* – table of US Dollar rates with selected key cross rates [3]
http://www.bloomberg.com/markets/

▓ *CNNfn* – table of US Dollar rates updated around the clock [4]
http://cnnfn.com/markets/currencies.html

▓ *Information Internet* – real-time foreign exchange prices through proprietary Windows program; comparison graphs to illustrate currency movements over the past 24 hours [5]
http://www.info-int.com/

▓ *Currency Management Corporation* – (foreign exchange dealers, associated with the above Information Internet) information on forex dealing; daily market report with fundamental/technical outlook; FOREX glossary and market description [4]
http://www.forex-cmc.co.uk/

▓ *Forex Watch* – major cross-rate trading levels (updated every 5 min.) with support/resistance, MA, with intraday hourly technical charts; scrolling bulletin board of currency comments; trading signals from an automated technical system; European crossrates and ERM table (updated every 15 min.); description of charts and technical analysis [5]
http://www.forex.co.uk

▓ *INO Global Markets* – 24-hour quotes/charts
http://www.ino.com/marketquote/

▓ *Xenon Laboratories* – interactive cross-rate calculator for major currencies, daily data from Bank of Montreal [3]
http://www.xe.net/currency/

- *Lund Institute of Technology* – interactive cross-rate calculator for major currencies, updated once a day from the Federal Reserve Bank of New York, via the University of Michigan's gopher server [2]
  http://www.dna.lth.se/cgi-bin/kurt/rates

- *Olsen & Associates* – (analysis of foreign exchange rates) forecasts; historical analysis; overbought/oversold summary; trading model position; currency ranking analysis chart updated every hour; historical exchange rates from Jan 1990; research papers [4]
  http://www.olsen.ch/

Commodities

- *CNNfn* – 20 min. delayed data for: metals, livestock/meat, petroleum, lumber [4]
  http://www.cnnfn.com/markets/commodities.html

- *Info-Mine* – (information on mining) daily mining news; investment newsletters; event calendar; subscription for access to MIN-MET databases and search facility [4]
  http://www.info-mine.com/

- *Energy Net* – general information regarding energy prices [2]
  http://www.netxn.com/~rsasaki/energy.html

- *The Northern Miner* – (weekly newspaper covering North American-based mining companies) selection from the paper version: top stories, headlines, companies mentioned, meetings, coming events, most active stocks; subscription to full online version and archive of past issues [3]
  http://www.northernminer.com/

Gold and precious metals

- *Kitco* – (gold and precious metals) prices updated every 10 min. for: gold, silver, platinum, palladium, rhodium; daily London Fix; intraday to 10-year historical charts for gold/silver; links [5]
  http://www.kitco.com/

- *CPM Group* – (subscription precious metals research) [2]
  http://www.cpmgroup.com/

- *EagleWing Asset Management* – analysis of gold funds; general reference info; links; subscription newsletter [4]
  http://www.eaglewing.com/

- *The Alchemist* – (monthly newsletter); precious metals news; technical analysis; general reference info [3]
  http://www.investools.com/cgi-bin/Ideas/alch.pl

- *GoldLGN* – gold FAQ [2]
  http://www.goldwww.com

▓ *Goldsheet* – quarterly newsletter on 400 mining stocks; links [3]
http://www.he.net/~gold/

▓ *Goldstock Letter by David Marantette* – (subscription paper newsletter) sample issue online [1]
http://www.goldstock.com/index.html

▓ *Chamber of Mines of South Africa* – press releases; facts and figures; info on kruggerand; online mining directory; daily news and archive; daily economic indicators: intl gold prices, other precious metal prices, kruggerand, currencies, Johannesburg SE indices, commodity links [5]
http://www.bullion.org.za/

Futures and options

▓ *Chicago Mercantile Exchange (CME)* – daily digest of futures industry news; futures reference/educational articles; futures glossary [5]
http://www.cme.com/

▓ *MarketPlex* – (at the CBOT, umbrella site for a collection of futures-related services) technical charts, research reports; select articles from journals; access to subscription MRI service: daily charts/data; access to MJK closing prices for commodity exchanges worldwide [4]
http://www.cbot.com/mplex.htm

▓ *INO Global Markets* – (umbrella site for many futures-related services) Options Industry Council; CTAs; Stark Research: performance tracker of CTAs; intraday/daily/weekly charts/data for the world's major futures and options markets; journal articles; conference calendar; reference articles; bookshop [5]
http://www.ino.com/

▓ *Office for Futures and Options Research (OFOR)* – (research into futures, options, and derivative markets at the University of Illinois) faculty research; working papers [2]
http://gopher.ag.uiuc.edu/ACE/ofor/aboutofor.html

▓ *Futures Magazine* – selection of articles from current issue; daily hot market news; educational resources; managed money news [4]
http://www.futuresmag.com/

▓ *Futures & Options World* – details of upcoming training courses; weekly futures industry headlines [2]
http://www.fow.com/

▓ *Prophetdata* – (futures data supplier) daily updated back-adjusted continuous futures contracts; data from 1959 [4]
http://www.prophetdata.com/futures.html

▓ *Gibbons Burke* – (author of the 'The Computerized Trader' column in *Futures Magazine*) archive of past articles; links [4]
http://www.io.com/~gibbonsb/

- *Troutman* – (Defender of Sticks) trading philosophy; reviews of books and trading systems [3]
  http://www.teleport.com/~troutman/
- *Futures and Options Bibliography* – (from the *Journal of Futures Markets*) [2]
  http://www.fiu.edu/~daiglerr/bib.htm

ECONOMY

- *The CIA World Factbook* – details on geography, people, government, economy (overview, key statistics and sector analyses), transportation, communications [5]
  http://www.odci.gov/cia/
- *World Bank* – quarterly Finance and Development report (IMF/WB); WB briefs; research reports; Development Economics database; speeches/press releases; site search facility [3]
  http://www.worldbank.org
- *United Nations* – umbrella site for UN agencies including: International Monetary Fund, International Trade Centre, United Nations Industrial Development Organization, World Bank, World Trade Organization [4]
  http://www.unicc.org/
- *Euro-Info-Sources* – central access point for a number of different European Union information sources including: ISPO (Information Society Project Office), I'M EUROPE, CORDIS (R&D activities), EUROBASES, EUROSTAT (Statistical Office of the European Union), EUR-OP (Publications Office of the Union) [3]
  http://www.cec.lu/en/info.html
- *Morgan Stanley* – daily economic reports; information about MSCI indices with daily update [4]
  http://www.ms.com/
- *Bankers Trust* – global economic research: newsletters/reports [4]
  http://www.bankerstrust.com/global/global.html
- [*Pasi Kuoppamäki* – jokes about economists and economics]
  http://www.etla.fi/pkm/pkm.html

Economics links

- *FINWeb* – links to economics and finance-related topics [4]
  http://www.finweb.com/
- *WebEc* – links to WWW economics resources including list of economics journals [3]
  http://www.helsinki.fi/WebEc/
- *Bill Goffe* – resources for economists on the Internet [4]
  http://netec.wustl.edu/EconFAQ/EconFAQ.html

■ *NetEc* – bibliography of printed working papers in economics, including finance from 250 institutions with search facility; collection of computer programs that are useful for economists [3]
http://netec.mcc.ac.uk/NetEc.html

SERVICES

Funds

■ *Fidelity International* – daily updated fund prices; market comments; investment reference information [4]
http://www.fid-intl.com/

■ *Flemings* – daily fund prices; weekly market update [3]
http://www.flemings.lu/

■ *GAM* – fund performance statistics/charts; fund asset allocation and top five holdings; manager information; market comment [3]
http://www.ukinfo.gam.com/

■ *Invesco* – [2]
http://www.invesco.com/

■ *Gartmore Investment Management* – [1]
http://www.iii.co.uk/gartmore/

Asset pricing and analysis

■ *Barra* – (analytical models and software) Barra market indices [3]
http://www.barra.com/

■ *Wilshire Associates* – [1]
http://www.wilshire.com/

■ *Ibbotson Associates* – (financial consulting, training, software, data and presentation products) research reports [3]
http://www.ibbotson.com/

Risk management

■ *J.P. Morgan* – RiskMetrics volatility and correlation data sets [5]
http://www.jpmorgan.com/

■ *Leland O'Brien Rubenstein Associates* – (designer of dynamic asset and currency hedging products) description of equity protection strategies; interactive Financial Simulator to analyse different investment strategies; option calculator [3]
http://lor.com/lor

- *Lindquist, Stephenson & White* – (risk management boutique specializing in fixed-income derivatives) [1]
  http://www.mkts.com/LSW.htm
- *Risk Information Service Center (RISC)* – (Price Waterhouse) [2]
  http://www.inect.co.uk/pwrisc/
- *Peartree Limited* – (risk management consultancy) [1]
  http://www.peartree.co.uk/
- *Courant Institute, NYU* – papers in Mathematical finance and course materials for risk-management in finance [3]
  http://math.nyu.edu/faculty/avellane/

Risk technology

- *C·ATS Software Inc.* – (technology products for derivatives and risk management) [1]
  http://www.cats.com/
- *Integral Development Corporation* – (software developer, products: Integral Derivatives Framework IDF, RiskNet) [1]
  http://www.integral.com/about.html
- *Infinity Financial Technology* – (applications for financial trading and risk management) [1]
  http://www.infinity.com/
- *Brady plc* – (treasury trading and risk management systems) download demo module [2]
  http://www.bradyplc.co.uk/
- *Algorithmics Incorporated* – (software applications and financial engineering services for risk management) [1]
  http://www.algorithmics.com/
- *Glassco Park* – (risk management systems technology for MS Windows, product: FinancialCAD) download demo; technical support [2]
  http://www.financialcad.com/
- *Ristek* – (risk management software) risk management competition [1]
  http://www.ozemail.com.au/~ristek/
- *Cambridge Risk Dynamics* – (risk management software, product: Risk Explorer) [1]
  http://www.riskex.com/
- *Redpoint Software* – (financial risk management technology, products: TotalRisk, FinWorks) [1]
  http://www.rpsi.com/

Derivatives

▓ *NumaWeb* – (general information on derivatives) calendar of courses/conferences; directory of software and journals; educational articles; online calculators: options, CBs, warrants; bookshop; links
http://www.numa.com/

▓ *DERIVATIVES 'R US* – series of articles providing a non-technical treatment of various topics in derivatives [5]
http://www.vt.edu:10021/business/finance/dmc/DRU/contents.html

▓ *Applied Derivatives Trading* – (monthly cyber magazine) product focus; educational articles; trade gossip; book/software reviews; issue archive [4]
http://www.adtrading.com/

▓ *Sumitomo Bank Capital Markets* – site includes educational articles, weekly commentaries and historical rates database [3]
http://www.sbcm.com/

▓ *Center for International Security and Derivative Markets (CISDM) (University of Massachusetts)* – research in international asset management especially as related to derivative markets; outline of faculty research [1]
http://www.umass.edu/som/cisdm/

▓ *Oxford Financial* – exotic option pricing software; courses on risk management, pricing and hedging derivatives, and mathematical finance; financial consultancy [2]
http://www.compulink.co.uk/~mathmax/

▓ *International Swaps and Derivatives Association* (ISDA) – educational information; market survey; details of conferences [3]
http://www.isda.org/

▓ *TermFinance* – a four-language glossary on derivative instruments [2]
http://Finance.Wat.ch/TermFinance/

Derivatives technology

▓ *Financial Engineering Associates* – (analytical tools for derivative products) [2]
http://www.fea.com/

▓ *Layer Eight Systems* – (derivatives pricing software systems) [2]
http://www.eight.com/

▓ *Monis Software* – (derivatives modelling software, product Optimum range) [2]
http://www.monis.co.uk/

▓ *Montgomery Investment Technology* – (spreadsheet and database add-ins for financial modelling) [2]
http://www.wallstreetnet.com/

▓ *May Consulting* – (software for derivative instruments, product: MicroHedge) [1]
http://www.may.com/

- *IRIS Investment Support Systems* – (decision support systems for futures and options) [1]
  http://www.iris.nl/
- *Robert's Online Pricers* – online calculators for: commissions, derivatives, options [4]
  http://www.intrepid.com/~robertl/
- *Derivatives Software Vendors* – (directory from InterNect) [3]
  http://www.inect.co.uk/cgi-bin/db/int0027.html

Subscription trading systems

- *Conductor* – (subscription quantitative financial research service, provides traders with forecast data based on proprietary financial models) [5]
  http://www.HHConductor.com/
- *Perception Knowledge Systems* – (weekly/monthly neural network market predictions) sample charts of weekly signals [2]
  http://www.perception.co.nz/
- *Burmese Tiger Technical System* – (offers buy/sell trading signals 24 hours a day, from NiTo) [2]
  http://nito.com/
- *Commodex* – (daily futures trading system) download performance records from 1982 [2]
  http://www.commodex.com/
- *Trend Analysis* – (technical analysis of major foreign exchange, financial futures and commodities markets) daily/weekly reports [3]
  http://www.trend-analysis.co.uk/index/
- *Preferred Trading Solutions* – (daily stock recommendations) past issues and sample of subscription page [1]
  http://www.trading-solutions.com/

General software/technology

- *Mathworks* – (interactive engineering and scientific software, product: MATLAB) technical support/tips; FTP library of software [3]
  http://www.mathworks.com/
- *Intuit* – (personal finance software, product: Quicken) Quicken Financial Network, Investor Insight: download news stories and five years of price histories [3]
  http://www.intuit.com/
- *Microsoft* – (product: MS Money) information about online banking; links to banks (Money Partners) [2]
  http://www.microsoft.com/

▒ *Bob Browning's Guide to Treasury Technology* – ordered by topic/vendor/product with site search facility [4]
http://www.textor.com/markets/guide/

▒ *Waters Information Services* – (publisher specializing in information technology in the financial markets) WAHOO Index of WWW technology sites; news articles/headlines about the Internet and technology in the financial markets [3]
http://www.watersinfo.com/

Trading software/technical analysis

▒ *Equis International* – (products: Metastock, Technician) collection of market comments from various 'gurus'; weekly investment events calendar; Hot Stock Lists generated by Metastock; download program demos/upgrades; archive of quarterly newsletter; technical support [4]
http://www.equis.com/

▒ *Omega Research* – (financial analysis software for the PC: TradeStation, OptionStation, SuperCharts, Wall Street Analyst) product demos for download; technical support; upgrade patches; data refresh libraries [2]
http://www.omegaresearch.com/

▒ *OptionVue* – (PC options trading software) downloadable demos/upgrades; reference articles on options; technical support; discussion forums [3]
http://www.optionvue.com/

▒ *Nirvana Systems* – (technical analysis software, products: OmniTrader) market commentary; recommended trades; download demo [3]
http://www.nirv.com/

▒ *Technical Tools* – (technical analysis software, product: TT ChartBook) [2]
http://www.techtool.com/

▒ *Center for Elliott Wave Analysis* – introduction to Elliot Wave analysis; Elliott Wave Analyser software with downloadable demo [3]
http://www.cewa.com/

▒ *International Pacific Trading Company* – (candlestick chart software, product: Candlestick Forecaster) download demo; trading hotline; technical support [2]
http://www.iptc.com/

▒ *Liberty Research Corporation* – (technical analysis software) weekly market comment with annotated charts; demo program; subscription newsletter [2]
http://www.libertyresearch.com/

▒ *i-Soft* – ('data-mining' software) download demo; discussion forum; FTP site for quotes [3]
http://www.i-soft.com/

▒ *TCM Trading Systems* – (financial futures predictive trading programs) historical performance; download demo program [2]
http://www2.interaccess.com/home/

- *Science in Finance* – (computational and artificial intelligence applications for trading, product: Fuzzy Candlesticks) academic papers; download program demo [2]
  http://www.i-way.co.uk/scifi/
- *BioComp Systems* – (neural network systems for market forecasting) [2]
  http://www.bio-comp.com/
- *International Federation of Technical Analysts* – directory of member countries [2]
  http://www.ifta.org/~ifta/
- *Computerized Trader* – collection of articles from *Futures* magazine about trading and technology; links [3]
  http://www.io.com/~gibbonsb/ct-index.html
- *Anderson Investor's Software* – order investment/trading software/data online [3]
  http://www.invest-soft.com/

Education and training

- *Taylor Associates* – (in-house financial training for: derivatives, capital markets and treasury skills) [2]
  http://www.taylorassociates.co.uk/

Market simulations

- *Auditrack Inc.* – (subscription simulated brokerage operation) archive of simulated accounts review [4]
  http://auditrack.com/
- *Gigabucks Stock Market Simulation*
  telnet://GAMES@castor.tat.physik.uni-tuebingen.de/
- *Mammon Stock Market Simulation* – (Media Lab at Massachusetts Institute of Technology (MIT))
  telnet://mammon.media.mit.edu:10900/
- *Sierra On-Line Stock Market Challenge*
  http://smc.sierra.com/
- *Swiss Center for Scientific Computing* – Artificial Trading Room: research into simulating real-time trading in an artificial trading environment [2]
  http://yin.ethz.ch/

Bookshops

- *Wall Street Directory* – [4]
  http://www.wsdinc.com/
- *Financial Trading, Inc.* – books for traders [3]
  http://www.elder.com/

▪ *Amazon* – general bookstore, search facility [4]
http://www.amazon.com

▪ *Windsor Books* – commodities/futures trading; technical analysis [3]
http://ison.com/windsor/index.html

▪ *INO Global Markets* – [3]
http://www.ino.com/

▪ *The Internet Bookshop* – [2]
http://www.bookshop.co.uk/

Miscellaneous

▪ *Eco-Rating* – analysis of companies' environmental performance [2]
http://www.eco-rating.com/

▪ *Ethical Business* – introduction to, and directory of, ethical investment [3]
http://www.bath.ac.uk/Centres/Ethical/

Reference

▪ *Department of Finance (Ohio State University)* – Internet research and
educational resources in finance [5]
http://www.cob.ohio-state.edu/~fin/

▪ *Finance.Wat.ch* – futures/options contracts specs; world indices specs;
financial education/training resources; four-language glossary on derivative
instruments; IFCI Geneva papers on Derivatives and Risk Management [5]
http://finance.wat.ch/

▪ *misc.invest FAQ* – collection of FAQs from the misc.invest newsgroup [5]
http://www.cis.ohio-state.edu/hypertext/faq/bngusenet/misc/invest/top.html

▪ *Prof. William F. Sharpe* – select papers (including explanation of the Sharpe
Ratio) articles on macro-investment analysis; analyses of the performance of
the LS100 US mutual funds [3]
http://gsb-www.stanford.edu/~wfsharpe/home.htm

▪ *Investment Strategies for the 21st Century* – (at GNN Personal Finance Center)
cyber book about investment [4]
http://www.gnn.com/gnn/meta/finance/feat/21st/index.html

▪ *Roy Davies' Money Links* – (sources for: history of money, contemporary
developments and electronic money) [5]
http://www.ex.ac.uk/~RDavies/arian/money.html

▪ *Financial Encyclopaedia* – [2]
http://www.euro.net:8003/innovation/Finance_Base/Fin_encyc.html

Journals

[1] indicates that there are just details of: subscription, editorial board,
submission guidelines, table of contents and abstracts

- *Applied Financial Economics* – [1]
  http://www.thomson.com/routledge/default.html
- *Applied Mathematical Finance* – [1]
  gopher://Niord.SHSU.edu:70/00gopher_root%3A%5B_DATA.ECON-CFP%5D.AMF
- *Finance and Stochastics* – [1]
  http://addi.or.uni-bonn.de:1048/finasto.html
- *Financial Analysts Journal* – [1]
  http://www.aimr.com/aimr/pubs/faj/fajhome.html
- *Financial Economics Network (FEN)* – (collection of contact details for journals including: *Corporate Finance and Organizations, Banking and Financial Institutions, Capital Markets, Derivatives*) [1]
  http://www.ssrn.com/FEN/
- *Financial Management Association (FMA)* – (journals: *Financial Management, Financial Practice and Education, Financial Management Collection, FMA Survey and Synthesis* series [1]
  http://www.webspace.com/~fma/
- *International Journal of Intelligent Systems in Accounting, Finance and Management* – [1]
  http://www.bus.orst.edu/faculty/brownc/isafm/isafhome.htm
- *International Review of Economics and Finance* – [1]
  http://www.udayton.edu/sba/iref.htm
- *Journal of Applied Econometrics Data Archive* – archive of papers after Jan 1994 [3]
  http://qed.econ.queensu.ca:80/jae/
- *Journal of Finance* – full text version of papers (PDF) – [3]
  http://www.cob.ohio-state.edu/~fin/journal/jof.htm
- *Journal of Financial and Quantitative Analysis* – [1]
  http://weber.u.washington.edu/~jfqa/
- *Journal of Financial and Strategic Decisions* – download current and archive articles (PDF) [3]
  http://washington.xtn.net/~mag/jfsd/jfsd.html
- *Journal of Financial Economics* – [1]
  http://WWW.SSB.Rochester.edu/fac/JFE/JFE.htm
- *Journal of Financial Statement Analysis* – [1]
  http://equity.stern.nyu.edu/~bsarath/hompage.html
- *Pacific Economic Review* – [1]
  http://www.cuhk.edu.hk/eco/per/per.htm
- *Quarterly Journal of Economics* – [1]
  http://www-mitpress.mit.edu/jrnls-catalog/quart-econ.html
- *RAND Journal of Economics* – [1]
  http://www.rand.org/misc/rje/

- *Review of Economics and Statistics* – [1]
  http://www-mitpress.mit.edu/jrnls-catalog/review-econ.html
- *Review of Economic Studies* – [1]
  http://www.ecn.bris.ac.uk/Restud/revstud.htm
- *Review of International Economics* – [1]
  http://www.ag.iastate.edu/journals/rie/
- *ECONbase* – searchable database containing up-to-date information on new and published articles in 33 Elsevier/North-Holland economics journals [3]
  http://www.elsevier.nl/homepage/sae/econbase/
- *CMS Business Intelligence Catalogue* – searchable catalogue of newsletters/magazines/reports with price/contact details [3]
  http://www.textor.com/cms/

Online financial calculators

Commissions calculators

- *Royal Bank Financial Group*, Canada – calculates commissions for: Canadian/US equity, options, mutual funds, gold/silver certificates
  http://www.royalbank.com/english/adirect/ccalc.html
- *Robert's Online Pricers* – (Intrepid Technology Inc.) stock/option indicative commissions for over 30 brokers
  http://www.intrepid.com/~robertl/index.html

Options

- *Leland O'Brien Rubinstein Associates* – American/European call/put options calculation for: value, delta, gamma, theta, implied volatility
  http://emanate.com/lor/calc.cgi
- *Montgomery Investment Technology* – Black Scholes American/European, Whaley models for: implied volatility and value, delta, gamma, theta, vega
  http://www.wallstreetnet.com/miti/pro.html
- *Numa Financial Systems* – single/multiple option Black Scholes call/put calculation for: value, delta, gamma, theta, vega, rho, implied volatility
  http://www.numa.com/derivs/ref/calculat/option/calc-opa.htm
- *OptionVue Systems International* – Black Scholes call/put options calculation for: value, delta, vega, theta
  http://www.optionvue.com/cgi-shl/optcalc.pl
- *Robert's Online Pricers* – (Intrepid Technology Inc.) American/European call/put option calculation for: value, delta, gamma, theta [Java, CGI]; derivatives pricer [Java]
  http://www.intrepid.com/~robertl/index.html

Convertible bonds

▦ *Numa Financial Systems* – calculates: conversion price/premium, simple yield, YTM, straight value, downside risk, implied volatility, dividend growth table
http://www.numa.com/derivs/ref/calculat/cb/calc-cba.htm

Warrants

▦ *Numa Financial Systems* – calculates: premium, gearing, CFP, parity ratio, leverage, Giguerre, share price growth matrix
http://www.numa.com/derivs/ref/calculat/warrant/calc-wta.htm

Fixed income yield calculators

▦ *Department of Physics, Boston University* – computes a variety of fixed income securities [Java]
http://physics.bu.edu/~sth/forms/yield.html

▦ *Department of Physics, Boston University* – day counter: calculations are based on the methodology outlined in the Securities Industry Association's (SIA) Standard Securities Calculations Methodologies [to be used with the above yield calculator, Java]
http://miranda.bu.edu:80/~sth/forms/dayCounts.html

Statistics

▦ *Department of Statistics, UCLA* – models: normal, exponential, binomial, poisson, correlation coefficient
http://www.stat.ucla.edu/~jbond/HTMLPOWER/index.html

▦ *Department of Statistics, UCLA* – probability models for variation
http://www.stat.ucla.edu/textbook/singles/describe_single/probmodels/

▦ *Department of Statistics, University of Washington* – statistics tools/projects
http://bayes.stat.washington.edu/STAT390/390projects.html

▦ *OptionVue Systems International* – probability calculator: the probability of a stock being above, below, or between two specified price targets
http://www.optionvue.com/cgi-shl/probcalc.pl

Present/future value

▦ *Institute for Biomedical Computing, Washington University* – calculations for: mortgages, loans, investment yield, future value/tax-deferred annuities
http://ibc.wustl.edu/mort/annuity.cgi

▦ *Salem Five Cents Savings Bank* – savings and investments planner; mortgage potential; loan payments
http://www.salemfive.com/salemfive/savings

▦ *NASA* – inflation calculator: parametric cost estimating using the GDP Deflator [JavaScript]
http://www.jsc.nasa.gov/bu2/inflate.html

▨ *Bank Rate Monitor* – interest calculator: future payments [JavaScript]
http://www.bankrate.com/bankrate/publ/intcalc.htm

▨ *Money Magazine* – calculates the exact percentage return – both total and annualized – for any investment over any time period
http://pathfinder.com/@@w8Xr0aFCygEAQEqa/cgi-bin/Money/portfolioworksheet.cgi

Deposit calculators

▨ *Westpac Banking Corporation*, Australia
http://www.westpac.com.au/deposit.html

Loan payments

▨ *Robert's Online Pricers* – (Intrepid Technology Inc.)
http://www.intrepid.com/~robertl/index.html

▨ *Mycrowynn Corp.* – APR calculation and loan amortization
http://www.mycrowynn.com/apr/

▨ *Live Software* – loan calculator [JavaScript]
http://jrc.livesoftware.com/loancalc/

US savings bond calculators

▨ *FRB New York* – computes the redemption values for Savings Bonds
http://www.ny.frb.org/pihome/svg_bnds/sb_val.html

▨ *MMR Software* – computes the value of Series EE Savings Bonds
http://www.execpc.com/~mmrsoft/

General personal finance

▨ *Sallie Mae* – savings, net assets, cost of college, cost of a deferment, monthly budget calculator
http://www.salliemae.com/calculators/

▨ *Merrill Lynch* – calculates net worth (input assets/liabilities)
http://www.merrill-lynch.ml.com/investor/worthform.html

▨ *ITT Hartford* – estate tax calculator
http://www.itthartford.com/corporate/life/est_calc1.html

▨ *Gabelli Funds, Inc.* – dollar cost averaging and a periodic investment calculator
http://www.gabelli.com/Gab_phtml/mfund/saving1.html#perinv

▨ *Prudential Securities* – wealth accumulation calculator
http://www.prusec.com/wlth_cal.htm

▨ *First Citizens Bank* – investment yield
http://www.firstcitizens.com/investfm.html

▨ *Financenter* – collection of personal finance calculators
http://www.financenter.com/

■ *BayBank* – mortgage calculators
http://www.baybank.com/products/calculators/index.html

Retirement

Most of the following require inputs such as: current age, desired retirement age, amount already saved, estimated annual income, estimated years of retirement, assumed annual average rate of return on your savings.

■ *Altamira Investment Services, Inc.* – analyses RRSP savings and future contributions
http://www.altamira.com/altamira/rrsp_calc.html

■ *Douglas County Bank & Trust Co. (DCB&T)* – retirement savings planner
http://www.dcbt.com/FinCalc/Retirement.html

■ *Piper Jaffray*
http://www.piperjaffray.com/cgi-shl/dbml.exe?template=/pj2/retire_first_version.dbm

■ *Austin Municipal Federal Credit Union*
http://www.amcu.org/onlineserv/retirement.html

■ *Waddel & Reed*
http://www.waddell.com/fun_ill.htm

■ *Gabelli Funds, Inc.*
http://www.gabelli.com/Gab_phtml/mfund/saving3.html

Miscellaneous

■ *Dentritics* – precious metal calculators: primary/misc stones carat weight; gemstone specific gravity; units converter
http://www.dendritics.com/a-calcs.htm

OTHER URL LISTS

■ *Virtual Library of Finance and Investments* – (Dept of Finance, Ohio State University) [5]
http://www.cob.ohio-state.edu/~fin/overview.html

■ *Institute of Finance and Banking* – (University of Göttingen) links to: finance, banking, currency, money and payment systems [5]
http://www.wiso.gwdg.de/ifbg/ifbghome.html

■ *Wall Street Directory* – (information for computerized traders and investors) [4]
http://www.wsdinc.com/

■ *The Treasury Management Pages* – [5]
http://www.mcs.com/~tryhardz/tmp.html

Regional

Asia

- *Dow Jones Telerate* – daily stock market report; news bulletins; value and charts for: stock index, currency [4]
  http://www.djtelerate.com.hk/

- *AsiaOne* – incorporating Singapore *Straits Times*, *Business Times* with BT Stockwatch [5]
  http://www.asia1.com.sg/

- *Jardine Fleming Unit Trusts* – weekly economic and market outlook; suggested model portfolio [3]
  http://www.jfleming_ut.com.hk/

- *Dharmala Capital* – (financial services) daily HK market report: index levels, market review and outlook, company news, economics, calendar, trading recommendations; archive of daily reports from Aug 95 [3]
  http://www.dharmala.com.hk/

- *Credit Lyonnais International Asset Management* – weekly review of the markets; monthly regional strategy notes; monthly funds report [3]
  http://www.asiaonline.net/cliam/

East Europe

- *OMRI* – daily digest of news (with historical archive) and analytic briefs for Transcaucasia/Central Asia, Central and Eastern Europe, Southeastern Europe [2]
  http://www.omri.cz

Latin America

▓ *Latin American Newsletters* – (monthly subscription newsletter on political/economic affairs)
http://www.softopt.co.uk/latin/brazil.html

▓ *Center for Latin American Capital Markets Research* – links for: exchanges, economic data, research, news [3]
http://www.netrus.net/users/gmorles/

▓ *Journal of Latin American Perspectives* – [1]
http://wizard.ucr.edu/~asampaio/lap.html

Emerging markets

▓ *Internet Securities* – (subscription news and research covering Poland, Russia, the Ukraine, the Czech Republic, the Baltic States, Hungary, China and India) [3]
http://securities.com/

▓ *Emerging Markets Companion* – links [2]
http://www.emgmkts.com

Countries

Alphabetically ordered by country.

Note: besides the resources listed under the 'Markets' section for each country, it may be useful also to check the market reports at the sites of:

- *Wall Street Journal*
  http://update.wsj.com/
- *Financial Times*
  http://www.ft.com/
- *Knight-Ridder* at CNN*fn*
  http://www.cnnfn.com/

ARGENTINA

Domain code	ar
Currency	Nuevo peso argentino
GDP	$270.8bn
GDP/capita	$7990
GDP growth	6.0%
External debt	$73bn
Exports	$15.7bn (fob)
Imports	$21.4bn

News

- *La Nacion* – (Spanish) daily news
  http://www.lanacion.com/
- *Clarin* – (Spanish) daily news
  http://www.clarin.com/

Markets

■ *Mercantil Valores* – (stockbroker) daily closing Buenos Aires SE stock prices and index levels; daily closing prices for government bond with table of bond terms; reference articles on: the Buenos Aires Stock Exchange and the Depositary System, foreign investment in Argentina [3]
http://www.totalnet.com.ar/Mercval/

Economy

■ *Ministry of Economy and Public Works and Services* – quarterly economic report; reports from the government economic program; information on privatization [2]
http://www.mecon.ar/

■ *National Statistics Institute* – (Spanish)
http://www.indec.mecon.ar/default.htm

Miscellaneous

■ *Rava Sociedad de Bolsa* – (securities broker) [1]
http://www.rpas.com/rava.html

■ *Banco de Galicia* – (private bank, Spanish)
http://www.bancogalicia.com.ar/

■ *Externa* – directory of Argentine businesses [2]
http://www.externa.com.ar/

AUSTRALIA

Domain code	au
Currency	Australian dollar ($A)
GDP	$374.6bn
GDP/capita	$20 720
GDP growth	6.4%
External debt	$147.2bn
Exports	$50.4bn
Imports	$51.1bn

News

■ *The Australian* – daily general and business news; brief closing financial market data [3]
http://www.australian.aust.com/

■ *Sydney Morning Herald* – daily general and business news; archive of past one month's issues [3]
http://www.smh.com.au/

- *Australian Financial Review* – daily news stories; regular investment columns [3]
  http://www.afr.com.au/
- *The Age* – daily general and business news [2]
  http://www.theage.com.au/

Markets

- *Macquarie* – (financial services) daily data and comment for: equities, commodities and currencies; SPI technical comment with charts for download; weekly economic update; restricted access to: ASX stock prices, close of trade equity market summary, equity research report [4]
  http://www.macquarie.com.au/
- *Pont Securities* – (discount broker) bimonthly newletter; portfolio game; accepts overseas clients; offers 'ten per cent discount for all orders sent by e-mail' [3]
  http://www.pont.com.au/
- *Wilson HTM* – (securities broker) daily stock market comment; weekly economic update; occasional sector notes; quarterly economic overview and investment strategy; selected company reports; reference articles for investors [4]
  http://www.wilsonhtm.com.au/
- *Norwich Investment* – daily data and comment on: stocks, commodities, fixed interest markets; monthly: stock market review and economic outlook [3]
  http://www.norwich.com.au/
- *Burdett, Buckeridge & Young* – (institutional stockbrokers) daily closing stock/sector indices; restricted access to research [2]
  http://www.bby.com.au/
- *The Privateer* – (subscription newsletter) front page of newsletter; report on recommended portfolio performance; download sample issue; charts updated three times weekly: stock indices, gold index; point and figure charts updated weekly: stock index, gold; regularly updated gold report: prices for gold stocks, market comment, gold price charts, Australian gold index [3]
  http://www.the-privateer.com/
- *BankWest* – occasional economic commentary concerning western Australia); weekly financial markets update with comment and data: official cash rate, bank bills, commonwealth bonds, currency, gold; regularly updated bank rates [3]
  http://www.bankwest.com.au/
- *First Pacific Stockbrokers* – (allied with CS First Boston) daily market reports (PDF format): summary, indices, company news and prices; archive back to Sep 95 [2]
  http://csfbae.com.au/

■ *St. George Bank* – daily data and comments on interest rates and currencies
[2]
http://www.stgeorge.com.au/

Stocks

■ *Australian Stock Exchange (ASX)* – market indices updated every hour; daily
closing share prices [4]
http://www.asx.com.au/

■ *Weblink* – daily closing stock quotes with top ten increases/decreases for
industrial/mining stocks; guide to investment; links; subscription for: hourly
updated stock quotes, historical quote database [4]
http://www.weblink.com.au/

■ *NetQuote* – daily closing stock prices and colon-delimited ASCII file available
for download; daily closing index levels; create and monitor stock portfolio;
investment articles [4]
http://www.asxquote.interpro.net.au/

■ *Gerry Pauley* – (newsletter) analyses, charts and gossip for a selection of ASX
stocks [5]
http://www.wantree.com.au/~tpauleyg/shares.html

■ *Dicksons* – (private client stockbroker) daily statistics report: Australian
stocks, currencies, commodities, interest rates; company reports; monthly
recommended stock list; updated charts for: stock indices, 10-year bond
yields, currency, gold, copper, aluminium, nickel, crude oil, recommended
stocks of the week [5]
http://www.opennet.net.au/dicksons/

■ *Phillips Henderson Ward* – (stockbroker allied with HSBC) updated table of
140 ASX companies with: price, 2-year estimates for profit/PE/yield, brief
comment; occasional company report [4]
http://www.phw.com.au/

■ *Rivkin Croll Smith* – (discount broker) [1]
http://www.intersol.com.au/rivkin.html

■ *Australian Equities Research* – (subscription newsletter) sample copy of
Australian Sharemarket Investor Newsletter to download [1]
http://www.aer.com.au/

Futures and options

■ *Sydney Futures Exchange* – download comma-delimited ASCII files with all
daily price data with archive of previous days; download comma-delimited
ASCII files with complete daily price history from contract inception;
statistical tables and charts detailing daily average volumes, deals, volatilities,
efps, nominal values, open interest and non-traded volumes; free
subscription to monthly SFE *Australian Market Update*; educational articles [5]
http://www.sfe.com.au/

Economy

- ■ *Australian Bureau of Statistics* – key economic and social indicators; latest press releases; twice yearly Census Update newsletter [3]
  http://www.statistics.gov.au/

- ■ *Westpac* – (retail and commercial bank) monthly economic bulletin with economic forecasts and comment; monthly commodity outlook; custodian newsletter; history of Australian banking [3]
  http://www.westpac.com.au/

- ■ *State Bank of New South Wales* – weekly report of forthcoming statistics; monthly economic report; economic outlook [3]
  http://www.sbnsw.com.au/

Miscellaneous

- ■ *Australian Securities Commission* – company search database; overview of regulations [2]
  http://www.asc.gov.au/

- ■ *Infocast* – (information provider) [1]
  http://www.pont.com.au/~infocast/

- ■ *Pembroke Josephson Wright* – (securities brokers) – [1]
  http://www.pjw.interpro.net.au/

- ■ *Newsgroup*: aus.invest

Banks

- ■ *Bain & Company* – (Deutsche Bank Group) restricted access to research [1]
  http://www.bain.com.au/

- ■ *ANZ Bank* – [1]
  http://www.anz.com.au/

Other URL lists

- ■ *netScents* – [4]
  http://www.peg.apc.org/~netscents/

- ■ *Weblink* – [5]
  http://www.weblink.com.au/webinvestor/doc/hotlist/

- ■ *Warren Butt* – [3]
  http://www.pcug.org.au/~wbutt/stocks/stocks.htm

AUSTRIA

Domain code	at
Currency	Austrian schilling (S)
GDP	$139bn
GDP/capita	$17 500
GDP growth	2.5%
External debt	$22bn
Exports	$44bn
Imports	$54bn

News

▓ *WirtschaftsWoche* – (German), weekly news, market comment, news archive [3]
http://www.wirtschaftswoche.co.at/wirtschaftswoche/

▓ *Der Standard* – (German) [2]
http://www.derstandard.co.at/derstandard/

Markets

▓ *Kleinen Zeitung* – (German) daily stock quotes, currency rates [3]
http://www.styria.co.at/kleine/Boerse/

▓ *Creditanstalt* – (German) domestic and international market comments [3]
http://www.creditanstalt.co.at/home/pidindx.shtml

▓ *GiroCredit* – (German) daily closing prices for currencies, bond futures and swaps [3]
http://www2.telecom.at/gc/

Stocks

▓ *Vienna Stock Exchange* – (German – English introduction); daily company news, price and turnover data [3]
http://www.apa.co.at/boerse/

▓ *Vienna University of Economics* – daily closing prices for stocks and indices, historical data [4]
http://www.wu-wien.ac.at/cgi-bin/boerse1.pl

Futures and options

▓ *Austrian futures and options* – FTP site to download historic daily closing prices [3]
http://www2.telecom.at/gc/ftp/

Economy

▓ *Vienna University of Economics* [2]
http://www.wu-wien.ac.at/

Miscellaneous

Banks

▓ *Hypo Bank* – (German) [1]
http://www.VOL.at/Hypo/

▓ *Bank Austria* – (German) [1]
http://www.telecom.at/ba/

▓ *Allgemeine Sparkasse Oberösterreich* – (German) [1]
http://www.oon.at/aspk/welcome.html

▓ *P.S.K. Telebanking* – (German) [1]
http://www.psk.co.at/psk/

▓ *Austrian Lotteries* – (German, English introduction) [2]
http://www.lottery.co.at/

Other URL lists

▓ *Netwing* [4]
http://www.netwing.at/webindex/

BELGIUM

Domain code	be
Currency	Belgian franc (BF)
GDP	$181.5bn
GDP/capita	$17 040
GDP growth	2.3%
External debt	$31.3bn
Exports	$117bn (fob)
Imports	$120bn (cif)

News

▓ *Grenz-Echo* – (German, East Belgium) daily news [3]
http://www.euregio.net/ge/Index.html

▓ *Het Volk* (Flemish, French) weekly summary of news [2]
http://www.hetvolk.be/

Markets

■ *N.V. De Maertelaere & Co.* (Flemish, English introduction) monthly financial bulletin (bonds, currencies); stock market review; daily eurobond bond prices [3]
http://www.de-maertelaere.be/istinfuk.htm

Stocks

■ *Tijd NV* – (Flemish) daily closing prices, links to company information [3]
http://www.tijd.be/tijd/beurs/beurs01.html

Futures and options

■ *Belgian Futures and Options Exchange (Belfox)* – (English, Flemish, French) daily closing prices [3]
http://www.belfox.be/belfox/UK/L1/L1indUK.html

Miscellaneous

Banks

■ *BACOB* – (Flemish, French) daily review of the news [2]
http://www.bacob.be/bacob/fr/index.html

■ *Banque CERA* (Flemish, French) [2]
http://www.Bank.CERA.be/CERA/

■ *Bank Brussel Lambert* – (Flemish, French, English) [1]
http://www.bbl.be/

■ *MoneyNet* – daily international price data for currencies, bonds, stock market indices [3]
http://moneynet.lrt.be/

Other URL lists

■ *Webrider*
http://www.webrider.be/

BRAZIL

Domain code	br
Currency	Real (R$)
GDP	$886.3bn
GDP/capita	$5580
GDP growth	5.3%
External debt	$134bn
Exports	$43.6bn
Imports	$33.2bn

News

- ▓ *Jornal do Brasil* – (Portuguese) daily general/economic news
  http://www.jb.com.br/
- ▓ *Agência Estado* – (Portuguese) daily financial news
  http://www.agestado.com.br/
- ▓ *O Estado de S. Paulo* – (Portuguese, English digest) daily news [2]
  http://www.estado.com.br/
- ▓ *Radiobras* – (Portuguese) daily digest of news from the newspapers
  http://www.cdsid.com.br/radiobras/sinopse.htm
- ▓ *Brazzil* – monthly magazine with general and economic news; archive of past issues from 1993 [2]
  http://www.brazzil.com/
- ▓ *Real Brazil* – bi-monthly journal on Brazil affairs [2]
  http://lanic.utexas.edu/project/ppb/rb/
- ▓ *Latin American Newsletters* – (monthly subscription newsletter on political/economic affairs)
  http://www.softopt.co.uk/latin/brazil.html

Markets

- ▓ *Banco da Bahia* – (investment bank) daily report with: updated charts of IBOVESPA and interest rates, inflation indices, IBOVESPA spot and futures prices, interest rates and futures prices, currency, gold, off-shore funds, fixed income; daily stock market report with closing prices; weekly inflation and macro-economics reports [4]
  http://www.bahiabank.com.br/

Stocks

- ▓ *Rio de Janeiro Stock Exchange* – daily closing prices, downloadable in zip format; 2-week archive of daily closing prices [3]
  http://www.embratel.net.br/infoserv/bvrj/index.html
- ▓ *São Paulo Stock Exchange* – BOVESPA – daily market report: closing share prices, forward market, options, index levels, major movers, most active; archive of previous ten daily reports; description of BOVESPA Index [4]
  http://www.bovespa.com.br/

Futures and options

- ▓ *Bolsa Brasileira de Futuros* – [2]
  http://www.embratel.net.br/infoserv/bbf/

Commodities

- *Bolsa de Mercadorias do Paraná* – (commodities exchange, Portuguese)
  http://www.mps.com.br/InfoServ/bmp/

- *A.Azevedo-Filho* – (Portuguese) information and links on commodities markets [3]
  http://am.esalq.usp.br/desr/market/mercados.html

Economy

- *Brazilian Embassy in London* – overview of the economy; key economic indicators; surveys on Brazil [4]
  http://www.demon.co.uk/Itamaraty/

- *Brazilian Institute for Geography and Statistics* – Census figures; key social/economic indicators [3]
  http://www.ibge.gov.br/

- *Institute for Applied Economic Research* – (Portuguese)
  http://www.ipea.gov.br/

- *Ministry of External Relations* – social/economic reference articles [2]
  http://www.dct.mre.gov.br/ndsg/ndsg1.htm

Miscellaneous

- *Câmara de Liquidação e Custódia* – (Brazilian Clearing and Custody) [1]
  http://www.embratel.net.br/infoserv/clc/index.html

Banks

- *Banco do Brasil* – [1]
  http://www.bancobrasil.com.br/

- *Bradesco* – [1]
  http://www.bradesco.com.br/

- *Banco do Estado do Rio Grande do Sul* – Banrisul – (state bank) [1]
  http://www.banrisul.com.br/espanol/ebergs.htm

- *Banco do Estado do Ceará* – BEC – (state bank) [1]
  http://www.bec.hosting.ibm.com/

- *Banco de Boston* – [1]
  http://www.bkb-br.com/

Other URL lists

- *Calor* – [3]
  http://charlotte.acns.nwu.edu/rio/brasil.html

- *Yaih* – [4]
  http://www.ci.rnp.br/si/index.html

▨ *Webra* – [4]
http://www.embratel.net.br/infoserv/webra/

CANADA

Domain code	ca
Currency	Canadian dollar (Can$)
GDP	$639.8bn
GDP/capita	$22 760
GDP growth	4.5%
External debt	$243bn
Exports	$164.3bn (fob)
Imports	$151.5bn (cif)

News

▨ *Financial Post* – (Toronto Sun) daily business/financial news; regularly updated rates: market indices, term deposits, currencies, economic stats, quarterly sector reports; weekly market comment from Argus Research; special market/sector reports; ranking of Canada's top 50 companies by: revenue, assets, net income, returns with details on growth, employees and ownership [4]
http://www.canoe.ca/FP/home.html

▨ *Globe* – daily general/business news; company briefs; business comment [3]
http://WWW.GLOBEANDMAIL.ca/

▨ *24 HR News* – news stories updated through the day [4]
http://www.canoe.ca/News/home.html

▨ *CBC Radio News* – headline news updated through the day [4]
http://radioworks.cbc.ca/radio/programs/news/

▨ *Daily News* – (Nova Scotia) daily general/business news [3]
http://www.hfxnews.com/

▨ *The Canadian Press (CP)* – daily news digest [3]
http://xenon.xe.com/canpress/hlines.htm

▨ *Canada NewsWire* – (press release database) daily company and Government of Quebec press releases; search facility on release archive [3]
http://www.newswire.ca/

▨ *Canadian Corporate News* – company press release database, archive and search facility [3]
http://www.cdn-news.com/

▨ *The Northern Miner* – (weekly newspaper covering North American-based mining companies) selection from the paper version: top stories, headlines, companies mentioned, meetings, coming events, most active stocks; subscription to full online version and archive of past issues [3]
http://www.northernminer.com/

Markets

- *Telenium* – (quote and information service) daily closing share prices from: Alberta, Montreal, Toronto, Vancouver Exchanges; subscription for: 15 min. delayed stock quotes from the TSE, MSE, VSE and ASE, 100-day and 100-week historical graphs, end-of-day trading summaries for download to graphing packages, 10 min. delayed futures and options quotes from the WCE, CME, CBOT, and COMEX, Reuters newswire [4]
  http://www.telenium.ca/

- *Toronto-Dominion Bank* – daily morning market update for: currencies/money/bonds with economic stats summary; weekly digest of economic and financial developments; proprietary funds description and daily prices; quarterly economic/automotive updates; commentary on federal and provincial Budgets; archive of reports and search facility [5]
  http://www.tdbank.ca/tdbank/

Stocks

- *Montreal Exchange* – daily market summary: indices, most active, major movers, futures settlement/vol/OI; description of XXM and sub-indices; details of training programs [4]
  http://www.me.org/

- *Vancouver Stock Exchange* – daily closing market summary: brief review and most active stocks; weekly trading summary: most active, major moves; 3-month VSE Index/turnover charts; brief information on listed companies [3]
  http://www.vse.com/

- *Canada Stockwatch* – company news bulletins; daily closing prices and 1-year stock charts; downloadable daily stock prices; subscription service for: search facility on bulletin archive from 1984, historical stock prices from 1986, e-mailed bulletins for select companies [4]
  http://www.canada-stockwatch.com/

- *Security APL* – 15 min. delayed quotes [4]
  http://www.secapl.com/cgi-bin/qs

- *CT Securities* – EasyLine Brokerage – 15 min. delay quotes on Canadian stocks/indices; portfolio facility [3]
  http://www.ctsecurities.com/

- *Digital Ink* – (information on Vancouver Stock Exchange) daily closing prices; brief company details; insider trading reports; VSE Notices [4]
  http://204.174.18.3/financial/main_idx.html

- *Canadian Stock Market Reporter* – subscription service for: stock quotes delayed 15 min., indices, most active, major movers, portfolio monitor, 2-year historical stock charts, company profile
  http://canstock.com/

- *Stock Research Group* – daily market report on selected companies: closing prices, stock chart, company information and news, indices, currencies;

company news bulletin; subscription newsletter [3]
http://www.stockgroup.com/

▓ *Hot Stocks Review* – (subscription newsletter and fax service for high risk, speculative small cap stocks) archive of previous issues
http://www.hot-stocks.com/

▓ *Carlson On-line Services* – (source for Canadian investor relations and corporate communications information) search for company information; links for press releases, quotes, charts [3]
http://www.fin-info.com/

▓ *MarketMasters* – subscription trading model for penny stocks
http://www.aurex.com/

Futures and options

▓ *Yaletown Futures Group* – (partnership of commodities trading advisers) [2]
http://web20.mindlink.net/yaletown/

Economy

▓ *Bank of Canada* – (central bank) current market rates (PDF format): Bank of Canada rate, exchange rates, money market yields, Government bond yields; weekly financial statistics (PDF format); press releases and speeches, various reports and working papers [3]
http://www.bank-banque-canada.ca/

▓ *Department of Finance, Canada* – transcript of annual Federal Budget; quarterly report on economic performance (PDF format); monthly report on the Government's fiscal performance (PDF format); quarterly update on the Federal Government's debt programme; archive of previous year's publications; press releases and speeches [4]
http://www.fin.gc.ca/

▓ *Government of Canada* – economic overview [3]
http://canada.gc.ca/

▓ *Statistics Canada* – updated social/economic statistics; daily report of latest released figures with archive and search facility – [5]
http://WWW.StatCan.CA/start.html

▓ *Royal Bank of Canada* – twice daily updated, and a weekly, currency and credit markets report (PDF format); review of the Federal Budget [3]
http://www.royalbank.com/

▓ *Scotiabank* – weekly economic commentary; occasional economic essays; daily proprietary funds prices [2]
http://www.scotiabank.ca/

▓ *Ernst & Young (Canada)* – Budget and tax analysis [3]
http://tax.ey.ca/ey/

Miscellaneous

- *Invest Network Canada* – (general Canadian investment information) e-mail newsletter with archive from Apr 95; participating company profiles; fund profiles [2]
  http://www.islandnet.com/invest/homepage.html
- *Newsgroup*: misc.invest.canada

Funds

- *Dynamic Mutual Funds* – daily proprietary fund prices; annual market outlook; introduction to funds [2]
  http://www.dynamic.ca/
- *Scudder Investor Services* – (fund management) [2]
  http://www.scudder.ca/
- *Ascot Financial Services* – [2]
  http://www.ascot.com/
- *Fund Library* – information on participating funds; monthly Fund Watch newsletter; daily funds prices [4]
  http://www.fundlib.com/
- *First Canadian Fund News* – daily economics report; weekly markets summary; North American economic calendar; monthly economic indicators; daily proprietary funds prices; introduction to funds
  http://www.fcfunds.bomil.ca/
- *FundWatch* – links [3]
  http://www.blvl.igs.net/~dmcateer/

Banks

- *Canada Trust* – (retail bank and fund manager) twice-daily market data summary: stocks, fixed income, money, currencies; monthly capital markets review; investor newsletter; daily proprietary fund prices [3]
  http://www.canadatrust.com/
- *Canadian Imperial Bank of Commerce* – quarterly investing newsletter; occasional economic updates [2]
  http://www.cibc.com/
- *Bank of Montreal* – [1]
  http://www.bmo.com/
- *Laurentian Bank* – [1]
  http://www.mortgagestore.com/laurent/laurent.html

Other URL lists

- *Canadian Finance Network* [3]
  http://www.CanadianFinance.com/cdnbase.htm

CHILE

Domain code	cl
Currency	Chilean peso (Ch$)
GDP	$97.7bn
GDP/capita	$7010
GDP growth	4.3%
External debt	$20bn
Exports	$11.5bn (fob)
Imports	$10.9bn (fob)

News

■ *Chip News* – daily general, mining and business news; archive of previous issues with search facility [4]
http://www.chip.cl/

■ *Diario Oficial de Chile* – (Spanish)
http://200.0.148.7/doficial.html

■ *La Epoca* – (Spanish)
http://www.reuna.cl/laepoca/

Markets

■ *Santiago Stock Exchange* – daily market summary: share indices, volumes traded and major price movers; list of Chilean ADRs in the US; calendar of market holidays [3]
http://www.bolsantiago.cl/

■ *Bolsa Electrónica de Chile* – (Spanish) real-time index charts
http://www.bolchile.cl/

Economy

■ *Chilean Government's Network* – (Spanish, English introduction) economic overview and statistics [2]
http://www.presidencia.cl/

■ *Banco Central de Chile* – (Spanish)
http://www.bcentral.cl/

Miscellaneous

■ *Alfa Corredores de Bolsa* – (stockbroker, Spanish)
http://www.alfa.corredores.cl/

Banks

■ *Banco Sud Americano* – (Spanish)
http://www.bsa.cl/

- *Banco O'Higgins* – (Spanish)
  http://www.boh.cl/
- *Banco Concepción* – (Spanish)
  http://www.bconce.cl/
- *Banco de Crédito e Inversiones* – (Spanish)
  http://www.bci.cl/

Other URL lists

- *Chilnet*
  http://www.chilnet.cl/

CHINA

Domain code	cn
Currency	Yuan (Y)
GDP	$2.978tr
GDP/capita	$2500
GDP growth	11.8%
External debt	$100bn
Exports	$121bn (fob)
Imports	$115.7bn (cif)

News

- *Singapore Business Times* – daily news stories; articles [3]
  http://www.asia1.com.sg/biztimes/
- *China News Digest* – regular general news digest with archive of past issues [2]
  http://cnd.org/
- *Beijing Review* – weekly digest of general and economic news [3]
  http://china-window.com/edu/books/bjreview/BJREVIEW.HTML
- *Asia, Inc. Online* – weekly economic review [3]
  http://www.asia-inc.com/thisweek/index.html
- *Guangzhou Rebao* – daily news for Guangzhou [2]
  http://www.asia1.com.sg/gzbao/
- *China News Service* – (subscription news service)
  http://www.chinanews.com/
- *Fox* – directory of news sources [3]
  http://www.inetworld.net/~fox/info.html
- *James Miles* – directory of news sources [4]
  http://www.hk.super.net/~milesj/

Markets

- *Dow Jones Telerate* – daily stock market report; news bulletins; value and charts for: stock index, currency [4]
  http://www.djtelerate.com.hk/

- *China Business Net* – stock quotes for: Shanghai A/B, Shenzhen A/B, Hong Kong H; futures quotes for exchanges: Beijing, China, Dalian, Guangdong, Shanghai, Shenyang, Shenzhen, Zhengzhou; RMB exchange rates; weekly business news briefs [3]
  http://www.business-china.com/index.htm

Stocks

- *Pacific ComNex* – daily closing prices for Shanghai SE with price and vol charts; customizable portfolio program [4]
  http://www.comnex.com/

- *Great Trend Internet Services* – (information about the Shenzhen SE)
  http://www.cninfo.co.cn/...

- *Dharmala Capital* – brief market report with prices and news [2]
  http://www.dharmala.com.hk/securities/regional_daily.shtml

Economy

- *Political and Economic Risk Consultancy* – regularly updated political/economic outlook; key economic indicators [4]
  http://asiarisk.com/china.html

- *US Department of Commerce* – key economic indicators; emerging sector analysis [3]
  http://www.stat-usa.gov/bems/bemschi/bemschi.html

- *ChinaNet* – (Government server, Chinese, English introduction) [1]
  http://www.bta.net.cn/

Miscellaneous

- *Nong Xiang Investment Consulting* – (software developers) [1]
  http://www.comnex.com/business/nongxiang.htm

Banks

- *Bank of China* – [1]
  http://bocwww.bta.net.cn/

- *UCC (Shanghai)* – directory of foreign banks in Shanghai [2]
  http://www.sh.com/public/branches.htm

Other URL lists

- *Marco Polo* – [4]
  http://www.calweb.com/~marcop/marco.htm
- *Weiqing Huang* – [4]
  http://www.aimhi.com/VC/nankai/chinasit.html
- *China Internet Yellow Pages* [3]
  http://china.webshop.net/
- *Australian National University* – [3]
  http://coombs.anu.edu.au/WWWVLAsian/China.html

CROATIA (HRVATSKA)

Domain code	hr
Currency	Croatian kuna (HRK)
GDP	$12.4bn
GDP/capita	$2640
GDP growth	3.4%
External debt	$2.9bn
Exports	$3.9bn (fob)
Imports	$4.7bn (cif)

News

- *HRT News* – daily Croatian radio news reports [4]
  http://www.hrt.hr/vijesti/hrt/index_eng.html
- *Hina Newsline* – Croatian News Agency, daily digest of news [3]
  http://www.hina.hr/
- *Banka* – business and finance magazine from Zagreb [3]
  http://www.zse.com.hr/banka/index.html

Markets

- *Zagreb Stock Exchange* – daily prices, CPF (Croatian Privatization Fund) auction reports, rules for foreign investment, description of Croatian banking and finance, list of financial institutions in Croatia, links [4]
  http://www.zse.com.hr/

Economy

- *Government of the Republic of Croatia* – list of government departments with contact numbers [2]
  http://www.vlada.hr/
- *Croatian Chamber of Economy* [2]
  http://alf.tel.hr/hgk/enmenu.htm

▓ *Faculty of Electrical Engineering and Computing* – short review of the economy [2]
http://rafael.zvne.fer.hr/HR/hr-intro.html

Miscellaneous

▓ *Croatia Banka* (Croatian)
http://open.cc.etf.hr/com/crobanka/

▓ *Zagrebacka banka* (Croatian)
http://open.cc.etf.hr/com/zaba/

Other URL lists

▓ *Tel.Fr* [4]
http://www.zse.com.hr/banka/index.html

CZECH REPUBLIC

Domain code	cz
Currency	Koruna (Kc)
GDP	$76.5bn
GDP/capita	$7350
GDP growth	2.2%
External debt	$8.7bn
Exports	$13.4bn (fob)
Imports	$13.3bn (fob)

News

▓ *CTK Czech News Agency* – daily news reports, daily survey of Czech press [3]
http://www.ios.com/

▓ *OMRI* – daily digest of news (with historical archive) and analytic briefs for Transcaucasia/Central Asia, Central and Eastern Europe, Southeastern Europe [2]
http://www.omri.cz/

▓ *Radio Prague E-News* – (Czech, English, French, German, Spanish) daily news with historical archive [3]
gopher://voskovec.radio.cz:70/11/radio

Markets

▓ *Komero Brokerage House* – proprietary daily stock and sector indices, risk/reward data for selected stocks [3]
http://www.anet.cz/komero/komero.htm

Stocks

- *Internet CZ, Alvera* – daily stock prices from the Prague Stock Exchange, daily market summary, historic prices [4]
  http://infox.eunet.cz:5555/cgi-bin/alvera1.pl/ea/
- *VOL* – (Czech) information about the Prague Stock Exchange
  http://www.vol.cz/BURZA/

Currencies and money

- *Internet CZ* – daily historical exchange rates from Czech National Bank [3]
  http://info.eunet.cz/cnbkalen_e.html

Economy

- *Czech National Bank* – comprehensive economic overview [4]
  http://www.czech.cz/infosrc/ff/economy.htm
- *CzechInvest* – information for inward foreign investment [4]
  http://www.czech.cz/infosrc/czinv/00-menu.htm
- *Czech Embassy in Washington* – economics report; contact information for Czech Ministries, investment organizations, Czech companies and banks; general business information [3]
  http://www.czech.cz/washington/ekon/ekon.htm

Miscellaneous

- *broKING, s.r.o.* – broker for the Czech capital markets [1]
  http://www.bohemia.net/broking/
- *Credittax* – (Czech, with English introduction, general financial services company) [1]
  http://www.infima.cz/creditax/

Other URL lists

- *Ministry of Foreign Affairs* [4]
  http://www.czech.cz/
- *Cesnet* [3]
  http://www.cesnet.cz/

DENMARK

Domain code	dk
Currency	Danish krone (DKr)
GDP	$103bn
GDP/capita	$19 860
GDP growth	4.5%
External debt	$40.9bn
Exports	$42.9bn (fob)
Imports	$37.1bn (cif)

News

▦ *Dagbladet Borsen* – monthly market and economics report [2]
http://www.borsen.dk/dagblad/Monthly.html

Markets

▦ *Jyske Bank* – stock and bond markets review, market outlook, stock recommendations [3]
http://www.jyske-bank.dk/

Stocks

▦ *Aktienyt* – (Danish) daily closing stock prices, daily stock news [3]
http://www.danielsen.com/aktier.shtml

Economy

▦ *Den Danske Bank* – half-year economic report [2]
http://www.DanskeBank.dk/3912inet/english.htm

Miscellaneous

▦ *Realkredit Danmark* (Danish, English introduction with information on the Copenhagen Stock Exchange, mortgage bonds) [2]
http://www.rd.dk/indny2.htm

▦ *Unibank* – (Danish)
http://www.unibank.dk/

Other URL lists

▦ *Jubii* (Danish)
http://www.jubii.dk/oekonomi/

ESTONIA

| Domain code | ee |
| Currency | Estonian kroon (EEK) |

GDP	$10.4bn
GDP/capita	$6460
GDP growth	4.0%
External debt	$650m
Exports	$1.65bn (fob)
Imports	$1.0bn (cif)

News

▨ *Baltic News Service* – general and business news updated through the day; weekly business journal; related news from AP, Reuters and PAP (headlines available free, subscription required for full access to newswire) [4]
http://www.bns.ee/

▨ *The Baltics Online* – daily news and archive from the Estonian News Agency; occasional securities markets reports and economic stats [4]
http://www.viabalt.ee/

▨ *Estonian Foreign Ministry* – weekly review of Estonian affairs; press releases of the Ministry, information and statistics on Estonia
http://www.vm.ee/

Markets

Currencies and money

▨ *Institute of Baltic Studies* – daily rates from the Bank of Estonia [2]
http://www.ibs.ee/cgi-bin/lastrate

Economy

▨ *Bank of Estonia* – economic bulletins, overview of banking regulation, reference articles on the Estonian economy [4]
http://www.ee/epbe/

▨ *Estonian Investment Agency* – general information on the economy, investment regulations [3]
http://www.vm.ee/eia/index.html

▨ *CIESIN* – brief overview and many links [3]
http://www.ciesin.ee/ESTCG/EandT/

Miscellaneous

▨ *North Estonian Bank* – occasional currency rate posting [1]
http://www.pep.ee/inglise/engnew.html

■ *Estonian Forexbank* [1]
  http://www.forex.ee/

■ *Estonian Savings Bank* (Estonian) [1]
  http://www.esb.ee/

Other URL lists

■ *Institute of Baltic Studies* [4]
  http://www.ibs.ee/

FINLAND

Domain code	fi
Currency	Markka (FMk)
GDP	$81.8bn
GDP/capita	$16 140
GDP growth	3.5%
External debt	$30bn
Exports	$23.4bn (fob)
Imports	$18bn (cif)

Markets

■ *Finnish Securities and Derivatives Exchange (SOM)* – derivatives prices updated every 15 min.; daily closing prices for the Helsinki Stock Exchange [5]
  http://www.som.fi/

Stocks

■ *Finstocks* – Finnish stock charts updated daily; flexible format: compare relative stock performance, detailed technical analysis on single stocks, create portfolio [5]
  http://finstocks.uwasa.fi/index.html.en

Economy

■ *Statistics Finland* – national statistical institute of Finland with comprehensive database of Finnish stats, latest released (and timetable for) economic stats [4]
  http://www.stat.fi/sf/genpres.html

■ *Research Institute of the Finnish Economy* – regularly updated financial markets overview; quarterly economic forecasts [3]
  http://www.etla.fi/

■ *TaT* – general economic data [2]
  http://www.tat.fi/finnfact/finnfact.htm

■ *Ministry of Finance* – economic bulletin; charts and statistics [3]
http://www.vn.fi/vn/vm/english/mof.htm

Miscellaneous

■ *Aktia Mutual Funds* – information on funds available, occasional fund reports [1]
http://www.aktia.fi/rahasto/fundsenglish.html

■ *Municipal Finance* – credit institution, collection of financial articles [1]
http://www.keva.fi/kura/english/welcome.htm

■ *Nedecon* – list of top 100 Finnish companies [2]
http://www.nedecon.fi/top-100/default.htm

Other URL lists

■ *Finnish Finance Network* [3]
http://www.shh.fi/ffn/

■ *Finland Online* [2]
http://www.finland.fi/pohja3.htm

FRANCE

Domain code	fr
Currency	French franc (F)
GDP	$1.080tr
GDP/capita	$18 670
GDP growth	2.4%
External debt	$300bn
Exports	$249bn (fob)
Imports	$238bn (cif)

News

■ *Dernières Nouvelles d'Alsace* – (French) daily general/economic news [3]
http://www.sdv.fr/dna/

■ *Le Monde* – (French) download daily version in PDF format
http://www.lemonde.fr/

■ *Le Revenu Français* – (French) weekly economics/financial journal with selected articles to download; guide to SICAVs [2]
http://www.calvacom.fr/lerevenu/

■ *Investir* – (weekly financial journal, French) subscription service to download in PDF format
http://www.edelweb.fr/Guests/Investir/

■ *Liberation* – (French) download daily version in PDF format
http://www.liberation.fr/

■ *Agence France-Presse* – (subscription customized e-mail service)
http://www.afp.com/

■ *Tocqueville Connection* – weekly general/political/financial news [2]
http://www.AdeTocqueville.com/index.htm

Markets

■ *Finacor* – (broker) regularly updated Matif charts with technical comment
for: CAC40, Pibor, Notionnel; daily European markets report with:
performance of recommended strategies, Government bond and forex
spreads, yield curve spreads; digest of the French press; weekly calendar of
economic announcements; futures hedge ratios [4]
http://www.finacor.fr/

■ *Crédit Lyonnais* – weekly economic analysis; macro-economic forecasts;
monthly reports on: economic outlook, exchange rates, monetary policy,
bond/equities, market forecasts; monthly technical analysis comments on:
currencies, short/long term bonds, indices, international economic outlook
[4]
http://deef.creditlyonnais.fr/

Stocks

■ *Bourse de Paris* – (Paris Stock Exchange) daily index levels; monthly
performance data on indices and sectors; annual statistics highlights;
description of indices; info on MONEP (equity/index options) [3]
http://www.bourse-de-paris.fr/

■ *Le Nouveau Marché* – (Paris market for high-growth companies) [2]
http://www.nouveau-marche.fr/

■ *Netfund* – monthly stock market bulletin: quotes and charts, analysis of
CAC40, buy/sell stock recommendations, trading recommendations [3]
http://www.fastnet.ch/NETFUND/home.html

Futures and options

■ *MATIF* – (Paris futures and options exchange) monthly/year-to-date/yearly
stats on volume/open interest; downloadable historical data; calendar of
banking holidays [3]
http://www.matif.fr/

Economy

■ *Ministry for Foreign Affairs* – daily review of the French press; overview of the
economy and sectors; Government press releases; daily exchange rates [4]
http://www.france.diplomatie.fr/

- *Ministère de l'Économie et des Finances* – various reports released mainly in French [3]
  http://www.cri.ensmp.fr/dp/
- *French Embassy in Washington* – brief economic overview; bi-weekly summary of French news, archive from Jan 1995 [3]
  http://www.info-france.org/
- *Banque Paribas* – monthly economic report [2]
  http://www.paribas.com/
- *Actufax* – French Economic Report – weekly report: economic policy, government action, company news, Europe, key economic indicators [3]
  http://www.actufax.com/

Miscellaneous

- *Siparex* – (private equity investment) [2]
  http://www.siparex.com/
- *Paris Corporate Finance* – list of venture capital/investment banks/consulting firms [2]
  http://www.paris-corporate.fr/
- *Jérôme Rabenou* – record of bond issues [2]
  http://www.fdn.fr/~rabenou/obligation/index.html

Banks

- *Banque Nationale de Paris* – BNP – [1]
  http://www.calvacom.fr/BNP/
- *Credit Commercial de France* – CCF – [1]
  http://www.calvacom.fr/ccf/
- *Credit Local de France* – (local development financing) [1]
  http://www.clf.fr/

Other URL lists

- *AdmiNet* – [5]
  http://www.ensmp.fr/~scherer/adminet/min/fin/
- *IWay* – [3]
  http://www.iway.fr/

GERMANY

Domain code	de
Currency	Deutsche mark (DM)
GDP	$1.344tr
GDP/capita	$16 580
GDP growth	2.9%
External debt	$NA
Exports	$437bn (fob)
Imports	$362bn (fob)

News

■ *German Information Center New York* – weekly subscription newsletter covering politics/economics; Government press releases; archive of past issues
http://www.germany-info.org/

■ *Die Welt* – (German) daily closing stock prices
http://www.welt.de/

■ *Die Zeit* – (German)
http://eunet.bda.de/bda/int/zeit/

■ *BR-Online* – (German) stock/economic bulletins
http://www.br-online.de/geld/

■ *Spiegel* – (German)
http://www.spiegel.de/

Markets

■ *Deutsche Börse* – (comprising Deutsche Terminbörse – DTB and Frankfurter Wertpapierbörse – FWB) subscription for historical DTB data from 1990 [3]
http://www.exchange.de/

■ *Financial Information Warehouse* – (German) daily closing stock prices; weekly market outlook; software; bookshop
http://www.financial.de/

■ *Helaba Trust* – (bank) interest rate and forex forecasts; quarterly investment strategy report; bi-weekly report and comment on stock/bond markets; sector reports; earnings forecasts for major companies [3]
http://www.helaba-trust.de/

■ *Landesgirokasse* – (German) weekly reports: bund/DAX futures; FAZ information on top 500 companies: address, SIC codes, turnover, net profit
http://www.lgbank.de/

■ *Adrian Schwegler* – (German) historic database of funds prices and other financial data [2]
http://www.hamburg.netsurf.de/~adrian.schwegler/boerse/index1.htm

Stocks

- *Deutsche Bank* – daily closing prices and company information for selected shares [2]
  http://www.deutsche-bank.de/

- *Bank24* – (stockbroker, German) company summary information for DAX stocks from Datastream (financial data and relative chart)
  http://www.bank24.de/

- *M W B* – (German) stock prices
  http://www.mwbonline.de/

- *Hoppenstedt Börseninformationen* – (German) daily closing DAX100 stocks; subscriptions service for charts and analysis [3]
  http://194.121.27.25/

- *Bayerische Börse* – (German) [1]
  http://www.financial.de/partner/brboerse/welcome.htm

Economy

- *Press and Information Office of the Federal Government* – overview of the economy [3]
  http://www.bundesregierung.de/

- *Federal Statistical Office* – key social/economic statistics for Germany [3]
  http://www.statistik-bund.de/

- *Federal Ministry of Economics* – (information on German information infrastructure projects) [1]
  http://www.kp.dlr.de/BMWi/gip/index_e.html

- *Deutscher Bundestag* – (German Government, German)
  http://www.bundestag.de/

- *Frankfurt Money Strategist* – (subscription newsletter) archives
  http://www.helix.net/fms/

Miscellaneous

- *Financial Network* – (German)
  http://www.fnet.de/

- *Consors* – (discount broker, German)
  http://www.consors.de/

- *BUTZN Börsen* – (German)
  http://www.boerse.de/

Investment funds

- *Dresdner Bank Investment Group* – (fund management, German) fund descriptions and current prices
  http://www.dit.de/

■ *DWS* – (fund management, German) fund descriptions and current prices
http://www.dws.de/

■ *ADIG* – (fund management, German) fund descriptions and current prices
http://www.adig.de/

■ *infos GMBH* – information on funds with prices and charts [3]
http://www.infos.com/english/

Banks

■ *Commerzbank* – (German) discount broker services, daily market comment
http://www.comdirect.de/

■ *Westdeutsche Landesbank* – (German)
http://www.westlb.de/

■ *Volksbank Hannover* – (regional bank for Hannover, German, English
introduction)
http://www.vbhan.de/

■ *HYPO BANK* – (German)
http://www.nord.hypo.de/news/

■ *Stadtsparkasse München* – (German)
http://www.sskm.de/

■ *Franken WKV Bank* – (German)
http://www.frankenwkv.de/

■ *Direkt Anlage Bank München* – (bank offering discount brokerage services,
German, English introduction)
http://www.diraba.de/

Other URL lists

■ *Cinetic* – [3]
http://vroom.web.de/

GREECE

Domain code	gr
Currency	Drachma (Dr)
GDP	$93.7bn
GDP/capita	$8870
GDP growth	0.4%
External debt	$27bn
Exports	$9bn (fob)
Imports	$19bn (fob)

News

■ *Athens News* – daily general news, economic news, currency rates; archive of back issues [3]
http://www.dolnet.gr/Athnews/Athnews.htm

■ *Athens News Agency* – daily general news and currency rates [3]
http://www.forthnet.gr/ape/

■ *Ministry of Press and Mass Media* – Government briefings [1]
http://web.ariadne-t.gr/

Markets

■ *Dow Jones Telerate* – subscription service for information on: Greek and Cypriot stocks, currency, money and bond markets and financial news
http://www.gsc.net/business/telerate/tlrdemo.htm

Stocks

■ *Athens Stock Exchange* – exchange statistics [2]
http://www.ase.gr/

■ *Thessaloniki Stock Exchange Center* – (joint venture between Athens Stock Exchange, the Chamber of Commerce and Industry of Thessaloniki and various banks) [1]
http://www.ase.gr/thessgb.htm

Economy

■ *Ministry of Foreign Affairs* [1]
http://www.mfa.gr/

Miscellaneous

■ *Alpha Credit Bank* [1]
http://www.gsc.net/business/alpha/

■ *Xios Bank* – brief explanation of local currency and money market [1]
http://www.gsc.net/business/xios/

Other URL lists

■ *Atlas* [4]
http://www.gsc.net/atlas/

■ *Forthnet* [4]
http://www.forthnet.gr/ape/

HONG KONG

Domain code	hk
Currency	Hong Kong dollar (HK$)
GDP	$136bn
GDP/capita	$24 530
GDP growth	5.5%
External debt	none
Exports	$169bn
Imports	$160bn (cif)

News

■ *Hongkong Standard* – daily: general/business news, stock market report, closing stock prices, index values at 15 min. intervals, most active shares; weekly market summary report [4]
http://www.hkstandard.com/

■ *ASIA, INC. Online* – (business magazine) daily business/financial news; special business/financial articles; daily HK stocks review (from Knight-Ridder); daily market comment and major stock moves (from Lippo Secs); daily currency technical comment; archive of past issues with search facility [3]
http://www.asia-inc.com/

■ *South China Morning Post* – (subscription e-mail daily news report)
http://www.scmp.com/

■ *Hong Kong Government's Economic and Trade Office in San Francisco* – daily summary of news; Government speeches/press releases; occasional economic reports – [2]
http://www.hongkong.org/

Markets

■ *Dow Jones Telerate* – daily stock market report; news bulletins; value and charts for: stock index, currency [4]
http://www.djtelerate.com.hk/

■ *Hong Kong Star* – daily closing stock prices, tables of most active and major movers; indices and futures values updated every 30 min. with intraday chart; currency rates updated every 30 min. with intraday chart; archive of past month reports [4]
http://www.hkstar.com/starinfo/stock/home.html

■ *Jardine Fleming Unit Trusts* – weekly economic and market outlook; suggested model portfolio [3]
http://www.jfleming_ut.com.hk/

- *Dharmala Capital* – (financial services) daily HK market report: index levels, market review and outlook, company news, economics, calendar, trading recommendations; archive of daily reports from Aug 95 [3]
  http://www.dharmala.com.hk/

- *Credit Lyonnais International Asset Management* – weekly review of the markets; monthly regional strategy notes; monthly funds report [3]
  http://www.asiaonline.net/cliam/

- *Regent Fund Management* – quarterly markets review; fund prices [2]
  http://www.asiaonline.net/regent/

Stocks

- *InTechTra* – brief information on: HKSE, warrants Mid Cap 50, HK ADRs; subscription reports for: market commentary, Hang Seng Index Shares report, MidCap 50 shares report, China H shares, warrants; archive of old summary reports [2]
  http://www.ganet.net/~ITTI/hkrpt.html

Futures and options

- *Hong Kong Futures Exchange* – daily contract closing prices; downloadable historical data [4]
  http://www.hkfe.com/

Economy

- *Hong Kong Government Information Centre* – overview of HK economy; social and economic statistics; annual budget speech; Government press releases and speeches [3]
  http://www.info.gov.hk/

Miscellaneous

- *BZW Investment Management* – monthly funds report: price, review and outlook [2]
  http://www.barclays.com.hk/

- *Fidelity Investments* – investment analysis calculators, market comments [2]
  http://www.fidelity.com.hk/

- *Gemini Financial Group* – (financial services) [1]
  http://www.glink.net.hk/~gemfin/

- *AF Dragon* – (information on accounting and finance in HK and China) [3]
  http://accounting.greatwall.com.hk/index.html

- *Compucharts* – (data provider and technical charting programs) [1]
  http://www.hk.super.net/~lcm/

Banks

▦ *Bank of China* – [1]
http://202.96.12.165/

▦ *Dao Heng Bank* – [1]
http://www.daoheng.com/

▦ *International Bank of Asia* – [1]
http://www.iba.com.hk/

▦ *Jardine Fleming Bank* – [1]
http://www.jardinefleming.bank.com.hk/

Other URL lists

▦ *Momentum*
http://www.momentum.com.hk/

HUNGARY

Domain code	hu
Currency	Forint (Ft)
GDP	$58.8bn
GDP/capita	$5700
GDP growth	3.0%
External debt	$27bn
Exports	$10.3bn (fob)
Imports	$14.2bn (fob)

News

▦ *Hungary Report* – weekly news and analysis; searchable index; archive of past issues [4]
http://www.isyshu.net/hrep/

▦ *Pro-Reference* – occasional articles from the *Budapest Business Journal* [1]
http://www.eps.hu/prorefhm.html

Markets

▦ *Fornax* – price data and statistics from the Budapest Stock Exchange and Budapest Commodity Exchange; real-time and historical daily record of BUX stock index; historical daily record of Daiwa Treasury Bill Index and Central European Stock Index; daily closing prices and background issuer data for: stocks, treasury bills, Government bonds, corporate bonds, compensation notes, investment funds; contact details for brokers [5]
http://www.fornax.hu/english/index.htm

Economy

- *The Hungarian Economy* – selected articles from a paper quarterly economic and business review [2]
  http://www.iqsoft.hu/economy/
- *Prime Minister's Office* – link to the Finance Ministry with occasional economic overviews [1]
  http://www.meh.hu/

Other URL lists

- *Hungary Network* [3]
  http://www.hungary.com/
- *Hungarian American Association* (at University of Maryland) [2]
  http://mineral.umd.edu/hir/

INDIA

Domain code	in
Currency	Indian rupee (Re)
GDP	$1.254tr
GDP/capita	$1360
GDP growth	5.0%
External debt	$89.2bn
Exports	$24.4bn (fob)
Imports	$25.5bn (cif)

News

- *News India-Times* – daily general and business news [3]
  http://www.newsindia-times.com/
- *Rediff* – daily general, economic and business news; daily market comment and chart for: stocks, currency, money; review of the IPO market; weekly fund prices [4]
  http://www.rediff.co.in/
- *Indolink* – daily general and business news stories and archive; business news weekly bulletin [3]
  http://www.genius.net/indolink/
- *The Times of India* – daily news [3]
  http://www.cyberindia.net/timesofindia/home.htm
- *IndiaWorld* – (subscription news services includes: selected articles from *Business India*, *Express Investment Week*, update on Indian markets, quotes from the Bombay Stock Exchange, analysis of new issues)
  http://www.indiaworld.com/

Markets

▓ *Dow Jones Telerate* – daily stock market report; news bulletins; currency rates [4]
http://www.djtelerate.com.hk/

▓ *India Market Access* – (subscription services for market prices) [1]
http://ns.uunet.in/montage/

Stocks

▓ *National Stock Exchange of India (NSE)* – daily closing stock prices and index level; view current stock quotes for up to 5 stocks [5]
http://www.nseindia.com/

Miscellaneous

▓ *LA Funds Investments* – (investments for non-resident Indians) [1]
http://www.lwbbs.com/lafunds/Welcome.html

▓ *Kotak Mahindra Finance* – (financial services) [1]
http://www.indiaworld.com/open/biz/kotak/index.html

Banks

▓ *Bank of India* – (state bank) [1]
http://www.bankofindia.com/

▓ *State Bank of India* – [1]
http://www.webindia.com/sbi/

INDONESIA

Domain code	id
Currency	Indonesian rupiah (Rp)
GDP	$619bn
GDP/capita	$3090
GDP growth	6.7%
External debt	$87bn
Exports	$41.3bn (fob)
Imports	$31.4bn (fob)

News

▓ *Indonesia Times* – daily general/business/finance news [4]
http://www.indocon.com/indotimes/

▓ *Economic & Business Review Indonesia* – weekly journal covering: capital markets, banking, business and general news [3]
http://web3.asia1.com.sg/~ebri/index.html

- *Indonesia Media Network* – daily general news [2]
  http://www.imn.co.id/
- *Embassy of the Republic of Indonesia*, Washington DC – news updates; Government press releases; monthly magazine including an economics section [2]
  http://www.newsindonesia.com/
- *Department of Foreign Affairs* – Government press releases [1]
  http://www.dfa-deplu.go.id/

Markets

- *Dow Jones Telerate* – daily stock market report; news bulletins; currency rates [4]
  http://www.djtelerate.com.hk/

Stocks

- *BT Stockwatch* – (*Singapore Business Times*) daily stock market report
  http://www.asia1.com.sg/btstocks/

Currencies and money

- *Bank Internasional Indonesia* – daily currency rates; regularly updated interest rates; occasional economic overview [3]
  http://www.bii.co.id/

Economy

- *Central Bureau of Statistics* – annual economic census; monthly summary of the macro-economic statistics; social and economic statistics [4]
  http://www.bps.go.id/
- *Indonesia Today* – brief economic overview [2]
  http://www.indonesiatoday.com/business/index.html

Miscellaneous

- *Indonesia Business Online* – selection of occasionally updated financial/economic data: stock prices, JSX statistics, currency rates, ranking of largest corporate and individual taxpayers [2]
  http://www.indobiz.com/news_fin.htm

Banks

- *PT Bakrie Nusantara Corporation* – (financial services, part of the Bakrie group, incorporates PT Bakrie Securities) [1]
  http://www.rad.net.id/bakrie/capitan.html

Other URL lists

■ *Indocon*
http://www.indocon.com/

ISRAEL

Domain code	il
Currency	New Israeli shekel (NIS)
GDP	$70.1bn
GDP/capita	$13 880
GDP growth	6.8%
External debt	$25.9bn
Exports	$16.2bn (fob)
Imports	$22.5bn (cif)

News

■ *Globes Business Arena* – daily: economic and business news, summary of trade on TASE; weekly: stock review, macro-economic review; occasional articles on the markets and economy [4]
http://www.globes.co.il:80/

■ *Jerusalem Post* – daily: news, stock market report, closing prices of Israeli stocks on Wall Street; occasional articles on companies [3]
http://www.jpost.co.il/

■ *Ministry of Foreign Affairs* – daily survey of Israeli press; official press releases; facts about Israel including overview of the economy [3]
http://www.israel.org/

Markets

■ *United Mizrahi Bank* – weekly Tel-aviv stock market review, monthly capital markets review: shares, bonds, unlinked shekel bonds, Maof option, new corporate and Government bond issues; monthly economic review [4]
http://www.mizrahi.co.il/

Stocks

■ *Tel-Aviv Stock Exchange (TASE)* – daily closing index and share prices; daily price data files for download for: shares, convertible bonds, bonds and bills; further data downloads possible with subscription; 4-year index and trading volume charts for shares and bonds [4]
http://www.tase.co.il/

■ *Walla* – daily closing index and share prices from TASE [3]
http://www.walla.co.il/

▓ *Meitav* – (financial services) company information on Israel's 25 major companies [2]
http://www.ventura.co.il/m/meitav/meitav.htm

Economy

▓ *Ministry of Finance* – economic overview; latest state budget; foreign investment policy; information on privatization programme [3]
http://www.macom.co.il/Government/MOF/

▓ *Israel Information Service* – general information [2]
gopher://israel-info.gov.il/

Miscellaneous

▓ *Genesis* – venture capital advisers for hi-tech companies [1]
http://www.interage.co.il/genesis/genesis.htm

▓ *Bank Leumi* – [1]
http://www.bll.co.il/

Other URL lists

▓ *Walla*
http://www.walla.co.il/

ITALY

Domain code	it
Currency	Italian lira (Lit)
GDP	$998.9bn
GDP/capita	$17 180
GDP growth	2.2%
External debt	$67bn
Exports	$190.8bn (fob)
Imports	$168.7bn (cif)

News

▓ *Corriere della Sera* – (Italian) daily general and financial news [5]
http://globnet.rcs.it/

▓ *Capital* – (Italian) monthly financial magazine [4]
http://globnet.rcs.it/

▓ *La Stampa* – (Italian) daily general and financial news [5]
http://www.lastampa.it/ls_home.html

■ *Milano Finanza* – (Italian) PMF financial news updated through the day; daily: largest stock moves, currency rates, funds prices; paper frontpage to be downloadable in PDF format [3]
http://www.milanofinanza.it/

Markets

■ *BorsaOnWeb* – (Italian) stock, index prices and charts updated though the day (prices recorded every minute); bond prices; news bulletins through the day [5]
http://www.telematica.it/borsa/BorsaOnWeb.html

■ *TexNET* – daily closing prices (and historical archive) for stocks, funds, currencies [3]
http://robot1.texnet.it/finanza/

■ *Banca Commerciale Italiana* – (Italian) weekly economic and markets comment [1]
http://www.bci.it/mflunedi.html

■ *Banco di Roma* – (Italian) weekly money/currency markets comment [1]
http://www.bancaroma.it/comfin.htm

Stocks

■ *Linknet* – updated daily charts on Italian stocks and indices [4]
http://www.linknet.it/borsa/

■ *Banca di Credito di Trieste* – daily currency rates [2]
http://www.bctkb.it/bctkb/

Economy

■ *Ministry of Finance* – (Italian) [1]
http://www.finanze.interbusiness.it/

Miscellaneous

■ *Gestnord Fondi* – (funds management) [1]
http://www.galactica.it/gestnord_fondi/

Other URL lists

■ *BOL-Invest* – (Italian) [3]
http://www.comm2000.it/bol-invest/

JAPAN

Domain code	jp
Currency	Yen (Y)
GDP	$2.527tr
GDP/capita	$20 200
GDP growth	0.6%
External debt	$NA
Exports	$395.5bn (fob)
Imports	$274.3bn (cif)

News

■ *Nikkei* – daily stories: news, economy, finance, companies; daily closing values: Nikkei Index, currency, bond yield; summary of news in the *Nikkei Weekly*; archive of past 30 issues of daily and weekly Nikkei; links [4]
http://www.nikkei.co.jp/enews/

■ *Kyodo News* – news headlines updated through the day; daily closing stock index and currency prices; daily updated 50-day N225 chart; stories from *Japan Weekly* with historical archive [4]
http://www.kyodo.co.jp/

■ *Asahi News* – daily news stories [3]
http://www.asahi.com/

■ *Japan Times* – news stories updated through the week; news archive; weekly news round-up [3]
http://shrine.cyber.ad.jp/~jtinter/home.html

■ *Mainichi* – weekly news stories [2]
http://www.mainichi.co.jp/index-e.html

■ *Gateway Japan* – searchable archive of news stories [2]
http://www.gwjapan.org/

■ *Kanzaki* – twice weekly listing of headlines from Japan newspapers; guide to Japan's newspapers and magazines [2]
http://www.kanzaki.com/

Markets

■ *Daiwa Institute of Research Limited* – daily closing Nikkei index; monthly economic report; quarterly economic outlook; investment strategy reports; monthly indices: bonds, CBs, warrants [3]
http://www.dir.co.jp/

■ *Nomura Research Institute (NRI)* – latest daily/monthly figures and charts for proprietary indices: equity market, multimedia sector, bonds, CBs; occasional research reports [2]
http://www.nri.co.jp/

▓ *Nikko* – (incorporating: Nikko Securities, Nikko Research Center, Nikko Investor relations) monthly update and historical database of Nikko Stock/Bond/CB Performance Indices; summaries of reports on: economic and earning forecasts, equity investment strategy [2]
http://www.nikko.co.jp/index.html

▓ *Yamaichi Securities* – outlook reports: economic, company earnings, market, investment strategy
http://www.yamaichi.com/

Stocks

▓ *Nagoya Stock Exchange* – daily closing share prices; weekly margin balance report; monthly report on most active stocks; daily CB prices [4]
http://www.iijnet.or.jp/nse-jp/e-home.htm

▓ *Corporate Information Bank* – (Daiwa Securities) daily updated announced company results; index of companies with Web sites
http://www.dir.co.jp/cib/[4]

Commodities

▓ *Tokyo Grain Exchange* – hourly updated market prices; historical data; record highs/lows [5]
http://www.toppan.co.jp/tge/

▓ *Mitsubishi Corporation Futures* – information on: commodity futures funds, Tokyo Commodity Exchange (TOCOM) and futures market in Japan [3]
http://www.mmjp.or.jp/mcfutures/index-e.html

Economy

▓ *Ministry of Foreign Affairs* – latest Government press releases; archive of documents, speeches and press releases; economic statistics [3]
http://www.nttls.co.jp/infomofa/

▓ *Statistics Bureau* – monthly data released; full statistics for Japan [3]
http://www.stat.go.jp/1.htm

▓ *Japan Economic Foundation* – economic reports and information from MITI [3]
http://www.jef.or.jp/

▓ *Sakura Bank* – monthly economic review; economic outlook report on the Asian economies [3]
http://www.sakura.co.jp/

▓ *Economic Planning Agency* – economic articles and statistics [3]
http://www.epa.go.jp/

▓ *Dai-Ichi Kangyo Bank* – monthly economic report; economic outlook report; occasional articles [3]
http://www.infoweb.or.jp/dkb/welcom-e.html

■ *Japan Research Institute* – occasional economic reports [2]
http://www.jri.co.jp/

Miscellaneous

■ *Daiwa Securities* – (Japanese) [1]
http://www.daiwa.co.jp/

■ *Nomura Securities* – (Japanese) [1]
http://www.nomura.co.jp/

■ *New Japan Securities* – [1]
http://www.iijnet.or.jp/njs/

Banks

■ *Asahi Bank* – [1]
http://www.asahibank.co.jp/

■ *Sumitomo Bank* – [1]
http://www.jri.co.jp/sumitomobank/sumitomo.html

■ *Tokai Bank* – [1]
http://www.csweb.co.jp/TBK/

■ *Fuji Bank* – [1]
http://www.fujibank.co.jp/eng/fb/home.html

■ *Japan Development Bank* – (Government financial institution) – occasional economic notes; summaries of research reports [2]
http://www.thejdb.go.jp/index_e.html

Other URL lists

■ *NTT*
http://www.ntt.jp/

KOREA (SOUTH)

Domain code	kr
Currency	South Korean won (W)
GDP	$508.3bn
GDP/capita	$11 270
GDP growth	8.3%
External debt	$44.1bn
Exports	$96.2bn (fob)
Imports	$102.3bn (cif)

News

▦ *Korea Herald* – daily general/business/finance news; search facility on previous 5 issues [4]
http://zec.three.co.kr/koreaherald/

▦ *Korea Economic Weekly* – daily updated news headlines, economy, money [4]
http://eco.ked.co.kr/text/website.html

▦ *Korean Press Service* – daily news headlines, with archive and search facility from Jan 1985 [3]
http://203.254.53.1/News/Kps/

▦ *Joong-ang Ilbo* – daily general news [2]
http://168.126.70.2/joongang/joong-e.html

Markets

▦ *Dow Jones Telerate* – daily stock market report; news bulletins; value and charts for: stock index, currency [4]
http://www.djtelerate.com.hk/

▦ *Korea Directory* – daily closing index and stock prices; currency rates [3]
http://korea.directory.co.kr/daily/daily.html

▦ *LG Securities* – daily market comment; occasional economic review; occasional market analysis; brief history of the stock market [2]
http://203.248.135.75/

▦ *Daewoo Securities* – (Korean)
http://www.securities.co.kr/

Stocks

▦ *Dongwon Securities* – database of 600 listed Korean companies with: company profile, financial ratios, balance sheet, earnings record; reports on the economy and stock market [4]
http://www.dws.co.kr/

Economy

▦ *Korean Overseas Information Service* – facts about Korea including economic overview [3]
http://www.kois.go.kr/Explore/Facts/index.html

▦ *Korea Development Bank* – (Government financial institution) quarterly economic research magazine [3]
http://www.kol.co.kr/~kdbmst/kdb.html

▦ *Kotra* – (Korea Trade Investment Promotion Agency) [1]
http://www.kotra.or.kr/

▓ *Korean Economy 5% Society* – (subscription newsletter) monthly report: Korea Economic Trend
   http://www.wisedb.co.kr/

Miscellaneous

▓ *Daehan Investment Trust* – (fund manager) review of the Korean economy and stock market; charts of KOSPI index, trading volume, CB index, total market value; brief explanation and listing of international trust funds [2]
   http://www.wisedb.co.kr/corp/ditc/ditc.html

▓ *Korea Investment Trust Co.* – (fund manager) 6-monthly review of funds; brief overview of: economy, stock and bond markets [2]
   http://www.wisedb.co.kr/corp/kitc/kitcindex.html

Banks

▓ *Industrial Bank of Korea (IBK)* – [1]
   http://www.cybernet.co.kr/business/ibk/index.htm

▓ *Hana Bank* – [1]
   http://www.wisedb.co.kr/corp/hana/hana.html

▓ *Daedong Bank* – [1]
   http://www.wisedb.co.kr/corp/ddbank/ddbank.html

▓ *Shinhan Bank* – [1]
   http://www.wisedb.co.kr/corp/shinhan/shinhan.html

Other URL lists

▓ *Korea Directory* – address information for all companies [3]
   http://korea.directory.co.kr/

▓ *Wisedb* [2]
   http://www.wisedb.co.kr/korea.html

▓ *Korean Media Networks* – [2]
   http://www.korean.com/

LUXEMBOURG

Domain code	lu
Currency	Luxembourg franc (LuxF)
GDP	$9.2bn
GDP/capita	$22 830
GDP growth	2.6%
External debt	$800m
Exports	$6.4bn (fob)
Imports	$8.3bn (cif)

News

▪ *Wort Online* – (French, German)
http://www.europeonline.com/lux/provider/lonline/wort/wohome.htm

Markets

▪ *Banque et Caisse d'Epargne de l'Etat* – (French) daily: currency, Luxembourg gold fixing rate and deposit rates [2]
http://www.bcee.lu/

Miscellaneous

▪ *Banque UCL* – updated deposit rates [1]
http://www.banqueucl.lu/
▪ *Credit Lyonnais Luxembourg* [1]
http://www.creditlyonnais.lu/
▪ *Finlink* – list of banks registered in Luxembourg with addresses [2]
http://www.finlink.lu/fin_data/luxstat/banks/default.htm
▪ *Flemings* – daily fund prices, weekly global market review [1]
http://www.flemings.lu/

Other URL lists

▪ *National Network for Education and Research* [3]
http://www.restena.lu/luxembourg/lux_welcome.html
▪ *Europeonline* [2]
http://www.europeonline.com/lux/

MALAYSIA

Domain code	my
Currency	Ringgit (M$)
GDP	$166.8n
GDP/capita	$8650
GDP growth	8.7%
External debt	$35.5bn
Exports	$56.6bn (fob)
Imports	$55.2bn (cif)

News

▪ *The Star* – daily general/business news; daily closing levels: KLSE stocks, indices, table of most active stocks, sector analysis, KLOFFE contracts; currency rates, Kuala Lumpur Interbank Offer Rates (Ringgit, S$, US$, HK$),

unit trust quotes; downloadable text file of daily record of shares transacted; daily updated KLSE Index charts; daily KLSE/financial news; archive of previous 6 issues with search facility; annual economic report [5]
http://www.jaring.my/star/

- *Asia Connect* – daily general/business news [3]
http://www.asiaconnect.com.my/utusan/

Markets

- *Dow Jones Telerate* – daily stock market report; value and charts for: stock index, currency [4]
http://www.djtelerate.com.hk/

Stocks

- *Kuala Lumpur Stock Exchange* – database of all listed companies with: capitalization, background, principal activities [3]
http://www.klse.com.my/

- *BT Stockwatch* – (*Singapore Business Times*) real-time KLSE prices: stocks, sectors, indices; table and chart of 15 min. values for key indices; table of major moves and turnover; daily KLSE market report [5]
http://www.asia1.com.sg/btstocks/

- *Malaysia Online* – MOL Java Stock Ticker: beta test for leading stock prices updated every minute; KLSE values updated 8 times every day: stock prices, sector/market indices; subscription service for: real-time stock quotes, company database with annual reports [4]
http://www.mol.net.my/molfinan/molfinan.html

- *Malaysian On-Line* – occasional posting of closing KLSE prices [3]
http://www.mol.com.my/news/klse/home.htm

- *Dynaquest Stock Market Report* – (subscription newsletter) sample report and company analyses [2]
http://www.mol.com.my/dynaques/home.htm

- *Dynaquest Monthly Digest* – (subscription newsletter) month delayed: market comment, company news [3]
http://www.mol.com.my/dynaques/mdigest/home.htm

- *Expertise Software* – occasionally updated charts for a selection of KLSE stocks [2]
http://www.mol.com.my/exsoft/home.htm

- *Malaysian Central Depository* – handbook and guides to the Central Depository System [2]
http://www.mol.net.my/~mcd/

Currencies and money

■ *Arab–Malaysian Bank* – daily rates: currency, Ringgit deposit rates, Ringgit bills, government securities, MYR forwards; ranking of top Malaysian banks; quarterly reviews: economy, money market [3]
http://www.mol-usa.com/ambg/arabbank/html/ambg.html

Economy

■ *Jaring* – (Government server) annual budget report with comment; review and outlook for Malaysian economy; basic economic statistics [4]
http://www.jaring.my/msia/economy/eco.html

Miscellaneous

■ *FISH*NET* – (subscription service for financial information) [1]
http://www.mol.net.my/fishnet/

Banks

■ *Pacific Bank* – (subsidiary of OCBC) [1]
http://www.pacbanc.com.my/pacific/

■ *Southern Bank* – (commercial bank with investment and broking services) [1]
http://www.sbbgroup.com.my/

Other URL lists

■ *Malaysia Online* [3]
http://www.mol.com.my/

■ *Jaring* [3]
http://www.jaring.my/

MEXICO

Domain code	mx
Currency	New Mexican peso (Mex$)
GDP	$728.7bn
GDP/capita	$7900
GDP growth	3.5%
External debt	$128bn
Exports	$60.8bn (fob)
Imports	$79.4bn (fob)

News

- *Excélsior* – (Spanish) daily general news and comment on financial markets
  http://www.excelsior.com.mx/
- *El Norte* – (Spanish) daily news
  http://www.infosel.com.mx/elnorte/
- *La Jornada* – (Spanish) daily news; archive from Nov 1995
  http://www.nuclecu.unam.mx/~jornada/
- *Spin* – (Spanish) daily index/currency levels
  http://www.spin.com.mx/noticias.html

Markets

- *Infosel* – (Spanish) daily prices for: shares, money, Peso; latest news bulletins updated through the day
  http://www.infosel.com.mx/infosel/if/
- *Grupo Financiero Serfin* – market analysis and outlook; weekly company comment and company results; derivatives information: options volatilities, betas, correlation, daily closing option prices [3]
  http://www.infosel.com.mx/serfin/
- *Nafinsa Securities Inc.* – daily rates for: interest rates, inflation, Government secs, currency, Peso futures; daily updated chart of stock market index and Peso spot [3]
  http://www.quicklink.com/mexico/nafinsa.htm
- *Grupo Financiero Banorte* – (retail/commercial bank with brokerage service) daily markets analysis with prices for: spot/forward currencies, futures, time deposits [2]
  http://www.gfnorte.com.mx/

Stocks

- *Bolsa Mexicana de Valores* (NY office)
  http://www.quicklink.com/mexico/bmv/bmv1.htm

Economy

- *US Treasury Secretary's Report to Congress on Mexico* – economic overview [3]
  http://www.ustreas.gov/treasury/mexico/top.html
- *Inter-American Development Bank (IDB)* – press releases for Mexico [2]
  http://ww2.iadb.org/prensa/prmex.htm

Miscellaneous

- *Caratula de Vector Casa de Bolsa* – (securities broker) [1]
  http://www.vector.com.mx/

■ *InverMexico* – (financial services) [1]
http://www.invermexico.com.mx/

■ *Mexican Commentary* – selection of company news stories and stock charts; forecast and chart of Peso; subscription newsletter [2]
http://ourworld.compuserve.com/homepages/mexcom/

■ *MexAssist* – (monthly subscription newsletter with financial information about Mexico, downloadable sample version in PDF format) [1]
http://www.mexassist.com.mx/finance/index.html

■ *MexFAX* – (weekly subscription business newsletter) [1]
http://www.castle.net/~shapiro/mexfax/

■ *Clasificadora de Riesgos* – (Spanish) debt rating service
http://www.infosel.com.mx/mercado/clase/

Banks

■ *Banco de Mexico* – (Spanish)
http://www.banxico.org.mx/

■ *Bancomext* – (Government bank for foreign trade) [1]
http://lince.dgsca.unam.mx/bancomext/

■ *Grupo Financiero Bital* – (Spanish, English introduction)
http://www.bital.com.mx/

■ *Grupo Financiero Banamex-Accival* – (Spanish)
http://www.banamex.com/texto/index.htm

■ *Banco Regional de Monterrey* – (Spanish)
http://www.banregio.com

Other URL lists

■ *Mexico Online* – [4]
http://mexicool.com/

■ *Trace* – link to many economic and financial articles [3]
http://www.trace-sc.com/

■ *Portillor* [2]
http://spin.com.mx/~portillor/mexico.html

NETHERLANDS

Domain code	nl
Currency	Netherlands guilder, gulden, or florin (f)
GDP	$275.8n
GDP/capita	$17 940
GDP growth	2.0%
External debt	$0
Exports	$153bn (fob)
Imports	$137bn (fob)

News

▓ *NOS Teletekst* – (Dutch) real-time financial news and price information
http://www.omroep.nl/cgi-bin/tt/nos/page

▓ *De Telegraaf* – (Dutch)
http://www.telegraaf.nl/

▓ *HANDELSBLAD* – (Dutch)
http://www.nrc.nl/Web/welkom.html

Markets

▓ *Amsterdam Stock Exchange* – real-time AEX stock index; index of listed securities [2]
http://wwwaeb.econ.vu.nl/

▓ *Remark* – (Dutch, subscription service with demo pages) technical analysis of Amsterdam bourse stocks [4]
http://www.bedrijfsnet.nl/~remark/

Economy

▓ *Rabobank* – overview and biweekly review of Dutch economy [3]
http://rabobank.info.nl/

▓ *Central Bureau of Statistics* – annual yearbook of statistics and latest statistics press releases [4]
http://www.cbs.nl/index.htm

▓ *Ministry of Finance* – (Dutch, some English pages on taxation and investment in the Netherlands) [1]
http://www.minfin.nl/

▓ *Ministry of Economic Affairs* – economic policy of the Netherlands [1]
http://www.minez.nl/aep/

▓ *ING Bank* – brief economic reports; highlights from the most recent issue of *Investment Strategy*
http://www.ingbank.com/

Miscellaneous

▪ *ABN AMRO* – [1]
http://www.abnamro.nl/

▪ *Rabobank Wijchen/Beuningen* – (Dutch) [1]
http://www.tref.nl/1586/rabobank/rabo1586.htm

▪ *Postbank* – (Dutch) [1]
http://www.postbank.nl/

▪ *Mama Cash Foundation Fund* – (financial support to companies and cultural projects of women) [1]
http://www.xxlink.nl/mamacash/0/

Other URL lists

▪ *Finnet-NL* [3]
http://www.bedrijfsnet.nl/~finnet/

▪ *Dutch Yellow Pages* [3]
http://www.markt.nl/dyp/index-en.html

NEW ZEALAND

Domain code	nz
Currency	New Zealand dollar (NZ$)
GDP	$56.4bn
GDP/capita	$16 640
GDP growth	6.2%
External debt	$38.5bn
Exports	$11.2bn
Imports	$10.4bn

News

▪ *The Press On-Line* – daily general/business news; archive of stories from Sep 95 [4]
http://www.press.co.nz/

▪ *Infotech Weekly* – (weekly information technology news) archive of past issues; site search facility [4]
http://www.infotech.co.nz/current/

Markets

▪ *Henley Market Watch* – (subscription financial market information) market data: currencies, interest rates, equities, commodities, market comment; historical data
http://www.henley.co.nz/

- *Program Traders* – (subscription technical analysis charting service with buy/sell signals)
  http://mail.inhb.co.nz/shares/

Stocks

- *Iguana Information Services* – (PC reports, charts and data on NZ share market) daily closing market summary with stock prices; subscription for real-time data [3]
  http://www.iguana.co.nz/
- *Global Register* – daily closing prices and index levels for NZSE stocks; updated chart of the NZSE40 Index; daily closing sharemarket statistics; daily NZ$ rates; information service for subscribing companies: overview, annual reports; weekly calendar of stock exchange news [5]
  http://www.globalregister.co.nz/
- *New Zealand Investment Center* – selection of company final results; occasional share prices, interest/exchange rates [2]
  http://www.charm.net/~lordhill/
- *Registry Managers (NZ) Limited* – (largest registry operating in New Zealand) taxation notes [2]
  http://www.globalregister.co.nz/rmnz/rmnz.htm
- *Akiko International* – occasional posting of stock prices with archive from Jul 95 [2]
  http://nz.com/NZ/Commerce/Stocks/

Economy

- *Reserve Bank of New Zealand* – statistical overview of the NZ economy; summary of economic projections; latest monetary policy statement; articles on: inflation, exchange/interest rates; news releases; speeches; list of registered banks [4]
  http://www.rbnz.govt.nz/
- *New Zealand Treasury* – NZ Budget and Budget policy statements; economic and fiscal update; monthly Government financial statements; Departmental Forecast of the Treasury; press releases; speeches [4]
  http://www.treasury.govt.nz/
- *New Zealand Government* – (official NZ Government Web server) information about NZ; links to Government agencies [2]
  http://www.govt.nz/
- *New Zealand Companies Office* – (companies database) free basic level access to search database for company; charged service for access to: charges and chargeholders, shareholders, company officers, document history, and official addresses [3]
  http://www.companies.govt.nz/

■ *New Zealand North American Investment Promotion Unit* – general economic/political information [2]
http://kiwiusa.com

Miscellaneous

■ *Money Managers* – (retail financial planning company) monthly economic overview; excerpts from monthly newsletter; details of investment seminars [3]
http://www.moneymanagers.co.nz/

■ *Deloitte Touche Tohmatsu* – (accountants) [1]
http://www.clearfield.co.nz/deloitte/

■ *New Zealand Investment Journal* – occasional investment articles [2]
http://ourworld.compuserve.com/homepages/reuhmanc/

Law firms

■ *Prince & Partners* – (chartered accountants and business consultants) information on: Government economic and fiscal policy, Government and business, taxation [3]
http://www.clearfield.co.nz/prince_partners/

■ *Russell McVeagh McKenzie Bartleet* – (commercial law firm) introduction to investment in New Zealand: taxation, investment in banking/financial sector; legal updates: taxation, banking, company and securities; legal papers; links [4]
http://www.rmmb.co.nz/

■ *Bell Gully Buddle Weir* – (commercial law firm) Budget tax report; library of publications [2]
http://www.bgbw.co.nz/

■ *Buddle Findlay* – (commercial law firm: banking/finance, capital markets, company law, investment services) articles on: Internet commerce, securities dealing on the Internet [3]
http://www.budfin.co.nz/

Banks

■ *ANZ Banking Group* – [1]
http://www.anz.com.au/

■ *ASB Bank* – weekly economic report; quarterly releases [3]
http://www.asbbank.co.nz/

■ *Trust Bank New Zealand* – [1]
http://www.trustbank.co.nz/

■ *Countrywide Bank* – public Disclosure Statement [1]
http://countrywide.co.nz/

Other URL lists

- *Lincoln University Library* – [4]
  http://www.lincoln.ac.nz/libr/nz/
- *New Zealand Business Directory* – [3]
  http://www.webworkshop.co.nz/nzbd/nzbd.html

NORWAY

Domain code	no
Currency	Norwegian krone (NKr)
GDP	$95.7bn
GDP/capita	$22 170
GDP growth	5.5%
External debt	$NA
Exports	$36.6bn (fob)
Imports	$29.3bn (cif)

News

- *Ministry of Foreign Affairs* – daily bulletin of news, editorials and commentaries from the major Norwegian daily newspapers [3]
  http://odin.dep.no/ud/publ/daily/
- *Norway Now* – twice monthly magazine of Norwegian business and community affairs [2]
  http://odin.dep.no/ud/publ/nn/
- *Norwaves* – weekly news about Norway; historical archive and search facility [3]
  http://www.nki.no/~morten/norwaves.html
- *Kapital* – (Norwegian, financial magazine)
  http://www.telepost.no/kapital/

Markets

- *Oslo Stock Exchange* – daily prices and charts for: stocks, sector indices, options and bonds; currency rates [3]
  http://nettvik.no/finansen/oslobors/
- *ABSNET* – Oslo bourse quotes updated every 5 min.; currencies and bond prices [3]
  http://www.absnet.no/finance/
- *Delphi Economics* – (Norwegian) updated daily charts and price data (by sector) of Oslo bourse stocks; daily market, sector and technical comment; macro-economic comment
  http://www.sn.no/delphi/

Stocks

▥ *HUGIN Online* – quarterly and annual reports, press releases and financial statements on companies listed on the Oslo Stock Exchange [4]
http://www.hugin.no/

▥ *Association for Norwegian Share Promotion* – (Norwegian)
http://www.intergate.no/aksjenorge/

Economy

▥ *ODIN* – (Norwegian Government Web server) facts and figures about Norway, including economic data: national accounts, fiscal budget, insurance, balance of payments, current accounts [2]
http://odin.dep.no/html/english/

▥ *Statistics Norway* – key economic figures (updated every Thursday); weekly bulletin (with historical excerpts); monthly stats on external trade [2]
http://www.ssb.no/www-open/index_en.html

Miscellaneous

▥ *Kreditkassen Bank* – [1]
http://www.kreditkassen.no/

Other URL lists

▥ *Nettvik*
http://nettvik.no/finansen/

▥ *HUGIN Online*
http://www.hugin.no/norden_e.html

▥ *Internet Systems AS*
http://www.telepost.no/sws/osloeng.html

PHILIPPINES

Domain code	ph
Currency	Philippine peso (P)
GDP	$161.4bn
GDP/capita	$2310
GDP growth	4.3%
External debt	$40bn
Exports	$13.4bn (fob)
Imports	$21.3bn (fob)

News

- *BusinessWorld Online* – daily general/business news; daily currency comment and rates; daily interest rate charts; archive of old issues from Nov 95 [4]
  http://bizworld.globe.com.ph/

- *Balita-L* – daily general/business news including currency rates [3]
  http://www.mabuhay.com/Balita-L/

- *The Journal Group* – daily general/business news; archive of previous few days [3]
  http://www.eiger.ch/eiger/pbo/pji/

Markets

- *Dow Jones Telerate* – daily stock market report; value and charts for: stock index, currency [4]
  http://www.djtelerate.com.hk/

Stocks

- *Philippine Stock Exchange (PSE)* – subscription access to stock prices [2]
  http://pdx.rpnet.com/pse/index.htm

- *Asian Capital Equities* – (stockbroker) daily closing PSE prices for: stocks, sectors, indices and tables for major moves, most active stocks; PSE announcements; downloadable daily and historic data for Metastock [4]
  http://www.portalinc.com/~ace/

- *Philippine StockWatch* – occasional stock prices with charts for: stocks, sectors, indices [3]
  http://is.eunet.ch:80/astarte/pbo/stock/mainstck.html

- *BPI Capital* – (investment bank) daily market brief; regularly updated table of recommendations and company financial ratios [4]
  http://www.globe.com.ph/~bpicapr/

Futures and options

- *Portalinc* – (information about the *Manila International Futures Exchange*) – [1]
  http://www.portalinc.com/mife/index.html

Economy

- *National Economic & Development Authority* – review of: GNP, inflation, interest rates, exchanges rates, fiscal position, international reserves; year end report on Philippine economy; economic outlook report [3]
  http://www.ph.net/neda/neda.html

- *GSI link* – information about Bangko Sentral ng Pilipinas (the central monetary authority of the Philippines); occasional updates including:

currency rates and history from 1987, T-bill, SDR, economic financial indicators [3]
http://www.gsilink.com/~bsp/

■ *Association of Development Finance Institutions in Asia and the Pacific (ADFIAP)* – list of Philippine bank members [2]
http://www.orion2000.com/philippi/prof_pi.html

Other URL lists

■ *RPNet* [3]
http://pdx.rpnet.com/rpnet/homepage/news.htm

POLAND

Domain code	pl
Currency	Zloty (Zl)
GDP	$191.1bn
GDP/capita	$4920
GDP growth	5.5%
External debt	$47bn
Exports	$16.3bn (fob)
Imports	$18.1bn (fob)

News

■ *Donosy* – daily general brief news; historical archive from 1993 [3]
http://info.fuw.edu.pl/donosy-english/

■ *Internet Securities* – (subscription) financial and industrial market information; searchable index [3]
http://www.securities.com.pl/

Markets

■ *Yogi* – (Polish, some English) daily stock prices from the Warsaw stock exchange ('najnowsze notowania'); stock tick data through day; ranking of stock price changes; 5-year and 6-month stock and index charts updated daily ('zbiorcze plansze'); daily trust fund prices; daily currencies rates ('waluty') [5]
http://yogi.ippt.gov.pl/gielda/wyniki/dogrywki/

Stocks

■ *Warsaw University* – (Polish) daily closing prices from the Warsaw stock exchange, TXT or HTML format, historical archive back to 1991 [4]
http://sunsite.icm.edu.pl/~jarek/

■ *Warsaw University* – daily stock prices from the Warsaw stock exchange [2]
gopher://plearn.edu.pl:71/00/roznosci/ekonomia/WGPW-Wa/ra/ost-wyn

Currencies and money

■ *Institute of Fundamental Technological Research (IPPT)* – daily currency rates
('waluta') [3]
http://yogi.ippt.gov.pl/gielda/waluta.txt

Economy

■ *Government Information Centre* – economic reports: weekly bulletin and
monthly newsletter; information from the Ministry of Privatization; brief
report on the stock exchange [3]
http://www.urm.gov.pl/welcomee.html

■ *US Department of Commerce* – economic overview [2]
http://www.stat-usa.gov/bems/bemspol/bemspol.html

■ *Municipality of Cracow City* – economy of Cracow [1]
http://www.cyf-kr.edu.pl/asc/KRAKOW/UM/ang/economy/index.shtml

Miscellaneous

Banks

■ *PPA Bank* – [1]
http://www.cyf-kr.edu.pl/com/PPABank/

■ *Bank Gospodarstwa Krajowego* – (Polish) [1]
http://www.atm.com.pl/~bgk/

Other URL lists

■ *Pol-Net*
http://www.pol-net.com/

■ *Warsaw University*
http://info.fuw.edu.pl/pl/

PORTUGAL

Domain code	pt
Currency	Portuguese escudo (Esc)
GDP	$107.3bn
GDP/capita	$10 190
GDP growth	1.4%
External debt	$20bn
Exports	$15.4bn (fob)
Imports	$24.3bn (cif)

News

■ *Publico Online* – (Portuguese) full text of daily newspaper
  http://www.publico.pt/publico/hoje/

■ *The News* – English language newspaper [2]
  http://www.nexus-pt.com/news/index.hts

■ *Jornal de Notícias* – (Portuguese)
  http://www.jnoticias.pt/

Markets

Stocks

■ *Lisbon Stock Exchange* – BVL30 stock index updated every 5 min.; archive of
  daily charts for BVL30; daily turnover and closing bond prices; monitor of
  top ten price changes for bonds and stocks over previous close – updated
  every 10 min.; monthly review of trading [3]
  http://www.bvl.pt/

Economy

■ *ICEP* – brief economic overview [2]
  http://www.portugal.org/

Miscellaneous

■ *Banco Nacional Ultramarino* (Portuguese) [1]
  http://www.EUnet.pt/bnu/

■ *Tecninvest* [1]
  http://www.tecninvest.com/

Other URL lists

■ *SAPO* – search engine and index
  http://sapo.ua.pt/

RUSSIA

Domain code   ru
Currency   Ruble (R)

GDP $721.2bn
GDP/capita $4820
GDP growth   15%
External debt $95bn
Exports $48bn (fob)
Imports $35.7bn (fob)

News

■ *Emerging Markets Navigator* – (information on Russian financial markets) daily newswire with archive and search facility; database of company profiles [3]
http://www.emn.ru/

■ *St. Petersburg Times* – weekly news review with business section [3]
http://www.spb.su/times/160/index.html

■ *OMRI* – daily digest of Russian news [3]
http://www.omri.cz/Publications/Digests/DigestIndex.html

■ *Russia Today* – daily news with digest of TV news [2]
http://www.ceo.cz/rtoday/

■ *Russia Portfolio* – (subscription journal with business, economic, financial news about Russia) – [1]
http://www.world.std.com/~rusport/

■ *Russia-On-Line* – (subscription for *Ivzestia* and other journals) [1]
http://www.online.ru/

Markets

■ *Russian Exchange* – (incorporating the Russian Commodities and Raw Materials Exchange) occasional weekly markets review; occasional daily auction results [2]
http://www.fe.msk.ru/infomarket/rtsb/ewelcome.html

■ *Federal Commission on Securities and the Capital Market* – latest press releases; official documents; search of documents [2]
http://www.fe.msk.ru/infomarket/fedcom/ewelcome.html

■ *REDGAR* – (Russian) disclosure project of data about securities issuers
http://www.fe.msk.ru/infomarket/redgar/ewelcome.html

■ *AK&M* – daily AKM stock market indices (general and sector); daily OTC prices with archive; poll results, rating: privatized companies, brokers, registrars [4]
http://www.fe.msk.ru/infomarket/akm/

■ *Vash Finansovy Popechitel* – (Russia and Ukraine investment adviser) daily stock bid/offer prices; daily closing index and stock prices with archive; daily updated charts of selected stocks; stock and industry reports; search facility [3]
http://www.yftrust.ru/

Stocks

■ *RINACO Plus* – (securities broker) updated daily prices/charts for stocks and indices; daily stock bid/offer prices; summaries of industry analysis reports; overview of the stock and fixed income markets; institutional investors guide to emerging market funds in Russia [4]
http://www.fe.msk.ru/infomarket/rinacoplus/rplus.html

■ *Lenstroymaterialy* – (financial broker and investment adviser) daily bid/offer stock prices; occasional stock reports; information on investment portfolio [2]
http://www.fe.msk.ru/infomarket/lenstroy/welcome.html

■ *Federal Stock Corporation* – (official privatization broker) information on forthcoming state stock auctions [2]
http://www.fe.msk.ru/infomarket/ffk/ewelcome.html

Futures and options

■ *St. Petersburg Futures Exchange* – [2]
http://ft.rcom.spb.su/

Miscellaneous

■ *Institute for Commercial Engineering* – umbrella site for many financial services [5]
http://www.fe.msk.ru/

■ *Alpha-RINACO* – (securities broker) [1]
http://www.fe.msk.ru/infomarket/alpharinaco/erinhis.html

■ *Russian Legal Server* – information about Russian law [2]
http://solar.rtd.utk.edu/~nikforov/main.html

Banks

■ *Rossiyskiy Kredit Bank* – rating of Russian banks [1]
http://www.roscredit.msk.su/eng/

■ *Petersburg-Invest* – (investment bank) [1]
http://www.peterlink.ru/ads/petinvest/

■ *The Directory of Banking & Financial Institutions in Russia* – lists of all Russian banks, simple search to find bank addresses (more complete information available with subscription); brief overview of Russian banking system [2]
http://www.wfi.fr/icp/

Other URL lists

- *West's Research* [3]
  http://www.eskimo.com/~bwest/rerc.html
- *Palm's Portal* – [3]
  http://www.aa.net/~russia/

SINGAPORE

Domain code	sg
Currency	Singapore dollar (S$)
GDP	$57bn
GDP/capita	$19 940
GDP growth	10.1%
External debt	$20m
Exports	$96.4bn (fob)
Imports	$102.4bn (cif)

News

- *Business Times* – daily business news; articles; company news; daily SIMEX market report and closing prices; daily currency rates; archive of past issues with search facility [4]
  http://www.asia1.com.sg/biztimes/
- *Straits Times* – daily general news; archive of past issues with search facility [3]
  http://www.asia1.com.sg/straitstimes/

Markets

- *Dow Jones Telerate* – daily stock market report; news bulletins; value and charts for: stock index, currency [4]
  http://www.djtelerate.com.hk/
- *OUB* – weekly forex commentary; weekly financial review with data and comment covering: economy, stocks, currencies and interest rates [3]
  http://www.oub.com.sg/

Stocks

- *Stock Exchange of Singapore (SES)* – daily report: indices, major movers, most active stocks, sector analysis [4]
  http://www.ses.com.sg/
- *BT StockWatch* – daily stock market summary data page; real-time SES stock prices, with history of all day trades; table of most active stocks and major moves; indices with 15 min. values through the day; daily market comment; market gossip; daily warrant comment; customized stock portfolio (up to 30

stocks with prices updated every 3 min.); companies earnings analysis with ranking table [5]
http://www.asia1.com.sg/btstocks/

■ *Financial Interactive Services Hub (FISH)* – daily stock prices with technical charts: HiLo, RSI, candlestick, MACD, OBV; stock indices: 15 min. intraday values and chart, 1-year historical chart; company announcements; news bulletins from Television Corporation of Singapore; users' gossip forum; subscription service for live quotes [5]
http://www.infront.com.sg/

■ *Stock Web* – real-time SES market indices and stock prices, with history of all day trades; major price moves (customizable); most active stocks [5]
http://www.livewire.ncb.gov.sg/stockweb/

■ *Singapore Press* – (subscription service for Singapore company research)
http://www.asia1.com.sg/company/

Futures and options

■ *SIMEX* – daily settlement prices for futures contracts; daily updated futures contract charts: daily OHLC, vol, OI; vol, OI charts for options contracts [4]
http://www.simex.com.sg/

Economy

■ *Statistics Singapore* – (national statistical authority) key social and economic statistics; quarterly economic survey; press releases on the economy [3]
http://www.ncb.gov.sg/stats/

■ *Singapore Government* – description of Government bodies; Government press releases and speeches [1]
http://www.gov.sg/

Miscellaneous

■ *United Overseas Bank (UOB)* – [1]
http://www.uob.com.sg/

■ *DBS Bank* – [1]
http://www.dbs.com.sg/dbs/

■ *Oversea-Chinese Banking Corporation (OCBC)* – [1]
http://www.singnet.com.sg/customers/ocbc/index.html

Other URL lists

■ *Admall* – [2]
http://www.admall.com.sg/money.htm

SOUTH AFRICA

Domain code   za
Currency   Rand (R)

GDP $194.3bn
GDP/capita $4420
GDP growth   2.0%
External debt $18bn
Exports $25.3bn (fob)
Imports $21.4bn (fob)

News

- *Mail and Guardian* – weekly newspaper; daily news bulletins; searchable index of articles back to July 1994 [4]
  http://www.mg.co.za/mg/

- *Financial Mail* – weekly newspaper; economic, business and investment sections; archive of back issues with search facility [4]
  http://www.atd.co.za/fm/

- *Independent Online* – daily news including business section [4]
  http://www.inc.co.za/

- *Finance Week* – business articles [3]
  http://africa.com/mags/finweek/

- *Star and SA Times* – daily news headlines [2]
  http://www.satimes.press.net/

Markets

- *Rand Merchant Bank* – (investment bank) daily digest of SA news; weekly market data: money, FRA, NCD, bond, forex, swaps, equity; articles on: share, bond and futures markets [4]
  http://www.rmb.co.za/

Stocks

- *Johannesburg Stock Exchange (JSE)* – weekly exchange statistics; monthly review of trading [3]
  http://www.jse.co.za/

- *Virtual Africa* – (overview of the companies listed on the African stock exchanges) summary company information [3]
  http://africa.com/pages/jse/index.htm

- *McGregor Information Services* – (information on African stock exchange quoted companies) [1]
  http://africa.com/pages/mcgregor/index.htm

▪ *Sharenet* – (subscription data download service for 6-month historical data and daily data: SFE shares, unit trust, gilts, currencies, metals; live price feeds offered) [1]
http://www.nis.za/sharenet/index.html

Futures and options

▪ *South Africa Futures Exchange* – daily data: contract prices, potato, maize, beef cash indices and prices; historical and volatilities; advice on futures; SA public holidays [3]
http://www.safex.co.za/

Commodities

▪ *Chamber of Mines of South Africa* – press releases; facts and figures; information on krugerrand; online mining directory; daily news and archive; daily economic indicators: international gold prices, other precious metal prices, krugerrand, currencies, Johannesburg SE indices, commodity links [5]
http://www.bullion.org.za/

Economy

▪ *South African Reserve Bank* – monthly report of economic data; list of authorized foreign exchange dealers; exchange control manual; latest press releases [3]
http://www.resbank.co.za/

▪ *ABSA* – (including Allied Bank, Trust Bank, United Bank, Volkskas Bank) daily economic report: currencies, interest rates, bonds, economic stats; economic weekly report; quarterly economic review; occasional economic articles [3]
http://www.absa.co.za/

▪ *Sanlam* – (financial services) bimonthly economic survey; comment on the SA Budget [3]
http://os2.iafrica.com/sanlam/index.htm

▪ *M. Brey and Assocs.* – guide to the SA Budget [2]
http://www.aztec.co.za/exinet/budget/budget.htm

▪ *KPMG* – (accountants) summary of the latest SA Budget [2]
http://www.kpmg.co.za/

Miscellaneous

▪ *Stones* – (unit trust information) beginners guide; sort trust performance; individual trust descriptions [3]
http://stones.co.za/ut/index.html

■ *TMA Investment Products Services* – (financial services) weekly data: unit trust prices, money market rates [2]
http://www.atd.co.za/tma/tmahm.html

■ *Standard Equities (Pty) Ltd.* – (stockbroker) [1]
http://os2.iafrica.com/anderwil/

■ *Robert J. Kiggins* – (business and finance adviser) business newsletter [2]
http://africa.com/pages/kiggins/index.htm

Banks

■ *NBS Bank* – [1]
http://www.nbs.co.za/

■ *Standard Bank* – (retail and commercial bank) selection of financial articles: Trading in Repo and Securities Lending in SA, A Foreigner's Guide to Investment in SA, Directory of Financial Markets in Africa [2]
http://www.sbic.co.za/

Other URL lists

■ *Marques Systems* [3]
http://minotaur.marques.co.za/index.htm

SPAIN

Domain code	es
Currency	Peseta
GDP	$515.8bn
GDP/capita	$13 120
GDP growth	1.8%
External debt	$90bn
Exports	$72.8bn (fob)
Imports	$92.5bn (cif)

Markets

■ *Argentaria* – weekly money/bond/stock/currency market data and brief markets comment; weekly brief economic comment and summary of main indicators; economic forecasts [2]
http://www.argentaria.com/

■ *Banesto* – weekly market comment; analysis reports on stocks [3]
http://www.banesto.es/

■ *Fincorp* – daily exchange rates, money and bond rates, stock indices; brief market news [2]
http://www.servicom.es/fincorp/

Stocks

▧ *Madrid Stock Exchange* – IBEX35, sector indices and IBEX35 constituent stock prices updated every 15 min., updated daily chart of IBEX35, quarterly key figures on IBEX35 constituent companies [4]
http://www.bolsamadrid.es/

▧ *Stock Research* – (Spanish) technical analysis newsletter
http://www.servicom.es/stockresearch/

Futures and options

▧ *MEFF Renta Fija* – (Spanish fixed income financial futures and options exchange) daily closing prices; historic data download (flexible format, including record of every trade for a specific contract, daily total market data in zip format); explanation of hedging using bond contracts [4]
http://www.meff.es/

Economy

▧ *la Caixa* – monthly economic report [3]
http://lacaixa.datalab.es/homecxan.html

▧ *BBV* – monthly economic report
http://www.bbv.es/

Miscellaneous

▧ *Banco Santander* – overseas contact addresses for Santander Investment [1]
http://www.bsantander.com/

▧ *Banco Central Hispano* [1]
http://www.offcampus.es/bch/

Other URL lists

▧ *BIWE* [4]
http://biwe.cesat.es/

▧ *El Indice* [3]
http://www.globalcom.es/indice/

SWEDEN

Domain code   se
Currency   Swedish krona (SKr)

GDP $163.1bn
GDP/capita $18 580
GDP growth   2.4%
External debt $NA
Exports $59.9bn (fob)
Imports $49.6bn (cif)

News

- *Dagens Industri* – daily business headlines [3]
  http://www.di.se/
- *Bergwester Scandinavian Financial Review* – brief financial news updated weekly; annual Nordic economic outlook [3]
  http://www.bergwester.se/

Markets

- *Aragon Fondkommission* – (fund manager) daily equity newsletter; fixed income newsletter; occasional stock research [4]
  http://www.aragon.se/
- *SVT Text* – (Swedish Teletext economics page) economic data, currencies, stocks [2]
  http://www.svt.se/texttv/200.html
- *Aktievision AB* – (information vendors) updated daily charts of Swedish OMX Index, Swedish SX General Index [1]
  http://www.aktievision.se/indexen.htm

Stocks

- *Stockholm Stock Exchange* – stock and index quotes delayed 30 min.; weekly summary of trading [5]
  http://www.xsse.se/
- *Affärsvärlden* – (business weekly journal) stock prices delayed by 30 min. from the Stockholm Stock Exchange; sorted lists by: top gainers/losers, trading volume; company information (including ten largest shareholders); Affärsvärlden's Generalindex index calculated with monthly historical data back to 1949; stock guide (sort stocks by: ytd price change, yield, PER) [5]
  http://www.et.se/
- *Finanstidningen* – database of company information: latest news, financial data and contact details [3]
  http://www.fti.se/ir/fti/

▧ *Linewise Information Services* – stock and index quotes from the Stockholm Stock Exchange delayed 30 min. [4]
http://www.public.se/english/

▧ *BolagsFakta* – (Swedish) annual reports, press releases, share prices for Stockholm stocks
http://www.bolagsfakta.se/

▧ *Stock Market Outlook* – (newsletter by Lars Sorensen) stock recommendations; model portfolio; market calendar; list of Swedish companies trading in the US; links [3]
http://www.geocities.com/WallStreet/1889/

Currencies and money

▧ *Teledata Sweden* – daily currency rates from Swedish Postal Giro [2]
http://www.teledata.se/valuta.html

Futures and options

▧ *OM Group* – (OM Stockholm and OMLX London futures exchanges) daily closing prices of options [3]
http://www.omgroup.com/

Economy

▧ *SCB* – (Sweden's national statistics body) comprehensive database of country statistics including economic indicators; latest statistical press releases [3]
http://www.scb.se/

Miscellaneous

▧ *Trygg-Hansa* – (financial services company) [1]
http://www.trygghansa.se/

▧ *Deriva Securities* – (Swedish) model portfolio
http://www.deriva.se/

▧ *Investor AB* – (industrial holding company) information on main holdings, historic headlines, review of its share price [2]
http://www.investor.se/

Banks

▧ *SE Banken* – [1]
http://www.sebank.se/sebank/

▧ *JP Bank* – [1]
http://www.jpbank.se/jpbank.html

Other URL lists

- *SUNET* – [3]
  http://www.sunet.se/sweden/business_stocks_and_finance.html
- *Nikos* [2]
  http://www.algonet.se/~nikos/wwwreg/finans.html

SWITZERLAND

Domain code	ch
Currency	Swiss franc (SwF)
GDP	$148.4bn
GDP/capita	$22 080
GDP growth	1.8%
External debt	$NA
Exports	$69.6bn (fob)
Imports	$68.2bn (cif)

Markets

- *UBS Bank* – daily fund prices; daily Zurich bourse comment (German); weekly markets comment (German); daily bond markets comment from Geneva (French); daily currency report (French) with cross rates, support/resistance levels, IVs on currency options, interest rates and comment; dictionary of banking/finance terms; excerpts from economic reports [3]
  http://www.ubs.com/
- *Credit Suisse Bank* – weekly stock prices for Swiss market; sample research documents; monthly Swiss derivatives report [2]
  http://www.ska.com/
- *Surge Trading* – (brokers for futures, options, forex) daily forex report: price ranges, support/resistance levels, comment; daily commodity reports for corn, wheat, sugar, cocoa, coffee [3]
  http://www.surgetrd.com/
- *Quoteline* – (quote vendor) sample weekly charts including Swiss SMI Index; Nestle, Roche, SBCI; downloadable file of daily closing quotes of Dow Jones Index since 1900 [2]
  http://www.ping.ch/quoteline/

Stocks

- *Geneva Stock Exchange* – compilation of Basle, Geneva, Zurich bourse daily and historic data: daily summary report of closing prices of all stocks; tick data for individual stocks; twice daily stock market comment (French); top ten advance/declines report [5]
  http://www.bourse.ch/

Currencies and money

▦ *Olsen & Associates* – (forex advisers) historic currency rate database; hourly proprietary 'currency ranking' chart; currency forecasts, historical analysis and trading model position [4]
http://www.olsen.ch/

Futures and options

▦ *Swiss Commodities Futures and Options Association* – [1]
http://Finance.Wat.ch/scfoa/

Economy

▦ *BSI-Banca della Svizzera Italiana* – research reports: quarterly investment outlook (asset allocation, currencies, bonds, equities), semi-annual economic outlook (Global, Europe, Swiss), monthly financial letter (various topics) [3]
http://www.tinet.ch/bsi/bsien00.htm

Miscellaneous

▦ *Matterhorn Investment Corp* – (financial services company) [1]
http://www.matterhorn.ch/

▦ *Intercom* – (trust company adviser) [1]
http://www.firmnet.ch/intercom/

▦ *BFI* – (financial services company) [1]
http://www.firmnet.ch/bfi/

Banks

▦ *Maerki, Baumann and Co.* – (private bankers)
http://www.mbczh.ch/welcome.htm

▦ *Zürcher Kantonalbank* – [1]
http://www.zhkb.ch/english/index.html

▦ *SW Consulting* – (banking software consultants) directory of addresses and a FAQ for Swiss banks [2]
http://www.swconsult.ch/

Other URL lists

▦ *Firmindex* – [3]
http://www.firmnet.ch/firmindex/

TAIWAN

Domain code	tw
Currency	New Taiwan dollar (NT$)
GDP	$257bn
GDP/capita	$12 070
GDP growth	6.0%
External debt	$620m
Exports	$93bn (fob)
Imports	$85.1bn (cif)

News

▓ *Taipei Economic and Cultural Office in New York* – daily general/business news from China News Agency with brief stock market summary [4]
http://www.taipei.org/

▓ *Sinanet* – daily Taiwan headline news from Central News Agency: brief stock market summary, currency rates; archive of four previous issues [4]
http://ww3.sinanet.com/

▓ *China Times* – (Chinese)
http://chinatimes.com.tw/

Markets

▓ *Dow Jones Telerate* – daily markets report; news bulletins; value and charts for: stock index, currency [4]
http://www.djtelerate.com.hk/

Stocks

▓ *Taiwan Stock Exchange* – daily closing stock prices and index; brief listed company information: address, turnover, operating profit, EPS [5]
http://www.tse.com.tw/

▓ *Taisec Securities* – daily stock market: data, sector performance chart, commentary, recommendation, analysis of trading activity; archive of daily market reports from Dec 1985 [4]
http://www.taisec.com.tw/

Economy

▓ *Government Information Office* – political and economic overview; annual yearbook of statistics including: economy, banking and finance, with reviews of the currency/money/bond/stock markets; online journals with news on business and the economy; latest Government press releases [4]
http://gio.gov.tw/

Miscellaneous

■ *Fidelity Investments* – (Chinese)
http://www.fidelity.com.tw/

■ *Asia Pacific Advisor* – (investment services) [1]
http://www.asiannet.com/asia-pacific

Banks

■ *Citibank Taiwan* – [1]
http://www.citibank.com.tw/

■ *Taipei Business Bank* – [1]
http://fakeindy.linkease.com.tw/tpbb/

■ *Chinatrust Commercial Bank* – [1]
http://www.chinatrust.com.tw/

Other URL lists

■ *Asianet*
http://www.asiannet.com/taiwan/taiwan

THAILAND

Domain code	th
Currency	Baht
GDP	$355.2bn
GDP/capita	$5970
GDP growth	8.0%
External debt	$64.3bn
Exports	$46bn (fob)
Imports	$52.6bn (cif)

News

■ *Business Day* – general and company news [3]
http://www.loxinfo.co.th/~bday/index.html

Markets

■ *The Stock Exchange of Thailand* – list of all quoted companies; monthly economic statistics from BOT; real-time prices by stock or whole sector; real-time market index; news reports on companies [5]
http://www.set.or.th/

■ *Thai Farmers Bank* – research articles, including: interest rate outlook; interest rates review, stock market review [3]
http://www.tfb.co.th/

Currencies and money

▧ *Siam Commercial Bank* – interest and currency rates [2]
   http://www.scb.co.th/

Economy

▧ *Board of Investment of Thailand* [1]
   http://www.bangkoknet.com/boi.html
▧ *Bangkok Bank* – guide to Thai economy; economic review and outlook [2]
   http://www.bbl.co.th/main.html
▧ *Note Printing Works* [2]
   http://www.npw.or.th/
▧ *Thailand Development Research Institute* [1]
   http://www.nectec.or.th/users/pong/TDRI/index.html

Miscellaneous

▧ *First Bangkok City Bank* [1]
   http://www.fbcb.co.th/
▧ *Citibank* [1]
   http://www.citibank.tnet.co.th/

Other URL lists

▧ *Trade On-Line* [1]
   http://www.sino.net/index.html
▧ *SiamWeb* [2]
   http://www.eskimo.com/~putt/siam/

TURKEY

Domain code	tr
Currency	Turkish lira (TL)
GDP	$305.2bn
GDP/capita	$4910
GDP growth	−5.0%
External debt	$66.6bn
Exports	$15.3bn (fob)
Imports	$27.6bn (fob)

News

▧ *Embassy of the Republic of Turkey*, Washington, DC – daily digest of news;
   selected articles; Government press releases; weekly exchange rates; business

and economic reference sources: Turkish capital markets, investment opportunities, privatization program, economic overview [4]
http://www.turkey.org/current.htm

Markets

■ *Tütünbank* – analyst summary report with charts on selected companies; occasional economic review and statistics [2]
http://www.tutunbank.com.tr:1100/tbhome.html

■ *Global Trade and Communication* – daily prices for: currencies, gold, stock market indices; daily new headlines
http://www.guide2turkey.com/

Economy

■ *Central Bank of Turkey* – daily currency rates; daily Government bond prices; weekly money and credit statistics bulletin; weekly press bulletin; monthly statistical bulletin; quarterly bulletin [4]
http://www.tcmb.gov.tr/

■ *Ministry of Foreign Affairs* – list of brokers; information on banks; library of national documents; economic reviews and statistics [3]
http://www.mfa.gov.tr/

■ *WIRE* – EBA economic report [2]
http://wire.co.uk/turkey/

Other URL lists

■ *Business Turkey Interactive Marketing Group* [3]
http://www.nwrain.net/~koray/

■ *Embassy of the Republic of Turkey*, Washington, DC [3]
http://www.turkey.org/

UNITED KINGDOM

Domain code	uk
Currency	British pound (BP)
GDP	$1.0452tr
GDP/capita	$17 980
GDP growth	4.2%
External debt	$16.2bn
Exports	$200bn (fob)
Imports	$215bn (cif)

News

- *Financial Times* – daily general/business news with updated bulletins through the day; major stock market indices updated during the day with a 30 min. delay; daily closing share prices for UK and other major markets, major movers calculated for market or sector, with basic stock data (yield, PER, div, earnings, sales, year high/low); daily valuation of UK Unit Trusts, pensions, life insurance funds, and offshore funds; daily reports on most major stock markets; regular: editorial, comment, analysis; diary of the forthcoming week's world political/economic/business/financial events; articles on economics and personal finance; weekly summary of main news stories available by e-mail; search facility on articles [5]
  http://www.ft.com/

- *The Times* – daily general/business/financial news; City gossip and comment; search facility on current issue [4]
  http://www.the-times.co.uk/

- *FTVision* – daily business/economics headlines; daily major stock market index levels and comment; company news and focus on hot stocks [3]
  http://www.ftvision.com/

- *Electronic Telegraph* – daily general/business news; daily UK stock market report; daily market data: major stock moves, major stock indices, popular shares, inflation/interest/Sterling rates, business comment; search facility on archive of past issues from Nov 94 [4]
  http://www.telegraph.co.uk/

- *London Evening Standard* – daily general/business news, market summary data; forthcoming company result and statistics announcements; stock prices; index of companies mentioned in articles; City gossip; archive of 5 past issues [3]
  http://www.standard.co.uk/

- *Weekend City Press Review* – summary of the economic, financial and corporate news in UK's leading weekend newspapers; archive from Jun 95 [4]
  http://www.news-review.co.uk/

Markets

- *PC Quote Europe* – (European representatives for PC Quote Inc.)
  http://www.pcquote-europe.co.uk/

Stocks

- *Electronic Share Information* – (London share market data) free service: top 400 stock prices updated 8 times a day, full LSE market prices updated after midnight, FTSE 100 Index updated through the day; base subscription service: personalized portfolio for tracking up to 100 shares, portfolio valuation e-mailed overnight, stock charts for 4500+ shares, top 400 stock prices updated 8 times daily, Unit Trust daily prices, downloadable 5-year

OHCLV price histories, news stories from AFX, company profiles from Hemmington Scott, access to trading gateway; higher level subscription includes also: unlimited real-time prices, a self-updating page of real-time prices for up to 25 different stocks, real-time multiple portfolios evaluation, stockwatch limit minding [5]
http://www.esi.co.uk/

▨ *Infotrade* – (Mitsubishi Electric Group) share information and dealing for retail investors by PC over private network; services include: real-time prices on all SEAQ UK shares, 3-year historical company results, 2-year results forecasts, 2 years' price history, company activities' descriptions and directors' dealings, FTSE indices and charting facilities [4]
http://infotrade.co.uk/

▨ *Hemmington Scott* – (information from Hemmington Scott's Corporate Information Database, updated weekly) for each company: activities, financials, directors, capital structure, 4-year share price chart relative to FTA, outlook (from company's annual/interim reports), consensus broker forecasts, contacts; key dates; registrar details; selected annual reports; ranking of corporate advisers: auditors, financial PR, solicitors, stockbrokers; regularly updated mergers and acquisitions table; list of companies with ADRs/options; index of AIM companies [5]
http://www.hemscott.co.uk/hemscott/

Brokers

▨ *Sharelink* – (discount broker, part of Charles Schwab Corporation) offers dealing and safe custody service for shares, investment trusts, unit trusts, corporate bonds, gilts, and cash by PC through the ESI Bronze Service [5]
http://www.esi.co.uk/sharelink/

▨ *Fidelity Brokerage* – (international discount brokers) summary of client dealing activity with comment; direct dealing software for retail clients; glossary of investment terms; guide to global markets [2]
http://www.fidelity.co.uk/

▨ *Barclays Stockbrokers* – occasional financial and economic overview; stock review; list of shareholder benefits for different companies; stock exchange settlement calendar; calendar of new issues pending; introduction to the stock market [2]
http://www.barclays.co.uk/stock/home.htm

▨ *Charles Stanley & Co.* – latest FTSE100 index level; London market prices [3]
http://www.charles-stanley.co.uk/

▨ *Durlacher* – traded options newsletter with recommended strategies; archive of previous issues; investment report about the Internet; extracts from research reports on multimedia [2]
http://www.durlacher.co.uk/

▨ *Killik & Co* – daily market news [3]
http://www.killik.co.uk/

- *Redmayne Bentley* – daily market comment; daily listing of 'interesting' shares [2]
  http://www.redmayne.co.uk/redmayne/
- *InvestNet* – (division of Cheviot Capital Ltd.) open account online; display portfolio at last night's prices [1]
  http://epsilon.mkn.co.uk/help/invnet/info/

Currencies and money

- *Information Internet* – real-time foreign exchange prices; comparison graphs to illustrate currency movements over the past 24 hours
  http://www.info-int.com/
- *Currency Management Corporation* – (associated with the above Information Internet) information on forex dealing [2]
  http://www.forex-cmc.co.uk/

Futures and options

- *London International Financial Futures and Options Exchange (LIFFE)* – daily update of downloadable file with settlement prices; downloadable files of Span risk arrays; downloadable files (5-day rolling daily update, in CSV format) of: high, low, close, estimated volume, previous day's official volume and previous day's open interest data on all contracts and time-stamped bids, asks and trades on all financial contracts; vol/OI records by contract; vol/OI charts for each contract from inception; series of technical articles to download in PDF format; reference guidelines on managing derivatives risk; information on training courses; glossary [5]
  http://www.liffe.com/
- *Phillip Alexander Securities and Futures* – explanation of futures/options markets/trading/risks; charts on stock indices, interest rates, currencies, commodities [3]
  http://www.bogo.co.uk/pasf/
- *Options Direct* – (options broker) daily future/options market report; monthly market review; client service: morning trading signals on all the LIFFE equity options [3]
  http://www.options-direct.co.uk/

Economy

- *HM Treasury* – annual debt management report; minutes of the Chancellor's monthly monetary meetings with the Governor of the Bank of England, with updated background economic information; annual Summer economic forecast; occasional economic papers and briefs; reports of the Panel of Independent Forecasters with archive from Oct 93; annual Budget information; record of speeches [5]
  http://www.hm-treasury.gov.uk/

▓ *Bank of England* – press releases [1]
http://www.bankofengland.co.uk/

▓ *CCTA Government Information Service* – Government departments online;
search facility for Government servers (including HM Treasury) [3]
http://www.open.gov.uk/

▓ *Central Office of Information (COI)* – Government press releases (including
departments: Bank of England, Department of Trade and Industry, HM
Treasury, Monopolies and Mergers Commission, Office of Fair Trading,
Securities and Investments Board) search facility on date [4]
http://www.coi.gov.uk/coi/

▓ *Institute for Fiscal Studies (IFS)* – (microeconomic policy research) surveys and
reports on economic policy; analysis of the budget; interactive programs:
'What the Budget Means to You', 'Be Your Own Chancellor' [4]
http://www1.ifs.org.uk/

Miscellaneous

▓ *MoneyWorld* – (general personal finance reference) information on:
unit/investment trust managers, IFAs, stockbrokers, regulatory bodies; daily
personal finance news; daily economic/market/company news report; series
of reference guides to investment; data on: daily share prices (from DBC),
unit/investment trust performance (from HSW), PEP performance (from
Allenbridge), savings/borrowings rates, tax and inflation rates; glossary of
financial terms; links [4]
http://www.moneyworld.co.uk/

▓ *MoneyWeb* – (general personal finance reference) large collection of links to
financial articles; FAQs from uk.finance newsgroup [4]
http://www.demon.co.uk/moneyweb/

▓ *Interactive Investor* – umbrella site for information on: IFAs, UK unit trusts,
investment trusts, PEPs, and offshore funds, with pages maintained by fund
managers; news service with the following journals: *Financial Adviser*, *Product
Adviser*, *Investment Adviser* and *Offshore Financial Review*; Micropal fund
performance figures; site search facility; links [5]
http://www.iii.co.uk/autif/

▓ *Venture Capital Report* – (subscription newsletter) monthly synopsis of new
opportunities [2]
http://www.demon.co.uk/vcr1978/

▓ *AAA Investment Guide* – reference work on all types of UK investment [3]
http://www.wisebuy.co.uk/

▓ *Ethical Business* – introduction to, and directory of, ethical investment [3]
http://www.bath.ac.uk/Centres/Ethical/

▓ *Offshore.net* – (guide to the Island of Jersey's international offshore financial
services industry) [2]
http://www.offshore.net/

Funds and trusts

▨ *GAM* – fund performance statistics/charts; fund asset allocation and top five holdings; manager information; market comment [3]
http://www.ukinfo.gam.com/

▨ *Fidelity International* – daily fund prices; regular market comments; interactive program to determine investment; guide to fund investing [2]
http://www.fid-intl.com/uk/home_e.html

▨ *Prolific* – monthly review of world's major stock markets [2]
http://www.iii.co.uk/prolific/

▨ *Cazenove Unit Trust Management Limited* – monthly updated UK sector and global market performance tables; charts updated twice-weekly: currencies, major stock markets, short term interest rates, bond markets, UK house price index, gold, silver and commodity price index; constituents of the FTSE100; guide to UK tax; guide to global stock exchanges [3]
http://www.cazenove.co.uk/

▨ *ECU Group* – (forex mortgages/deposits, fund management) similar charts available to those on the Cazenove site [3]
http://www.bogo.co.uk/ecu/home.htm

▨ *M&G* – daily fund prices [1]
http://www.iii.co.uk/m_g/

▨ *Gartmore Investment Management* – [1]
http://www.iii.co.uk/gartmore/

▨ *Culross Global Management* – (institutional fixed income management) explanation of its investment process and procedure [2]
http://secure.londonmall.co.uk/culross/

General fund sites

▨ *Micropal* – (investment performance tables for: unit/investment trusts, PEPs and authorized offshore funds) Micropal awards for best performing funds; review top performing funds over 1, 3, 5 years; subscription service for further analysis [2]
http://www.iii.co.uk/micropal/

▨ *Association of Unit Trusts and Investment Funds (AUTIF)* – explanation of trusts and PEPs; directory of members with brief profiles; glossary [3]
http://www.iii.co.uk/autif/

▨ *Association of Investment Trusts Companies* – explanation of investment trusts; directory of members with brief profiles; glossary [3]
http://www.iii.co.uk/aitc/

▨ *TrustNet* – directory of investment trusts and offshore funds with: fund details, capital structure, portfolio summary; directory of fund managers with contact details and funds managed; investment trust prices and warrant performance tables [4]
http://www.trustnet.co.uk/

Independent Financial Advisers (IFA)

■ *Online Independent Financial Advisers* – personal financial report from online form; e-mail quote request; reference articles on investing and investments [2]
http://www.onlineifa.co.uk/online/

■ *Pronoia Financial Consultancy* – brief descriptions of investment vehicles (e.g. unit trusts) [2]
http://www.vossnet.co.uk/company/pronoia/

■ *IFA Direct* – (discount IFA) [1]
http://www.ftech.net/~ifadirec/

■ *GÆIA* – (ethical investment adviser) [2]
http://www.u-net.com/~gaeia/

■ *Garrison Investment Analysis* – (discount brokerage) [1]
http://www.garrison.co.uk/

■ *Coombe Financial Services* – (discount dealing service) [1]
http://www.objcomputing.co.uk/nettgain/nettgain.htm

■ *Advisa Financial Services* – (off-shore IFA) [1]
http://www.offshore.net/advisa/

General IFA sites

■ *IFA Association* – [2]
http://www.ifaa.org.uk/

■ *Interactive Investor's IFA service* – geographical search on database of 6000 IFAs; financial questions answered by DBS Financial Management [3]
http://www.iii.co.uk/ifa/

■ *FT Magazines* – (incorporating *Financial Adviser, Investment Adviser, Product Adviser*) investment industry news and surveys for advisers [2]
http://www.iii.co.uk/ftmags/

■ *Investment Week* – (magazine for IFAs) investment industry news; feature articles; global markets review and comment [2]
http://www.invweek.co.uk/

Banks

■ *Barclays Bank* – [1]
http://www.barclays.co.uk/

■ *Barclays Offshore Banking Services* – [1]
http://www.offshorebanking.barclays.com/

■ *Lloyds Bank* – [1]
http://www.lloydsbank.co.uk/

■ *Midland Bank* – [1]
http://www.midlandbank.co.uk/midlandbank/

■ *InterNect* – list of UK banks with telephone numbers and Web links if existing [2]
http://www.inect.co.uk/

Software

■ *Synaptic Systems* – (software for financial advisers) downloadable demo version of Compliance Manager [1]
http://www.synaptic.co.uk/

Other URL lists

■ *UKDirectory* – [4]
http://www.ukdirectory.com/

■ *Yell* – [4]
http://www.yell.co.uk/

UNITED STATES

Domain code	us
Currency	United States dollar (US$)
GDP	$6.738tr
GDP/capita	$25 850
GDP growth	4.1%
External debt	$NA
Exports	$513bn (fob)
Imports	$664bn (cif)

News

■ *CNNfn Financial News* – business/financial news updated through the day; daily market reports; daily calendar of economic data releases and world holidays; global market news from Knight-Ridder; continually updated prices for: commodities, currencies, interest rates, US/global stock indices (with rankings of: most active, major moves); 15 min. delayed individual quotes available for: stocks, mutual/money market funds; business/financial glossary; search facility on news archive [5]
http://www.cnnfn.com/

■ *Wall Street Journal* – daily business/financial news; personalized: news facility, stock portfolio monitor; 20 min. delayed stock quotes; daily market reports; brief company profiles: background, financial overview, stock performance, last 20 news articles and press releases; calendars: US/international economic, securities offerings; economic indicators archive; search facility on previous 14 issues [5]
http://update.wsj.com/

▓ *Bloomberg Personal* – updated business/financial news; market reviews; market data: equities, treasuries, Muni bonds, futures; digest of top headlines from world newspapers; mutual funds news; market holidays [5]
http://www.bloomberg.com/

▓ *Investor's Business Daily* – daily general/business/economic news; market summary; search facility on news archive [3]
http://ibd.ensemble.com/

▓ *Barrons Online* – news, articles, archive of past issues [4]
http://www.barrons.com

▓ *Nando Times* – daily general/business news [3]
http://www2.nando.net/

▓ *Reuters News (via Yahoo)* – general/business news updated through the day; archive of previous week's issues [3]
http://www.yahoo.com/headlines/

▓ *San Jose Mercury News* – daily general/business news; headlines updated through the day [2]
http://www.sjmercury.com/

▓ *Crayon* – experimental personalized news digest from other sources [2]
http://crayon.net/

▓ *Electronic Newstand* – links to business magazines [2]
http://www.enews.com/monster/business.html

Markets

Regulators

▓ *US Securities and Exchange Commission (SEC)* – reference articles for investors; access to EDGAR Database of Corporate Information; directory of State Securities Regulators; SEC rules and enforcements; press releases; site search facility [5]
http://www.sec.gov/

▓ *Commodity Futures Trading Commission (CFTC)* – commitments of traders and other statistical reports from the division of economic analysis; reference articles; press releases; futures glossary [3]
http://www.cftc.gov/

Associations

▓ *Securities Industry Association (SIA)* – press releases; conference calendar; publications; briefing papers [3]
http://www.sia.com/

▓ *Public Securities Association (PSA)* – (bond market trade association) legislative/regulatory issues; market practices; conferences; research

reports/stats; press releases; site search facility [4]
http://www.psa.com/

■ *National Association of Investors Corporation (NAIC)* – investors' reference articles; order: software/books/magazines; site search facility [3]
http://www.better-investing.org/

■ *Association for Investment Management and Research* – [2]
http://www.aimr.com/aimr.html

■ *Managed Futures Association* – [2]
http://www.mfahome.com/

■ *New York Society of Security Analysts* – details of seminars/conferences; educational services for CFA candidates [2]
http://www.nyssa.org/

■ *Market Technicians Association* – Capital Growth newsletter; monthly index charts; technical analysis software files for FTP; MTA newsletter [3]
http://www.mta-usa.org/~lensmith/

■ *Technical Securities Analysts Association of San Francisco (TSAA)* – [1]
http://www.teleport.com/~ifta/TSAA/tsaahome.html

■ *American Association of Individual Investors (AAII)* – [1]
http://www.spectra.net/mall/aaii/

Exchanges

■ *Chicago Mercantile Exchange (CME)* – summary quote page for most contracts updated every 10 min.; intraday currency prices updated every 10 min.; daily settlement prices with vol/OI for all contracts; daily summary report of all trading activity; calendar of economic/agricultural reports; daily digest of futures industry news; futures reference/educational articles; futures glossary [5]
http://www.cme.com/

■ *Chicago Board of Trade (CBOT)* – (financial/agricultural products) midday and closing market comment and data; daily bulletin of trading activity and notices; agricultural/financial calendar; educational articles; links [5]
http://www.cbt.com/

■ *Chicago Board Options Exchange (CBOE)* – daily market statistics with archive from Aug 95; introduction to options [5]
http://www.cboe.com/

■ *New York Stock Exchange (NYSE)* – daily market summary; daily updated list of all issues traded with: stock symbol, company name, specialist name, trading post, and trading panel; historical data archive of daily market volume (from 1879) and daily closing values for the NYSE indices (from 1966) [3]
http://www.nyse.com

■ *The American Stock Exchange (AMEX)* – (New York, stocks, options) daily market summary: most active, major moves with archive from Jun 95;

explanation of Derivative Securities [3]
http://www.amex.com

▓ *Nasdaq* – 15 min. delayed stock quotes; index/sector activity; most active stocks [3]
http://www.nasdaq.com/

▓ *Philadelphia Stock Exchange (PHLX)* – (stocks, stock options, sector index options, currency options) daily settlement values for customized currency options; weekly currency options review: week/year spot price range, IV/vol/OI; weekly charts of PHLX sector indices [3]
http://www.libertynet.org/~phlx/

▓ *Kansas City Board of Trade (KCBT)* – subscription for historical data [1]
http://www.kcbt.com/

▓ *The Arizona Stock Exchange (AZX)* – (Phoenix, open screen call market for equity trading) daily summaries: open book orders, trade report information; monthly summaries of volume statistics [3]
http://www.azx.com/

▓ *New York Mercantile Exchange (NYMEX)* – (energy/financial/metal futures exchange) contract charts and data [2]
http://www.nymex.com/

▓ *Coffee, Sugar and Cocoa Exchange (CSCE)* – (New York) daily market report by contract: OHLC, settlement/vol/OI; 1-month historical price data by contract (WK1); contract charts and data; economic overview of individual commodity markets [3]
http://www.csce.com/

▓ *New York Cotton Exchange (NYCE)* – contract charts and data [3]
http://www.nyce.com/

▓ *The Mid-America Exchange (MIDAM)* – (Chicago) daily OHLC prices; daily charts; trading simulation program; glossary [4]
http://www.midam.com/

▓ *Minneapolis Grain Exchange (MGE)* – links to cash markets [2]
http://www.mgex.com/

Quotes, charts and information

▓ *DBC Online* – (market data from the major global exchanges) 15 min. delayed stock quotes, 10 min. delayed futures quotes; portfolio monitor; news headlines updated through the day; market index summary pages updated through the day; market reports through the day; stock rumours; financial glossary; subscription for real-time data [5]
http://www.dbc.com/

▓ *Quote.com* – 15 min. delayed US/Canadian stock quotes; 10 min. delayed futures; daily closing international stocks; stock data: earnings, P/E, yield, 52-week price range; portfolio with up to 7 securities; real-time and

historical news headlines; charts [4]
http://www.quote.com/

▓ *NETworth Quote Server* – 15 min. delayed US/Canadian stock quotes; charts with custom graph facility; monitor up to 50 stocks/mutual funds/S&P500 with a portfolio program [4]
http://quotes.galt.com/

▓ *Security APL Quote Server* – 15 min. delayed US/Canadian stock quotes; 1-year price charts; daily closing prices for: mutual and money markets funds; 20 min. delayed market watch page with summary of indices [4]
http://www.secapl.com/

▓ *StockMaster* – 15-20 min. delayed stock and fund quotes/charts; report of popular stocks [4]
http://www.stockmaster.com/

▓ *Charter Media* – news updated through the day: stock/bond markets, companies, dollar, economic; daily updates: political/market briefs, market forecasts/calendar, economic/political forecasts; bond quotes updated every 15 min. [5]
http://www.briefing.com/

▓ *PC Quote* – 20 min. delayed stock quotes; subscription service for: real-time quotes, charts, portfolios [4]
http://www.pcquote.com/

▓ *Interquote* – up to 5 intraday quotes; unlimited closing quotes; subscription for delayed and real-time quotes [4]
http://www.interquote.com/

▓ *Holt Report* – daily market report: indices, international markets, new highs/lows, currency, gold, interest rates, most active; archive from Feb 95 [3]
http://207.67.198.21/holt/

Company research

▓ *Edgar Online* – up-to-the-minute SEC electronic corporate filings [4]
http://www.edgar-online.com/

▓ *Smart Edgar* – (joint venture of DBC and IFN) subscription for real-time SEC Edgar filings
http://dbc.smart-edgar.com/

▓ *Hoover's Corporate Database* – brief company profiles, with subscription service for further details (also available at CNN*fn* and *WSJ* sites) [4]
http://www.hoovers.com/

▓ *Zacks Investment Research* – index and search facility of current brokerage research; directory of company Web sites; subscription research reports and portfolio watch [3]
http://www.zacks.com/

▩ *Dun & Bradstreet Information Services* – (subscription service for Business Background Reports: information on a US company's history and operations, business background of its management, special events and recent newsworthy items)
http://www.dbisna.com/

▩ *Disclosure* – (source for global public company information) [1]
http://networth.galt.com/www/home/equity/disclosure/

▩ *I/B/E/S* – (supplier of earnings forecasts to investment professionals) – [1]
http://networth.galt.com/www/home/equity/ibes/home.html

▩ *Investor Relations NetSources* – (Rein Nomm & Associates, Inc.) links [3]
http://users.aol.com/netir/rna-ir1.htm

Online trading

▩ *Lombard Institutional Brokerage* – 15 min. delayed index/stock/option/funds quotes and charts; intraday charts; registered client service: real-time quotes; online trading via WWW; updated account information [5]
http://www.lombard.com/

▩ *e.Schwab Online Investing* – (discount brokerage) online trading with proprietary software
http://www.eschwab.com/

▩ *ETrade* – (online discount brokerage) online trading of stocks/options; portfolio tracking; 20 min. delayed stock quotes [5]
http://www.etrade.com/

▩ *National Discount Brokers* – (discount brokerage, online service with PAWWS)
http://pawws.secapl.com/Broker/Ndb/

▩ *Jack White & Company* – (discount brokerage, online service with PAWWS) place trades, view positions, receive confirmations online
http://pawws.com/Broker/Jwc/wso.shtml

▩ *Aufhauser & Co.* – online trading via the firm's WealthWEB system
http://www.aufhauser.com

▩ *CompuTEL Securities* – online trading
http://www.rapidtrade.com/rapidtrade/

Futures and options

▩ *MarketPlex* – (at the CBOT, umbrella site for a collection of futures-related services) technical charts, research reports; select articles from journals; access to subscription MRI service: daily charts/data; access to MJK closing prices for commodity exchanges worldwide [4]
http://www.cbot.com/mplex.htm

▩ *INO Global Markets* – (umbrella site for many futures-related services) Options Industry Council; CTAs; Stark Research: performance tracker of CTAs; intraday/daily/weekly charts/data for the world's major futures and options markets; journal articles; conference calendar; reference articles;

bookshop [5]
http://www.ino.com/

- *FutureSource* – (real-time data vendor for the futures/options/cash markets) 6-hour delayed Futures World News feed; intraday quotes on selected contracts [3]
http://www.futuresource.com/

- *Lind-Waldock* – (discount futures brokerage) daily market update; real-time futures information for registered clients [3]
http://www.ino.com/broker/home.htm

- *Ira Epstein & Company* – historical data; occasional market reports; demo version of IraChart program; bulletin board system [2]
http://www.iepstein.com/

- *Jack Carl Futures* – (discount futures brokerage) daily market comment; daily settlement prices on 30 actively traded futures contracts; commodity calendar; contract specs; margin requirements [3]
http://www.jackcarl.com/

- *Futures & Options Trading Group* – previous 10 days closing futures prices for major US exchanges; educational articles on futures trading [4]
http://www.teleport.com/~futures/

- *Jake Bernstein's FuturesWeb* – weekly market report; articles on futures [3]
http://www.trade-futures.com/

- *ISON's Futures Links* – (collection of newsletters and trading systems) [3]
http://ison.com/futures/

- *STA Futures* – economic/agricultural research [3]
http://stafutures.com/

- *The Option Page* – (guide to educational and trading resources for options) archive of educational articles; reviews of options products [3]
http://optionpage.com/

Bonds

- *GovPX* – daily GovPX benchmark prices and Treasury report [3]
http://www.panix.com/~govpx/

- *Bloomberg Personal* – Treasury yield curve; National Muni bond yields [3]
http://www.bloomberg.com/markets/

- *Strategic Investment Consultants* – daily/historical bond market analysis with charts/tables [4]
http://www.well.com/user/tonydelo/

- *Federal Reserve Bank of New York* – daily quotations for US Government securities [3]
gopher://una.hh.lib.umich.edu/00/ebb/monetary/quotes.txt

■ *Bonds-Online* – (information on: treasuries, corporates, municipals, funds) reference articles; links [4]
http://www.bonds-online.com/

■ *Municipal Resource Center (MRC)* – (RR Donnelley Financial) issuers' data; library of resource materials; market analysis links [4]
http://www.municipal.com/

■ *The Blue List* – (Standard & Poor's, municipal/corporate bonds) weekly commentary; municipal yield scales; today's issue par value; browse issues for bond description, coupon, and maturity date; subscription for full access with dynamically updated ticker service [3]
http://www.bluelist.com/

■ *Bondtrac* – (information on the municipal and corporate bond markets) subscription service for access to bond offerings [3]
http://www.bondtrac.com/

Funds

■ *NETworth* – mutual fund information from Morningstar: search facility for funds, fund rankings, prospectus database, articles and market outlooks; directory of company Web sites [5]
http://networth.galt.com/

■ *Mutual Funds Magazine* – (subscription journal for articles and fund evaluations)
http://www.mfmag.com/

■ *Mutual Funds Interactive* – market analyses, opinions, and mutual fund recommendations; features; educational articles; site search facility [3]
http://www.brill.com/

■ *Mutual Fund Research* – ranking of top performing funds: daily/weekly/ monthly/previous year; fund news; fund links; directory of downloadable shareware and freeware programs for mutual fund investing; glossary [4]
http://www.webcom.com/~fundlink/

Technical analysis, graphs

■ *Stock Room* – graphs/quotes of US and international market indices, bond yields, metals, currencies, advance/decline and breadth indicators, interest rates, producer price indices, Fidelity Sector Fund Relative Strength, and custom graphing options [5]
http://loft-gw.zone.org/jason/

■ *Kuber's Trading Desk* – intraday/end-of-day charts for: stocks/indices/futures/options/funds; with technical indicators: moving average stochastics, MACD, and DMI [5]
http://www.best.com:80/~mwahal/invest/

Financial services

▧ *Fidelity Investments* – (fund management, discount brokerage) daily updated fund prices; investment reference information [4]
http://www.fid-inv.com/

▧ *Merrill Lynch* – key indices and most active stocks updated through the day; 20 min. delayed stock quotes; daily midday/closing comments; selection of sector research; weekly Washington Watch; general personal finance articles [3]
http://www.ml.com/

▧ *Prudential Securities* – daily stock/bond market commentaries; weekly update of market data; personal finance reference articles; selection of investment reports to be ordered online [3]
http://www.prusec.com/

▧ *PaineWebber* – selection of investment/economic reports [2]
http://www.painewebber.com/

▧ *Gruntal & Co* – investment newsletter; monthly economic calendar [2]
http://www.gruntal.com/

Newsletters

▧ *Silicon Investor* – quotes, charts, discussion forums, and links for technology stocks [5]
http://www.techstocks.com/

▧ *WebFinance* – (from *Investment Dealers' Digest*, newsletter covering financial companies) weekly headlines; archive of past articles; links [3]
http://nestegg.iddis.com/webfinance/

▧ *Jag Notes* – (subscription newsletter, digest of morning comments from the major Wall Street research firms) individual stock quotes [2]
http://www.jagnotes.com/

▧ *Pitbull Investor* – (subscription newsletter: stocks, shorting, options)
http://com.primenet.com/pitbull/

▧ *Blue Sky Mining Company* – BSM Market Studies newsletter; historical S&P500 futures data; information on managed futures [2]
http://www.pernet.net/~capital1/

▧ *Envision Capital* – (bond market newsletter) [3]
http://www.directnet.com/bonds/

▧ *SGA* Goldstar Research – (subscription newsletter, stocks/options/futures) [1]
http://sgagoldstar.com/sga/

▧ *Investment Crossroads* – (subscription newsletter with weather information for trading)
http://www.investaweather.com/investaweather/

▧ *Wall Street Online* – (umbrella site for collection of subscription newsletters: Prostock, Instant Advisor, IPO Outlook, The Pristine Day Trader, Pristine's

Small Cap Review)
http://www.wso.com/wso/

■ *H$H Investment Club* – (subscription newsletter, penny stocks) [2]
http://hh-club.com/

■ *Growth Stock Gazette* – (subscription bimonthly paper newsletter) excerpts
from previous issues [2]
http://home.navisoft.com/gsg/

■ *Newsletter Network* – umbrella site for many market analysis newsletters [4]
http://www.margin.com/

Economy

■ *US Department of the Treasury* – tax policy; information from the Bureau of
the Public Debt; T-bill, Note and Bond auction results; press releases [3]
http://www.ustreas.gov/

■ *STAT-USA* – (US Department of Commerce) daily economic news; selected
documents: Survey of Current Business, Global Trade Outlook, Economic
Report of the President, Budget of The United States; subscription required
for access to databases [4]
http://www.stat-usa.gov/

■ *Federal Reserve Board* – (Washington DC) statistical releases; links to FRB sites
[2]
http://www.bog.frb.fed.us/

■ *US Census Bureau* – [3]
http://www.census.gov

■ *FedWorld* – (central access point for US Government servers) search facility
[3]
http://www.fedworld.gov/

■ *Economic Bulletin Board (University of Michigan)* – data from the Department
of Commerce; monetary stats; Treasury auction results; economic indicators
[3]
gopher://una.hh.lib.umich.edu:70/11/ebb

■ *National Bureau of Economic Research* – gopher with search facility to find
specific working papers [2]
gopher://nber.harvard.edu/1

Miscellaneous

■ *GNN Personal Finance Center* – (cyber finance magazine) regular investment
articles; links [5]
http://gnn.com/gnn/meta/finance/index.html

■ *PAWWS Financial Network* – (subscription general investment resources:
brokerage and research services)
http://pawws.com/

- *Nest Egg* – (umbrella site for financial services) Smith Barney Wall St Watch: daily market information; New York Institute of Finance Center; general articles on equities/funds [4]
  http://nestegg.iddis.com/

- *Thomson MarketEdge* – (subscription investment resources for: stocks, mutual funds, municipal bonds) daily newsletter: company headlines, debt markets; research centre; company reports [4]
  http://www.marketedge.com/

- *Pathfinder* – (Time's umbrella site for: Fortune, Hoover's Business Profiles and Money) general information on personal finance and investment [5]
  http://www.pathfinder.com/

- *INVESTools* – collection of investment newsletters; news/research resources; charts; Morningstar reports; bookstore; investment articles [4]
  http://investools.com/

- *Research* – (resources for investing and financial planning) stocks, mutual funds, charts, corporate profiles, research reports, Wall Street analysis, shareholder news [3]
  http://www.researchmag.com/

- *The Motley Fool* – (financial forum for individual investors) daily market comments; portfolio updates; educational articles [5]
  http://fool.web.aol.com//fool_mn.htm

- *Equity Analytics* – technical analysis and short-term trading recommendations; markets comments; reference articles on: stocks, options, bonds, futures, commodities, technical analysis, mutual funds; daily sector charts; glossaries; software downloads [4]
  http://www.e-analytics.com/

- *Investor's Galleria* – (source for financial products/services) collection of investment product advertisements; reference articles; links [3]
  http://centrex.com/

- *Streetnet!* – (general stocks resources) investment ideas; industry profiles with recommended stocks; details of selected newsletters; corporate information on subscribing companies [4]
  http://www.streetnet.com/

- *Investment SIG* – (investment club) links [2]
  http://cpcug.org/user/invest/

- *Consumer Information Catalog* – (US General Services Administration) consumer articles on money and investing [4]
  http://www.pueblo.gsa.gov/

- *Financial World* – general investment site with newsletters – *Financial World* and *Brand Names* [3]
  http://www.financialworld.com/

■ *M&A Marketplace* – database of businesses for sale/wanted; general information/resources about M&A [2]
http://www.webcom.com/~cfnet/

■ *Iowa Electronic Markets* – (futures markets on economic and political events) prospectus; quotes; charts [2]
http://www.biz.uiowa.edu/iem/

Investment banks

■ *J.P. Morgan* – daily updates to: Government bond indices, Emerging Markets Bond Index Plus, currency indices, and RiskMetrics volatility and correlation data sets; monthly analysis reports; reference outline on Government bond markets; glossary; world holiday and time guide [5]
http://www.jpmorgan.com/

■ *Morgan Stanley* – daily economic reports; information about MSCI indices with daily update; excerpts from selected research reports [4]
http://www.ms.com/

■ *Salomon Brothers* – access to Bond Market Roundup: Abstract for registered clients [1]
http://www.salomon.com/

■ *Goldman Sachs* – [1]
http://www.goldman.com/

■ *Bankers Trust* – global economic research; description of RAROC; Depositary receipt services [3]
http://www.bankerstrust.com/

■ *CS First Boston* – access to research for registered clients
http://www.csfb.com/

■ *First Chicago Capital Markets* – economic forecasts [2]
http://www.fccm.com/

■ *Hambrecht & Quist* – H&Q Internet/Growth/Technology indices; occasional research reports [3]
http://www.hamquist.com/

■ *Montgomery Securities* – review prospectus documents [2]
http://www.montgomery.com/

Venture capital

■ *FinanceHub* – listing and search facility on ventures; links to pages on banking, law, investing, VC consultants and advice [3]
http://www.FinanceHub.com/welcomef.html

Other URL lists

■ *Wall Street Research Net* – [5]
http://www.wsrn.com/

- *NETworth* – [4]
  http://networth.galt.com/www/home/insider/insider.html
- *Wall Street Directory* – (information for computerized traders and investors)
  [4]
  http://www.wsdinc.com/

VENEZUELA

Domain code	ve
Currency	Bolivar (Bs)
GDP	$178.3bn
GDP/capita	$8670
GDP growth	−3.3%
External debt	$40.1bn
Exports	$15.2bn (fob)
Imports	$7.6bn (fob)

News

- *El Nacional* – (Spanish) daily general, economic and business news; brief
  share market report with selected share prices
  http://ourworld.compuserve.com/homepages/nacional/
- *Venezuela Analitica* – (monthly review of Venezuelan affairs) covers foreign,
  national and economic affairs [2]
  http://www.internet.ve/analitica/
- *El Universal* – (Spanish) daily news
  http://venezuela.mit.edu/universal/

Markets

- *Caracas Stock Exchange* – daily report: stock and sector index levels with
  chart; stock prices; mutual fund prices; archive of daily report from Dec 95
  [4]
  http://www.caracasstock.com/english.htm

Economy

- *Office of Economic Studies* – weekly Venezuelan Economic Review covering:
  banking, finance, commerce, industry, petroleum, government, politics [3]
  http://www.cyberven.com/rev/indexing.html
- *Venezuela Embassy in Washington* – economic information and statistics;
  year-end economic review from the Central Bank of Venezuela [3]
  http://venezuela.mit.edu/embassy/

■ *CONAPRI* – (Venezuelan Council for Investment Promotion) investment information; privatization information [2]
http://lanic.utexas.edu/la/venezuela/conapri/venezuela_now.html

■ *University of Texas* – selected 5 year economic data [3]
gopher://lanic.utexas.edu/00/la/region/aid/Economy/country/VENSAM.TXT

■ *Petróleos de Venezuela* – oil and gas information; general political and economic articles [1]
http://www.pdv.com/

Other URL lists

■ *Venezuela at MIT* [4]
http://venezuela.mit.edu/

■ *University of Texas* [2]
http://lanic.utexas.edu/la/venezuela/conapri/

Stock and
futures exchanges

Alphabetically ordered by continent. For further details on the Web sites, *see* the respective listings in the 'Countries' section (Resources marked with an asterisk indicate a reference about the stock market, but not provided by the Exchange itself).

AFRICA

South Africa

 *Johannesburg Stock Exchange (JSE)*
   http://www.jse.co.za/

 *South African Futures Exchange (SAFEX)*
   http://www.safex.co.za/

Swaziland

 *Swaziland Stock Exchange*
   http://mbendi.co.za/mbendi/exsw.htm

AMERICA (NORTH)

Canada

- ▓ *Montreal Exchange*
  http://www.me.org/
- ▓ *Vancouver Stock Exchange*
  http://www.vse.ca/

Jamaica

- ▓ Jamaica stock prices *
  http://www.infochan.com/jamex/jam-lite/jxl-hp.htm

Mexico

- ▓ *Bolsa Mexicana de Valores* (NY office)
  http://www.quicklink.com/mexico/bmv/bmv1.htm

United States

- ▓ *American Stock Exchange*
  http://www.amex.com/
- ▓ *Arizona Stock Exchange*
  http://www.azx.com
- ▓ *Chicago Board of Trade*
  http://www.cbot.com/
- ▓ *Chicago Board Options Exchange*
  http://www.cboe.com/
- ▓ *Chicago Mercantile Exchange*
  http://www.cme.com/
- ▓ *Coffee, Sugar and Cocoa Exchange*
  http://www.csce.com
- ▓ *Iowa Electronic Markets*
  http://www.biz.uiowa.edu/iem/index.html
- ▓ *Kansas City Board of Trade*
  http://www.kcbt.com/
- ▓ *Mid-American Commodity Exchange*
  http://www.midam.com/
- ▓ *Minneapolis Grain Exchange*
  http://www.mgex.com/

- ▓ *New York Cotton Exchange*
  http://www.nyce.com/
- ▓ *New York Mercantile Exchange*
  http://www.nymex.com/
- ▓ *New York Stock Exchange*
  http://www.nyse.com/
- ▓ *Philadelphia Stock Exchange*
  http://www.libertynet.org/~PHLX/

AMERICA (SOUTH)

Brazil

- ▓ *Bolsa de Mercadorias do Paraná*
  http://www.mps.com.br/InfoServ/bmp/
- ▓ *Bovespa*
  http://www.bovespa.com.br/
- ▓ *Bolsa Brasileira de Futuros*
  http://www.embratel.net.br/infoserv/bbf/index.html
- ▓ *Rio de Janeiro Stock Exchange*
  http://www.embratel.net.br/infoserv/bvrj/bolsa.htm

Chile

- ▓ *Santiago Stock Exchange*
  http://www.bolsantiago.cl/

Peru

- ▓ *Bolsa de Valores de Lima*
  http://www.bvl.com.pe/homepage.html

Venezuela

- ▓ *Bolsa de Valores de Caracas*
  http://www.caracasstock.com/

ASIA-PACIFIC

Australia

▧ *Australian Stock Exchange (ASX)*
http://www.asx.com.au/

▧ *Sydney Futures Exchange (SFE)*
http://www.sfe.com.au/

Hong Kong

▧ *Hong Kong Futures Exchange*
http://www.hkfe.com/

India

▧ *National Stock Exchange of India (NSE)*
http://www.nseindia.com/

Israel

▧ *Tel-Aviv Stock Exchange (TASE)*
http://www.tase.co.il/

Japan

▧ *Nagoya Stock Exchange*
http://www.iijnet.or.jp/nse-jp/e-home.htm

▧ *Tokyo Grain Exchange*
http://www.toppan.co.jp/tge/

Kuwait

▧ *Kuwait Stock Exchange*
http://www.kuwait.net/~exchange

Lebanon

▧ *Beirut Stock Exchange*
http://www.lebanon.com/financial/stocks/index.htm

Malaysia

■ *Kuala Lumpur Stock Exchange*
http://www.klse.com.my/

Philippines

■ *Manila International Futures Exchange**
http://www.portalinc.com/mife/index.html

■ *Philippine Stock Exchange (PSE)*
http://pdx.rpnet.com/pse/index.htm

Singapore

■ *Singapore International Monetary Exchange (SIMEX)*
http://www.simex.com.sg/

■ *Stock Exchange of Singapore (SES)*
http://www.ses.com.sg/

Sri Lanka

■ *Colombo stock prices**
http://www.lanka.net/lisl2/business/stocks/slstock.html

Taiwan

■ *Taiwan Stock Exchange*
http://www.tse.com.tw/

Thailand

■ *Thailand Stock Exchange*
http://www.set.or.th/

EUROPE

Austria

■ *Vienna Stock Exchange*
http://www.apa.co.at/boerse/

Belgium

▓ *Belgian Futures and Options Exchange (Belfox)*
http://www.belfox.be/belfox/UK/L1/L1indUK.html

Croatia

▓ *Zagreb Stock Exchange*
http://www.zse.com.hr/

Finland

▓ *Finnish Securities and Derivatives Exchange (SOM)*
http://www.som.fi/

France

▓ *Bourse de Paris*
http://www.bourse-de-paris.fr/

▓ *Le Nouveau Marché*
http://www.nouveau-marche.fr/

▓ *MATIF*
http://www.matif.fr

Germany

▓ *Deutsche Terminbörse*
http://www.exchange.de/gdb.html

▓ *Frankfurt Stock Exchange*
http://www.exchange.de

Greece

▓ *Athens Stock Exchange*
http://www.ase.gr

Netherlands

▓ *Amsterdam Stock Exchange*
http://wwwaeb.econ.vu.nl/

Norway

▓ *Oslo Stock Exchange*
http://nettvik.no/finansen/oslobors/

Portugal

- *Bolsa de Valores de Lisboa*
  http://www.bvl.pt/

Russia

- *Russian Exchange*
  http://www.fe.msk.ru/infomarket/rtsb/ewelcome.html
- *St. Petersburg Futures Exchange*
  http://ft.rcom.spb.su/

Slovenia

- *Ljubljana Stock Exchange*
  http://www.ljse.si

Spain

- *Bolsa de Madrid*
  http://www.bolsamadrid.es
- *MEFF Renta Fija*
  http://www.meff.es

Sweden

- *OM Group (OM Stockholm futures exchanges)*
  http://www.omgroup.com/
- *Stockholm Stock Exchange*
  http://www.xsse.se

Switzerland

- *Geneva Stock Exchange*
  http://www.bourse.ch/

United Kingdom

- *London Commodity Exchange*
  http://www.netbenefit.co.uk/lce/
- *London International Financial Futures Exchange (Liffe)*
  http://www.liffe.com/

APPENDICES

INDEX TO THE APPENDICES

APPENDIX A

Internet Access Providers (IAPs) worldwide

The great strength of the Internet is that the best reference material about it is on the Internet itself. But this is not very useful if you are looking for information on how to access the Net in the first place. Therefore, a list is included here of a selection of IAPs in various countries. (The US and Canada are not included, as there is no shortage of Internet magazines to refer to in those countries). Inclusion in this list does not imply any recommendation of the service.

If you do have access – albeit temporarily – to the Internet, the best source for IAPs around the world is **http://www.thelist.com**, and also look at the Yahoo directory:

Business and Economy | Companies | Internet Services | Internet Access Providers at **http://www.yahoo.com/**

In addition to the country-specific IAPs below, a few companies either have, or are developing, broader international services. This includes: IBM Global Network, CompuServe and AOL.

Andorra

Calvacom
Tel: +33 1 34 63 19 19
Fax: +33 1 34 63 19 48

IMAGINET
Tel: +33 43 38 10 24
Fax: +33 43 38 42 62

Argentina

Comint-ar
Tel: +54 1 813 8706

SatLink SA
Tel: +54 1 474 4512
Fax: +54 1 474 4512

SiON Online Services
Tel: +54 1 656 9195
Fax: +54 1 469 1335

Australia

AUSNet Services Pty Ltd.
Tel: +61 2 241 5888
Fax: +61 2 241 5898

Nettech AU Pty Ltd.
Tel: +61 6 254 8322

OzEmail
Tel: +61 (02) 391 0480
Fax: +61 (02) 437 5888

Austria

Net4You GmbH
Tel: +43 4242 257367
Fax: +43 4242 257368

PING – Personal InterNet Gate Austria
Tel: +43 1 319 43 36
Fax: +43 1 310 69 27

Vianet Austria Ltd.
Tel: +43 1 5892920
Fax: +43 1 58929220

Belgium

EUnet Belgium
Tel: +32 (0)16 23 60 99
Fax: +32 (0)16 23 20 79

Link Line
Tel: +32 2 644 25 13
Fax: +32 2 644 26 41

PING Belgium
Tel: +32 56 615894
Fax: +32 56 615958

Brazil

DGLNet
Tel: +55 192 360058
Fax: +55-192 313446

MPS Informatica – Curitiba PR
Tel: +55 41 322 4744
Fax: +55 41 224 6288

Bulgaria

EUnet Bulgaria
Tel: +359 52 259135
Fax: +359 52 234540

Caribbean

[see below]

Chile

IUSATEL CHILE SA
Tel: + 56 2 2469155
Fax: +56 2 2469164

Netup Ltda.
Tel: +56 2 2510346
Fax:+56 2 2510347

Reuna
Tel: +56 2 274 0403
Fax: +56 2 274 09 28

Costa Rica

TicoNet Costa Rica
Tel: +506 290 3344
Fax: +506 290 3355

Cyprus

Cyprus Telecommunications Authority (CYTA)
Tel: +357 2 486633

EUnet Cyprus/Cylink Information Services Ltd.
Tel: +357 2 369 114
Fax: +357 2 459 852

Czech Republic

Czech Educational and Scientific NETwork (CESNET)
Tel: +42 2/2435 2974
Fax: +42 2/2431 0271

Denmark

CyberCity
Tel: +45 3333 9496
Fax: +45 3333 9406

Cybernet
Tel: +45 3325 2282
Fax: +45 3888 2527

Danadata
Tel: +45 7010 8080
Fax: +45 8930 7510

Ecuador

Ecuanex
Tel: +593 2 227 014

Egypt

RitseCom
Tel: +20 2 340 3538
Fax: +20 2 3412139

Finland

Clinet Ltd.
Tel: +358 0 437 5209
Fax: +358 0 455 5276

EUnet Finland Oy
Tel: +358 0 400 2060
Fax: +358 0 478 4808

Net People
Tel: +358 81 5515 000
Fax: +358 81 5515 001

France

Calvacom
Tel: +33 1 34 63 19 19
Fax: +33 1 34 63 19 48

IMAGINET
Tel: +33 43 38 10 24
Fax: +33 43 38 42 62

MicroNet
Tel: +33 40 59 46 68
Fax: +33 45 79 39 71

Germany

EUnet Germany
Tel: +49 231 972 00
Fax: +49 231 972 1111

NET Network Expert Team GmbH
Tel: +49 711 976 8921
Fax: +49 711 976 8933

Noris Network
Tel: +49 911 995 9621
Fax: +49 911 598 0150

SpaceNet GmbH
Tel: +49 89 324 683 0
Fax: +49 89 324 683 51

Ghana

Chonia Informatica
Tel: +233 21 669 420
Fax: +233 21 669 420

Greece

FORTHnet
Tel: +30 81 391 200
Fax: +30 81 391201

Hellas On Line S.A.
Tel: +30 1 620 3047

Guam

Kuentos Communications, Inc.
Tel: +671 477 5750
Fax: +671 477 4218

Hong Kong

HKIGS
Tel: +852 2527 4888
Fax: +852 2527 4848

Hong Kong Supernet
Tel: +852 2358 7924
Fax: +852 2358 7925

Vision Network Limited
Tel: +852 2311 8855
Fax: +852 2311 8881

Hungary

EUnet Hungary
Tel: +36 1 269 8281
Fax: +36 1 269 8288

Iceland

IntIS/ISnet
Tel: +354 525 4747
Fax: +354 552 8801

India

Live Wire! BBS
Tel: +91 22 577 1111
Fax: +91 22 578 7812

STATUS INDIAGATE
Tel: +91 11 698 5111
Fax: +91 11 698 5111

Indonesia

IndoInternet, PT (INDONET)
Tel: +62 21 470 2889
Fax: +62 21 470 2965

Indonesia Online Access – Indonesia
Tel: +62 21 230 2345
Fax: +62 21 230 3883

Ireland

Eirenet
Tel: +353 21 274141
Fax: +353 21 271635

HomeNet
Tel: +353 1 679 7355
Fax: +353 1 454 6659

Israel

ACTCOM – ACTive COMmunication Ltd.
Tel: +972 4 676 115
Fax: +972 4 676 088

elroNet
Tel: +972 4 545 042
Fax: +972 4 551 166

Shani Technologies Ltd.
Tel: +972 3 639 1288
Fax: +972 3 639 1287

Italy

DSnet
Tel: +39 51 521 285
Fax: +39 51 522 109

FASTNET SRL
Tel: +39 71 2181 081
Fax: +39 71 2181 233

ITnet
Tel: +39 10 6503 641
Fax: +39 10 6563 400

Japan

Bekkoame Internet
Tel: +81 3 5610 7900
Fax: +81 3 5610 7901

Internet Initiative Japan, Inc. (IIJ)
Tel: +81 3 5276 6241
Fax: +81 3 5276 6239

Twics
Tel: +81 3 3351 5977
Fax: +81 3 3353 6096

Kuwait

Gulfnet Kuwait
Tel: +965 242 6728
Fax: +965 243 5428

Liechtenstein

EUnet AG
Tel: +41 1 291 45 80
Fax: +41 1 291 46 42

Ping Net
Tel: +41 21 641 13 39

Luxembourg

Europe Online S.A.
Tel: +352 40 101 226
Fax: +352 40 101 201

Malaysia

Jaring Net-Malaysia
Tel: +60 3 254 9601
Fax: +60 3 253 1898

Mexico

Ashton Communications Corporation
Tel: +210 668 6000
Fax: +210 668 6001

Soluciones Avanzadas de Redes
Tel: +52 5 420 5900
Fax: +52 5 420 5909

Nepal

Mercantile Communications Pvt. Ltd.
Tel: +977 1 220 773
Fax: +977 1 225 407

Netherlands

bART Internet Services
Tel: +31 70 345 5349
Fax: +31 70 364 5062

EuroNet Internet bv
Tel: +31 20 625 6161
Fax: +31 20 625 7435

Stichting DataWeb
Tel: +31 70 381 9218
Fax: +31 70 383 5168

New Zealand

Internet Company of New Zealand
Tel: +64 9 358 1186
Fax: +64 9 300 3122

Wave Internet Services
Tel: +64 7 838 2010
Fax: +64 7 838 0977

Nicaragua

UniComp
Tel: +505 2 783142

Norway

MultiNet AS
Tel: +47 72 55 59 66
Fax: +47 72 55 73 38

PowerTech Information Systems Inc.
Tel: +47 2220 3330
Fax: +47 2220 0333

Vestnett
Tel: +47 5554 3787
Fax: +47 5596 2175

Pakistan

Brain Computer Services
Tel: +92 42 541 4444
Fax: +92 42 758 1126

Panama

Servicio Nacional Internet SA
Tel: +507 227 2222
Fax: +507 227 4612

Paraguay

Digital Electronics Laboratory (LED)
Tel: +595 21 334 650
Fax: +595 21 310 587

Peru

Red Cientifica Peruana
Tel: +51 1 445 5168
Fax: +51 1 444 7799

Philippines

i-Way Services
Tel: +63 2 634 1963
Fax: +63 2 634 1963

IPhil Communications Network, Inc.
Tel: +63 2 893 9705
Fax: +63 2 893 9710

Poland

MALOKA
Tel: +48 22 630 5004
Fax: +48 22 630 5004

Polska OnLine
Tel: +48 22 663 5086
Fax: +48 22 663 5281

Portugal

EUnet Portugal
Tel: +351 1 294 2844
Fax: +351 1 295 7786

Telepac
Tel: +351 1 790 70 00
Fax: +351 1 790 70 01

Romania

EUnet Romania SRL
Tel: +40 1 312 6886
Fax: +40 1 312 6668

Singapore

Pacific Internet (Singapore) Pte Ltd.
Tel: +65 1800 872 1455
Fax: +65 773 6812

Singapore Telecom
Tel: +65 730 8079
Fax: +65 732 1272

Slovak Republic

EUnet Slovakia
Tel: +42 7 725 306
Fax: +42 7 728 462

South Africa

Aztec Information Management
Tel: +27 21 419 2690
Fax: +27 21 251 254

Internet Africa
Tel: +27 21 683 4370
Fax: +27 21 683 5778

Spain

Goya Servicios Telematicos – EUnet Spain
Tel: +34 1 413 4856
Fax: +34 1 413 4901

SARENET
Tel: +34 4 420 9470
Fax: +34 4 420 9465

Sri Lanka

Information Laboratories (PvT) Ltd.
Tel: +94 1 61 1061

Lanka Internet Services, Ltd.
Tel: +94 71 30 469
Fax: +94 1 343 056

Sweden

NetG
Tel: +46 31 280 373
Fax: +46 201 934 1445

Bahnhof Internet Access
Tel: +46 18 100 899
Fax: +46 18 103 737

Switzerland

EUnet AG
Tel: +41 1 291 45 80
Fax: +41 1 291 46 42

Worldcom
Tel: +41 21 802 51 51
Fax: +41 21 803 22 66

Taiwan

Hinet
Tel: +886 2 344 3143–8

WOWNET Network Service Co., LTD.
Tel: +886 2 998 3268
Fax: +886 2 998 5069

Thailand

INTERNET THAILAND SERVICE
Tel: +66 2 642 7065
Fax: +66 2 642 7065

KSC Commercial Internet Co. Ltd.
Tel: +66 2 719 1948
Fax: +66 2 719 1945

Turkey

EgeNET
Tel: +90 232 388 1080 x 278

United Kingdom

Demon Internet Ltd.
Tel: +44 181 371 1234
Fax: +44 181 371 1150

PIPEX
Tel: +44 1223 250 120
Fax: +44 1223 250 121

U-NET Limited
Tel: +44 1925 633 144
Fax: +44 1925 633 847

Venezuela

Internet Comunicaciones, c.a.
Tel: +58 2 959 9550
Fax: +58 2 959 4550

NetPoint Communications, Inc.
Tel: +305 891 1955
Fax: +305 891 2110

Vietnam

NetNam Telematic Services
Tel: +84 4 346 907
Fax: +84 4 345 217

Zambia

ZAMNET Communication Systems Ltd.
Tel: +260 1 290 358
Fax: +260 1 290 358

For the following Caribbean countries:

Antigua and Barbuda, Bahamas, Barbados, Bermuda, Cayman Islands, Dominica, Dominican Republic, Grenada, Jamaica, Montserrat, Puerto Rico, Virgin Islands

All America Cables and Radio, Inc.
Tel: +809 221 3211
Fax: +809 686 2385

Caribbean Internet Service, Corp.
Tel: +809 728 3992
Fax: +809 726 3093

Caribbean Resources International Inc.
Tel: +809 431 0415
Fax: +809 429 5903

Internet (Bermuda) Limited
Tel: +809 296 1800
Fax: +809 295 7269

APPENDIX B

Country
Domain Names

Besides the high-level Domain Names (the final part of an Internet address) such as, .com, .net or .org, the other names used in the Domain Name System are two-letter country identifiers. A comprehensive list is given below. (Inclusion in this list does not imply that the country is actually connected to the Internet – indeed, it's possible that some may not even have a telephone system yet.)

Example

If you receive an e-mail from somebody with the address: ydobon@ynapmoc.at, the last two letters of the address (at) indicate that this is from Austria. A Web site with the address **http://www.ynapmoc.za** is based in South Africa.

ad	Andorra	ba	Bosnia and Herzegovina
ae	United Arab Emirates	bb	Barbados
af	Afghanistan	bd	Bangladesh
ag	Antigua and Barbuda	be	Belgium
ai	Anguilla	bf	Burkina Faso
al	Albania	bg	Bulgaria
am	Armenia	bh	Bahrain
an	Netherlands Antilles	bi	Burundi
ao	Angola	bj	Benin
aq	Antarctica	bm	Bermuda
ar	Argentina	bn	Brunei Darussalam
as	American Samoa	bo	Bolivia
at	Austria	br	Brazil
au	Australia	bs	Bahamas
aw	Aruba	bt	Bhutan
az	Azerbaijan	bv	Bouvet Island

bw	Botswana	gh	Ghana
by	Belarus	gi	Gibraltar
bz	Belize	gl	Greenland
ca	Canada	gm	Gambia
cc	Cocos (Keeling) Islands	gn	Guinea
cf	Central African Republic	gp	Guadeloupe
cg	Congo	gq	Equatorial Guinea
ch	Switzerland	gr	Greece
ci	Cote D'Ivoire (Ivory Coast)	gs	South Georgia and South Sandwich Islands
ck	Cook Islands		
cl	Chile	gt	Guatemala
cm	Cameroon	gu	Guam
cn	China	gw	Guinea-Bissau
co	Colombia	gy	Guyana
cr	Costa Rica	hk	Hong Kong
cs	Czechoslovakia (former)	hm	Heard and McDonald Islands
cu	Cuba	hn	Honduras
cv	Cape Verde	hr	Croatia (Hrvatska)
cx	Christmas Island	ht	Haiti
cy	Cyprus	hu	Hungary
cz	Czech Republic	id	Indonesia
de	Germany	ie	Ireland
dj	Djibouti	il	Israel
dk	Denmark	in	India
dm	Dominica	io	British Indian Ocean Territory
do	Dominican Republic	iq	Iraq
dz	Algeria	ir	Iran
ec	Ecuador	is	Iceland
ee	Estonia	it	Italy
eg	Egypt	jm	Jamaica
eh	Western Sahara	jo	Jordan
er	Eritrea	jp	Japan
es	Spain	ke	Kenya
et	Ethiopia	kg	Kyrgyzstan
fi	Finland	kh	Cambodia
fj	Fiji	ki	Kiribati
fk	Falkland Islands (Malvinas)	km	Comoros
fm	Micronesia	kn	Saint Kitts and Nevis
fo	Faroe Islands	kp	Korea (North)
fr	France	kr	Korea (South)
fx	France, Metropolitan	kw	Kuwait
ga	Gabon	ky	Cayman Islands
gb	Great Britain (UK)	kz	Kazakhstan
gd	Grenada	la	Laos
ge	Georgia	lb	Lebanon
gf	French Guiana	lc	Saint Lucia

li	Liechtenstein	pg	Papua New Guinea
lk	Sri Lanka	ph	Philippines
lr	Liberia	pk	Pakistan
ls	Lesotho	pl	Poland
lt	Lithuania	pm	St Pierre and Miquelon
lu	Luxembourg	pn	Pitcairn
lv	Latvia	pr	Puerto Rico
ly	Libya	pt	Portugal
ma	Morocco	pw	Palau
mc	Monaco	py	Paraguay
md	Moldova	qa	Qatar
mg	Madagascar	re	Reunion
mh	Marshall Islands	ro	Romania
mk	Macedonia	ru	Russian Federation
ml	Mali	rw	Rwanda
mm	Myanmar	sa	Saudi Arabia
mn	Mongolia	sb	Solomon Islands
mo	Macau	sc	Seychelles
mp	Northern Mariana Islands	sd	Sudan
mq	Martinique	se	Sweden
mr	Mauritania	sg	Singapore
ms	Montserrat	se	St Helena
mt	Malta	si	Slovenia
mu	Mauritius	sj	Svalbard and Jan Mayen Islands
mv	Maldives	sk	Slovak Republic
mw	Malawi	sl	Sierra Leone
mx	Mexico	sm	San Marino
my	Malaysia	sn	Senegal
mz	Mozambique	so	Somalia
na	Namibia	sr	Suriname
nc	New Caledonia	st	Sao Tome and Principe
ne	Niger	su	USSR (former)
nf	Norfolk Island	sv	El Salvador
ng	Nigeria	sy	Syria
ni	Nicaragua	sz	Swaziland
nl	Netherlands	tc	Turks and Caicos Islands
no	Norway	td	Chad
np	Nepal	tf	French Southern Territories
nr	Nauru	tg	Togo
nt	Neutral Zone	th	Thailand
nu	Niue	tj	Tajikistan
nz	New Zealand (Aotearoa)	tk	Tokelau
om	Oman	tm	Turkmenistan
pa	Panama	tn	Tunisia
pe	Peru	to	Tonga
pf	French Polynesia	tp	East Timor

tr	Turkey	ve	Venezuela
tt	Trinidad and Tobago	vg	Virgin Islands (British)
tv	Tuvalu	vi	Virgin Islands (US)
tw	Taiwan	vn	Vietnam
tz	Tanzania	vu	Vanuatu
ua	Ukraine	wf	Wallis and Futuna Islands
ug	Uganda	ws	Samoa
uk	United Kingdom	ye	Yemen
um	US Minor Outlying Islands	yt	Mayotte
us	United States	yu	Yugoslavia
uy	Uruguay	za	South Africa
uz	Uzbekistan	zm	Zambia
va	Vatican City State (Holy See)	zr	Zaire
vc	Saint Vincent and the Grenadines	zw	Zimbabwe

Appendix C

Directory of investment programs

▓ Portfolio management

Computer Associates Intl.
One Computer Associates Plaza
Islandia, NY 11788
US
Tel: 800 225 5224
Program: *Simply Money*

Dow Jones & Company
PO Box 300
Princeton, NJ 08543
US
Tel: +1 609 520 8349
Program: *Market Manager Plus*

Fairshares Software Ltd.
56a High Street
Epsom
Surrey, KT19 8AP
UK
Tel: +44 (0)1372 741 969
Fax: +44 (0)1372 739 883
Program: *Fairshares*

Hamilton Software, Inc.
6432 East Mineral Place
Englewood, CO 80112
US
Tel: +1 303 795 5572
Program: *Portfolio Analyzer*

Intuit, Inc.
66 Willow Place
PO Box 3014
Menlo Park, CA 94026
US
http://www.intuit.com/
Program: *Quicken*

Microsoft Corporation
One Microsoft Way
Redmond, WA 98052-6399
US
http://www.microsoft.com/
Program: *MS Money*

TechServe, Inc.
PO Box 9
Issaquah, WA 98027
US
Tel: +1 206 747 5598
Program: *CapTool*

Telescan, Inc.
10550 Richmond, #250
Houston, TX 77057
US
Tel: +1 713 952 1060
Program: *Telescan Portfolio Manager*

Technical analysis

AIQ Incorporated
916 Southwood Boulevard
PO Box 7530
Incline Village, NV 89452
US
Tel: +1 702 831 2999
Program: *AIQ TradingExpert*

Avco Financial Corp, US
8 Grigg Street
Greenwish
CT 06830
US
Tel: +1 203 622 8566
Program: *Recurrence III*

CompuCharts
1003 East Town Building
41 Lockhart Road
Wanchai
Hong Kong
Tel: +852 2866-2404
http://www.hk.super.net/~lcm/
Program: *CompuChart/Genesis*

Dow Jones & Company
PO Box 300
Princeton, NJ 08543
US
Tel: +1 609 520 8349
Program: *Market Analyzer Plus*

Center for Elliott Wave Analysis
8 Davenport Road
Booargoon
Perth, 6154
Australia
Tel: +61 9 316 1499
http://www.cewa.com/
Program: *Elliott Wave Analyser*

Equis International
3950 South 700 East, Suite 100
Salt Lake City, UT 84107
US
Tel: 800 882 3040
http://www.equis.com/
Program: *Metastock*

i-Soft, Inc.
1201 4th Avenue South, 3rd floor
Seattle, WA 98134
US
Tel: 800 909 4218
Program: *StockWiz*

Indexia Research
Berkhampsted House
121 High Street
Berkhampsted
Herts HP4 2DJ
UK
Tel: +44 1442 878015
Program: *Indexia II*

International Pacific Trading Co.
1050 Calle Cordillera, Suite 105
San Clemente, CA 92673
US
Tel: +1 714 498 4009
http://www.iptc.com/
Program: *Candlestick Forecaster*

Linn Software Inc.
8641 Pleasant Hill Road
Lithonia, GA 30058
US
Tel: +1 404 929 802
Program: *TickerWatcher*

MarketsArts, Inc.
1810 N. Glenville Drive, Suite 124
Richardson, TX 75081
US
Tel: 800 998 8439
Program: *Windows on Wall Street*

Meridian Software
Amberley House
The Park
Sidcup, DA14 6AL
UK
Tel: +44 181 309 5960
Program: *Stockmarket 3*

N-Squared Systems
6821 Lemongrass Loop S.E.
Salem, OR 97306
US
Tel: +1 509 391 5929
Program: *CandlePower*

Nava Development Corporation
251-A Portage Road
Lewiston, NY 14092-1710
US
Tel: 800 532 0041
Program: *NavaPatterns*

Nirvana Systems
3415 Greystone Drive, Suite 205
Austin, TX 78731
US
Tel: 800 880 0338
http://www.nirv.com/
Program: *OmniTrader*

Omega Research
US
Tel: +1 305 270 1095
e-mail: Sales@omegaresearch.com
http://www.omegaresearch.com/
Program: *Tradestation, SuperCharts*

Synergy Software
Brittannic House
20 Dunstable Road
Luton LU1 1ED
UK
Tel: +44 1582 424282
Program: *Sharemaster 2*

Technical Tools
980 North Federal Highway
Suite 304
Boca Raton, FL 33432
US
Tel: +1 415 948 6124
http://www.techtool.com/
Program: *TT ChartBook*

Telescan, Inc.
10550 Richmond, #250
Houston, TX 77057
US
Tel: +1 713 952 1060
Program: *Telescan Analyzer*

Trading Techniques, Inc.
677 W. Turkeyfoot Lake Road
Akron
OH 44319
US
Tel: +1 216 645 0077
Program: *Advanced GET*

Worden Brothers, Inc.
4905 Pine Cone Drive, Suite 12
Durham, NC 27707
US
Tel: 800 776 4940
Program: *TeleChart 2000*

▓ Options

Essex Trading Company
Tel: +1 708 682-5780
US
http://www.essextrading.com/
Program: *Options Pro*

Institute for Options Research, Inc.
PO Box 6586
Lake Tahoe, NV 89449
US
Tel:+ 702 588 3590
Program: *Options Master*

London International Financial Futures Exchange
Cannon Bridge
London, EC4R 3XX
UK
Tel: +44 171 623 0444
http://www.liffe.com/
Program: *Options Trademaker 2*

May Consulting Inc.
Suite 1400
401 S. LaSalle Street
Chicago, Illinois 60605
US
Tel: +1 312-786-5065
http://www.may.com/
Program: *Microhedge*

OPA Software
PO Box 90658
Los Angeles, CA 90009
US
Tel: +1 310 545 3716
Program: *Option Pricing Analysis*

The Options Institute
Chicago Board Options Exchange
LaSalle at Van Buren
Chicago
Illinois 60605
US
Tel: +1 312 786 7760
http://www.cboe.com/
Program: *The Options Toolbox*

OptionVue Systems International, Inc.
1117 South Milwaukee Avenue
suite C10
Libertyville
IL 60048-9860
US
Tel: +1 708 816 6610
http://www.optionvue.com/
Program: *OptionVue IV*

Radix Research Limited
PO Box 91181
West Vancouver, BC V7V 3N6
Canada
Tel: +1 604 926 5308
Program: *OVM/Focus*

Sharefinder Limited
PO Box 3004
Birmingham
B4 6DQ
UK
Tel: +44 121 200 4600
Program: *Sharefinder Options*

Telescan, Inc.
10550 Richmond, #250
Houston, TX 77057
US
Tel: +1 713 952 1060
Program: *Options Analyzer*

■ AI / neural networks

AND Corporation
1033 Bay Street, Suite 208
Toronto, Ont.
Canada
M5S 3A5
Tel: +1 416 920 8260
http://web.idirect.com/~andcorp/

BioComp Systems
2871 152nd Ave.
NE, Redmond, WA 98052
US
Tel: +1 206-869-6770
http://www.bio-comp.com/
Program: *NeuroGenetic Optimizer*

California Scientific Software
10024 Newtown Road
Nevada City
CA 95959
US
Program: *Brainmaker*

Epic Systems
PO Box 277
Sierra Madre
CA 91025-0277
US
Tel: +1 818 355 2988
Program: *Neuralyst*

Future Wave Software
1330 S. Gertruda Avenue
Redondo Beach
CA 90277
US
Tel: +1 310 540 5373
Program: *Stock Profit*

Intelligent Market Analytics, Inc.
US
Tel: 800 477 5530
Program: *MarketMind*

The Math Works, Inc.
24 Prime Park Way
Natick, MA 01760
US
Tel: +1 508 653 1415
http://www.mathworks.com/
Program: *MATLAB Neural Network Toolbox*

NeuralWare Inc.
Penn Center West IV
Pittsburgh
PA 15276
US
Tel: +1 412 787 8222
Program: *NeuralWorks Professional II/PLUS*

Predictive Technologies Group
25941 Apple Blossom Lane
Wesley Chapel
FL 22544
US
Tel: +1 813 973 0496

Scientific Consultant Services Inc.
20 Stagecoach Road
Selden
NY 11784
Tel: +1 516 696 3333
Program: *N-TRAIN*

Teranet IA Inc.
US
Tel: +1 604 754 4223
Program: *Neural Edge*

Ward Systems Group Inc.
Executive Park West
5 Hillcrest Drive
Frederick
MD 21702
US
Tel: +1 301 662 7950

Reference – investment programs

Reviews and advertisements for investment programs can be found in the following journals:

Technical Analysis of Stocks & Commodities
3517 SW Alaska St.
Seattle
WA 98126-2700
US
Tel: +1 206 938 0570
Fax: +1 206 938 1307

Investors Chronicle
Greystoke Place
Fetter Lane
London
EC4A 1ND
UK
Tel: +44 171 405 6969
Fax: +44 171 405 5276

NeuroVe$t Journal
Finance & Technology Publishing
PO Box 764, Haymarket, VA 22069 US
Tel: +1 703-754-0696
Fax: +1 703-753-2634
E-mail: 72672.261@compuserve.com

On the Web:

http://www.wsdinc.com/ – Wall Street Directory, a good list of programs with online ordering.

■ **FIG C1**

APPENDIX D

Financial shareware programs

This appendix contains a list of financial shareware and freeware programs. All the programs listed should be available at one or more of the following download sites:

Financial shareware download sites

Shareware.com **http://www.shareware.com**
Simtel.Net **http://oak.oakland.edu/simtel.net/**
Coast to Coast Software Repository **http://www.coast.net/SimTel/**
Jumbo **http://www.jumbo.com/**

For more information about financial programs available on the Internet, *see* the section on investment software (page 250)

Stocks, charts and technical analysis

Program name/description	File name	File size (K byte)
Stocks, Charts, Moving Averages, Trade Signals	anal141.zip	328
SmartBroker v2.0: Stock and Options analysis	broker2.zip	846
Util. for MetaStock & MegaTech stock charting	cu1a.zip	336
ECON v2.0: Stock market forecasting/analysis	econ2.zip	432
Elliott Wave stock price prediction tutorial	ewa41.zip	1205
Compare 2 investments w/graphs. Excel add-in	icxla.zip	44
MarketEdge: Stock Market trend/timing analysis	mes1.zip	586
Master investor for Windows Ver 1.21	mi121.zip	1257
Market Master: analyse stocks, bonds, mutuals	mkmst431.zip	272
Momentum Trader v1.21: Tracks/plots stocks	mtrad121.zip	269
Stock market timing buy/sell expert	oexbse11.zip	87
Parity 1.5: Stock charting/analysis for Win3.x	parity15.zip	704
QTRADER: Chart/analyse stocks/commodities	qtdem309.zip	881
RSA/2 for Windows: Stock Analysis v2.2a	rsa2w22a.zip	187
Fundamental analysis of stock balance sheets	sa251a.zip	35
Stock Selection By Filtering and Ranking	select11.zip	896
Stock analysis tool	sman_f4.zip	209
Stable Technical Graphs – Stock Market Analysis	stab220.zip	375
Stock Trader v7.11: Stock history, buy, sell	stckt711.zip	415
StockQuest v2.20: Stock price analyser	stckwz22.zip	90
Powerful stock analysis/charting program	stkan110.zip	148
Stock Tracker 2.1 – Stock Tracking Software	stktrk21.zip	555
Stock charting/technical analysis; w/train mode	sview10.zip	156
Create historical graphs of financial data	sym.zip	493
Scans and analyses stock market data	tas605.zip	708
The Wall Street Utilities 2.7	tracut27.zip	529
Value Trend Indicator v2.62	vtid262.zip	280
The Wall Street Tracker 7.1d	walst71d.zip	350
Investment Projection utility, w/QBasic source	werks112.zip	56
Wall Street Simulator Fo 1.1	wssw11.zip	422
Wall Street stock-tracker/analyser	wwallst1.zip	395

Futures and options

Program name/description	File name	File size (K byte)
Evaluate call/put options (Black Scholes model)	black2.zip	5
Black Scholes option pricer add-in for Excel	bsopt161.zip	41
Future Commodities Graphs and Analysing 4 win	fcg10g.zip	105
Options Analyser: Stock market calculator	option10.zip	68

Bonds

Program name/description	File name	File size (K byte)
Tracks US savings bonds	bonds20.zip	195
Bond Calculator	bondsjdz.zip	75
Predict movement in the Treasury Bond yield	pbond10.zip	77
Winbond 6.1 for Series EE bonds	wbd61.zip	509
Winbond-E 6.1 for Series E bonds	wbe61.zip	494

Mutual funds

Program name/description	File name	File size (K byte)
Fund manager with graphs and reports	afmw9513.zip	398
Fund manager with graphs and reports	fundmn86.zip	366
InvesTrax 1.6g Mutual Fund tracker DEMO	invtr16g.zip	608
Monocle: Mutual Fund Analysis For Windows	mcdemo.zip	586
Dalton Mutual Fund Model v1.2	mfswap12.zip	56
MFTC32: Mutual fund tax calculator v1.0 32-bit	mft3210.zip	2200
MFTC: Mutual fund tax calculator v2.1	mftc21.zip	592
The Mutual Fund Tracker 3.6e	mftra36e.zip	436
The Wall St. Mutual Tracker 2.7	trcut27.zip	530

Quote retrievers and data converters

Program name/description	File name	File size (K byte)
EZ-MYMWin for Prodigy Windows	ezm02s.zip	406
EZ-Quicken for Prodigy Windows	ezq04s.zip	404
MetaStock to Quicken data conversion program	ms2q11.zip	22
Converts MYM4Windows data to Quicken	mw2q14.zip	1151
Translates MYM data to Quicken QIF format	mymd2q45.zip	60
Convert AOL/CIS prices to Quicken's CSV format	oqckn17.zip	59
Downloads quotes from CIS, DJNS, Dial Data	ptt323.zip	498
Display 15min Stock Quotes (CompuServe, Win3.1)	qtrack21.zip	166
Convrt AOL/CIS prices to Quicken's CSV format	toqckn17.zip	59

Neural nets

Program name/description	File name	File size (K byte)
Artif. neural network; exe+manual+examples	ainet110.zip	720
Brain Construction Kit, neurotrans. based ANN	bck01.zip	101
Neural network simulator based on backprop	brain12.zip	77
Multi-Pass Instance-Based Learning	mpil10.zip	138
Backprop network for Win3.1 w/TP source & docs	neural22.zip	191
Neuro Developer's Kit for Win3/Win95	neurokit.zip	302
NeuroForecaster/GA	nfga5.zip	814
NeuroSolutions Demo v2.0 (NN Simulator)	ns2demo1.zip	1040
Qnet: 32-bit Neural Net modelling under Windows	qnetv2t.zip	1141
Neural net data preprocessor	vida2.zip	656
Build (neural net)	wneu10.zip	246

Financial calculators

Program name/description	File name	File size (K byte)
Financial Calculations – Lending/Investments	fincalc3.zip	1372
Hi, Finance! 2.18	hifi218b.zip	342
Financial calculator and cash flow analyser	mathwz22.zip	110
Money Math Financial Calc v2.0	momath3.zip	196
SolveIt v4.2 financial calculator	slvit42.zip	299

Personal finance

Program name/description	File name	File size (K byte)
Windows amortization program	amortw29.zip	184
Financial Freedom GOLD 2.00	ffgold.zip	430
FINANCE 101: Comprehensive Financial Adviser	fin10127.zip	257
Loans, annuities, investments, retirement	finaut13.zip	960
Financial investment strategy planning tool	invst_20.zip	43
Saving, investing, retirement, stocks, funds	itkd144.zip	312
Mortgage Modeller	mtgml3_0.zip	342
Personal Money 1.1	permon11.zip	1117

▶

Personal finance continued

Program name/description	File name	File size (K byte)
WinPrice 1.00: home finance price evaluation utility	price_10.zip	92
Financial Analysis For Windows	winfin43.zip	701
Wealth Management System 8.38	wmsd838.zip	303

Retirement

Program name/description	File name	File size (K byte)
Tracks & analyses 401K Retirement Plan savings	401k_11.zip	193
Forecast and display future retirement income	invest07.zip	114
Retirement funds projections, with 4 payouts	nestegg.zip	253
Low-Risk Strategies for Retirement Investing	ow_risk.zip	78
Retirement Strategizer for Excel	retire2c.zip	168

Miscellaneous

Program name/description	File name	File size (K byte)
Econometric stock market/economy forecasting	econ.zip	64
Investment Guide 2.0	iguide20.zip	504

APPENDIX E

Financial data providers worldwide

The following lists companies that provide computerized financial data.

Australia

AAP Information Services
Tel: +61 2 322 8000

Hutchison Telecommunications (Australia) Ltd.
Tel: +61 2 9964 4630
Fax: +61 2 9964 4656
http://www.hutch.com.au/home/
e-mail: newspager@hutch.com.au

Market Data Corporation
Tel: +61 2 233 6822

Research Technology Corp.
Tel: +61 2 233 6822

Telestra Multimedia
Tel: +61 2 903 3333

Belgium

F I A International
Tel: +32 3 286 0393

Interfinance SA
Tel: +32 2 763 0960

Brazil

Agencia Estado Ltda
Tel: +55 11 856 2003/2009
Fax: +55 11 857/5037
http://www.embratel.net.br/
infoserv/agestado
e-mail: agestado@oesp.com.br

Agencia Oglobo-Meca
Tel: +55 11 259 0888
Fax: +55 11 256 1070

CMA Engenharia de Sistemas (CMA)
Tel: +55 11 887 5544

Momento Information
Tel: +55 11 851 5222

Canada

Autobyte Technologies
Tel: +1 514 637 6232

Dow Jones Telerate Canada
Tel: +1 416 365 7171

Glance Market Data Services
Tel: +1 604 926 8830

North American Quotations
Tel: 800 465 4300
Fax: +1 519 657 3331
e-mail: naq@fonorola.net

Star Data Systems Inc.
Tel: 800 387 8123

Telenium
Tel: +1 204 957 2807
http://www.telenium.ca

Denmark

Tenefore International BV
Tel: +45 38 34 7070

France

GL Consultants SA
Tel: +33 42 78 82 82

S D I B
Tel: +33 14 729 4799

Germany

boersen-informations-systeme Gmbh
Tel: +49 211 830 7111

Euro American Group Inc.
Tel: +49 69 44 00 71
Fax: +49 69 44 60 07

News Net
Tel: +49 76 153 0914

Sharework
Tel: +49 05321 279 6

Teledata Boersen Informationen
Tel: +49 69 7148 122

VWD – Vereinigte Wirtschaftdienste Gmbh
Tel: +49 6196 405 274

Greece

Profile Systems
Tel: +30 1 3223 8153

Hong Kong

Hong Kong Data Communications Ltd.
Tel: +852 2 522 0045

Telequote Data International Limited
Tel: +852 856 0878

India

DART
Tel: +91 283 5830

Israel

InfoSat Financial Services
Tel: +972 2 244 963

Italy

Fainex spa
Tel: +39 444 964 220

Japan

Quick Corporation
Tel: +81 3 690 0916

Netherlands

Ed Van der Ende Commodity Consultancy
Tel: +31 5787 2152

New Zealand

Micom
Tel: +64 9 528 3164

Singapore/Malaysia

Key Computers
Tel: +65 271 7075

Sweden

Folkes Data
Tel: +46 175 13658

Switzerland

DataTrade Services S.A.
Tel: +41 22 347 3636

Digicall S.A.
Tel: 41 22 802 2211

Fides Informatik
Tel: +41 1 298 6832

Quoteline GmbH
Tel: +41 01 709 20 70
Fax: +41 01 709 20 75
e-mail: quoteline@ping.ch

Portmann Bureau
Tel: +41 22 732 6040

Telekurs AG
Tel: +41 1 123 8135

Taiwan

Rosenthal & Co. Taiwan Ltd.
Tel: +886 2 775 8278
Fax: +886 2 731 3633
e-mail: rcgtw@hntp2.hinet.net

Systex Corporation
Tel: +886 2 356 9008

Thailand

BisNews PLC
Tel: +66 2 535 0009

Funtecon
Tel: +66 2 390 0154

Turkey

Bogazici Data Paralama
Tel: +90 1 275 9007

UK

Commodity Market Services Ltd.
Tel: +44 171 702 0202

CQGI Ltd.
Tel: +44 171 827 9500

DataStream International Ltd.
Tel: +44 171 250 3000

Futures Pager, Ltd.
Tel: +44 171 895 9400

New Prestel
Tel: +44 171 591 9008
http://www.prestel.co.uk

Sprintel Communications
Tel: +44 149 444 4415

Tradermade International
Tel: +44 181 313 0992

US

Note: a large list of US data providers can be found in *The Individual Investor's Guide to Computerized Trading* [American Association of Individual Investors, Chicago, 1995.]
http://www.spectra.net/mall/aaii/

America Online
Tel: 800 827 6364
http://www.aol.com/

Automatic Data Processing (ADP)
Tel: 800 669 0660

Bloomberg Inc.
Tel: +1 212 318 2000
http://www.bloomberg.com/

BMI
Tel: 801 532 3400

Bridge Market Data
Tel: +1 314 567 8100

Commodity Info. Services Co. (CISCO)
Tel: +1 312 922 3661
http://www.cisco-futures.com/

CompuServe
Tel: 800 848 8199
http://www.compuserve.com

CQG, Inc.
Tel: 800 525 7082

Data Broadcasting Corp.
Tel: +1 415-571-1800
http://www.dbc.com

Data Transmission Network
Tel: 800 475 4755
Fax: +1 402 255 3750
e-mail: support@dtn.com

Dial Data/Track Data
56 Pine Street
New York, NY 10005
Tel: 800 935 7788

Dow Jones/Retrieval
Tel: +1 609 520 8349

FutureSource
Tel: 800 621 2628
e-mail: trade@futures-tech.com
http://www.futuresource.com

GEnie
Tel: +1 301 340 4442

Knight-Ridder
Tel: +1 312 454 1801

Market Vision Corporation
Tel: +1 212 227 1610
Fax: +1 212 233 1430
http://www.mvision.com

PC Quote
Tel: 800 225 5657
http://www.pcquote.com

Quote Com Inc.
Tel: +1 415 812 7740
http://www.quote.com/
e-mail: info@quote.com

Quotron Systems (Reuters)
Tel: +1 312 435 8500

Reuters Money Network
Tel: +1 215 277 7600

S&P Comstock
Tel: +1 914 381 7000

Signal
Tel: +1 415 571 1800

Telerate Systems, Inc.
Tel: +1 201 938 4000

Venezuela

Infoven (Venezuela)
Tel: +582 285-7944
Fax: +582 283 9958

APPENDIX F

US financial bulletin board systems

When people first started connecting their PCs to the telephone, one of the first services to appear were bulletin board systems (BBSs). These bulletin boards are computers linked to a telephone, whereby users can dial into the bulletin board (strictly, a program running on a computer) and send/view messages and upload/download files. The computer running the BBS might be a large Government mainframe, or a small PC. Both America Online and CompuServe can be regarded as BBSs – albeit of a rather grand nature. These BBSs became very popular in the US, where there are now over 10 000 of them, covering all varieties of function: software companies for technical support; businesses for their employees; the Government for distributing public information and also private individuals running a BBS as a hobby in a special interest area.

The popularity of BBSs has waned of late with the growth of the Internet and particularly the World Wide Web.

Listed below are BBSs that specialize in finance. All these systems will be slightly different; some are free, some will require a subscription. To log onto these systems, a general communications program will be required (MS Windows Terminal is sufficient in most cases). The telephone number given is the access number that must be dialled by the computer. After logging onto the system, the BBS will give instructions as to what to do.

AAII Computerized Investor : 312 280 8764
AGCNJ : 908 753 9758
American Assoc. Indiv. Inv. : 312 280 9043
Bits & Bytes : 708 953 0396
Boardwatch Online HST : 303 933 2286
Bull Stocks Milwaukee : 414 546 1761
Business and Financial : 215 643 7711

Canadian Investor : 416 897 8583
Capps Remote : 708 672 7611
Census Bureau : 301 763 4576
Channel One : 617 354 8873
Chicago Megaphile : 312 283 4035
Computer Connections : 202 547 2008
Data Base : 201 943 5419
Data Bit Network : 703 719 9648
DC Metro : 301 855 0339
Denver Computer Investors : 303 499 8852
DLM Consulting BBS Dallas : 214 596 5121
Dollars & Bytes : 619 483 5477
Dr. Young's Market Rpt : 212 543 9033
E. KY College (Prof BBS) : 606 269 1565
Eastern Kentucky College : 606 269 1565
Economic BBS : 202 377 3870
Ed Hopper's BBS : 713 782 5454
Exec PC : 414 789 4210
Executive Network : 914 667 4567
Executive Region : 312 267 4749
Export Import Bank : 202 566 4699
FABulous : 407 277 3449
Farpoint (Historical Data) : 312 274 6128
Fed Reserve Economic Data (FRED) : 314 621 1824
Fed Reserve FED FLASH : 214 220 5169
Fed Reserve KIMBERELEY : 612 340 2489
Federal Bank of Minneapolis : 612 340 2489
Financial Software Exchange New York : 212 697 7171
FlexsoftOakland : 510 829 2293
Free Financial Network : 212 697 7171
Fun Investing BBS Wilton : Ct. : 203 834 0490
IBM PC Info Exch. (IBBS) : 708 882 4227
InveStment Club San Diego : 619 476 0692
Investor's Exchange : 818 281 2537
Investors On Line : 206 285 5359
Jack's Emporium Fredericksburg : 703 373 8215
Keith's Little SW Shop : 713 277 5465
Lynn Western Newswires : 408 778 9656
Manhattan South : 212 432 7288
Market Research Language : 609 985 9783
Market Technicians New York : 914 478 7311
McAffee : 408 998 4004
Microcomputer Investor's : 703 373 8215
MULTI COMM : 702 362 9224

PBS BBS : 317 856 2087
PC Magazine Information : 212 696 0360
Pisces Financial : 312 281 6046
Pitstar Chicago : 708 687 4413
PK Ware : 414 354 8670
PPC Bulletin Board Service Long Beach : 310 978 0024
Profit Margin : 708 356 7895
Public Brand Software : 317 856 2087
Quadratic Financial Minneapolis : 612 475 4188
Quant IX Software : 414 961 2592
RAD Software : 805 962 8206
Random Walk BBS Mississauga : 416 274 2381
Real Estate Board : 301 384 9302
Ret tech : 708 246 1385
San Jose Business : 408 745 0880
Short's BBS : 319 381 1591
Sleepy Hollow : 213 859 9334
Sonshine Inn : 415 651 4147
Sound of Money : 619 461 2521
Stock Exchange : 515 226 0680
Stock Forecasts Online : 408 733 9341
Stocks & Such : 201 377 2526
syslink tbbs : 312 622 4442
Tech Books : 503 760 1473
Telestock One : 12 338 4591
The Bank Board : 305 742 2187
The Exchange : 214 517 8553
The Guild : 407 777 6603
The List : 516 938 6722
The Market : 301 299 8667
The Market Newark : 201 467 3269
The Palace Gates : 516 698 6182
The Windmill : 312 232 1250
US Dept. of Commerce : 202 377 1986
Viking Magic : 617 354 2171
Wall Street BBS Des Moines : 515 223 1113
Wall Street Connection Honolulu : 808 521 4356
Wall Street On Line : 212 344 5195
WalStreet : 515 223 1113
Zeitgeist : 713 530 1166

APPENDIX G

US market and sector indices

The table below lists market and sector indices (with ticker symbols) that are available at the Web site of Data Broadcasting Corporation (which offers free current index levels and historic charts).

The ticker symbols are fairly standard, with indices usually beginning, as below, with a '$' sign. However, some quote providers may use slightly different symbols. For example, Quote.com sometimes adds an '.x' at the end of the symbol, so '$SPX' (for the S&P500 Index) becomes '$SPX.X'; but $INDU remains the same for both. As can be seen, it is best to check the symbol guide for each site.

Note: brackets after an index name indicate that options are trading on that index at the exchange specified.

TABLE G.1 Market and sector indices at the DBC Web site

Ticker Symbol	Index
$TNX	10 Year T-Note Interest Rates (CBOE)
$TYX	30 Year T-Bond Interest Rates (CBOE)
$FVX	5 Year T-Note Interest Rates
$XAL	Airline (AMEX)
$PLN	Airline (PHLX)
$ADR	AMEX ADRs
$ADVA	AMEX Advancing Issues
$XAT	AMEX Atlantic Region
$XCP	AMEX Capital Goods
$XCI	AMEX Computer Technology (AMEX)

Ticker Symbol	Index
$XCS	AMEX Consumer Goods
$TICKA	AMEX Cumulative Tick
$DECLA	AMEX Declining Issues
$DVOLA	AMEX Down Volume
$XFN	AMEX Financial
$XFR	AMEX Foreign Region
$XHT	AMEX High Technology
$XHC	AMEX Housing And Construction
$XII	AMEX Institutional Investors (AMEX)
$XLT	AMEX Long Term 20 (Leaps)
$XAM	AMEX Market Value
$XMN	AMEX Mountain Region
$XNG	AMEX Natural Gas (AMEX)
$XNR	AMEX Natural Resources
$XNC	AMEX North Central Region
$XNE	AMEX Northeast Region
$XOI	AMEX Oil And Gas (AMEX)
$XPI	AMEX Pacific Region
$XRI	AMEX Retail
$XSI	AMEX Services
$TRINA	AMEX Short Term Trading Index
$XSA	AMEX South Atlantic
$XSC	AMEX South Central
$TVOLA	AMEX Total Volume
$UCHGA	AMEX Unchanged Issues
$XVOLA	AMEX Unchanged Volume
$UVOLA	AMEX Up Volume
$EAX	Asian Emerging Markets (CBOE)
$MKT	Big Cap
$BTK	Biotech (AMEX)
$BGX	Biotech (CBOE)
$CWX	Computer Software (CBOE)
$KAK	Cotation Assis. En Continue 40 (France)
$XCB	Cust. Upside Basket Sec. (Bear Stearns)
$COMP	Dow Jones Composite
$INDU	Dow Jones Industrials
$DJ	Dow Jones Indus. (Actual Highs & Lows)
$TICKI	Dow Jones Industrials Tick
$TRAN	Dow Jones Transportation

Ticker Symbol	Index
$UTIL	Dow Jones Utilities
$EVX	Environmental
$TOP	Euro Top 100
$EUR	Eurotop 100 (AMEX)
$ERT	Eurotrack 100 (British Stocks Excluded)
$ETI	Eurotrack 200 (Stocks From $FTI & $ERT)
$ERI	Financial Times–Actuaries Europe
$FTI	Financial Times–Stock Exchange (FT-SE)
$FPP	Forest 7 Paper Products Sector
$GAX	Gaming (CBOE)
$GTX	Global Telecommunications
$XAU	Gold And Silver
$PSE	High Technology Index
$HKO	Hong Kong 30 (40)(AMEX)
$HKX	Hong Kong 30 (AMEX Warrants)
$HKL	Hong Kong 30 (AMEX Leaps)
$IIX	Internet (AMEX)
$ISX	Israel (CBOE)
$JPN	Japan (AMEX)
$LTX	Latin 15 (CBOE)
$XMI	Major Market (AMEX)
$VIX	Market Volatility (CBOE)
$MXY	Mexico (AMEX)
$MEX	Mexico (CBOE)
$CYC	Morgan Stanley Cyclical (AMEX)
$CMR	Morgan Stanley Consumer (AMEX)
$MSH	Morgan Stanley High Tech 35 (AMEX)
$NDX	Nasdaq 100 (CBOE)
$ADVQ	Nasdaq Advancing Issues
$BANK	Nasdaq Banking
$IXBT	Nasdaq Biotech
$IXC	Nasdaq Chicago Regional
$COMPQ	Nasdaq Composite
$IXCO	Nasdaq Computer
$TICKQ	Nasdaq Cumulative Tick
$DECLQ	Nasdaq Declining Issues
$DVOLQ	Nasdaq Down Volume
$IXF	Nasdaq Financial
$INDS	Nasdaq Industrial

Ticker Symbol	Index
$INSR	Nasdaq Insurance
$IXA	Nasdaq Int'L Market
$IXL	Nasdaq Los Angeles Regional
$NCMP	Nasdaq National Market Composite Index
$NIND	Nasdaq National Market Industrial Index
$IXN	Nasdaq New York Regional Index
$IXS	Nasdaq San Francisco Regional Index
$TRINQ	Nasdaq Short Term Trading Index
$IXTC	Nasdaq Telecommunications Index
$TVOLQ	Nasdaq Total Volume
$TRANQ	Nasdaq Transportation Index
$UCHGQ	Nasdaq Unchanged Issues
$XVOLQ	Nasdaq Unchanged Volume
$UVOLQ	Nasdaq Up Volume
$IXW	Nasdaq Washington DC Regional
$XOC	National OTC (PHLX)
$NIK	Nikkei 300 (CBOE)
$ADV	NYSE Advancing Issues
$NHB	NYSE Beta
$NYA	NYSE Composite
$TICK	NYSE Cumulative Tick
$DECL	NYSE Declining Issues
$DVOL	NYSE Down Volume
$NF	NYSE Financial
$ND	NYSE Industrial
$TRIN	NYSE Short Term Trading Index
$TVOL	NYSE Total Volume
$NV	NYSE Transportation
$UCHG	NYSE Unchanged Issues
$XVOL	NYSE Unchanged Volume
$UVOL	NYSE Up Volume
$NNA	NYSE Utilities
$OFIN	Other Financials
$DRG	Pharmaceutical (AMEX)
$BKX	PHLX/Kbw Bank (PHLX)
$PNX	Phone (PHLX)
$RIX	Reit (Real Estate) (CBOE)
$RUI	Russell 1000
$RUT	Russell 2000 (CBOE)

Ticker Symbol	Index
$RUA	Russell 3000
$OEX	S&P 100 (CBOE)
$SPIN	S&P 400 Industrials
$MID	S&P 400 Midcap (AMEX)
$SPX	S&P 500 (CBOE)
$SGX	S&P 500 Barra Growth
$SVX	S&P 500 Barra Value
$SXD	S&P 500 Cum. Quarterly Dividend Payment
$PREM	S&P 500 Futures Minus Cash Spread
$SML	S&P 600 Small Cap
$BIX	S&P Bank (CBOE)
$CEX	S&P Chemical (CBOE)
$SPFN	S&P Financial
$HCX	S&P Health Care (CBOE)
$IUX	S&P Insurance (CBOE)
$RLX	S&P Retail (CBOE)
$SRX	S&P Super Composite
$SPRA	S&P Transportation
$TRX	S&P Transportation (CBOE)
$SPUT	S&P Utilities
$XBD	Securities Broker/Dealer (AMEX)
$SOX	Semiconductor
$IRX	Short-Term Interest Rate
$HFX	Super Cap Sector
$TKX	Tech 50
$TXX	Technology (CBOE)
$PSE	High Technology Index
$TCX	Telecommunications (CBOE)
$TPX	US Top 100
$UTY	Utility Index
$XVL	Value Line Index (Arithmetic)
$XVG	Value Line Index (Geometric)
$WSX	Wilshire Small Cap Index

Source: Data Broadcasting Corporation

APPENDIX H

Ticker symbols for US stock and index options

Ticker symbols for stock and index options are formed by combining:

option symbol + month code + strike code

Tables for the month codes and strike codes are given below. For example:

EKEP   : Eastman Kodak May 80 call
TXTO   : Texaco August 75 put
MRKFR   : Merck June 90 call

Stocks listed on the NYSE and AMEX always have a one, two or three letter stock symbol – and for these stocks this same symbol is used as the option symbol.

In the case of Nasdaq, the general rule is to take the first two letters of the stock symbol and add a 'Q'; thus Microsoft [MSFT] has an option symbol MSQ. But this is not alway the case (for example, Cisco [CSCO] has the option symbol CYQ), so always check first.

Month codes

These codes serve the dual role of indicating the expiry month of the option and also whether it is a put or call.

■ TABLE H.1 Month codes for US stock and index options

Month	Call	Put
January	A	M
February	B	N
March	C	O
April	D	P
May	E	Q
June	F	R
July	G	S
August	H	T
September	I	U
October	J	V
November	K	W
December	L	X

Strike prices

This may not be a very elegant method, but it solves the problem of representing a wide range of possible strikes with just one character. Thus, the code 'C' can equally represent strikes of 15, 115, 215, or 815.

■ TABLE H.2 Strike price codes for US stock and index options

Strike			Code	Strike			Code
5	105	205 ...	A	65	165	265 ...	M
10	110	210 ...	B	70	170	270 ...	N
15	115	215 ...	C	75	175	275 ...	O
20	120	220 ...	D	80	180	280 ...	P
25	125	225 ...	E	85	185	285 ...	Q
30	130	230 ...	F	90	190	290 ...	R
35	135	235 ...	G	95	195	295 ...	S
40	140	240 ...	H	100	200	300 ...	T
45	145	245 ...	I	7.5	37.5	...	U
50	150	250 ...	J	12.5	42.5	...	V
55	155	255 ...	K	17.5	47.5	...	W
60	160	260 ...	L	22.5	52.5	...	X
65	165	265 ...	M	27.5	57.5	...	Y
70	170	270 ...	N	32.5	37.5	...	Z

Appendix I

Ticker symbols for US futures

Ticker symbols for futures are formed by combining:

contract code + month code + last digit of year

Tables for these codes are given below. For example,

EDU7   : Eurodollar (CME), September 1997
SPH6   : S&P500 (CME), March 1996
HGG7   : Copper (COMEX), February 1997
WZ7   : Wheat (CBOT), December 1997

The *month code* 'Y' is used to signify the cash or spot price (or index), for example,

SFY   : Swiss Franc, cash

However, although the codes are fairly standardized, their combination is not – and not all quote providers use the same system. For example, some may put the year *before* the month code; in which case the first example above would become, ED7U. Because of this, the rules for each quote provider should be checked. (For further details, *see* Section 2, 'Futures and options', page 196).

Month codes

Each contract must have a one letter code indicating its expiry month.

▥ TABLE I.1 **Month codes for US futures**

Month	Code
January	F
February	G
March	H
April	J
May	K
June	M
July	N
August	Q
September	U
October	V
November	X
December	Z
Cash (or spot)	Y

Contract codes

The table below gives a fairly comprehensive list of all contracts on US futures exchanges. Some notes about the columns:

- **Contract**: name of the contract (note, similar contracts may trade on more than one exchange).
- **Exchange**: a table of exchanges and their abbreviations can be found in the box below.
- **Trading months**: the valid expiry months for each contract (if looking up a contract, ensure that it does actually trade the month).
- **Symbol**: the one or two letter contract code.
- **Option symbol**: some futures contracts have options on them, and where they do, their contract code is given here. (The symbol scheme for these options on futures codes is not given here, as they are even less consistent than for ordinary futures. Again, check with the respective quote provider.)
- **Spot index**: the code for the spot price or index (if existing).

■ TABLE I.2 Contract codes for US futures

Contract	Exchange	Trading months	Symbol	Option Symbol	Spot/ Index
Aluminium	CEC-COMEX	current month, next two months, jan/mar/may/jul/sep/dec	AL		
Anhydrous Ammonia	CBOT	mar/jun/sep/dec	NZ		
Australian Dollar	CME-IMM	mar/jun/sep/dec plus serial months for options	AD	AD	ADY
Australian Dollar	PBOT	mar/jun/sep/dec plus 2 near-in months	ZA		
Barge Freight Rate Index	CBOT	mar/may/jul/dec	BF		
British Pound	CME-IMM	mar/jun/sep/dec plus serial months for options	BP	BP	BPY
British Pound	MIDAM	mar/jun/sep/dec	XP		
British Pound	PBOT	mar/jun/sep/dec plus 2 near-in months	ZB		
Canadian Dollar	CME-IMM	mar/jun/sep/dec plus serial months for options	CD	CD	CDY
Canadian Dollar	MIDAM	mar/jun/sep/dec	XD		
Canadian Dollar	PBOT	mar/jun/sep/dec plus 2 near-in months	ZC		
Cattle, Feeder	CME	jan/mar/apr/may/aug/sep/oct/nov	FC	FC	
Cattle, Live	CME	feb/apr/jun/aug/sep/oct/dec	LC	LC	
Cattle, Live	MIDAM	feb/apr/jun/aug/oct/dec	XL		
Cheddar Cheese	CEC-CSCE	feb/may/july/sep/nov	EZ	EZ	
Chickens, Broiler	CME	feb/apr/may/jun/july/aug/ oct/dec	BR	BR	
Cocoa	CEC-CSCE	mar/may/jul/sep/dec	CC	CC	

Contract	Exchange	Trading months	Symbol	Option Symbol	Spot/ Index
Coffee 'C'	CEC-CSCE	mar/may/jul/sep/dec	KC	KC	
Brazil – Differential Coffee	CEC-CSCE	mar/may/jul/sep/dec	KB		
Commodity Research Bureau Index	NYFE	mar/may/jul/sep/dec	CR	CR	CRY
Copper, High Grade	CEC-COMEX	all months	HG	HG	
Corn	CBOT	mar/may/jul/sep/dec	C	CO	
Corn	MIDAM	mar/may/jul/sep/dec	XC	XC	
Cotton, No. 2	CEC-CTN	mar/may/jul/oct/dec	CT	CT	
Cotton, Cotlook World	CEC-CTN	mar/may/aug/oct/dec	CI	CI	
Crude Oil, Light Sweet	NYM	all months	CL	CL	
Crude Oil, Sour	NYM	all months	SC		
Currency Cross Rates	CME-IMM	mar/jun/sep/decDMark/Yen, Yen-settled	DJ	DJ	
Deutsche Mark	CME-IMM	mar/jun/sep/dec plus serial months for options	DM	DM	DMY
Deutsche Mark	MIDAM	mar/jun/sep/dec	XM		
Deutsche Mark	PBOT	mar/jun/sep/dec plus 2 near-in months	ZD		
Diammonium Phosphate	CBOT	mar/jun/sep/dec	FZ		
Eurodollar	CME-IMM	mar/jun/sep/dec plus serial months for options	ED	ED	
Eurodollar	MIDAM	mar/jun/sep/dec	UD		
Euromark, 3 month	CME-IMM	mar/jun/sep/dec plus serial months for options	EK	EK	
European Currency Unit	CEC-CTN	mar/jun/sep/dec plus serial months for options	EU	EU	

European Currency Unit	PBOT	mar/jun/sep/dec	ZE	ZEY	
Eurotop 100 Index	CEC-CTN	mar/jun/sep/dec plus serial months for options	ER	ER	ERY
French Franc	PBOT	mar/jun/sep/dec	ZF		
FT-SE 100 Share Index	CME	mar/jun/sep/dec	FI	FI	FNX
Gasoline, Gulf Coast, Unleaded	CEC-NYM	all months	GU		
Gasoline, Unleaded	NYM	all months	HU	HU	
Gas, Natural	NYM	all months	NG	NG	
Gold, 100 troy oz.	CEC-COMEX	current month, next two months, feb/apr/jun/aug/oct/dec	GC	GC	
Gold, 100 troy oz.	CEC-COMEX	weekly option	GW		
Gold, 3rd & 4th year, 100 troy oz.	CEC-COMEX	jun/dec	GM		
Gold, 5th & 6th year, 100 troy oz.	CEC-COMEX	jun/dec	LD		
Gold, 100 oz.	CBOT	current month, next two months, feb/apr/jun/aug/oct/dec	GH		
Gold, 1 Kilo	CBOT	feb/apr/jun/aug/oct/dec	KI		
Gold, NY 33.2 troy oz.	MIDAM	all months	XK	XK	
Goldman Sachs Commodity Index	CME-IOM	feb/apr/jun/aug/oct/dec, all months for options	GI	GI	GNX
Heating Oil, No. 2	NYM	all months	HO	HO	
Hogs, Live	CME	feb/apr/jun/jul/aug/oct/dec	LH	LH	
Hogs, Live	MIDAM	feb/apr/jun/jul/aug/oct/dec	XH		
Insurance, Catastrophe	CBOT	mar/jun/sep/dec	UE (Eastern) UM (Midwestern) UN(National)		
Interest Rate, 30-day	CBOT	/FF	FFY		
Japanese Yen	CME-IMM	mar/jun/sep/dec plus serial months for options	JY	JY	JYY

Contract	Exchange	Trading months	Symbol	Option Symbol	Spot/ Index
Japanese Yen	MIDAM	mar/jun/sep/dec	XJ	XJ	
Japanese Yen	PBOT	mar/jun/sep/dec	ZJ	ZJ	
Kansas City Value Line	KCBOT	mar/jun/sep/dec	KV	KV	KVY (arith),KVA (geo)	
Libor, One-month	CME	3 months in mar/jun/sep/dec cycle plus 4 additional serial months	EM	EM	
Lumber, Random Length	CME	jan/mar/may/jul/sep/nov	LB	LB	
Major Market Index	CBOT	3 month cycles starting dec/mar/jun/sep	BC	BC	BCY
Milk, Nonfat Dry	CEC-CSCE	feb/may/july/sep/nov	MU	MU	
Mini Value Line Index	KCBOT	mar/jun/sep/dec plus serial months for options	MV	MV	KVA (arith), KVS (geo)
Municipal Bond Index	CBOT	mar/jun/sep/dec	MB	MO	MBY
NIKKEI 225 Index	CME-IOM	mar/jun/sep/dec plus serial months for options	NK	NK	
NYSE Composite Index	NYFE	mar/jun/sep/dec plus serial months for options	YX	YX	YXY
Oats	CBOT	mar/may/jul/sep/dec	O	OO	
Oats	MGE	mar/may/jul/sep/dec	OM	OM	
Oats	MIDAM	mar/may/jul/sep/dec	XO		
Orange Juice, Frozen Concentrated	CEC-CTN	jan/mar/may/jul/sep/nov plus serial monthsfor options	JO	JO	
Palladium	NYM	mar/jun/sep/dec	PA		
Platinum	NYM	jan/apr/jul/oct	PL	PL	
Platinum	MIDAM	current month & jan/apr/jul/oct	XU		

Pork Bellies, Frozen	CME	feb/mar/may/jul/aug	PB	PB	
Propane Gas, Liquid	NYM	all months	PN		
Rice, Rough	MIDAM-CRCE	jan/mar/may/jul/sep/nov	NR	NR	
Russell 2000 Index	CME	mar/jun/sep/dec plus serial months for options	RL	RL	IUX
S&P 100 Index	CME-IOM	OEX			
S&P MidCap 400 Index	CME-IOM	mar/jun/sep/dec plus serial months for options	MD	MD	IDX
S&P 500 Index	CME-IOM	mar/jun/sep/dec plus serial months for options	SP	SP	INX
Shrimp, Frozen, White	MGE	mar/jun/sep/dec	SH	SH	
Silver, 1000 oz.	CBOT	feb/mar/apr/jun/aug/oct/dec	AG	AG	
Silver, 5000 oz.	CBOT	current month, next 2 months & feb/mar/apr/jun/aug/oct/dec	SV		
Silver, 5000 oz.	CEC-COMEX	current month, next 2 months & jan/mar/may/jul/sep/dec	SI	SI	
Silver, 5000 oz.	CEC-COMEX	weekly option	SW		
Silver, New York	MIDAM	all months	XY		
Sorghum, Grain	KCBOT	mar/may/jul/sep/dec	GS		
Soybeans	CBOT	jan/mar/may/jul/aug/sep/nov	S	SO	
Soybeans	MIDAM	jan/mar/may/jul/aug/sep/nov	XS	XS	
Soybean Meal	CBOT	jan/mar/may/jul/ aug/sep/oct/dec	SM	SM	
Soybean Meal	MIDAM	jan/mar/may/jul/ aug/sep/oct/dec	XE		
Soybean Oil	CBOT	jan/mar/may/jul/ aug/sep/oct/dec	BO	BO	
Steel, Ferrous Scrap	CBOT	mar/jun/sep/dec	SK		
Sugar, White	CEC-CSCE	jan/mar/may/jul/oct	WS		

Contract	Exchange	Trading months	Symbol	Option Symbol	Spot/ Index
Sugar, No. 11 World	CEC-CSCE	jan/mar/may/jul/sep/oct plus serial months for options	SB	SB	
Sugar, No. 14 Domestic	CEC-CSCE	jan/mar/may/jul/sep/oct	SE		
Swiss Franc	CME-IMM	mar/jun/sep/dec plus serial months for options	SF	SF	SFY
Swiss Franc	MIDAM	mar/jun/sep/dec	XF		
Swiss Franc	PBOT	mar/jun/sep/dec	ZS		
US Dollar Index	CEC-CTN	mar/jun/sep/dec plus serial months for options	DX	DX	DXY
US Dollar Index, Large Lots	CEC-CTN	mar/jun/sep/dec	DL		
US Dollar Composite Index	CBOT/MIDAM	mar/jun/sep/dec	IX	IXY	
US Treasury Bills, 90-day	CME-IMM	mar/jun/sep/dec	TB	TB	
US Treasury Bills, 90-day	MIDAM	mar/jun/sep/dec	XT		
US Treasury Bonds, Long-Term, 15–30 year	CBOT	mar/jun/sep/dec	US	UO	
US Treasury Bonds, 15 year, 1st & 2nd year	MIDAM	mar/jun/sep/dec	XB	XB	
US Treasury Notes, 2 year	CBOT	mar/jun/sep/dec	TU	TU	
US Treasury Notes, 2 year Yield Based	CBOT	mar/jun/sep/dec	NU		
US Treasury Notes, 2 year Yield Based	CEC-CTN	mar/jun/sep/dec plus 2 nearest calendar months	TW		
US Treasury Notes, 5 year	CBOT	mar/jun/sep/dec	FV	FW	
US Treasury Notes, 5 year Yield Based	CEC-CTN	mar/jun/sep/dec plus 2 nearest calendar months	FY	FY	
US Treasury Notes, 10 year	CBOT	mar/jun/sep/dec	TY	YF	

US Treasury Notes, 10 year	MIDAM	mar/jun/sep/dec	XN	
Wheat	CBOT	mar/may/jul/sep/dec	W	WO
Wheat	MIDAM	mar/may/jul/sep/dec	XW	XW
Wheat, Spring, American Exercise	MGE	mar/may/jul/sep/dec	MW	MW
Wheat, Spring, European Exercise	MGE	mar/may/jul/sep/dec	EW	
Wheat, White	MGE	mar/may/jul/sep/dec	NW	NW
Wheat, Winter	KCBOT	mar/may/jul/sep/dec	KW	KW
Wilshire Small Cap Index	CBOT	mar/jun/sep/dec plus serial months for options	WI	WI
				WIY
Zero Coupon Bond	CBOT	mar/jun/sep/dec	ZO	
Zero Coupon Note	CBOT	mar/jun/sep/dec	ZN	

Source: PC Quote

US Futures Exchanges and their abbreviations

US Futures Exchanges

CBOT	Chicago Board of Trade
CME	Chicago Mercantile Exchange
CME-IOM	Chicago Mercantile Exchange, Index & Option Market
CME-IMM	Chicago Mercantile Exchange, International Monetary Market
CEC-CSCE	Commodity Exchange Center, Coffee, Sugar & Cocoa Exchange
CEC-COMEX	Commodity Exchange Center, New York Commodity Exchange
CEC-CTN	Commodity Exchange Center, New York Cotton Exchange
NYFE	Commodity Exchange Center, New York Futures Exchange
KCBOT	Kansas City Board of Trade
MIDAM	MidAmerica Commodity Exchange
MIDAM-CRCE	MidAmerica Commodity Exchange, Chicago Rice & Cotton Exchange
MGE	Minneapolis Grain Exchange
NYM	New York Mercantile Exchange
PBOT	Philadelphia Board of Trade

APPENDIX J

American Depositary Receipts (ADR)

Because there can be problems in dealing in unfamiliar foreign markets, Depositary Receipts were devised as a method of trading international securities (equity or debt) within the US. This involves depositing the ordinary securities from the foreign market with a bank (called the *depositary*), which will then issue certificates in the US that represent (and are backed by) the deposited securities. These certificates are freely traded and are commonly called American Depositary Receipts (or Depositary Receipts for short, or sometimes Global Depositary Receipts for marketing purposes).

The attractions of ADRs

- The main appeal is that they are **US securities**: this means that they are covered by US securities regulations; trade and settlement is similar to any other US security; and quoted prices and dividends are in US Dollars.

- Because of the above, investment by various **funds and institutions** is possible, where perhaps they would otherwise be prevented from investing directly in foreign markets.

- Investing directly in international securities may incur **global custodian fees** – these are not required with ADRs.

- ADR **prices and liquidity** will track very closely the underlying security as any deviation will be quickly corrected by traders exploiting an easy arbitrage opportunity.

Although ADRs may have been devised originally for US investors, all of their attractions can be equally applicable for foreign investors. For example, an investor in Kuwait may be interested in buying shares in Telefonica De Argentina, in which case the US traded Depositary Receipts may be more attractive than dealing direct in the Argentine market. In addition to the advantages above, the investor would be able to look at price history charts and follow real-time prices (as with any other US security), transaction fees could be less and the foreign currency investment may be more competitive than converting funds to Argentine Dollars directly.

The types of ADR

A similarity obviously exists between ADRs and covered warrants (or OTC options). As with the latter, there is frequently nothing to stop anybody buying some shares in a company and then issuing Depositary Receipts representing those shares – without consulting, or acting with the accord, of the company itself. These are termed *unsponsored* Depositary Receipts, and in the early days of the ADR market they were quite common. Today, however, nearly all ADRs are sponsored, whereby companies sign a Deposit Agreement with a bank acting as the depositary.

There are then a few different types (or levels) of ADR:

- **Sponsored Level 1**: this is the simplest method for foreign companies to issue tradeable securities in the US markets. The ADRs are not listed, and are traded over-the-counter (OTC). The attraction to the companies of not listing is that they do not have to adapt any reporting procedures to comply with US Generally Accepted Accounting Principles (GAAP) or Securities and Exchange Commission (SEC) disclosure.

- **Sponsored Level 2**: if the company wishes the shares to be listed then it has to satisfy the procedures mentioned above, and further comply with the listing rules of whichever exchange it chooses. This stage actually comprises many different levels, depending on the type of visibility the company desires – and therefore the type of listing they choose.

- **Private placement (144A)**: instead of publicly traded securities, a company may wish to make a private placement to large institutional investors in the US (which will not require SEC registration).

The ADR market

There are now over 1500 ADRs from over 50 countries; and the majority of these are OTC (Level 1 type). In many cases the ADRs may constitute 5–15 per cent of the total shareholder base for a company.

The depositaries for the ADRs tend to be concentrated among a very few banks; the most active of which is the Bank of New York, which acts as a depositary for approximately 60 per cent of all issues.

The Bank of New York maintains a list of all ADRs on the Web, which can be found at the *Research* magazine site. On its pages there is also an overview of Depositary Receipts and a monthly fact sheet with details of new issues. The DBC Web site collates a list of ADR prices and displays them by underlying country.

Table of technology-related ADRs

From the total market of 1500 ADRs, the table below lists 80 technology-related issues that are all Level 2, and thus listed on an exchange (in this case either the NYSE or Nasdaq). As they are listed, the prices should be as readily accessible as any other US security. For example, if one wants to see a current price and historical chart for Tele Danmark, the code TLD can be input as the ticker symbol when using DBC, NETworth, StockMaster or any of the other quote services.

The depository abbreviations in column 7 are:

BNY   : Bank of New York
BT   : Bankers Trust
CIT   : Citibank
MGT   : J.P. Morgan

All the ADRs in the table are sponsored except Sanyo Electric and Telefonos De Mexico 'A'.

■ TABLE J.1 Level 2 technology-related issues

Issue	Exchange	Symbol	Ratio	Country	Industry	Depositary
(1)	(2)	(3)	(4)	(5)	(6)	(7)
Alcatel Alsthom Cie Generale	NYSE	ALA	05:01	France	TEL	CIT
Asea AB 'B'	NASD	ASEAY	01:01	Sweden	EEI	CIT
ASM Lithography Holding, NV	NASD	ASMLF	01:01	Netherlands	EEI	CIT
Automated Security (Holdings) PLC	NYSE	ASI	01:02	UK	SER	BNY
Baan Company NV	NASD	BAANF	01:01	Netherlands	SER	CIT
BE Semiconductor Industries	NASD	BESIF	01:01	Netherlands	CLE	BNY
Bell Cablemedia PLC	NASD	BCMPY	01:05	UK	PUB	CIT
British Sky Broadcasting Group PLC	NYSE	BSY	01:06	UK	PUB	CIT
British Telecommunications PLC	NYSE	BTY	01:10	UK	TEL	MGT
Business Objects S.A.	NASD	BOBJY	01:02	France	OFF	BNY
Cable and Wireless PLC	NYSE	CWP	01:03	UK	TEL	BNY
Canon Inc	NASD	CANNY	01:05	Japan	OFF	MGT
Carlton Communications PLC	NASD	CCTVY	01:02	UK	PUB	MGT
CBT Group PLC	NASD	CBTSY	01:01	Ireland	OFF	BNY
Compania De Telecom. De Chile 'A'	NYSE	CTC	01:17	Chile	TEL	BNY
Cordiant PLC	NYSE	CDA	01:03	UK	PUB	BNY
CSK Corporation	NASD	CSKKY	01:01	Japan	SER	BNY
Danka Business Systems PLC	NASD	DANKY	01:04	UK	OFF	BNY
Elsevier NV	NYSE	ENL	02:01	Netherlands	PUB	CIT
Empresas Telex-Chile Common	NYSE	TL	01:02	Chile	TEL	BNY
Ericsson Telephone (LM) Debenture	NASD	ERICZ	01:01	Sweden	TEL	CIT
Ericsson Telephone Company 'B'	NASD	ERICY	01:01	Sweden	TEL	CIT

Company	Exchange	Ticker	Ratio	Country		
Futuremedia PLC	NASD	FMDAY	01:01	UK	PUB	BNY
Futuremedia PLC Warrant	NASD	FMDYW	01:01	UK	PUB	BNY
General Cable PLC	NASD	GCABY	01:05	UK	TEL	BNY
Great Wall Electronics	NASD	GWALY	01:50	Hong Kong	CLE	CIT
Grupo Iusacell Series 'D'	NYSE	CELD	01:10	Mexico	TEL	BNY
Grupo Iusacell Series 'L'	NYSE	CEL	01:10	Mexico	TEL	BNY
Grupo Radio Centro, S.A. De C.V.	NYSE	RC	01:09	Mexico	PUB	CIT
Hitachi Limited	NYSE	HIT	01:10	Japan	EEI	CIT
Hong Kong Telecommunications	NYSE	HKT	01:10	Hong Kong	TEL	BNY
Insignia Solutions PLC	NASD	INSGY	01:01	UK	DAT	BNY
Integrated Micro Products PLC	NASD	IMPTY	01:01	UK	DAT	CIT
ISS-International Service System A	NYSE	ISG	02:01	Denmark	SER	CIT
KPN (Royal PTT Nederland NV)	NYSE	KPN	01:01	Netherlands	TEL	CIT
Kyocera Corporation	NYSE	KYO	01:02	Japan	CLE	CIT
Learmonth & Burchett Management SYS Inc.	NASD	LBMSY	01:02	UK	DAT	MGT
M.A.I.D. PLC	NASD	MAIDY	01:04	UK	DAT	BNY
Makita Corporation	NASD	MKTAY	01:01	Japan	EEI	BNY
Matsushita Electric Industrial Co., Ltd	NYSE	MC	01:10	Japan	EEI	MGT
Memorex Telex N.V.	NASD	MEMXY	01:01	Netherlands	CLE	MGT
Micro Focus Group PLC	NASD	MIFGY	01:01	UK	DAT	BNY
NEC Corp.	NASD	NIPNY	01:05	Japan	CLE	BNY
Nera A.S.	NASD	NERAY	01:01	Norway	TEL	BNY
News Corporation Limited	NYSE	NWS	01:08	Australia	PUB	CIT
News Corporation, Preferred	NYSE	NWS+	01:04	Australia	PUB	CIT
Nice Systems Ltd	NASD	NICEY	01:01	Israel	CLE	BNY

Issue	Exchange	Symbol	Ratio	Country	Industry	Depositary
(1)	(2)	(3)	(4)	(5)	(6)	(7)
Nippon Telegraph and Telephone Corp.	NYSE	NTT	1:200	Japan	TEL	MGT
Nokia Corporation	NYSE	NOKIA	02:01	Finland	TEL	CIT
Nynex Cablecomms Group PLC & Inc	NASD	NYNCY	01:10	UK	TEL	BNY
P.T. Indosat	NYSE	IIT	01:10	Indonesia	TEL	BNY
P.T. Telkom	NYSE	TLK	01:20	Indonesia	TEL	BNY
Philippine Long Distance Telephone	NYSE	PHI	01:01	Philippines	TEL	CIT
Philippine Long Distance Telephone Pref	NYSE	PHIA	01:01	Philippines	TEL	CIT
Philips N.V.	NYSE	PHG	01:01	Netherlands	EEI	CIT
Pioneer Electronic Corporation	NYSE	PIO	01:01	Japan	CLE	CIT
Polygram N.V. 'New York shares'	NYSE	PLG	01:01	Netherlands	PUB	CIT
Portugal Telecom	NYSE	PT	01:01	Portugal	TEL	BNY
Reed International PLC	NYSE	RUK	01:02	UK	PUB	CIT
Reuters Holdings PLC	NASD	RTRSY	01:06	UK	PUB	MGT
Sanyo Electric Co., Ltd	NASD	SANYY	01:05	Japan	CLE	BNY BT CIT MGT
Saville Systems PLC	NASD	SAVLY	01:01	Ireland	DAT	BNY
SGS-Thomson Microelectronics NV	NYSE	STM	01:01	Netherlands	EEI	BNY
Sony Corporation	NYSE	SNE	01:01	Japan	CLE	MGT
Stet (Societa Finanziara Telefonica)	NYSE	STE	01:10	Italy	TEL	MGT
Stet – Non Conv. Savings Shares	NYSE	STEA	01:10	Italy	TEL	MGT
TDK Corporation	NYSE	TDK	01:01	Japan	CLE	MGT
Tele Danmark A	NYSE	TLD	02:01	Denmark	CLE	BNY
Tele West Communications PLC	NASD	TWSTY	01:10	UK	TEL	BNY
Telebras Preferred Shares	NYSE	TBR	1:1000	Brazil	TEL	BNY

Telecom Argentina Stet-France Telecom	NYSE	TEO	01:10	Argentina	TEL	MGT
Telecom Corporation of New Zealand LTD	NYSE	NZT	01:16	New Zealand	TEL	BNY
Telefonica De Argentina S.A. GDR	NYSE	TAR	01:10	Argentina	TEL	CIT
Telefonica De Espana SA	NYSE	TEF	01:03	Spain	TEL	MGT
Telefonos De Mexico 'A'	NASD	TFONY	01:01	Mexico	TEL	BNY CIT MGT
Telefonos De Mexico S.A. De C.V. SER L	NYSE	TMX	01:20	Mexico	TEL	MGT
Thomson-CSF	NASD	TCSFY	01:01	France	CLE	MGT
United News & Media PLC	NASD	UNEWY	01:02	UK	PUB	BNY
Videotron Holdings PLC	NASD	VRONY	01:05	UK	TEL	CIT
Vodafone Group PLC	NYSE	VOD	01:10	UK	TEL	BNY
WPP Group PLC	NASD	WPPGY	01:10	UK	PUB	CIT

Source: Bank of New York

APPENDIX K

US technology stocks

This appendix presents a list of 180 US technology-related stocks. There is no strict selection criteria, beyond concentrating on the larger and better known companies. These are not all the technology stocks in the US, *Red Herring* magazine has a technology index of 250 stocks and Silicon Investor follows nearly 400 companies. Hopefully the listing here will provide a ready reference for the ticker symbols (in the square brackets), and some data for an interesting comparative analysis of the technology market in July 1996.

A few notes on the following table:

1 All data is for **closing values 17 July 1996**.
2 **Exchange abbreviations**: AMEX – American Exchange, NASD – Nasdaq, NYSE – New York Stock Exchange.
3 The **sector classification** is neither rigorous nor necessarily correlates with any other classification system. It is meant merely as an indication of the principal activity of the company. In 90 per cent of cases the designated categories will be appropriate, but in a few others such a simple classification may not be possible.
4 The **source for the data** in columns 4 to 8 is *Data Broadcasting Corporation* (DBC).
5 Table columns:
   Column 4 – stock market capitalization
   Column 5 – dividend yield
   Column 6 – the price/earnings ratio
   Column 7 – stock volatility
   Column 8 – stock price.
6 A **zero** appearing in columns 4, 6 or 7 implies that the data is not available.

For up-to-date figures for any company see the Web sites of DBC, CNN or Security APL, and for more detailed information on any of the stocks below a good source is Silicon Investor.

TABLE K.1 US technology-related stocks

Company [ticker symbol]	Exchange	Sector	Mkt-Cap ($m)	Div-Yld	P/E Ratio	Volatility	Price 17/07/96
(1)	(2)	(3)	(4)	(5)	(6)	(7)	(8)
3Com [COMS]	NASD	hardware	7186	0.0	37.5	46.5	40.3
3DO [THDO]	NASD	software	221	0.0	0.0	65.1	8.5
ACT Networks [ANET]	NASD	hardware	155	0.0	0.0	0.0	25.5
Adaptec [ADPT]	NASD	hardware	2491	0.0	23.0	58.4	47
ADC Telecommunications [ADCT]	NASD	hardware	2899	0.0	39.7	52.3	45.3
Adobe Systems [ADBE]	NASD	software	2382	0.6	25.8	55.6	31.5
Adtran [ADTN]	NASD	hardware	2404	0.0	68.6	59.1	62.3
Advanced Logic Research [AALR]	NASD	hardware	93	0.0	10.2	0.0	7.75
Advanced Micro Devices [AMD]	NYSE	hardware	1606	0.0	12.2	47.9	11.9
Altera [ALTR]	NASD	hardware	1310	0.0	13.3	48.7	30
Amati [AMTX]	NASD	hardware	202	0.0	0.0	142.4	13.8
Amdahl [AMH]	AMEX	hardware	1078	0.5	0.0	52.6	9
America Online [AMER]	NASD	service	3587	0.0	189.7	81.3	32.3
American Power Conversion [APCC]	NASD	hardware	854	0.0	12.9	51.6	9.13
Analog Devices [ADI]	NYSE	hardware	2267	0.0	15.8	37.2	19.6
Ancor [ANCR]	NASD	hardware	104	0.0	0.0	0.0	12.6
Apple [AAPL]	NASD	hardware	2087	0.0	0.0	43.9	16.9
Applied Magnetics [APM]	NYSE	hardware	238	0.0	6.9	85.5	10
Applied Materials [AMAT]	NASD	hardware	4686	0.0	7.3	53.4	26.1
Applix [APLX]	NASD	software	305	0.0	292.1	85.8	32.1
Ascend [ASND]	NASD	hardware	6251	0.0	84.4	77.0	50.6

Company [ticker symbol]	Exchange	Sector	Mkt-Cap ($m)	Div-Yld	P/E Ratio	Volatility	Price 17/07/96
(1)	(2)	(3)	(4)	(5)	(6)	(7)	(8)
AT&T [T]	NYSE	service	90 525	2.3	234.9	17.4	56.4
Autodesk [ADSK]	NASD	software	1033	1.1	13.0	35.3	21.3
Banyan Systems [BNYN]	NASD	software	113	0.0	0.0	92.5	6.75
Bay Networks [BAY]	NYSE	hardware	4453	0.0	21.3	46.8	22.4
Boca Research [BOCI]	NASD	hardware	135	0.0	13.3	91.1	15
Bolt Beranek & Newman [BBN]	NYSE	service	325	0.0	0.0	52.2	18.3
Boole & Babbage [BOOL]	NASD	software	246	0.0	17.1	0.0	22.5
Borland [BORL]	NASD	software	227	0.0	15.0	82.5	6.75
Broadband Technology [BBTK]	NASD	hardware	356	0.0	0.0	94.8	27
Broderbund [BROD]	NASD	software	683	0.0	14.4	65.2	31.9
Brooktree [BTRE]	NASD	hardware	241	0.0	17.3	103.8	14.4
C-Cube Microsystems [CUBE]	NASD	hardware	932	0.0	28.3	113.6	28.3
Cabletron Systems [CS]	NYSE	hardware	4445	0.0	24.7	40.1	61.5
Caere [CAER]	NASD	software	144	0.0	43.5	55.7	10.9
Cambridge Technology Partners [CATP]	NASD	software	1178	0.0	93.8	89.0	26.3
Camelot [CAML]	NASD	software	29	0.0	0.0	0.0	2
Cascade [CSCC]	NASD	hardware	5970	0.0	177.1	69.5	63.8
Catalyst Semiconductor [CATS]	NASD	hardware	47	0.0	12.6	0.0	5.56
Check Point Software [CHKPF]	NASD	software	0	0.0	0.0	0.0	16.5
Cheyenne Software [CYE]	AMEX	software	681	0.0	24.5	50.7	18.1
Cirrus Logic [CRUS]	NASD	hardware	983	0.0	0.0	55.6	15.4
Cisco Systems [CSCO]	NASD	hardware	30 459	0.0	41.5	38.2	53.5

Company	Exchange	Type					
Citrix Systems [CTXS]	NASD	software	703	0.0	174.4	121.2	34.9
Coherent [CCSC]	NASD	hardware	225	0.0	28.5	62.6	15.1
Compaq [CPQ]	NYSE	hardware	12 303	0.0	15.6	30.9	45.9
Compression Labs [CLIX]	NASD	hardware	77	0.0	0.0	91.4	5
Compuserve [CSRV]	NASD	service	0	0.0	0.0	65.7	13.5
Computer Associates [CA]	NYSE	software	16 885	0.2	0.0	38.3	46.5
Computer Sciences [CSC]	NYSE	software	3789	0.0	27.3	19.8	67.6
Corel [COSFF]	NASD	software	556	0.0	62.1	54.9	9.31
Cray Research [CYR]	NYSE	hardware	616	0.0	0.0	28.1	24.1
Cybercash [CYCH]	NASD	service	273	0.0	0.0	0.0	38.3
Cypress Semiconductor [CY]	NYSE	hardware	854	0.0	7.4	45.3	10.8
Cyrix [CYRX]	NASD	hardware	305	0.0	0.0	101.9	15.3
Data Broadcasting [DBCC]	NASD	service	247	0.0	21.5	49.4	7.94
Data General [DGN]	NYSE	hardware	388	0.0	0.0	46.9	10
Dell [DELL]	NASD	hardware	4306	0.0	16.1	57.9	47.6
Dialogic [DLGC]	NASD	software	392	0.0	16.4	50.2	25.3
Diamond Multimedia Systems [DIMD]	NASD	hardware	267	0.0	0.0	80.4	7.75
Digital Equipment [DEC]	NYSE	hardware	5400	0.0	12.0	39.3	35.1
Digital Link [DLNK]	NASD	hardware	153	0.0	38.6	0.0	17
Disney [DIS]	NYSE	service	35 224	0.7	28.1	19.7	56
Documentum [DCTM]	NASD	software	385	0.0	209.6	0.0	27.3
DSC Communications [DIGI]	NASD	hardware	3156	0.0	19.8	47.6	27.3
DSP Group [DSPG]	NASD	hardware	86	0.0	14.5	93.8	9.13
Dun & Bradstreet [DNB]	NYSE	service	9715	4.6	32.4	13.9	57.3
Eastman Kodak [EK]	NYSE	hardware	24 747	2.2	19.7	18.6	72.9

Company [ticker symbol]	Exchange	Sector	Mkt-Cap ($m)	Div-Yld	P/E Ratio	Volatility	Price 17/07/96
(1)	(2)	(3)	(4)	(5)	(6)	(7)	(8)
Excite [XCIT]	NASD	service	72	0.0	0.0	0.0	6.75
FastComm [FSCX]	NASD	hardware	142	0.0	0.0	100.3	15
Fore Systems [FORE]	NASD	hardware	2947	0.0	304.6	94.4	33.5
FTP Software [FTPS]	NASD	software	180	0.0	23.1	72.5	6.69
Gandalf [GANDF]	NASD	hardware	241	0.0	0.0	124.6	5.63
Gateway 2000 [GATE]	NASD	hardware	2696	0.0	14.7	62.3	34.6
General Datacomm [GDC]	NYSE	hardware	241	0.0	0.0	76.1	11.6
General Magic [GMGC]	NASD	software	146	0.0	0.0	110.6	5.63
Global Village [GVIL]	NASD	hardware	113	0.0	13.8	83.9	6.75
Gupta [GPTAE]	NASD	software	56	0.0	0.0	89.8	4.56
Hewlett-Packard [HWP]	NYSE	hardware	43 964	1.1	16.3	27.6	43
IBM [IBM]	NYSE	hardware	50 796	1.4	14.5	24.7	94.1
IMP [IMPX]	NASD	hardware	237	0.0	43.8	138.2	8.75
Informix [IFMX]	NASD	software	3209	0.0	30.4	57.6	21.9
Integrated Device Technology [IDTI]	NASD	hardware	697	0.0	6.3	60.3	9
Intel [INTC]	NASD	hardware	58 875	0.2	17.7	31.4	71.6
Intergraph [INGR]	NASD	hardware	498	0.0	0.0	56.0	10.6
Interleaf [LEAF]	NASD	software	75	0.0	225.0	55.7	4.5
Intuit [INTU]	NASD	software	1642	0.0	0.0	48.3	36.3
Iomega [IOMG]	NASD	hardware	3110	0.0	163.3	152.5	26.1
Level One [LEVL]	NASD	hardware	245	0.0	21.6	67.5	19
Logic Devices [LOGC]	NASD	hardware	22	0.0	14.8	0.0	3.69

Company	Exchange	Type					
LSI Logic [LSI]	NYSE	hardware	2479	0.0	10.7	55.4	19.3
Lucent [LU]	NYSE	hardware	22 802	0.8	0.0	35.3	35.9
Lycos [LCOS]	NASD	service	115	0.0	0.0	0.0	8.38
Macromedia [MACR]	NASD	software	646	0.0	30.1	115.5	17.8
Madge [MADGF]	NASD	hardware	503	0.0	0.0	104.2	11.5
McAfee [MCAF]	NASD	software	2236	0.0	75.8	77.8	47.8
MCI [MCIC]	NASD	service	13 458	0.2	28.2	30.7	24.3
Mecklermedia [MECK]	NASD	service	132	0.0	0.0	0.0	15.8
Microcom [MNPI]	NASD	hardware	157	0.0	12.5	130.3	10
Micrografx [MGXI]	NASD	software	105	0.0	58.8	63.2	11.8
Micron Technology [MU]	NYSE	hardware	3728	1.1	4.5	47.2	17.9
Microsoft [MSFT]	NASD	software	69 689	0.0	37.3	24.6	117
Motorola [MOT]	NYSE	hardware	32 338	0.8	20.2	23.8	54.6
National Semiconductor [NSM]	NYSE	hardware	1911	0.0	10.2	49.1	13.9
Netcom [NETC]	NASD	service	251	0.0	0.0	65.0	21.9
NetManage [NETM]	NASD	software	435	0.0	19.2	89.0	10.4
Netscape [NSCP]	NASD	software	4300	0.0	0.0	74.2	51.4
Network Computing Devices [NCDI]	NASD	hardware	62	0.0	0.0	172.0	3.81
Network Express [NETK]	NASD	hardware	85	0.0	0.0	47.6	8.38
Network Peripherals [NPIX]	NASD	hardware	151	0.0	0.0	58.7	12.9
Newbridge Networks [NN]	NASD	hardware	4564	0.0	30.1	43.6	54.1
Northern Telecom [NT]	NYSE	service	13 216	1.0	26.8	21.1	51.6
Novell [NOVL]	NASD	software	4093	0.0	25.8	36.0	11.6
nView [NVUE]	NASD	hardware	20	0.0	0.0	0.0	4.13
Oak Technologies [OAKT]	NASD	hardware	326	0.0	5.1	77.2	7.63

Company [ticker symbol]	Exchange	Sector	Mkt-Cap ($m)	Div-Yld	P/E Ratio	Volatility	Price 17/07/96
(1)	(2)	(3)	(4)	(5)	(6)	(7)	(8)
Open Text [OTEXF]	NASD	software	0	0.0	0.0	0.0	8.25
Optical Data Systems [ODSI]	NASD	hardware	341	0.0	24.1	51.7	20.3
Oracle [ORCL]	NASD	software	25 187	0.0	41.7	43.5	37.5
PairGain [PAIR]	NASD	hardware	1909	0.0	56.4	85.8	53
PC Quote [PQT]	AMEX	service	42	0.0	28.0	78.1	5.88
Phoenix Technologies [PTEC]	NASD	software	264	0.0	26.0	62.5	16.6
PictureTel [PCTL]	NASD	software	1288	0.0	57.4	59.8	39
Pixar [PIXR]	NASD	software	593	0.0	103.3	56.5	15.5
Premisys [PRMS]	NASD	hardware	1017	0.0	72.9	69.7	38.6
Presstek [PRST]	NASD	service	950	0.0	225.0	264.2	63
PSINet [PSIX]	NASD	service	388	0.0	0.0	94.7	9.94
QLogic [QLGC]	NASD	hardware	56	0.0	82.3	0.0	9.88
Qualcomm [QCOM]	NASD	hardware	2858	0.0	86.7	21.9	40.8
Quantum [QNTM]	NASD	hardware	711	0.0	0.0	56.8	13.1
Quarterdeck [QDEK]	NASD	software	257	0.0	95.3	81.8	7.63
Raptor Systems [RAPT]	NASD	software	0	0.0	0.0	0.0	22.8
Rockwell [ROK]	NYSE	hardware	11 039	2.2	13.9	23.6	50.9
S3 [SIII]	NASD	hardware	570	0.0	14.1	79.9	12.1
Santa Cruz Operation Inc. [SCOC]	NASD	software	236	0.0	0.0	56.2	6.38
Seagate [SEG]	NYSE	hardware	4347	0.0	15.0	48.6	41.3
Secure Computing [SCUR]	NASD	software	127	0.0	0.0	0.0	19.5
Security Dynamics [SDTI]	NASD	software	1057	0.0	141.8	85.2	78

Company	Exchange	Sector					
Sequent [SQNT]	NASD	hardware	393	0.0	13.4	49.2	11.8
Sequoia Systems [SEQS]	NASD	hardware	39	0.0	0.0	0.0	2.52
Shiva [SHVA]	NASD	hardware	2123	0.0	0.0	79.0	70.3
Sierra Semiconductor [SERA]	NASD	hardware	246	0.0	10.7	85.8	9.13
Silicon Graphics [SGI]	NYSE	hardware	3735	0.0	18.5	38.4	22.9
Silicon Valley Group [SVGI]	NASD	hardware	512	0.0	8.4	71.5	17.5
Sprint [FON]	NYSE	service	13 094	2.6	13.0	28.9	37.4
Spyglass [SPYG]	NASD	software	0	0.0	0.0	63.8	19.1
Stac [STAC]	NASD	software	275	0.0	0.0	70.8	9
Storage Technology [STK]	NYSE	hardware	1825	0.0	0.0	57.4	34.3
Stratacom [STRM]	NASD	hardware	4656	0.0	0.0	39.2	57.3
Stratus Computer [SRA]	NYSE	hardware	595	0.0	25.4	28.0	23.1
Structural Dynamics Research [SDRC]	NASD	software	611	0.0	0.0	84.3	20.5
Sun Microsystems [SUNW]	NASD	hardware	10 123	0.0	22.5	48.7	55
Sybase [SYBS]	NASD	software	1245	0.0	0.0	51.8	16.6
Symantec [SYMC]	NASD	software	522	0.0	0.0	80.4	9.75
Synopsys [SNPS]	NASD	software	1376	0.0	133.7	58.5	34.8
SyQuest [SYQT]	NASD	hardware	72	0.0	0.0	183.0	6.38
Tandem Computer [TDM]	NYSE	hardware	1175	0.0	325.0	45.2	9.75
Telebit [TBIT]	NASD	hardware	140	0.0	0.0	119.2	10.4
Tellabs [TLAB]	NASD	hardware	5157	0.0	42.7	54.2	58
Tencor Instruments [TNCR]	NASD	hardware	498	0.0	7.1	76.3	16.3
Teradyne [TER]	NYSE	hardware	1104	0.0	5.7	43.4	13
Texas Instruments [TXN]	NYSE	hardware	9195	1.5	8.2	28.2	43.3
Time Warner [TWX]	NYSE	service	14 389	0.9	0.0	18.9	36.6

Company [ticker symbol] (1)	Exchange (2)	Sector (3)	Mkt-Cap ($m) (4)	Div-Yld (5)	P/E Ratio (6)	Volatility (7)	Price 17/07/96 (8)
Touchstone Software [TSSW]	NASD	software	22	0.0	0.0	0.0	3
Tricord Systems [TRCD]	NASD	hardware	44	0.0	0.0	103.1	3.38
Unisys [UIS]	NYSE	hardware	1045	0.0	0.0	51.0	6
US Robotics [USRX]	NASD	hardware	6440	0.0	43.8	74.2	73.5
UUNET [UUNT]	NASD	service	1924	0.0	0.0	31.0	59.8
VeriFone [VFI]	NYSE	software	1036	0.0	29.3	28.7	41.1
ViewLogic Systems [VIEW]	NASD	software	183	0.0	57.2	73.2	10.9
VLSI Technology [VLSI]	NASD	hardware	562	0.0	14.9	77.8	12.4
VTEL [VTEL]	NASD	hardware	1270	0.0	56.3	73.4	9
Wall Data [WALL]	NASD	software	165	0.0	22.4	61.3	17.3
Westell [WSTL]	NASD	hardware	0	0.0	0.0	108.6	26
Western Digital [WDC]	NYSE	hardware	1152	0.0	12.2	50.0	22.8
Xcellenet [XNET]	NASD	software	88	0.0	26.2	0.0	11.3
Xerox [XRX]	NYSE	hardware	15 710	2.3	14.1	30.7	48.5
Xircom [XIRC]	NASD	hardware	267	0.0	0.0	77.2	13.8
Yahoo! [YHOO]	NASD	service	509	0.0	0.0	0.0	19.3
Zilog [ZLG]	NYSE	hardware	458	0.0	10.7	59.6	23.4
Zoom Telephonics [ZOOM]	NASD	hardware	57	0.0	8.0	0.0	9.25
Zycad [ZCAD]	NASD	hardware	94	0.0	0.0	91.5	4.75
Averages:			4486		48.7	65.7	

APPENDIX L

Internet
Index options

To invest in Internet-related stocks, an easy method is to trade the cash-settled index options. Two such options exist: one trading at AMEX and another at CBOE. The contract specifications for both of these contracts is given below. The component stocks for each Index are listed in Table 2.50 page 307.

Contract specifications for options on the Inter@ctive Week Internet Index, trading on AMEX

Trading Unit	The minimum trade size is one option contract. The notional value underlying each contract equals $100 multiplied by the Index value.
Expiration Cycle	Three consecutive near-term months plus two additional further-term months in the January cycle. Long-term options or LEAPS® may be available on either the full or reduced value of the Index.
Expiration	The Saturday following the third Friday of the expiration month.
Limited Exercise of Options	European style exercise – options may be exercised only on the last business day prior to expiration. Writers are subject to assignment only at expiration.
Last Trading Day	Two business days prior to expiration (normally a Thursday).
Final Index Settlement Value	Determined on the last business day prior to expiration, based on the first (opening) reported sale price for each component stock.

Delivery Method if Exercised	Cash settlement based on the dollar difference between the final settlement valuation of the Index and the strike price of the contract multiplied by $100.
Exercise Price Intervals	Exercise (strike) prices are set at 5-point intervals, bracketing the current Index value, when the Index is above 200; otherwise the interval will be 2½-points.
Option Premium Quotations	Stated in points and fractions. One point equals $100. Minimum tick for series trading below 3 is 1/16 ($6.25); for all other series, 1/8 ($12.50).
Settlement	Next business day following expiration.
Position Limits	12 000 contracts on the same side of the market.
Minimum Customer Margin for Uncovered Writers	Premium plus 20 per cent of the aggregate Index value (Index value × $100) reduced by any out-of-the-money amount to a minimum of premium plus 10 per cent of the aggregate Index value.
Trading Hours	9:30 a.m. to 4:10 p.m., New York time.
Trading System	Specialist/Registered Options Trader.
Index Base Reference Point	200
CUSIP Number	1982107
Trading Symbol	IIX
Final Settlement Valuation Symbol	IIV

Contract specifications for options on the CBOE Internet Index

Symbol	INX
Underlying	The CBOE Internet Index is an equal-dollar weighted index composed of 15 companies involved in providing Internet access services, as well as the design and manufacture of software and hardware that facilitates Internet access. The Index will be re-balanced quarterly after the close of trading on the third Friday of March, June, September and December.
Multiplier	$100.00
Strike Price Intervals	Five points.

Strike (Exercise) Prices	In-, at- and out-of-the-money strike prices are initially listed. New series are generally added when the underlying trades through the highest or lowest strike price available.
Premium Quotation	Stated in points and fractions. One point equals $100. The minimum tick is 1/16 ($6.25) for series trading below 3 and 1/8 ($12.50) for all other series.
Exercise Style	European – INX options generally may be exercised only on the last business day before expiration.
Expiration Date	Saturday immediately following the third Friday of the expiration month.
Expiration Months	Up to three near-term months plus up to three additional months from the March quarterly cycle (March, June, September and December).
Settlement of Options Exercise	The CBOE Internet Index exercise-settlement value, ITS is calculated using the first (opening) reported sales price in the primary market of each component stock on the last business day (usually a Friday) before the expiration date. If a stock in the index does not open on the day on which the exercise-settlement value is determined, the last reported sales price in the primary market will be used in calculating the exercise-settlement value. The exercise-settlement amount is equal to the difference between the exercise-settlement value and the exercise price of the option, multiplied by $100. Exercise will result in delivery of cash on the business day following expiration.
Position Limit	The position limit is 12 000 contracts on the same side of the market.
Margin	Uncovered writers must deposit 100 per cent of the option proceeds plus 20 per cent of the aggregate contract value (current index level multiplied by $100) minus the amount by which the option is out-of-the-money, if any. Minimum margin is 100 per cent of the option proceeds plus 10 per cent of the aggregate contract value. Long puts or calls must be paid in full.
CUSIP Number	12483S
Last Trading Day	Trading in INX options will ordinarily cease on the business day (usually a Thursday) preceding the day on which the exercise-settlement value is calculated.
Trading Hours	8:30 a.m. – 3:10 p.m. Central Time (Chicago time).

APPENDIX M

WWW portfolio monitor I

Source HTML code for a Web page that customizes links for specific companies to the major news and data sources on the Internet. (For further details *see* page 296.)

```
<html>
<head><title>INVESTING ONLINE - WWW Portfolio Monitor
I</title></head>
<body>

<h1>WWW PORTFOLIO MONITOR I</h1>
<h2>PORTFOLIO NAME: <i>Monde-01</i></h2>


<!------- PORTFOLIO STOCK NO. 1 --------->
<hr>
<b>Telebras [TBR]</b> :
<a href="http://qs.secapl.com/cgi-bin/qs?tick=TBR">Quote</a> |
<a href="http://www.stockmaster.com/sm/g/T/TBR.html">Chart</a> |
<a href="http://cnnfn.com/markets/knight-
ridder/americas.html">Market Report</a> |
<a href="http://biz.yahoo.com/news/TBR.html">Company News</a> |
<a href="http://search.dejanews.com/dnquery.xp?query=Telebras">
Usenet</a>


<!------- PORTFOLIO STOCK NO. 2 --------->
<hr>
<b>News Corp [NWS] </b> :
<a href="http://qs.secapl.com/cgi-bin/qs?tick=NWS">Quote</a> |
<a href="http://www.stockmaster.com/sm/g/N/NWS.html">Chart</a> |
<a href="http://cnnfn.com/markets/knight-ridder/asia.html">Market
Report</a> |
<a href="http://biz.yahoo.com/news/NWS.html">Company News</a> |
<a href="http://search.dejanews.com/dnquery.xp?query=News+Corp">
Usenet</a>


<!------- PORTFOLIO STOCK NO. 3 --------->
<hr>
<b>Philips [PHG]</b> :
<a href="http://qs.secapl.com/cgi-bin/qs?tick=PHG">Quote</a> |
<a href="http://www.stockmaster.com/sm/g/P/PHG.html">Chart</a> |
<a href="http://cnnfn.com/markets/knight-ridder/europe.html">Market
Report</a> |
<a href="http://biz.yahoo.com/news/PHG.html">Company News</a> |
<a href="http://search.dejanews.com/dnquery.xp?query=Philips">
Usenet</a>


<!------- PORTFOLIO STOCK NO. 4 --------->
<hr>
<b>Xerox [XRX] </b> :
<a href="http://qs.secapl.com/cgi-bin/qs?tick=XRX">Quote</a> |
<a href="http://www.stockmaster.com/sm/g/X/XRX.html">Chart</a> |
<a href="http://cnnfn.com/markets/knight-ridder/americas.html">
Market Report</a> |
<a href="http://biz.yahoo.com/news/XRX.html">Company News</a> |
<a href="http://search.dejanews.com/dnquery.xp?query=Xerox">
Usenet</a>

<hr>
</body>
</html>
```

APPENDIX N

WWW portfolio monitor II

Source HTML code for a Web page that customizes links for specific companies to the major news and data sources on the Internet. This is a more sophisticated development of the Web page than was given in the previous appendix.

```
<html>
<head><title>INVESTING ONLINE - WWW Portfolio Monitor
II</title></head>
<body>

<table cellspacing=4 cellpadding=6 width=100% border=8>

<!--------- HEADER BOX ----------->
<tr>
  <td>
    <center><font size=+3>WWW P</font><font size=+2>ORTFOLIO</font>
    <font size=+3>M</font><font size=+2>ONITOR</font> <font
    size=+3>II</font></center><hr width=50%>
    <font size=-1>PORTFOLIO NAME:</font> <i>Monde-01</i>
  </td>
<!--------- GENERAL MARKET --------->
  <td>
    <a href="http://www.bloomberg.com/cgi-bin/tdisp.sh?bbn/
    snapshot.html">World market snapshot</a><br>
    News: <a href="http://cnnfn.com/news/">CNN</a> | <a
    href="http://www.yahoo.com/headlines/">Reuters</a><br>
    <a href="http://www.bloomberg.com/cgi-bin/tdisp.sh?bbn/
    papers.html">World newspaper headlines</a><br>
    <a href="http://www.briefing.com/dollar.htm">FX ticker with
    comment</a>
  </td>
<tr>
</table>
```

```html
<p>
<table width=100% cellspacing=0 cellpadding=4 border=4>

<!-------- PORTFOLIO HEADINGS --------->
<tr>
  <th>Company</th>
  <th>Quotes</th>
  <th>Charts</th>
  <th>Markets</th>
  <th>Company<br>News</th>
  <th>WWW /<br>Usenet</th>
  <th>Currencies</th>
</tr>
<!--------- PORTFOLIO STOCK NO. 1 ----------->
<tr valign=top>
  <td>
    Telebras<br>[TBR]
  </td>
  <td>
    <a href="http://www.dbc.com/cgi-bin/htx.exe/squote?SOURCE=dbcc&
    TICKER=TBR&tables=table">DBC</a></td>
  <td>
    <a href="http://www.lombard.com/cgi-bin/PACenter/Graph/graph?
    TYPE=I&SIZE=S&BACKGROUND=W&COUNT=30&PERIOD=Days&SYMBOL=TBR">
    Intraday</a><br>
    <a href="http://quotes.galt.com/cgi-bin/stockclnt?stock=
    TBR&action=1&period=100&periodunit=0&sectype=0">100 Day</a>
  </td>
  <td>
    <a href="http://cnnfn.com/markets/knight-ridder/americas.html">
    Knight-Ridder</a><br>
    <a href="http://interactive2.wsj.com/edition/current/articles/
    Brazil.htm">WSJ</a>
  </td>
  <td>
    <a href="http://www.briefing.com/cgi-bin/webfind.exe?
    Keywords=TRB">Briefing</a> |
    <a href="http://cnnfn.com/cgi-bin/searcher?terms=Telebras&all=
    on&number=50">CNN</a><br>
    <a href="http://www.ft.com/cgi-bin/pft/wwwwais?keywords=
    Telebras">FT</a> |
    <a href="http://biz.yahoo.com/news/TBR.html">Yahoo</a>
  </td>
  <td>
    <a href="http://www.altavista.digital.com/cgi-bin/query?
    pg=aq&what=web&fmt=.&q=telebras&r=&d0=1%2FOct%2F96&d1=">Alta
    Vista</a><br>
    <a href="http://search.dejanews.com/dnquery.xp?query=~g+misc.
    invest*+%26+(TBR+|+Telebras)">DejaNews</a>
  </td>
  <td>
    <a href="http://www.bloomberg.com/cgi-bin/tdisp.sh?markets/
    wcv1.html">Bloomberg</a>
  </td>
```

```
</tr>
<!--------- PORTFOLIO STOCK NO. 2 ---------->
<tr valign=top>
  <td>
    News Corp<br>[NWS]
  </td>
  <td>
    <a href="http://www.dbc.com/cgi-bin/htx.exe/squote?SOURCE=
    dbcc&TICKER=NWS&tables=table">DBC</a>
  </td>
  <td>
    <a href="http://www.lombard.com/cgi-bin/PACenter/Graph/graph?
    TYPE=I&SIZE=S&BACKGROUND=W&COUNT=30&PERIOD=Days&SYMBOL=NWS">
    Intraday</a><br>
    <a href="http://quotes.galt.com/cgi-bin/stockclnt?stock=
    NWS&action=1&period=100&periodunit=0&sectype=0">100 Day</a>
  </td>
  <td>
    <a href="http://cnnfn.com/markets/knight-ridder/asia.html">
    Knight-Ridder</a><br>
    <a href="http://interactive2.wsj.com/edition/current/articles/
    Australia.htm">WSJ</a>
  </td>
  <td>
    <a href="http://www.briefing.com/cgi-bin/webfind.exe?
    Keywords=NWS">Briefing</a> |
    <a href="http://cnnfn.com/cgi-bin/searcher?terms=News+Corp&all=
    on&number=50">CNN</a><br>
    <a href="http://www.ft.com/cgi-bin/pft/wwwais?keywords=
    News+Corp">FT</a> |
    <a href="http://biz.yahoo.com/news/NWS.html">Yahoo</a>
  </td>
  <td>
    <a href="http://www.altavista.digital.com/cgi-bin/query?
    pg=aq&what=web&fmt=.&q=News+Corp&r=&d0=1%2FOct%2F96&d1=">Alta
    Vista</a><br>
    <a href="http://search.dejanews.com/dnquery.xp?query=~g+misc.
    invest*+%26+(NWS+|+News+Corp)">DejaNews</a>
  </td>
  <td>
    <a href="http://www.ino.com/cgi-bin/c?symbol=AUDUSf&range=
    intra">INO chart</a>
  </td>
</tr>

</table>
</body>
</html>
```

GLOSSARY

As with the world of investment, the jargon of the Internet can initially be rather intimidating. However, the following glossary should cover most of the common terms found with reference to the Internet; and should therefore help with the reading of this book, and also hopefully in the understanding of investment reports about the Internet.

Reference – glossaries

New terms are always appearing, so the following online glossaries may also prove useful:

- **http://www.matisse.net/files/glossary.html** – Internet glossary maintained by *Internet Literacy Consultants*
- **http://wwwli.com/translation/netglos/net-glos.html** – multilingual glossary
- **http://wombat.doc.ic.ac.uk** – the best general dictionary of computer terms (at Imperial College, London)

2600

Famous underground magazine for the *hacker* community. (There is also a newsgroup: alt.2600.)

7-bit

Data is described to be in 7-bit format if it just contains *ASCII* characters.

8-bit

Binary files are said to be 8-bit format.

ActiveX (OCX)

Microsoft's system for embedding and viewing OLE linked objects in *Web* pages. (Will run *Java applets* as well as *VBScript*.)

ADN

Advanced Digital Network: usually refers to a 56Kbps *leased line*.

ADSL

Asymmetric digital subscriber line: using similar technology to *T1* over ordinary telephone lines, ADSL has a capacity up to 6Mbps. Originally developed to compete with cable TV for delivering video-on-demand services. *Asymmetrical*, as the line has more bandwidth in one direction – unlike a similar technology, *HDSL*, which is symmetric. (A stage up from the 1.54Mbps of T1 and below the 45Mbps of *T3*.)

America Online (AOL)

The largest *commercial online service* in the US, now expanding operations in Europe.
http://www.aol.com

analogue (analog)

A continuously variable signal (unlike a discrete, or *digital*, signal). The term may equally be applied to the circuit carrying such a signal. (For example, human speech on telephone lines is analogue.) The term is frequently used to distinguish services and devices that are analogue based (e.g. an ordinary *modem*) from those that are digital (e.g. *CSU/DSU*).

anonymous FTP

FTP is the method of transferring files between two computers over the Internet. Occasionally, when logging on to a remote computer to download a file, a password will be required. In the case of *anonymous FTP* sites, the login name is 'anonymous', and the password can be your e-mail address. (Note: most FTP programs will use these values automatically – so it is rarely necessary to actually input them manually.)

AOL

[*See America Online*]

API

Application programming interface: the interface by which an application program accesses an operating system and other services.

applet

A small program written in *Java* to be downloaded over the Internet and run on a *client browser*.

arc

An *archive* format using the compression program PKARC.

Archie

A system of finding publicly available files for download by *anonymous FTP*. (However, in most cases nowadays it is probably easier to use one of the general Net search engines – for example, Alta Vista – or **http://www.shareware.com** or **http://www.zdnet.com**)

archive

To aggregate two or more files into one file. In addition, some archive programs may also compress the data to form a smaller aggregate file. The resulting aggregate file can be called an 'archive', and the constituent files are said to have been 'archived'. (Common archive formats are *arc, gz, lha, tar, z, zip*.)

ARPA

Advanced Research Projects Agency: part of the US Department of Defense.

ARPAnet

The initial network (*backbone*) in the US upon which the Internet was based.

ASCII

American Standard Code for Information Interchange: world-wide computer standard for representing Latin letters, numbers and punctuation by the numbers 0–127. (Files containing solely ASCII characters are sometimes, loosely, referred to as *text* files – to distinguish them from *binary* files.)

asynchronous

Not *synchronous*; proceeding independently. A method of transferring data between communication devices – for example, modems. (Transmission of data is not based on some predefined timing pattern, but rather dealt with irregularly as required.)

AT

[*See Hayes*]

ATM

Asynchronous transfer mode: a cell relay protocol using fixed-size cells of 53 bytes. (The expected future underlying Internet protocol, managing voice, data and variable resolution video.)

backbone

The high-speed data connections that form the core (or 'major pathway'), of a network. *IAPs*, governments, educational institutions and other major networks will connect to the backbone to join together.

bandwidth

The range of frequencies possible over a communications medium (e.g. the medium might be twisted-pair telephone lines or fibre optic cable). The greater the range of frequencies, the greater the quantity of data that can be transmitted using that medium.

baud

The rate at which data is transmitted between devices (e.g. modem to modem or computer to printer). Technically, it measures the number of signal changes per second, and will sometimes be equal to the *bps*, and sometimes not. (Because of this there can be confusion with its use, and it is best to always use the term *bps* instead which is unambiguous.)

BBS

Bulletin Board System: a computer system that allows people to dial in and carry on discussions (by posting messages – so that users do not have to be logged on simultaneously), and to *upload/download* files. There are thousands of BBSs around the world – some may be very small (just one PC and a telephone line) while at the other end of the scale, *CompuServe* might also be described as a BBS.

binary

A system having two states, (e.g. 1/0, on/off).

binary file

A file – for example a graphics file, or a formatted document – that is 8-*bit*. (The term is used to distinguish these files from 7-bit *ASCII* files – ordinary text files. Some Internet procedures only work with *ASCII* files.)

Binhex

*Bin*ary *Hex*adecimal: a method of converting non-text files to text files for the purposes of transmission by Internet email. [*See also* **MIME**]

bit

Binary digit: a single digit in base 2 (binary). (For example, the binary number, 101, contains 3 bits.) Seven bits are required to represent all the *ASCII* characters, while *binary* files require 8-bit characters. The speed of data communication is usually measured in *bits-per-second*. [*See also* **byte**]

BITNET

An early network of education computers (distinct from the Internet) where *Listservs* first appeared.

bits per second (bps)

The standard unit for measuring the speed of transmitting data. (A 14 400 modem will move 14 400 *bits* every second, while a *T1* Internet connection is capable of 1.54 Mbps, or 1 048 576 bits every second.) [*See also* **baud**]

body (as in *message body*)

E-mail messages and newsgroup postings are composed of two parts: the first part is called the *header* (containing information about the message), and the second part is the body – the actual text of the message itself.

bounce

E-mail messages that cannot be delivered are bounced back to the sender.

bps

Abbreviation for *bits per second*.

broadband

Not strictly defined, but usually taken to mean transmission speeds above 45 Mbps.

broadcast

To transmit specified data packets to multiple hosts at the same time.

browser

A *WWW client* program. (For example, Netscape Navigator or Microsoft Explorer.)

BTW

Forum abbreviation for 'by the way'.

bulletin board system

[*See BBS*]

byte

There are 8 *bits* in one byte. As an 8-bit binary number can represent up to 256 ASCII and extended *ASCII* characters, one byte can be thought of as being equivalent to one character. [*See also bit*]

cable modem

A device for connecting a computer to a fibre-optic cable. (A normal *modem* connects a computer to the *twisted-pair copper* wire of ordinary telephone lines.)

Capstone Project

The Capstone Project is the US Government's attempt to develop a set of standards for publicly available encryption. The project is controlled by the *NIST* and the *NSA*, and involves the *Skipjack* algorithm on the *Clipper* chip.

CATALIST

MS Windows version of *Hytelnet*.

CCITT

Consultative Committee on International Telegraph and Telephone: was the main standards body for telecommunications, now replaced by the *ITU-T*.

Cello

One of the first MS Windows *Web browsers*. (Developed at Cornell University.)

CERN

European Particle Physics Laboratory: birthplace of the *Web*.

CGI

Common Gateway Interface: the standard interface between *HTTP* servers and other programs. (This allows *Web browsers* to communicate with programs – for example, a database – running on a Web *server*.) [*See also Perl*]

character

A binary (0 and 1s) representation of a single letter, number or symbol.

CIS

CompuServe Information Service.

CIX

Compulink Information Exchange: a large *BBS* in the UK.

CIX

Commercial Internet Exchange: the network of major US commercial Internet providers – a major part of the US Internet *backbone*. (Originally set up so that commercial traffic could avoid the *NSFnet*.)

ClariNet

An electronic news service company that uses Usenet newsgroups to deliver the articles.

client

A program that runs on your local computer that interacts with, and/or extracts data from, a remote *file server*.

clickable map

[*See imagemap*]

Clipper

An encryption microchip that includes the *Skipjack* data encryption algorithm. (Part of the US Government's *Capstone* project.)

CMC

Computer-mediated communication: incorporating all the means of communicating via a computer.

Commercial online services

Private networks that frequently offer access to the Internet, but also require a subscription to access specialized services with proprietary content (examples of these services are *CompuServe, AOL* and *Prodigy*.)

compress

[*See data compression*]

CompuServe (CServe)

A worldwide *commercial online service*.
http://www.compuserve.com

cookies

A Netscape-devised method of tracking a user's path on the *Web* by means of modifying a file on the *client* system.

cps

Characters per second. (In most cases a *character* will be equivalent to a *byte* of data, in which cases *cps* will be the same as bytes per second.)

cracker

A person who deliberately tries to break into computer systems where they have no permission for access. [*See also hacker*]

cross-post

Sending the same message simultaneously to more than one *newsgroup*. (Quite a common procedure, but if cross-posted to too many newsgroups, it might be considered *spamming*.)

cryptography

[*See* encryption]

CSU/DSU (DSU/CSU)

Channel service unit/digital service unit: a DSU is a device in digital communications for connecting a CSU to a *DTE* (e.g. a computer). A DSU therefore acts in a similar fashion to a *modem* in *analogue* communications.

cybercafe

Café offering the use of computer terminals linked to the Internet.

cyberpunk

Not well defined, but generally taken to mean a person living in the culture of a future digital world (including virtual reality etc.).

Cyberspace

Not well defined, but generally taken to mean the collective domain of all connected computers, and incorporating the new 'life' that can develop within that domain – being distinct from the ordinary world. (The term was first used by William Gibson in his novel *Neuromancer*.)

DARPA

The Defence Advanced Research Projects Agency: responsible for the development of *ARPAnet*.

data compression

The compression of data to decrease the total file size that must be transferred. (Examples of data compression standards are, MNP5 and V.42bis.)

DCE

Data communication equipment: the devices and connections of a communications network that connect *DTE*s (e.g. a *modem* is a type of DCE). DTEs and DCEs are most commonly connected with a *RS-232* serial line.

dedicated line

[*See* **leased line**]

DES

Data Encryption Standard: a *secret key* cryptosystem using a 56-bit key. (An encryption cipher using a method developed at IBM, that was endorsed by the US Government in 1977 as an official standard.)

dialup

A method of accessing a network using an ordinary telephone line or *ISDN*, where access is made afresh each time by dialling in. (The other method of connection is a permanent link using a *leased* – or *dedicated* – *line*.)

digital signature

A method of authenticating authorship of digital documents (i.e. similar to the role played by handwritten signatures for paper documents.)

DNS

[*See Domain Name System*]

Domain Name

A unique text address of a computer connected to the Internet. (These Domain Names are not used directly by *Internet protocols* but are used to represent *IP addresses* using the *DNS*.)

Domain Name System (DNS)

Domain Name System: the system of translating text *Domain Names* (e.g. yahoo.com) to *IP addresses* (e.g. 205.216.162.12) that incorporates a collection of *nameservers* distributed around the Internet.

download

The transfer of a file *from* a remote computer *to* your computer.

DSA

[*See DSS*]

DSS

Digital Signature Standard: a proposal made by *NIST* and *NSA* as the US Government's standard for digital authentication. It specifies a Digital Signature Algorithm (DSA), and is part of the *Capstone* project.

DSU/CSU

[*See CSU/DSU*]

DTE

Data terminal equipment: a device that acts as the source or destination of data, and additionally controls the data communication channel (e.g. a personal computer). [*See also DCE*]

ecash

Abbreviation for electronic cash, incorporating all systems for transferring money in a digital world.

ECHO

East Coast Hang Out: an online community conference system. (New York's answer to the *WELL*.)

EDI

Electronic data interchange.

EFF

Electronic Frontier Foundation: an organization founded to protect civil liberties in *Cyberspace*.
http://www.eff.org

e-mail/Email/E-mail

Electronic mail: a method of sending text messages from one computer to another computer on a connected network. (Internet e-mail is defined as e-mail sent over the Internet using one of the Internet mail protocols – the most common being *SMTP*.)

emoticons

ASCII characters used in e-mail or newsgroup messages to denote emotion. (For example, :-) to denote a smile; as such sometimes referred to as *smileys*.)

encryption

The process of coding a message so that only certain people can understand it. [*See also secret-key* and *public-key* encryptions]

escrow agencies

Independent bodies designated by the US Government to look after the keys for the *Clipper* chip system. (Part of the *Capstone Project*.)

Ethernet

A common method of linking computers together to form a network called a *LAN*.

FAQ

Frequently Asked Questions: a document containing all the most commonly asked question on a particular topic. There are hundreds of FAQs available on the Internet.

FDDI

Fibre Distributed Data Interface: a standard for optical fibre cable data transmission at 100 000 000 *bps*.

file server

A *host* that stores files making them available to other computers on the network.

FidoNet

One of the earliest personal computer *bulletin boards*. (Formed in 1983 in San Francisco.)

finger

A method of finding out information about a user on a local or remote network.

firewall

A security system to restrict access to computers on a *LAN* from outside networks that the LAN is connected to. (For example, to restrict access to computers that are linked to the Internet.)

flame

Abusive e-mail or *newsgroup* message. Sometimes received by a *newbie* if they ignore *netiquette*. If the flame is responded to in like manner, a *flame war* can ensue.

forum

A special interest message area on *CompuServe* (equivalent to a *newsgroup* on *Usenet*).

frame relay

A standard specification for connecting *LAN-LAN* or *LAN-WAN*. Frame relay can be used to connect *dedicated lines* and *X.25* to *ATM* or *SMDS*.

freeware

A software program for which there is no charge.

FTP

File Transfer Protocol: a standardized procedure for transferring files from one computer to another across the Internet.

gateway

A combination of hardware and software that allows data to be passed between two different networks. (For example, *CompuServe* is a private network, using its own internal protocols, but a gateway exists to allow communication with the different system of the Internet.)

Gbyte

Abbreviation for *gigabyte* (1 073 741 824 bytes).

gif

Graphics interchange format: a standard format for image files (first used extensively on *CompuServe*).

gigabyte (Gbyte)

1 073 741 824 *bytes*.

GNN

Global Network Navigator: one of the pioneer large Web sites. (Bought by *AOL* in 1995.)

gopher

A method for organizing and retrieving documents on a network through a hierarchical system of menus. The collection of all files referenced by gopher menus is called *gopher space*. (Now largely replaced by HyperText and the *WWW*, and most *Web browsers* can read gopher menus.)

GUI

Graphical User Interface: pioneered by Xerox at Palo Alto, developed by Apple and then also adopted by Microsoft in Windows. (An interface system where the user points and clicks at icons or hot spots on the screen, rather than typing commands.)

.gz

File extension that indicates the file has been *archived* using the GNU Zip (*Gzip*) program.

Gzip

GNU Zip: a *UNIX* archive program – the *UNIX* (incompatible) answer to the popular DOS *zip* utility.

hacker

A person who enjoys exploring computer systems. (The term is frequently applied in a narrower sense to refer to exploration of non-public systems where such exploration is unwelcome – which more appropriately describes a *cracker*.)

handshaking

The process of establishing, or maintaining, contact between two communicating devices (e.g. the whoops and squeals made by *modems* when they initially try to connect).

Hayes

One of the pioneer *modem* manufacturers, whose command set (Hayes AT) has become an industry standard for passing commands from a computer to a modem.

HDSL

High-speed digital subscriber line: similar technology as that for *ADSL*, although this is fully symmetrical.

header

Part of a *packet* which precedes the actual data and contains source, destination and error checking information. The term is also used to refer to the first part of *e-mail* messages, or *newsgroup* postings, that contains information about the message.

hit

A single request to a *Web* server is called a *hit*. (The popularity of a Web service is usually measured by the number of hits it receives. But this can lead to some confusion: if a Web page contains many graphic images, then the retrieval of each single image will be registered as a hit.)

Home page

Refers to a *Web* page that is designated as the entry point (or main, or index page) for a collection of Web pages.

host

A computer on a network that provides services for other computers. (Commonly used to describe *Web* servers, *FTP* servers etc. on the Internet.)

HTML

HyperText Mark-up Language: the standardized language used on the **WWW** for the processing and presentation of text. Hence, **Web** pages are written in HTML. (To see examples of the underlying HTML for a Web page, select View | Document Source from the menu bar of a **browser** program.)

HTTP

HyperText Transfer Protocol: the Internet **protocol** that is used to enable Web **clients** (**browsers**) retrieve files from Web **servers** (i.e. the rules that govern the transmission of Web pages from one computer to another).

hyperlink

An area within a document that when clicked on will cause the **browser** to search for and retrieve a specified linked file.

hypermedia

An extension of **HyperText** to include graphics, video and sound as linked components.

HyperText

A document presented on a screen that contains links (**hyperlinks**) to other files (these other files may be documents, images, sound etc.). Clicking on the links will cause the computer to search for, and retrieve, the linked file.

Hytelnet

Short for **Hyper**Text browser for **Telnet** accessible sites. **Hypertext** interface for a database of **Telnet** sites with access instructions.

IAB

Internet Architecture Board: charged with researching and deciding Internet standards, governed by the **Internet Society**.

IANA

Internet Assigned Number Authority. Part of the **IAB**, the central registration authority for values used in Internet **protocols**.

IAP

Internet Access Provider: the terms **IP** and **ISP** are also sometimes used. (This book always uses the term **IAP** to cover all those straight services offering plain Internet access as distinct from the **commercial online services**.)

IDEA

A **secret-key encryption** system (an alternative to **DES**). Used by **Pretty Good Privacy**.

IETF

Internet Engineering Task Force. Working groups which design and update protocols for the Internet.

imagemap
An image that contains one or more *hyperlinks*, so that a linked file will be retrieved by the *browser* depending on the area of the image that is clicked on.

IMHO
Forum abbreviation for 'in my humble opinion'.

internet
The description of a system when two or more networks connect together.

Internet
The collection of interconnected networks around the world that all use the *TCP/IP protocols* to communicate with each other. Sometimes abbreviated to the *Net*.

Internet address
[*See IP address*]

Internet protocols
Describes the collection of *protocols* that make up and define the Internet. This includes the foundation *TCP/IP* protocols, and then the higher level protocols such as *SMTP, HTTP, NNTP, FTP*.

InterNIC
Internet Network Information Center: Internet resource centre, looking after, among other things, the allocation of *IP addresses* and .com *Domain Names* in the US.

Internet Society
An international organization that exists to support the Internet (the closest thing to an Internet governing body).

intranet
The description of a system of interconnected computers **within** an organization that use the Internet's *TCP/IP protocols* to communicate with each other. An organization's intranet may or may not be connected to the *Internet*.

IP
Internet provider. [*See also IAP*]

IP
Internet Protocol: one of the fundamental Internet *protocols* that looks after the addressing of data *packets* (to enable them to arrive at the correct destination). [*See also TCP/IP*]

IP address
Internet Protocol address: a unique number that identifies each computer connected to the Internet, and a fundamental part of *Internet Protocol* (*IP*). (Sometimes expressed in dotted decimal notation, for example, 205.216.162.12). [*See also Domain Name System*]

■ **IPhone**

Internet telephone: the process of using the Internet for real-time telephone conversations.

■ **IPng (IP next generation, IPv6)**

Internet Protocol next generation: IP version 6 is a candidate to replace the existing *Internet Protocol* (IP) to address current shortcomings (particularly those involving the shortage of **IP addresses**).

■ **IRC**

Internet Relay Chat. A method for direct person-to-person (or rather, keyboard-to-keyboard) 'conversation' over the Internet.

■ **ISAPI**

Internet Server Application Program Interface: the standard for applications written to run on a Microsoft Internet Server. (Microsoft's answer to Netscape's **NSAPI**.)

■ **ISDN**

Integrated Services Digital Network: a method of transmitting data over standard telephone lines. As the process is *digital*, no **modem** is required to convert the computer data to **analogue**. Speeds of up to 128Kbps (or in practice 64Kbps) are possible.

■ **ISO**

The International Organization for Standardization.

■ **ISP**

Internet service provider (*see also* **IAP**); generally not a well-defined term, but recently has increasingly been used to denote a provider that offers some level of support above that offered by a plain vanilla *IAP*.

■ **ITU-T**

International Telecommunications Union: the international organization that ratifies the world's telecommunication standards (formerly called the **CCITT**). **http://www3.itu.ch/**

■ **JANET**

Joint Academic Network: major network in the UK that is linked to the Internet.

■ **Java**

A new object-oriented programming language invented by Sun Microsystems. It can operate on many different platforms, thereby making it attractive for Internet applications. [*See also* **applet**]

■ **JavaScript**

A simple, cross-platform, World Wide Web scripting language that was developed by Sun Microsystems, and has been adopted by Netscape and other **browsers**. Formerly called LiveScript, it is a competitor to Microsoft's **VBScript**, and entirely different from *Java*.

JPEG

Joint Photographic Experts Group: a team comprising *ISO* and *CCITT* that developed a file compression standard for grey-scale or colour still images (very popular format on the Net).

.jpg

File extension for a compressed image file using *JPEG*.

Jughead

An index method for *gopher*.

K byte

Abbreviation for *kilobyte* (1024 *bytes*)

Kerberos

An authentication system used to maintain security on networks (ensures that the entity accessing the service is actually the authorized user).

kermit

A common error-correcting file transfer protocol used on *BBSs*.

kill file

A method of automatically filtering out messages from people that you do not want to read (increasingly common for newsgroups). The kill file contains a list of e-mail addresses; messages from those addresses will be deleted by the newsreader program.

kilobyte (K byte)

1024 *bytes*.

Knowbot

A *robot* that is programmed to find specified resources.

LAN

Local area network: a collection of computers in a closed environment (typically an office or a building) that are connected together by cable, and can communicate with each other. [*See also Ethernet*]

leased line (dedicated line)

A dedicated telecommunications link that can be permanently open (as distinct from a *dialup* connection).

lha

File extension for files created by the MS-DOS data *compression* and *archive* program LHARC.

Listserv

An automated mailing list distribution system.

login

The process of connecting to a remote computer – and thereby accessing, for example, an online service. (Usually a two-stage procedure requiring first the input of a user name and then a password.)

LOL

Forum abbreviation for 'laughing out loud'.

lurker

Somebody who reads newsgroups or mailing lists but who does not contribute any postings themselves.

Lynx

One of the most common text-only (non graphical) Web *browsers*.

.lzh

File extension for files created by the MS-DOS data *compression* and *archive* program LHARC.

mail gateway

A computer that translates messages using one e-mail system to another. (For example, translating between a *LAN* mail system and the *SMTP* mail system used by the Internet.)

mailing list

An e-mail address that is a group alias for many other e-mail addresses. Used loosely, it can refer to some publication that is distributed via e-mail to many recipients. It can also refer to the group of people who actually receive e-mail and whose addresses are in the mailing list.

Matrix

The set of all computer networks that can exchange e-mail messages – either directly or through *mail gateways*. (The Internet is a sub-set of the Matrix. The term was coined by J.S. Quarterman in his book, *The Matrix*.)

MBONE

Multicasting backbone. A network superimposed on top of the Internet *backbone* to enable multi-channels of audio and video to transmit across the Net. (Can be used for *broadcasting* and voice/video-conferencing.)

M byte

Abbreviation for *megabyte* (1 048 576 *bytes*).

megabyte (M byte)

1 048 576 *bytes*.

MIME

Multi-Purpose Internet Mail Extensions: an attempt to establish a standard method for attaching *binary files* to Internet *e-mail*. Internet e-mail is designed to send only *7-bit files* (printable *ASCII* text characters) whereas *binary files* (non-text files such as graphics or sound files) are *8-bit*. Various different methods are available (e.g. *uuencode* or *Binhex*) to convert 8-bit files to 7-bit. MIME provides a way of specifying what type of file is being transmitted, and what should be done with it.

▨ MIPS

Million instructions per second: the rate at which a processor executes instructions (i.e. a measure of the calculation speed of a computer).

▨ mirror

Some Web *servers* and *anonymous FTP* sites are so heavily used that they set up mirror sites on other computers (frequently on other continents) to relieve the load.

▨ MNP

Microcom Network Protocol: a *modem* error correction system.

▨ modem

MOdulator/DEModulator: a device that converts the *digital* information of a computer into an *analogue* signal (sound waves) that can be transmitted over ordinary telephone lines, and then converts back again.

▨ moderate

Some Internet *newsgroup*s and all *CompuServe forums* are moderated, whereby somebody actually reads all the messages posted and filters out those thought unsuitable.

▨ MOO

Abbreviation of MUD Object Oriented: a text-based multi-user role-playing environment (a next stage development beyond the original *MUD*s).

▨ Mosaic

The first widely used Web *browser*. (The name can be a little confusing: it was the name for the Web browser developed at the *NCSA*, which then licensed it to other institutions and companies – for example, to Spry, which developed AirMosaic. One of the NCSA developers, Marc Andreesen, left in April 1994 to set up a company, with Jim Clark, called *Mosaic Communications Corporation*, whose first product was the Web browser *Netscape* – briefly referred to as Mosaic Netscape. In November 1994, the company changed its name to *Netscape Communications Corporation*, but traces of the Mosaic name survive in numerous old *hyperlink*s to the Netscape home page – **http://home.mcom.com**)

▨ MUD

Multi-User Dungeon: an online role-playing adventure game.

▨ MUG

Multi-User Game: an online game involving two or more players.

▨ multimedia

Not a well-defined term, but generally taken to mean the integration of text, image, sound, video – and recently, communication – technologies.

multiplexer

A device for managing the bandwidth for networked applications.

name resolution

The *DNS* process of translating text *Domain Names* to numerical *IP addresses*. (For example, to translate from sales@ynapmoc.com to sales@123.123.1.1)

nameserver

A *host* that carries out *name resolution* under the *DNS*. (These are computers scattered around the Internet that act as directories for the *Domain Name System*.)

NCSA

The National Center for Supercomputing Applications: located at the University of Illinois (developer of the *Mosaic browser*).

Net

Generally, an abbreviation for the Internet; although more loosely used occasionally to refer to *Usenet* or the whole of *Cyberspace*.

netiquette

A 'code of behaviour' for users of the Internet.

Netscape

May equally be used to refer to the company, *Netscape Communications Corporation*, or its popular *Web browser*, Netscape Navigator. **http://home.netscape.com**

network

A collection of computers that can communicate with each other.

newbie

A new user of the Internet. (Commonly applied to somebody new to the *newsgroups* who has ignored *netiquette*.)

newsgroup

An Internet discussion forum, where people can read and post messages on a certain topic. The collection of all newsgroups is called *Usenet*.

news server

A *host* that acts as a *server* for *Usenet*. (A computer that receives, stores and transmits *Usenet* articles.)

NIC

Network Information Centre: any office that holds information about a network. [*See InterNIC*]

NIST

National Institute of Standards and Technology: US Government's standards body for computer systems (including cryptographic routines). In charge, with the *NSA*, of the *Capstone Project*.

■ **NNTP**

Network News Transfer Protocol: the *protocol* used between *news servers* to transfer *Usenet* articles.

■ **node**

Any single computer connected to a network is called a node. (One measure for the size of a network is to count the nodes, which is why one will see the size of the Internet sometimes expressed as a number of nodes. However, the problem is that one node, being one computer, may be a *gateway* to another network, and hence to many other computers.)

■ **NSA**

National Security Agency: the US Government communications security body (engaged in classified research into encryption).

■ **NSAPI**

Netscape Server Application Program Interface: standard specifications for applications written to run on *Netscape*'s server. [*See also **ISAPI***].

■ **NSFnet**

National Science Foundation Network: one of the main *backbones* of the Internet in the US.

■ **off-line reader (OLR)**

A program that enables *e-mails* and *newsgroup* articles to be downloaded and then read off-line, thereby saving the communication charges incurred while online.

■ **OHLC**

Open, high, low, close: common format for daily price data.

■ **OI**

Open interest: referring to the number of futures or options contracts outstanding at the end of a trading day.

■ **OLR**

[*See **off-line reader***]

■ **OSI**

Open Systems Interconnect: an international standard for computer communications.

■ **Pack**

UNIX file compression program.

■ **packet**

Discrete 'small' bundles of data (*see **packet-switching network***).

■ **packet-switching network**

A method of transmitting data around a network in small discrete units called packets. (The method used on the Internet – under the *TCP/IP* protocols – and thus the Internet is a 'packet-switching network'.)

■ **PBX**

Private branch exchange.

■ **PCMCIA**

Personal Computer Memory Card International Association: a standard interface for portable computers and peripherals.

■ **PDF**

Portable Document Format: a proprietary format developed by *Adobe* as a means of displaying documents on different platforms. (Many *Web* sites have PDF documents: these must be downloaded on to a local hard disk, and then read using *Adobe Acrobat Reader*.)

■ **PEM**

Privacy Enhanced Mail: a proposed Internet standard for securing e-mail using encryption techniques.

■ **Perl**

Practical Extraction and Report Language: an interpreted programming language optimized for scanning text files, and useful for many system management tasks. (Perl is popular as a *CGI* scripting language and will run on many different platforms – for example, *UNIX* or DOS.)

■ **PGP**

[*See* ***Pretty Good Privacy***]

■ **phreak**

To make a phone call while avoiding the charging system.

■ **PING**

Packet Internet Gropher: a program used to test if destination addresses are working (or, more precisely, first if your *host* is a valid hostname and then if the destination address is reachable from your host).

■ **PKZIP**

Popular DOS *archive* program.

■ **plug-ins**

Originally devised by *Netscape* as a method of allowing third-party developers to add functionality to *Web browsers*. The system is now supported by Microsoft as well. (An example of a plug-in is Macromedia's Shockwave.)

■ **PoP**

Point of Presence: a telephone access number where local users can connect to a network over *dialup* telephone lines.

POP3

Post Office Protocol 3: a method for e-mail programs to retrieve e-mail from a mail server.

port (port number)

Computers running *TCP/IP protocols* can use different ports (referenced by numbers) for different services. Sometimes it may be necessary to include a port number in a *URL*. (For example, **http://www.ynapmoc.com:80/** will use port 80 on the computer www.ynapmoc.com.)

post

To send a message either by e-mail or to an Internet *newsgroup* or *CompuServe forum*.

POTS

Plain old telephone system.

PPP

Point to Point Protocol: a *protocol* for *IP* connections over *synchronous* or *asynchronous* communication links. (Largely superseding the older *SLIP*.)

Pretty Good Privacy

Public key-encryption software that uses the *RSA* algorithm. (A program used to send encrypted messages, without the sender and recipient having to share a common encrypting key, thereby avoiding the major problem of *secret-key encryption*.)

printable ASCII

Characters with *ASCII* codes 10, 13, and 32-126 – a subset of the ASCII character set – that (as the name suggests) can be printed on most common printers.

protocol

An agreed standard for communicating computers for a particular activity. (For example, *FTP* for transferring files between computers, or *SMTP* for sending e-mail messages.)

PSTN

Public Switched Telephone Network (i.e. the ordinary telephone system).

PTT

Poste de Telephony et Telegraph: refers to the operators of an individual country's public telephone systems.

public domain

Files placed in the public domain are free for use with no charge. (However, there is some discussion over the legal aspects of this and exactly how a file is placed, and identified as being, in the public domain.)

public-key encryption

A method of encryption that uses two keys: one key (public) to encrypt a message, and a *different* key (private) to decrypt. (Also called an asymmetrical system.) An example of this type of encryption is *RSA*, which is used by *PGP*. [*See also secret-key encryption*]

RBOC

Regional Bell operating company.

RFC

Request for comment: the method for establishing a new standard for the Internet. A proposal document is generally circulated, and if thought a good idea will be implemented.

RIPEM

Riordan's Internet Privacy Enhanced Mail: a *public-key encryption* mail program that uses the *RSA* algorithm (similar to *PGP*).

robot

A program that automatically traverses the Web scanning pages and indexing *URL*s. Similar to a *spider*.

ROFL

Forum abbreviation for 'rolling on the floor laughing'.

router

A hardware/software device that connects different networks to exchange data *packets* between them, and can additionally determine the quickest route for sending a packet to its destination address.

RS-232

A standard for transmitting two-way, *asynchronous* serial data (via a serial port).

RSA

Public-key encryption algorithm used by *PGP* and *RIPEM* (developed at MIT by Rivest, Shamir and Adleman).

RSA Data Security

The company set up by the *RSA* algorithm developers to exploit their patent on it. (The company was bought by Security Dynamics in 1996.) **http://www.RSA.com**

search engine

A program used on a network to find files using keywords to search on. (For example, on the Internet, Infoseek and Lycos.)

secret-key encryption

The classic encryption method that uses the same key to encrypt and decrypt messages (and therefore called a symmetric system). Examples are *DES, IDEA*. [*See also public-key encryption*]

serial line (serial cable)

A cable used to connect devices through a computer's serial port. [*See also RS-232*]

server

A combination of hardware and software that provides a service to *client* software on another computer.

SGML

Standard Generalized Mark-up Language: a system for describing mark-up languages defined by an ISO standard. (*HTML* is formally defined as an SGML document type definition.)

Shareware

A method of marketing and distributing programs best summarized as 'try, before you buy'. Such programs can frequently be downloaded free from the Internet, *BBS*s or can be supplied on floppy disks; the programs might be full working versions or crippled in some ways. After trying the programs for a period (usually 30 days) users are expected to pay the registration fee, or otherwise erase the files from their computer.

SIG

Special Interest Group: an area for messages talking about a particular topic. (An old name for *forums* on *CompuServe*.)

signal-to-noise ratio

A term frequently used with reference to Internet *newsgroups* or *CompuServe forums* to describe the ratio of useful, interesting discussions to the rubbish. (A high signal-to-noise ratio is preferred.)

signature

[*See digital signature*]

signature file

A file containing a brief message that will be appended to all *e-mail* or *newsgroup* messages sent.

site

Refers to a service on the Internet, or, more specifically, to the computer hosting the service. (One can refer to a *gopher* site or *FTP* site, but the term is usually applied to the *Web* and a collection of pages on a server. The term is slightly anachronistic as site conveys an impression of place – which has little meaning on the Internet.)

Skipjack

The encryption algorithm contained in the *Clipper* chip, which is part of the *Capstone Project*. The algorithm was designed by the *NSA*, uses an 80-bit key and can only be implemented in hardware.

▒ SLIP

Serial Line Internet Protocol: a *protocol* for enabling computers to use the *Internet protocols* over standard telephone lines (one of the methods used to connect a PC to an *IAP*, but now largely being superseded by *PPP*).

▒ SMDS

Switched Multimegabit Data Service: a new standard for very high-speed data transfer.

▒ smileys

[*See emoticons*]

▒ SMTP

Simple Mail Transfer Protocol: the *protocol* used to transfer *e-mails* between computers using the *TCP/IP protocol* system (e.g. the Internet).

▒ SNA

System network architecture (network architecture from IBM).

▒ SOHO

Small office/home office. (Categorization invented to describe a consumer market segment for technology products – although doubts are now emerging as to whether this is in fact a homogeneous group.)

▒ SONET

Synchronous optical network: a protocol for high-speed transmission over *WAN*s of fibre optic where speeds are denoted in multiples of 51.84Mbps. (A stage up from the 45Mbps of *T3*.)

▒ spam

To *cross-post* a message simultaneously to a large number of *newsgroups*. (The favoured method for the 'MAKE MONEY FAST' posters.)

▒ spider (or crawler)

A program that automatically scans and indexes pages across the entire Web. Similar to a *robot*. (For example, Alta Vista, Lycos and WebCrawler are all Internet *search engines* that will use *spiders* to create their index databases.)

▒ SQL

[*See structured query language*]

▒ SSL

Secure sockets layer: a protocol designed by *Netscape* Communications Corporation to provide secure communications on the Internet.

▒ structured query language (SQL)

An international standard language for defining and accessing relational databases.

synchronous

A standardized method of communications between devices (e.g. *modems*) based on a standard timing signal. (The other type of communication is *asynchronous*.)

SysOp

Systems operator: a person who runs a *BBS*. Also used in the narrower sense to describe those who *moderate CompuServe forums*.

T1

A *leased line* data connection offering 1.54Mbps over ordinary telephone lines – *twisted-pair copper wires*. (A stage up from the 128Kbps of *ISDN*, and below the 6Mbps of *ADSL* or the 45Mbps of *T3*.)

T3

A fibre-optic connection for *WAN*s that supports 45Mbps. (A stage up from the 1.54Mbps of *T1* or 6Mbps of *ADSL* and below the 51.84Mbps and over of *SONET*.)

.tar

File extension for a tar format *UNIX archive* file (but this does not include any file compression).

.tar.gz, .tgz

File extensions for a *UNIX* file that has been tarred and then *Gzipped*.

.tar.Z, .tZ, .tarZ

File extensions for a *UNIX* file that has been tarred and then *data compressed*.

TCP

Transmission Control Protocol: one of the fundamental *Internet protocols* (along with *IP*). This protocol looks after the organization of splitting data into discrete *packets*, that will then be addressed and routed under *IP*.

TCP/IP

Describes the combination of the fundamental *Internet protocols* (*TCP* and *IP*). This label can be used to distinguish the mechanism of the Internet from other networks, and is therefore the defining characteristic of the Internet.

telco

Abbreviation for telephone company. (Often used in a pejorative sense to describe them as large and arrogant.)

Telnet

An *Internet protocol* that enables logging on to remote computers.

text

In its loosest sense, used to refer to what you are reading here (without the formatting), as distinct from pictures. It may be used to refer more strictly to just the defined *ASCII* characters, or yet more strictly to just *printable ASCII* characters. (A file containing solely ASCII characters may be called a *text file*, to distinguish it from a *binary file*.)

■ **thread**

A continuing discussion in a *newsgroup* or *forum* under one heading. Once a message has been posted with a particular heading, other posters may reply; and the discussion can be read by following the thread. If someone replies to a post by changing the message *header*, the discussion cannot be followed and this is called 'breaking the thread'.

■ **Trumpet**

Software company developing Internet applications; famous for its Trumpet Winsock program. [*See* **Winsock**]

■ **TTFN**

Forum abbreviation for 'ta ta for now'.

■ **twisted-pair copper wires**

Describes the wiring of ordinary telephone lines.

■ **.txt**

File extension for an ordinary text file comprising *ASCII* text.

■ **UNIX**

A computer operating system – the most widely used by computers on the Internet.

■ **UNIX system**

A computer using the *UNIX* operating system.

■ **upload**

The transfer of files *from* your computer to a remote computer.

■ **URL**

Uniform Resource Locator: a standard *WWW* system for identifying the nature of, and location for, an Internet resource. (For example: **http://www.yahoo.com** – the initial 'http://' identifies the resource type as being a WWW page and the location is at www.yahoo.com.)

■ **Usenet**

Describes the collection of discussion areas on the Internet – the individual messages of which are passed between computers using *NNTP*. There are over 10 000 of these discussion areas, called *newsgroup*s.

■ **UUCP**

Unix-to-Unix-copy: a method of transferring files between *UNIX systems*.

■ **uuencode**

A method of encoding *binary files* as *ASCII* text files which can then be sent as *e-mail* messages. [*See also* **MIME**]

■ **V-Series**

A set of *ITU-T* standards for *modem* communications (governing matters such as speed of transfer and error correction).

- **VBScript**

  Microsoft's programming language answer (with Visual Basic) to *Java* and *JavaScript*.

- **Veronica**

  Very Easy Rodent Oriented Net-wide Index to Computerized Archives. An aid for finding resources in *gopher* space.

- **virus**

  A program designed to enter a computer and change or destroy data outside the control of the computer administrator.

- **vol**

  Volume: number of securities or contracts traded.

- **VRML**

  Virtual Reality Modelling Language.

- **WAIS**

  Wide Area Information Server. A tool for indexing information on computers that can then be searched over networks.

- **WAN**

  Wide area network: similar to a *LAN*, but a network encompassing a larger area (outside a building).

- **Web**

  Abbreviation for the *World Wide Web*.

- **WELL**

  Whole Earth 'Lectronic Link: an early example of a *bulletin board system* that developed in San Francisco in 1985. Going beyond ordinary BBSs, the WELL has become something of an experiment in evolving online communities.

- **WHOIS**

  An Internet program used to find the *e-mail* address of someone.

- **Winsock**

  A socket interface specification standard (WinSocket API), that allows MS Windows applications to interface with *TCP/IP* software. (In other words, the essential software bridge between Windows applications and the Internet.)

- **Wintel**

  Windows-Intel: an abbreviation used to describe the system combination of Intel processors and Microsoft Windows – providing an 'intelligent machine on every desktop'. (Used frequently in a pejorative sense to indicate the unhealthy dominance of Intel and Microsoft. Recently, the Wintel system has been challenged by the Network Computer idea proposed by Larry Ellison of Oracle.)

■ World Wide Web (WWW)

A file presentation system for computer networks that uses *HTML* as the authoring language and *HTTP* as the transport *protocol*. In slightly less technical language: a collection of standardized files on a network that can be read with a *Web browser*; the browser can jump between files by means of *hyperlinks* (inter-file references).

■ WWW

[*See World Wide Web*]

■ WYSIWYG

What you see is what you get: commonly used to describe a feature of word processors if the printed document is close to what is displayed on the screen.

■ X.25

A *CCITT* standard for communications devices to access the public *packet-switched network*.

■ X.400

An open standard for electronic mail systems defined by the *ITU-T*.

■ X.500

An OSI defined directory server (a standard directory system for addresses on a network).

■ X-MODEM

A protocol for transferring files between two computers (usually via a *modem*).

■ Y-MODEM

A protocol for transferring files between two computers (usually via a *modem*).

■ .z

File extension for a *UNIX* file compressed using *Pack*.

■ Z-MODEM

A protocol for transferring files between two computers (usually via a *modem*).

■ zip

To zip a file is to *archive* it using the DOS *PKZIP* program.

■ .zip

File extension for an *archived* DOS file created by *PKZIP*. (Note: not compatible with the UNIX *Gzip* method.)

INDEX

INVESTING ONLINE

Feedback

To inform the author of any corrections – or of new Internet resources – for future editions of this book send an e-mail to:

info@global-investor.com

or complete the forms available on the GLOBAL INVESTOR Web site which has been established in conjunction with the publication of this book:

http://www.global-investor.com

About the disk included with this book

All the references from this book's *Financial Internet Directory* – plus some general Internet resources – are included as hyperlinks on the accompanying disk.

The disk contains 60 Web pages that can be loaded on to your local hard disk. These Web pages provide an extensive, off-line guide to the financial Internet: clicking on a reference will cause the browser to connect to the Internet and retrieve the desired site.

Requirements

The disk has been designed for Windows systems running a Web browser. The Web pages can be viewed off-line, but an Internet connection will be required for the hyperlinks to work.

Installing

To install the Web pages: insert the disk into the disk drive, select File Run from Windows Program Manager, and type `a:setup`.

Viewing the Web pages

1   Run your Web browser (e.g. Netscape Navigator or Microsoft Internet Explorer).
2   Load the file 'index.htm', from the new directory, into the browser (i.e. select File Open from the menu bar of the browser).

If you did not change the default installation directory, the file will be found at c:\global-i\index.htm. This will load the home page of the Directory.

3   Having loaded this page once, it is then recommended to bookmark the page, to return to it easily.

If you have any problems with the disk or the files please contact:

Numa Financial Systems Ltd

E-mail: info@numa.com   Web: **http://www.numa.com**